The Encyclopedia of Japanese Horror Films

National Cinema Series

Series Editor: Cynthia J. Miller

The Encyclopedia of Japanese Horror Films, edited by Salvador Murguia, 2016

The Encyclopedia of Japanese Horror Films

Edited by
Salvador Murguia

ROWMAN & LITTLEFIELD
Lanham • Boulder • New York • London

Published by Rowman & Littlefield
A wholly owned subsidiary of The Rowman & Littlefield Publishing Group, Inc.
4501 Forbes Boulevard, Suite 200, Lanham, Maryland 20706
www.rowman.com

Unit A, Whitacre Mews, 26-34 Stannary Street, London SE11 4AB

British Library Cataloguing in Publication Information Available

Library of Congress Cataloging-in-Publication Data

Names: Murguia, Salvador, 1977– editor.
Title: The encyclopedia of Japanese horror films / edited by Salvador Murguia.
Description: Lanham : Rowman & Littlefield, [2016] | Includes bibliographical
    references and index.
Identifiers: LCCN 2016010203 (print) | LCCN 2016019009 (ebook) | ISBN
    9781442261662 (hardback : alk. paper) | ISBN 9781442261679 (electronic)
Subjects: LCSH: Horror films—Japan—Encyclopedias.
Classification: LCC PN1995.9.H6 E53 2016 (print) | LCC PN1995.9.H6 (ebook) |
    DDC 791.43/6164—dc23
LC record available at https://lccn.loc.gov/2016010203

Printed in the United States of America

Contents

Acknowledgments

A project like this is not an individual endeavor, but rather a group effort. I would like to acknowledge, therefore, the professionalism and hard work of Rowman & Littlefield's senior editor of arts and literature, Stephen Ryan, and his staff. Additionally, National Cinema Series editor Dr. Cynthia Miller of Emerson College has been, and continues to be, an invaluable resource for wisdom and expertise in developing both the potential for meaningful writing ventures as well as individual career options for those that propose to write them.

Within my own academic institution of Akita International University I would also like to acknowledge the director of Liberal Arts Studies, Dr. Marcin Schroeder; vice president of Academic Affairs, Dr. Peter McCagg; and executive registrar, Mrs. Yukiko Suda for their understanding, cooperation, and support for my research agendas.

Within my close circle of family and friends, I would also like to acknowledge Hide Murguia; Kohaku Francisco Murguia; Kiseki Concepcion Murguia; Polito Jin Murguia; Yoko Naganishi; Paul Jimenez; Jan Jimenez; and my mother, Olivia Jimenez, for their help with everything from translation assistance and personal advice to time to think, reflect, and write—arigatou, thank you, and gracias!

Finally, I am indebted to those individuals who contributed to this volume, whose combined output makes this work rich with diversity and perspective. They, along with the producers, directors, actors, and fans of Japanese horror films, are the most valuable part of *The Encyclopedia of Japanese Horror Films*.

Introduction

Japan's film industry is not only one of the oldest, but perhaps one of the more prominent in the world of motion picture production. Among its many genres, horror films have had a real impact on global popular culture. From the eerie storylines incorporating a fascination with violence and death like *Suicide Circle* and *Ichi the Killer* to the science fiction terrors of *Godzilla* and *Tetsuo*, horror plays a major role among Japanese film genres. While some of these films are rather poor productions, others, such as the *Ringu* movies, have been major hits in Japan and have influenced other horror productions in both Asia and the United States.

Accessible for general audiences and academics alike, this volume is one of the more comprehensive reference texts, covering virtually every major horror film production made in Japan from the past century to date. Additionally, this text also includes entries for notable writers, directors, producers, actors, and film festivals, as well as several cultural and literary influences that have helped to engender J-horror material.

To be sure, there are a number of texts on the market that serve as important tools for both obtaining a general understanding of the J-horror genre, as well as conducting advanced scholarly research on this topic. For example, it is important to acknowledge Colette Balmain's (2008) *Introduction to Japanese Horror Film*, as it is an invaluable guide to establishing how the J-horror genre fits into the rest of Japanese cinema. Indeed, Balmain's work has been an incredibly useful reference since the inception of the project, especially with regard to arranging the larger framework for how this volume would come to be. Additionally, Jay McRoy's (2005) *Japanese Horror Cinema* and Jim Harper's (2009) *Flowers from Hell: The Modern Japanese Horror Film*, are both seminal works in the field of J-horror studies and have been instrumental in guiding the interpretations and analyses of the vast majority of the authors whose works appear in this text. Incidentally, this volume features several contributions from both McRoy and Harper. Moreover, Valerie Wee's (2013) timely exploration of the cross-cultural adaptations and revisions of J-horror productions situates this entire field study within a transnational context—a truly important analysis for understanding the horror niche within popular culture in an era of globalization.

Notwithstanding these valuable works, this volume has several unique features that contribute to the larger body of literature on Japanese horror films. In addition to being—at the time of the writing—the only *encyclopedia* on the English-speaking market that takes up the specific content of the J-horror genre, there are also certain features about the way this text is written that are exclusive to this volume. First, this text adopts a rather basic definition of horror as merely content intended to disturb, repulse, unnerve, or unsettle an audience. For example, although emphasizing horror as a general theme, this encyclopedia also includes other genres that fit this definition, inclusive of Japanese comedy horror, science fiction horror, hyper-violence, Japanese cyberpunk horror, ero guru (erotic grotesque), *tokusatsu* horror (live-action special effects), and anime horror. In this way, the scope of this work stretches beyond the conventional parameters of the horror film genre, offering readers a broad, and hopefully novel, perspective on the intersection between popular culture and the commercial production of horror.

In addition to this broad definition and the amount of flexibility to incorporate content outside of the typical J-horror genre that it allows for, perhaps the most distinctive contribution of this text is the corpus of essays written by such an international assemblage of authors. Spanning the globe, this international and multicultural team engenders a variety of different interpretations, explanations, and points of views—all of which should offer the reader some new insight into the horror genre in general and Japanese horror cinema in particular. To this end, this compilation of essays provides a window, albeit certainly limited, through which readers may view how Japanese horror films are received in different parts of the world—a feature that may prove as interesting as it is significant to understanding the transnational context of film today. For example, while some authors have incorporated notes on political and social constraints that have limited the pervasiveness of the films globally, others have picked up on controversial tropes associated with race, class, sex, and gender that steer some of these films away from traditional horror to a subtext of the socially horrific. Of course, as an encyclopedic endeavor, the contributors have made every attempt to produce objective output, yet in important places and, more *importantly*, important ways their critical thinking and interpretations are a valuable addition to this volume.

In an effort to integrate the different writing styles and nuances of interpretation into a much more streamlined product, I have made several standardizations and revisions with this coherency in mind. To be consistent with the English format of this text, I have indexed as much of the content as possible with English-version titles, followed by—in the case of films—the Japanese titles under which they were originally released. Additionally, Japanese names, which traditionally begin with the surname followed by the given name (e.g., Kurosawa Akira), have been reversed. Finally, although the contributors have worked diligently to provide as much accurate information as possible within their essays, some content, in particular birthdates for various individuals and release dates of a few films have been omitted—due to the unavailability of such information.

In the *Encyclopedia of Japanese Horror Films*, readers will find an enormous breadth of detailed material. With such wide-ranging content delivered through the insights of international authors, this collection is certain to draw attention to the J-horror genre. It is with great hope and anticipation that readers come to appreciate the topic, the encyclopedia, and the efforts of those that contributed to this important and timely work.

• A •

ALL NIGHT LONG films

All Night Long (1992)
DIRECTOR: Katsuya Matsumura
SCREENPLAY: Katsuya Matsumura
SPECS: 90 minutes; color

All Night Long: Atrocity (1995)
DIRECTOR: Katsuya Matsumura
SCREENPLAY: Katsuya Matsumura
SPECS: 76 minutes; color

All Night Long: The Final Chapter (1996)
DIRECTOR: Katsuya Matsumura
SCREENPLAY: Katsuya Matsumura
SPECS: 76 minutes; color

All Night Long (*Ooru naito rongu*) is a trilogy of "dove-styled" rape-revenge films (viz. *House at the Edge of the Park* [1980] and *I Spit on Your Grave* [1978]). The trilogy profiles teenage characters as they look to cure their boredom or despair via violent acts of bullying or revenge. Each film ends with a protagonist committing large-scale vengeful murders.

The first *All Night Long* film revolves around three male teenagers: (1) Tetsuya Tanaka, a socially awkward brainy student, (2) Shinji Saito, a student motivated by his unfulfilled dreams to become a pilot, and (3) Kensuke Suzuki, an overly confident rich student. The film separately traces the failing love lives of each student. However, the teenagers' lives intersect when they witness a random stabbing of a woman at a train crossing. Via the common traumatic experience, the murder creates solidarity between these three peers—and they become friends. After Saito's girlfriend is gang-raped and beaten by a street gang, the group of friends led by Tanaka, now armed and determined to reclaim a sense of agency, exacts revenge by torturing and killing the gang.

The first *All Night Long* film is often considered the mildest of the three films. The second film, *All Night Long: Atrocity*, also concerns revenge; however, the cast of characters differs from the first film. The characters' motivations and attitudes are less developed, and the violence is more graphic. Rather than exclusively depicting heterosexual relationships and desires, *All Night Long: Atrocity* explores the desires—and the subsequent violent choices—between homosexual and heterosexual groups of friends. *All Night Long: Atrocity* is often considered the most disturbing and excessive in the trilogy, but also the most complex.

All Night Long: Atrocity follows Shinichi, a socially awkward teenage bookworm, as he wrestles with his own isolation while craving female interaction. In the beginning of the film, it becomes clear that Shinichi owes a large sum of money to a gang of violent homosexuals who proceed to torture Shinichi for the money. While torturing Shinichi, the leader of the violent gang ambivalently expresses apologetic and tender remarks to Shinichi, overtly desiring him in a sexual manner. Once free from the gang's clutches, Shinichi combats his alienation by befriending two peers on the Internet. Their friendship develops and Shinichi is introduced to a common female acquaintance named Sayaka, with whom he is immediately smitten. While the new friends are at Shinichi's residence, the violent gang shows up at the house demanding their money from Shinichi. When the gang realizes that a female is at Shinichi's house, they invade the house and torture Shinichi's friends as well as Sayaka. During these violent scenes, the leader isolates Shinichi and sexually pursues him. Shinichi fights back against him and the entire gang. With the aid of one of his new friends, Shinichi vengefully murders the homosexual gang including the leader. In celebration of their survival, Shinichi's friend has sex with Sayaka. Frustrated by their sexual relationship (similar to the sexual frustration that was depicted by the leader of the gang), Shinichi kills his friend and Sayaka with a samurai sword.

The third *All Night Long* film, *All Night Long: The Final Chapter*, focuses on nihilism and misanthropy more explicitly than the other two films in the trilogy. Much like the first *All Night Long* film, the bleak urban environment is foregrounded; however, whereas the first and second films reveal occasional glimmers of optimism, this last film discloses no such optimism. The central theme "people as disposable garbage" pervades numerous scenes, punctuating the film's overall despairing and futile tone.

All Night Long: The Final Chapter accentuates teenage alienation through the central character of the film: Kikuo Sawada. Sawada, a janitor and voyeur at a "love hotel," maintains an ardent curiosity toward the objectification, examination, and possession of women. The overall plot spotlights Sawada's obsession with his attractive neighbor, Hitomi Nomura. As an introvert, Sawada does not talk to Nomura but rather comes to know her through her trash. Sawada forages Nomura's trash, collecting bags of disposed intimate artifacts, including her half-eaten food, which he proceeds to eat as a means of communing with her. With these items, he attempts to reconstruct Nomura via physical compositions of her trash and realistic computer-graphic representations. He also captures a disabled woman, whom he imprisons as a hostage. He experiments on this woman, presumably trying to understand how Nomura "works." Unlike protagonists from the previous volumes of the trilogy, Sawada never finds companionship in others. In fact, he meets a "dusthunter" (or garbage scavenger) who shares a common philosophy of trash-voyeurism; instead of building this relationship, Sawada kills the dusthunter merely to gain ownership of more garbage artifacts. As with the previous films, this one ends in blood-soaked revenge. At the end of the film, Sawada's colleagues from the love hotel abduct Nomura and Nomura's lover—presumably looking to rape them. Sawada arrives to the scene and kills everyone, including Nomura after he realizes the futility of the "conquest."

In sum, each film follows initially powerless teenage characters as they exact final revenge on teenage peers who initially possessed the power, thus reversing the power relations. However, unlike rape-revenge narratives such as *Last House on the Left* (1972) and *I Spit on Your Grave* (1978), men are the protagonists rather than women. Woman empowerment is not a chief concern for director, Katsuya Matsumura; instead, Matsumura seems more interested in character reclamation and assertion of masculinity. The trilogy also heavily depicts themes of urban alienation and nihilism, in both style and content. Based on these expressions and themes, the films cohesively work with each other, despite being three separate stories involving different characters. Alongside the *Guinea Pig* films, the *All Night Long* films are considered to be some of the most violent and controversial Japanese films. According to Tom Mes's review of *All Night Long 2: Atrocity*, it has been rumored that Japan's official censorship board, Eirin, "condemned" the second and third *All Night Long* films.

Although the original trilogy is his most celebrated *All Night Long* work, Matsumura wrote and directed *All Night Long 4* (*Ooru naito rongu R*) in 2002, *All Night Long 5* (*Ooru naito rongu: Inisharu O*) in 2003, and *All Night Long: Anyone Would Have Done* (*Ooru naito rongu: Daredemo yokatta*) in 2009. These supplementary films are less well known and not widely distributed/translated. In the tradition of the series, the films also navigate love, nihilism, and revenge.—Gavin F. Hurley

AOYAMA, SHINJI (1964–)

With strong interests in music, novels, and cinema, Shinji Aoyama graduated from Rikkyo University in 1989, majoring in American literature. While Aoyama cites the experience of watching Jean-Luc Godard's *Pierrot le Fou* (1965) and *Two or Three Things I Know about Her* (1967) in his high school years as inspiring him to consider making films, it was at Rikkyo that he was influenced by eminent film critic Shigehiko Hasumi, and began making his first films in 8 mm.

Following graduation, he worked as assistant director on Kiyoshi Kurosawa's slasher *The Guard from Underground* (1991), as well as with Go Riju, Swiss director Daniel Schmidt, and the Icelander Fredrik Thor Fridriksson. Aoyama made his directorial debut with the V-cinema project *It's Not in the Textbook!* (1995), followed by his first theatrical film *Helpless* (1996).

Aoyama entered the cinematic landscape of post-bubble-economy Japan following the watershed events of 1995: the massive Kobe Earthquake and several months later the Tokyo subway sarin gas attacks by Aum Shinrikyo. *An Obsession* (1997), marks his first entry into horror-thriller territory, departing from the premise of Akira Kurosawa's *Stray Dog* (1949) to tell the story of a detective (Ryo Ishibashi), whose gun is stolen in the midst of a cult leader's assassination and then used for murder. As his fixations grows, his relationship with his wife deteriorates.

The director's filmography reflects the development of a unique cinematic articulation of the politics of individuality, steeped in art and popular media. His work expands commercial entertainment's received boundaries of genre film and art film, and he wears his influences on his sleeve, experimenting in different recognizable genres, whether that be Yakuza, documentary, mystery, youth film, or horror.

Often emphasizing individualistic striving instead of collective, socially integrated struggle, Aoyama's films could be mistaken for popular culture's general trend toward self-centered isolation in a time of social malaise and frustrated youth culture. However, his work offers meaningful interrogations of communication, politicizing relationships between self and other. As critics such as Aaron Gerow have pointed out, Aoyama's formal innovations in camerawork and editing are characterized by long-take, long-shot scenes that avoid shot-reverse-shot psychologization (courtesy of regular cinematographer Masaki Tamura) and preclude characters' merging into the social and literal landscape while foregrounding their tension with it.

Filmmakers of the period typically dealt with death and history, however the loss or trauma Aoyama's characters suffer often mediates postwar historical amnesia. Narratives often feature unlikely strangers coming together forming improvised domestic arrangements and surrogate families against prescribed social mores and blood ties. While his most gory horror entry is *E.M.: Embalming* (1999), in which a corpse leads embalmer Miyako (Reiko Takashima) into a world of organ harvesting and cults, he is perhaps best known for the sepia-toned, over-three-and-a-half-hour-long *Eureka* (2000), which was awarded the "FIPRESCI Prize" and "Prize of the Ecumenical Jury" at the 2000 Cannes Film Festival. The film tells the story of a bus hijacking with three survivors—middle-aged bus driver Makoto (Koji Yakusho), and young brother Naoki (Masaru Miyazaki) and sister Kozue (Aoi Miyazaki)—who initiate a road trip to overcome the trauma and sense of victimhood that links them. *Eureka* extended the stories of characters from the earlier *Helpless*, later joined by *Sad Vacation* (2007) to form the "Kitakyushu Saga" set in the area of Aoyama's birth. Via *Eureka*, Aoyama's films may be regarded for their periods of near silence; however, they are just as notable for loud music and always-inventive soundtracks (which Aoyama participates in scoring).

Rather than nihilism, his films foreground creation amid the limits of communication and the impenetrability of people's interiority in life and cinematic representation. Such as in *Eli, Eli, Lema Sabachthani?* (2005), a lo-fi sci-fi tale of a near future in which a pair of noise musicians (Tadanobu Asano and Masaya Nakahara) are found to produce frequencies capable of curing the "Lemming Syndrome" that is causing a wave of suicides across the world. Throughout his career as a director, Aoyama has continued writing about film in print and online, publishing a book of film theory and criticism and collections of interviews with directors and writers and editing a book on Wim Wenders. In addition, he has also written several novels, including the novelization of *Eureka* in 2001, which was awarded the "Yukio Mishima Prize." Aoyama has taught at the Film School of Tokyo, Tokyo University, and Tama Art University, and he is married to Maho Toyota, star of his *Desert Moon* (2001).—Joel Neville Anderson

APARTMENT 1303 (2007)
DIRECTOR: Ataru Oikawa
SCREENPLAY: Ataru Oikawa, Kei Oishi, Takamasa Sato
SPECS: 94 minutes; color

Based on Kei Oishi's (b. 1961) novel of the same name, *Apartment 1303* tells the story of a determined young woman who investigates the apparent suicide of her sister and the horrible secrets she finds.

The film opens with a woman unpacking boxes in an upscale, seaside condo. After a quick phone call with her boyfriend on his way there, she hears a strange noise in the tatami room along with a gust of wind. There is also a foul smell coming from a closet, which she opens, and screams in terror at an unseen threat. As her boyfriend arrives, a little girl and her mother pass him. The girl grabs his hand and shows him his girlfriend hanging from the balcony, then falling to her death.

A month after this apparent suicide, Sayaka, played by Aki Fukada (b. 1983), moves into the same apartment. She is enjoying her newfound freedom with her friends, and she jokingly tells them the building is famous for ghosts, especially one who asks for the thirteenth floor looking for her eyes. The real reason she got the apartment for a good price is because it is located far from town, or at least this is what the real estate agent told her.

One of Sayaka's friends goes looking for her dog, and finds it in the tatami room. She smells something foul and Sayaka goes to investigate the closet. When she comes out, she acts strangely and eats the dog's food. To her friends' horror, she then puts on a motorcycle helmet, grabs her teddy bear, and jumps off the balcony. A little girl takes the teddy bear from Sayaka's dead grasp.

At her funeral, Sayaka's sister Mariko, played by Noriko Nakagoshi (b. 1979), talks to Sayaka's boyfriend, who doesn't believe her death was a suicide, and Mariko sees an apparition of a bloodied Sayaka revealing that their mother pushed her. When Mariko returns home, she finds her mother, played by Naoko Ōtoni (b. 1950), grief stricken and resentful that Sayaka was the one who died, since Mariko seems emotionless over her sister's death. Mariko is hurt and baffled over the suicide, as she remembers the day when Sayaka left for the new apartment.

She is tasked with packing up Sayaka's apartment and is met by the little girl in the elevator who tells her that the "big sister" next door gave the teddy bear to her. They exit the elevator and the girl goes into the apartment next to Sayaka's. As Mariko packs, she remembers tender moments and memories of her sister from a photo album she finds. She also steps on an earring that is not Sayaka's, and when a gust of wind blows through the balcony window, Sayaka's phone rings. Mariko picks it up and finds texts telling of Sayaka's excitement over the apartment, asking her boyfriend to move in with her, and a photo of her with the teddy bear. She goes next door to ask the girl once more about the teddy bear and her "big sister next door" but is interrupted by the girl's mother arriving home, who looks annoyed that they were talking.

Mariko sees her sister's mute ghost again and is soon overcome with grief over her loss. Looking at more pictures on Sayaka's phone, she finds one with an apparition in the background. She then hears a noise in the closet and when the lights flicker and the room shakes she realizes it's a minor earthquake and not the paranormal.

On her way out, Detective Sakurai, played by Arata Furuta (b. 1965), waits for her. He has a report listing five suicides, including Sayaka's, in the same apartment, as well as articles about a mother and daughter who died there as well. He gives her a book about the murder/suicide and after Mariko argues with her hysterical mother, who says hurtful things to her, goes off to read the book. Apparently, a girl named Yukiyo, played by Eriko Hatsune (b. 1982) and her mother, played by Shion Machida (b. 1971) moved into the apartment, where over the years her mother drank, abused Yukiyo, and went mad. When she attacks Yukiyo over her newly pierced ears, Yukiyo stabs her, and she dies in the tatami room closet where she decayed for months as Yukiyo "cared" for her corpse. Haunted by her mother's ghost, Yukiyo finally took her own life after realizing she had no money and nowhere else to go, jumping off the balcony. Mariko sees a picture of the teddy bear in the book, realizing Sayaka and the little girl had the same toy. She has a terrifying dream within a dream after finishing the book, and is startled awake by Sayaka's presence.

The apartment has been quickly rented out to some young men, and they plan a party. When Mariko finds out there are new tenants, she is enraged and confronts the deceitful real estate agent, who plays dumb. Once again, Sayaka appears, frightening Mariko. At the party in 1303, the jealous entity strikes again. She is only interested in punishing women, and grabs the girls by their hair, throwing them to their deaths. Mariko and the detective drive past the condo after a heart-to-heart and see the aftermath. In a series of scenes, we see Mariko go to the apartment, where she finds her mother, who has been missing all day, in a trance; the mummified corpse of Yukiyo's mother; and Yukiyo's ghost, who tricks Mariko when she asks her why she killed her sister, appearing as the little girl hanging from the balcony rails.

When Mariko tries to help her up, she is attacked by Yukiyo's ghost; Mariko tries to bargain with her, even offering to be her sister. Yukiyo vanishes and Mariko goes to the balcony, where the ghost reappears and startles her, and she falls, hanging onto the balcony railing. Yukiyo tells her that there is only one girl for her mother. The detective looks up in time to see Mariko fall to her death.

This 2007 mother-daughter vengeful ghost story is a generic, albeit disjointed, J-horror film reminiscent of *Ringu* and *Ju-on*. Director Ataru Oikawa, who also directed three films from the Tomie series, follows the onryō and the long-haired spirit trope with both the mother and daughter doing ghostly damage, as well as the grimly popular topic of suicide in Japanese culture. There are a few suspenseful moments, and while the film is more compelling in the second half, critics have charged that it is not Oikawa's best. *Apartment 1303* had a North American remake called *Apartment 1303 3D* released in 2013 that was unanimously panned.—Carolyn Mauricette

See also Ju-on series; Oikawa, Ataru; *Ringu*

Bibliography

"*Apartment 1303*." IMDb. Accessed 29 May 2015. http://www.imdb.com/title/tt0841993/.

"*Apartment 1303 3D*." Michael Taverna, dir. *Rotten Tomatoes*. Accessed 29 May 2015. http://www
.rottentomatoes.com/m/apartment_1303_3d/.

Balmain, Colette. "Haunted Houses and Family Melodramas." In *Introduction to Japanese Horror Film*, 136–37. Edinburgh: Edinburgh University Press, 2008.

Meyer, Matthew. "Onryo." Accessed 29 May 2015. http://yokai.com/onryou/.

Oikawa, Ataru, dir. *Apartment 1303*. Amuse Inc./T.O. Entertainment Inc., 2007. DVD.

Traphagan, John W. "Japan's Suicide Problems: Searching for Answers." *Diplomat*, 16 January 2013. Accessed 29 May 2015. http://thediplomat.com/2013/01/searching-for-answers-japans
-suicide-epidemic/1/.

ARAI, RYŌHEI (1901–1980)

Born on 22 October 1901, Ryōhei Arai was, as an actor, screenwriter, and Japanese director, a pioneer in the Japanese motion picture industry. From the 1930s to

1950s, he directed some forty-seven films, by and large specializing on *jidaigeki* (period drama) and *kaidan eiga* (tales of ghosts), both steeped in traditional folktales. The former more often involved familiar tales of disenfranchised samurai warriors and revenge, while the latter focused on the *kaidan* classics of the Edo and Meiji periods and, in particular, *bakemono* (ghostly apparitions). Because films from the prewar period competed directly with other popular entertainments, especially the lively antics found in Kabuki performances, his works rely upon the stylization of elaborate sets and dramatic techniques, often incorporating into the action accepted conventions from the stage. Among these, aerial acrobatics and unexpected, exaggerated, and improbable images are central to much of his work.

Notable among his early films is *Tsubana(ri) Ronin* (1939), a typical *jidai geki* first released by Nikkatsu Film Company on 30 December 1939, just in time for movie-going crowds eager to celebrate the New Year. Based on a story by Tsunoda Kikuo (1906–1994) and developed as a screenplay by Hisa Yoshitake (1904–1981), the film stars such prominent Kabuki-trained actors as Bandō Tsumasaburō (1901–1953) and Hara Kensaku (1905–2002)—as well as newcomers to the stage, Japanese film actress and singer, Ichikawa Haruyo (1913–2004), for example. There is an extraordinary amount of attention paid to the costuming of the major characters. Hardly the typical rank-and-file military drama, the performance, recalling Kabuki, is highly dependent upon great shows not of strength but of agility, while the plot depends upon a particular group of ronin samurai, bent on avenging their master's honor. In turn, the ronin were themselves obliged to commit *seppuku* (traditional samurai suicide) for committing the crime of murder.

The major characters are *tsubanari*, extremely loyal samurai warriors known for their mastery of *iaijutsu*, a combative quick-draw sword technique characterizing the Japanese *koryū* martial art disciplines. The slightest movement in the peripheral vision of these individuals leads them to perceive a threat. Because their reflexes are so highly developed to the point of overkill, they automatically strike at anything in their way. Swift and often unforeseeable, their involuntary reflex actions often form the basis of exaggerated fight scenes where they kill and re-sheath their sword before anyone realizes what has taken place. It is, then, less their action than the resulting gore and bloodletting that catch and hold the attention of the audience. They devote their full power to the strike as they strike, but it is in hindsight that anyone might take notice that their swords were in some way damaged. The *tsubanari* appear aloof and distanced from the action, often appearing not to see the carnage before them. This true story was popularized in Japanese culture as emblematic of the loyalty, sacrifice, persistence, and honor that people should preserve in their daily lives. The popularity of the film coincides with a rapidly modernized Japan already involved in an escalating Fifteen Years War (1931–1945), and in this sense it contributes to an ongoing discourse of the larger issues, national heritage and identity. So very popular was the first film that its sequel, *Zoku Tsubanari ronin* (1940), was released less than a month later.

Following the end of the Second World War, Arai refocused his attentions on the ghost tales, in particular on the well-known legends of ghosts having taken the form of cats. Historically, there had been a long-held prohibition on the selling of cats, and as a result feral cats could be found roaming the streets. Traditional folktales quickly associated these with the *bakeneko*, or cat demon, known for their supernatural abilities to walk on their hind legs and to fly, to speak, and in many instances to individuals, to shape-shift and even to resurrect the dead. As expressions of the horror of the demonic, for example, their powers also expressed an abiding awareness of the supernatural. The first of these works, *Ghost-Cat of Arima Palace* (1953, *Kaibyō Arima goten*), stars Japanese actress Irie Takako (1911–1995). Later that year, Arai released *Ghost of Saga Mansion* (1953, *Kaidan Saga yashiki*), further expanding the already-popular tales. Both works were successful, if largely because they elicited negative emotional reactions from the audience by playing on their most primal of fears, while simultaneously captivating and entertaining at the same time in a cathartic experience. Cats remain a familiar feature in the Japanese horror film.

The following year, Arai would return to the *jidai geki* and familiar tales of disenfranchised warriors with the release of *Virtuous Men of Akō* (1954, *Akō gishi*), based upon the popular tales of the forty-seven samurai as they decide to take revenge of their master's death. Noted actors from the genre Kurokawa Yatarō (1910–1984), Bandō Kōtarō (1911–1981), Sanjo Miki (1928–2015), and Shindō Eitarō (1899–1977) were cast as *Ako Gishi*, or retainers of the Ako-han Domain. Well-received as a vehicle for revenge and battle certainly, in this instance there is a renewed focus on scenes of blood and gore, as well as dismembered corpses all around, moving the *jidai geki* even closer to an increasingly popular genre of horror films.

Thereafter, Arai continued to direct but with less and less financial success as audiences abandoned his outmoded depictions for the spectacle, as well as the turmoil and uncertainty, of the 1960s. Some two decades later, he passed—even as his works passed into increasing obscurity—on 22 October 1980.—James A. Wren

Bibliography

"Arai Ryōhei." Nihon eiga jinmei jiten: Kantoku hen. *Kinema Junpō.*

Arai, Yoshio. *Chichi to eiga to watakushi.* Tokyo: Shinjusha, 1981.

Leiter, Samuel L., ed. *Rising from the Flames: The Rebirth of Theater in Occupied Japan, 1945–1952.* Lanham, MD: Lexington Books, 2009.

Sharp, Jasper. *Historical Dictionary of Japanese Cinema (Historical Dictionaries of Literature and the Arts).* Lanham, MD: Scarecrow Press, 2011.

Worland, Rick. *The Horror Film: An Introduction.* London: Blackwell Publishing, 2006.

ASATO, MARI (1976–)

There have been some notable female filmmakers working within the modern Japanese horror scene over the years: Shimako Satō, director of the quintessential teen horror films *Wizard of Darkness* (1995) and *Birth of the Wizard* (1996); Kei Fujiwara, former associate of Shinya Tsukamoto and director of challenging body-horror meditations *Organ* (1998) and *ID* (2005); and Kayoko Asakura, director of postmodern slasher flick *It's A Beautiful Day* (2013). One of the most successful is Mari Asato, director of the recent genre hit *Bilocation* (2012) and the live-action adaptation of the Fatal Frame (aka Project Zero), survival horror game franchise. One of several young would-be filmmakers recruited as crew members (in her case, as photographer) on Kiyoshi Kurosawa's *Barren Illusion* (1999), Asato also served as Hiroshi Takahashi's assistant director on *Sodom the Killer* (*Sodomu no Ichi*, 2004).

Okinawa-born Asato made her debut in 2004 with *Samurai Chicks* (*Dokuritsu shōjo gurentai*), a politically charged martial arts movie that takes place against the backdrop of "The Kingdom's" struggle for independence from its powerful neighbor. Undercut somewhat by its English title, it's a well shot and occasionally inventive movie hampered by budgetary constraints and a weak cast. Asato's second release of 2004 was *Boy from Hell* (*Jigoku Kozō*), the first installment in a series of low-budget features based on the works of horror manga icon Hideshi Hino, Hideshi Hino's Theater of Horror. One of the best episodes of the series, *Boy from Hell* manages to capture the weird, psychedelic feel of the source material, as well as Hino's grotesque sense of humor.

Since then Asato has become a prominent part of the horror scene, contributing to a number of established franchises. She was one of two directors (the other being Ryūta Miyake) selected to helm the first of a pair of new *Ju-on* films to commemorate the tenth anniversary of the series, *Ju-on: Black Ghost* (*Ju-on: Kuroi Shōjo*) and *Ju-on: White Ghost* (*Ju-on: Shiroi Rōjo*), both released in 2009. Scripted by each director, the films develop a new mythos but maintain a connection to their predecessors by using the Gary Ashiya score of the original V-Cinema installments. Asato also directed *Twilight Syndrome: Dead Go Round* (2008), a blackly humorous adaptation of the Nintendo DS game franchise; coincidentally, the second movie in the series would be handled by Takeshi Furusawa, director of *Another* (2012) and an assistant director on *Barren Illusion*.

In 2011 Asato's career entered its most active (and successful) phase. As well as helming three sequels to Issei Shibata's surprise sci-fi/horror hit *The Chasing World* (*Real onigokko*, 2008) and *Cellular Girlfriend* (*Keitai kanojo*, 2011), a V-Cinema sequel to Shinju Funabiki's *Cellular Boyfriend* (*Keitai kareshi*, 2009), Asato also directed *Ring of Curse* (*Gomen Nasai*, 2011), a multimedia project featuring *idoru* (idol) group Buono! playing the primary roles. Although nominally another "cursed item" knock-off (this time a notebook), it develops beyond that as class pariah Kurohane finds new ways to punish her victimizing classmates and her callous family. A sizeable hit in Asian markets, *Ring of Curse* is considerably better than the majority of *idoru* projects, mainly because Asato manages to get surprisingly decent performances from the three Buono! members.

With *Ring of Curse* raising Asato's profile and bringing her films to new audiences, the director moved on to her most ambitious project so far, an adaptation of Haruka Hōjō's best-selling novel, *Bilocation*. With Asami Mizukawa (*Dark Water*, *The Locker*) taking the lead role, *Bilocation* (2013) is the story of artist Shinobu who discovers that her life is being sabotaged by her "bilocation," a *doppelgänger* determined to replace her. With the help of a group of people in the same situation, Shinobu struggles to understand what is happening and keep hold of the best parts of her life—her husband and her career—before her bilocation steals them permanently. Although *doppelgängers* are not uncommon in horror, *Bilocation* avoids recycling the clichés and provides a series of well-thought-out plot developments to keep the viewer's interest right up to the unusual but entirely appropriate ending. Hailed as one of the best Japanese horror films of recent years, *Bilocation* picked up a number of favorable reviews at film festivals.

Thanks to the success of *Bilocation*, Asato was hired to direct a live-action adaptation of the lucrative Fatal Frame survival horror franchise, also known as

Project Zero. The games are an intensely atmospheric experience, one that transfers well to the predominant style of contemporary Japanese horror. Adapting a novelization written by Eiji Ōtsuka, creator of the Multiple Personality Detective Psycho series, Asato's film has performed well on its domestic release and is expected to be a substantial hit in foreign markets.—Jim Harper

ATTACK GIRLS' SWIMTEAM VS. THE UNDEAD (2007)
DIRECTOR: Koji Kawano
SCREENPLAY: Satoshi Owada
SPECS: 78 minutes; color

Attack Girls' Swimteam vs. the Undead, alternately titled *Undead Pool* and known as *Joshikyōei hanrangun* in Japanese, is a 2007 erotic-horror film that incorporates strong grindhouse thematic elements. The film is directed by Koji Kawano (b. 1972). The storyline revolves around the hapless students and faculty of a high school that is unwittingly infected with a virus that transforms nearly everyone into rapacious zombies. This flesh-driven film follows the few immune survivors through a festival of carnage.

The film opens with the solitary scene of a young lady swimming laps in a pool. She is troubled throughout with a sequence of premonitory hallucinations of being followed and grasped by someone.

The film then cuts to the swim team discussing an upcoming meet. The coach is a hard-boiled masochist that brooks no excuses and abuses his athletes. Meanwhile, the school is suffering from an unknown virus. Amid this, "Aki," played by Sasa Handa (b. 1985), a new transfer, is just arriving to the all-girl school and gaining her bearings.

Aki wanders the school and decides to visit the swimming pool. As Aki gazes into the pool, "Sayaka," played by Yuria Hidaka (b. 1983), arrives and decides to playfully push this new transfer into the water. Aki and Sayaka proceed to shower together and discover that they have matching birthmarks on their breasts.

The swim coach hears water running and enters the shower to find it empty. As he angrily grumbles about showering protocol, he is stabbed to death by an unseen assailant. This first scene of graphic violence sets the tone for the remainder of the film.

Despite exhortations that students and faculty report to the nurse's station for mandatory vaccinations, Aki and Sayaka decide to retreat to the roof. Sayaka asks Aki to join the swim team and Aki ignores the request. In another intimate moment, Aki notes a mole identical to her own on Sayaka's neck and pauses perplexedly.

The swim team discovers the body of their coach. They abandon the body and meet in the locker room to discuss how to proceed. At this moment the coach appears in the locker room unscathed and assures his team that he is perfectly healthy and that he will report the assault to the authorities after the swim meet. The coach is uncharacteristically upbeat and smiles maniacally.

The film quickly erupts into gratuitous violence as the students and faculty succumb to the virus. Decapitations, dismemberments, and sexually driven violence ensue throughout the campus. Soon everyone, except the swim team, is dead or infected and festooned with gore.

Amid the mayhem, Aki discovers that it was the inoculations that caused the virus. She also concludes that some property about swimming in the pool has made the swim team immune.

The swim team decides to convene in the locker room when they are waylaid on their path by an infected teacher. Aki nearly dies saving Sayaka. When she awakens, Sayaka is serving Aki food and reassures her that everything will be fine. Aki blames the entire incident on herself and commences to confide in Sayaka that she is a trained assassin and a genetically modified human created by a virologist, geneticist, and assassin known to her only as "Doctor." Aki explains that after her training she decided to abscond to a high school in search of a normal life. She fears that she is the harbinger of the current bedlam caused by Doctor and his search for her. Emotionally driven by the conversation, the two engage in a passionate sexual encounter. Immediately after the sexual interlude, they discuss the possibility that because they are both orphans that they could be twins based upon their matching birthmarks. This fact is almost immediately dismissed except that Sayaka now wants to privately refer to Aki as "Big Sister."

Aki and Sayaka rejoin the swim team to fight the zombie scourge. They begin to douse the infected with pool water and discover that the chlorine is a cure for the student body. The faculty, however, was treated with a different virus and is unaffected by the chlorine.

A flashback is then inserted of Aki masturbating to Doctor playing the flute. The flute seems to have some mysterious power over her; she is incapacitated by it, which allows him to have intercourse with her. This scene seemingly motivates Aki to try to solve the zombie problem unassisted.

Upon Aki's departure, Sayaka rallies the swim team to help Aki. Dressed in their swimsuits, they launch a full offensive against the zombies. The swim coach reappears, seemingly uninfected and inexplicably joins his swim team against the zombies only to turn on them shortly thereafter. The entire team is summarily dispatched leaving only Sayaka and the coach. With only Sayaka left unharmed, the coach removes an elaborate mask to reveal that he is "Doctor."

Aki is found by Doctor and he attempts to render her into a helpless state of sexual arousal with his flute. Aki manages to resist him with earplugs. In a state of rage he injects himself with both zombie virus strains and mounts an attack. Aki manages to overcome and kill him, and then runs off to find Sayaka.

Sayaka is tied up outside of the school. Aki unties and resuscitates Sayaka only to discover that Sayaka was part of an elaborate ruse. As it turns out, Sayaka was another student of Doctor. Sayaka was tasked by Doctor to lay in wait at a nearby high school in anticipation of Aki's eventual defection.

Sayaka has managed to dose Aki with a paralyzing agent during the resuscitation. Moments before Sayaka can plunge a knife into Aki, Doctor reemerges and shoots Sayaka. Doctor explains to Aki that she has killed his twin brother. To his delight, he reveals to Aki that there have always been two persons acting as Doctor unbeknownst to her.

This identical, yet physically less imposing, twin takes advantage of Aki's paralysis and begins to sexually assault her. Aki manages to regain some of her movement and turns the tables by seducing him. While the twin is enraptured by her tantalizing behavior, she shoots a laser beam from a device inserted in her vagina. This other Doctor explodes into a bloody mass of body parts.

Naked and blood soaked, Aki walks to the pool and strikes Sayaka's name from the swim team's list in blood; after which, she decides to take a dip. An incoming call, recorded on the school's answering machine, informs the swim team that they have been disqualified from the swim meet. Aki then drowns in the pool due to a side-effect of the paralyzer.

The film received mixed to mostly negative reviews. Its nearly pornographic nature has a limited appeal. Moreover, the fragmented plot disrupts the narrative. For die-hard erotic-horror fans, this film might have an appeal; otherwise, it represents a footnote in an overwrought genre.—Evan Marmol

Bibliography

Kawano, Koji, dir. *Attack Girls' Swimteam vs. the Undead.* Switchblade Pictures, 2007. Film.

AUDITION (1999)

DIRECTOR: Takashi Miike
SCREENPLAY: Daisuke Tengan
SPECS: 115 minutes; color

Audition is a 1999 psychological horror film directed by Takashi Miike and adapted from a novel by Ryū Murakami. It is arguably Miike's most famous work among Western audiences and can be credited for launching his international cult following and ongoing reputation as a vulgar auteur. Despite its controversial content, the film received positive critical reviews and is regarded highly among other horror directors as well as genre aficionados.

The film's protagonist is "Aoyama," played by Ryō Ishibashi, a middle-aged widower and successful video producer who, at the urging of his teenage son, played by Tetsu Sawaki, decides it is time to remarry. When Aoyama confesses he is unsure of how to find the ideal bride, a colleague devises a scheme to host a fake casting call for the female lead in a romance film, during which Aoyama can meet and interview the candidates during their auditions. Aoyama is ambivalent at first, but agrees to participate. Sifting through the candidates' profiles, he finds himself intrigued by "Asami Yamazaki," played by Eihi Shiina, a young woman whose application essay recounts her struggles with depression after a hip injury shattered her dreams of becoming a professional dancer. At her "audition," Asami proves to be beautiful and demure, and Aoyama is instantly smitten. They begin a courtship, and Asami expresses her excitement at having someone take an interest in her.

During a weekend getaway, Asami disappears after a night of lovemaking. A frantic Aoyama searches for her, but his investigation grows increasingly disturbing as he learns that Asami's professional acquaintances have long since been murdered or have gone missing. Aoyama returns home to process his findings when he begins to lose focus; his liquor has been drugged. Falling unconscious, he hallucinates details from Asami's past: we learn that, as a child, Asami was sexually molested by her ballet instructor and has since been enacting violent revenge on the men who have wronged or lied to her. She is also holding one of her mutilated victims captive in her apartment, having sewn him into a large sack and treating him like a feral pet.

As Aoyama lies paralyzed on his living room floor, Asami arrives and explains that she knows the audition was a ploy to lure and manipulate women for sex; at this point, it is unclear if she understands that Aoyama was searching for a romantic partner. She tortures him, stabbing him in the stomach and eyes with needles and then severing one of his feet with piano wire. Eventually, she is interrupted by the arrival of Aoyama's son, and after a struggle, he manages to knock her down a flight of stairs. As Asami lies dying from a broken neck, she looks across the floor at the incapacitated Aoyama and repeats her earlier statement of joy at having found someone to care for her. The film's final image is a flashback to Asami as a child, lacing up her ballet slippers.

Audition is concerned thematically with gender politics and issues of trust and power between men and women, exemplified most by Aoyama's moral ambiguities—he is presented as a lonely, sympathetic character, and by all measures a thoughtful and caring father, who nevertheless participates in orchestrating the fraudulent audition. The film's hallucinatory sequences also reveal his subliminal evaluations of women based on sexual criteria, as he is haunted by fantasies of the various women in his life, including a colleague, his housekeeper, and even one of his son's classmates. Some interpret the film as a tale of female revenge against male chauvinism, particularly in professional settings, and that Asami's acts of torture are symbolic of castration.

The film is noteworthy for its abrupt tonal shift midway through the narrative; the first act plays like a sentimental romance, and it is not until approximately forty minutes into the film that we learn Asami is not all she claims to be. There are also extended sequences in which it is uncertain whether Aoyama's experiences are real or hallucinated, rendering many of the plot's details unreliable; this includes a momentary possibility that all of the horrors of the final act have been just a dream. These surreal characteristics, combined with disturbing content and grisly images, have spurred comparisons to the works of David Cronenberg or David Lynch, which have continued to frame analyses of Miike's auteurism.

Upon its release, *Audition* gained immediate notoriety for its climactic torture sequence, which reportedly caused audience members to flee from theaters during festival screenings. *Audition* is also one of the seminal films of the so-called "Asia Extreme" brand, popularized by the DVD company Tartan, which distributes contemporary East Asian genre films in the West.—Mike Dillon

See also Miike, Takashi

• B •

BAKENEKO

A *bakeneko* or "ghost cat" is a type of Japanese *yōkai*, a monster from traditional folklore. According to legend, a cat that laps the blood of a murder victim has the power to take on the person's *urami* or hatred, giving the animal the ability to seek revenge against those responsible for the crime. Ghost stories and woodblock prints from the Edo Period (1600–1868) occasionally depict them as cats grown to enormous size, although the portrayal of *bakeneko* by actors in the Kabuki theater popularized the notion of the creature taking on the form of the (usually female) murder victim. *Bakeneko* tales were the single most popular subject of Japanese horror films from the dawn of cinema through the 1960s, with more than sixty such pictures released by 1970.

The half-feminine, half-feline werecat version of the *bakeneko* quickly found its way from the Kabuki stage to Japanese cinema screens in the early years of the twentieth century. No fewer than twenty-nine *bakeneko* pictures were made during the silent era. Although none of these films survive, written evidence suggests they were likely rather straightforward adaptations of their theatrical counterparts, with the important addition of trick photography to portray the ghost cat's supernatural powers. As was the industry norm at the time, male actors who specialized in female impersonation portrayed the female humanoid *bakeneko* onscreen. Japan's first movie star, Onoe Matsunosuke played a *bakeneko* at least once.

By the end of the 1920s actresses had replaced the female impersonators on film, and the main site of spectacle in *bakeneko* pictures and other horror films of the day shifted from trick photography special effects to the body of the actress, who typically underwent a beauty-to-beast transformation from suffering heroine to vicious *bakeneko* or hideous ghost halfway through the picture. The most popular of this new breed of monster movie actresses was Sumiko Suzuki (1904–1985), a onetime vamp whose career found a second wind in the 1930s via her many appearances in Shinkō Studio's *kaidan* ghost story adaptations and *bakeneko* movies. Dubbed "the *bakeneko* actress," Suzuki's large, coquettish eyes, intense gaze, and onscreen physicality combined alluring femininity and fearsome monstrosity in a manner that bewitched prewar audiences. Although only one of Suzuki's prewar *bakeneko* performances—the 1937, *The Cat of Arima (Arima neko)*—survives, her striking portrayal of the titular monster makes it easy to see why she was the most popular Japanese horror movie star of her time. Following Suzuki's retirement from film in 1941 and the subsequent years of war and occupation that saw horror films suppressed by government policy, the *bakeneko* returned to Japanese movie screens in the early 1950s in the persona of the second great "*bakeneko* actress," Takako Irie (1911–1995). Appearing in a series of remakes of the prewar Sumiko Suzuki *bakeneko* pictures produced by Shinkō's successor studio, Daiei, Irie's on-screen transformations from beautiful maiden to savage monster were even more extreme than Suzuki's, featuring more elaborate and grotesque makeup. The films themselves, however, were generally panned by critics, who found their dated, Kabuki-derived antics less than frightening for postwar audiences.

One such antic was the *neko jarashi* or "cat toying" scene, a hallmark of the Suzuki and Irie *bakeneko* films in which the ghost cat possesses the body of one or more of its victims, forcing them to perform a series of acrobatics before sinking its teeth into their throats. A direct holdover from Kabuki *bakeneko* plays, the *neko jarashi* typically begins with a servant discovering her mistress is actually a *bakeneko* by witnessing her lap the oil from a lantern, the silhouette of a cat's head cast by the flickering light. The extended acrobatics that follow interrupt the narrative flow for a sequence of marked-off spectacle, with professional acrobats and contortionists doubling for the monster's possessed victims and traditional shamisen musical accompaniment that broke sharply from the films' otherwise Western orchestral scores. Daiei's *neko jarashi* increased in complexity with each subsequent entry in the series, but despite the venerable tradition behind them, they were more whimsical than bone-chilling.

Two of the most successful postwar *bakeneko* films were Nobuo Nakagawa's *Mansion of the Ghost Cat* (*Bōrei kaibyō yahsiki*, 1958) and Yoshihiro Ishikawa's *The Ghost Cat of Otama Pond* (*Kaibyō Otama ga ike*, 1960). Made at the struggling Shintōhō studio, which was Daiei's main rival in horror film production during the 1950s, both films lacked a star actress in the *bakeneko* role but compensated with the technical innovations of widescreen and color, along with an emphasis on moody, atmospheric suspense over elaborate makeup and Kabuki theatrics. The Shintōhō *bakeneko* films also mark an important shift in the development of the Japanese horror film, featuring contemporarily set prologues and epilogues that pluck the monster out of the fairy tale Edo past to haunt present-day Japan. The invasion of traditional ghosts and monsters into the mundane, modern world would become one of the defining motifs of the J-horror movement decades later, and Nakagawa's and Ishikawa's films prefigure this turn from classic *kaiki* ("strange" or "bizarre") films to contemporary *horā* ("horror") pictures.

The production of horror films declined sharply in Japan after 1970, and apart from the 1975 porno *The Ghost Cat in the Turkish Bath* (*Kaibyō Toruko furo*) the once-omnipresent *bakeneko* subgenre of Japanese horror vanished from the silver screen. Nonetheless, *bakeneko* traditions continue to inform contemporary J-horror. Toshio, the little boy ghost at the center of the Ju-on franchise, howls and wails with the voice of a deranged feline to incredibly horrific effect, and the series hints that he is actually a *bakeneko*, with shots of the murdered boy's pet cat lapping the blood of its young owner. If the critics once deemed the Kabuki acrobatics of Sumiko Suzuki and Takako Irie laughable instead of frightening, in Toshio's terrifying form the *bakeneko* may have the last laugh.—Michael Crandol

See also The Ghost Cat of Arima Palace; The Ghost Story of Saga Mansion; Irie, Takako; Ju-on series; *Kuroneko;* Suzuki, Sumiko

BATTLE ROYALE (2000)
DIRECTOR: Kinji Fukasaku
SCREENPLAY: Kenta Fukasaku
SPECS: 114 minutes; color

Battle Royale is a 2000 gore-horror thriller film directed by Kinji Fukasaku (1930–2003). The film, based on the dystopian horror novel by the same title written by Koushun Takami and published in 1999, tells the story of a group of high school students who are forced by the government to kill all other classmates in three days, in a bizarre competition to become the only survivor.

The plot of the film revolves around a group of high school students of the same class, randomly chosen by the government to participate in a cruel game of survival. During a school trip they are induced by gas to sleep on the bus. They awake in an old school, which is located on an uninhabited island and realize that all of them have been fitted with an electronic collar that transmits information of the geographic position and the physical condition of the students. The collar is designed to automatically detonate the explosive it contains if the students try to take it off.

After they awake, "Kitano," played by Takeshi Kitano, a former teacher of these students, explains the situation to them: the "Battle Royale Law" establishes that every year one classroom of a high school has to participate in a game, which has been approved as a measure to reduce the increasing unemployment and combat teenagers' rebellions. The rules of the game establish that in three days students must fight between them until only one of them survives. To promote the fight and avoid students from hiding themselves, every six hours several danger zones are declared, so if a student remains in one of these zones, the collar will explode. Moreover, when the period of three days is over, if there is more than one survivor, all collars will explode. The students also find out that two students who participated and won the previous editions of the game will join the fight. When the game finally starts, all students receive a backpack with some food, water, a map, a compass and, in some cases, a defensive or offensive weapon.

After the game starts, the film shows how students respond to the situation in several different ways: a few of them who cannot bear the idea of killing or being massacred prefer to commit suicide; while some willingly participate by trying to take revenge for previous offenses they endured during their high school experiences. Others try to discuss the situation with fellow classmates and convince them not to participate in the killings; however, misunderstandings and lack of trust lead to murder after murder. Other groups try to survive without killing or attack the headquarters where Kitano and the army control the game.

The film caused controversies in Japan and other countries for its high level of cruelty and graphic fight scenes. However, it was shown in more than twenty countries and is considered one of the best movies directed by Kinji Fukasaku.—Alex Pinar

BIG MAN JAPAN (2007)
DIRECTOR: Hitoshi Matsumoto
SCREENPLAY: Hitoshi Matsumoto, Mitsuyoshi Takasu
SPECS: 113 minutes; color

Big Man Japan, known in Japanese as *Dai Nihonjin*, is a 2007 mockumentary written, directed, and starred in by the comedian Hitoshi Matsumoto. The story is about a man named "Masaru Daisatō"— of rather average character, divorced, and living a life of relative poverty in his filthy Tokyo apartment. Inheriting an ability to transform himself into a giant man with the help of high voltage electricity, Daisatō commits to a mission of protecting Japan against monster attacks. The film premiered at Cannes Film Festival and got a favorable reception by critics and audience. After Cannes Film Festival the film was shown in several international film festivals in Europe, East Asia, and the United States with huge success.

Hitoshi Matsumoto is a comedian known as *Macchan*, born in Amagasaki, Hyōgo prefecture. Matsumoto grew up in a poor family, a fact that, as he always remarks in television shows, helped him to become a comedian. When he was a teenager aiming to become a TV comedian he wrote a poem transformed in 2004 into a song, explaining how growing up in poverty influenced his decision to find alternative ways of entertainment and intensified his sense of humor. After graduating from a technical high school in 1982 he enrolled at the Yoshimoto Kōgyō, a major Japanese entertainment company based in Osaka. The same year, alongside his friend Masatoshi Hamada they formed the celebrated comedy duo called *Dauntaun* ("Downtown" in English), arguably one of the most famous comic duos in Japan today. After this first successful initiation in the film business he directed three more films, *Shinboru* (2009), a peculiar fantasy story about a man who wakes up in a white room with no doors or windows; *Saya Samurai* (2010), the comic adventures of a renegade samurai; and *R–100* (2013), the story of an ordinary man in an S&M club in Tokyo. The filmic style of Matsumoto's works is a heterogenic mixture of eccentric humor, oneiric environment, and science fiction.

The popularity gained in TV programs from as early on as the mid–1980s encouraged Matsumoto to write, direct, and perform in *Big Man Japan*, a film that combines the classic *kaijū* genre with the eccentric sense of humor of Matsumoto's style and a touch of contemporary drama. Conventional monster movies usually work around science fiction and horror genres, but Matsumoto's documentary perspective is an innovative element that amplifies a dramatic component. Matsumoto depicts the life of an ordinary man fighting against monsters, inclusive of aliens from outer space and marketing agents that have leased his body in a commercial enterprise to broadcast advertisements—a subtle metaphor of the excesses of capitalism. Additionally, the film forges a parallel story about Daisatō's attempts to reinstate a relationship with his daughter, as well as a struggle against his own lack of self-esteem.

The entire movie is recorded by an unnamed documentarian that peers into Daisatō's seemingly ordinary life vis-à-vis his all but ordinary battles against bizarre monsters. The style of the film is then a mockumentary about Daisatō; with the director following and interviewing him, as well as others he interacts with. This unique display of peering into the adventures of a quasi-superhero with a rather ordinary life suggests the delivery of a certain amount of social commentary on the part of Matsumoto—most of which is associated with alienation, estrangement, and a need to feel significant in an era steeped in the loss of individual autonomy. The elements of horror arrive prepackaged with humor and

creativity that arguably add something altogether new to the J-horror genre.—
Nieves Moreno Redondo and Fernando Ortiz-Moya

THE BIG O

The Big O is a twenty-six-episode giant robot anime series that incorporates elements of the film noir, detective, and science fiction genres. Produced by Sunrise, created by Keiichi Sato (b. 1965), and directed by Kazuyoshi Katayama (b. 1959), *The Big O* draws heavily upon classic American and Japanese films and television programs to spin a tale of giant robot battles, mass amnesia, and dangerous secrets set in a retro near future. Although not an initial success in Japan upon its premiere in 1999, international airings were well received and led to the commissioning of a second season in conjunction with Cartoon Network and Bandai.

The main character in *The Big O* is Roger Smith, a millionaire negotiator in Paradigm City and pilot of the titular Big O, a giant robot referred to as a "megadeus." Forty years prior to the beginning of the series, an unspecified catastrophe known as the "Event" took place that destroyed the world outside of "Paradigm City" and erased the memories of the surviving inhabitants. The disaster, which is later shown to be partly the result of an attack by an army of giant robots, gave Paradigm the nickname of the "City of Amnesia." As a negotiator, Smith takes on various jobs for the citizens of the city, many of which involve secrets of the past or the recovery of lost memories, which includes forgotten artifacts and technology as well as actual recollections of the time before the Event. He is assisted in his task by the usually dour and emotionless android R. Dorothy Waynewright, his butler Norman Burg, and military police chief Dan Dastun. A sometime-ally, sometime-adversary arrives in the third episode in the form of the mysterious Angel, who often crosses paths with Smith, much to the annoyance of R. Dorothy. As Smith plies his trade as a negotiator, he is often forced into the role of a detective and is drawn into conflict with sinister elements both within and without Paradigm City, which tend to end in a confrontation against another megadeus.

The series shifts tone in the second half, moving away from episodes chronicling Roger Smith's work as a negotiator to a connected story arc in which Roger works to uncover the secrets of Paradigm City, the Event, and of his own existence. A group of survivors from outside the city, named the Union, emerge as a threat, and Roger enters into direct conflict with Alex Rosewater, the shadowy ruler of Paradigm City. In the confusing series finale, Paradigm City is revealed to be a virtual reality construct either created or controlled by Angel. After Roger's final showdown with Alex Rosewater, Angel transforms into a megadeus, erasing existence as she moves through the city. As a manifestation of Angel views the Big O facing down her megadeus alter ego while listening to Roger's entreaties for her to forget the past and live in the present on monitors in a television studio control room, she is interrupted by another Roger and Dorothy. Reality within Paradigm City vanishes in a flash of light as the Angel megadeus and Big O collide. In the final moments of the series, Roger, Angel, and Dorothy reprise an altered initial scene from the first episode as the story loops back upon itself. The meaning of the ambiguous ending and the truth behind the mystery of Paradigm City has since been subject to multiple interpretations by fans.

The visual style of *The Big O* is similar to the American production *Batman: The Animated Series*, which Sunrise helped to animate. The series pays homage to a wide variety of influences, as Smith and his entourage bear marked similarities to Bruce Wayne, recurring villain Beck resembles *Lupin III*, and the giant robot battles are inspired by action sequences in *tokusatsu* (special-effects) films. Although set in a future complete with androids and giant robots, most of the technology, fashions, and architecture call to mind 1930s and 1940s America and classic film noir settings. The muddling of reality and the virtual that characterizes the end of the series is a hallmark of screenwriter Chiaki J. Konaka's (b. 1961) earlier series, *Serial Experiments Lain*. The anime also benefits from solid voice acting in both languages by industry professionals. *The Big O* enjoyed critical success, and Japan saw the publication of a short-lived manga. Although originally envisioned as a potential franchise, the series ultimately ended with the second season.—Daniel Fandino

BIG TITS ZOMBIE (2010)
DIRECTOR: Takao Nakano
SCREENPLAY: Takao Nakano
SPECS: 73 minutes; color

Big Tits Zombie (*Kyonyū doragon: Onsen zonbi vs. sutorippaa 5*) is a 2010 satirical horror film written and directed by Takao Nakano, based on the *Kyonyū Dragon* manga by Rei Mikamoto. Sora Aoi, Risa Kasumi, and Mari Sakurai star as performers in a gentleman's club who stumble upon a cursed tome that raises an army of the undead.

This film is ostensibly a satire, but to any casual viewer, *Big Tits Zombie* seems much more like a film that glorifies Japanese pop culture's idiosyncrasies instead of lampooning them. Writer-director Takao Nakano is known primarily as a producer and performer in *pinku eiga*. This film, like many of its kind, stars an adult video actress, lending to the film necessary degrees of eroticism and legitimacy. *Big Tits Zombie* represents an important milestone for star Sora Aoi, who, since the film's release, has gone on to star almost exclusively in mainstream roles in Japan, South Korea, and Indonesia.

Fans of the manga have noted a number of substantial differences between the film and its source material. The screen versions of Ginko/Rock and Maria differ greatly from their manga counterparts and the girls are revealed as the cause of the zombie outbreak, whereas in the manga, no explanation is offered. The zombies in manga and film alike are notable for retaining their memories and intellect, unlike most zombies featured in the genre.

The film's deliberately poor staging is likely intended as a jab at the pink films where Nakano made his name. Ramshackle sets, amateurish costuming, and papier-mâché monsters are punctuated with heavy splashes of computer-generated gore—the film revels in the absurd, a characteristic of many of Nakano's films. Scenes filmed in 3-D add to the B-movie atmosphere.

A group of zombies ambushes an exhausted Ginko, played by Risa Kasumi, in an abandoned restroom. Lena, played by Sora Aoi, wielding a chainsaw, arrives to save her. They fight their way through the zombies as Lena recounts how they got there.

A week earlier, Lena returns from a long trip abroad with no money. After breaking into a homeless man's shelter and sleeping with him, Lena accepts an offer from an old acquaintance to come dance at his gentleman's club. When she arrives, the club's bouncer, Yudai, played by Ini Kusano, picks her up and tells her the story of the derelict spa next to the club.

Lena settles in with the other strippers: Maria, played by Mari Sakurai, a well-read Goth complete with self-harm scars; Nene, played by Tamayo, an older performer with maternal instincts; Darna, played by Io Aikawa, who doesn't speak Japanese and just needs enough money to get home; and Ginko, a hardened woman with a shadowy past.

The girls make a regular habit of flirting with Yudai. One day they are able to force him to admit that the club will soon be closed, even though none of them have been paid. After confronting the owner, they're offered a temporary gig with a local massage parlor. When the girls arrive at the parlor, they realize that they have been hired as sex workers rather than masseuses. A group of wealthy men arrives and the girls perform their act for them. The leader of the group proposes that Ginko and Lena wrestle for their entertainment, with the loser forced to serve at a nude sushi bar. Lena manages to knock Ginko off balance and wins the match. The leader then propositions Lena; she declines but sleeps with him anyway after becoming extremely drunk.

The next day, Ginko berates Lena about her habit of sleeping around. The ensuing melee reveals a secret door to the basement, where the girls discover all kinds of intriguing artifacts, among them a "Book of the Dead"—from which Maria reads several of the incantations. Darna hides a box of yen in the basement. When she returns for it, she is ambushed and devoured by zombies.

Meanwhile, Nene and Ginko realize something has happened when their dinner reanimates. The town of Ikagawa and then the whole of Japan become infected as the girls try to escape. Maria betrays the others and returns to the secret room to reclaim the Book of the Dead. She recovers the book and discovers a way to control the zombies.

The others fight their way to the spa that they learned of the day prior. A mutated Darna tries to rape and kill Lena, but Lena manages to decapitate her. Ginko finds the zombified man who killed her sister and impales him with an umbrella, but she succumbs to her wounds after she and Lena fight their way to Maria. While Lena and Marie fight, an ogre emerges from the "Spirit Well" and pledges to return the dead to their rightful place. He drags Maria down into Hell. The film ends as Lena and Ginko's ghost extort their salary from their former club owner.

Alternately absurd and entertaining, *Big Tits Zombie* demonstrates the lengths to which some directors will go in order to incorporate the next novel idea into the zombie subgenre. The film is riddled with the objectification of females and the exploits that arise therein, yet somehow the gore that overlays the storyline obscures the potentially offensive nuances that *Big Tits Zombie* presents.—Boleyn Key

THE BIRTH OF JAPAN (1959)

DIRECTOR: Hiroshi Inagaki
SCREENPLAY: Ryuzo Kikushima, Toshio Yasumi
SPECS: 182 minutes; color

The Birth of Japan (literally translated to *Nippon tanjō* in Japanese, but also internationally known as *The Three Treasures*) is a *tokusatsu* (special effects) film directed by Hiroshi Inagaki and produced by Tōhō studios in 1959. Celebrated as Tōhō's one-thousandth production, the film offers a big-budget spectacle in color and *Tōhōscope* (the studio's version of CinemaScope) re-creating the indigenous mythology of the Japanese nation's origin. The original script is inspired by the historical records and myths found in the *Kojiki* and the *Nihon Shoki*—the two oldest accounts of the creation of Yamato (ancient name of Japan) and the fundamental texts for the Japanese national religion of Shinto. In particular, the narrative of *The Birth of Japan* combines the legendary story of Japan's so-called first national hero, Prince Takeru Yamato, with episodes of the "age of gods" such as the formation of the Japanese archipelago by the sibling deities *Izanagi* and *Izanami*; the reign of the sun goddess, *Amaterasu*; and the descent to Earth of the god of the sea and the storm, *Susanoo*. The famous actor Toshirō Mifune plays both Yamato Takeru, the main protagonist of the film, and the boisterous god, *Susanoo*.

In addition to Takeru, the film features a star-studded cast, inclusive of Kinuyo Tanaka, Kōji Tsuruta, Takashi Shimura, Kyōko Kagawa, Akira Takarada, Haruko Sugimura, and Setsuko Hara. The technical staff is equally impressive, involving many members of the team who made *Godzilla* films for Tōhō. In *The Birth of Japan*, Eiji Tsuburaya, the talented creator of the *kaijū* and science fiction classics, is the director of the special effects. Tsuburaya is accompanied by producer Tomoyuki Tanaka, art director Akira Watanabe, and music composer Akira Ifukube. Under the direction of Inagaki, this production staff contributes to some of the most famous fantasy and epic events of Japanese religious and popular traditions ever to materialize on screen. Perhaps the talents of this productions staff are most evident in such scenes as the fighting scene between *Susanoo* and the eight-headed dragon *Yamata no Orochi*, which was created by Tsuburaya and his team using a complex machinery structure to move and animate the giant monster—a true feat for its time in the history of filmmaking. Complementing the spectacular representation of this celebrated *kaijū*, some other scenes of the film also make remarkable use of special effects, creating, for example, a terrifying sea storm that threatens the hero's vessel and a volcanic eruption followed by a tsunami that destroys an entire army of men. These outstanding technical achievements of Tsuburaya in *The Birth of Japan* were celebrated with the "Best Special Effects Award" of the year, a prize conferred annually by *The Motion Picture and Television Engineering Society of Japan*. Additionally, the cinematography of Kazuo Yamada and the lighting of Seichiro Ijima also received awards, accompanied by critical acclaim.

The Birth of Japan was released in the autumn of 1959 and became a big box office success. Inagaki's film was the most profitable production for Tōhō in 1959 and was also ranked as the second-most-lucrative Japanese film of the year. Tsuburaya's special effects, the presence of many stars in the cast, and the appeal of a well-known traditional legend were surely decisive factors in the film's success. Moreover, being an epic spectacle film, *The Birth of Japan* was also conceived as a suitable production to be exported and the film was theatrically released in countries such as the United States (1960) and Spain (1972). More recently, Tōhō has released the film in different Japanese DVD editions, as a single DVD (2001), as a part of a DVD box set containing other *tokusatsu* science fiction films (*Tōhō tokusatsu-kūsōkagakubako*, 2007), and as an individual DVD of a Tōhō "special-effects films" collection (*Tōhō tokusatsu eiga DVD korekushon*, no. 37, 2011).—Alejandra Armendáriz Hernández

BLACK CAT MANSION (1958)
DIRECTOR: Nobuo Nakagawa
SCREENPLAY: Jiro Fujishima, Yoshihiro Ishikawa
SPECS: 69 minutes; black and white

Black Cat Mansion (aka *Mansion of the Ghost Cat*, original Japanese title: *Bōrei Kaibyō Yashiki*), is a 1958 ghost film that was directed by Nobuo Nakagawa (1905–1984), who is famous for his ghost and horror films of the 1950s and 1960s. The film tells the story of a possessed cat that is in pursuit of vengeance, making it a typical example of *bakeneko-mono* or ghost-cat tale. The film interlinks the encounter of a married couple with the spirit in contemporary Japan with events from the spirit's past during the Edo period. While the latter era is depicted in color, scenes set in the present are shot in black and white.

In the opening scene, we see Dr. Kuzumi on a night shift in a hospital, where the cries of a black cat mix with the sound of rain and thunder. Porters push a trolley carrying what appears to be the dead body of a man through the pitch-black corridors. The sound of footsteps of unknown origin cause Dr. Kuzumi to pause and reflect on the horrors of six years earlier, when he and his wife, Yoriko, were terrorized by a ghost.

Having moved to Yoriko's hometown seeking therapy for her tuberculosis, the couple moved into an old mansion that was rumored to be haunted. However, undeterred, the couple turn it into Dr. Kuzumi's new clinic. An ominous old lady frequently appears. She kills the family dog and uses her ability to speak in different voices to lure Dr. Kuzumi away from his wife before attempting to strangle her. Dr. Kuzumi learns the notorious story of the house from a local priest. The mansion is haunted by a cat ghost who is in search of vengeance for misdeeds committed by the former owner, samurai Lord Shogen.

Lord Shogen murdered the young gō master Kokingo after a dispute over a match and, with the help of his retainer Saheiji, hid his body behind a wall. Kikingo's blind mother, Lady Miyaji, knowing the short-tempered and aggressive character of Lord Shogen, feared the worst before a vision of her dead son confirmed her suspicions. When she confronted Lord Shogen, he raped her, which drove her to commit suicide; however, before doing so she asked her beloved cat Tama to seek vengeance. The vengeance spirit is able to enter the Lord's mansion and gain control of the body of Shogen's old mother, whom we recognize as the old woman from the earlier scenes of the movie. The spirit, now often in the form of an elderly woman/cat hybrid, spreads discord between Shogen and his son over their affection for the young servant girl Yae and haunts Lord Shogen with nightmares and visions of a blood-stained Kokingo. Shogen grows increasingly unstable and eventually kills Yae after mistaking her for the dead Lady Miyaji. He then attacks his son, believing him to be Kokingo. By the end of the priests' account, both the father and son are dead.

Having learned about the events of the past and discovered that Lord Shogen's retainer Saheiji was one of Yoriko's ancestors and thus an object of the spirit's vengeance, Dr. Kuzumi tries to protect his wife using a charm that was given to him by the priest. However, the following night the charm is carried away by the wind and, left unprotected, Yoriko is strangled by the spirit. When Dr. Kuzumi finds her lying lifeless on the floor, the wall of the living room opens and Kokingo's mummified body appears.

In the final scene, we return to the hospital and find Yoriko alive and visiting her husband. Their conversation informs us that the haunting ceased once the mummified body of Kokingo was buried. At the end of the film, Yoriko discovers a kitten in the laboratory and, despite her past fear of cats, decides to keep it as a pet.

While the director's choice to use both black and white and color was originally related to the need to reduce the budget, Nakagawa's use of gloomy monochromatic sets and images to depict the present and vivid color to portray the past is one of the most memorable elements of the film. This approach allows him to fully exploit the power of color through vivid depictions of blood-stained walls and clothes, and the use of swirling kaleidoscopic lighting effects that are designed to emphasize Shogen's unstable state of mind.—Till Weingärtner

See also Jigoku; Kaidan Kasane-ga-fuchi; Nakagawa, Nobuo; *Tokaido Yotsuya kaidan*

Bibliography

Nakagawa, Nobuo, dir. *Black Cat Mansion.* Shintōhō, 1958. Film.
Suzuki Kensuke, ed. *Jigoku de yōi hai! Nakagawa Nobuo. Kaidan kyōfu eiga no gōka.* Tokyo: Waizu Shuppan.
Takisawa Osamu and Yamane Sadao, eds. *Eiga kantoku Nakagawa Nobuo.* Tokyo: Liburo Bōto 1987.

BLIND BEAST VS. KILLER DWARF (2001)

DIRECTOR: Teruo Ishii
SCREENPLAY: Teruo Ishii
SPECS: 95 minutes; color

Blind Beast vs. Killer Dwarf, also known as *Mōju vs. Issun-bōshi,* is a 2001 erotic grotesque (or *ero guro*) mystery thriller film directed by Teruo Ishii (b. 1924). This film is Ishii's last directorial credit before his death in 2005. It is also the last low-budget film produced by Ishii's production company, Ishii Teruo Production. This film is an original screenplay written by Ishii based on a blend of three Edogawa Ranpo novels: *Blind Beast, Issun-bōshi* (One-inch boy), and *Odoru Issun-bōshi* (The dancing dwarf). The film was produced in 2001 and was screened at the 23rd Pia Film Festival, but was not officially released until 2004 (released by Slowrunner) due to difficulty in finding a distributor.

The film follows a struggling novelist, Monzo Kobayashi, played by Lily Franky (b. 1963) and his longtime friend and famous detective, Kogoro Akechi, played by Shinya Tsukamoto (b. 1960), trying to solve bizarre crimes committed separately by a dwarf, played by Little Franky, and a blind man known as the

"Blind Beast," played by Hisashi Hirayama. First, there is a series of crimes that seem to be completely unrelated: an amputated foot is found in the sewer; Kobayashi runs into a dwarf carrying an amputated arm; Michiko Yamano, played by Tomoko Matsumoto, goes missing; and Ranko Mizuki also goes missing. Kobayashi is approached by Yurie Yamano, played by Reika Hashimoto (b. 1980), to ask his longtime friend Akechi to help find her missing step-daughter, Michiko. During the investigation, Kobayashi and Akechi reason that the arm Kobayashi saw the dwarf carrying is Michiko's arm and conclude that she is dead. Shortly after learning of Michiko's death, Yurie encounters the dwarf, who threatens her in an attempt to coerce her into becoming his lover.

While Akechi and Kobayashi are trying to solve the mystery of Michiko's death, Ranko is held captive by a blind man in a white womb-like hidden room filled with plastered body parts. During her captivity Ranko is physically abused by the blind man and later stabbed to death by him. More amputated body parts are found and Akechi initially hopes these instances are connected to Ranko's disappearance; yet it turns out to be a prank set up by a Sanka (Japanese Gypsy) girl as an attempt to inflict revenge on a pawnshop owner.

Meanwhile, audiences learn that the blind man is a masseur who works at a bathhouse, luring his victims in with his massaging skills. Suddenly, a plastered woman's body is found by a statue and is identified as Ranko. With this discovery, Akechi gradually solves Ranko's mysterious death.

After a heated pursuit of the dwarf by Akechi and Kobayashi, the dwarf falls off the roof and suffers irreparable injuries. Akechi gathers everyone to reveal the truth behind Michiko's disappearance. He reveals that Michiko was fighting with Komatsu, the maid, played by Kaname Wakaba, over a driver named Fukiya, played by Mitsuhiro Oikawa, and in a fit of romantic jealousy accidentally killed Komatsu. Hoping to hide this truth, Yurie, with the help of Fukiya, disposes of Komatsu's body, allowing Michiko to disguise herself as a maid and ultimately carry on with Fukiya. Fukiya takes Komatsu's body to a local temple and asks the dwarf to help him dispose of the body. At this point, the dwarf, who had been enamored with Yurie, begins to pursue Yurie and coerce her into a romantic relationship.

In the end, the blind beast sends Akechi a letter confessing to the murders, promising to surrender to the police and release his three hostages under one condition: that art critic Tetsuro Tange, played by Testuro Tamba (b. 1922), witnesses what the beast calls "tactile art"—the preservation of the dead bodies he has plastered in clay. Akechi, Kobayashi, and the police are able to have Tange look at this art piece, but as Tange beats the work with his cane out of anger, they discover that the blind beast has committed suicide and become part of his art piece.

As the last film by Teruo Ishii, who is also frequently heralded as the "king of cult," the film engages with erotic desire that straddles the boundaries of beauty and the grotesque. Similar to many of his other films, the erotic and grotesque imagery is used as key components of character development or as a centralized visual/thematic motif rather than a device that propels the story. Indeed the storyline drives itself regardless of what characters find or what the audience knows. Ishii's playful engagement with narrative structure, character development, and *ero guro* imagery is visible in this film through the abrupt editing, limiting the grotesque imagery to select scenes, and framing it in ways that hide more than they reveal. Despite the low budget for production, the film features many famous actors and figures such as Sion Sono, who makes a cameo as a drunken man. The film is also known for featuring Mieko Tanaka nude before she was elected to Parliament as a representative of the Democratic Party.—Yuki Nakayama

See also ero guro nansensu genre

Bibliography
Ishii, Teruo, dir. *Blind Beast vs. Killer Dwarf.* Ishii Teruo Production, 2001. Film.

BLOOD: THE LAST VAMPIRE (2000)
DIRECTOR: Hiroyuki Kitakubo
SCREENPLAY: Kenji Kamiyama
SPECS: 48 minutes; color

In the land of media mix, in 2000, Production I.G. launched one of its largest franchises with *Blood: The Last Vampire*. Directed by Hiroyuki Kitakubo, known for *Roujin Z* (1991), the film revolves around a young vampire slayer named Saya, set in the High School of Yokota Air Base. Saya is charged with the mission of tracking down and destroying a lair of demonic creatures called "chiropterans"—a sort of humanoid bat—who have the ability to disguise themselves as humans. There is a secret international organization hunting down these creatures, although Saya seems to be the only one capable of following their trail and recognizing them.

The screenplay is cleverly deceptive in this respect because one never knows what or who Saya is exactly. The boundary between good and evil is blurred and part of the narration's terror lies in the unknown, giving audiences only a few hints to solve the mystery. Along these lines, Kitakubo was inspired by the themes created by David Fincher in his thriller *Se7en*, which the Japanese director watched prior to starting his own film.

The classic vampire storytelling of *Blood: The Last Vampire* is improved through technical innovations, as Production I.G. sought to create a new visual style. To do so, for the first time in Japan they created a film made completely of digital animation; that is, the staff refrained from the traditional use of cel animation throughout the production process. Moreover, the team combined this technique with computer-generated imagery to enrich the background, putting the studio at the forefront of innovative procedures applied to animation. As noted by the company's president, Mitsuhisa Ishikawa, this was the reason why the OAV (original animated video) lasts forty-eight minutes, because if it were extended, the quality of the anime would have been compromised. The movie rapidly acquired a cult following and it was the very first cross-platform piece created for one homonymous manga (2002), three light novels (*Blood: The Last Vampire* [2001]; *Blood: The Last Vampire: Night of the Beasts* [2002]; and *Blood: The Last Vampire: A Tragic Dream in Shanghai* [2005]), two video games in 2000 and 2006, two animated TV series spin-offs (*Blood+* [2005–2006] and *Blood C* [2011]), and one live-action adaptation namesake coproduced among Hong Kong, France, the United Kingdom, and Japan in 2009.

The OAV was the product of a series of sessions led by Mamoru Oshii. "Team Oshii," as it was dubbed, brought together the young talents from Production I.G. Of this effort, two ideas were produced: the first one, provided by Jun'ichi Fujisaku, involved an angry young woman wearing a schoolgirl's uniform and carrying a katana, while the second plot was called *The Last Vampire*, created by Kenji Kamiyama—today one of the studio's leading filmmakers. At that moment, the company was looking for a new project to produce, so Oshii proposed making a film combining both concepts. As a result, Fujisaku, Oshii, and Kamiyama began to craft the horror film together. The original plan involved a trilogy planned for release on video for the domestic market. However, in the end Production I.G. only developed the central installment of the proposal and did not adapt the other two stories. The film took care of every detail from the stunning design of characters by the artist Katsuya Terada to the bilingual English-Japanese dubbing that was needed due to the interaction of American and Japanese speakers in the film, although the English voice artists sound artificial and unnatural.

Although remarkably outstanding in its visual achievements, *Blood: The Last Vampire* is less original in its plot, especially in depicting the stereotyped young female in uniform—a suggestive trope often used to meet male *otaku* expectations. Throughout its history, anime has provided interesting works using themes of horror and vampires. The most prominent of these are: *Vampire Princess Miyu* (1997–1998); Yoshiaki Kawajiri's beautiful *Vampire Hunter D: Bloodlust* (2000), the second movie based on a Hideyuki Kikuchi novel; *Hellsing* (2001–2002); *Trinity Blood* (2005); *Dance in the Vampire Bund* (2010), and the comical and unclassifiable parody *Nyanpire* (2011).—Laura Montero Plata

BLOODTHIRSTY films

Legacy of Dracula (1970)
DIRECTOR: Michio Yamamoto
SCREENPLAY: Hiroshi Nagano, Ei Ogawa
SPECS: 71 minutes; color

Lake of Dracula (1971)
DIRECTOR: Michio Yamamoto
SCREENPLAY: Ei Ogawa, Masaru Takesue
SPECS: 82 minutes; color

Evil of Dracula (1974)
DIRECTOR: Michio Yamamoto
SCREENPLAY: Ei Ogawa, Masaru Takesue
SPECS: 87 minutes; color

Although it has been suggested that the *yuki onna* (snow woman) is essentially a Japanese vampire, the traditional bloodsucker is not indigenous to Japan. In the past they have either been imported from foreign parts or not really supernatural creatures at all, as in Nobuo Nakagawa's 1956 film, *Vampire Moth*, the very first Japanese vampire movie and an informal riff on the "old dark house" classic, *The Cat and the Canary*. When Nakagawa returned to the theme three years later in *Female Vampire* (1959), he took the more popular approach of making the Shigeru Amachi bloodsucker a European refugee. In keeping with this trend, Kimiyoshi Yasuda's special effects in the classic *Yokai Monsters: Spook Warfare* (1968) has a vampire from ancient Mesopotamia plaguing eighteenth-century Japan, while Hajime Satō's delirious cult classic *Goke, Body Snatcher from Hell* (1968) portrays Earth being invaded by a race of bloodsucking extraterrestrials. One of Shintoho's last releases, the notorious *Vampire Bride* (1960), directed by Kyōtarō Namiki, is also one of the few movies of the period to include a genuinely Japanese vamp.

Many Japanese vampire films can be unsatisfying for Western viewers, primarily because their creators are either unaware of or uninterested in the various aspects of Western vampire lore. With no indigenous traditions to draw upon (like China's "hopping vampires"), writers will often create their own mythos or take concepts from elsewhere (the creature in Nakagawa's *Female Vampire* only becomes a vampire during the full moon, for example). However, this unorthodox approach can sometimes be refreshing, bringing in welcome changes to the tradition-bound world of vampire legends. This is certainly the case with the Bloodthirsty films, as the Michio Yamamoto trio of vampire films has become known.

The first in the series is *Legacy of Dracula* (1970), released in the United States as *Vampire Doll* and *Night of the Vampire*, and also known as *Fear of the Ghost House: The Bloodthirsty Doll*. It was followed in 1971 by *Lake of Dracula*, also released as *Japula* (!), and often referred to as *Cursed House: Bloodthirsty Eyes*; and in 1974 by *Evil of Dracula*, aka *Bloodthirsty Rose*. All three films would be directed by Yamamoto and released by Toho.

Legacy of Dracula begins in classic gothic horror fashion, with a young man arriving at a desolate mansion in the middle of nowhere, on a dark and stormy night. Having been away on business for several months he is keen to see his girlfriend, but arriving at her home he is told that she died a short while ago. When the man himself disappears, his sister (Kayo Matsuo of *Lone Wolf & Cub: Baby Cart at the River Styx*) and her boyfriend go in search of him, convinced there is something very wrong at the foreign-style mansion deep in the countryside.

Of the three films, *Lake of Dracula* is the closest to a traditional (that is, Western) vampire movie, with very little that is Japanese about it. When a mysterious box is delivered to a house close to hers, artist Akiko, played by Midori Fujita, finds herself plagued by visions of a sinister black-clad figure with golden eyes. At the same time, local doctor (and Akiko's fiancé) Takashi, played by Chōei Takahashi, struggles to pinpoint the cause of a series of mysterious deaths in the area, all of them caused by loss of blood. The situation worsens when Akiko's sister falls prey to this unusual disease, only to return to life and attack her.

Like Jimmy Sangster's *Lust for a Vampire* (1971), *Evil of Dracula* is set in a girls' school, but it retains the same contemporary setting as the earlier films. Teacher Shiraki, played by Toshio Kurosawa, arrives at an isolated girls' school deep in the Hokkaido countryside to take up a position as psychology lecturer. A number of things strike him as somewhat unusual: the principal's wife was killed in a car crash a few days earlier, and her body lies in a coffin in the basement; the principal has already decided that Shiraki will be his successor, despite the fact that the two men have only just met; one of the students has mysteriously disappeared, soon to be followed by another one. Like many Euro-horror movies, the isolated girls' school setting in *Evil of Dracula* is a hothouse of sexual tension and adolescent hormones, with half the girls immediately in love with their new teacher, and happy to proposition him openly, while the French master has already picked up an unpleasant reputation for leering at his students.

Although not directly related, the three films share a number of common characteristics. All three take place in predominantly isolated locations: northern Honshu in *Lake of Dracula* and Hokkaido in *Evil of Dracula* (no specific location is named in the first film, although it is also a distant, rural area). A similar sprawling and a foreign-style gothic mansion features prominently in each of the films. Most important is the nature of the vampirism, which often relates back to a distinctly Western origin. *Lake of Dracula*'s vampire is a foreigner living in Japan, with the "curse of vampirism" carried on through his family's bloodstream, but only becoming active in the last descendant. In *Evil of Dracula* the vampire was a *gaijin* (foreigner or foreign) missionary who was forced to recant his religious beliefs. Having done so he was cursed by his God with a craving for human blood. Only *Legacy of Dracula*'s vampire is Japanese; but even so, she is part of a diplomat's family who maintained close links with foreigners in Japan, with the implication that they have been "infected" by their associations. The specific cause of her vampirism is actually an echo of the classic Edgar Allan Poe story "The Facts in the Case of M. Valdemar" with the victim having been hypnotized just before her death, allowing her to continue existing in a half-dead, half-alive state.

Often mischaracterized as lackluster attempts to relocate the Hammer film ethos into Japan, most of their bad reputation comes from the badly dubbed, cut, pan-and-scan versions that circulated on US television and later on VHS in the 1980s. While Yamamoto was clearly influenced by Hammer's gothic vampire tales, these three films are not quite the slavish, misguided knock-offs they have been frequently accused of being. For a start, they all present unusual, original portrayals of vampires and vampirism that avoid recycling many of the usual clichés. Yamamoto's bloodsuckers rarely behave like Christopher Lee or Bela Lugosi, preferring out-of-the-way locations where they can quietly and safely continue their existence. Dracula meets his end because he tries to relocate to London; in contrast, the principal in *Evil of Dracula* has lasted generations by keeping a low profile and taking as few victims as possible.

This is not to suggest that Hammer films were not an influence at all; it's most likely that *Lake of Dracula* was inspired by Terence Fisher's *Brides of Dracula*, with its lone vampire imprisoned by his own family, eventually escaping to pursue a specific female victim. It's also the only film in the trilogy to use the name Dracula. By the same token, it's unlikely that Hammer would conceive of a monster like the vampire in *Legacy of Dracula*: a miserable, unwilling creature that did not ask to be kept alive and plaintively begs its victims to kill her. When she dies, there is no Christopher Lee–style howl of frustration, just a welcoming resignation.

These three films form interesting additions to the early 1970s cycle of contemporary vampire films and deserve their place alongside Bob Kelljan's *Count Yorga, Vampire* (1970), William Crain's *Blacula* (1972), and the Dan Curtis–produced TV movie *The Night Stalker* (1972). It's also worth noting that (like the *Count Yorga* films), *Legacy of Dracula* and *Lake of Dracula* predate Hammer's own attempts to bring their vampires into the twentieth century, beginning with Alan Gibson's *Dracula A.D. 1972.*—Jim Harper

THE BLOODY SWORD OF THE 99TH VIRGIN (1959)
DIRECTOR: Morihei Magatani
SCREENPLAY: Jiro Fujishima, Susumu Takaku
SPECS: 82 minutes; black and white

The Bloody Sword of the 99th Virgin (*Kyūjūkyū-honme no kimusume*) is a 1959 film directed by Morihei Magatani about a remote mountain village in northern Japan which practices ritual human sacrifice. One of the Shintōhō Studio's most notorious releases, its current copyright holder, Hōei Kokusai, refuses to distribute the picture, giving rise to the mistaken belief that the film is banned in Japan. Savage, inbred mountain dwellers became a staple of the horror genre in films like *Deliverance* (1972), *The Hills Have Eyes* (1977), and even Japan's own *X-Cross* (2007), but *The Bloody Sword of the 99th Virgin*'s explicit use of the term *Burakumin* for its villains makes it particularly offensive for many Japanese. The nation's "untouchable caste," *Burakumin* were openly discriminated against well into the twentieth century and continue to face hardships, both economic and social, in Japanese society, making any future official release of the film unlikely.

The film begins *in media res* with two men in the woods capturing a deranged, feral-looking old woman, played by Satsuki Fujie, whom they bring to a rural police station in Iwate Prefecture. The woman slips away before they can make it inside, however, and the police disbelieve the men's tale of how the old crone abducted their two young female companions while camping in the mountains. Laying the matter aside, the chief of police later asks a relatively new recruit from Tokyo named Abe, played by Bunta Sugawara, to try and persuade the nearby mountain shrine's priest, Yugebe, played by Yoichi Numata, to adhere to the centuries-old custom of the upcoming "Fire Festival" and vacate the mountain for the duration of the observance. Tradition holds that any outsiders who remain on the mountain will be murdered for sacrilege, but the progressive Yugebe sees the festival as an opportunity to bridge the cultural gap between the mountain-dwelling *Burakumin* and the people who reside at the foot of the mountain, and refuses to leave the shrine. Accompanied by an admiring young woman from the *Burakumin* village named Azami, played by Namiji Matsura, Yugebe goes to see the village headman, played by Arata Shibata, and explain his intentions. The headman disapproves of Yugebe's plan, remarking that increased interaction between the *Burakumin* and the "city people" would be disastrous. Azami's betrothed, the half-wild Goromaru, also expresses his disapproval of Yugebe to Azami's mother, the old woman who has in fact kidnapped the two missing female tourists.

On the eve of the festival the love-struck Azami suddenly stabs Yugebe, explaining to the shocked priest that it was the only way to get him to leave the mountain and save his life. As Yugebe recovers in the hospital, the villagers conduct the once-in-a-decade Fire Festival ritual, during which the headman sacrifices the two abducted women and bathes a newly forged sword in their blood. Upon examining the sword, however, he proclaims the ritual a failure, citing the women's "impure blood." The following day Yugebe returns to the shrine with Abe and the other police, where they discover a hidden basement chamber that contains ninety-eight swords, many of which appear to be centuries old. The police later find the bodies of the two murdered women on the mountaintop, along with the skeletal remains of several other victims.

Learning that Yugebe has found the ninety-eight swords and given them over to the police, the enraged villagers capture and execute him, despite the tearful objections of Azami. Explaining that the ninety-ninth sword must still be bathed in the blood of a virgin to appease the mountain deity, the headman demands the life of Azami unless her mother can find a replacement within two days. The old woman ventures down off the mountain where the police soon arrest her for the abduction and murder of the two tourists. At the station the old woman catches sight of the chief's young daughter, and when Goromaru and others from the village come at night to break her out of the jail, they murder the chief's wife and take the girl back to the village to be sacrificed. Abe and the other police give chase and a bloody battle between the cops and the *Burakumin* ensues, with Abe shooting the headman just as he is about to sacrifice the chief's daughter. Failing to complete the ritual, the wounded headman commits suicide in front of an effigy of the mountain deity as the film comes to a close.

Although infamous today, Shintōhō's *The Bloody Sword of the 99th Virgin* caused little commotion at the time of its release. Like the portrayal of blacks and other ethnic minorities in classic Hollywood cinema, the negative stereotyping of *Burakumin* in motion pictures was an accepted practice at the time. The image of *Burakumin* as inbred, uneducated, superstitious, and murderous that was in part perpetuated by wholly fictional films like *The Bloody Sword of the 99th Virgin* had very real and unfortunate consequences, such as the 1963 murder conviction of a *Burakumin* based solely on shaky circumstantial evidence. Shintōhō's successor company Kokusai Hōei released *The Bloody Sword of the 99th Virgin* on VHS during the early days of home video, but increased awareness of the mistreatment of *Burakumin* and the spread of *Burakumin* rights groups during the 1980s and 1990s makes it a film that today the company would like to pretend doesn't exist. While rumors that the movie was banned by the government are untrue, few films are as securely locked away from the public. In 2010 the Udine Far East Film Festival in Italy requested a print for screening, which Kokusai initially declined. The company finally granted the festival permission to show the film, but with the mandate that all those in attendance were to be checked at the theater entrance for recording equipment, lest bootleg copies find their way back to Japan and Shintōhō's dirtiest secret be unleashed.—Michael Crandol

See also Okura, Mitsugu; *X-Cross*

Bibliography
Magatani Morihei, dir. *The Bloody Sword of the 99th Virgin.* Shintōhō, 1959. Film.

BOTAN DORO

Among *kaidan*, or Japanese ghost stories, that of *Botan Doro* (The Peony Lantern), the tale of a man who falls madly and strangely in love with a woman from the spirit world, is one of the most popular and familiar. It was the first *kaidan* to make it to celluloid in the early days of Japanese cinema and has spawned many film versions since, although the oldest of these versions are lost forever and even some of the more recent productions can be difficult to track down.

Botan Doro arrived in Japan from China in the 1600s in a translation of *New Tales Under the Lamplight* (*Jian Deng Xin Hua*), a Ming-era collection of ghost stories by Qu You. Later, and although a Buddhist monk himself, the writer Ryoi Asai played down the collection's Buddhist teachings concerning man's karma and transplanted *Botan Doro* to the urban Edo of his time.

Two hundred years later, the professional storyteller San'yūtei Enchō (also known as Jirokichi Izubuchi) modified and developed the characters, and made the tale a key part of his *rakugo* repertoire. In the 1880s, an edited shorthand transcription of the raconteur's reworking was published, further spreading its popularity. This version was soon adapted into a Kabuki play (first performed at the Kabuki-za in Tokyo in 1892), where the writer Lafcadio Hearn (Yakumo Koizumi) came across it, publishing the first English translation of the tale as *A Passional Karma*, in his collection of supernatural stories *In Ghostly Japan* (1899).

Satsuo Yamamoto's 1968 film *Kaidan Botan Doro* in many ways follows in this tradition, but also uses other sources and adds ideas of its own. Where Hearn painted Shinzaburo as selfish and detestable, he is now more heroic—no longer a student, he's an altruistic but struggling tutor to impoverished children, much to the shame of his proud samurai family.

This shift allows Yamamoto, a staunch Communist, to launch a dimly veiled criticism of Japan's feudal system, as Shinzaburo accuses the samurai class of caring only for their own glory and honor and having no compassion for the poor. He also refuses repeated entreaties to marry his widowed sister-in-law, a match that would be advantageous to his family, thus setting up the dynamic of obligation versus true love. It is also through the fickle selfishness of the elite that O-Tsuyu, the woman Shinzaburo becomes entranced by, loses her father and is left helpless and alone.

During the festival of O-bon (when spirits are believed to return briefly to Earth), the radiant O-Tsuyu makes the first of several nightly visits to Shinzaburo's home, accompanied by her faithful maid O-Yone, who carries a lantern decorated with peony flowers to light their way. In one particularly effective scene, Shinzaburo's curious servant is terror stricken to see Shinzaburo making love not to a beautiful woman but to a ghastly skeleton. As O-Tsuyu is revealed to have been a ghost from when she first met Shinzaburo, the film is actually closer to Asai's work on this point than the *kabuki/rakugo* version, which gave them a prior romantic relationship in the earthly realm.

Persuaded that he must drive the spirits away, Shinzaburo chants sutras and allows religious texts to be pasted on the outer walls of his home. A scene in which the ghosts arrive and are distraught to see these precautions in place opens one of the film's many atmospheric sequences, full of eerie lighting and ethereal voices and sound effects as well as dramatic camera movements sweeping in on the tormented man. Where the Shinzaburo of Asai's version breaks down and heeds the ghosts' pleas to allow O-Tsuyu to meet him once again, in the film he struggles but manages to overcome his desire out of concern to stay alive for the sake of his pupils and to help make the world a little better.

It is notable that in the film O-Tsuyu finally gets to be with Shinzaburo again not simply because of his own weakness, but also through the treachery of those close to him. In this regard, *Kaidan Botan Doro* conveys considerable psychological depth in its depiction of ordinary people coming undone through greed or desire. Or perhaps, without giving away any more, the ending is not so bleak for the two lovers after all.

Considering the flexibility the tale of *Botan Doro* allows for, there is no definitive version to speak of, including this filmic interpretation. That's all the more reason to explore how *Kaidan Botan Doro* plays freely with the many possibilities that can be gleaned from the ancient tales.—Jeff Hammond

BŪSU (2005)

DIRECTOR: Yoshihiro Nakamura
SCREENPLAY: Yoshihiro Nakamura
SPECS: 73 minutes; color

Būsu (The booth) was directed by Yoshihiro Nakamura (b. 1970) in 2005. At that time Nakamura was clearly familiar with J-horror, having scripted Hideo Nakata's popular *Dark Water* (*Honogurai mizu no soho kara*) in 2002, and seen Kiyoshi Kurosawa's psychological works. But Nakamura used this knowledge to deviate from genre conventions, as he has frequently done throughout his career. Containing elements of parapsychology and a female avenger, there are plot shifts that catch audiences off guard in his depiction of the psychological meltdown of *Būsu*'s DJ. Although one may readily predict the conclusion, anticipating the details leading there can be more baffling. While horrific elements advance its plot, they do not drive *Būsu*.

A prologue features an older, golden-voiced late-night radio talk show host. Its grainy black-and-white images highlight a lime-green telephone. His caller asks advice concerning a love suicide she and her boyfriend have planned. When he discourages them, she responds that they already attempted it thirty years earlier, but only she died. Although the DJ is initially amused, his expression grows more serious as she accuses him of being the boyfriend, and that "you . . . betrayed . . . me." Static partially drowns out her conversation. Following a close-up of a speaker on the wall, we see the DJ's body suspended from the ceiling of the broadcast area, Studio 6.

Būsu shifts to color as it jumps to "Tokyo Love Lines," a present-day radio talk show hosted by the overbearing Shingo Katsumata. His theme for the evening is "unpardonable words." Shingo, played by Ryuta Sato (b. 1980), informs his audience that the night's broadcast originates from a studio used in earlier days with an enjoyable retro feel. Once off the air, he immediately complains about the substitute studio's dinginess and mildewed headphones. When he leaves the booth, the camera draws back, focusing upon its Studio 6 sign. Upon his return, a cabinet top swings open, revealing a now well-used lime-green telephone.

The night's first caller is twelve-year-old, Nasty. A classmate whose family was about to move uttered the unpardonable "Stop staring, ugly!" just as she was about to tell him she had a crush on him. Shingo sympathizes with Nasty, confirming that those words were stinging and mean. He continues that his family moved a lot while he was young, and he had no interest in girls at that age. This is contradicted by a flashback in which the young Shingo holds a little girl's hand. A tracking shot following them awkwardly halts upon reaching the apparent edge of someone seated on a swing. Returning to the present, Shingo warmly consoles the girl. Suddenly an eerie creaking sound breaks in. As Shingo announces that there is a bad connection, the camera cuts to a wall speaker through which is broadcast the damning words "You liar," spoken by a scary disembodied voice familiar to the film audience. When the noise diminishes, Shingo, self-absorbed but doting, recovers. During the commercial break, the technicians, who had originally trained in this old studio, reluctantly inform Shingo about a rumor that it is haunted by a disc jockey that had committed suicide.

Momo, the next caller, tells Shingo that her husband told her that her husband's nasty complaint was that he should have married his ex-girlfriend. Momo doesn't feel she can talk back because the two had been engaged before she took him away. As Shingo responds, the screen image changes to an attractive woman speaking through a mike in a modern studio. The film's sound continues with Shingo and Momo's conversation, but there is a cut to Shingo, dressed differently, observing the new woman. Following several more quick cuts, the voice of the woman, "Mabuchi," played by Hijiki Kojima (b. 1976), announcing the day's news and sports, supplants the conversation as well. When Mabuchi wraps up and begins to head home, Shingo chases her down the hall and demands a date, even though she is already engaged. As Shingo forces himself upon Mabuchi in this flashback, the sound track returns to the present with Shingo assuaging Momo's guilt and justifying her actions. The eerie studio sounds again break in, and the woman's voice again brands Shingo a liar.

During the next call, an agitated Shingo's mind flashes back to earlier that day, with Mabuchi also calling him a liar. Mabuchi has broken up with her fiancé and is having an affair with Shingo, whom she accuses of cheating on her. He attempts to deflect her conversation and, blaming her, breaks their relationship. Shingo is jarred back into the present by further unexplained sounds, and his booth assistant, played by Makoto Ashikawa (b. 1960), must mime and scribble the caller's conversation on paper. Lost, he quickly introduces the song listed on his queue sheet only to hear a different one play. He demands that the program's director pay attention without acknowledging his own negligence, only to learn that Mabuchi has not shown up for her broadcast. His own inattentiveness continues, the film alternating between flashbacks and the present. He had fought with Mabuchi during their date, viciously pushing her out of his car. Her head struck a metal barrier, and she briefly lost consciousness. Struggling to reenter the car as Shingo attempted to drive away, her body was dragged, then pushed under a barrier leading to coastal waters. The evening newscast, done by a substitute, includes a story of an unidentified body being found in the water off the coast near where he and Mabuchi struggled. During the broadcast, Shingo believes he briefly glimpses a ghostly looking Mabuchi in back of the studio, and fears her relationship with the earlier phone interruptions.

As the evening continues, Shingo's despair intensifies. Two men dressed in business suits enter the studio, followed by a cut to the men examining the tires on the DJ's car. His mind further wandering, he quickly loses patience with his callers and yells abusively at his coworkers. Just before the sports news begins, a bloodied Mabuchi slowly walks ghost-like through the studio, further panicking Shingo, then calmly but coldly announces the sumo results. The two well-dressed men, we eventually learn, are sponsors, and the nonlinear scenes have occurred in Shingo's mind, some being actual flashbacks, others imagined consequences. The narcissistic DJ is forced to reflect, and comes to realize that the phone calls can all be related to his destructive actions and tendencies. As he signs off for the evening with all the phone lines off, the eerie sounds break in again. Shingo realizes that they echoed swings from his old school playground. The camera had halted during his earlier conversation with Nasty to block from his memory the same unpardonable words he had uttered to a little girl when he was twelve, and then physically abused her. The booth door suddenly closes, and Shingo meets his ghostly accuser.

Director Yoshihiro Nakamura used an old studio in the Nippon Building in Tokyo as a set for *Būsu* shortly before it was closed. Its cramped booth augments his film's claustrophobic atmosphere. While including certain elements from the J-horror genre, he twisted them to create his own style of thriller. While the paranormal sets the tone here with each conversation containing further incriminating associations, Shingo eventually realizes that he, rather than the chilling telephone voice, is the real monster. Many horror films include sympathetic protagonists struggling against supernatural elements. Here the protagonist is insensitive, and the audience is concerned with Mabuchi's fate. Rather than acting as an unknown to be unraveled, the uncanny serves to unlock the protagonist's character. Scenes in the film also include an interview with a former chess champion hoping to regain his title and a sports story about a sumo wrestler facing dethronement, foreshadowing that the popular DJ could be the next star to be uncrowned.

Unpardonable words, unnerving associations, and strong but previously unacknowledged memories merge to create powerful linkages. Throughout his career Nakamura has used such linkages—his acclaimed 2009 *Fish Story* (*Fisshu sutori*) depicts a 1975 band's obscure punk song eventually saving the world in 2012—but none as dauntingly as in *Būsu.*—Bill Thompson

Bibliography
Nakamura, Toshihiro. *The Booth*. Tartan Asia Extreme, 2005. DVD.

· C ·

COLD FISH (2010)

DIRECTOR: Sion Sono
SCREENPLAY: Sion Sono, Yoshiki Takahashi
SPECS: 146 minutes; color

Cold Fish, known as *Tsumetai nettaigyo* in Japanese, is a 2010 dark-comedy horror film directed by Sion Sono (b. 1961). The film tells the story of a heavy-handed tropical fish shop owner, his deranged wife, and a feeble associate who resolve a series of business deals gone wrong through violent murders and cover-ups. Roughly based upon actual events that took place in 1993 in a prefecture neighboring Tokyo, the film was critically acclaimed in Japan and received notable recognition internationally.

The plot of the film revolves around the lackluster life of a forty-something-year-old fish shop owner named Nobuyuki Shamoto, played by Mitsuru Fukikoshi (b. 1965). Possessing a frail personality to accompany what appears to be a struggling business, Shamoto is overrun by his teenage daughter and constantly overlooked by his attractive and much younger wife of a second marriage. Among other implications of Shamoto's failures, the bane of his existence is his family life, rife with jealousy and distrust between his daughter and his wife. The role of Shamoto is particularly important to achieving the type of desperation Sono intended to convey in the film. For Sono, it is this hopelessness that is lacking in Japanese cinema and Shamoto's character—in all of his anguish and failures—showcases this for audiences.

Shamato's life takes a turn for what appears to be the better when he is approached by another fish shop owner named Yukio Murata, played by Denden (b. 1950), a stage name. Murata offers a business proposal that would combine both of their stores into a partnership agreement and increase their revenue. Believing that more money will solve his problems, Shamoto accepts the deal and begins to work with Murata; yet almost immediately, Murata's tyrannical personality begins to show. Overtaking Shamato's business, seducing both his daughter and his wife, Murata eventually becomes another untenable problem in Shamato's life.

As the relationship between Murata and Shamoto increasingly sours, Murata effectively reduces Shamoto to a mere assistant, assigning him trivial and degrading jobs unrelated to anything discussed in their original agreement. Murata and his wife, Aiko Murata, played by Asuka Kurosawa (b. 1971), then gradually reveal a sinister side of their business to Shamoto, wherein the Muratas defraud and extort various customers out of money. In more than one instance, these cons go awry and the Muratas then begin killing their deceived customers. Forcefully enlisting Shamoto as a get-away-driver and labor-hand, the Muratas showcase their methodical procedure for executing their murders and disposing of the dead bodies.

Eventually Shamoto grows tired of the abuse and turns on the Muratas, first assaulting Yukio and then forcing Aiko to finish the job and dispose of his body. Shamoto then murders Aiko and attempts to pin the killings on the now deceased Muratas by calling the police and exposing their exploits.

Similar to several of Sono's horror films, *Cold Fish* is replete with lurid imagery. The murders and disposals of the deceased bodies are particularly gruesome. In the former, the killing scenes range from poisonings and violent sexual encounters to asphyxiation by rope and multiple stabbings to the neck with a ballpoint pen. In the latter, the disposals of the bodies include scenes akin to cattle butcher shops, inclusive of blood splattered floors and walls; large chunks of meat and bones set aside for dismemberment; as well as camera pans of meticulous jabbing, slicing, and ripping of flesh by the Murata couple. In both the murder and disposal scenes, the cast maintains an eerie and ever-present aloofness about them that really bolsters the gory images.

The film is loosely based upon the events surrounding four murders committed by Gen Sekine and his common-law wife Hiroko Kazama during the 1990s. According to the criminal investigations, Sekine and Kazama, pet shop owners and semi-famous dog breeders, frequently arranged dubious business agreements in which the couple would defraud customers and colleagues alike. When some of these business agreements broke down, similar to the film, Sekine and Kazama, portrayed by Denden and Kurosawa respectively, murdered, dismembered, and disposed of the bodies of various clients and business associates. Nearly a decade prior to the release of *Cold Fish*, Sekine and Kazama were tried, convicted, and sentenced to death.

The film received several positive reviews and was honored by premiering at the Sixty-Seventh Venice International Film Festival, as well as winning the Best Screenplay Award in the 2010 Fantastic Fest in Austin, Texas.—Salvador Murguia

See also ero guru nansensu genre; Sono, Sion.

Bibliography
Sono, Sion, dir. *Cold Fish*. Nikkatsu, 2010. Film.

CRAZY LIPS (2000)
DIRECTOR: Hioshisa Sasaki
SCREENPLAY: Hiroshi Takahashi
SPECS: 85 minutes; color

Crazy Lips, or *Hakkyōsuru kuchibiru* in Japanese, is a 2000 Japanese comedy-horror film directed by Hioshisa Sasaki (b. 1961). The film chronicles a young woman, Satomi, played by Hitomi Miwa (b. 1978), who lives with her sister and widowed mother. After Satomi's brother is accused of severing the heads of four young schoolgirls, she seeks the help of a mysterious psychic and her male assistant who insist that they can prove her brother's innocence. What ensues is a chaotic and seemingly unrelated sequence of events in which supernatural conjuring of the dead, cult worship, and secret agencies engaging in espionage, culminate into an epic Kung Fu battle. *Crazy Lips* was written by Hiroshi Takahashi, who also wrote the script for the 1998 international success *Ringu*. The film is known for its eclectic blending of genres, and its insanely wild and unexpected narrative.

Crazy Lips centers around the Kuramashi family, who have been in hiding for years because Satomi's father was sentenced to death as a serial killer and because Satomi's brother Michio, played by Kazuma Suzuki (b. 1968), has been accused of a similar killing spree of four young girls. Michio has gone into hiding, leaving his widowed mother, and sisters Satomi and Kaori, played by Hijiri Natsukawa to defend themselves from a continual onslaught of reporters and detectives who are looking for Michio. A police inspector, played by Ikko Suzuki (b. 1962), visits the women regularly to harass them and attempt to gain information on Michio's whereabouts, while strangers constantly throw rocks through the windows of the Kuramashi home.

In an act of desperation, Satomi contacts a psychic named Mamiya, played by Yoshiko Yura, in order to unveil the true identity of the serial killer. Mamiya and her sinister helper, Touma perform a séance within the Kuramashi home that awakens the spirits of the murdered school children and sends their decapitated bodies on a mission to find where the murderer has stowed away their heads, which in turn, will reveal the true killer.

The narrative structure of *Crazy Lips* begins to change tremendously through an eclectic blending of various nods to film genres. Once Mamiya and Touma enter the Kuramashi home, several graphic rape scenes ensue in which Touma either rapes Satomi's mother as a payment for their psychic services or, in a particularly graphic scene, forces Satomi to have sex with the hanging body of the police inspector, while Touma also has his way with Satomi in what appears to be a cult ritual. In another scene, Satomi unexpectedly breaks into song and dance in the tradition of a Bollywood musical after she is informed by mysterious secret agents Lucy, played by Tomomi Kuribayashi (b. 1972), and her partner Narimoto, played by Hiroshi Abe (b. 1964), that she has harmful psychic abilities. In surreal fashion, while also incorporating comedic elements into the film, an individual known as the Colonel who is the boss of Lucy and Narimoto, is able to communicate with Satomi via broadcast television in which he disguises himself as the host of a variety show and can speak only to Satomi through the TV set. Once Mamiya and Touma enter the room and the Colonel feels his cover will be blown, he dresses in a leotard and dances so as to avoid suspicion, pretending once more to be a part of the regular programing. Both Lucy and Narimoto, who work for a mysterious international agency along with the Colonel, are attempting to stop Mamiya and Touma from conjuring a type of monster-deity from the heavens that is enacted through their ceremonial raping of the Kuramashi women.

The bodies of the four school girls are finally able to find their missing heads, which leads to the unveiling that all three of the Kuramashi women decapitated the girls. This shocking revelation sets in motion a chaotic and surreal climax in which Michio, Mamiya, and Touma, along with the angered parents of the four girls, corner the Kuramashi women and threaten to beat them to death. The Kuramashi women are chased through the woods and defend themselves in a scene that plays out much like a traditional Kung Fu film, with Lucy and

Narimoto joining in the battle as well. The film concludes with a bloodbath in which nearly every character is violently killed while Mamiya tries to conjure a mysterious monster-god from space, but not before the viewer, in another odd turn of events, witnesses a love scene between Satomi and her brother Michio.

Although noted for its shock value and generally negative reviews from critics, *Crazy Lips* portrays Takahashi's efforts to write a script that appears completely uninhibited in its narrative approach, hence the film has garnered attention for its eclectic homage to various film genres.—Edwin Lohmeyer

See also Ringu

Bibliography
Sasaki, Hioshisa, dir. *Crazy Lips*. Omega Project, 2000. Film.

CRUEL RESTAURANT (2008)
DIRECTOR: Koji Kawano
SCREENPLAY: Koji Kawano, Satoshi Owada
SPECS: 75 minutes; color

Cruel Restaurant (*Zankoku hanten*) is a 2008 erotic comedy-horror film directed by Koji Kawano and written by Kawano and Satoshi Owada. The film features the adult video idol Mihiro as Ms. Lin, the owner of a popular dumpling restaurant, alleged to be using human meat in its famous Tougen Dumplings.

While not critically acclaimed, *Cruel Restaurant* is stellar evidence of a number of tropes in Japanese filmmaking, parody and the erotic being chief among them. Itself a parody of *The Eight Immortals Restaurant*, a Chinese film, *Cruel Restaurant* also pokes fun at a number of American franchises, using musical cues from *Mission: Impossible*, *Halloween*, and *Jaws*, as well as the infamous whispers from *Friday the 13th*. Most pronounced is *Cruel Restaurant*'s familiar juxtaposition of sex and violence, demonstrated by the way in which none of the film's three major sex scenes depict consensual actions, and yet, the way these scenes are filmed and the fact that a notable pornographic actress features prominently in all of them clearly suggests that these scenes are meant to titillate rather than repulse. During a rape scene, Shu, played by Toshiyuki Teranaka, spends several minutes of screen-time rubbing Lin's bare breasts with vegetable oil; the camera never wavers from her chest. The scene tries at humor by focusing on Shu's scrunched face and absurd squeaks of passion. Although not explicit, the film seems to suggest something about violent fantasy and sexual repression; especially in scenes such as the one in which Mr. Chin, played by Sakae Yamazaki, is unable to perform sexually.

According to the storyline, newspaper reporter Toshiko, played by Miho Funatsu, relaxes at Nakia Beach as a fisherman hooks a severed arm floating in the surf. She calls in the incident to her editor as a newsworthy story, yet the editor sends her to cover the lunch service at the mysterious Tougen Dumpling restaurant instead. While she samples the food, detectives Goro, played by Katsuya Naruse, and Iwanomoto, played by Yūsuke Iwata, launch their own investigation. Barely underway, the detectives' investigation is trumped by Tougen's head chef, Mr. Chin, and the painful beating he delivers to them, ultimately warning them not to interfere with his restaurant.

Inside, a famous food journalist named Hoemi, played by Chihiro Koganezaki, angrily demands the recipe for Lin's dumplings and is ejected from the restaurant. Toshiko follows her and questions her about the outburst. Hoemi reveals that her sister has been missing since writing about Tougen Dumplings, and Hoemi is certain she was killed and served. Toshiko then somehow realizes that the severed arm from that morning belonged to Hoemi's sister.

That evening, a former patron named Shu begs Lin and Mr. Chin to accept him as an apprentice, but Mr. Chin declines and threatens Shu. The next morning, Shu, in a strangely erotic revenge scene, attacks Lin during her morning exercises. However, Goro, who informs her about the rumors surrounding the restaurant, rescues her. Revolted by these rumors, Lin demonstrates her dismay and Goro seems to take her revulsion as proof of her innocence.

Scenes later, while Lin is alone in the restaurant, Shu sneaks in and begs for one more chance to accept him as an apprentice. When she refuses, he humiliates and rapes her. Losing consciousness, Lin awakes in her apartment, with no sign of Shu. In a peculiar twist, Lin is then haunted by visions of Shu's severed head.

In her nervous state, Lin begins to recall her training under "Dumpling Master Hoi," played by Kēsuke. In a moment of reminiscence, Lin remembers Master Hoi accepting her as an apprentice only after seeing her exposed thighs, and his training regime that involved watching her exercise in her underwear and masturbate while he accompanied her on guitar. Lin's reverie is interrupted when Hoemi ambushes her in the kitchen. Hoemi strangles Lin to unconsciousness. Yet, when Lin awakens on the floor, she finds Hoemi—with her head caved in—laying next to her. In a panic, Lin flees; returning later to find no sign of Hoemi's body.

Convinced she must have killed Shu and Hoemi, Lin turns herself in to the police. Goro explains that he trusts that she is innocent. Meanwhile, Toshiko and Iwanomoto execute a plan to find out the restaurant's secrets once and for all. Iwanomoto follows Mr. Chin, hoping to see where he buys the restaurant's meat, but Chin catches him and beats him to death with a steel pipe. During the murder, Toshiko hides in the kitchen, and later sees Lin using Master Hoi's secret technique. Chin then notices Toshiko, follows her home, and eventually kills her.

Learning of all the recent murders, Goro arrives at the restaurant to confront Chin, and although he admits to the killings, he denies ever having provided human flesh for the restaurant. In the midst of the admission, Chin attacks and defeats Goro, then professes his obsession with Lin and tries to rape her. In a rather bizarre set of scenes, Chin's rape attempt is stymied when he cannot become erect, and in frustration, bites into his own wrist and bleeds to death. The next morning, Goro, recovering from his beating, wakes up alone in Lin's apartment. At the climax of the film, Lin at last reveals Master Hoi's secret technique.—Boleyn Key

CURE (1997)
DIRECTOR: Kiyoshi Kurosawa
SCREENPLAY: Kiyoshi Kurosawa
SPECS: 111 minutes; color

Released by Daiei Film shortly before its purchase by Kadokawa Pictures in 1997, *Cure* was directed by Kiyoshi Kurosawa following a prolific output of shorts, V-Cinema (direct-to-video), and theatrical features; however, it was the first of his many films to receive wide international acclaim. Premiering at the 1997 Tokyo International Film Festival prior to its domestic release where star Koji Yakusho was awarded Best Actor, this breakthrough work was subsequently screened at the San Francisco International Film Festival and Toronto International Film Festival, among others. Following the international commercial success of Hideo Nakata's *Ring* (1998), *Cure* was also released theatrically in the United States in 2001. Thus it predates the popular J-horror phenomenon, while being received during its boom in the 2000s. Shot from Kurosawa's original screenplay by director of photography Tokusho Kikumura, with production design by Tomoyuki Maruo, Kurosawa also wrote a novelized version of the same story published by Tokuma Shoten in 1997.

Looking on at the videotaped confession of a man who had just bludgeoned a prostitute with a pipe then carved an *X* in her throat and chest, consulting psychologist Makoto Sakuma, played by Tsuyoshi Ujiki, remarks, "He looks okay to me." This is the third such case of random homicide and identical mutilation in two months, in which the perpetrator is found at the scene of the crime and admits an illogical intent to kill with no real motive, followed by shock and disbelief at his own actions, and Tokyo detective Kenichi Takabe, played by Koji Yakusho, is on the trail of the mysterious and elusive killer. But as the string of ordinary people inexplicably committing gruesome murders continues, the practical-minded detective appears to be less on the trail of one or more serial killers than a wave of amnesic rage sweeping society. Popular entertainment media—a usual suspect of linked crimes—provides no promising explanations, and Takabe searches for means of suggestion outside the realms of pulp mystery and horror plots.

Kurosawa's style itself plays around with genres, transforming from police procedural into psychological inquiry focused more on the motives of the hero detective and the contemporary society he is purportedly trying to protect. Here, the killer is not a monstrosity to be shunned by everyday society, but a mirror of society itself, a businessman, schoolteacher, policeman, and doctor. Producing an eerie atmosphere through Gary Ashiya's haunting score, detached observational representations of violence, and Kurosawa's signature derelict spaces, *Cure* delivers genre tropes in deadpan style, mixing comedic staging with suspense timing. Clever rear projection vehicle interior setups epitomize Kurosawa's brand of realism and reverence for commercial genre cinema, constructing transcendent commentaries on contemporary life.

Cure further demonstrates Kurosawa's fascination with myths and fables (often of a supernatural character), opening with Takabe's wife "Fumie," played by Anna Nakagawa, reading the French folktale Bluebeard while in a therapy session. The tale subtly foreshadows the film's enigmatic conclusion, while introducing Takabe's concern with his wife's undefined mental illness. Takabe's mental composure becomes increasingly strained when the investigation leads to a young drifter, played by Masato Hagiwara, who seemingly suffers from amnesia, and had encounters with perpetrators just prior to their crimes. Disoriented yet strangely calm, the man interacts with others through an aggravating stream of questions that proceed from a confused "Where am I?" to more forceful "Who are you?" The man turns out to be Kunio Mamiya, a former medical student who had been studying hypnosis, specifically experiments in "mesmerism" suggested to have been suppressed by the state a century earlier due to links to occultism. Takabe's practicality rams against Mamiya's philosophical pressure, leading to a breaking point that, rather than provide any satisfying solution to the mystery, serves to alienate and cause the viewer to reconsider everything that has just taken place.

By the film's end, there is little explanation for the crimes beyond Sakuma's weak initial conclusion that "the devil made them do it." The real horror *Cure* brings the viewer into contact with is the hypnosis of modern life, whereby Takabe's wife's clinical madness seems less bizarre than an anonymous businessman Takabe encounters in a Laundromat muttering to himself, and acts of violence are carried out with a regard tantamount to taking out the trash. Kurosawa's interrogation of existential questions in contemporary society and deconstruction of genre spills out onto the spectator's enjoyment of the film, posing Mamiya's question "Who are you?" in surprising ways.—Joel Neville Anderson

THE CURSE (2005)

DIRECTOR: Kōji Shiraishi
SCREENPLAY: Kōji Shiraishi, Naoyuki Yokota
SPECS: 115 minutes; color

The Curse (*Noroi*) is a Japanese horror movie from 2005 that was directed by Kōji Shiraishi. It belongs to the genre of found-footage films, because it was shot in the form of a documentary. At 115 minutes in length, it is rather unusual for a movie within the horror genre in Japan. *The Curse* also stands out with its main cast of more than twenty-five different characters and very complex story line; it is a rather atypical horror movie and does not rely on existing genre-based plots and techniques.

The plot of *The Curse* focuses on an ancient Japanese demon called "Kagutaba" that is connected to several paranormal activities. These events are investigated by Masafumi Kobayashi, who is an expert in paranormal activities. He begins his work by looking into a paranormal case involving a woman named Junko Ishii. She has disappeared, and dead pigeons are found outside her house. A few days later, her neighbors die in a mysterious car accident. Kobayashi also speaks to the parents of a girl, Kana Yano, who is portrayed as a master of psychic powers on television shows. He takes an interest in her because the powerful Yano has disappeared as well. A man named Mitsuo Hori eventually meets with Kobayashi. During the meeting, Hori claims that Yano has been taken away by a strange type of worm that is driven by ectoplasmic energy. He also wants to know what Kagutaba is and draws Kobayashi's attention to a mysterious blue building, which they set out to examine.

Osawa, a man who lives in this building, is captured on film taking pigeons into his apartment; however, he also disappears and is reported as a missing person. Marika Matsumoto, a real-life actress acting as herself, is haunted by an evil spirit at a shrine and sleepwalks through the night. Kobayashi records her doing this and is able to catch a deep voice on the video saying "Kagutaba." Matsumoto later confirms that she has heard the same voice at the shrine before. Finally, Kobayashi discovers that the voice belongs to an old Japanese demon that had been summoned by villagers in the past. As a consequence of his disobedience, the villagers later sent the demon into an underground prison, where he was appeased year after year with a ceremonial ritual. However, the ritual was not held in 1978, when the village was abandoned to build a dam. Kobayashi is able to access a recording of the final ritual where a priest's daughter is possessed by the demon. From there, he tries to uncover her current whereabouts. Kobayashi is able to determine that Ishii is actually the priest's daughter. He also learns that she had previously worked at a school for nurses where she supported illegal abortions and stole embryos.

During the next portion of the movie several people, who once worshiped Kagutaba, die, including Osawa. Kobayashi and Hori want to perform a ritual in the old village and try to save the possessed Matsumoto. While the two men are conducting the ritual, however, Hori pretends to see Yano and runs away; therefore, Marika is possessed by the demon again. The two men later discover mutilated animals in the shrine, and Kobayashi finds the deceased Yano, who is lying in a pile of living fetuses. In the next scene, the recovered Matsumoto as well as Hori are sent to the hospital, while Kobayashi locates Ishii; she has committed suicide by hanging herself at home. He decides to adopt Ishii's son, and with the help of a historian, Kobayashi learns that Ishii had been worshiping the demon by feeding Kana embryos in order to turn her into a medium for communication with Kagutaba. While Matsumoto begins healing in the hospital, Hori seemingly commits suicide after being sent to a mental institution.

In the last segment of the film Kobayashi also disappears, and it turns out that the evidence left on his video camera is the footage the audience has been viewing. Ishii's son is attacked by Hori, who thought that the boy was the demon. Before he disappears, Kobayashi recognizes the presence of Yano's ghost in his house. Shortly thereafter, his wife, Keiko, is possessed by Kagutaba and sets herself on fire. Then Hori is seen leaving the house with the demon. The film abruptly ends at this point, and it is unclear what has happened to Kobayashi.

The Curse is a very complex Japanese horror movie that weaves many characters into a very elaborate plot. Although such factors may have contributed to the film's poor reception, some critics did underline its worth by highlighting the new perspective that is offered when historical myths, which are often used in horror movies, are mixed with filming techniques such as the documentary approach. However, the film has remained a rather avant-garde piece within the Japanese horror genre, and traditional fans were left wanting more of their movie expectations to be fulfilled.—Frank Jacob

· D ·

DAIMAJIN films

Daimajin (1966)
DIRECTOR: Kimiyoshi Yasuda
SCREENPLAY: Tetsurō Yoshida
SPECS: 84 minutes; color

Daimajin Okoru [*The Wrath of Daimajin*] (1966)
DIRECTOR: Kenji Misumi
SCREENPLAY: Tetsurō Yoshida
SPECS: 79 minutes; color

Daimajin Gyakushuu [*The Return of Daimajin*] (1966)
DIRECTOR: Kazuo Mori
SCREENPLAY: Tetsurō Yoshida
SPECS: 79 minutes; color

The Daimajin trilogy is a saga of three films released in 1966. *Daimajin*, the first film of the trilogy, was directed by Kimiyoshi Yasuda (b. 1911). The second film, *The Wrath of Daimajin*, known as *Daimajin Okoru* in Japanese, was directed by Kenji Misumi (b. 1921). Kazuo Mori (b. 1911) directed the last installment in the series, *The Return of Daimajin*—*Daimajin Gyakushuu* in the Japanese version. Daiei produced this series of *daikaiju* (gigantic monsters with great powers) films. Unlike the more typical versions of *kaijū* lore, the Daimajin series portrays this *kaijū* as one that triumphs over evil, rather than working alongside it.

The three films follow the same narrative structure and have a similar storyline, despite being disconnected; each film is set in its own location and has different characters. *Daimajin*, the Great Demon God, unifies the saga, as he is the common element to all the films. Nonetheless, the plot is almost identical in all of them. In feudal Japan, a righteous lord is overthrown by a merciless and cruel individual that defies priests and others in their attempt to convince him of his wrongdoings. His oppressive manners and cruelty make the people yearn for their former leaders, and they attempt, to no avail, to overthrow this oppressive leader. Their faith and hope is thus placed in the giant, Daimajin, to avenge their former lord and vanquish the current tyrant.

The first film, *Daimajin*, opened to the public on 17 April 1966. According to the storyline, in feudal Japan, a series of earthquakes are believed to be caused by Majin, a god imprisoned in a rock statue at the top of a mountain. Lord Hanabasa and his chamberlain, Samanosuke, attend to the prayers at the local shrine to reduce Majin's rage. Yet, during the prayers, Samanosuke rebels against Lord Hanabasa and takes power by force. Lord Hanabasa and his wife are murdered, but their children Tadafumi and Kozasa escape with the help of Kogenta, a samurai faithful to Hanabasa. Samanosuke and his men interrupt the prayers and forbid these events in the future, defying the priests' warnings. Ten years later, the cruelty of Samanosuke and his men drives Tadafumi to attempt to recover his throne with the help of Kogenta. However, they are captured and condemned to die. At the same time, Samanosuke orders his men to destroy Daimajin's statue as proof of their fearlessness even toward the god itself. They capture Kozasa and begin destroying the idol, at which time Daimajin awakens and unleashes a murderous wrath on all. Kozasa's prayers convince Daimajin to destroy Samanosuke's palace, killing Samanosuke and saving Tadafumi and Kozasa. Although Daimajin then turns to punish the villagers, Kozasa's tears and faith in the god stem his rage and spare the village. Daimajin's spirit leaves the idol, engendering a new start for Tadafumi and his town.

The second film, *The Wrath of Daimajin*, was released on 13 August 1966. Here Daimajin's idol is placed on a shrine in an island in the middle of a lake, which is surrounded by three villages—Chigusa, Nagoshi, and Mikoshiba. The Lord of Mikoshiba is a cruel and irascible man, who is constantly threatening the other two villages—eventually executing his threat and taking over these villages. In order to avoid the wrath of Daimajin, Mikoshiba orders his men to blow up the idol. Nonetheless, once everything seems lost for the inhabitants of Chigusa and Nagoshi, Daimajin appears from the lake and kills Lord Mikoshiba and his men. Once again, Daimajin saves the helpless and oppressed villagers and frees them.

The last film of the saga, *The Return of Daimajin*, opened to the public on 21 December 1966. This last film focuses on a group of children that go to the nearby village in an attempt to rescue their fathers from the evil warlord Arakawa. Foiling their plans, Arakawa captures the children and forces them into slavery. The four children cross Majin's mountain, taking good care to pray in front of the god's statue and ask for protection. Nonetheless, Lord Arakawa and his men infuriate Daimajin, who awakens again with vengeance and kills them all. This allows the children and their parents to return to their village in peace.

Daimajin came back again in 2010 in a TV drama entitled *Daimajin Kanon*. The drama was broadcast on *TV Tokyo* and shared some of the characteristics of the original films.—Fernando Ortiz-Moya

DARK WATER (2002)

DIRECTOR: Hideo Nakata
SCREENPLAY: Ken'ichi Suzuki, Yoshihiro Nakamura
SPECS: 101 minutes; color

Yoshimi Matsubara and her daughter Ikuko move in to a dilapidated apartment building where they are haunted by a mysterious little girl with a red bag and a yellow raincoat, while an ominous dark stain on the ceiling spreads day by day. But for the viewer, it is less the simple story than the wet, monochrome, urban imagery that drags us into the dreary and suffocating atmosphere of *Dark Water* (*Honogurai mizu no soko kara*, 2002). It may have been director Hideo Nakata's *Ring* (*Ringu*, 1998) that kick-started the J-horror boom of the late 1990s to early 2000s, but it's his slow-burning *Dark Water* that best exemplifies the movement's aesthetic. The film has grainy footage of desolate city living spaces, a haunting ambiguously tied to a protagonist's personal inner torments, and a contemplative horror that stems less from an evil being than a tragic world. If one were seeking the archetypal J-horror film, all the key elements are to be found here.

Like *Ring*, *Dark Water* is an adaptation of a work of fiction by Koji Suzuki, though this time the source material is a short story rather than a novel. The practical matter of plot-length is presumably one reason why the story is told slowly, with plenty of attention to an atmospheric setting and believable characterization. Another similarity with *Ring* is that the main characters represent a "broken family." The implicit idea is one that circulates through many horror films and seems to be that a family is unstable and vulnerable (mostly to emotional and supernatural threats) without a patriarch. It's almost as though the "missing man" is a hole in the family, through which ghosts and psychological trauma can pass through. One of the ironic effects of this patriarchal framework in horror, as we see in *Dark Water*, is the centrality of women and children it bestows. While focusing on the relationship between Yoshimi and Ikuko, the film constantly reminds us that their world is threatened by the problem of "family" pushing in on them from the outside: running parallel to *Dark Water*'s ghost story is its divorce plot, in which an increasingly desperate Yoshimi risks losing custody of her child. In other words, the friction between family as a loving unit and family as a social unit is built into the film's pervasive sense of unease.

Despite their depressing situation, Yoshimi and Ikuko have a wonderful and convincing chemistry, and day-to-day moments of fun and playfulness (brushing teeth together, getting ready for school) shine brightly from within the film's deteriorating, claustrophobic world. The heartfelt love between parent and child is always overshadowed by something terrible—the ghost, Yoshimi's past, the divorce, or something that subsumes all these threats, a terrifying waterlogged pressure that we can't fully explain. As the fear that Yoshimi and Ikuko will be separated becomes more palpable, the dark patch on the ceiling spreads and the mother's desperate love intensifies—we begin to wonder, like Yoshimi, if perhaps she really is the best person to raise her daughter, and if her love might not be another driving force in the heavy pressure that weighs on us. Trapped by the camera in the subjectivities of Yoshimi and Ikuko, it is impossible for us to know if the ex-husband is as bad as Yoshimi asserts, and as her desperation increases, her worldview seems more and more suspect. The one thing that we can be completely assured of, however, is her painfully strong love for her daughter, and *Dark Water*'s major achievement is its ability to depict that love not as the moral goodness that opposes fear and oppression, but as a murky, viscous entity joining the fleeting happy moments to the grimness and suffering that surround them.

The lack of a moralized internal logic is another way that this film typifies J-horror, and yet, ironically, it owes more than a little of its visual power to Western predecessors. Both the use of water as a sensuous embodiment of oppressive horror, and the recurring image of a lost child in a strikingly colored raincoat are key components of *Don't Look Now* (1973), and one of *Dark Water*'s climactic images will be instantly familiar to anyone who's seen Stanley Kubrick's *The Shining* (1980). But what makes *Dark Water* (and J-horror in general) seem distinct from "Western horror" is its difference from contemporary Hollywood horror film tropes. In the Hollywood formula, whether it is applied in American or Japanese films, scares will come more or less predictably after a short period of atmospheric tension building, when a phone rings loudly or a monster pops up, hopefully making viewers jump, scream, or be viscerally affected in some other way. Structurally, *Dark Water* could be equated to one of these "jump scare" scenes, only drawn out to the length of an entire film. The atmospheric tension building continues relentlessly, without the release of on-screen violence or sudden bursts of loudness, building pressure until the heart-stopping finale. For some, trained to view high-speed thrillers as the norm, the slow pace will be too alien to accommodate: their concentration will flag after another long elevator trip or another gray corridor, and they will have escaped from Yoshimi's world enough times to not be viscerally affected by the ending. For those who are gripped by the lingering camera or the silent rainy flashbacks, and feel the tension rise without respite, the final blows will be devastating.—Seán Hudson

Bibliography

Nakata, Hideo, dir. *Dark Water*. Toho, 2002. Film.

DEATH AT AN OLD MANSION (1975)

DIRECTOR: Yōichi Takabayashi
SCREENPLAY: Yōichi Takabayashi
SPECS: 106 minutes; color

Death at an Old Mansion (*Honjin satsujin jiken*) is a 1975 mystery-horror film directed by Yōichi Takabayashi (1931–2012) and coproduced by the Art Theatre Guild (ATG). In addition to *Death at an Old Mansion*, the film's title has also been translated variously into English as *Murder in Honjin Manor House*, *The Murder in the Honjin*, or *The Honjin Murders*.

The story takes place almost entirely on the grounds of the old mansion of the once-prosperous Ichiyanagi family. The story begins with the wedding ceremony of Kenzō, played by Takahiro Tamura (1928–2006), the current head of the family, and his bride Katsuko, played by Yūki Mizuhara (b. 1953). That night, the family is awakened by the sound of a koto (a stringed instrument) and a blood-curdling scream. Rushing to the newlyweds' quarters, the rest of the family finds Kenzō and Katsuko brutally murdered. Three bloody fingerprints are smeared along the wall, and outside a bloody sword has been thrust upright into the newly fallen snow. There are no footprints in the snow, which lead the family to believe that the killer is still on the premises. After searching, however, they decide that the killer must have somehow escaped.

The next day, the survivors summon Kōsuke Kindaichi, played by Akira Nakao (b. 1942) to help solve the case. The local police investigator suspects a mysterious man with three fingers on one hand who appeared immediately before the wedding ceremony and who left an ominous letter in which he declared himself Kenzō's "nemesis for life." That night, Kenzō's younger brother Saburō, played by Akira Nitta (b. 1950) is apparently wounded in a repeat attack. On the following day, a friend of Katsuko's visits the mansion. She is convinced that the killer is Katsuko's delinquent former lover.

By this point, however, Kindaichi has uncovered the basic trick behind the mystery. The deaths of Kenzō and Katsuko were actually a murder-suicide. After Katsuko revealed to Kenzō that she was not a virgin, Kenzō, a man extreme in the rigidity of his ideals, resolved to kill himself and Katsuko. With the help of Saburō, an avid fan of detective novels who is driven by an inferiority complex to prove his wit to his older brother, Kenzō devised a system whereby the sword used for the suicide is transported out of the room and into the garden outside via a koto string, which has been attached to the water wheel on the premises. Having discovered by chance the body of an indigent man with three fingers on one hand, Kenzō used the dead man's clothes and fingerprints to disguise the suicide as a murder carried out by a fictitious nemesis. This denouement is revealed to the viewer through a direct depiction of what happened that night, combined with Kindaichi's explanations and narration by Saburō.

Death at an Old Mansion is not a horror film in the traditional sense, due to the fact that its focus is not the production of the effect of fear or horror in the audience, but instead the intrigue of an unsolved murder case. In other words, it is not an intentionally scary film. Nonetheless, it can still be classified within a larger horror framework by virtue of the fact that horror elements are central to its plot. The initial murder scene, for example, is endowed with a stylized gruesomeness that is at home in the genre of slasher films, and the atmospheric portrayal of an isolated Japanese-style mansion peopled by grotesque, shadowy characters is effective in creating a horror setting.

Death at an Old Mansion is an adaptation of the 1946 Seishi Yokomizo (1902–1981) novel, *Honjin satsujin jiken*. This novel was the first to feature Yokomizo's famous detective, Kindaichi Kōsuke, and established Yokomizo's trademark use of rural Japan as the site for his tales of mystery and horror. In addition to the 1975 film, the novel was also adapted as a feature film in 1947 under the title *Sanbon yubi no otoko* (The man with three fingers), starring Chiezō Kataoka (1903–1983) as Kindaichi and directed by Sadatsugu Matsuda (1906–2003); and it was adapted for television three times in 1977, 1983, and 1992. Kindaichi was played by Ikkō Furuya (b. 1944) in the 1977 and 1983 versions, and by Tsurutarō Kataoka (b. 1954) in the 1992 version.

Takabayashi's *Death at an Old Mansion* serves as an important precursor to the so-called "Yokomizo boom" of the 1970s, which began in earnest with the 1976 blockbuster *Inugami-ke no ichizoku* (The Inugamis or The Inugami clan). In fact, the publishing house Kadokawa Shoten, a driving force behind the "Yokomizo boom," helped publicize and advertise Takabayashi's *Death at an Old Mansion* in a first attempt to promote book and other media sales through a synergistic form of trans-media marketing known as the "media mix."

Death at an Old Mansion was shown in competition at the Twenty-Sixth Berlin International Film Festival, and was a financial success. It marks a turning point in the history of the Art Theatre Guild as the first ATG film to earn more than one hundred million yen at the box office, and was remarkable among ATG films at the time for blurring the line between art film—for which ATG was known—and a more commercially viable type of genre film, the murder mystery.—Peter Bernard

DEATH NOTE films

Death Note (2006)
DIRECTOR: Tetsuro Arake, Naohasu Hanyu, Tomohiko Ito, Hiroyuki Tsuchiya, Ryosuke Nakamura
SCREENPLAY: Gracie P. Aylward, Toshiki Inoue, Takeshi Obata, Tsugumi Obata
SPECS: 126 minutes; color

Death Note: The Last Name (2006)
DIRECTOR: Shūsuke Kaneko
SCREENPLAY: Tetsuya Oishi
SPECS: 141 minutes; color

The "Death Note" phenomenon manifests itself in a worldwide franchise including a full line of merchandising, including novels, manga and anime, video games, action figures, and much more. Directed by Shūsuke Kaneko (b. 1955), the live-action filmic adaptations, *Death Note* and *Death Note: The Last Name*, were released in 2006 and immediately became box-office sensations, reaching number one in the ratings. The two movies are based on the *Death Note* manga (2003–2006) and later anime series by *gensakusha* writer Tsugumi Ohba and illustrated by Takeshi Obata (b. 1969). The films primarily center on a university student who decides to rid the world of evil with the help of a supernatural notebook that kills anyone whose name is written in it. A spin-off thriller film directed by Hideo Nakata (b. 1961), entitled *L: Change the World* (2008), was released on 9 February 2008. The focus in this film shifts to the character "L."

In *Death Note*, Japanese college student Light Yagami finds his life forever changed when he discovers a mysterious notebook, known as the "Death Note," lying on the ground. The Death Note's instructions claim that if a person's name is written within while picturing that person's face, that person will die. Light is initially skeptical of the Death Note's authenticity, but after experimenting with it, he realizes it is real and has a meeting with the previous owner of the Death Note, a *Shinigami*, or "spirit of death," named Ryuk. These spirits belong to a race of extra-dimensional beings who survive by killing human beings in order to extend their own lives. Light seeks to become "god of the new world" by passing judgment on those he deems to be evil or who get in his way. He begins using the Death Note to kill scores of criminals, becoming a notorious serial killer known as "Kira."

As the Kira killings continue, some in Japanese society come to see Kira as a righteous figure. Interpol launches an investigation of the murders, but months pass without any fruitful lead. The case eventually attracts the attention of "L," a reclusive and world-famous detective. Working with Interpol and the Japanese police, L manages to confront Light through a television broadcast and demonstrates his deductive skills, correctly surmising Kira's residence in the Kanto region and that he can "kill without lifting a finger." The race begins between L and Light to discover each other's identity, and a game of cat and mouse ensues between the two geniuses.

After Light hacks into the police database to find information on acquitted criminals, L realizes that Kira is somehow related to the Kira task force led by Light's father, Soichiro. Light finds out that he is being followed by an FBI agent named Raye Penber and, through a series of events, kills him and his fellow agents. Penber's fiancée, Naomi Misora, takes it upon herself to uncover Kira's identity. Suspecting Light, she kidnaps his girlfriend, Shiori, and demands that he confess if he wants to save her. Light adamantly insists that he is not Kira. When Shiori tries to escape, Naomi shoots her and commits suicide. Shiori dies in Light's arms.

Ryuk finds that Light had actually engineered Naomi's death using the Death Note, as he had already found out her identity and written a scenario whereby Naomi would commit suicide after shooting Shiori. Ryuk is confused that Light would deliberately put Shiori in danger, but Light reveals that he had written her name in the Death Note as well. Using these events to foster hatred for Kira, Light asks to join his father's task force. While Soichiro is slightly reluctant, L immediately grants his wish and it is hinted that he is still certain that Light is Kira.

As a prequel to the second movie, Misa, an actress, is chased down an alley by a man wielding a knife, intent on killing her. As she screams for help, the man dies of a heart attack just like Kira's victims. A second Death Note lands beside her.

In *Death Note: The Last Name*, Misa receives a second Death Note from Rem, another Shinigami. As Light joins the task force after Shiori's funeral, Misa becomes the second Kira and forces a TV station into broadcasting her tapes. Through her TV screen Misa, using her Shinigami eyes, kills a critic of the original Kira, as well as Detective Mogi and two policemen who tried to break up a makeshift Kira supporters' rally. Light's younger sister Sayu is almost killed for not supporting Kira until Soichiro crashes into the festival wearing a motorcycle helmet. Light later arrives to comfort Sayu and Soichiro but is spotted by Misa as the family leaves the area. Misa correctly identifies Light as the original Kira.

Misa confronts him near his home, wishing to be his girlfriend and aid his quest for a crimeless society. Seeing that she has Shinigami eyes, Light accepts her help to eliminate L. Light sets up a meeting between L, Misa, and himself at Light's university so that Misa can learn of L's real name. However, Misa is arrested for being the second Kira and is detained. Fearing that she might crack, Rem asks Light to free her. In an elaborate plan, both Kiras lose their respective ownership of the Death Notes, and thus lose their memories of possessing them. Light orders Rem to give Misa's Death Note to Kiyomi Takada, a reporter covering the Kira case, while he buries his own Death Note elsewhere. Light would then prove he is not Kira by also being detained while Takada continues Kira's killing spree.

Light and Misa are released but still watched by L. Light finds a clue leading to Takada and the task force sets a trap to arrest her. As the team discovers the Death Note in Takada's possession and Rem's existence, Light kills Takada using a piece of the Death Note inside his watch to regain ownership of the Death Note and not be incriminated. When Misa is allowed to leave, Light asks her to find his buried Death Note and use it to kill L. After being told that the task force is flying to the United States to research the Death Note, Light tricks Rem into killing Watari and, seemingly, L; Rem herself dies for intentionally killing someone to help Misa, but burns her Death Note beforehand. To tie up loose ends, Light tries to use Misa's Death Note to kill his father, much to her horror.

It is revealed that L is alive and wrote his name in the Death Note with the intent to die almost a month in advance, thereby foiling Light. The task force did not leave for the United States but instead surveilled Light from another location, therefore hearing and observing Light's confession as Kira and replacing Light's Death Note with a decoy. Cornered, Light pleads with Ryuk to kill L and the task force. Instead, Ryuk writes Light's name in the Death Note, telling Light that anyone who uses the Death Note is banned from heaven and hell and will instead spend eternity as nothingness. Light dies in his father's arms, begging him to believe he acted as Kira to carry out justice.

Knowing that supernatural events were involved, the official line put out by L and the investigation team was that Light was killed by Kira. Twenty days later, Soichiro and L meet one last time before L dies peacefully. One year on (on Light's birthday) Soichiro keeps to the lie to Sayu and his wife, as Sayu adores Light but did not support Kira's actions. Misa also celebrates Light's birthday, still loving him, but has no recollection of the Death Notes.

Death Note was released in Hong Kong on 10 August 2006, in Taiwan on 8 September 2006, in Singapore on 19 October 2006, and in Malaysia on 9 November 2006, with English and Chinese subtitles. The world premiere was in the UA Langham Place cinema in Hong Kong on 28 October 2006, the first Japanese movie to premiere in Hong Kong. The film ended up earning $41 million (USD) in Japan and $1.9 million (USD) in Hong Kong. The film was released in the UK on 25 April 2008.

The second movie, *Death Note: The Last Name*, premiered on 3 November 2006, and instantly topped the Japanese box office, remaining at number one for four straight weeks, and grossed 5.5 billion yen in Japan by the end of the year, making it one of the year's highest grossing Japanese films.

The sequel was released in Hong Kong on 3 November 2006, in Taiwan on 24 November 2006, in Singapore on 28 December 2006, and in Malaysia on 25 January 2007. All have received limited theatrical screenings at art house venues around the world.

The core plot device of the story is the "Death Note" itself, which is a black notebook with instructions (known as "rules of the Death Note") written on the inside. Correctly used, it allows anyone to commit a murder, knowing only the victim's name and face.

A two-hour animated *Death Note Relight: Visions of a God* TV special aired on Nippon Television in Japan on 31 August 2007. It is a recap that takes place after the series end, where a Shinigami approaches Ryuk in the Shinigami realm in order to learn more about the human world. Ryuk tells him of all the events leading up to the last story arc, about Light Yagami and his rival L. Originally, this special was advertised as a retelling told from Ryuk's point of view, but it does not give a different point of view from what was originally told. However, it contains updated dialogue, as well as a few new scenes.—James A. Wren

DEATH POWDER (1986)
DIRECTOR: Shigeru Izumiya
SCREENPLAY: Shigeru Izumiya
SPECS: 63 minutes; color

Death Powder is an experimental, avant-garde, cyberpunk horror film that was released in 1986. Directed by Shigeru Izumiya, *Death Powder* is considered to be one of the major forerunners to the development of the cyberpunk and science fiction horror subgenre. The movie is written, directed, scored (most notable with the song "Scar People"), and produced by Izumiya, whose own "radical artistic vision" is bolstered by his involvement in films such as *Burst City* and *Crazy Thunder Road*.

Set in the "near future," the premise of the film is set around the discovery of a strange android creature, known as "Guernica," played by Mari Natsuki and Tomoko Ohtsu, who spews a strange "powder" on those who come near her; with a philosophically fueled narrative and eye-popping practical visual effects, *Death Powder*'s horror is less about shock value and more about addressing the idea of postapocalyptic destruction of the flesh.

The movie opens with Noris, played by Rikako Murakami, and Kiyoshi, played by Takichi Inukai, running through the bright neon signs of the city, attempting to escape unknown pursuers. Having come into possession of Guernica, whom they know next to nothing about, they have become targets of a shadowy organization. Having left Guernica in an abandoned building under the guard of the strange man Harima, played by director Shigeru Izumiya, they rush to check on him, worried as to what he may have done to the android in their absence. Harima eventually loses his mind, somehow affected by his exposure to Guernica, who lies dormant on a cage-like table, her face an odd mixture of human and machine.

When Kiyoshi and Noris enter an abandoned warehouse, they struggle with Harima, which ultimately leads to Kiyoshi being directly exposed to a large plume of Guernica's "death powder," which begins to melt and tear at his flesh. As Kiyoshi begins to suffer, Guernica communicates to him telepathically via a sequence of odd scenes. These scenes are actually Guernica's memories of her creation and her original purpose. Created by Dr. Loo, a hard rocking scientist played by Kiyoshiro Imawano, Guernica was intended to be used to open the human mind to the possibilities beyond the flesh. This experience opens Kiyoshi up to Guernica's consciousness.

As Kiyoshi begins his "transformation," the audience is made aware of the existence and goals of the shadow organization, known only as "Scar People," a group of deformed and strange individuals played by Kenichi Segawa, Isamu Izumiya, and Toshiro Nakamura. Led by Mr. Hacker, played by Tamio Kageyama, the Scar People attempt to gain possession of Guernica.

Emerging from his powder-induced journey into the past and into his mind, Kiyoshi has become enlightened to the reality of the world. While his flesh decays, he believes that he has moved beyond his human limitation and become an entirely different living being. It is here where Izumiya's bizarre narrative structure begins to drift into the realm of the philosophical, concerning itself with the nature of life and death and whether or not one can exist without the other. As Kiyoshi comes to terms, rambling on about madness, he begins to drift toward Noris and Harima to reengage in the struggle, which had begun before. They continue to struggle until the building is assaulted by the Scar People; in a final fight, Kiyoshi dispatches Mr. Hacker, while Noris and Harima deal with the rest of the gang.

The film is interrupted by a very lengthy montage of black-and-white photographs, many of which are inspired by a noire-type atmosphere. As the montage draws to an end, Kiyoshi seems to hear Guernica again as she speaks to him before he wakes up. Before him is a bandaged Harima, holding a rifle and trying to get his attention, while Noris stands off to the side, keeping watch. It appears that the strange powder caused Kiyoshi to have an episode of vivid hallucinations, which the audience is led to believe must have also occurred to Harima after his exposure to the death powder. Seeming to have resolved their difficulties, Kiyoshi, Noris, and Harima prepare for a final confrontation with the shadow organization that has been chasing them since their discovery of Guernica.

Just when it appears that everything caused by exposure to Guernica's death powder was a hallucination taking place inside the mind of the victim, the film closes on a scene where a group of delivery men break into a building and are eaten by a strange flesh creature, reminiscent of both the deformed Scar People and Kiyoshi's hallucinations.

Filled with highly visual sequences and strange imagery, Izumiya's *Death Powder* has become an underground cult classic; Izumiya's characteristic artistic rebellion has caused others to consider *Death Powder* to be an odd but meaningful entry in early science fiction and cyberpunk horror in Japan, opening the door for later films such as *Tetsuo, The Iron Man* (Shinyu Tsukamoto, 1989), and later films like *Tokyo Gore Police* (Yoshihiro Nishimura, 2008). Since its original release it has become hard to find, drifting in and out of the public domain; it only survives in grainy VHS quality, with distorted sound.—Megan Negrych

See also Izumiya, Shigeru

Bibliography
Izumiya, Shigeru, dir. *Desu pawuda*. Essen Communications, Media Mix Japan, 1986. Film.

DEMONS (1971)
DIRECTOR: Toshio Matsumoto
SCREENPLAY: Toshio Matsumoto
SPECS: 135 minutes; black and white and color

Demons, or *Shura* in Japanese, is a 1971 film directed by experimental filmmaker and theorist, Toshio Matsumoto. The film was produced by the *Art Theatre Guild*, a Japanese production company specializing in art films that commercial studios would normally not deal with (e.g., it produced Matsumoto's 1969 film, *Bara no Sōretsu*, a transvestite adaptation of *Oedipus Rex*). Although generic classification can often be difficult, *Demons* pertains to several genres, including *jidaigeki* (period drama), melodramas, and perhaps even psychological thrillers. However, many would argue that *Demons* is among the most horrific films ever produced in Japan.

The film is based on the Kabuki play, *Kamikakete sangotaisetsu*, by Nanboku Tsuruya IV, one of the most famous *Yotsuya kaidain* (Japanese ghost stories) writers in Japan. Yet, although the main protagonist, Gengobe, is played by Katsuo Nakamura (b. 1938) of Kabuki lineage, the film strays away from Kabuki tropes such as gaudy sets, exaggerated acting, lavish customs, and extensive use of music. Instead, *Demons* is composed of carefully crafted, often rather minimalistic, scenes separated by laconic intertitles. The cinematography includes repetitive shots, some taken from unusual camera angles, such as the floor or ceiling, exposing roof-less, most often barren interiors. In addition, the film is excessively dark. With the exception of the opening shot of a setting red sun, in color, the entire film is in black and white, while the action in the plot takes place entirely within the dark of evening. Furthermore, the way in which locations are lit, the importance placed on shadows within empty spaces, contrasts between dark and pale surfaces, all result in an exceptionally stark effect.

The narrative of the film is set at the background of the well-known tales associated with the forty-seven *rōnin*, (master-less samurai) who—after their leader was forced to commit suicide—sought to avenge him by killing the man they deemed responsible. Yet, given that the revenge is highly anticipated, before storming into the man's protected compound, the group disperses for several years, in order to give the impression that there is no such plot. Gengobe is one of these avengers waiting for the right day to regroup with his fellow *rōnin*, yet his real intents are actually a little too well camouflaged. He spends his entire family fortune on alcohol, and on the company of one geisha, Koman, played by Yasuko Sanjō (b. 1940), thereby falling into debt that forbids him from taking part in the vendetta. The day his loyal servant, Hachiemon, played by Masao Imafuku (b. 1921), returns after acquiring the amount of money required to redeem his master's reputation, Gengobe is deceived by Koman, and loses all of this fortune. The gruesome scenes to follow were already partially seen in an earlier sequence of the film, and future ones will appear again several times during the film, when Gengobe envisions bloody events. Yet, the full extent of violence unfolds gradually, culminating in a truly demonic, albeit all too human, scene.

Koman manipulates Gengobe to agree to marry her, leading him to believe that she truly loves him. Subsequently, fearing for her life when another man offers to buy her, he puts down the amount raised by Hachiemon. After making the payment, however, it is revealed that Koman is already married. Her husband, Sangorō—played by the renowned avant-garde stage director and playwright, Jūrō Kara (b. 1940)—had orchestrated this scheme with his friends who acted as the owners of Koman and as those who wished to purchase her. Soothed by his servant, Hachiemon, who also appears at the scene, Gengobe manages to control his anger and retreats without the geisha he thought he had just bought. Unable to sleep, however, he returns to Koman and Sangorō's house, where a celebration of the successful deception has just ended. He then kills everyone there, aside from Koman and Sangorō, who escape. The couple then head to their hometown, where Sangorō hopes to restore his relationship with his father, who has denounced him, and to reunite with their infant son, who is being adopted by a foster family. With the money acquired from Gengobe given to Sangorō's father, played by Kappei Matsumoto (1905–1995), the couple successfully make amends with the father and reunite with their son. The film closes with the couple establishing a new life in their new home, while Gengobe, who is now wanted for murder, hunted by both the authorities and the ghosts of the people he killed, is about to become their first visitor—a suggestion that no one will be spared.—Rea Amit

Bibliography

Matsumoto, Toshio, dir. *Demons*. ATG, 1971. Film.

DENSEN UTA (2007)

DIRECTOR: Masato Harada
SCREENPLAY: Masato Harada, Daisuke Habara
SPECS: 128 minutes; color

Densen Uta, also known as *Infectious Song, Contagious Song,* or *Suicide Song,* is a 2007 horror film by Masato Harada (b. 1949). The story revolves around an infamous song that is rumored to drive people to suicide. Under the influence of a shady magazine journalist, a group of high-school students perform the song and several of them soon meet a gruesome end.

Anzu, played by Yuko Oshima (b. 1988) is a student at an all-girls high school who is drawn to the auditorium following a haunting melody. She discovers it to be empty aside from her friend Kana, played by Atsuko Maeda, who stops singing, turns around to reveal a large knife in her hand, then apologizes and casually ends her life with it. The police and school administration are baffled by the abrupt suicide from a happy and otherwise normal girl, and Anzu and her friends quickly come under fire for suspected bullying. The girls themselves, along with other students, begin to speculate openly about rumors of a cursed song that can drive anyone who sings it to commit suicide shortly afterward. Some of them believe that this same song could be responsible for the growing number of un-explained suicides occurring to young people.

Meanwhile, when the employees of a tabloid magazine gather for a team-building survival game, the suicide song is brought up, and it is suggested that multiple high school girls have taken their lives because of it now. Two of the journalists, the reserved and curious Riku, played by Ryuhei Matsuda (b. 1983) and the brash and eccentric Taichi, played by Yusuke Iseya (b. 1976), express interest in researching the phenomenon and make the connection between Kana's inexplicable death and an online rumor about a particular song that is supposedly capable of inducing suicide.

After Kana's funeral, her remaining group of friends tries to process why she may have taken her life. They bring up a rumor that Kana was involved with a modeling scout, Koji, played by Takuma Sueno, who took her to karaoke, which is where she sang the song that may have led to her demise. They go to where he lives and discover evidence that he was involved in a group that drove women to suicide as part of a competition, including photographs, newspaper clippings, and a "suicide scoreboard" with pictures of extreme close-ups of women's eyes. They hear the noise of an approaching man calling for Koji and split up to hide around the apartment. While looking to hide, they encounter Taichi and Riku, both of whom had also followed leads to the same place and had arrived minutes before the girls. Unfortunately this lead proves to be a dead end as Koji's corpse is discovered submerged in his bathtub.

After discussing with the magazine chief, the employees and girls argue about how to proceed and if they should report the body to the police. Taichi, an ex-mercenary, wants to sing the song to test it, after arguing that he is so tough that he would never kill himself and hence would be able to resist the curse and protect everyone else. Taichi and five of the girls sing the song in a karaoke booth, and when Riku and Anzu catch up with them, they find the group acting dazed and immediately stop the song. The girls don't feel any ill effects but set up a system to check in with each other by e-mail every hour.

Taichi quickly succumbs to the song's power after drinking to excess in Koji's apartment and beating up one of Koji's associates from the suicide group. He stumbles to a police station to confess his crime and then pulls out a gun and begins shooting wildly into the air before putting it in his mouth and pulling the trigger while a station full of horrified officers watch. Soon afterward, one of the infected girls, Kiriko, commits suicide in a romanticized self-immolation with one of her teachers. It is revealed that the teacher was in love with Kana and had been humming the suicide song to himself while planning a double suicide with her. Kiriko offered herself as a substitute since they were now both under the effect of the song.

After these events, Anzu and Riku are forced to take the situation and the power of the song seriously if they are to have any hope of saving their remaining friends. Retreating to Riku's hometown, Anzu and her friends camp out at a *ryokan* (a traditional-style inn) operated by Riku's family and await an appointment to see a local spiritualist in search of help. Meanwhile, the remaining staff of Riku's magazine haphazardly digs up the origin of the fateful tune and the tragic events that befell its creator. They discover that the artist and numerous producers, including Anzu's parents, involved in the making of the song had tragic accidents shortly after its release. As they struggle to escape their fate, it slowly becomes clear that Anzu is more connected to the song than anyone realizes, and that Anzu is hiding a terrible secret of her own.

Loosely inspired by the real-life folklore surrounding an old Hungarian song from the 1930s, which has supposedly been banned from radio play in several countries as a matter of public safety, the "curse" premise is well-worn territory for J-horror. Harada succeeds in making the story his own, however, with a sometimes whimsical tone and nonlinear structure that set it apart from its more recognizable predecessors.

The bulk of the film's cast is taken from Japanese idol girl group AKB48, who make a cameo en masse as themselves early on in the film. Sayaka Akimoto (b. 1988) also makes a longer appearance as a fictional AKB48 member who happens to be Anzu's childhood friend.—Rebecca Bacheller

Bibliography
Harada, Masato, dir. *Densen Uta*. Kodansha, 2007. Film.

THE DISCARNATES (1988)
DIRECTOR: Nobuhiko Ōbayashi
SCREENPLAY: Shin'ichi Ichikawa
SPECS: 115 minutes; color

Although Taichi Yamada's source novel was a bestseller in Japan and the movie adaptation was a smash hit that reaped a staggering haul of awards and nominations (including two *Japanese Academy Awards* and a further nine nominations), Nobuhiko Ōbayashi's *The Discarnates* (1988) is almost entirely unknown outside Japan. Re-titled *The Strangers*, Yamada's novel was finally published in

English in 2003, while a solitary screening on BBC2 in 1992 helped to generate a small but devoted cult following. The only home video release outside of Japan is a single Hong Kong DVD release in 2004.

Harada is a forty-something screenwriter, divorced and living alone in an office that doubles as his flat. One night, the only other permanent resident of the building, a woman named Kei, knocks on his door. She's drunk and tries to convince Harada to finish the bottle of champagne with her, but he rebuffs her offer and closes the door. Several nights later Harada encounters Kei again, and the pair become lovers. Later on Harada is scouting locations for a script and finds himself in Asakusa, Tokyo's former "entertainment district" and the area he grew up in. A chance encounter leads him to meet a couple that closely resemble Harada's parents, who have both been dead since he was twelve. Although he knows they cannot be alive, Harada enjoys spending time with his parents, playing catch with his father and cooking with his mother, or just playing card games as a family. Unfortunately, over the course of the summer Harada has become haggard and pale, ageing unnaturally. Kei comes to suspect that Harada's visits to his parents are draining his vitality, and begs him to stop seeing them.

Like many of Ōbayashi's films, *The Discarnates* focuses on nostalgia and our view of the past, particularly our own. At the start of the film Harada sees his situation as a position of strength: he's successful, he's single and responsible only for himself. Through his meetings with his parents and his relationship with Kei, Harada comes to understand that his behavior is not strength but weakness, fleeing from any obligation that might cause him the same pain he felt when his parents were killed. He has become estranged to his own teenage son, subjecting him to the same abandonment and alienation that Harada himself experienced.

As befits a film about traditions and the way our past reflects and defines our lives, *The Discarnates* is based upon a number of traditional ghost stories, transposed into a contemporary setting. The most important one is the *Kaidan botan dōrō* (Ghost story of the peony lanterns). Originally of Chinese origin, this tale is one of the most popular ghost stories in Japan and has been retold and adapted a great many times over the centuries. In the story, a lonely samurai falls in love with a beautiful woman only to discover that she has been dead for several months. Realizing that his relationship with this woman is draining his life away, the samurai chooses to stay with her and the pair cross to the underworld, together for eternity.

The *Kaidan botan dōrō* is obviously the primary source for Harada's relationship with Kei, but it isn't the only one. In Yamada's novel Kei is an *onryō*, a vengeful spirit driven by feelings of anger and hatred against those responsible for the person's demise. Blaming Harada for rejecting her, after her suicide Kei returns to seek revenge. In Ōbayashi's adaptation she has become more like the *yuki-onna* or "snow woman," one of many supernatural beings found in Japanese folklore. In these stories the *yuki-onna* marries a human male, disguising her supernatural origin, but is forced to abandon her new life when her husband unknowingly breaks the conditions of their union. Likewise Kei must leave Harada when he discovers who she is and how she died, giving the film a more tragic ending than Yamada's novel.

Despite drawing influence from traditional tales, *The Discarnates* has plenty to say about modern families and the downside of contemporary Japan's punishing work ethic. Harada is given a second chance to spend time with his parents, but for most working fathers they will only realize what they have lost when it is too late to bring it back, something that clearly rang true with Japanese audiences.—Jim Harper

DOOMED MEGALOPOLIS (1991)

DIRECTOR: Rintarō
SCREENPLAY: Rintarō
SPECS: 160 minutes; color

Doomed Megalopolis is a 1991 four-part animation directed by Rintarō (b. 1941). As an original video animation, it did not see a theatrical release. Its Japanese title, *Teito Monogatari* (The tale of the imperial capital) refers to the twelve-volume epic novel written by Hiroshi Aramata (b. 1947) upon which it is based. The novel—which boasts a great variety of both historical and fictional characters—is a retelling of the history of Tokyo during the twentieth century, but focuses heavily on occultism and magic.

Like its 1988 live-action predecessor, Akio Jissōji's (1937–2006) *Tokyo: The Last Megalopolis*, *Doomed Megalopolis* adapts most major events occurring within the first four volumes of the novel. Due to the difficulty in adapting such a wealth of source material, *Doomed Megalopolis* is also the victim of a disjointed narrative. However, running at less than three hours total, it seems to adapt the material in a more cohesive manner than its 1988 counterpart.

While undoubtedly influenced by the live-action adaptation, Rintarō chose to focus heavily on the supernatural elements of the novel, knowing that the medium of animation could bring them to life in a way that the cinematic special effects of the time could not. Further, the darker and more sexual elements of the novel are further emphasized in this adaptation, perhaps owing to the heightened influence of *ero guro nansensu* in animated works such as *Urotsukidōji: Legend of the Overfiend* (1987–1989) and *Wicked City* (1987).

Doomed Megalopolis focuses on a powerful sorcerer (*onmyōji*, or "master of yin-yang") named Yasunori Katō (his voice reprised by actor Kyūsaku Shimada, b. 1955) and his attempts to destroy the megalopolis of Tokyo by reawakening the spirit of Taira no Masakado (d. 940), a revolutionary who almost overturned the Japanese government in ancient times. Katō plans to realize Masakado's initial ambitions, focusing his attention on the Tatsumiya family. The Tatsumiyas join forces with other fictional and historical characters in an attempt to defeat Katō and save Tokyo.

The first episode begins in 1907, demonstrating an unsuccessful attempt on the part of Katō to awaken the spirit of Masakado. The next several scenes introduce the principal characters—Yukari Tatsumiya (voiced by Keiko Han, b. 1953), Yōichirō Tatsumiya (voiced by Kaneto Shiozawa, 1954–2000), Junichi Narutaki (voiced by Kōichi Yamadera, b. 1961), and Yasumasa Hirai (voiced by Naya Gōrō, 1929–2013). Other historical figures, such as the industrialist Eiichi Shibusawa (1840–1931), voiced by Osamu Saka (b. 1930), and the architect Torahiko Terada (1878–1935), voiced by Naoki Tatsuta (b. 1950), are also introduced.

This adaptation focuses much more on Yukari's character. She sees a vision of Tokyo's incoming destruction and remembers her brother Yōichirō attempting to strangle her and then relenting. She is targeted by Katō early on, as he slips her a curse via a kiss. She is kidnapped by Katō during the night and it is the onmyōji Hirai that must detect her location. Hirai finds her with Katō, and the two of them duel with magic. Yukari is recovered by the author Rohan Kōda (1867–1947), who is given a minor role in this adaptation, but is a major character in the novel. Shortly thereafter, Yukari vomits a large phallic insect-like creature—the physical manifestation of Katō's enchantment on her.

Disguised as Yukari's nurse, Katō's assistant, Feng Hong, gives Yukari a second dose of the spell, also via a kiss. Katō appears to kidnap her again, but she is under the protection of Hirai and a group of onmyōji—identical in the film adaptation. Katō's demons attack, penetrating the sacred seals on the temple. Inside, Hong's skin molts away, revealing a gigantic insect creature that controls her body. Hirai attacks it, and it explodes in a mess of juices and pus, killing Hong. With the temple breached, Katō walks in and kidnaps Yukari. Hirai attempts to strike Katō with an arrow, but it is magically reflected back upon him, causing critical injury. Katō escapes with Yukari and the episode ends.

The second episode begins with Katō casting a spell on the defenseless Yukari so that she may operate under his control. He brings her to Masakado's grave, where the still-sleeping Masakado speaks through her voice, warning Katō to let him sleep. Katō urges Masakado to join him, but ultimately fails to resurrect him. Katō then sees that Yukari is pregnant. He declares that their child will serve as a better medium through which to reawaken Masakado.

Abandoned by Katō, Yukari is recovered by Narutaki. Her companions understand that she is pregnant with Katō's child. She wakes from sleep being choked by her brother Yōichirō, just as he did many years ago. He relents, and she gasps for air. Yōichirō then initiates sexual intercourse with her. Meanwhile, Emperor Meiji (r. 1852–1912) dies, and Hirai kills himself as an act of *junshi* (suicide through fidelity). Hirai bleeds out and his blood forms a character indicating the year 1923. While Hirai's death does provide the year in which Katō will attack, its divinatory aspect is downplayed in this version. Further, Hirai also leaves a will containing all of the information he had obtained regarding Katō prior to his death.

The next scene, now in 1923, introduces a young girl—Yukari's daughter Yukiko. By this time, Tokyo has suffered from several minor earthquakes that happen to have Masakado's grave as the epicenter. Terada explains to Narutaki that the Chinese city of Dalian shows a similar pattern, and thus, the two cities have a similar vibrational frequency—earthquakes at Dalian would then resonate at Tokyo. The film version fills in the gap here, showing Katō at Dalian, attempting to initiate an earthquake in Tokyo.

Kamo—another onmyōji that largely takes over Hirai's role—predicts the day that Katō will return. Narutaki and the others prepare in an attempt to save both Yukiko and Masakado's grave from Katō. Katō succeeds in luring Yukiko away from her protectors. The two then fall into a magical trap set by Kamo. Believing that Yukiko's life is at stake, Narutaki disarms the trap, allowing Katō to arrive at Masakado's grave. Kamo challenges Katō and is quickly slaughtered.

Masakado again warns Katō not to interrupt his sleep—this time through Yukiko. Using Yukiko as a medium, Masakado's energy retrieves Kamo's blade and plunges it through Katō's neck. When he tears out the knife to strike back, he is electrocuted. Masakado then releases Yukiko and a shocked Katō can no longer move. The next day, September 1, at nearly noon, begins with the Great Kantō Earthquake. The devastation is wide and unprecedented. While Yukari laughs in madness, having seen this in her vision, Yukiko watches the endless flames in silence.

During the third and fourth episodes, Yukari and the Tatsumiyas slip farther into the background so that a new protagonist can be highlighted: Keiko Mekata, a shrine maiden at Omokage Shrine. The third episode opens with Keiko dreaming of an elegant white horse. Her father, the shrine priest, interprets this as a sign that Masakado has chosen Keiko to take up arms against Katō. In time, she marries Yōichirō, entering into the Tatsumiya family. Since then, Katō rears his head from time to time, possessing Yukari for example.

As Tokyo recovers from the earthquake, Shibusawa, the feng shui (Chinese geomancy) master Shigemaru Kuroda, and other historical figures begin to plan to create an underground railroad to facilitate travel in the capital. Kuroda in particular uses his skills to keep the vast energies underneath Tokyo from manifesting as major earthquakes. However, the underground workers encounter demons manipulated by Katō that stall their progress. Between the demons and a cave-in incident, the workers become too scared to proceed. Terada enlists the aid of Makoto Nishimura (1883–1956), more specifically that of his artificial robot Gakutensoku, which can do the work without fearing the demons.

Finally, Katō attacks the Tatsumiyas in full force, spiriting away with Yukiko, with Keiko closing in quickly. Katō reveals that he plans to sacrifice Yukiko to stimulate the underground spirits in releasing their energy. Simultaneously, the underground demons do their best to repel Gakutensoku. Nishimura rigs Gakutensoku to explode, destroying the demons and tearing the underground energy away from Katō. Keiko chooses this moment to strike, burying a dagger through his palm and deep into his left eye. With Katō defeated again, Yukiko is rescued and the work on the underground railway can continue unhindered.

The fourth and final episode begins with a thirteen-year-old Yukiko ardently working on quintic equations under Yukari's guidance with the moon very large in the sky. These are revealed to be Lagrange equations, given to Yukiko from her mother, who is possessed by Katō, and feeding Yukiko's answers to him. It is determined that the moon is becoming closer to the Earth, that there is some connection to Yukiko's equations, and that the background culprit is likely Katō.

Meanwhile, Yōichirō is tormented by memories of Yukari. It is revealed that her brush with death at his hands directly led to her sensitivity to the supernatural, and thus made her Katō's first target. He is troubled so much that he attempts to commit suicide. When he fails, in his madness, he attempts to strangle Yukiko. Once she is freed, Yukiko reveals that she is *his* daughter—a product of incestuous rape—not Katō's.

In the meantime, the moon has traveled so close to the Earth that it obscures 90 percent of the sky. Determining with Kuroda where Katō is hiding, Keiko rides to challenge Katō for good. Demons attempt to stop her left and right, but she slices through all of them. As Keiko nears Katō's lair, the moon arrives at its closest point and "bounces" back toward space.

When Keiko enters the building, she drops her sword. Katō sends further demons to attack her as she advances toward him, but her radiant power causes them to vanish. It is revealed that she is an incarnation of Avalokiteśvara, the bodhisattva of compassion; rather than attacking these beasts, she is pacifying them. Katō uses all of the magic he can muster to stop her, but she continues to advance, step by step. Finally, Katō falls to his knees in defeat. Keiko embraces the dark onmyōji and they kiss. A great power surges between them, wrecking the building.

While neither Keiko nor Katō are seen again, it is assumed that Keiko was able to pacify even Katō's troubled spirit. His damage is reversed and the moon returns back to its initial position. Masakado's grave remains silent and the film ends, with a famous quote from the real Rohan Kōda.

Doomed Megalopolis was quite successful in Japan, but its reputation among Western audiences tends to gravitate from average to extremely negative. Rather than the lack of familiarity with the original novel, most of the negativity stems from the incestuous rape of Yukari and the unsympathetic representation of Yōichirō. This is often worsened by *Doomed Megalopolis*'s lack of a true protagonist, which causes Western audiences that are used to young male protagonists to incorrectly identify Yōichirō as such.

This incorrect identification also leads to a misinterpretation of Yukari's rape—one of the most crucial parts of the narrative to appear in this adaptation. Because the rape is part of a side plot, it receives little attention in *Doomed Megalopolis*. However, if Yōichirō is viewed as the main character, the rape scene feels improvised, even shoehorned into the plot just for the shock factor. Of course, nothing could be further from the truth: the revelation of Yukiko's father's identity serves as a critical plot twist in the final episode.

Westerners also have a difficult time reconciling the juxtaposition between the fearsome representation of supernatural chaos and the uneventful day-to-day life of Tokyo's inhabitants. Viewers expecting a supernatural fright fest have trouble justifying the transition between fast-paced action scenes and the general mundaneness of events while Katō is off-screen; the dichotomy between the two has often been criticized as a production flaw. However, these divergences are quite crucial to the work as a whole. While *Tokyo: The Last Megalopolis* is particularly good at demonstrating the rise of a modernized Tokyo from the ashes of the slowly dying supernatural hub it once was, this contrast is only hinted at in Rintarō's adaptation. Katō is part of a dying breed, and it is Shibusawa's new modernized Tokyo that defies him, blooming into the megalopolis that still exists today.—Joseph P. Elacqua

See also ero guro nansensu genre; *Onmyōji; Teito Monogatari Gaiden; Tokyo: The Last Megalopolis*

Bibliography
Jissōji, Akio, dir. *Tokyo: The Last Megalopolis.* Takashige Ichise, 1988. Film.
Rintarō, dir. *Doomed Megalopolis.* Takashige Ichise, 1991. Original video animation.

DOPPELGÄNGER (2003)
DIRECTOR: Kiyoshi Kurosawa
SCREENPLAY: Ken Furusawa, Kiyoshi Kurosawa
SPECS: 107 minutes; color

Produced in the production committee system and distributed by Amuse Pictures in 2003, Kiyoshi Kurosawa's *Doppelgänger* was featured at the Busan International Film Festival and International Film Festival Rotterdam among other festivals following its domestic release in Japan. It later received a DVD release under the Palisades Tartan "Asia Extreme" UK/USA DVD label in 2005. Noriyuki Mizuguchi's expert cinematography masks the complex setups allowing the fluid appearance and interaction of the film's doubles, and Takayuki Nitta's subtle art direction extends Kurosawa's constant interests in deserted, run-down spaces. An appropriately inventive score by Yusuke Hayashi supports the film's unpredictable careening between suspense and levity, engineering and subverting audience expectations. The film represents a cathartic reworking of Kurosawa's long-standing interest in popular genres, playing with his popular association with horror, and more thoroughly embracing his unappreciated flair for comedy. It is also a kind of reflective climax of the collaboration between Kurosawa and actor Koji Yakusho, who had served as Kurosawa's own double or onscreen avatar in a successful string of films, collaborating on at least one film per year between 1997 and 2000. Only a few months apart in age, their critically acclaimed work together represents one of the great director-actor partnerships, which *Doppelgänger* pushes to the limit. It may begin as a horror movie, but it becomes something else entirely along the way.

Doppelgänger tells the story of Michio Hayasaki, played by Yakusho, an engineer developing a potentially groundbreaking mind-controlled robotic wheelchair for disabled people. Stressed out by his company's difficult deadlines, the first scenes exhibit Hayasaki as a meek workaholic. Without warning, his doppelgänger appears. Their interactions are rendered with seamless composite image doubling, allowing for Yakusho's impressive double performance in which the visually identical characters clash, revealing nearly opposite personalities. Hayasaki is warned of the danger with doubles by Yuka Nagai, played by Hiromi Nagasaku, whose brother's own doppelgänger caused him to commit suicide before it took his place. While the sight of one's double is normally an omen of death, here the event signals an injection of comedy. The double is not stoic or expressionless, but instead shockingly casual and laid-back, convincing Hayasaki he's nothing to be afraid of, and they should band together to reach his goals. However similar their appearance, Hayasaki soon learns they are opposite in nature, and their relationship slowly leads him toward madness. His crisis of identity is accented by split screens, as the question of what precisely constitutes one's identity is posed through their relationship. This existential problem is also communicated through Hayasaki's obsessive goal of designing the bionic wheelchair, a machine made to replace functions of the human body, designed to give people with spinal injuries who have lost control of their body mastery over their environment. Hayasaki loses his job, but continues to work on the chair with his double, hiring Kimishima, played by Yusuke Santamaria—a not entirely trustworthy assistant—at the same time he's tracked by corrupt businessman Murakami, played by Akira Emoto. Soon the double is found to be shockingly amoral, and mayhem ensues by turns disturbing and hilarious.

Doppelgänger pushes Kurosawa's propensity for physical comedy (foregrounded in much of his early V-Cinema work) to the extreme. This comes to a head at the conclusion of the film with the appearance of a giant tumbling ball (a gag à la Indiana Jones, which was improvised on set with one of Kurosawa's assistant directors), as well as characters appearing in the final scenes as if in a video game, attempting to stop Hayasaki from reaching his goal of delivering his robot prototype. This comic treatment, and an un-cynically happy, if not jarring, ending comes, following the apocalyptic plot and tone of *Pulse* (2001), in which a kind of virus or possession is passed through computers and the Internet feeding upon people's loneliness. The change was signaled in the persistence of human connections beyond technology found in *Bright Future* (2003) and is extended here in provocative and surprising ways. At the same time, it also represents Kurosawa's increasing willingness to subvert the genre expectations of not only horror and comedy but the confines of the art house film, taken to further extremes in *Seventh Code* (2013) and the accompanying short *Beautiful New Bay Area Project* (2013).

While *Doppelgänger* may disappoint those viewers looking only for scares (perhaps misled by the Tartan Asia Extreme release, which overemphasized those elements in its promotional material and copywriting), it again proves Kurosawa as one of the most inventive filmmakers to work in the genre, if only along its fringes.—Joel Neville Anderson

• E •

EKO EKO AZARAK films

Eko Eko Azarak: Wizard of Darkness (1995)
DIRECTOR: Shimako Sato
SCREENPLAY: Shiniki Koga, Shimako Sato
SPECS: 80 minutes; color

Eko Eko Azarak II: Birth of the Wizard (1996)
DIRECTOR: Shimako Sato
SCREENPLAY: Shiniki Koga, Shimako Sato
SPECS: 83 minutes; color

Eko Eko Azarak: Misa the Dark Angel (1998)
DIRECTOR: Katsuhito Ueno
SCREENPLAY: Sotaro Hayashi
SPECS: 95 minutes; color

Eko Eko Azarak: Awakening (2001)
DIRECTOR: Suzuki Koosuke
SCREENPLAY: Hirotoshi Kobayashi
SPECS: 89 minutes; color

Eko Eko Azarak: R Page (2006)
DIRECTOR: Taichi Ito
SCREENPLAY: Hiromitsu Amano
SPECS: 80 minutes; color

Eko Eko Azarak: B Page (2006)
DIRECTOR: Taichi Ito
SCREENPLAY: Hiromitsu Amano
SPECS: 83 minutes; color

Eko Eko Azarak is a series of six live-action films stretching from 1995 to 2006 and based on manga of the same name. The series centers on Misa Kuroi, played by various actresses, who is a powerful dark witch who uses her abilities for mostly good as she tries to stop various evil forces from summoning evil powers while protecting herself and those close to her.

The first film, *Eko Eko Azarak: Wizard of Darkness*, was directed by Shimako Sato (b. 1964) and released in 1995. It opens with a group of hooded figures chanting in a ritualistic manner around a pentagram, while elsewhere a frightened woman runs in terror down the street from an unseen assailant. Once the ritual is complete, a large metal beam falls from above, killing her. These hooded figures explain that although the sacrifice is now complete, more are needed to cleanse their sanctuary. In a high school, a male student explains his theory that a string of recent accidents is actually part of a magical ritual to summon the Devil, showing that the incidents can be connected on a map to form a pentagram. Soon, a new transfer student is introduced to the class, Misa Kuroi, played by Kimika Yoshino (b. 1975).

It quickly becomes apparent that Misa is no ordinary student when one of her fellow students, Mizuki Kurahashi, played by Miho Kanno (b. 1977), collapses and Misa immediately recognizes her fall as the result of a magic spell. Breaking the spell, she runs to the basement of the school to find a recently used altar, but no sign of the perpetrator. While in search of a culprit, Misa encounters a group of students who wish to curse a teacher that has been molesting female students. It quickly becomes clear that they don't know how to perform the curse and Misa agrees to show them the proper ritual for harming someone using a voodoo doll. The following day the cursed teacher falls ill and is absent—a point at which students begin to take Misa's use of black magic more seriously. The rumors turn to fear when the cursed teacher later has a serious accident and becomes hospitalized. Misa knows that this couldn't be the original curse and concludes that the real perpetrators put an additional curse on the teacher to frame Misa.

Miss Shirai, played by Mio Takaki (b. 1960), is having an affair with one of her female students. One night she has a number of students stay late for a makeup test, but then leaves the room for an extended period of time to be with her girlfriend and never returns. The students eventually try to leave but find themselves unable to escape the school building. Windows won't open, and when they try to step outside they are transported instantly back into a classroom. The number 13 also appears magically on the blackboard, seemingly representing the number of students in the room. One student mysteriously drowns while in the bathroom by herself, and the number on the board instantly changes to 12. While trying to contact the outside world, five students become trapped in the teacher's lounge and are killed by an unseen force and the number changes to 7. As the numbers continue to dwindle, Misa reveals that this isn't the first occasion where people near to her have died and that the magic boundary that is trapping them in the school is also blocking the use of her powers. Unable to save her friends, Misa finds herself alone and is abruptly attacked by Miss Shirai. Cloaked in a robe, Miss Shirai informs her that she is the final sacrifice. In the ensuing fight, Misa manages to overpower and kill Miss Shirai, only to realize that the fight may still not be over.

The second film, *Eko Eko Azarak II: Birth of the Wizard*, was also directed by Shimako Sato, and was released in 1996. It is a prequel to the first film and explores the origin story of Misa Kuroi, again played by Kimika Yoshino (b. 1975), as she first discovers her powers. In 1880 an entire village was massacred for unknown reasons. In modern times, a professor and student are investigating the site, when they uncover a mummy. The mummy comes to life, brutally murders the student, and possesses her body.

Misa is having a small party at her house when several strange occurrences begin. When going out to buy beer, she notices a man following her and when she returns home, she is attacked by someone who has murdered all of her friends in a gruesome fashion. The man following her, Saiga, played by Wataru Shihodo (b. 1962), arrives in time to save Misa and escape. He struggles to protect her as multiple assailants, who are possessed by the same evil spirit, relentlessly pursue her and brutally kill anyone in their way. Saiga tells Misa the story of the aforementioned village and reveals that all of the residents were magic users. A resurrection spell went awry and created an evil spirit that is now trying to possess Misa's body to gain power and a permanent physical form. Saiga was one of the few remaining survivors of the village and was tasked with finding Misa and preventing the spirit from taking her. As they flee from their attackers, Saiga desperately tries to prepare Misa for the road ahead of her, and Misa struggles to find the strength within herself to accept her destiny and confront the evil spirit.

The third film, *Eko Eko Azarak: Misa the Dark Angel*, was directed by Katsuhito Ueno and released in 1998. This film introduces a new character, Misa Kuroi's uncle Satoru, played by Bang-ho Cho (b. 1956), an eccentric morgue worker who refers any supernatural incidents he comes across to his niece for further investigation. Following a lead provided by her uncle, Misa, who is now played by Hinako Saeki (b. 1977), heads to a nearby all-female high school and successfully infiltrates the drama club. After becoming close with the other members of the club, she discovers too late that the play they are rehearsing has the power to initiate a Lovecraftian ritual that transports all its participants to a parallel dimension full of lumbering robed figures.

After being trapped in the alternate universe, Misa and the other members of the drama club begin to get killed off one at a time by a malevolent force that preys on their worst fears. Misa uncovers a plot by the former head of the school to create a "homunculus," an artificial person free from sin and imperfection, through the use of human sacrifice. As the ritual continues, Misa is forced to confront the fact that some of her classmates are keeping dark secrets of their own.

The 2001 entry is *Eko Eko Azarak: Awakening*, directed by Suzuki Koosuke (b. 1961). The story opens with Misa, now played by Natsuki Kato (b. 1985), being taken to the hospital from the site of an unseen violent incident. The police are baffled by the gory scene they find, and suspicious that Misa, although unconscious, seems to be completely unharmed. Meanwhile, a sleazy and ambitious tabloid reporter named Maeda, played by Kenichi Endou (b. 1961), frantically attempts to dig up any salacious details about Misa's life.

After a series of mysterious incidents result in the death of a nurse and a medical examiner, Misa flees the hospital and goes into hiding as her story begins to gain momentum in the national news. Maeda is overjoyed at the attention the story is receiving, and continues to dig deeper, using increasingly unethical means. When Misa receives word that her parents have died in a sudden murder-suicide while overseas, she is at first despondent but then resolves to do whatever it takes to reconnect with what is left of her old life. Upon returning to school, her classmates panic at the sight of her, before slowly beginning to realize the degree to which they have been manipulated by the news media.

Maeda, desperate to maintain the momentum of his story, hires an actress to impersonate Misa for a televised interview. Confused by what they're seeing,

Misa's classmates then immediately turn on her, with the exception of her friend Hitomi, played by Mitsuho Ootani (b. 1982), who remains loyal. Rushing to the studio to intervene, Misa and her friends arrive just in time to see the look-alike inexplicably stab herself to death on live television. The trauma of seeing this appears to reawaken Misa's powers, leading to a final showdown between her and her accusers.

The final two films, *Eko Eko Azarak: R Page* and *Eko Eko Azarak: B Page*, were released direct-to-video in 2006. Both films are directed by Taichi Ito (b. 1971) and feature Narumi Konno (b. 1988) as Misa.

In *R Page*, a reporter travels to a small town investigating a string of bizarre deaths. He soon encounters Misa, who has been sent there by the leader of a cabal of black-magic wizards who have foreseen the rebirth of a demon called "Ezekiel." Along the way, the two of them befriend a young girl named Saeko, played by Nana Yanagisawa (b. 1987) and an orphan boy named Wataru, who are in the care of a local nun, played by Yuko Ito (b. 1974).

B Page follows after the end of *R Page*, retaining certain story elements, including the return of Saeko and Wataru and the ongoing threat of the demon Ezekiel. In this final (to date) installment, Misa crosses paths with Ryo, a wheelchair-bound photographer who was injured in an accident that also killed a model named Mirisu. Ryo wants to use Misa's black magic to bring Mirisu back to life, but may also have set things in motion that are beyond her control.

The films are generally only loosely connected, and the timeline remains extremely vague. The only constant element is Misa herself, and even she is barely recognizable at times. Although the films vary significantly in tone, they generally share a remarkably bleak worldview. Misa is able to reliably fend off the apocalypse, but is almost completely unable to protect the people close to her, often emerging as the sole survivor at the end of each film.

Whereas much of the J-horror canon relies heavily on local superstition, the Eko Eko Azarak series prefers to borrow as much as it can from Christian and satanic imagery, as well as exoticized Western mysticism in general. *Yuurei* and *yokai* are nowhere to be found, having been replaced by pentagrams and horned beasts.—Rebecca Bacheller

Bibliography

Sato, Shimako, dir. *Eko Eko Azarak: Wizard of Darkness*. GAGA, 1995. Film.

———. *Eko Eko Azarak II: Birth of the Wizard*. GAGA, 1996. Film.

Suzuki, Koosuke, dir. *Eko Eko Azarak: Awakening*. GAGA, 1995. Film.

E.M.: EMBALMING (1999)

DIRECTOR: Shinji Aoyama

SCREENPLAY: Izo Hashimoto, Shinji Aoyama

SPECS: 96 minutes; color

Shinji Aoyama (1964) gained considerable international fame when his three-and-a-half hour-long *Eureka* (2000) won the Ecumenical Jury Prize at the Cannes Film Festival. One year before this international success he made a strange, morbid thriller *E.M.: Embalming* (1999), adapted from Saki Amemiya's novel.

Amemiya, a penname of Michiko Matsuda (b. 1949), the former wife of the late cult actor Yūsaku Matsuda (1949–1989), is a prolific screenwriter and novelist, notorious for, among other works, having written the original story on which the anti-PC *Perfect Education* (1999) was based. Her novel, *E.M.*, incorporates into itself the familiar pattern of the "peeking behind the taboo curtain" nonfiction genre, devoting a large proportion of its content to detailed description of the work methods and routines of its protagonist, the embalmer Miyako Murakami. In comparison, less attention is paid to the central plot involving the alleged suicide of a seventeen-year-old boy, Yoshiki Shindō. Despite the novel's lukewarm reception among hardcore mystery fans, and the criticism that in real life the embalmer's job would be closer to a beautician than a medical examiner, thus undermining the novel's plot contrivances in which Miyako would notice clues in a cadaver somehow overlooked by professional forensic specialists, the embalmer was popular enough to be given her own franchise, starring in three sequels as of January 2015.

In the film, like the novel, Miyako, played by Reiko Takashima (b. 1964) investigates Yoshiki's murder. Aided by the cynical and outspoken cop named Hiraoka, played by Yutaka Matsushige (b. 1963), the film pushes the plot into an increasingly bizarre and convoluted direction. The background for the original's multiple personality disorder is expanded to touch on such issues as collusion between political fat cats and religious cults, Japan's historical involvement in medical experiments on human subjects, and the modern society's problematic view of death as a process of physical decay, rather than of spiritual transition.

Aoyama, whose ironic, intellectual, yet committed approach to the horror and thriller genres links him to his contemporary Kiyoshi Kurosawa (b. 1955), is seemingly less interested in telling a straightforward narrative than creating a particular atmosphere of *fin-de-siècle* moral breakdown. The flagrantly fake-looking rear projection background for a driving scene, the bizarrely prosaic, almost nonchalant shoot-out between cops and criminals, and the utter lack of affective delivery in the overtly melodramatic exposition of the relationship between Dr. Fuji, played by Toshio Shiba (b. 1949), and Miyako, are some of the deliberately distancing mechanisms Aoyama employs. Unfortunately, instead of inducing a feeling of uneasy foreboding, they merely serve to prevent viewers from emotionally investing in the characters.

Of course, this does not mean that *E.M.* is badly made or even boring: the film, while obviously suffering from budgetary limitations, maintains a strikingly consistent look that might be characterized as "antiseptic noir," swathed in sickly, yellowish light or conversely displaying windy, barren urban spaces, through which the characters devoid of emotional anchors drift around. Aside from Shiba as the chain-smoking and intensely hateful Dr. Fuji, recalling William Burroughs's Dr. Benway as he hacks away at technically-still-not-dead bodies in his lab *cum* abattoir, few actors leave strong impressions. Reiko Takeshima is very attractive, but her character is annoyingly passive, considering her alleged professional skills.

E.M.'s initial reputation in the North American market was to a great extent based on its in-your-face, clinical depiction of the process of embalming. Currently, however, mainstream TV shows such as *CSI* and *Bones* routinely show naked bodies cut open and laid out on the autopsy table, disgustingly realistic flesh wounds and half-rotten organs, and other outcomes of bodily mayhem on a weekly basis. In this way, *E.M.* appears totally tame and almost abashed.—Kyu Hyun Kim

See also Aoyama, Shinji; Kurosawa, Kiyoshi

Bibliography
Aoyama Shinji, dir. *E.M.: Embalming*. GAGA Productions, 1999. Film

ERO GURO NANSENSU GENRE

The term *ero guro nansensu* (erotic grotesque nonsense), frequently shortened to *ero guro* or *guro*, refers to a literary and artistic movement originating in the quotidian culture of Japan from the 1920s and 1930s, the focus of which is the erotic, the sexually corrupt, and the decadent. Mirroring the events in the first half of the twentieth century, in particular extreme catastrophes alternating with an urgent love affair with all aspects of the modern, "grotesqueness" refers to the malformed, unnatural, or horrific. Significantly impacting the mind-set of the period were first and foremost the Great Kantō Earthquake (1 September 1923) and the mass bombing of Japanese cities in 1944 to 1945, culminating with the dropping of the atomic bombs on Hiroshima and Nagasaki. In both instances, much of the urban centers of Tokyo had to be rebuilt, but it was the earthquake that in the Japanese mind marked the big break with the traditional and signified the arrival of the modern.

During the two decades preceding the events of Pearl Harbor, the new gestures, relationships, and humor of *ero guro nansensu* came into use to express a self-consciously modern ethos that challenged state ideology and expansionism already in place. The "new" and immediate suddenly overwhelmed all else—with public spaces, familial relationships, and an ironic and "modern" sensibility of newfound Japanese capitalism commercialized and consumed in the face of tradition, on the one hand, and an internationalization arising from the mobilization of a nation for war, on the other. From a historical perspective, the term speaks to a period of time in modern cultural history divisible into three distinct parts of the whole.

The first, arising in the second decade of the twentieth century and including the beginnings of the Fifteen Years' War, reflects a "prewar, bourgeois" cultural phenomenon devoting itself by and large to intense and imminent explorations of the deviant, the bizarre, and the ridiculous.

The second period includes the Fifteen Years' War (1931–1945), where newspaper articles on fashion and new American films, for example, combined with the immediacy and the fleeting nature of gossip on sexual questions relating to its stars, might deflect attention from political and military developments. The Japanese invasion of Manchuria in 1931 was neglected and ostensibly rendered moot, in favor of transient discussions of sexual activity on the big screen that would sway the attentions of the public only up to and until they dictated the imagined lives of those seated and watching. Thus, popular culture, although frowned on by the increasingly militaristic authority of the state, served to silence the details of their own aggression from further public scrutiny. Rather than report on activities of the League of Nations' Lytton Report on Japanese encroachments onto the Asian continent, the media refocused the attentions of its readers with a minute—certainly heretofore insignificant—examination of the sensational, the mass consumption of the two-touch tease of such public images as the American Tarzan, clad in no more than a loosely fitting loincloth, and Jane, his woman, stripped down to her bare legs. Put differently, what was at one moment condemned as erotic, grotesque nonsense could at another hide inconvenient truths of the world beyond. The Sada Abe incident of 1936, where a woman strangled her lover and castrated his corpse, for example, struck a chord with latent public sensibilities, and would come to represent the genre for the second half of the century, even as it referred to all such personal behaviors and larger social movements unleashed among the Japanese public—while the details of what those beyond her borders had already perceived as the Second World War were concomitantly suppressed.

The third, the *apure*, or postwar period (from the French *après-guerre*, "postwar generation") is further inscribed with the re-emergence of such matters, especially in manga and music, and sometime later in the literary, performing, and visual arts. The *ero guro* shifted from the peripheral, as an element of many Japanese horror films, to dictate the very definition of *pinku eiga*, particularly of the 1960s and 1970s. *Shogun's Joys of Torture* (1968, Tokugawa Onna Keibatsushi), directed by Teruo Ishii (1924–2005), is the quintessential exemplary of a new style of public nudity included under the rubric of pink films. In fact, from the late 1960s and early 1970s, Japanese studios produced their own variations of the *pinku eiga*, increasingly made comfortable with brutal attitudes toward—if not the actual depictions of—sex and violence taken together. Both *Horrors of Malformed Men* (1969, Kyofu Kikei Ningen), again directed by Ishii, and *Blind Beast* (1969, Moju), directed by Masumura Yasuzo (1924–1986) represent the nature of the genre as it gained in popularity.

Also signaling what would emerge at Toei Studios as the "pinky violent" style in the early 1970s and was billed as Ishii's splatter film "sequel," appropriately titled *Shogun's Sadism* (1976, Tokugawa Onna Keibatsu-emaki: Ushi-zaki no Kei), is hardly so, directed instead by Makiguchi Yūji (b. 1936). Less overtly political than extremely misogynistic, female abuse and rape become a mainstay of the genre, dramatizing the uneven relationship between men and woman in Japan at the time. Despite scenes of violation, the finer details of which are pixelated out, the Makiguchi's film managed to strike a peculiar balance between horror and humor with equal amounts of torture, best illustrated by the detail behind the castration scene, of feet being hammered to a bloody pulp, or of the slow and excruciatingly torturous beheading with a blunt saw. While there is plenty here for a fan of extreme cinema, what with intense scenes of torture and obligatory amounts of sexual sadism, the film is at the same time an exhaustive meditation on the ethical nature of violence. Consider, for example, the still images of the dead and dying in the aftermath of the atomic bomb in Hiroshima and Nagasaki, their very presence underscoring that all such atrocities, great or small, are not merely a fact of the past but continue into the present. That the film is set in Nagasaki makes this explicit, as does the fact that two of the actors from the first story appear in the second in different narrative roles, the position of power reversed, suggesting that the weak can indeed become the strong within a circular karmic understanding of life.

The genre continues to gain in popularity, even now, as with *Strange Circus* (2005, Kimyō na Sākasu), directed by Sion Sano (b. 1961), where the structure of the family is redefined as it were by incest, suicide, and murder.

In fact, modern *guro* artists, some of whom cite erotic grotesque nonsense as an influence on their work, explore the macabre intermingled with sexual overtones. Among the leaders in the industry are such directors as Hideshi Hino (b. 1946), Toshiharu Ikeda (1951–2010), Shinji Imaoka (b. 1965), Teruo Ishii (1924–2005), Atsushi Kaneko (b. 1966), Yasuzō Masumura (1924–1986), Rintaro Mayuzumi (b. 1953), Satoru Ogura (b. 1957), Okuyama Kazuyoshi (b. 1953), Hisayasu Satō (b. 1969), Sone Chūsei (b. 1937), and Noboru Tanaka (1937–2006).

Often the erotic element of such productions, even when not explicit, merges with the grotesque. Others view *ero guro* as a low-budget genre of decidedly Japanese pornography and *hentai* (loosely meaning "strange" or perverted), making the most of blood and gore, disfiguration and violence, enemas and excrements. This tradition of morbid eroticism continues in the work of such respected contemporary Japanese illustrators and manga artists, Takato Yamamoto (b. 1960) and Suehiro Madruo (b. 1956). With the former—in dreamlike scenes involving themes of darkness and bondage; of vampires, decay, and metamorphosis; of love and death betrayed in bondage and torture—the often naked, effeminate protagonists are frequently depicted as calm, even aloof and eerily detached. The horror depicted in illustrations by the latter, adopting an illustrative style highly reminiscent of World War II–era Japanese propaganda posters, are typically somewhat gorier in detail. The oft-used motif of a youthful couple frozen in an intimate embrace, with penetration, in fact, serves his work well, insofar as it, likewise, disrupts with another insertion—of gore. In both instances, we revel in a celebration of the more grotesque, far more salacious elements that we now associate with all things *ero guro*.—James A. Wren

See also pink films

Bibliography
Aguilar, Carlos, ed. *Bizarre Sinema! Japanese Ero Gro & Pinku Eiga 1956–1979*. Florence, Italy: Glittering Images, 2005.
Boscaro, Adriana, Gatti, Franco, and Raveri, Massimo. *Rethinking Japan Vol 1: Literature, Visual Arts & Linguistics*. London: Routledge, 2013.
Buruma, Ian. *Inventing Japan, 1853–1964*. New York: The Modern Library, 2003.

EVIL DEAD TRAP (1988)
DIRECTOR: Toshiharu Ikeda
SCREENPLAY: Takashi Ishii
SPECS: 102 minutes; color

Despite the success of films like *Friday the 13th* (1980) and *A Nightmare on Elm Street* (1984) in Japan, the slasher movie never really became a significant part of the Japanese horror scene. This is partly because of timing; when those films made it into Japanese cinemas and video stores, domestic horror was at a low ebb, surviving mainly through big-budget movies like Nobuhiko Obayashi's *Ijintachi to no natsu* (1988) or Akio Jissōji's *Tokyo: The Last Megalopolis* (1988). The low-budget sexploitation arena produced a handful of genre films, including Gaira's *Entrails* movies and the notorious Guinea Pig series, but these were not widely seen and profited more from their reputation than any degree of popularity. However, in this period the underground scene did produce one bona fide cult classic, Toshiharu Ikeda's *Evil Dead Trap* (1988). As well as being Japan's first true slasher movie, Ikeda's film also prefigured and influenced the splatter boom of the late 1990s, not to mention the cyberpunk-splatter and "torture porn" waves of the following decade.

TV host Nami Tsuchiya, played by Miyuki Ono, presents a show that specializes in *mondo*-style material for late night audiences. Every week she puts out a request for the fans to send her videos, but most of it is junk she can't use. That changes when she receives a tape that appears to show a woman being murdered, graphically and realistically. The video also gives directions to an abandoned military-industrial site where the killing was apparently carried out. Accompanied by her regular production team, Nami heads off to investigate the location, only to find her friends disappearing one by one.

It's a classic slasher movie setup, and on that score *Evil Dead Trap* certainly delivers, providing a slew of brutal murders. Scripted by *Flower and Snake* (2004) director and longtime Ikeda associate Takashi Ishii, *Evil Dead Trap* is informed by the writer's passion for European horror films, and in particular the works of Dario Argento, whose complex and bloody murders were a clear influence on the film. Likewise, Tomohiko Kira's synth-flavored score carries echoes of Claudio Simonetti and Goblin's work on Argento's movies. Technically, *Evil Dead Trap* is a high-quality film, but it is visually outstanding, due to the talents of veteran cinematographer Masaki Tamura. A key figure in the Japanese independent cinema scene in the 1980s and 1990s, Tamura's excellent work goes a long way in elevating *Evil Dead Trap* above its contemporaries.

Although it fits well into the slasher ethos, *Evil Dead Trap* is not simply a straightforward *Friday the 13th* clone, bringing together a number of outside influences and concepts, both Japanese and Western. With the exception of Miyuki Ono and a few others, the bulk of the cast came from the AV (adult video) world and *pinku eiga* (soft-core theatrical pornography), where Ikeda and Ishii predominantly worked. Ikeda also stages some low-level tracking shots through fog-bound woodland that seem inspired by *Evil Dead* director Sam Raimi, but similar black-and-white shots through abandoned industrial land are immediately reminiscent of the works of Sōgo Ishii, and in particular *Halber Mensch*, his 1986 collaboration with German industrial collective Einstürzende Neubauten (like Ikeda, Sōgo Ishii was an associate of Director's Company, the independent production company that produced both *Evil Dead Trap* and *Halber Mensch*). In retrospect they also seem to prefigure *Tetsuo: The Iron Man*, the 1989 debut feature of Shinya Tsukamoto, a director very much influenced by the films of Sōgo Ishii. In the last thirty minutes *Evil Dead Trap* takes a turn into body-horror territory equally inspired by Ridley Scott's *Alien* (1979) and David Cronenberg, leading to a climax that is unexpected, to say the least; whether it's entirely successful is another question, but Ikeda and Ishii cannot be accused of playing things by the numbers.

In a career spanning two decades, *Evil Dead Trap* remains one of Ikeda's most well-known films. Two sequels followed. Scripted by Chiaki Konaka, Izo Hashimoto's *Evil Dead Trap 2: Hideki* (1991) has no connection to its predecessor, being an overtly psychedelic splatter movie that follows overweight film projectionist Aki as she murders a string of sex workers in the garish, overcrowded Tokyo urban sprawl. Ikeda returned to the series in 1993 to direct *Evil Dead Trap 3: Broken Love Killer*, an understated psycho-thriller about the battle of wills between an inexperienced female detective and a brilliant sociopath who may have murdered his wife.—Jim Harper

EXTE (2007)

DIRECTOR: Sion Sono
SCREENPLAY: Sion Sono, Masaki Adachi, Makoto Sanada
SPECS: 108 minutes; color

Exte, also released as *Exte: Hair Extensions*, is a 2007 horror comedy from director Sion Sono (b. 1961). The film revolves around the vengeful spirit of a victim of human trafficking whose hair torments and kills people following her death at the hands of her captors. An aspiring young hairdresser named Yuko, played by Chiaki Kuriyama (b. 1984), who is best known for her roles in *Battle Royale* and *Kill Bill*, gets inadvertently drawn into the hair's rampage after unknowingly receiving a batch of hair extensions harvested from the stolen corpse. Long a staple of the J-horror genre, the vengeful *yuurei* ghost with long, dark hair obscuring her face has become an iconic image. In this film, Sono effectively "cuts out the middleman" and has the hair itself committing gruesome murders.

Officials are called in to inspect a shipping container found to be suspicious due to its peculiar smell, later revealing that the container is completely full of human hair extensions. Initially the smell is thought to be associated with the hair itself, but later a dead female appears holding a small silver bell in her hand. An autopsy on the corpse reveals a large gash in her midsection that had been clumsily stitched together. Upon cutting the stitches, her midsection is revealed to be full of hair. She also has mysterious tattoos on her bald head and evidence of past surgeries that lead the doctors performing the autopsy to conclude she was a victim of human trafficking. A deranged but affable hair-obsessed morgue employee named Yamazaki, played by Ren Osugi (b. 1951), discovers that hair is beginning to grow on her head and from her mouth and steals the body in order to harvest its hair for use in his ghoulish hobby of collecting hair from dead women and reselling it.

Meanwhile, Yuko is working tirelessly to pursue her lofty aspirations as a hair stylist in a small town, only to have her life repeatedly interrupted by her vicious and irresponsible sister Kiyomi, played by Tsugumi (b. 1976). Kiyomi's drunken and abusive antics grate on Yuko, culminating in Kiyomi unapologetically abandoning her eight-year-old daughter Mami, played by Miku Sato (b. 1998) at Yuko's apartment with no warning. Seeing evidence that Kiyomi has been physically abusing Mami, Yuko reluctantly allows her to stay, despite feeling unprepared to deal with the presence of a child.

Yamazaki, who is fixated on women's hair with fetishistic intensity, is delighted to find that the corpse he brought home is continuing to grow hair at a prodigious rate. Driven by an unknown force, hair that Yamazaki judges to be of the absolute highest quality begins to extrude not just from the body's scalp, but from the eyes and a variety of open wounds as well. Treating both the hair and the corpse with an almost religious reverence, he seems unconcerned with its supernatural nature and enthusiastically encourages the girl's spirit to produce as much hair as possible. The corpse's hair grows visibly quickly now from all visible orifices and past wounds. A business plan is hatched when he cuts it while apologizing and speaking lovingly to the corpse. He packages the trimmed hair as hair extensions to sell to hair salons and each extension has a bell tied to it reminiscent of the bell the corpse was found with. The first victim is a hair stylist who attached portions of the cursed extensions to her own head. Shortly after she begins hallucinating about what must have been the fate of the female corpse. It is revealed that she was captured, drugged, operated on, and shaved. The hair stylist screams in pain, cries, and reenacts the corpse's fate by murdering her customer by stabbing her in the ear before taking her own life. The morgue attendant watches a news report on television of the incident and concludes that her spirit is very angry.

Later, when Mami has an accident at home and wanders into town in search of Yuko, she is spotted by Yamazaki, who has donned a bizarre outfit and gone out to record video footage of passing women while remarking on the quality of their hair. Drawn in by the quality of Mami's hair, he helps her find Yuko's salon and ends up providing her and her coworkers with "samples" of his handmade hair extensions. The sister returns to Yuko's house and convinces Mami to let her in, only to abuse her, steal clothing, and then flee to her boyfriend's house. Unfortunately for her, the hair extension sample was among the objects she stole. She locks Mami in a small closet, which inadvertently spares Mami. The couple is not as fortunate, as the man rolls onto the hair sample, which attaches itself to him and then goes on the offense. From Mami's closet, she can only hear screams, see splashes of blood, and glimpses of hair wildly lashing around the room. Once the commotion dies down, Mami explores the devastation, finding another room full of hair that becomes aggressive once it identifies her presence. Mami escapes with only minor injuries by jumping off a balcony.

Yuko later identifies her sister's body and visits Mami in the hospital who tells the police that a hair monster killed her mother. The forensics of the mysterious deaths are so far-fetched, that the police find the story too unbelievable. Hair fibers found at each death match that of the body they had found in the shipping container, which is still missing. The amount of hair found at the scene is also unbelievable, as it is enough to be the hair of thirty women yet is determined to all come from the same person. The police then begin questioning salons about extensions used and Yuko realizes that she gave Mami pieces from the questionable hair earlier that day. Yuko rushes home, but the attack is already underway against Mami and her roommate, Yuki. Yuko arrives home to an apartment covered in hair, her roommate's body, and an unconscious Mami. As she tries to free her, the hair also attacks Yuko and she falls unconscious to the ground. Yamazaki arrives in time to plead with the hair to spare the girls and takes them to his house where they awaken in a room completely covered in hair for the final confrontation between the girls, the fetishist, and the vengeful corpse.

Although the visual style is well within Sono's usual range, the straightforward plot and structure make this one of the director's most accessible works. Despite the gruesome premise, much of the more horrific action takes place offscreen, and the visible action is remarkably restrained compared with many of Sono's films.—Rebecca Bacheller

See also Sono, Sion

Bibliography
Sono, Sion, dir. *Exte*. Toei, 2007. Film.

EXTREMELY SCARY STORY A: DARK CROW (2004)

DIRECTOR: Yoshihiro Hoshino
SCREENPLAY: Yoshihiro Hoshino, Hirotoshi Kobayashi
SPECS: 80 minutes; color

Extremely Scary Story A: Dark Crow, known as *"Chō" Kowai Hanashi A: Yami no Karasu* in Japanese, is a low-budget 2004 horror film by first-time director Yoshihiro Hoshino. The story focuses on a haunted convenience store and its doomed customers. It is an adaptation of a Yumeaki Hirayama (b. 1961) short story and is the first in the Extremely Scary Story series. Of particular note, this film was renamed *Cursed* for distribution to Western audiences. Unfortunately, in renaming this film, much of the crow imagery scattered throughout the work becomes somewhat obfuscated.

The film opens cold at a train crossing. A cutaway shows a murder of crows cawing on the wires above. Two schoolgirls exit a bus and walk toward a Mitsuya Mart. As the students near the store, one refuses to enter. Terrified, this young woman walks backward into traffic and is instantly killed. The opening credits play. Reflecting the film's actual title, a rotating graphic of a dead crow fills the screen for the credit's duration. Unbeknownst to the viewer, the film now backtracks several days and will ultimately be bookended with this opening scene.

Nao Shingaki, played by Hiroko Satō (b. 1985), is a mild-mannered young woman who is employed part-time at the Mitsuya Mart. She has worked at this store for only a month. Ryouko Kagami, played by Kyōko Akiba (b. 1975), is a representative for Cosmos Mart. She arrives to assist the store owner's transition into the franchise. Ryouko's business partner Tejima initially procured this contract but soon met with "an accident," losing both feet. The responsibility for successfully turning this independently owned store into a Cosmos Mart is now hers. Unfortunately, Ryouko encounters immediate, hostile resistance from the store's owners. This sadistic pair, who are frequently shown as unresponsive and blankly staring at nothing, are later revealed to be possessed. With the owners unwilling to cooperate in the store's changeover, Ryouko must do the work alone since she fears disappointing her superiors. She tells Nao that she will be there for about three days.

As Ryouko focuses on cataloging inventory in an alleyway, a hooded figure in an anorak and orange track pants enters the store. Later revealed to be an evil spirit, he/she stands at the magazine rack, reading a sports feature and silently laughing. Meanwhile, Nao rings up a bespectacled customer. His total is "666 yen." A close-up of the register's display and an alarming sound effect solidify the number's importance. As the man exits the store, the camera follows. From a shadowy alleyway, a white ball bounces toward him in slow motion. The disembodied voice of a child asks for the ball. Though fearful, the man carries it into the darkness. Viewers are left to assume that he succumbs to the curse.

The next day, Nao finds Ryouko in the stockroom, continuing inventory. After Ryouko inquires about the negative energy she feels at the store, Nao concurs that she too has the same sentiment. As the film reveals, both women see and hear spirits. And, while Ryouko has accepted this fate, Nao struggles with her horrific visions.

Returning to the sales-floor, Nao spies a menacing, bandaged man in the security mirror. She investigates but finds no one. Shortly thereafter, a crow flies into the storefront's window. A spattering of blood marks its demise. As Nao and Ryouko assess the situation, another crow slams into the window, instantly perishing. Ryouko asks Nao to return inside while she cleans the carnage. Before Ryouko can begin disposing of the birds, the store's owners giddily spray at the gory scene with a hose. Laughing manically, the owners seem to revel in horrifying Ryouko. The scene fades out.

Komori, played by Takaaki Iwao, relieves Nao for the nightshift. He rings up a woman's order. The total is "999 yen." A close-up of the number and sound effect serve as a warning to the viewer. The camera follows her as she walks home. Behind her trails the bandaged man Nao saw in the mirror earlier. He is dragging a sledgehammer. As the woman waits for the elevator in her apartment complex, she finally notices this ominous figure and flees to her floor. After a heart-pounding showdown in the hallway, the woman locks herself in her apartment. In the blackness of her home, the television turns on. The terror of this moment is punctuated with the eerie sound and glow of static. The woman's cell-phone rings and that, too, betrays her. She is greeted by a growl and a view of the bandaged creature silhouetted behind her curtains. Her death is also left to the viewer's imagination as the scene cuts to black.

The next evening, Nao sees a pair of foreboding eyes staring at her from inside the beverage cooler. She tells Komori, who then tries to comfort her with a bag of food that he bought for her dinner. Though he is portrayed as having a crush on Nao, he proclaims that his Christian faith inspires him to do good deeds for others. As Nao changes in the back room, the hooded figure makes a purchase from Komori. The total is "44.4444 yen." The previously established close-up and sound effect are repeated. The hooded figure then mesmerizes Komori and envelopes his head into her/his hood. In the stockroom, Ryouko hears his scream and runs to assist. She find Komori sitting on the floor, one eye wildly protruding from his face. In an instant, it appears normal again. A female customer emerges on the opposite side of the counter and waits for Ryouko to check her out. The order totals "666 yen." The requisite close-up and sound effect indicate this woman's doom. Meanwhile, Nao emerges from the stockroom and finds Komori on the floor. She is distraught and wants to help, but Ryouko asks her to go home. The store's owners watch this grim tableaux with glee. Immediately, a man enters the store and purchases toiletries. His total is "907 yen." However, the siren song of steamed buns proves irresistible. His new total is "999 yen" (accompanied by close-up and sound effect).

At this juncture, the narrative divides into three parts. Cross-cutting shows the female customer arriving home, Nao walking home, and the male customer visiting a sentō (communal bath house). All three parts are tied together by a news anchor delivering the day's top stories. (The news anchor is played by Yumeaki Hirayama, the author of this work.) The screen then noticeably splits into thirds, showcasing each potentially cursed victim. Ultimately, cross-cutting reveals the fate for each. The male customer is murdered by an evil spirit who slams his head into a marble shelf in the bath house. The female customer finds a different evil spirit in her refrigerator and, in an attempt to protect herself, stabs her boyfriend by accident. This woman is next seen with a plastic bag over her head, sitting next to her dead boyfriend. And, Nao is seen struggling with the infamous hooded figure that is trying to push her in front of a train. Finally, the evil spirit disappears and Nao is left alone to process this moment. All instances are cross-cut to Bach's "Air On the G String" (this same piece was previously used to similar effect in Kinji Fukasaku's *Battle Royale*).

The next day, Nao arrives at work and finds Komori flanked by the store's owners. He wears their same vacant stare. She weeps at his obvious transformation. A middle-aged woman, who has been watching the shop throughout the film, approaches Nao. She cannot speak in such close proximity to the Mitsuya Mart so they walk to a park. Nao spots Ryouko and beckons her over. The older woman explains that the original owner would steal money from his employees' paychecks or arrange to have them injured for the insurance money. She also reveals that the local people believe the store's foundation is the ground-up tombstones of those without a family. Since this woman appears mentally unstable, the viewer remains skeptical. The older woman leaves. Ryouko and Nao engage in a frank discussion. Nao worries that she will always see spirits. Ryouko explains that though it has been a constant in her life, she has elected to ignore it. She said that if one dwells on it, it becomes a curse. The swings on the playground begin moving on their own. Ryouko tells Nao that she should leave the store. The swings then violently entangle.

Walking home, Nao is haunted by the image of Komori and runs toward the store. The viewer sees him in the Mitsuya Mart's bathroom, transfixed by a pair of eyes peering at him from under the toilet-tank lid. Nao breaks the evil spirit's hold on Komori by physically dragging him out of the lavatory. He is next found in the river, purifying himself and purged of his work shirt. He and Nao sit on the riverbank, Nao's jacket wrapped around him. The two walk away together, finally free.

On the journey from the park to the market, Ryouko receives a call from Tejima. She sees him in the distance. She knows that he is now a spirit. He is at peace. Ryouko bravely thanks him for all he has done for her and says good-bye. She walks away from his spirit and does not look back. As Ryouko passes the Mitsuya Mart, the film returns to the two girls exiting the bus. The viewer now sees what caused the young girl to back into traffic: the trapped spirits of all the customers, pressed against the storefront's glass in abject desperation.

Of significance, the word for the number four in Japanese ("shi") is the same as the word for death. Likewise, in Japanese, the number nine shares the same pronunciation as the word for suffering. And while the number 666 is frequently considered as good fortune in Asian cultures, Komori's declaration of his Christianity allows the number's use a degree of significance, as in some branches of Christianity "666" is considered the nefarious "number of the beast." With this in mind, it becomes clear that each customer is unknowingly risking their soul with each transaction. In fact, the film teases the audience with totals such as 699 yen (which, in the context of this film, do not seem to elicit the curse).

Several scholars note echoes of contemporary Japanese horror cinema in *Extremely Scary Story A: Dark Crow*. For instance, Kim Newman asserts that it is "heavily indebted to [Hideo Nakata's] *Ringu*." While there are clear strains of *Ringu* in the film, intended to be playful nods, in *Flowers from Hell*, Jim Harper deems *Extremely Scary Story A: Dark Crow* a "collection of *Ring* and *Juon* spoofs"—a slightly more accurate description of the film. For instance, *Juon's* exploitation of so-called "safe spaces" is taken to a nearly absurd degree in this film. Here, the refrigerator, the toilet-tank, an oki-gotatsu all become areas of fear. Nonetheless, *Extremely Scary Story A: Dark Crow* is, by all means, a horror film that distinguishes itself from other works. While it clearly acknowledges its predecessors, it also expands on the genre by moving it from a more private sphere to a public one.

This is director Yoshihiro Hoshino's only full-length film.—Erica Joan Dymond

Bibliography

Harper, Jim. *Flowers from Hell*. Hereford, UK: Noir, 2008.
Hoshino, Yoshihiro, dir. *Extremely Scary Story A: Dark Crow*. Tokyo Shock, 2005. Film.
Newman, Kim. *Nightmare Movies: Horror on Screen since the 1960s*. London: Bloomsbury, 2011.

4444444444 (1998)

DIRECTOR: Takashi Shimizu
SCREENPLAY: Takashi Shimizu
SPECS: 71 minutes; color

Originally aired as a short-segment on Kansai Television's *Gakkō no kaidan G* in 1998, *4444444444*, and its accompanying feature *Katasumi*, marked director Takashi Shimizu's entry into the J-horror genre. In this three-minute experimental piece, Shimizu begins the development of two ghost-figure characters— the young boy Toshio Saeki, played by Sawada Daiki and his accompanying cat—that later become central to his Ju-on franchise. Although never explicitly stated, Shimizu's direction and cinematography seem to convey some sort of social commentary about the deterioration of responsibility and morality as they relate to modern familial conventions. In particular, Shimizu fleshes this commentary out vis-à-vis the supernatural hauntings of this tortured ghost-figure, Toshio, throughout *4444444444*, as well as in his subsequent films in the Ju-on series. The implication is that such hauntings are a form of posthumous retaliation, generated by some type of neglect or abuse inflicted upon Toshio before his death. By extension, Shimizu's other characters also appear to represent a symbolic reference to such social commentary, as they too are often depicted as victims of both societal ills, as well as the hauntings of Toshio.

The film opens with the appearance of a male teenager named Murakami Tsuyoshi, played by Kazushi Ando, who happens upon a ringing mobile phone, suspiciously left abandoned alongside a deserted housing complex. Upon picking up the handset, Murakami locates the source of the call as the number "4444444444." As the number 4 often carries an ominous connotation in several Asian cultures, this series of ten consecutive 4s foreshadows the tenor of fear and unease throughout the film.

Answering the phone, Murakami is greeted only by the sound of a moaning cat, while his precarious position is showcased in the framing of the shot, the phone's centrality accentuating its importance. Puzzled by the sound of the cat and attempting several greetings to no avail, Murakami explains how he found the phone on the street to the irresponsive caller, insisting that he merely happened upon the phone by chance in nothing more than an innocent encounter with an abandoned object. After several more attempts at communication, Murakami terminates the call in frustration. Yet shortly thereafter, he receives another call and again is unable to converse with the caller, as only the cat's moans can be heard.

With the onset of howling and rustling leaves terminating in the eerie sound of a slowly dripping faucet, Murakami is overwhelmed by the feeling that he's not alone, but rather in the company of some supernatural presence. Making one last attempt at communication, Murakami questions, "Can you see me?" This time the caller responds with "I'm looking at you." The camera then pivots to expose Toshio, who opens his mouth to release a cat-like moan before, audiences may assume, taking the life of Murakami.

Despite its short length, Shimizu manages to encompass elements of familial decay and social abandonment, in addition to the utter inescapability of their effects, all of which are central themes in the Ju-on series. From this perspective, both Murakami and Toshio are representative of normative deviations. Though the fate that had befallen Toshio remains a mystery, audiences are left to guess that in some way, he had lacked the care and protections accorded to children— a concept developed extensively in Shimizu's later works.—Jason Christopher Jones

FRANKENSTEIN VERSUS SUBTERRANEAN MONSTER BARAGON (1965)
DIRECTOR: Ishiro Honda
SCREENPLAY: Reuben Bercovitch, Takeshi Kimura, Jerry Sohl
SPECS: 87 minutes; color

Frankenstein versus Subterranean Monster Baragon (*Furankenshutain tai chitei kaijū Baragon* in Japanese and known in North America as *Frankenstein Conquers the World*) is a *kaijū*/horror film released in 1965 in Japan and 1966 in the United States. It was directed by Ishiro Honda, with special effects by Eiji Tsurubaya under the auspices of Toho Company Ltd. The film follows two converging plots as Frankenstein's monster is resurrected in Hiroshima after the atomic bombing and a prehistoric *kaijū*, Baragon, is awaked from hibernation to terrorize Japan. The storylines come together in a climactic battle, in which Frankenstein's monster ultimately defeats Baragon before both are swallowed up by a fissure in the Earth. Initially intended as *Frankenstein versus Godzilla*, the film went through a number of changes over its production period, resulting in Godzilla being replaced with a new monster. The production is notable as an early joint Japanese-US production and includes both Japanese and American cast and crew.

The film begins in World War II as Nazi operatives steal the heart of Frankenstein's monster from the laboratory of "Dr. Reisendorf," played by Peter Mann (b. 1934), and transport it to Japanese forces in the Pacific. The Japanese then store the heart in Hiroshima, where it is presumed destroyed after the 1945 bombing. It then flashes forward to 1960s Hiroshima, where a feral street boy is capturing and consuming any and every animal he can find. An American scientist named James Bowen, played by Nick Adams (b. 1931), and his two Japanese lab assistants, Sueko Togami (Kumi Mizuno, b. 1937) and Yuzo Kawaji (Tadao Takashima, b. 1930), hear about the child and go searching for him. They save the boy from an angry mob, which has backed him into a cave, and bring him first to a hospital, then to their laboratory. It is discovered that the child is actually Caucasian and that his body is immune to radiation.

Meanwhile, Mr. Kawai, played by Yoshio Tsuchiya (b. 1927), former captain of the ship that transported the monster's heart, is working in a factory in Akita, part of which is destroyed in an earthquake. Wading through the rubble,

Kawai is horrified to find an enormous monster. Back in Bowen's lab facility, the rescued boy is being kept in a cage and his body grows at an extraordinary rate, causing an insatiable desire for protein. The scientists surmise that the boy may have somehow sprung from the heart of Frankenstein's monster, and Kawaji is dispatched to visit Dr. Reisendorf for further information. Reisendorf explains that the monster is nearly indestructible and suggests testing the captive child by amputating a limb to see if it grows back. Kawaji is in favor of this, while Togami, who has grown attached to the boy, argues vehemently against it. A film crew arrives to produce a story on the child, but the bright lights enrage the now-formidable creature and he escapes. Following an emotional scene in which the creature visits Togami's home, he then wanders the countryside, consuming meat and growing ever larger.

While the authorities and Bowen's team search for Frankenstein's monster, the dinosaur awakened by the earthquake in Akita burrows underground, demolishing towns. The public assumes that Frankenstein's monster is to blame and the hunt intensifies with military involvement. Kawai then arrives to inform the scientists that the destruction may be the fault of the prehistoric creature from Akita, called Baragon. When the team manages to track down Frankenstein's monster, Kawaji attempts to kill it, against Bowen's wishes. He plots to use a shock grenade to render it blind, and then remove its heart. Instead, the scientists stumble across Baragon, which tries to eat Togami. Frankenstein's monster arrives at the last moment to save her. This results in the film's climactic battle, which causes enormous destruction and Frankenstein's creature ultimately proves the victor, killing Baragon. Another earthquake opens a fissure, into which both titular creatures fall, leaving the cast unsure about the fate of Frankenstein's creation.

A famous extended ending was filmed in which, after defeating Baragon, Frankenstein's monster battles a giant octopus. The producers felt that this scene was unnecessary and nonsensical given the plot, and it was not utilized in the Japanese release. Benedict Pictures, the American production company with which Toho cooperated, later insisted on reshooting the scene for the film's sequel, *War of the Gargantuas* (1966).—Jared Miracle

Bibliography

Honda, Ishiro, dir. *Frankenstein versus Subterranean Monster Baragon*. Toho, 1965. Film.

Hood, Robert. "Divided Kingdom." In *King Kong Is Back!*, edited by David Brin and Leah Wilson, 173–86. Dallas, TX: Benbella Books, 2005.

Ryfle, Steve. *Japan's Favorite Mon-Star: The Unauthorized Biography of "The Big G."* Toronto: ECW Press, 1998.

FRANKENSTEIN'S MONSTERS: SANDA VS. GAIRA (1966)

DIRECTOR: Ishirō Honda
SCREENPLAY: Takeshi Kimura (as Kaoru Mabuchi)
SPECS: 92 minutes; color

Not much respected but enjoying a cult following among fans of Japanese monster romps, this US-Japanese coproduction (1966) between the Toho Studio and Henry G. Saperstein's UPA is better known to American viewers as *War of the Gargantuas*. Some of the movie's problematic reputation stems from its confusing story setting, which results in different origins for the film's monsters in the domestic and US import versions. In the original Japanese version, Sanda and Gaira are supposed to have cloned themselves out of the body parts of Franken-stein's monster, seen to be buried underground at the end of the 1965 film, *Frankenstein versus Subterranean Monster Baragon* (aka *Frankenstein Conquers the World*). In the US version, this reference is dropped: they are simply two variants of a Yeti-like cryptozoological species called Gargantua. For once, the English-language storyline makes more sense, as these two beasties look nothing like Toho's Frankenstein's monster (whose design is closely based on the makeup of Boris Karloff in the Universal series).

Written by Takeshi Kimura (1911–1987, writing as Kaoru Mabuchi) and adapted for the screen by director Ishirō Honda (1911–1993), *Sanda vs. Gaira* closely follows the Toho monster film templates of the 1950s and early 1960s: a mysterious opening, usually set in the sea, where the viewers get the first glimpse of the monster; scientists putting clues together as to the identity of the creature; a major monster attack on the human population at about the one-third point of the running time; panoramic depictions of the Self-Defense Forces being mobilized against the threat; disagreements among human characters regarding the best way to capture/kill the creatures; a climactic death match between an-tagonistic monsters; and so on. Honda's direction is solid, although a bit work-manlike compared to the almost phantasmagorical touches he brought to his masterpieces *Rodan* (1956) and *Mothra* (1961).

Due to the fact that the monsters look distinctively humanoid, unlike usual dinosaur-based monsters of the Toho stable, they must have required extra care in maintaining the illusion of gigantic scale. Considering this, Sanda and Gaira are by and large imposing creatures, the stunt actors beneath the suits (Godzilla-suit veterans Hiroshi Sekida [b. 1932] for Sanda, Haruo Nakajima [b. 1929] for Gaira) are able to convey their essential characters quite well via facial snarls and gestures under Honda's expert guidance. Indeed, the unsuspecting viewers get a jolt of gruesomeness when Sanda at the Haneda airport grabs a screaming office worker, à la King Kong getting hold of a Manhattan lady in her bedroom, and proceeds to eat her up, nonchalantly spitting out his prey's chewed-up gar-ment—*Sanda vs. Gaira* was domestically released as children's fare paired with the theatrical version of the animated *Kimba the White Lion* (1965); one can imagine the trauma likely suffered by the unsuspecting children in the audience.

As for the human cast, Russ Tamblyn (b. 1934) fails to display the kind of energy and enthusiasm he had shown in even nonmusical films such as *The Fast-est Gun Alive* (1956). He may have been a better actor than Nick Adams (star of *Frankenstein versus Subterranean Monster Baragon*), but here he never rises above what is required of a generic *gaijin* (foreigner) role in a Japanese monster movie. Kenji Sahara (b. 1932) proves a reliable presence, as expected, and Kumi Mizuno (b. 1937), famous for her role as the alien femme fatale from Planet X in *Invasion of the Astro-Monster* (1965), is a pleasant sight to behold. Special effects supervised by Tsuburaya Eiji (1901–1970) are most impressive in the scenes of the nighttime battle between Gaira and the Self-Defense Forces deploying the Maser Cannon, a parabola-dish blaster mounted on a tank firing lethal beams of microwave, which makes for a gorgeous light show and many explosions. The film also features the superb talents of Akria Ikufube (1914–2006) and his majestic score, illustrating Sanda's savagery, Gaira's grandiosity, and the Self-Defense Force's martial spirit and determination with thrilling, pounding music.

While not included among the top tier of the Toho special-effects extravaganzas, *Sanda vs. Gaira* nonetheless continues to claim a substantial fan base on both sides of the Pacific, if mostly for nostalgic values. Stateside, as of January 2015, one can view the film through Media Classic's DVD (2008), which includes both the domestic and the US import versions. Toho released a Blu-ray disc in 2010, but it is only the Japanese release version and contains no English subtitles.—Kyu Hyun Kim

See also Frankenstein vs. Subterranean Monster Baragon; Godzilla

Bibliography

Galbraith, Stuart, IV. *Japanese Science Fiction, Fantasy and Horror Films*, Jefferson, NC: McFarland, 1994.
Honda, Ishirō, dir. *Frankenstein's Monster: Sanda vs. Gaira* [*Furankenshutain no kaijū Sandatai Gaira*], Toho-UPA, 1966. Film.

FUJIO A, FUJIKO (1934–)

Motoo Abiko, better known as Fujiko Fujio A, is one of the best-known Japanese cartoonists alive. Along with his creative partner Hiroshi Fujimoto (1933–1996), Abiko created a number of memorable characters during the postwar period under the alias of Fujiko Fujio. Although they are arguably best known for enormously popular comedies, such as *Obake no Q-tarō, Ninja hattori-kun, Kaibutsu-kun,* and *Doraemon,* they have also penned horror stories and black comedies, such as *Warau sērusuman* and *Matarō ga kuru!!,* many of which are the creations of Abiko. Although they worked separately, their productive partnership lasted until 1987. The pair remain an inspiration for new generations of cartoonists.

Abiko was born to a Buddhist monk in Toyama prefecture. As a child, he started penning cartoons and befriended Fujimoto, also a cartoon enthusiast, in elementary school. At the age of seventeen, the pair made their professional debut in 1951. The twenty-six episodes of the four-cell comic strip *Tenshi no tama-chan* were serialized in a Japanese newspaper for children, *Mainichi shōgakusei shimbun.* After graduation from a local high school, Abiko worked as a writer-cum-illustrator for a local newspaper company, although he did not abandon his career as a cartoonist. A few years later, Abiko was approached by Fujimoto to pursue a full-time career as cartoonists together. Abiko eventually accepted Fujimoto's invitation and quit his job to move to Tokyo in 1954. Their early years as struggling cartoonists in Tokyo are depicted in an autobiographical comic *Manga-michi* (*The Way of Manga,* 1970–2013) and in Abiko's autobiography, *78-sai imada mangamichi o* (2012). They lived in a cramped apartment called Tokiwa-sō in Toshima ward, Tokyo, along with other aspiring cartoonists, including Shōtarō Ishinomori, Fujio Akatsuka, and Jirō Tsunoda. The pair rose to fame after *Obake no Q-tarō* (1964–1976), and continued to create other memorable cartoon series like *Ninja hattori-kun* (1964–1968, 1981–1988) and *Kaibutsu-kun* (1968–1969, 1980–1982). Although their works had been published under the alias of Fujiko Fujio, the pair in fact worked separately after *Obake no Q-tarō*. For example, *Ninja hattori-kun* and *Kaibutsu-kun* were created by Abiko while *Doraemon* (1969–1996) and *Parman* (1967–1968, 1983–1984) were created by Fujimoto. However, they officially announced the termination of their creative partnership after Fujimoto's illness in 1987. Abiko started using a new pen name, Fujiko Fujio while Fujimoto used Fujiko F. Fujio.

Abiko represents the more serious and darker side of Fujiko Fujio. After the 1980s, he turned to black comedy, occult, and *gekiga* genres. In *Warau sērusuman* (*The Laughing Salesman*, 1968–), a mysterious salesman Fukuzō Moguro exposes the greed and hypocrisy of ordinary people. From 1989 to 1992, the animation series were broadcast as a part of a television show, *Give Me a Break*. In an occult story, *Matarō ga kuru!!* (1972–1975), he created another memorable character, Urami Matarō. Although scrawny and bullied at school, he can turn into a wizard at night to take revenge on his enemies. *Black shōkai henkirō* (1976–1977) is a horror story about a boy who punishes wrongdoers by supernatural power, whereas the *Shiroi dōwa* series (White fables) consist of six horror stories, which were published in legendary comic magazine *COM* in 1971. Many of Abiko's black comedies are compiled into Chūōkōronsha's black humor anthologies.

Apart from being a cartoonist, Abiko is known as a movie lover. In 1990, he wrote the film script of *Shōnen jidai* (Childhood days), which is based on Hyōzō Kashiwabara's novel *Nagai michi* (Long road). Some of his works, such as *Ai nusubito* (Thief of love, 1974) and *Kaibutsu-kun* (2011), have been dramatized.—Senjo Nakai

Bibliography
Fujio A, Fujiko. *Black Humor tanpenshu* [Black humor anthologies] (Volume 1). Tokyo: Chūōkōronsha. 1989.
———. *Black Humor tanpenshu* [Black humor anthologies] (Volume 2). Tokyo: Chūōkōronsha. 1990.
———. *Black Humor tanpenshu* [Black humor anthologies] (Volume 3). Tokyo: Chūōkōronsha. 1994.
———. *Fujiko Fujio A no black humor 1: Kuroi salesman* [Fujiko Fujio A's black humor 1: The black salesman]. Tokyo: Shōgakkan. 2011.
———. *78-sai imada mangamichi o* [At 78 years old, I am still on manga road]. Tokyo: Chūōkōronsha. 2012.
Shinoda, Masahiro, dir. *Shōnen Jidai*. Toho, 1990. Film.

FUJIWARA, KEI (1957–)
Kei Fujiwara, born in March 1957, was initially a Japanese actress who transitioned into working as a cinematographer, movie director, editor, and writer. Fujiwara first appeared on the movie screen in 1973 in the American science fiction production *The Neptune Factor*, which was directed by Daniel Petrie. However, she is best known for her role in the Japanese cyberpunk movie *Tetsuo: The Iron Man* (1989), which was directed by Shinya Tsukamoto. It was later in her career that Fujiwara became a director herself and created violent horror films such as *Organ* (1996) and *Ido* (2005).

While Fujiwara only had a minor role in *The Neptune Factor*, a film that is rather unknown except for its use of underwater photography that incorporates miniatures and living marine life, her part in *Tetsuo* made her well known in the science fiction genre. After its release, *Tetsuo* became an international cult movie, not just a Japanese phenomenon. The movie opens with a man who has a fetish for metal being hit by a car that is being driven by a businessman. The businessman's girlfriend, played by Fujiwara, is also present at the time of the accident, and they work together to get rid of the body in order to cover up the incident. Although they dump the body, the metal fetishist is not actually dead. He recovers and seeks revenge during the course of the movie by transforming the businessman into metal. This process begins with a small piece of metal embedded in the businessman's cheek; it steadily grows throughout the movie and transforms him into a metal man. *Tetsuo* is known for its impressive chase scenes, including a segment where a woman, whose body has been taken over by the metal fetishist, is hunting the businessman through one of Japan's underground train stations. In this particular situation, the businessman is able to get rid of the woman even though he himself transforms even further.

After the hunt sequence, a bad dream ensues where Fujiwara has transformed into a burlesque-like exotic dancer and rapes her lover, the businessman, with a metal probe. Once the couple wakes up, they have sex and eat; at this time, Fujiwara's chewing sounds like metal being scraped together. Consequently, the businessman falls into a violent rage against her. Additional parts of his body transform into metal, and he ultimately kills his girlfriend. The businessman, who has finally become an "Iron Man," meets the fetishist in person and receives a vision of a future metal world. However, the former businessman does not want to accept this outlook and a final battle between the two characters ends with them being fused into a metal monster with two heads. The pair then decides to transform the world, and the movie ends with the statement: "Game Over."

Even if *Tetsuo* is only a genre-specific "success," Fujiwara, as an actress, is mainly known for her role in this science fiction movie. Despite the fact that her acting career never brought her a significant breakthrough, she was able to transition into directing movies, starting with *Organ* (*Orugan*) in 1996, which she also wrote, produced, and starred in as one of the organ thieves. In *Organ*, the one-eyed "Yoko," played by Fujiwara, and her brother, a teacher named Saeki, cut open their living victims in order to steal their organs. Two detectives immerse themselves in an undercover operation in an effort to find the organ thieves and learn that Saeki began this brutal practice because his mother bit off his genitals during his youth. Overall, Fujiwara's movie was criticized for its bizarre depiction of violence, and it never became a great success. However, like *Ido* (2005), *Organ* is a recognized part of the Japanese horror movie genre.

In *Ido*, Fujiwara describes the wanderings of a man, simply known as "the Murderer," through a forest. He is driven crazy by the sound of water that is flowing underground and in his "id," which resembles his personal subconscious. An unidentifiable voice drives the Murderer to a steel factory located close to a river. After the Murderer arrives, people who work at the factory slowly begin to disappear, and eventually the boss's body is found outside the building. As it turns out, a woman who was full of hate and therefore orchestrated the killings had summoned the Murderer. The combined hatred and sadness from the woman and the Murderer ultimately cause the "human-hog" monster to appear, further complicating the situation. An ex-detective who had already been hunting the Murderer before he was summoned to the factory then discovers the monster. Like Fujiwara's first movie, *Ido* never gained great fame or became a box-office hit; however, it must be taken into consideration when one talks about Japanese horror movies, even if the concept of the subconscious control of a murderer who happens to be wandering through the woods stretches the genre over its existent edges.—Frank Jacob

• G •

THE GHOST CAT OF ARIMA PALACE (1953)
DIRECTOR: Ryōhei Arai
SCREENPLAY: Tokichi Kinoshita
SPECS: 49 minutes; black and white

The Ghost Cat of Arima Palace (*Kaibyō Arima goten*) is a 1953 *bakeneko* or "ghost cat" film starring Takako Irie (1911–1995) and directed by Ryōhei Arai (1901–1980). The second in a slew of *bakeneko* features produced by the Daiei studio during the 1950s, the film's slim running time of less than fifty minutes and recycled cast, crew, costumes, and sets from the same year's *The Ghost Story of Saga Mansion* suggest the project was hastily completed to fill out the studio's schedule of program pictures. Although the sometimes outrageous special effects were derided as laughable on the film's release, today they make *The Ghost Cat of Arima Palace* one of the more enjoyably campy entries in the *bakeneko* subgenre of classic Japanese horror cinema.

Irie stars as Otaki, a maiden in the harem of Arima Palace. Her favored status with the Arima lord earns her the ire of her senior, Okoyo (Kitami Reiko), who resents that a mere grocer's daughter has bested her for the *daimyo*'s affections. Okoyo vents her anger on Otaki's pet cat, Tama, accusing the animal of causing trouble and demanding it be killed. Otaki pleads for Tama's life, and Okoyo relents, demanding her attending ladies strip Otaki naked as punishment instead. The humiliation is halted by the entrance of the *daimyo*, and later Otaki and her faithful attendant, Onaka (Michiko Ai), turn Tama loose to spare the animal from Okoyo's wrath.

Following further unsuccessful attempts to humiliate Otaki, Okoyo performs a taboo midnight ritual, the *ushi no koku mairi*, to curse her rival. The rite is interrupted by passers-by and Okoyo flees before she can be identified. The crafty Okoyo uses the situation to accuse Otaki of performing the *ushi no koku mairi* against her, framing her for the crime. Once again, Otaki is spared punishment via the intervention of the lord of Arima, who refuses to believe she is the culprit. Thwarted at every turn, Okoyo finally has her henchwomen murder Otaki, attempting to make it look like a suicide. Onaka finds the body, whereupon Tama suddenly returns and laps the blood of its mistress—which, according to convention, will cause the cat to take on the wrath of the murder victim and transform into the monstrous *bakeneko* to wreak vengeance on her behalf.

Concurrent with Onaka's investigation into her mistress's murder, the *bakeneko* takes the form of Otaki and begins to attack Okoyo's accomplices one by one, turning them into her undead minions. In the climax of the film, the *bakeneko* and its ghostly slaves come for Okoyo, but the attack is interrupted by the lord's brother, Daigaku (Kōtarō Bandō). Following a protracted battle between the cat monster and the guards of Arima Palace, Daigaku succeeds in decapitating the beast, but its still-living head flies magically through the air and with its final breath sinks its fangs into Okoyo's neck, killing her.

Like the same year's *The Ghost Story of Saga Mansion*, Daiei's *The Ghost Cat of Arima Palace* was a remake of a prewar Shinkō Studios *bakeneko* picture, *The Cat of Arima* (*Arima neko*, 1937). While most prewar Japanese horror films did not survive the devastation of World War II, damaged but more-or-less complete prints of *The Cat of Arima* still exist. Comparing the earlier picture to *The Ghost Cat of Arima Palace* suggests that Daiei's *bakeneko* pictures of the 1950s were indeed close remakes of their 1930s Shinkō counterparts. The Shinkō pictures were built around the star persona of Suzuki Sumiko, the "*bakeneko* actress" famous for her onscreen beauty-to-beast transformations. Although Suzuki plays the maidservant Onaka in the 1937 film, it is her form the cat monster takes in the picture's climax, not Otaki's. As with Suzuki's films, much of the appeal in the Daiei *bakeneko* pictures relied on the spectacle of seeing the aging beauty Irie morph into a ferocious half-woman, half-feline monster onscreen, and Irie's makeup is even more grotesque and outré than Suzuki's. Both films conclude with strikingly similar *tachimawari* fight scenes, the latter film re-creating the earlier picture's elaborate battle between the monster and a host of warriors up several flights of stairs and scaffolding.

Although *bakeneko* and other B-grade Japanese horror films of the prewar and early postwar eras typically received negative reviews from the critics of the day, reception of *The Ghost Cat of Arima Palace* was particularly harsh. *Kinema junpō* complained that the film had "not even one genuinely creepy idea," and that "before it would frighten the children in the audience, it would more naturally induce howls of laughter." The over-the-top finale, in which Irie's decapitated but still-alive head goes whizzing through the air, is just as laughable today, but also perfectly captures the sense of fun with which these pictures were made.—Michael Crandol

See also Arai, Ryōhei; *bakeneko*; *The Ghost Story of Saga Mansion*; Irie, Takako; Suzuki, Sumiko

Bibliography

Arai Ryōhei, dir. *The Ghost Cat of Arima Palace*. Daiei, 1953. Film.
Kinema Junpō, February 15, 1954, 65.

THE GHOST STORY OF CHIBUSA ENOKI (1958)

DIRECTOR: Gorō Kadono
SCREENPLAY: Torao Tanabe, based on a novel by Enchō San'yūtei
SPECS: 48 minutes; black and white

The Ghost Story of Chibusa Enoki (*Kaidan Chibusa Enoki*), also known in English as *The Mother Tree*, is a 1958 film directed by Gorō Kadono. Released on a double bill with Nobuo Nakagawa's widescreen color horror movie, *Mansion of the Ghost Cat* (*Bōrei kaibyō yashiki*), Kadono's forty-seven-minute black-and-white film was produced as the B-picture for the Shintōhō studio's annual "monster cavalcade" release during the summer *obon* festival of the dead. While not quite measuring up to the level of Nakagawa's horror masterworks, Kadono made *The Ghost Story of Chibusa Enoki* one of the finer Shintōhō ghost-story pictures and demonstrated that the studio's other directors were also capable of producing quality work in the genre.

Like most *kaidan* (traditional Japanese ghost stories), *The Ghost Story of Chibusa Enoki* takes place in the Edo Period (1600–1868) and concerns the revenge of murdered spirits on their oppressor. Shigenobu Hishikawa, played by Akira Nakamura, is a renowned artist, commissioned by the head of the Nanzo-in temple to paint a pair of dragons. A vagabond ronin named Namihei, played by Asao Matsumoto catches sight of Shigenobu with his wife Kise, played by Katsuko Wakasugi and their infant son, and begins to lust after the woman. Convincing a mutual acquaintance to recommend him to Shigenobu as an apprentice, Namihei infiltrates the Hishikawa household and, while Shigenobu works on his commission at Nanzo-in, forces Kise into a sexual relationship by threatening to murder her young child. When the Hishikawas' maid, Hana, discovers the affair, Namihei strangles her and presses Shigenobu's elderly manservant Shosuke into fearful complicity. Namihei and the reluctant Shosuke next lure Shigenobu to a remote location in the country, where the treacherous pupil stabs his master to death.

Shosuke reports to the head of Nanzo-in that bandits murdered Shigenobu on the road, to which the surprised monk replies that Shigenobu only just returned to complete the dragons. Shosuke flees in terror upon seeing the bloody and disheveled ghost of his master at work before his unfinished painting. After the other monks discover Shigenobu's body and news of the famous painter's murder spreads, the despondent Kise becomes unable to nurse their baby. Hana's ghost appears to her mistress and silently beckons her to the Rokusho Shrine and its sacred tree, Chibusa Enoki (literally "The Breast Tree"). Seeing milk drip from its branches, Kise begins suckling the infant from the tree, swearing to her departed husband their son will live to seek revenge for his father's murder. Shigenobu's ghost appears from behind the tree and says that only then will he be able to finish the eyes of the dragons and complete his final work of art.

Meanwhile Namihei orders Shosuke to kill the child. Unable to go through with it, he instead abandons the baby under Chibusa Enoki, telling Namihei he drowned the baby. Namihei then kills Shosuke to cover up the crime, telling Kise he sent the child to a wet nurse in the city. Now plagued by the ghosts of Shigenobu, Hana, and Shosuke, Namihei flees the Hishikawa estate with Kise, driven by their vengeful spirits toward the Rokusho Shrine. Kise hears her baby crying under the tree and, realizing the full extent of Namihei's wickedness, attacks him with her hair pin even as Namihei draws his sword to finish off the mother and child. With the aid of the three ghosts, Kise stabs Namihei to death, but she herself is fatally wounded in the struggle. With her last strength, Kise takes the baby to Nanzo-in, leaving him in the care of the head monk, who subsequently discovers that the eyes of the dragons have been inexplicably finished.

Screenwriter Torao Tanabe adapted *The Ghost Story of Chibusa Enoki* from a ghost story of the same name by Sanyūtei Enchō (1839–1900). Not as well known as Enchō's other classic, often-filmed ghost stories *The Peony Lantern* (*Botandōrō*) and *The Ghost Story of Kasane's Swamp* (*Shinkei Kasane ga fuchi*), Shintōhō head Mitsugu Okura chose *Chibusa Enoki* as the accompanying feature for Nakagawa Nobuo's more ambitious *Mansion of the Ghost Cat*. Nakagawa and *Chibusa Enoki* director Kadono Gorō had each helmed one half of Shintōhō's *obon* double feature for the previous year, *The Ghost Story of Kasane's Swamp* and *The Ghost Story of the Seven Wonders at Honjo* (*Kaidan Honjo nana fushigi*). Nakagawa's take on *Kasane* being the better-received of the two, Okura next put the elder director in charge of the studio's first color, widescreen horror picture, leaving the comparatively fresh Kadono to fill out the bill with a slim, forty-five-minute black-and-white quickie. The results occasionally betray the picture's C-grade production at a B-grade studio, particularly in shots of the ghostly, floating *hi no tama* fireballs attached to plainly visible strings and sticks. Kadono's film has much to commend it, however, especially in its atypically restrained portrayal of the three ghosts. While it does resort to some of the usual fun-house tricks common in 1950s Japanese horror films like double-exposure, see-through wraiths, for the most part *The Ghost Story of Chibusa Enoki* conveys the understated menace of its vengeful spirits by letting them stand concretely in frame with the human characters, unmoving, silent, with only darkened circles around the eyes or a trickle of blood from the mouth to suggest their otherworldly state.—Michael Crandol

See also Kaidan Kasane-ga-fuchi

Bibliography

Kadono, Gorō, dir. *The Ghost Story of Chibusa Enoki.* Shintōhō, 1958. Film.

THE GHOST STORY OF SAGA MANSION (1953)

DIRECTOR: Ryōhei Arai
SCREENPLAY: Tokichi Kinoshita
SPECS: 97 minutes; black and white

The Ghost Story of Saga Mansion (*Kaidan Saga yashiki*) is a 1953 *bakeneko* or "ghost cat" film directed by Ryōhei Arai (1901–1980). One of numerous film versions of the famous "Ghost Cat of Nabeshima" legend, the story concerns a wicked *daimyo* who is haunted by the spirit of a blind man he murdered over a game of *gō*, as well as the victim's pet cat, which imbibes human blood and transforms into the half-woman, half-feline *bakeneko* to seek revenge for its master. The Daiei studio's first postwar *bakeneko* picture, the film reestablished this popular subgenre of Japanese horror following a decade of war and occupation during which horror films were suppressed by the government, and ensured that its star, Takako Irie (1911–1995), would be typecast as a "*bakeneko* actress" for the remainder of her career.

The film's action revolves around the Lord of Nabeshima, played by Kunitarō Sawamura, and three brother-sister pairings: the blind Mata-ichirō (Shintarō Nanjō) and the beautiful Ofuyu (Kazuko Fushimi); the noble retainer Hanzaemon (Kōtarō Bandō) and the resourceful Otsuyu (Yōko Wakasugi); and the wicked Buzen (Shōsaku Sugiyama) and his sister Otoyo (Irie). When the lord expresses his desire for a concubine to produce an heir, Buzen tries to impress his sister Otoyo upon the *damiyo*, but the master only has eyes for Ofuyu. Mata-ichirō is invited to the lord's Saga Mansion to discuss his sister's future, but declines to offer her hand to the lord, as both Ofuyu and their mother hold out hope for a proper marriage. Sensing an opportunity, Buzen suggests to the lord that the real motive behind the refusal is a lingering resentment on the part of Mata-ichirō's family, who used to hold a higher rank but is now subservient to the Nabeshima clan. He then arranges for Otoyo to dance for the lord, and he accepts her as his concubine.

The tension between the lord and Mata-ichirō comes to a head over a game of *gō*, during which Buzen convinces the lord to cheat against his blind opponent. Mata-ichirō nonetheless notices the attempt and, in a fit of anger at being called out for cheating the lord, strikes him with his sword. Buzen finishes the unfortunate Mata-ichirō off, then orders his body dumped down a well. Mata-ichirō's mother is later visited by the spirit of her son, who recounts the crime and implores her to take revenge on his behalf. Before committing ritual suicide, the mother instructs the family cat, Koma, to lap her blood, recalling the legend that a cat that imbibes the blood of the deceased will assume their wrath and be transformed into a *bakeneko*.

Mata-ichirō's ghost and the *bakeneko* begin to torment the lord, and the retainer Hanzaemon, who has been investigating the disappearance of Mata-ichirō, also begins to hunt the cat spirit. He tracks the creature's bloody paw prints to the house of Buzen, where the trail ends. Buzen's wife later discovers that the *bakeneko* has possessed the body of her mother-in-law and falls victim to its magic, whereupon Buzen strikes his mother dead. The *bakeneko* spirit next possesses Otoyo, but Hanzaemon, with the help of his sister Otsuyu, exposes Otoyo as the monster. Taking on a grotesque, half-feline appearance, Otoyo kills Buzen, and then engages in a spectacular battle with a small army of Nabeshima samurai, with Hanzaemon finally slaying the *bakeneko*-possessed concubine. The film concludes with the lord of Nabeshima repenting his actions, restoring Ofuyu's family legacy, and honoring Hanzaemon and Otsuyu as heroes.

Bakeneko pictures had been a staple of the B-movie market in prewar Japan, with Daiei's precursor studio, Shinkō, producing several each year during the latter half of the 1930s. The Shinkō films' success was built largely around the persona of their star actress, Sumiko Suzuki (1904–1985), a onetime vamp who found renewed fame by becoming the "ghost cat actress" and Japan's first horror movie star. Suzuki's and the *bakeneko* genre's success was cut short, however, by the 1939 Film Act, which effectively turned the Japanese film industry into a propaganda machine under direct government control. In the ensuing years Shinkō would merge with Nikkatsu and Daito to form Daiei; Japan would lose the war; and Occupation censorship would continue to suppress *bakeneko* and *kaidan* (ghost story) adaptations, which were rife with themes of the defeated and vanquished seeking revenge.

When the Occupation ended in 1952, Daiei almost immediately put the once popular and profitable ghost cat pictures back into production. The studio was minus an essential ingredient to the *bakeneko* formula, however, with star attraction Sumiko Suzuki having retired from the movie business in 1941. Fortunately for Daiei, another fading screen beauty, Takako Irie, had recently come under contract with the studio. Irie was given the role of the monster in *The Ghost Story of Saga Mansion* and proved an effective successor to Suzuki, in part due to the impressive makeup effects, which utilized lighting techniques to show Irie transform in close-up from a beautiful maiden into a hideous cat creature in a single take. The picture minted Irie as the second great "*bakeneko* actress," and she would go on to appear in four more ghost cat pictures for Daiei throughout the 1950s.—Michael Crandol

See also Arai, Ryōhei; *bakeneko*; *The Ghost Cat of Arima Palace*; Irie, Takako; Suzuki, Sumiko

Bibliography
Arai Ryōhei, dir. *The Ghost Story of Saga Mansion*. Daiei, 1953. Film.

GODZILLA

Godzilla (known in Japan as Gojira) is the eponymous monster from Tōhō Studios' Godzilla franchise and one of the most internationally iconic and enduring characters of all Japanese pop culture. Since its inception, the character has appeared across a variety of media, including cartoons, comic books, and video games, although its closest association remains with film. The Godzilla series is the prevailing archetype of the *kaijū* (giant monster) genre and has spawned numerous sequels, remakes, and imitations. It is generally regarded as one of the primary influences for any narrative in which a city is besieged by a giant monster, such as the American films *Cloverfield* (Reeves, 2008) and *Pacific Rim* (Del Toro, 2013). Owing to this character, the slang suffix "-zilla" is used in English to denote size, destructiveness, or monster-like qualities.

The original name "Gojira" is popularly rumored to be a portmanteau of the Japanese words for "gorilla" (*gorira*) and "whale" (*kujira*), though Godzilla's physical appearance is mainly reptilian. Despite variations in character design over the decades, the monster has maintained a specific set of characteristics, including black or gray skin, a standing posture, anthropomorphic forearms, long tail, and large, white spikes on its back. Godzilla always emerges from the ocean and walks upright on land, and its design is partially inspired by several types of dinosaurs as well as the fictitious "Rhedosaurus," a monster featured in *The Beast from 20,000 Fathoms* (Lourié, 1953). Most versions of the monster also preserve its unique and thundering roar, which has become a recognizable sound effect. Godzilla is typically portrayed by an actor in a latex suit, though the series has increasingly come to rely on animatronic effects to make the monster's face more expressive. Recent American productions have rendered Godzilla primarily through computer imagery.

In addition to its physical strength and near-invincibility against conventional military weapons, Godzilla also possesses an "atomic breath," most famously represented as a powerful stream of blue fire that the creature can expel toward its enemies. In subsequent films and media, Godzilla has been given additional capabilities, such as increased speed or the ability to fly or generate magnetic fields. While American versions typically refer to the monster with the pronoun "he," Godzilla's sex is usually unspecified in Japan; in the 1968 sequel *Son of Godzilla*, however, he/she gives birth to the child-friendly character "Minilla," suggesting that the creature is female, at least in some iterations.

However, Godzilla is never seen alongside another adult creature of its species in the same film.

Godzilla was first featured in the 1954 *tokusatsu* film directed by Ishirō Honda and produced by Tomoyuki Tanaka. The film begins with a Japanese fishing vessel being destroyed at sea by an unseen force, igniting rumors among villagers of an ancient monster called "Gojira." The paleontologist Yamane, played by Takashi Shimura, is sent in to investigate a mysterious set of giant footprints when he witnesses the enormous Gojira firsthand. He concludes that the monster is a prehistoric creature that had been lying dormant under the sea until it was awakened by repeated H-bomb tests. Early attempts to kill the monster with depth charges in the ocean fail, and Gojira eventually surfaces outside of Tokyo, proceeding to destroy the city and its defense forces. In the following days, many of those who survived the attack have become eradiated by the radioactivity Gojira has left in its path.

In a subplot, Yamane's daughter Emiko, played by Momoko Kochi, is caught in a romantic triangle: she is in love with Ogata, Akira Takarada, a shipping captain, but is engaged to Serizawa, Akihiko Hirata, a brilliant but enigmatic scientist. Serizawa has sworn Emiko to secrecy about a device he has created—the "Oxygen Destroyer"—which can kill underwater organisms almost instantly by disintegrating the oxygen in their atoms. Upon surveying the spectacular devastation Gojira has left behind, Emiko enlists Ogata's help to convince a reluctant Serizawa to use his technology against the monster. Serizawa agrees, but fearing his doomsday device may fall into the wrong hands, deliberately sacrifices himself to deploy his Oxygen Destroyer onto the ocean floor. He is killed, and Gojira is disintegrated. The film ends with Yamane issuing an ominous warning that Gojira may not be the only one of its kind, and that continued nuclear testing may give rise to future monsters.

The original film was produced less than ten years after the atomic bombings of Hiroshima and Nagasaki, and it is generally well known that the Godzilla character (played by Haruo Nakajima), is a metaphor for the apocalyptic dangers of nuclear weapons and nuclear fallout. The capsizing of a Japanese ship during the opening sequence, for instance, purposefully alludes to a 1954 incident involving the fishing boat *Lucky Dragon 5* (*Daigo Fukuryū Maru*); in a tragic accident, the crew was contaminated by radiation from a nuclear test on the Bikini Atoll, a controlled detonation whose danger radius proved much larger than expected. The attack on Tokyo, the film's greatest sequence, contains several striking images of the monster stomping through a burning cityscape, invoking comparisons to the atomic bombings (possibly also the American fire-bombings). Subsequent scenes in the city's overcrowded hospitals place a grim focus on the small children who have lost their parents and now are testing positive for radiation.

Although most of the film's miniature sets and special effects are crude, and there is undeniably a campiness to Godzilla's anachronistic appearance and clumsy movements, the film takes its subject matter seriously, and its tone is never hokey or ironic. Upon the film's initial release, these overt allegorical references to nuclear weapons were not universally well received in Japan, as some critics believed *Gojira* exploited the real-life traumas of war and the atomic bombings. Nevertheless, the film was commercially successful and received award nominations for best film and best special effects by the Japanese Movie Association, winning the latter. The film has since been lauded as a classic of Japanese cinema.

In 1956, *Gojira* was released in the United States as *Godzilla: King of the Monsters!*, also to financial success. The American version replaced many of the human scenes with new footage, altering the story to make an American journalist (Raymond Burr) the central character and narrator. Some of the Japanese dialogue has been dubbed into English, while other scenes integrate the American character into the original film through clever editing and the use of acting doubles dressed to resemble members of the original Japanese cast. This version also downplays the film's antinuclear—and implicitly anti-American—themes. In 2004, the original, unedited film was given a limited release in the United States to coincide with its fiftieth anniversary; during this year, the Godzilla character received a star on the Hollywood Walk of Fame. In May 2014, the film was rereleased again, this time to promote the simultaneous release of the American remake *Godzilla*, directed by Gareth Edwards.

Capitalizing on the original film's popularity, Tōhō soon turned Godzilla into its flagship series and has since produced twenty-seven more films starring the titular monster. The long-standing franchise is commonly divided into three distinct periods, distinguishable largely by their respective tonal and stylistic approaches. The immediate decades following the 1954 original is known as Godzilla's Shōwa phase (so named for Japan's Shōwa period), lasting until 1975. Nakajima continued to portray Godzilla in the majority of films from this period; he retired in 1972.

Targeting younger audiences, much of the Shōwa series abandoned the melancholy tone of the original in favor of a more playful one, incorporating slapstick humor into the action sequences. The addition of other, rival monsters also became a standard feature after *Godzilla Raids Again*, the second film in the series, in which Godzilla battles the dinosaur "Anguirus." This model was solidified with the next sequel, *King Kong vs. Godzilla*, a crossover film in which Godzilla is pitted against the eponymous giant ape from the Hollywood classic *King Kong* (Cooper and Schoedsack, 1933). The film was reedited and released in the United States a year later, and still remains the most commercially successful film in the Godzilla franchise. There is a prevailing myth that there are two versions of the film (one in which Kong defeats Godzilla, and vice versa) that were produced for the respective American and Japanese markets; in reality, the film's sole ending shows Kong emerging victorious, with Godzilla's ultimate fate left ambiguous.

As the Shōwa series progressed, the stock "Godzilla vs. . . ." formula provided Tōhō with opportunities to introduce a host of new monsters into their expanding *Godzilla* universe. Some of these costars were short-lived, while others have become staple characters throughout the series—these include "King Gidorah," the three-headed dragon, and "Mechagodzilla," Godzilla's robotic doppelgänger. Still others, like "Mothra," the giant moth, and "Rodan," a Pteranodon, originated from their own *kaijū* films before becoming absorbed into the Godzilla series. The "vs." formula also fundamentally altered Godzilla's antagonistic nature. While still depicted as a destructive force, Godzilla is no longer necessarily an enemy of humanity, and in some instances, it allies with Japan's Self-Defense Force against the greater threat posed by one of the other creatures.

The Shōwa series, the most prolific era of existing Godzilla films, includes *Godzilla Raids Again* (*Gojira no gyakushū*; Oda, 1955); *King Kong vs. Godzilla* (*Kingu Kongu tai Gojira*; Honda, 1962); *Mothra vs. Godzilla* (*Mosura tai Gojira*; Honda, 1964); *Ghidorah, the Three-Headed Monster* (*San daikaijū: Chikyū saidai no kessen*; Honda, 1964); *Invasion of Astro-Monster* (*Kaijū daisensō*; Honda, 1965); *Godzilla vs. the Sea Monster* (*Gojira, Ebira, Mosura nankai no daikettō*; Fukuda, 1966); *Son of Godzilla* (*Kaijū-tō no kessen Gojira no musuko*; Honda, 1968); *Destroy All Monsters* (*Kaijū sōshingeki*; Honda, 1968); *All Monsters Attack* (*Gojira-Minira-Gabara: Oru kaijū daishingeki*; Honda, 1969); *Godzilla vs. Hedorah* (*Gojira tai Hedora*; Banno, 1971); *Godzilla vs. Gigan* (*Chikyū kogeki meirei: Gojira tai Gigan*; Fukuda, 1972); *Godzilla vs. Megalon* (*Gojira tai Megaro*; Fukuda, 1973); *Godzilla vs. Mechagodzilla* (*Gojira tai Mekagojira*; Fukuda, 1974); and *Terror of Mechagodzilla* (*Mekagojira no gyakushū*; Honda, 1975). Godzilla also appeared in numerous Japanese manga throughout this period, and in the late 1970s, Marvel Comics published a comic book series in which the monster encounters major Marvel characters, such as *The Avengers* and the *Fantastic Four*. A *Godzilla* cartoon series, coproduced by Tōhō and Hanna-Barbera Productions, aired between 1978 and 1979.

In 1984, *The Return of Godzilla* (coproduced with the United States) launched a new phase in the franchise, the Heisei series. Ignoring all of the sequels produced in the previous decades, this new film returned the series to its serious roots. In a manner similar to *King of the Monsters!*, the film underwent reediting to incorporate new footage before reaching American audiences. It was released in the United States one year later as *Godzilla 1985*.

Among the Heisei films, *Godzilla vs. King Ghidorah* was the subject of some controversy and alleged anti-Americanism: the film contains a sequence in which Godzilla vanquishes invading US soldiers during World War II. Like the Shōwa series, the Heisei films featured Godzilla battling some new enemies, while also resurrecting specific fan favorites, such as Mechgodzilla and Mothra. The series lasted until 1995, and includes *The Return of Godzilla* (*Gojira*; Hashimoto, 1984); *Godzilla vs. Biollante* (*Gojira tai Biorante*; Omori, 1989); *Godzilla vs. King Ghidorah* (*Gojira tai Kingu Gidora*; Omori, 1991); *Godzilla vs. Mothra* (*Gojira tai Mosura*; Okawara, 1992); *Godzilla vs. Mechagodzilla II* (*Gojira tai Mekagojira*; Okawara, 1993); *Godzilla vs. Space Godzilla* (*Gojira tai Supēsu Gojira*; Yamashita, 1994); and *Godzilla vs. Destoroyah* (*Gojira tai Desutoroia*; Okawara, 1995). Since the 1980s, Godzilla has also been the subject of numerous video games produced for the major consoles, including Game Boy, NES, SNES, Playstation, and Xbox. Starting in 1987, Godzilla was also featured in a number of Dark Horse Comics series and miniseries. In addition, Random House published a series of English-language novels between 1996 and 1999, each authored by Marc Cerasini. Most of these ancillary media consist of independent stories with no connections to the films.

After a four-year hiatus, the series was relaunched again in 1999 with the release of *Godzilla 2000: Millennium*, kick-starting Godzilla's third phase, the "Millennium" series. Once again, films in the new series ignored what had come before, "rebooting" many of it classic characters and villains. However, unlike the Heisei films, which maintained narrative continuity throughout its sequels, most of the Millennium films share no overlapping storylines. The series concluded in 2004 with *Godzilla: Final Wars*. As of this writing, Tōhō has announced yet another domestic reboot of the franchise, with a new Godzilla film slated for 2016. The project is reportedly being developed independently from ongoing American productions.

Godzilla films in the Millennium series include *Godzilla 2000: Millennium* (*Gojira Nisen: Mireniamu*; Okawara, 1999); *Godzilla vs. Megaguirus* (*Gojira tai Megagirasu: Jī shōmetsu sakusen*; Tezuka, 2000); *Godzilla, Mothra and King Ghidorah: Giant Monsters All-Out Attack* (*Gojira, Mosura, Kingu Gidora: Daikaijū sōkōgeki*; Kaneko, 2001); *Godzilla against Mechagodzilla* (*Gojira tai Mekagojira*; Tezuka, 2002); *Godzilla: Tokyo S.O.S.* (*Gojira Mosura Mekagojira Tōkyō Esu ō Esu*; Tezuka, 2003); and *Godzilla: Final Wars* (*Gojira: Fainaru wōzu*; Kitamura, 2004).

To date, *Godzilla* has been adapted into two Hollywood productions, including a widely ridiculed 1998 film, in which the monster rampages through New York City. Directed by Roland Emmerich, this film marks the first in the franchise to be produced entirely by an American studio. It was panned by critics for its script and performances and earned multiple nominations for Golden Raspberry Awards. Following this negative reception, plans for a sequel were scrapped. Instead, an animated series was produced that continued the film's storyline; it aired from 1998 to 2000.

This 1998 film sparked some controversy over the creative licenses taken in producing the new creature's sleek, iguana-like design and increased speed and agility, which caused an uproar among fans of the series. These characteristics departed drastically from Godzilla's classical appearance and lumbering movements, prompting allegations that the filmmakers modeled their monster on a Tyrannosaurus Rex in an attempt to capitalize on the popularity of *Jurassic Park* (Spielberg, 1993) and its sequel, *The Lost World* (1997). Distaste for the new creature was such that Tōhō rebranded it as "Zilla," formally recasting the character as a separate monster within the Godzilla franchise. The character has since made appearances in other related media, including *Final Wars* in 2004. The American film is also noteworthy for depicting the creature as explicitly female, as the protagonists discover late in the story that she has chosen Manhattan as a nesting ground and has laid countless eggs; an action sequence featuring the hatchlings chasing the human characters spurred further unfavorable comparisons to *Jurassic Park*.

The above-mentioned 2014 remake marks Hollywood's second attempt at the franchise, this time starring Godzilla as an ancient predator that awakens to hunt down a pair of monsters that terrorize Japan, Hawaii, and eventually San Francisco. Here, the computer-generated Godzilla adheres closely to the creature's original features and sound design. The film was released in 3-D and IMAX formats and was met with positive reviews, though some questioned the filmmakers' decision to withhold Godzilla's arrival until an hour into the film, resulting in limited screen time for the character. Legendary Comics—a division of Legendary Pictures, which produced the film—published a graphic novel, written by Max and Greg Borenstein and illustrated by Eric Battle, to tie in with the film. A sequel, tentatively titled *Godzilla 2*, is scheduled for a 2018 release.—Mike Dillon

GODZILLA films

Godzilla (1954)
DIRECTOR: Ishirō Honda
SCREENPLAY: Ishirō Honda, Takeo Murata
SPECS: 98 minutes; black and white

Godzilla King of the Monsters (1956)
DIRECTOR: Ishirō Honda, Terry Moore
SCREENPLAY: Shigeru Kayama, Al C. Ward
SPECS: 80 minutes; black and white

Godzilla, known as *Gojira* in Japanese, is the first film to feature Godzilla and the prototype for the postwar Toho monster (*kaijū*) genre. The story intertwines a romance, a monster mutated by nuclear radiation, and a moral dilemma over the use of a scientific discovery that could potentially become a weapon of mass destruction. It was directed in 1954 by Ishirō Honda (1911–1993) and produced by Tomoyuki Tanaka (1910–1997) for Toho Company. Beginning with *Godzilla*, the team of Honda, Tanaka, special-effects director Eiji Tsuburaya (1901–1970), and composer Akira Ifukube (1914–2006) created many of the enduring narrative and stylistic elements that define the Toho Godzilla series, comprising twenty-eight films as of 2004.

Godzilla King of the Monsters is the 1956 reedited version of *Godzilla* with new scenes shot with US actor Raymond Burr (1917–1993), dubbed English language dialogue, and additional sound effects. A small production company, Jewell Enterprises, Inc., acquired the rights to the US theatrical release of *Godzilla* after Toho sold them for $25,000. *Godzilla* was reworked to better conform to the formula of the predominantly low-budget, atomically mutated, giant creature films targeted at and popular with young adult audiences during the 1950s. Terry O. Morse (1906–1984) was in charge of direction and editing. The film's final credits list Morse and Honda as directors.

Godzilla was inspired by actual events, including the nuclear bombing of Hiroshima and Nagasaki and the more recent irradiation of a Japanese fishing boat, the *Lucky Dragon No. 5* (*Daigō Fukuryū Maru*), by the US nuclear test shot Bravo in the Bikini Atoll on 1 March 1954. Additional influences include the 1952 worldwide rerelease of *King Kong* (1933) in the context of contemporary science fiction/monster films, and *The Beast from 20,000 Fathoms* (1953), about a dinosaur awoken by a nuclear test at the North Pole that swims to New York City, where it emerges at the city docks to terrorize the population.

Godzilla King of the Monsters retains *Godzilla*'s basic plot elements of a romance, a monster, and a dangerous scientific discovery, but twenty minutes of new footage was added and forty minutes of the original film were cut. *Godzilla King of the Monsters* is approximately eighty minutes long compared to *Godzilla*'s ninety-eight minutes. Two new lead characters were added: American news reporter Steve Martin, played by Burr and Japanese Service Officer Iwanaga, played by Frank Iwanaga, who becomes Burr's guide and translator. Scenes of Martin and Iwanaga, along with Martin's voice-over narration, replace some of the interaction between the original film's lead characters. Through skillful editing and the use of body doubles, Burr appears to interact with these characters: the scientists Dr. Kyohei Yamane, played by Takashi Shimura (1905–1982); Dr. Daisuke Serizawa, played by Akihiko Hirata (1927–1984); Yamane's daughter Emiko, played by Momoko Kōchi (1932–1998); and her romantic interest, Hideto Ogata, played by Akira Takarada (b. 1934).

Godzilla opens by acknowledging the Japanese Coast Guard's collaboration in the film's production, followed by rolling white credits against a solid black background. They are strikingly similar to those of Akira Kurosawa's *Seven Samurai* (1954), which Toho released while *Godzilla* was in the early stages of preproduction planning. Ifukube's original score and the signature sound effects that will signal Godzilla's presence in the film—sounds resembling a monster's deep, throaty roars and heavy footsteps—accompany the credits. The film's opening sequence directly refers to the fate of the *Lucky Dragon No. 5*. The crew of a small fishing ship, the *Eikō Maru*, is relaxing on deck when the sailors are startled by bright flashes of light, a loud sound, and a shot of what appears to be an underwater explosion. Shots of their terrified reaction are the first of many reaction shots that continue to generate a sense of horror throughout the film.

The ship's radioman frantically attempts to send an SOS as waves crash into the cabin. The signal reaches its destination, but the ship sinks. In the aftermath, the South Seas Salvage Company, owners of the *Eikō Maru*, telephone a young company employee, Ogata, and summon him to company headquarters. Ogata reluctantly breaks his date with his girlfriend, Emiko Yamane.

The *Eikō Maru* is the first of several South Seas Salvage Co. ships that suddenly disappear at sea under mysterious circumstances. Emotionally distraught relatives press company officials for news of survivors as the officials rally forces in an attempt to make sense of the disasters. News arrives that a fishing ship from Odo Island is returning to the island with three survivors, but it also sinks under similar circumstances. There is a lone survivor, an Odo Island fisherman named Masaji, but that same night he is killed when his house is crushed during a violent storm. His brother Shinkichi, now an orphan, survives. A delegation from Odo Island, including Shinkichi and Hagiwara, a reporter present on the island during the storm, travel to Tokyo to inform a government assembly that the damage on the island was caused by a force more powerful than a typhoon. A renowned paleontologist, Dr. Kyohei Yamane (Emiko's father), testifies that many mysterious natural phenomena have occurred throughout history that humankind is unable to explain.

An expeditionary force including Yamane, Emiko, Ogata, Shinkichi, and Hagiwara leave by boat to investigate the situation on Odo Island. Dr. Daisuke Serizawa, a colleague of Dr. Yamane who has been engaged to Emiko since childhood, solemnly sees them off. At this point, approximately fifteen minutes into the film, all major characters except Godzilla have been introduced.

On Odo Island, Dr. Yamane, Emiko, and another scientist, Dr. Tanabe, discover what appear to be giant, radioactive footprints. Dr. Yamane is excited to discover a trilobite, thought to be extinct, in one of the footprints. In a dynamically edited sequence, a villager rings a bell in warning and villagers and the expedition members run toward the hills to seek safety. In the ensuing melee,

Godzilla's head appears behind a hilltop ridge for the first time. Dr. Yamane snaps a photo as evidence.

The narrative that unfolds from this point bears traces of *Godzilla*'s generic roots in the jungle adventure film genre (e.g., *The Lost World* and *King Kong*) and such post-Hiroshima science fiction "creature features" as *The Beast from Twenty Thousand Fathoms*. After Odo Island villagers liken Godzilla to a mythical force of nature that must be appeased, Godzilla surfaces in Tokyo Bay. In two subsequent night attacks on the city, Godzilla is enraged by attacks launched by artillery tanks and other weapons, and wreaks havoc on iconic landmarks and the city's terrified inhabitants. The Self-Defense Forces' reliance on weapons and Ogata's conviction that the monster must be destroyed to prevent further human casualties clashes with the idealistic pursuit of human advancement through scientific knowledge, represented by Yamane and Serizawa. The relationships between Ogata and Emiko, who are in love, and Serizawa, Emiko's fiancé in an arranged engagement, play out in parallel to this conflict and Godzilla's rampages.

Emiko's actions turn the narrative around when she discloses that Serizawa has a secret invention, the "Oxygen Destroyer," which could be used to defeat Godzilla. Pressured by Ogata and Emiko, Serizawa reluctantly agrees to its use only after destroying his research to prevent it from falling into the wrong hands. After confirming the weapon's fatal effect on Godzilla, he tells Ogata to enjoy a happy future with Emiko. He severs his lifeline, ensuring that he will never be coerced to re-create the Oxygen Destroyer for evil ends. The film closes with Yamane's somber warning that if atomic tests continue, it is likely that more monsters like Godzilla will reappear.

Godzilla significantly differs from preceding generic formulas. Later testimony by Ifukube and members of the special-effects team reinforce Honda's later recollection that the production team took the film seriously as an antiwar statement. Returning to Tokyo after having lived in China during the war, Honda witnessed the aftermath of Hiroshima's nuclear obliteration. Meeting with Tanaka and Tsuburaya a few months before the film went into production, he and his colleagues agreed to proceed as if they were filming an actual event rather than an implausible story about a radioactive monster.

The film's focus on human relationships and specific temporal references are realistic details. The role of media during a national crisis (commercial TV broadcasting began in Japan in 1953); recognizable Tokyo locations (the Diet building, Nichigeki Theater, the Ginza shopping and entertainment district, and the iconic Seiko Building clock tower) add a sense of familiarity and immediacy. This is reinforced by dialogue references to personal wartime experiences unique to Japan, a sense of national unity (maps of Japan are ubiquitous on walls in the background of several scenes, newspaper headlines infer popular speculation), and an emerging sense of Japan's unique role in the postwar international world order.

By Japanese standards, *Godzilla* was an expensive production. The $250,000 budget compared favorably to the $75,000 cost of the average film. It is less extravagant compared to Hollywood standards at the time. Special-effects director Eiji Tsuburaya admired the stop-motion animation in *King Kong* by special effects pioneer Willis O'Brien (1886–1962), but *Godzilla*'s budget precluded this option. Tsuburaya instead relied on a stage technique now commonly referred to as "suitmation." This was to become a signature Toho special effect.

As Godzilla, Haruo Nakajima (b. 1929) wore a heavy, cumbersome suit consisting of a wire and bamboo framework padded with cotton and covered by molten synthetic rubber treated with oil. To convey Godzilla's lumbering, massive size, scenes were shot at four times the normal speed. Miniature sets of Tokyo with built in structural weaknesses where they were meant to crumble were built on a scale of 25:1 to further increase the illusion that Godzilla towered over the city. Composite and matte shots were used extensively. The film was shot on studio sets as well as on location.

The use of Godzilla's targeted breath blasts as a physical manifestation of lethal radiation was achieved by running a pipe up through Nakajima's suit and pumping propane gas through the mouth opening. It was an innovative effect not only in terms of technique. The threat of radiation exposure permeates the film. As recently as 1950, US civil defense films assured viewers that they "could beat radiation," but incidents like the contamination of the *Lucky Dragon No. 5* helped erode this misconception.

The *Eikō Maru* incident is not the narrative point of departure in *Godzilla King of the Monsters*. The film begins with the corporate logos of Toho and Transworld Pictures, the film's US distributor, accompanied by the resonant sounds resembling Godzilla's footsteps as they are heard in the original film. We see the sea and what appears to be an underwater explosion; we hear Godzilla's roars from the original film as the title *Godzilla King of the Monsters* flashes on screen.

The story opens with a pan across a devastated landscape without signs of human life. Voice-over narration identifies this as "Tokyo, once a city of six million people." The next shot and continuing narration introduces the narrator, lying in a pile of rubble. This is Steve Martin, played by Raymond Burr.

This opening sequence establishes Steve Martin as the film's central character. The next sequence situates Martin among the victims of a night of horror that has turned Martin's stopover in Tokyo on a social call into "a visit to the living hell of another world." Shots of Martin bandaged and lying on a stretcher alternate with shots of Godzilla's victims, but Godzilla is not yet mentioned. Martin and Emiko Yamane recognize one another: Martin is revealed to be friends with Dr. Yamane. Like the other original lead characters, Emiko is portrayed here by dubbed shots from *Godzilla* of Emiko played by actress Momoko Kōchi, and a body double similarly dressed and shot from behind. Emiko asks Martin why he is in Tokyo.

The flashback that follows in answer to this question begins with Martin's arrival to pay a visit to his old college friend, Dr. Serizawa. His arrival coincides with the disappearance of the South Seas Salvage ships. Security Officer Iwanaga questions Martin at the airport to learn whether he noticed anything unusual during his flight. His curiosity piqued, Martin is drawn into the ensuing plot.

Martin and Iwanaga act as a team throughout the film. Shots of them together are inserted into *Godzilla*'s events. These events do not necessarily occur in their original order, and continuity is largely dependent on Martin's expository voice-over narration. Some key scenes in the original film are cut, such as an argument among officials about whether or not certain news should be made public. Martin's presence is consistent, but he remains an observer despite attempts to make it appear that he interacts with the original lead characters.

Martin's flashback ends approximately one hour into the film; he is once again recovering on his stretcher, ostensibly among other victims of Godzilla's most recent attack. He then sets in motion the events leading up to Godzilla's death by compelling Emiko to urge Dr. Serizawa to use his Oxygen Destroyer to put an end to Godzilla's reign of terror. After Godzilla's death and Serizawa's self-sacrifice, Martin's narration brings the film to an end with the observation that now "the whole world could wake up and live again."

The "Americanization" of *Godzilla* is interpreted as a reflection of different Japanese and US cultural attitudes in the 1950s, particularly popular attitudes toward nuclear power. The centrality of the Steve Martin character, intended to act as a narrative bridge making *Godzilla* more accessible for US audiences, and the dependence on dubbing and expository narration, all affect the characterization of and dynamics between *Godzilla*'s lead characters. Specific topical references, particularly references to the Japanese wartime and postwar experience, are lost in translation through omission or generalization.

Beyond a comparison between *Godzilla* and *Godzilla King of the Monsters* as Japanese and US productions, the different circumstances of their reception and distribution further complicate attempts to definitively pinpoint the origins of Godzilla and the Japanese *kaijū* film genre. *Godzilla* was a box office success in Japan upon its release, but critical reception was mixed, with some critics asserting that the film trivialized the actual events that inspired it. A subtitled print of *Godzilla* was included in a series of Toho films shown in select US venues in 1982 to commemorate the company's fiftieth anniversary, but it was not released theatrically in the United Satates until its fiftieth anniversary in 2004, when a newly re-struck print was billed as *Godzilla: The Uncut Japanese Original*. *Godzilla King of the Monsters* was a financial success when it opened in the United States in 1956, establishing a fan base for subsequent, similar Japanese imports. In addition to successful runs in Europe and South America, *Godzilla King of the Monsters* was released in 1957 as *Kaijū ō Gojira* with Japanese-language subtitles in Japan, where it was also popular. For the next fifty years, *Godzilla King of the Monsters* continued to displace the original film, introducing Godzilla to audiences worldwide.—Joanne Bernardi

See also Godzilla

Bibliography
Honda, Ishiro. *Godzilla*. Toho, 1954. Film.
Honda, Ishiro, and Terry O. Morse. *Godzilla King of the Monsters*. Toho and Jewell Enterprises, Inc., 1956. Film.
Tucker, Guy Mariner. *Age of the Gods: A History of the Japanese Fantasy Film*. Brooklyn, NY: Daikaiju Publications, 1996.

GOMENNASAI (2011)
DIRECTOR: Mari Asato
SCREENPLAY: Yoichi Minagawa
SPECS: 94 minutes; color

Released on 29 October 2011 in Japan, *Gomennasai* (literally "I'm sorry"), also known as *Ring of Curse*, is a Japanese horror (J-horror) film. Directed by Mari Asato with a screenplay by Yoichi Minagawa, this 94-minute movie is based on a popular mobile phone novel by scriptwriter Yuka Hidaka. The structure of this film's storyline is divided into three diary entries, which portray the perspectives of the two central characters. The movie features three members of the Buono, a Japanese pop girl unit that is a part of the Hello! Project and is managed by the Up-Front Agency. These three stars, who are in the film's lead roles are Momoko Tsugunaga (age nineteen, as Shiori Sonoda) and Miyabi Natsuyaki (age nineteen, as Hinako Kurohane) from Berryz Workshop, and Airi Suzuki (age seventeen, as Yuka Hidaka) from Cute. All three girl-group idols are high school students originally from the Chiba prefecture.

The story of *Gomennasai* revolves around a girl named Hinako, who puts a curse on any person who gives her trouble. Hinako has a hard life at home due to her parents' neglect—as they favor her younger sister, Kana. Jealous of Kana, Hinako curses her sibling, who is then diagnosed with cancer and dies shortly thereafter. As Hinako is blessed with literary talent, she receives good grades in school, but in her social life she struggles as a victim of bullying. Having the ability to deliver curses through the written word, including texting, Hinako goes on a killing rampage, creating text messages that her unsuspecting victims read and then die from.

Mari Asato's *Gomennasai* begins with a typical storyline of the strange student in class being bullied, yet it takes a scarily fresh turn when the bullied one turns out to be an obsessed writer who transforms the script of a school play into spooky death sentences for her tormentors. However, only at the end is the mysterious sentence shown at the opening revealed to be indeed a curse, and the audience understands the actual meaning of the film's title.

The film presents a plot that explores the power of words to curse and kill. Although the film's scare tactics are somewhat underdeveloped, its creepy tone certainly resonates throughout the film and the genre clichés and predictable plot points are kept to a minimum. Moreover, it uses humor to good effect. Even though *Gomennasai* failed to attain large-scale success, it did well enough on the strength of its screenplay as well as the realistic performances of the actors.

Gomennasai exhibits originality, something seldom found in the contemporary horror genre, but in addition it is a timely story. Set at a high school in Japan's Kanagawa Prefecture, the film presents audiences with real-life horror situations, as bullying is a rather crucial social issue in Japan today.—Monir Hossain Moni

Bibliography
Galloway, Patrick. *Asia Shock: Horror and Dark Cinema from Japan, Korea, Hong Kong and Thailand*. Berkeley, CA: Stone Bridge, 2006.
McRoy, Jay. *Nightmare Japan: Contemporary Japanese Horror Cinema*. Amsterdam: Rodopi, 2007.

GOZU (2003)
DIRECTOR: Takashi Miike
SCREENPLAY: Sakichi Satō
SPECS: 129 minutes; color

Film director Takashi Miike has always been regarded as a wildly audacious and experimental filmmaker. Dabbling in the yakuza, science-fiction, and action genres, many of Miike's films have strong satirical undercurrents. Miike's unorthodox methodologies and taboo-bashing extreme violence mark him as an intensely influential and iconoclastic artist of the past twenty years. With *Gozu*, Miike blends yakuza stories with ghost stories, urban legends, and bizarre vignettes to create a magical blend of grotesque imagery and creative exploration.

Gozu boasts one of the most outrageous and startling opening scenes in all of Japanese cinema, wherein a yakuza henchmen tells the boss that a dog of a small breed outside the restaurant at which they are meeting is really a vicious yakuza dog and a spy. The yakuza clan stand with trepidation and fear as they gaze at this innocuous looking creature, and finally our protagonist goes outside to pulverize the dog in a horrific and nauseatingly humorous moment. So begins the elaborately satirical and absurd film very much in the vein of other Miike vehicles such as *The Happiness of the Katakuris* (2001) and *Visitor Q* (2001).

Minami, the central protagonist drives his beloved brother, Ozaki, to be assassinated and to be disposed of in a "company" depot. The "hit" is ordered by the head of the Azamawari clan, as result of Ozaki's increasingly irrational and demented behaviors. As the two progress further into this nightmare, Ozaki snaps his own neck in Minami's car, saving Minami the trouble. When his body disappears, Minami is left with a series of labyrinthine puzzles and odd encounters.

Gozu borrows source material from Greek mythology, and Minami's episodic quests are similar to challenges Ulysses might have faced, only updated to a small town in modern Japan. The disorienting puzzles and a miscellaneous array of surrealist horrors such as the closet full of yakuza "skin suits" literarily made of human skin, and freshly pressed, make for the exhilarating type of bewilderment we've come to expect from Miike. Perhaps of note, also, is when Ozaki reappears as a woman. She persuades Minami to engage in sex and she ultimately gives birth to the male Ozaki.

Gozu has been subtitled "a yakuza ghost story." Among the bizarre characters are an overly lactating innkeeper, a unpredictable and abrasive bigot, and a man with a cow's head—from which the title is derived. These types of characters are grotesque pieces of Miike's surrealist/absurdist machine, which may make little sense to general audiences, but have truly fueled highly involved analyses among film and cultural critics. Miike has constantly pushed the envelope of viewer's expectations and arguably, of good taste, but in *Gozu* he manages to incorporate a wide range of genre influences and create new ground. Although *Gozu* may be construed as less graphically violent or gratuitous, there are still deeply unsettling depictions of massacre and carnage.

Gozu was originally slated for release straight to DVD. However, at the 2003 Cannes Film Festival, it stirred its share of controversy and accolades. The New York Times, BBC, and Washington Post commented on both Miike's fragmented filmmaking structure, as well as its unique nuances. Miike, whose career spans thirteen years and over sixty films, is a powerful force in Japanese filmmaking. All of the staples that audiences have come to expect from a Miike film are present in *Gozu*. Miike smashes sexual taboos, transcends gruesome violence, and attempts to leave the audience bewildered, confused, and disturbed. The film lingers long after it is over. Although it is disturbingly violent, it is a creative and unique example of a visionary director's attempt to add to the tapestry of worldwide cinema. While many regard *Audition* (1999) to be the quintessential Miike film, *Gozu* serves as a minor classic of the genre Miike, himself, has created.—William Blick

THE GREEN SLIME (1968)
DIRECTOR: Kinji Fukasaku
SCREENPLAY: Bill Finger, Colin Sinclair
SPECS: 90 minutes; color

The 1968 science fiction–action adventure *The Green Slime* (*Gamma 3: Operation Outer Space*) follows in a long tradition in Japanese folklore where Nature suddenly gives way to demonic forces—docile animals mutate into gruesome beasts, insects become ravenously carnivorous, and wayside plants grow into cold-blooded killers. An international collaboration, it was spearheaded by Ivan Reiner (1911–1997) and Walter Manley (1918–1996), directed by Kinji Fukasaku (1930–2003) in Japan at Toei Studio, and produced in the United States by MGM Studios. It was filmed for the wide screen and in color. Not a single member of the main cast is of Japanese descent.

A group of astronauts set out on a mission to stop a giant asteroid, codenamed "Flora," on a collision course with the planet Earth. Landing on the asteroid, they plant explosive charges and successfully destroy it. Afterward they return to Gamma 3, a space station in orbit around the Earth. One scientist from the mission has unwittingly brought aboard a luminous-green slime on the leg of his spacesuit. Once in place, the alien substance begins to grow and undergoes a transformation into gigantic one-eyed monsters with eight tentacles, capable of discharging lethal bolts of electricity. The crew fends off the aliens with laser-based weaponry, only to discover that they feed off the energy: as they bleed, new creatures spout from their blood. However much these creatures overrun the station, the crew continues their fight, against increasingly poor odds, ultimately to preserve life and all that they hold dear on Earth.

As if the battle of man against alien were not enough, interwoven into the storyline is a second battle—between two commanding officers for the affections of the voluptuous, if tempestuous and fiery, Thunderball. Eventually all realize that they must set aside their personal interests and the ensuing romantic rivalry for the larger good, the salvation of humanity.

In hindsight, the film appears more a clever satire of the sci-fi movie/horror genre, but one must not lose sight of the fact that it is itself a cultural artifact of the times in which it was produced, the turbulent sixties. Such an understanding perhaps justifies the Jimi Hendrix–like psychedelic rock theme song—the commercial success of the film was, in fact, bolstered by the release of the soundtrack widely distributed as 45 RPM singles. It may explain the wildly imaginative and outlandish costumes (e.g., inventive, if unconvincing, potato-shaped monster suits, or motor-cycle-helmet-clad astronauts), the outrageously naive sets (a plastic toy likely inspired by the space station seen in the 1968 sci-fi epic *2001: A Space Odyssey*, produced and directed by Stanley Kubrick, 1928–1999) and props (insubstantial, unmistakably plastic pistols and miniature projectiles meant to be missiles ready for interplanetary combat). It perhaps does less to justify the frequency with which clichés passed for—replaced—serious dialogue. Taken together, however, the result is what has, rightly so, been called "one of the funniest made-in-Japan sci-fi monster movies ever."

Later, portions of the film were used to pitch the pilot of the made-for-television series *Mystery Science Theater 3000*, although the entire film was never lampooned. A single episode, "The Green Slime," appeared in 1988.—James Wren

Bibliography
Fukasaku, Kinji, dir. *Green Slime*. Warner Home Video, 2010. DVD.

GROTESQUE (2009)
DIRECTOR: Kōji Shiraishi
SCREENPLAY: Kōji Shiraishi
SPECS: 73 minutes; color

Grotesque, or *Gurotesuku* in Japanese, is a 2009 splatter film written and directed by Kōji Shiraishi (b. 1973), who stated that he set out to make a modern day version of the notorious film *Guinea Pig*. The film is notable for being banned in the UK due to the presentation of humiliation, brutality, sexual violence, and sadism in combination with minimal narrative justification or character development. In the film an unnamed man, played by Shigeo Ōsako (b. 1974), abducts a young couple and without explanation subjects them to various forms of torture. Although never explicitly mentioned, he tends to their wounds throughout and appears to be a doctor. Despite being considered devoid of narrative, the film maintains a theme of how far you would be willing to go to save someone that you supposedly love.

The film opens with a man sitting in a van watching a young couple, Aki, played by Kotoha Hiroyama (b. 1985) and Kazuo, Hiroaki Kawatsure (b. 1977). He hits them with a hammer and when they wake up they are bound and gagged in a basement. The man stabs Kazuo with a metal pole, and licks Aki's face before asking if she would die for him. A flashback reveals the couple on their first date, where Kazuo tells Aki that it was love at first sight for him. Aki asks if he would die for her, and when she receives no answer insists that she is just kidding. Kazuo says that he will do his best, and it is at that point that they are snatched.

Scenes later, set in the basement, the man informs the couple that they will both die there, but that there is one way out. If they excite him sexually with their will to survive he will release them. He then sexually assaults them both and tells him that the real pain will now begin. The couple reawaken to find themselves restrained on flat tables. Using a chainsaw the man cuts off Kazuo's fingers and threads them onto a necklace that he hangs around Aki's neck as "a gift." He cuts the fingers from Aki's left hand, removes her nipples with scissors and cuts off her right arm. The man then says that he will kill Kazuo after torturing him, but that if he is brave and doesn't break down he will spare Aki. He hammers nails into Kazuo's testicles, takes out his eye, and removes his penis. As he holds Kazuo's severed penis in his hand, the kidnapper declares that he has deeply felt the sexual stimulation he was seeking.

The couple then wakes up in what appears to be a recovery room. The man brings them flowers and asserts that he will release them when they have recovered. He also says he will turn himself in and give them his seven-hundred-million yen assets. Although unsure of whether they should trust him, Kazuo and Aki tentatively make plans for a life together once they are released. The man continues to tend to their wounds over several days. However, after informing them that they will be free in two to three days, they awake once more in the torture chamber.

The man tells them that he wasn't excited enough to release them yet. He wants to see their survival will again, and for Kazuo to prove that he really is willing to die for Aki. He attaches the end of Kazuo's intestine to a hook, informing him that he must cross the room to cut Aki's ropes, effectively disemboweling himself. Kazuo stumbles to a pair of scissors halfway across the room and cuts his own intestine, before crawling to Aki and freeing her feet. He manages to stand up and attempts to cut the rope around her wrists. However, the rope is revealed to contain wire that could never be cut with scissors.

Kazuo collapses to the ground and Aki spits in the kidnapper's face, calling his mother a prostitute and pointing out his foul body odor, saying that if anyone had ever really loved him then they would have told him about it. In anger he attacks her with a chainsaw before cutting off her head with an axe. Her decapitated head bites down hard on his shoulder and with his last energies Kazuo stabs the scissors into the man's foot. The couple die looking into each other's eyes.

Sometime afterward, the kidnapper now walks with a limp. Outside, he hangs the scissors across two posts, which function as makeshift graves. Multiple other posts suggest that he has done this many times before. The scene then cuts to him waiting in a van once more, this time applying deodorant. As a young woman walks past he clutches his hammer, assumedly to kidnap again.—Aimee Richmond

See also ero guro nansensu genre; Guinea Pig series

Bibliography
Ogura, Satoru, dir. *Guinea Pig*. Sai Enterprise, 1985. Video.
Shiraishi, Kōji, dir. *Grotesque*. JollyRoger, 2009. DVD.

GUINEA PIG films

Infamously known as *Ginī Piggu*, the Guinea Pig series contains some of the goriest, most violent, senseless, and bizarre horror films to come out of the early "shock horror'" subgenre in Japan. Comprised of six short films, a "worst of" clips compilation show, and a behind-the-scenes special, the Guinea Pig films pride themselves on their masochistic and sadistic content. Typically low budget, they were released between 1985 and 1988 with a variety of directors and actors (both credited and uncredited). The series gains much of its infamy as a result of two known incidents: first, the collection was found to be showcased by serial killer Tsutomu Miyazaki, which led to the series as a whole being removed from production in Japan; the second incident involved American actor Charlie Sheen, who, after viewing *Chiniku no Hana* (*Flower of Flesh and Blood*) in 1991, believed the film to be a real incident and called the FBI, prompting an investigation of the filmmakers by the Japanese authorities.

The first two entries, *Akuma no Jikken* (*Devils Experiment*), directed by Satoru Ogura, and *Chiniku no Hana* (*Flower of Flesh and Blood*) by Hideshi Hino (b. 1946) were both released in 1985, and virtually share the same premise: a young woman is abducted and subjected to torture at the hands of her captors. *Akuma no Jikken* is an "adventure" in the discovery of the human body's ability to tolerate pain. Its plot centers on the premise that it is a "found-footage film," in which three men subject a single woman to a series of increasingly inhumane torture techniques; beginning with being repeatedly punched, each scene is punctuated by a black screen and a single word to describe what will follow. Satoru takes the audience through an uncomfortable hour of film, with is nearly dialogue and story free. It includes scenes in which the woman is kicked and demeaned, is spun around in a chair while forced to ingest alcohol, has her fingernails removed, is kept awake for a long period of time by uncomfortable sounds, and is further scalded with hot oil. Finally, the woman has a pin forced through the side of her eye, which emerges from her pupil, and though her murder is not shown, she is put on display in a swinging net. To add to the unease—and force the trope of found-footage—none of the actors are credited.

Hideshi Hino's *Chiniku no Hana* is quite similar, though with an added script which details the torture process and indicates a certain amount of madness on the part of the tormentor; based on one of Hino's manga creations, and rumored to feature the director as the torturer, it is framed as a "re-creation" of a fictitious torture film sent to the director Hino by a fan. To create his atmosphere of discomfort, Hino admits to abandoning all narrative structure and to forgoing the moral overview of character motivation in his antagonist, a florist who abducts and kills women in order to use their bodies in his displays. In an almost clinical manner, the film progresses through the dismemberment and vivisection of an innocent female, played by Kirara Yūgao, who is first heavily drugged, and remains in a form of induced ecstasy. Beginning with her hands, the florist utilizes dull implements to cut her apart; each new removal is interrupted by the florist explaining how he is revealing the most beautiful part of the woman, and drawing her closer to blooming. After removing her arms and legs, he proceeds to cut her open and lay her organs over her body in a slow and almost reverent exposure, before decapitating her. Hino closes the film by having the florist display his collection of parts, all of which are treated and incorporated in plant-like displays and in various stages of decay.

Both *Akuma no Jikken* and *Chiniku no Hana* conclude with a brief bout of text designed to further push the audience into a suspension of their disbelief, stating that while the victims and the perpetrators remain unknown, the Japanese authorities are conducting investigations in order to determine the nature of the footage. Both films are drawn from the mid-1980s urban legend in Japan, which held that in the underground film circuit, there were such snuff films that could be purchased, showing the real life death of unnamed individuals at the hands of gore and violence enthusiasts.

After switching production houses, the Guinea Pig series underwent a dramatic shift, becoming slightly more plot driven and less reliant on torture to create horror. They retained their "shock and gore" focus, but set themselves up so as to be readily identified as film experiences rather than actual footage of violence committed against innocent people. Masayuki Kusumi's *Senritsu! Shinanai otoko* (*He Never Dies!*, 1986), tells the story of Hideshi, played by Masahiro Satō, a young office worker who finds his life meaningless after a series of humiliating let-downs, in which his work ability and personal relationships seem to fall apart. In a moment of depressed boredom, Hideshi accidentally cuts his wrist, but instead of bleeding out he finds that he feels no pain and is unable to die. After a series of increasingly drastic attempts to commit suicide, Hideshi decides to use his condition to affect the only individuals he can think of, his office coworkers Nakamura, played by Shinsuke Araki, and Kyoko, played by Ivu/Eve. He invites them over under the guise of needing tools to take care of his home; in a series of increasingly gruesome "shock and awe" scenes, Hideshi cuts open his stomach and throws all of his internal organs over Nakamura who has been reduced to a screaming pile on the floor. In the final scene, Hideshi sets out to shock Kyoko by decapitating himself and leaving his head on the table to speak to her when she comes to check on Nakamura; instead of being frightened, Kyoko is instead appalled at the mess that Hideshi has created, and urges Nakamura to join her in attempting to clean up the blood and gore, all while admonishing Hideshi's lack of consideration in making such a mess. Hideshi then confides that he now feels able and ready to return to work. Classified as a gore-comedy rather than strict horror film, Kusumi frames the whole story as a series of scientific footage, seemingly questioning viewers about how they would handle being unable to die.

The fourth entry in the series is *Pītā no Akuma no Joi-san* (*Devil Doctor Woman*), directed by Hajime Tabe in 1986, and despite being chronologically labeled as the fourth in the series, it is often referred to as the final film. In the film, the Devil Doctor, played by Shinnosuke Ikehata, is a type of physician that examines and consults on very strange medical cases that exist outside the confines of actual science and drift into the realm of the paranormal. Each vignette scene is short and self contained, as the director guides the audience through a series of increasingly incredible scenarios, which include a family whose heads explode if they experience any type of "fiery" emotions; a man whose right side is attempting to kill him; a yakuza-type with a polite talking tumor; a recently deceased man who continues to rot and decay while taking part in daily life activities with his young wife; a warning to be aware of abandoned human organs that chase any unwary pedestrian; a moving tattoo removal that results in the complete skinning of the patient; and a group of four men who showcase an increasingly bizarre set of symptoms in order to prove that their illness is the worst. Regarded as the least composed and shocking of the shock and gore series, *Pita no Akuma no Joi-san* steps away from the single plot structure utilized by the rest of the series.

For the fifth installment in 1988, Hideshi Hino returns with another piece based on one of his manga, *Manhōru no naka no ningyo* (*Mermaid in the Manhole*). It is considered to be the most artistic of the series, following a fully structured narrative about obsession and madness, but returning to the gore and shock for which the series is infamous. Hino returns to an intimate story and creates an atmosphere of unease, centering the story on an artist, played by Shigeru Saiki, who recently lost his wife, and a mermaid, played by Mari Somei, that has been rescued from a sewer near his home—which, incidentally, used to be a beautiful waterway where the artist played as a child. Since the water and the environment became polluted, the mermaid has developed a spreading infection. At the mermaid's telepathic pleading, the artist begins to paint her, pouring all of his energy and focus into providing her with fish and keeping her comfortable while he works. As the infection begins to spread, it opens up pigment and fluid oozing boils on her body, which the artist uses in order to continue painting his masterpiece. With mounting obsession, the artist abandons all things, save for his painting, and as the mermaid's condition continues to get worse, the painting changes, reflecting the decay and the ugly truth of the mermaid's condition instead of the initial dream-like quality it had once conveyed. Eventually the mermaid succumbs to the infection and her boils break out, spewing worms and leeches into the porcelain tub where the artist had placed her. The artist obsessively continues to paint, pausing only to pull handful after handful of worms from her body, until she dies. In his sadness, he decides to discard her as one would a fish, dismembering her body. Below, his neighbors have begun to notice an odd smell, and call the local authorities when blood begins leaking down onto their kitchen table. When the police arrive they discover that the artist has killed and dismembered his ill wife and infant son. The tale of obsession moves between the oddly fantastical and heartbreaking fairytale, and the all too poignant macabre story of obsession and madness.

The final entry in the Guinea Pig series is Kazuhito Kuramoto's *Nōtorudamu no andoroido* (*The Android of Notre Dame*, 1988/89), an endeavor into the philosophical and experimental horror of the mad scientist persuasion. Utilizing computer technology, DNA sequencing, and a variety of experiments in revivification, Karazawa, played by Toshihiko Hino works tirelessly to find a way to save his sister, played by Mio Takaki, who suffers from a weak heart. Supported financially by Kato, played by Tomorowo Taguchi, Karazawa is backed into a corner through blackmail, as his programming is stolen and Kato blackmails him. Flipping the tables, Karazawa lures Kato into his lab, where he kills and decapitates him in order to continue his experiments, while his sister's heart slowly begins to give out as she willingly avoids taking her medication. Through his computer programming, Karazawa is able to revive Kato's head, controlling him through his computer and expanding on his grotesque creation by adding mechanical arms, which Kato is only somewhat able to control and at great expense to his already deteriorating flesh. In a truly emotionally destructive turn, Karazawa turns his experimentations on himself, prolonging his life indefinitely as he contemplates the nature of creation and playing god, and becoming the android he sought to create to keep his sister alive.—Megan Negrych

See also Hino, Hideshi

Bibliography
Hino, Hideshi, dir. *Ginī Piggu 2: Chiniku No Hana.* Sai Enterprise, 1985. Film.
———. *Ginī Piggu 5: Manhōru no naka no Ningyo.* Japan Home Video, 1988. Film.
Kuramoto, Kazuhito, dir. *Ginī Piggu 6: Nōtorudamu no andoroido.* Japan Home Video, 1988/89. Film.

GUROZUKA (2005)
DIRECTOR: Yōichi Nishiyama
SCREENPLAY: Ao Murata, from a story by Tadayoshi Kubo
SPECS: 85 minutes; color

Released in Japan in October of 2005, *Gurozuka* is a slasher film directed by Yōichi Nishiyama. Ao Murata adapted the screenplay from an original story by Tadayoshi Kubo. The title refers to the name of a video watched by the film's main characters. The video features a figure in a *deigan* mask committing a murder and throughout *Gurozuka*, the same figure systematically kills the members of an all-girl drama club who are staying at the same secluded lodge at which the cursed video was created. *Gurozuka* follows in a tradition of horror films such as *Ring* (1998), *The Manual* (2003), and *One Missed Call* (2003) featuring at the plot's center technology such as videos, DVDs, and cell phones.

Gurozuka opens with two girls, Maki, played by Yoko Mitsuya, and Ai, played by Chisato Morishita, watching the titular video. The images are grainy, but a masked figure is seen killing someone and then chopping up their body with a hatchet, though little blood is actually seen. While *Gurozuka* does contain violent scenes, graphic blood and gore is actually minimal. In the video, the figure walks toward the camera and then a dissonant screech accompanies a close-up of one of the girls. The screech continues into the opening credits. This is the first of many instances in which the film follows the generic tradition of the "jump-scare," pairing sudden sounds and startling images.

Maki and Ai are members of an all-girl drama group and at the beginning of the film are leaving for a trip to a secluded, wooded lodge in order to work on a film project. In addition to the group's three other members, Yuka, played by Yukari Fukui; Natsuki, played by Yuko Kurosawa; and Yayoi, played by Keiko Saito, Yoko, a teacher and former club member, played by Yuko Ito, and Takako, played by Nozomi Ando, a student and the teacher Yoko's alleged lover, are also traveling. As a former member, the girls question Yoko, who denies rumors that the club originally disbanded when one member went missing and another insane.

When the group reaches Yuai House, their destination, odd events begin almost immediately. Natsuki's attention is broken during her meditation when a dark figure, the one from the video, is seen crawling on the ground. Later, when she is taking a shower, the figure passes behind a pane of frosted glass and is accompanied by a loud musical hit. Later in the evening, Ai has a dream in which a *deigan*-masked figure jumps out at her.

At dinner, Maki shows the other girls an old 8 mm film, which Ai explains is derived from a song called "Kurotsuka" (Black tomb) that tells the story of a *kijo* who eats a group of traveling monks. Though Yoko denies it, the girls surmise that the video was made at the lodge by the previous incarnation of the drama club. Further, the girls are upset to find out that Maki and Ai want to film a horror movie based on the video instead of the love story originally planned.

Strange events continue at the lodge when the girls awake the next morning to find their food gone and suspicion among the girls also begins when Takako is accused of the theft. More horror tropes are exhibited such as a low-angle POV shot of Natsuki seen through the woods and a jump scare when Ai has a vision of the *koji* crawling on the ground and grabbing her leg. The video, dreams, and reality all blur together for the girls.

When the group reconvenes at the lodge, they find their wallets, phones, the *deigan* mask, and props for their film are all missing. This time the girls blame Yoko. Meanwhile, Natsuki's dead body is revealed as Yayoi is searching for her. Paranoia and accusations continue after Yuka and Takako are poisoned at dinner with Maki stating, "I think it is Yayoi." This appears plausible when Yayoi is shown in the woods eating the stolen food.

The girls continue to try to determine the cause of these strange events, whether it is one of them or something else. Watching a video shot earlier of Natsuki, Ai, Maki, and Yuka see the *deigan*-masked killer. When Ai and Maki go outside to search for the other girls, they find Natsuki's burned body and Yayoi's body surrounded by flowers. These are representations of two of the five parts of the Noh story that is referenced in the *Goruzuka* video. Running back to the lodge, the girls decide to stay until morning, but turn their suspicions toward Yoko and Takako.

While the girls are waiting out the night in the lodge, Yoko, covered in blood, knocks at the front door but is denied entry. When she leaves, another jump scare occurs when a *deigan* mask pops up in front of the window. The masked killer proceeds to stalk the girls through the darkened lodge, breathing heavily through the mask and brandishing a cleaver stained in blood. Yuka and Takako are both killed, with the latter confessing with her dying breath that she meant for Ai to eat the poisoned mushrooms at dinner.

The climactic chase continues into the woods with the killer finally catching Ai. Pulling off the mask, Maki reveals herself as the killer and explains how she had developed a taste for killing after watching the *Gurozuka* video. Yoko runs to the rescue, and after hitting her in the head with the cleaver, Maki states that she loves Ai, wants to be her, and is therefore going to eat her. Ai escapes after plunging a large nail, which the girls had found earlier attached to a wooden effigy, into Maki's chest.

Following traditional horror motifs, the film concludes with a twist ending. Though Yoko and Ai escaped from Maki, the next morning Yoko is featured watching the *Gurozuka* video again. Mirroring Maki's statement, Yoko tells Ai that she wants to be her. The final shot is a POV from Yoko, seeing Ai in the same grainy imagery as the video.

The use of the video as a viral source of corruption or evil is a theme present among contemporary Japanese horror. However, while a supernatural element may be present in the form of a ghost in a film such as *The Ring*, there is none in this story, save the ability of the video to corrupt the viewer. No ghost or spirit is murdering these girls; the killer is actually one of *them*.—Jeffrey Bullins

• H •

THE H-MAN (1958)

DIRECTOR: Ishirō Honda
SCREENPLAY: Takeshi Kimura, Hideo Unagami
SPECS: 87 minutes; color

Between 1958 and 1960, Japan's Toho company's ace producer Tomoyuki Tanaka (1910–1997) and special-effects supervisor Eiji Tsuburaya (1901–1970) collaborated on a trio of SF-horror films focusing on the theme of human transformation, remarkable in the sense that they eschewed oversized beasties demolishing miniature city blocks and instead featured mutant creatures strikingly different from other classical humanoid monsters such as vampires, werewolves, or zombies. Their origins were firmly grounded in the misuse of science and immoral human experiments. These films are *The H-Man* (1958), *The Secret of the Telegian* (1960), and *The Human Vapor* (1960), often blocked under the designation "Weird Science Fiction Cinema Series" (*Kaiki kūsō kagaku eiga siriizu*) that occasionally includes the more popular *Attack of the Mushroom People* (1963).

The H-Man, whose Japanese title is *The Beauty and the Liquefied Man*, is unique in two aspects. First, it is a rather strange genre hybrid, in the sense that a large chunk of the movie plays like a crime thriller or a gangland-set potboiler: in an interesting reversal of their usual roles, the stalwart Kenji Sahara (b. 1932) plays the atomic scientist Masada, and the suave, aristocratic-looking Akihiko Hirata (1927–1984), Dr. Serizawa from the original *Gojira* (1954), plays the skeptical detective Tominaga, pursuing baffling cases of gangsters disappearing into thin air (as it turns out, into the sewer along with rainwater) leaving their raincoats, hats, and shoes behind. Second, the "monster" is a truly original creation: unfortunate sailors liquefied by the radiation shower produced by a US hydrogen bomb experiment into slithering puddles of eerily fluorescent slime (*The H-Man*'s "amoebic liquid monster" predates a similarly formless outer-space menace in *The Blob* [1958]). The hapless gangsters have been absorbed by the original group of Liquefied Men: yet one gangster victim seems to retain some memory of his previous existence, and begins to stalk his "moll," a cabaret singer "Chikako," played by Yumi Shirakawa (b. 1936), the striking heroine of *Rodan* (1956).

The unusual mixture of the gangster/crime thriller genre and SF-horror certainly renders a unique texture to the film, including a certain kind of film noir–like grittiness and existential despair found in the climactic getaway attempt by the main villain, Uchida, played by Makoto Satō (1934–2012) taking Chikako as a hostage. The sparely used special effects are, considering the ambitiousness of the concept, surprisingly effective: the scenes in which the actors are consumed alive by the glowing glops of radioactive mutant, screaming and suddenly deflating as if being drained from within, are genuinely creepy even by early twenty-first-century standards. On the downside, the film is too talky, with a bit too much of earnest expositions involving the (in truth, extremely hokey) "science" behind the liquefying of living organisms via massive doses of radiation. Satō Masaru's jazz-inflected music likewise works hard but is less effective in conveying the mystery and terror of the Liquefied Men than an Akira Ifukube score might have been.

Not as beautifully sublime or awe-inspiring as the original *Gojira* (1954) or *Rodan* (1956), *The H-Man* is nonetheless a solid Toho special-effects extravaganza with a welcome message against the abuse of nuclear power and some dark atmosphere to savor.

Aside from *Attack of the Mushroom People*, *The H-Man* has so far received the best representation among the "Weird Science Fiction Cinema" trio in the North American DVD market, in the form of Sony Columbia's *Icons of Sci-Fi: Toho Collection* DVD (2009) that gathers together *H-Man*, *Battle in Outer Space* (1959), and *Mothra* (1961). The motion picture included in this DVD collection is the domestic release version, with Japanese-language dialogues and restoration of whatever cuts were made for the US import version.—Kyu Hyun Kim

See also The Human Vapor; The Secret of the Telegian

THE HAPPINESS OF THE KATAKURIS (2001)
DIRECTOR: Takashi Miike
SCREENPLAY: Kikumi Yamagishi
SPECS: 113 minutes; color

A 2001 film directed by Takashi Miike, *The Happiness of the Katakuris* (*Katakuri-ke no kofuku*) is a remake of a Korean production, Jee-woon Kim's solid debut *The Quiet Family* (1998). Miike's film tells of the multigenerational Katakuri family, consisting of husband Masao, played by Kenji Suwada and wife Terue, played by Keiko Matsuzaka; their son Masayuki, played by Shinji Takeda; daughter Shizue, played by Naomi Nishida; and the grandfather, played by Tetsuro Tamba. The Katakuris have decided to operate a guesthouse in the countryside, but because their house is accessible only to wayward hikers and a promised road has yet to be built, business is sluggish. They eagerly await their first guests, and when one does show, played by film critic Tokitoshi Shiota, he commits suicide in his room. Knowing that such a scandal could irreparably hinder their new venture, Masao insists that they bury the body on the grounds. The body count and proximate interment rises, however, as more guests inexplicably die under their roof, including a sumo wrestler who suffers a heart attack while climaxing, crushing his tiny girlfriend under his enormous bulk.

The story of a hotel owner who buries his guests has certainly been done before, such as the American horror film *Motel Hell* (1980), but of course *The Happiness of the Katakuris* has more in common with the film it remade, *The Quiet Family*. (The story would again be recycled in 2003 as the Hong Kong production *A Mysterious Murder*.) Still, noticeable differences between the two films arise. Perhaps surprising considering Miike's reputation for pushing the boundaries of taste, *The Happiness of the Katakuris* adopts a lighter tone than its predecessor, with more comic moments, a lowered body count, and a happier ending. The Japanese remake also removed the horror-film conventions that the

Korean original employed, including the ominous soundtrack. The Katakuris are less complicit in the deaths of their guests and not as smug with their ability to hide the corpses, while a subplot about an assassination attempt was removed. Miike's film has also been more enduring than Kim's, carefully balancing the horrific and comic elements from *The Quiet Family*, while also adding claymation scenes and, perhaps most critically, transforming it into a musical. Kikumi Yamagishi's script also changed the family structure, replacing teenagers and an uncle with a little girl and a grandfather for added comic relief. Miike also added unexplained phenomena, whether astronomical (solar eclipse), meteorological (typhoon), or geological, in the volcanic eruption in the film's climax that acts as a blessing, sparing the Katakuris from police involvement and depositing their home in a more suitable location.

The Happiness of the Katakuris was released during a productive year for Miike, as he also released some of his most memorable films, *Visitor Q* and *Ichi the Killer*, as well as *Agitator*, *Family*, and two more minor productions. Although much less disturbing than *Visitor Q* and *Ichi the Killer*, *The Happiness of the Katakuris* has in common with *Visitor Q* its emphasis on the family unit, a dominant theme for Miike, particularly a family moving from disintegration toward unity and happiness.

Among the more impressive elements of the film were the three claymation scenes, lasting over six minutes altogether, animated by Hideki Kimura. These sequences were intentionally designed to recall the work of Czech animator Jan Svankmajer and stand out within Miike's oeuvre. Making the film a musical perhaps inspired the choices in casting, including casting Sawada (lead singer of 1960s rock band the Tigers) and one of the most popular Japanese rock stars, Kiyoshiro Imawano, in the role of the broken-Japanese-speaking con man who seduces Shizue by claiming to be British royalty. Released around the same time as other significant international forays into the musical genre, such as *Dancer in the Dark* (2000) and *Moulin Rouge* (2001), *The Happiness of the Katakuris* was more eclectic in its musical choices, featuring a variety of musical styles, from rock musical to more traditional, Hollywoodesque musical numbers; indeed, its bucolic setting and overwhelmingly cheerful final number inspired critics to actually compare the film to *The Sound of Music* (1965). There is even a duet between Masao and Terue that turns into a karaoke number, complete with on-screen lyrics.

The Happiness of the Katakuris debuted at the Tokyo International Film Festival in October 2001. Originally intended to be a New Year's Film, it was not released nationwide until February 2002 and would later screen at numerous festivals around the world. Internationally, the film was not as popular as some other Miike films (like *Audition* and *Ichi the Killer*), but it has since become a cult hit, occupying a worthy place in Miike's extensive filmography.—Zachary Thomas Ingle

See also Miike, Takashi

Bibliography

Mes, Tom. *Agitator: The Cinema of Takashi Miike*. Surrey, UK: FAB Press, 2003.
Miike, Takashi, dir. *The Happiness of the Katakuris*. Shochiku, 2001. Film.

HAUNTED SCHOOL 2 (1996)

DIRECTOR: Hirayuki Hadeyama
SCREENPLAY: Satoko Okudera
SPECS: 103 minutes; color

One of the most popular Japanese "horror" film series is the family-friendly *Haunted School* (*Gakko no Kaidan*, literally School ghost stories) film series. Released between 1995 and 1999, all of the films take place in a school and feature young protagonists dealing with a seemingly endless variety of ghosts and monsters.

The Haunted School series began as a collection of ghost stories compiled by middle school teacher Toru Tsunemitsu. The 1990 book, which included more than 160 ghost stories, most of them set in a school, became a bestseller. Following a typical book-TV-movie-TV trajectory, Haunted School became a live action series in 1994. The first film was released in 1995, and an anime series was created in 2000.

The ghost stories, many of which are depicted in the films, included classic urban legends like "Toire no Hanako-san" (Hanako in the toilet), a sort of Japanese version of "Bloody Mary." Hanako is said to haunt the third stall on the third-floor girls' bathroom of any school, and when someone knocks on the door and calls her name, she will answer, "I'm here."

Though some of the ghosts and monsters depicted in the *Haunted School* films are associated with violence and death, the films are still "horror light." The jumps and scares are more slime-and-spiders, not so much the excessive gore and ominous tone that characterize so many contemporary Japanese horror films. There are some genuinely creepy moments, but the overall feeling is of a campfire ghost story.

Haunted School 2 is directed by Hirayuki Hadeyama, who also directed the first and fourth movies in the series (there are a total of four live-action films). In the second film, the elementary school students in question are on an overnight school trip to a countryside shrine that just happens to be situated next to an abandoned schoolhouse. The shrine priest tells them the story of the schoolmistress who mysteriously disappeared from the school one day at 4:44 PM—an hour when strange events seem to occur. After some rudimentary establishment of location and characters, the children enter the schoolhouse and accidentally jam the clock tower so that it's stuck at 4:44. Ghosts and monsters roam freely, and the children (plus a cat burglar disguised as a monk who's been stealing shrine treasures) spend the next hour running and screaming through the halls of the school. The monsters are many and varied—there's the disappeared schoolmistress who has an impossibly long neck, a stone statue that comes to life, a monster lurking in a toilet, and a floating, pink creature with giant teeth and purple hair.

Like the films that came before and after it, *Haunted School 2* is a good introduction to a plethora of traditional Japanese ghost stories. For Japanese film buffs, it also contains brief appearances by legendary performers. The long-necked schoolmistress is played by Kyoko Kishida, of *The Woman in the Dunes*, in a performance that provides the movie with one of its few genuine chills. The shrine priest is played by stage actor and playwright Yonekura Masakane, who also appears as a dog with a human face.

Given its origins as a bestselling book for young children, it's not surprising that the Haunted School series was designed as family-friendly entertainment. Though *Haunted School 2* was made in 1996, its visual effects seem even more dated. Multiple shots of the school and the night sky are clearly still shots, some of the monsters have the look of Ray Harryhausen figures, and other monsters are obviously cartoons. At one point the children look out the window to see neon-green *hitodama* (will o' the wisps) floating and dancing through the air, a cinematic image that goes back as far as Saito Torajiro's 1934 silent film *Bakudan hanayome*. Besides lending the film an overall tone of goofiness, the lack of realism is clearly meant to keep the film grounded in a not-too-realistic world. Beyond a few shots of blood dripping onto a piano and a slightly darker sequence in which soldiers with worm-covered faces march upside down across a ceiling, there really isn't anything here that older children would find intolerable.—Lindsay Nelson

Bibliography

Tsunemitsu, Toru. *Gakko no Kaidan 2*. Tokyo, Japan: Kodansha, 1990.

HEARN, LAFCADIO [KOIZUMI, YAKUMO] (1850–1904)

Lafcadio Hearn, also known by his Japanese name Yakumo Koizumi, was a writer whose life and career spanned three continents. Born on the Greek island of Lefkada to a Greek mother and an Irish father, Hearn would spend time as a child in Ireland, go to school in France and England, and work as a journalist in the United States and the Caribbean before settling in Japan in 1890, where he would remain until his death.

Today, Hearn is best remembered in English as a chronicler of the customs and tales of a Japan that was rapidly growing obsolescent even during his own lifetime. Hearn's fascination with an old, unfamiliar, ghostly Japan—a place that was just as much the offspring of his own fanciful imagination as it was reflective of a historical, geographical reality—reflects the central idiosyncrasy of his aesthetic system: Hearn was a writer who was journalistic in approach and hyper-Romantic in sensibility. In this regard, Hearn's writings often read as engaging in problematic racializing or Orientalizing discourses, and Hearn is to be rightly faulted for contributing to a culture of Romantic essentializing, directed especially but not solely toward East Asia, from the perspective of Anglophone writers and readers. Without denying or trivializing this aspect of Hearn's writing, however, a close reading of Hearn, when juxtaposed with the particulars of his life and historical contexts, reveals that oftentimes Hearn subverts and undercuts such essentializing just as much as he reinforces it by constructing a narrative relationship between writer and the written that is radical in its private particularity and instability. When viewed in this light, the tension between journalistic and Romantic tendencies mentioned above was for Hearn a productive one, and allowed his best writing to move beyond simple reportage or essentializing Orientalism and to become the performative enactment of a relationship with Japan and elsewhere that was extreme in its self-conscious subjectivity in a way that foreshadows Roland Barthes's *Empire of Signs* seven decades later.

A corollary of this hybrid aspect of Hearn's output is that his works can be exceedingly difficult to classify. Not only did Hearn write in a number of different modes, but many of his individual works seem to be an amalgamation of these different modes—fiction, travelogue, translation, journalism—within a single text. In an attempt at classification, then, two major systems may be proposed: classification by geographical focus and classification by type of work. In terms of geographical focus, the most obvious division is between works written about America and works written about Asia. The former may be further subdivided into works dealing with Cincinnati, where Hearn first worked as a journalist at the *Cincinnati Enquirer* from 1872 to 1875 and later the *Cincinnati Commercial* from 1875 to 1877; works dealing with New Orleans, where he lived from 1877 to 1887, publishing widely in local and national venues during that time; and works based on his time in the Caribbean (principally Martinique) from 1887 to 1889. The majority of Hearn's works about Asia are on Japanese topics, although his first work of literary retellings, *Stray Leaves from Strange Literature* (1884), draws from a wide range of sources including Egyptian, Polynesian, Indian, and Arabic legends and folktales, and his lyrical treatment of Chinese ghost stories, *Some Chinese Ghosts* (1887), is a masterpiece of his early period.

But this system of classification leaves out major parts of Hearn's output, such as his work in literary translation. A classification by type of work thus proves most useful when surveying Hearn's oeuvre. The following are the major genres, broadly speaking, in which he worked:

1. *Journalism.* Although not as widely read today as his more famous works on Japan, Hearn's journalism, especially the work he produced during his time in Cincinnati and New Orleans, is remarkable for its high literary merit. Hearn would turn his reportage of often grotesque and ghastly subjects into little gems that read more like short stories than they do newspaper articles. His use of dialogue, often in dialect, and the sympathetic ear he lends his often liminal interlocutors—murderers, prostitutes, gravediggers, the impoverished—are particularly striking. Hearn's journalism has been collected piecemeal numerous times after his death; important collections include *An American Miscellany* (1924), edited by Albert Mordell; *Period of the Gruesome: Selected Cincinnati Journalism of Lafcadio Hearn* (1990), edited by Jon Christopher Hughes; and The Library of America's collection of Hearn's work, *American Writings* (2009).

2. *Retellings.* This is the category for which Hearn is best known today. He reworked folktales, legends, ghost stories, and the like from Japan and throughout the world and rendered them in his own idiosyncratic prose style as "stories of strange things," as the title of his most famous collection, *Kwaidan: Stories and Studies of Strange Things* (1904), aptly suggests. In addition to *Kwaidan*, other major collections include *Stray Leaves from Strange Literature* and *Some Chinese Ghosts*, both mentioned above; *In Ghostly Japan* (1899); *Shadowings* (1900); and *Kottō: Being Japanese Curios, with Sundry Cobwebs* (1902).

3. *Japanology*. This category intersects significantly with the category of Hearn's literary retellings, and indeed examples of both are often contained within a single published volume. If the retellings are the "stories," these are the "studies of strange things" of *Kwaidan*'s title. Hearn wrote broadly on his experiences in Japan in multiple different modes, from personal reminiscences to more scholarly and researched treatises on particular cultural and historical subjects. *Shadowings*, for example, which also follows the "stories" and "studies" dichotomy in its table of contents, includes writings on "Japanese Female Names" and "Old Japanese Songs." Texts in this category include *Glimpses of Unfamiliar Japan* (1894); *Out of the East: Reveries and Studies of New Japan* (1895); *Kokoro: Hints and Echoes of Japanese Inner Life* (1896); as well as In Ghostly Japan, Shadowings, Kottō, and Kwaidan, all mentioned above.

4. *Original fiction*. In addition to reworking old tales, Hearn also wrote original works of fiction. The two major texts in this category are the novellas *Chita: A Memory of Last Island* (1889) and *Youma: The Story of a West-Indian Slave* (1890). Both are included in The Library of America's *American Writings* collection.

5. *Travelogues*. Since Hearn's life was one marked by itinerancy, virtually all of his writings can be classified as travelogues, if the term is defined broadly enough. The fact that he repeatedly used the word "glimpses" to describe his writings is telling: this stance allowed him to cast himself as a rover and a passerby, allowed only a few poignant glimpses of the scene at hand before moving on. When read as a whole, his work is a fascinating enactment of a very particular relationship between the artist-subject and the artistic object—a relationship defined by restlessness and incessant dislocation. Put another way, in virtually all of Hearn's writing, nonfiction or fiction, the implied author assumes the voice of a traveler relating sights he has seen on his journey. Hearn thereby transforms the very act of writing into an instantiation of melodrama, something made possible by the tension between the journalistic and hyper-Romantic aspects of his artistic identity. That being said, some works fall more clearly under the purview of this category than others. The major example of a coherent travelogue in Hearn's oeuvre is his *Two Years in the French West Indies* (1890), included in The Library of America's *American Writings* collection; in addition, *Glimpses of Unfamiliar Japan* is a work from his Japan period that can be read in this mode, as can, to a more limited degree, many of the other works on Japan mentioned above.

6. *Translations*. Hearn was an accomplished translator of French literature. He translated Theophile Gautier (*One of Cleopatra's Nights and Other Fantastic Romances*, 1882); Anatole France (*The Crime of Sylvestre Bonnard*, 1890); Gustave Flaubert (*The Temptation of Saint Anthony*, 1910); Guy de Maupassant (*Saint Anthony and Other Stories*, 1924; and *The Adventures of Walter Schnaffs*, 1931); and Pierre Loti (*Stories from Pierre Loti*, 1933).

7. *Lectures*. After Hearn's death, the notes of Hearn's students at Tokyo Imperial University were used to reconstruct Hearn's lectures on Anglophone literature that he gave as a lecturer there. These have been

published piecemeal in collected form numerous times throughout the twentieth century, and show Hearn's skill as a sensitive reader and interpreter of literature.

8. *Letters.* Much like his lectures, Hearn's letters have been published in collected form multiple times after his death.

9. *Other.* Hearn's output was diverse enough that there are works that yet fall under none of the categories above. Although comparatively minor works from a literary standpoint, examples include the cookbook *La Cuisine Créole: A Collection of Culinary Recipes* (1885) and the lexicon *"Gombo Zhèbes": Little Dictionary of Creole Proverbs, Selected from Six Creole Dialects* (1885).

As has already been hinted at above, a major theme that runs throughout Hearn's career, from his time as a young journalist in Cincinnati in the 1870s to works published on Japan right before his death, is an interest in the gruesome, the weird, and the supernatural. Hearn is unique in that his contributions in this regard left an important mark on the traditions of weird literature in both Japan and the United States. In Japan, his endeavors to collect and retell old Japanese folktales that took up dark, frightening, or supernatural themes—often drawn from medieval literature but sometimes coming from more ephemeral, oral sources—make him one of the first individuals in modern Japan to show a sustained interest in such material. As such, he is an important precursor to figures like Kunio Yanagita (1875–1962) and Kizen Sasaki (1886–1933), whose *Tōno monogatari* (1910) is a landmark achievement in a folkloristics of the weird. In addition, through his lectures at Tokyo Imperial University and his more scholarly studies, Hearn was one of the first individuals to systematically introduce the terminology and characteristics of Gothic and supernatural fiction as coherent literary genres to Japan. His works have been translated into Japanese in multiple different "complete works" series after his death, making his writings widely accessible to the Japanese reading public.

In the American context, his writings during his time in Cincinnati and New Orleans make him one of the most important practitioners of an American Gothic mode in the period between the death of Nathaniel Hawthorne (1804–1864) and the emergence of Ambrose Bierce (1842–c. 1914) as a fiction writer. Twentieth-century America's preeminent practitioner of weird fiction, H. P. Lovecraft (1890–1937), praised Hearn in his *Supernatural Horror in Literature*, noting among others *Kwaidan* and Hearn's translation of *The Temptation of Saint Anthony* as particularly effective works in this genre.

Hearn's influence on Japanese horror cinema is most directly manifested in *Kwaidan*, a 1964 film directed by Masaki Kobayashi (1916–1996). *Kwaidan* is an omnibus film composed of adaptations of four of Hearn's retellings. The first, "Kurokami," is based on "The Reconciliation" from *Shadowings*; "Yukionna" is based on "Yuki-Onna" from *Kwaidan*; "Mimi-nashi Hōichi no hanashi" is based on "The Story of Mimi-Nashi Hōichi" from *Kwaidan*; and "Chawan no naka" is based on "In a Cup of Tea" from *Kottō*. It is therefore worth noting that only two out of the four stories actually come from Hearn's *Kwaidan*—not all four, as is commonly assumed.

In addition to Kobayashi's *Kwaidan*, Hearn's indirect influence on cinema, through his popularization of old Japanese tales and thereby his impact on Japanese-language weird literature in the twentieth century, is profound. To cite but one of many examples, Shūji Terayama's (1935–1983) 1979 film *Kusameikyū* (translatable as *The Grass Labyrinth*), which is primarily based on the 1908 novel of the same name by Kyōka Izumi (1873–1939), prominently borrows imagery from the Mimi-nashi Hōichi legend. Since this imagery is absent from Kyōka's novel, it is safe to assume that Terayama is quoting a motif brought into the modern popular consciousness by Hearn. Such is the nature of Hearn's impact on the culture of weird literature and horror stories in modern Japan: it is through his treatment of the theme that the story moves beyond local legend or specialized antiquarian interest and becomes nationally recognized.—Peter Bernard

See also Kwaidan

HELLDRIVER (2010)
DIRECTOR: Yoshishiro Nishimura
SCREENPLAY: Yoshishiro Nishimura, Daichi Nagisa
SPECS: 117 minutes; color

This slice and dice zombie action comedy was directed and cowritten by Yoshishiro Nishimura along with Daichi Nagisa. In his usual gore-splattered fashion, Nishimura tells the tale of a meek and abused schoolgirl who becomes a zombie-fighting warrior intent on saving Japan and fulfilling a personal vendetta.

A man clad in a textured rubber bondage suit rides a bicycle in the night and climbs a wall that encases horned zombies. He lures them with human body parts and starts to harvest their heads for the horns, but he is intercepted by one and falls into the zombie fray. A truck comes hurtling through the night, and a girl equipped with a chainsaw samurai sword, rescues him and kills the zombies.

In a flashback, we find out that she is Kika Miyata (Yumiko Hara b. 1986), a schoolgirl that was bullied by her abusive mother, Rikka (Eihi Shiina b. 1976) and uncle Yasushi (Kentaro Kishi b. 1973). They tortured Kika's invalid father, and are also wanted for over twenty cannibal murders. As they set Kika's father on fire, brutally kill two policemen, and beat Kika, an asteroid hits Rikka as she strangles her daughter. It blows her heart out leaving a cartoon hole in her chest, and annoyed, she rips out Kika's heart for herself. They both become crystallized, but not before Rikka becomes a host to a strange alien attached to her head that sprays a weird ash all over Japan. This ash turns unsuspecting citizens into bloodthirsty horned zombies. Thirty-six hours later, six million people have become zombies and a wall is built to divide Japan and contain the infected. Through a darkly comedic montage, society declines financially, socially, and physically, with people being divided on whether the zombies should have rights or be killed. We find out that the zombie horns are a sought-after illegal narcotic that is lethal because of its explosive nature, tying in the opening scene of the film.

Kika has been found in her crystal cocoon by government scientists and is experimented on. She now has a mechanical heart and great strength, but officials dump her for fear of being arrested for the unorthodox modifications. She awakens at the wall that separates humans from zombies and immediately goes into fight mode as zombies attack two horn smugglers. They battle soldiers (in armor reminiscent of *Silent Hill*'s Pyramid Head) that guard the wall as well as zombies, and Kika helps the smugglers escape. They take her in, and Taku (Yūrei Yanagi b. 1963) tells her about their mission to find Mai, his silent partner "No-Name's" (Mizuki Kusumi b. 1987) sister. That night, Kika dreams of a terrible birthday with her uncle and mother, and has horrible chest pains. At the same time, her mother has burst from her cocoon, now an evil zombie queen who controls all zombies and wants world domination. They are both connected through Kika's heart.

Rivals, opposition leader Osawa, and the prime minister set up a news conference for zombie rights in front of the wall where Osawa rigs an explosion. His goal to get rid of the zombie-sympathizing prime minister is fulfilled as the zombies spill forth and attack. At the same time, Osawa's army raid the drug boss Andou, as Kika, Taku, and No-Name make a delivery of horns. They are to be put to death under Osawa's new dictatorship unless they choose to find and kill the zombie queen. They take the mission, avoiding a bloody iron maiden death, and set off to find her.

Their adventure starts with the queen sending zombie head missiles that kill Andou and her bodyguard. The others are rescued by a cowboy named Kaito (Kazuki Namioka b. 1978). He has lost his family to the zombies and agrees to help find Mai and defeat the queen. He takes them to what he called the "Zombie Bar," a den of debauchery that reveals the zombies are getting smarter as they are now capturing humans for food. Many fights occur as Kika's uncle, who is now a zombie minion for his sister the queen, tortures Mai, feeding her spraying blood to surrounding zombies. The team fights a zombie geisha, zombie babies, and a many-limbed zombie prostitute that culminates in a car chase with Kika's uncle driving a car made of zombie body parts. Taku sacrifices himself in order to kill zombie uncle and save Kika; Mai succumbs to her injuries; and the remaining team, Kaito, No-Name, and Kika are even more determined to kill the queen.

The final battle is complete chaos. As Osawa's army readies for war, the zombies create a giant of their bodies with the zombie queen serving as the head. Kika climbs to the top to face her mother, and No-Name uses a trigger gun that would prompt Osawa to release a missile. It hits and momentarily disables the giant, but the zombie queen regroups, and the next two missiles become jet engines as the giant morphs into a zombie plane. Zombie uncle's head survives, and he is catapulted into the fray, acquiring a new body. Kika, her uncle, and mother battle to the death, with a nod to Takashi Miike's *Audition*, as the zombie queen sadistically pokes at Kika's heart. Osawa suffers a zombie attack in his bunker and is killed by his own army when mistaken for a zombie. Kika eventually rules triumphant, and lops off the zombie queen's head. It soars into space as Kika, No-Name, and Kaito stand in front of the defeated zombie hoard. In a strange twist, the queen's head travels through galaxies to land on an alien planet and kill its blue-skinned inhabitants.

Helldriver provides a fast paced, rag-tag filming style that includes the opening credits in the middle of the film, combined computer-generated imagery and a ton of practical makeup effects, and lots of base comedy. Nishimura wanted to revive the Japanese zombie film with *Helldriver* and also broaches the subject of discrimination and human rights through zombie segregation. He was also the character designer for the film.—Carolyn Mauricette

See also Audition; Miike, Takashi

Bibliography

Leung, James. "Director's Cut of *Helldriver* with Yoshihiro Nishimura and Eihi Shiina." *Random Access Information*, 30 April 2011, http://raiwebs.com/?p=1200.
Nishimura, Yoshihiro, dir. *Helldriver*, Uncut Director's Edition, Sushi Typhoon, 2010. Film.

HELLS (2008)

DIRECTOR: Yoshiki Yamakawa
SCREENPLAY: Kazuyuki Fudeyasu, Yoshiki Yamakawa
SPECS: 117 minutes; color

Hells is a supernatural/horror anime based on the manga *Hells Angels* by Sin'Ichi Hiromoto (b. 1966). The movie was directed by Yoshiki Yamakawa (b. 1968) for Madhouse animation studio. It tells the story of Rinne Amagane, a girl who goes to Hell and makes friends, and whose encouragement and hope help thwart a plot to destroy life on Earth. The manga was serialized in *Ultra Jump* from 2002 to 2004. It premiered at the Tokyo International Film Festival in 2008.

The movie begins as Rinne is running to school. She sees an odd-looking cat in the middle of the road and is struck by a bus while trying to save it. She suddenly finds herself again running to school, only to discover when she finds her classroom that she is in Hell and her classmates are demons and supernatural creatures. She quickly learns that all souls go to Hell and must attend the River Styx Academy, run by Headmaster Helvis, a large demon modeled after Elvis Presley. The only way anyone can return to Earth is by graduating from the Academy. Always optimistic, Rinne slowly befriends her new classmates and develops a close friendship with her roommate Steela, a creature who looks like she was stitched together by Dr. Frankenstein.

Shortly after starting classes, the Student Council, led by School Council President Ryu Kutou, tells Rinne that she is not actually dead. Kutou noticed that Rinne's nose bled the last time they ran into each other; he thinks that she was brought to Hell forcibly and that she hasn't died yet. The Student Council members are all alive, like her, and they want to defeat Helvis so they can go home. They explain that Helvis is Cain, mankind's first murderer, and that he plans to disrupt the cycle of reincarnation by never letting any soul return to Earth to be reborn. In a minor romantic storyline, "Mario," a Council Member, becomes interested in Rinne.

Helvis declares a sports day and will grant the wish of each team member of the volleyball tournament. The Student Council members and Rinne see this as a way to wish themselves back to Earth. Fueled by her grit and determination, Rinne earns the respect of her classmates and they work together to win the competition. Helvis grants all the wishes but Rinne's, who wished to go home to her mother. He reminds her that the only way to leave Hell is by graduating. Rinne tries to find Helvis later that night to ask him again about the wish when she finds a room containing God. God, who is also the cat she tried to save, tells her that the sibling rivalry between Cain and Abel is still playing out in Hell. After Abel died, he waited near the River Styx for Cain to arrive. Now Abel is known as "Ryu Kutou." Abel's grudge against Cain and his parents, Adam and Eve, is embodied by a blade embedded in a dark mass that is the physical representation of Abel's insanity. Rinne pulls the blade out to confront Helvis, only to realize that she has played straight into Kutou's hands as his madness grows and threatens to destroy Hell and everyone in it. Kutou physically begins to change into a demon, and he explains that he is the one who wants to end reincarnation and life on Earth, not Helvis.

Rinne tries to use the blade to stop the madness from hurting her friends but it gets past her and infects Steela. Steela's heart is filled with Abel's insanity, creating a vacuum that begins pulling everyone into a void of nothingness. Kutou tells Rinne that she is the reincarnation of Eve, his and Cain's mother, and he brought her to Hell to destroy her and everyone in Hell. A small group fights back against Kutou, including Rinne, Mario, God, and the reincarnation of Adam, Eve's husband. Fighting with Kutou are Rinne's former classmates and friends as the embodiment of the Seven Deadly Sins. Rinne and Mario fight against her former friend Phantoma to save Rinne's mother, whom Kutou brought to Hell to further torment Rinne.

During the battle Mario loses part of his arm and Rinne's mother falls into nothingness. Rinne willingly follows and once she is absorbed by the void, realizes that she is still conscious and must therefore exist. She sees everyone who had disappeared, including Steela, who tells Rinne to reject the nothingness. Working together, they break through the image of the void and return to Hell. Rinne explains to Mario that she wished herself back, and if everyone believed in themselves without any doubts, their wishes would also come true. As Mario wishes his arm back, Kutou tries to destroy everyone's self-confidence. Mario and Rinne fight against him until eventually Kutou begins to feel the pain his betrayal caused Mario. Rinne tells everyone to believe in themselves and together they break the darkness.

Rinne begins to fly toward Earth, encouraging the others to follow, but they are overcome with doubt fed to them by Kutou. Kutou then collects and force-feeds the doubt into his followers, who enlarge and attack both physically and psychically with projected doubt. Helvis saves Kutou from one of these attacks but Kutou allows himself to slip out of his brother's grasp and plummet to the ground, deciding that he wants to die. Mario and Rinne's unflagging encouragement and support makes Kutou realize that he wants to live. Pillars of light shine from them as pathways back to Earth. They have to fight against "Kiki," another former friend, as she tries to keep them from leaving, filled with anger and sadness from the doubt she has inside her. Rinne's love for her friend removes the doubt forced into her by Kutou, but the doubt physically manifests. Steela fights it to save Rinne and sacrifices herself in the process. She turns into a tall crucifix-like statue of herself; Rinne is devastated by this loss.

All the creatures want to go back to Earth but Rinne refuses to leave Steela's side. Steela's spirit visits Rinne, reminding her that they will always be together. Mario and Rinne convince everyone to rebuild the school, emphasizing the power of a group working toward the same wish. When they are done, Helvis informs Rinne that she has graduated and she returns to Earth, retaining only her feelings about her time in Hell but not her memories.

Rinne wakes up in a hospital bed and sees her mother sitting next to her. When she is again running to school, she sees a little girl who looks like Steela in the middle of traffic. She quickly runs to her, pulling her out of the way of a car. They are then both saved from another oncoming truck by the human versions of Kutou and Phantoma while human versions of her former classmates look on. Rinne feels happy as the spirit of Steela watches her take the little girl's hand and walk her to school.

The animation style has a macabre aesthetic. It is filled with high energy, occasionally looking like it was sketched quickly. Yasushi Nirasawa (b. 1963) designed the monsters for the manga and the anime. Kazuto Nakazawa (b. 1968) was responsible for the character design.—Paula S. Kiser

Bibliography
Yamakawa, Yoshiki, dir. *Hells*. Madhouse, 2008. Film.

HELLSING

The mysterious "Hellsing Organization" is a clandestine British agency, the Royal Order of the Protestant Knights, whose mission is to hunt down and destroy vampires, ghouls, and other undead forces. Hellsing employs vampires including the macabre Alucard, certainly among the coolest vampires anywhere, to help in its investigations. Its stealthy activities were first chronicled in the vehement manga series *Hellsing* (*Herushingu*), written and drawn by Kauta Hirano (b. 1973). The ninety-five episodes were published in the manga magazine *Young King OURs* from 1997 thru October 2008. This gave rise to the thirteen "order" (episode) TV series *Hellsing*, directed by Umanosuke Iida (1961–2010) and others. The series was originally released during 2001–2002, with each installment running around twenty-two minutes. An OVA (original video animation) simply titled *Hellsing* in Japan and *Hellsing Ultimate* elsewhere, followed. It consisted of ten episodes made between 2006 and 2012, with running times ranging between forty-two and sixty-four minutes, and was directed by Tomokazu Tokoro (episodes 1–4), Hiroyuki Tanaka (ep. 5–7, 9, and 10), and Yasuhiro Matsu (ep. 8). All three feature many of the same characters and settings. The intent of the OVA was to more closely approximate the original manga than did the TV series.

The Hellsing Organization was founded by Abraham Van Helsing, the Dutch doctor and vampire hunter most renowned for his pursuit and defeat of Count Dracula in Bram Stoker's celebrated *Dracula*. Sir Integra Fairbrook Wingates Hellsing, the collected matriarch and committed head of the mysterious organization, is his direct descendant. After her father died from a sudden illness, she became Hellsing's leader when she was just twelve years old. Her uncle defied her father's wishes and attempted to usurp control of the organization. Seeking refuge in the mansion's subterranean dungeon, she was rescued by Alucard, a vampire originally rendered dormant by her father. After she liberated him, he chose to serve her devotedly.

Hellsing is primarily set in the present. The first episode in each series introduces Sir Integra as she battles with governmental bureaucracy as well as demonic forces. Several people have disappeared in the village of Cheddar, including the investigating police swat team. Integra must convince the military that these events are the handiwork of a vampire, and that Hellsing must lead the investigation. She deploys Alucard, who first encounters groups of zombie-like ghouls, created after villagers were bitten by a vampire serving as the village priest. Alucard easily crushes them, but appears to be destroyed while battling the vampire. No ordinary vampire, Alucard possesses the ability to regenerate himself. He then kills the vampire priest with a silver bullet, but must shoot it through the chest of Seras Victoria, a shapely young police officer and the only surviving member of the initial law enforcement team sent to the village.

The free-spirited Alucard ("Dracula" spelled backwards) more closely resembles Francis Ford Coppola's Dracula than Bram Stoker's more formal Transylvanian vampire. There are allusions that he is the original Count Dracula. Kauta Hirano imbues him with certain talents not possessed by most vampires. In addition to being able to reconstruct himself, for example, he is able to survive daylight, he simply doesn't like it.

In this telling of supernatural lore, a new vampire can be created only when an old one bites a virgin of the opposite sex. Impressed by the virginal Seras Victoria's determination as the only surviving constable, Alucard lets her pick between joining him as a vampire and death. She chooses the former. As Alucard's assistant, Seras does play a major role in the manga and the OVA renderings, but she is the soul of the anime. Her attempts to retain her human qualities as long as possible and her reluctance to incorporate vampire features into her life play a central function in the anime. In its early episodes, for example, she refuses to even drink hospital blood initially, finally doing so only when she realizes she is unable to imbibe anything else to replenish herself. In the last episode she finally sips Alucard's red juices, but still refuses to draw human blood. Through her sparkling personality, the anime possesses considerable warmth and an upbeat quality not found in the other two renderings.

Walter C. Dornez also serves Sir Integra; aka "The Angel of Death," the dutiful family butler and former Hellsing Elite Trash Disposal soldier is deadly when manipulating string-like wires. He must occasionally join with Alucard to fight demonic forces. After Hellsing's security forces are decimated in the manga and the OVA, he hires the Wild Geese, mercenary soldiers headed by Captain Pip Bernadotte, to reinforce Hellsing. Alucard, Seras Victoria, Walter C. Dornez, and the Wild Geese are the key members of Integra's team.

Only some of the anime episodes are derived from the original manga, including an adventure featuring Leif and Jessica, a teenage couple getting highs from their newly acquired vampire powers, and another in which the Valentine Brothers lead a heavy contingent of ghouls to attack the seemingly impenetrable Hellsing Mansion, decimating most of Hellsing's security forces. Sir Integra Hellsing notes an increasing number of incidents involving supernatural beings and warns the Round Table, another elite group of a dozen British aristocrats, Parliament and military leaders, that she anticipates a rising force about to challenge them. The anime rapidly deviates from the original after the twelfth manga chapter, forging several episodes of its own. In them, Integra correlates progressively increasing violence to the activation of implanted chips. The Hellsing Organization must track down their mysterious origin, in part by creating a ruse in which its operatives are deployed at the Tower of London. In the final anime episode Alucard must defeat an ancient vampire from Africa calling himself "Incognito" who is on a mission to destroy London. The anime ends with many unresolved issues.

A tall, gaunt, sinister-looking Catholic priest named Alexander Anderson is introduced as an opposing force in all three media. Genetically modified and given extraordinary powers, this fanatical man of God represents the Iscariot Division, also known as Section XIII, a secret division of the Vatican named after Jesus's betrayer that actively pursues supernatural beings. Anderson's religious obsessions contrast strongly with Seras's warmth and innocence, particularly in the anime. Both he and Enrico Maxwell, his former student who now heads Section XIII, occasionally find themselves forced to work with Hellsing, but more often are bitter enemies of the British organization. Hellsing serves the Anglican Church, the Queen, and Great Britain, and considers their protection to be its paramount task, while Iscariot supports the Catholic Church and the Vatican, their traditional rivals.

The plot of both the manga and the OVA primarily focuses upon the wars between Hellsing and Iscariot and the Millennium, a bitter enemy of both that does not appear in the anime. Begun by Nazis near the end of World War II, the Millennium coerced the Vatican to provide primary assistance at that time. Its name referencing Hitler's anticipated thousand-year empire, it initially shipped substantial resources to South America to fund future activities. Its members hid there after the war while its leading scientists developed the "*Letztes Battalion*" (Last Battalion), a Nazi vampire army with one thousand members, former elite Waffen-SS militia. The leader, simply called "The Major," is a short, pudgy psychopath appointed by Hitler who now simply seeks blood, endless war, and chaos. After destroying London Tower and devastating much of the city, he divulges that the primary purpose of his attack is to destroy Alucard, who, together with Walter C. Dornez, had defeated his group during World War II. Among The Major's assistants is The Doctor, an eccentric whose knowledge of technology and physiology has allowed him to develop many of Millennium's projects. His glasses have several lenses on each side, his sinister appearance frequently augmented by his bloodstained lab coat and four-fingered gloves. Some of his vampire knowledge has come from digging up graves. The Major has several additional assistants, some created by The Doctor.

Although *Hellsing* is set in the present, it is strongly linked to the past, as the air is filled with zeppelins and dirigibles used by the Nazis. Dreams, particularly those of past glory, and the past itself play prominent roles in the sanguine episodes of monsters and never-ending battles. At one point The Major remarks that all three groups are fighting for the restoration of a dream: the Catholics to restore the creed of God, the Nazis to win the war and defeat Alucard, Alucard to re-create the bloodlust of past battles. Enrico Maxwell, the head of Section XIII, becomes a power-hungry archbishop who turns the war into a religious crusade for the Vatican. Although unstated, Hellsing represents an old notion of traditional Britain, which it wishes to protect.

Monsters likewise figure prominently in *Hellsing*. The Nazi vampires and ghouls are strongly linked with the war. The Major, who sometimes longs to be immortal himself, is the greatest of all the monsters even though he is not a vampire. Alucard revels in warfare, feeling a sense of nostalgia toward it. Late in the story it is implied that he was originally Vlad the Impaler. Raised by Turks and abused by the sultan as a child, he became hardened, and survived due to his fixation with blood. As a vampire, Alucard is considered to be a monster by his opponents. In his final confrontation with the priest Alexander Anderson, his strongest rival, he wistfully recalls images of desecrated Ottoman Empire warriors, their strung-up bodies elevated. Alucard fought equally with Anderson several times, both eventually restrained by their masters, but always looking forward to their next encounter. As the tale winds down, the Bible-quoting assassin breaks from Enrico Maxwell, fearing his religious zeal. At the same time, Alucard's control restrictions are released, and they engage in a final all-out combat. Anderson ingests Helena's Nail, a remnant from Christ's crucifixion venerated by the Catholic Church, to gain even stronger powers for the final battle. In doing so he loses his self-identity, transforming himself into a "monster . . . of God."

Blood and blood allusions play equally prominent roles as well. Zorin Blitz, The Major's first lieutenant who leads a later assault against the Hellsing Mansion, creates a fearsome presence. Bedecked with spiky orange hair and sinister tattoos, she possesses the power to cast illusions. Seras Victoria and Captain Pip Bernadette of the Wild Geese, initially rivals who have since bonded, must overcome her. When Seras, the stronger of the two, weakens while struggling to break Zorin's spells, Bernadette sacrifices his life to protect her. As Bernadette dies, he encourages Seras, still an innocent, to drink his blood and bond with him. By doing so, Seras absorbs his soul and his memories in addition to restoring her own strength, and the two merge to defeat the imposing Nazi. Afterward, as Seras is leaving, the surviving Wild Geese soldiers salute, recognizing their captain within her. Although she had physically become a vampire some time earlier, she became a real vampire only by feasting on Bernadette's blood.

Alucard eventually becomes a victim of his own bloodlust. The Major has manipulated a confluence of blood to gather near Alucard in central London. The gluttonous vampire gulps it down, continually fusing with other souls as he synthesizes the blood. Warrant Officer Schrödinger, a cat-like creation of the Doctor with the power to be "everywhere and nowhere" while jumping around the world (he is based on a principle in quantum theory proposed by Erwin Schrödinger), slits his own throat. His blood joins the river that Alucard is absorbing, his essence being dissolved into that of the collective. By ingesting him, Alucard is no longer able to distinguish between himself and the millions of lives he has imbibed, and he enters a state in which he is not alive but also not dead. The Major now believes that he has succeeded in destroying his nemesis. When Integra and Seras break through his compound and shoot him, he feels that he has won a great war and can now die happily. Only thirty years later, at *Hellsing*'s denouement, does Alucard reappear. He has been constantly killing those millions of lives within him until only one remains. In addition to his previous powers, he has now obtained the ability of omnipresence, being everywhere and nowhere simultaneously.

The manga *Hellsing* and the OVA *Hellsing Ultimate* are as dark and somber as the anime *Hellsing* was bright, and they may have benefitted from additional humor. But the manga fans desired an OVA that closely reflected the original work and its shadowy characters. Like the manga, *Hellsing Ultimate* has acquired a cult following, visible at fantasy conventions and through websites that provide detailed analysis of its characters and trivia. At one point Kauta Hirano started both a manga and an OVA entitled *Hellsing: The Dawn*, a prequel featuring Alucard and Walter C. Dornez doing battle against Nazi forces in Poland in 1944, but it was discontinued after several episodes. Meanwhile cosplay, prints, and other products have generated a minor market among its fans. Like Alucard, *Hellsing* continues to live for them.—Bill Thompson

Bibliography

Hirano, Kauta. *Hellsing* (manga). Accessed 15 January 2015. http://www.goodmanga.net/471/hellsing.

Iida, Umanosuke, et al. *Hellsing*. Geneon Entertainment Inc., 2002. DVD.

Tokoro, Hiroyuki, Hiroyuki Tanaka, and Yasuhiro Matsu. *Hellsing Ultimate*. Funimation, 2006–2012. DVD.

HENSHIN NINGEN films

Henshin Ningen series is a part of Tōhō's *tokusatsu* film cycle, an attempt to make use of the team behind *Gojira's* (1954) success. It includes three films: *The H-Man* (*Bijo to ekitainingen*, 1958), *The Secret of the Telegian* (*Densō ningen*, 1960), and *The Human Vapor* (*Gasu ningen daiichi-gō*, 1960). In addition, *Tōmei Ningen* (*The Invisible Man*, 1954) is often promoted as a prequel and *Matango* (1963) most certainly as a kind of spin-off sequel, an addition in which the theme of a transformation is taken ever further. Directors that worked with the trilogy were Ishirō Honda and Jun Fukuda. Honda was selected as the director of the first installment, having shown his skills with science fiction and horror films such as *Gojira* and *The Mysterians* (*Chikyū bōeigun*, 1957). He directed *The H-Man*, but was too busy to direct the following *The Secret of the Telegian*. Thus, Jun Fukuda, who had worked as an assistant director in *Rodan* (*Sora no daikaijū Radon*, 1956), was invited to direct the second part of the trilogy. Some of Honda's projects were postponed, though, and he was able to direct *The Human Vapor*. *The Secret of the Telegian* was released in April 1960, and *The Human Vapor* in December of the same year.

The trilogy also owes much to Eiji Tsuburaya and his never-ending vision of creating weird, scary, and wonderful special effects on screen. In this trilogy Tsuburaya was faced with the challenge of creating human-sized monsters. The H-Men were created by using translucent organic glass. For example, the final scene in which the liquid human beings are destroyed by blazing fire was given only one opportunity to shoot—after which the miniature set would have been burned and useless. Similar techniques were used in *The Human Vapor*, in which Tsuburaya used an inflatable rubber doll and a miniature set in the final scene, concluding with an explosion. In *The Secret of the Telegian*, Tsuburaya was first and foremost interested in showing the disappearance into and emergence from the teleport machine. The images Tsuburaya creates look almost like digital special effects, using neon color and acrylic to create the appearance of an electric human being. In all three films the music, too, enhanced the strange and horrific atmosphere, with all of the transformed human beings having a unique melody or sound of their own.

The Henshin Ningen trilogy was aimed at an adult audience. Spectacular scenes of horror are often contrasted with spectacular scenes of (erotic) dance. Indeed, the main characters endlessly flirt with their girlfriends, demonstrating their rather conspicuous love and affection. This semi-erotic feature is a huge difference when compared with the larger context of *tokusatsu* films, which often include monsters with an aim to impress a much younger and male audience. Henshin Ningen films, in turn, represent the *ero guro* of the postwar times. All of the films in the trilogy are explicitly concerned with the issue of good/bad science. This is by no means exclusive to this series—rather, Honda was known for his tendency to employ various tropes from science and science fiction in the service of conveying social commentary. In *The H-Man* everything starts with a nuclear test gone awry. Radiation falls from the sky in the form of "ash of death" which turns people into blueish "H-men" or liquid human beings with the power to kill by mere touch. Or rather, the touch of an H-man transforms the victims into H-men themselves, much like a vampire bite. *The Secret of the Telegian*, as well, incorporates this science/science fiction theme, especially with the incorporation of teleportation. This is also the only film in the series in which the antagonist does not undergo a bodily transformation as such, instead just using scientific means to move his body from place A to place B. The final installment employs the motif of a mad scientist who conducts experiments on human beings. The result of such an experiment is the human vapor, who, at will, can turn into a gas being, all the while maintaining his identity, thoughts, and human heart. This is what the horror of the Henshin Ningen is all about: fear of another human being who—through science—gains an ever greater subversive existence and who is superior to the normal citizen in every means.

The H-Man begins with a scene straight from hell: an explosion, a flash of orange light, and then a news announcement of the many lives this nuclear experiment has taken in the South Pacific Sea. The film cuts to Tokyo, where the rain is pouring down in the dark. When a car suddenly hits a man, Misaki, played by Hisaya Itou, there is no describing the surprise of both the driver and the police, as there is absolutely no body to be seen—just empty clothes. They find, however, a stash of drugs among Misaki's bag. The event leads police to Mizaki's girlfriend, cabaret singer Chikako Arai, played by Yumi Shirakawa.

The cabaret scenes create a decadent atmosphere for the unraveling mystery. When Detective Tominaga, played by Akihiko Hirata, sees his old friend from the university, Masada, played by Kenji Sahara, approaching Chikako, he goes on to interrogate them both. Masada, who is currently a professor at a local university, explains that he is not interested in drugs, but rather in the strange effect hydrogen radiation might have on human beings. When he states that a human body might indeed melt under strange conditions, no one believes him—it is only after Masada takes Tominaga with other members of the police to meet two victims of the nuclear explosion, that they really believe him.

In the end Chikako, who has gotten closer to Masada along the way, is kidnapped and taken into the sewers. The police are planning on scorching the H-Men once and for all after luring them into the very same sewer system. It is up to Masada to save Chikako before she too will burn. After a high-intensity rescue scene, Tokyo is in flames yet again, reminding people both on and off screen of the horrors of the war and the bombings. The film ends with the ominous promise, that there is a possibility that the H-Men will return.

Similar themes are taken up in *The Secret of the Telegian*. When ex-soldier Tsukumoto, played by Shin Ootomo, is brutally murdered in an amusement park attraction, newspaper reporter Kirioka, played by Koji Tsuruta, and his girlfriend Akiko, played by Yumi Shirakawa, assist the police in trying to solve the homicide.

As the plot unfolds, a series of secrets and cover-ups are revealed that revolve around yet an earlier death involving Tsukumoto's fellow soldiers and their roles in the killing of Corporal Sudō, played by Tadao Nakamaru. Seemingly now a ghost, Sudō returns to haunt the soldiers that took part in his murder, seeking to ultimately take revenge by killing all those involved. Transitioning in and out of what appears to be the natural and supernatural dimensions, Sudō displays a certain amount of invincibility, which is explained through scenes of flashbacks to a time when he and his assailants were working at a military laboratory under the command of teleport and telekinesis specialist Dr. Niki, played by Takamaru Sasaki. When a plan to appropriate gold materials from the laboratory for profit emerges, soldiers turn on Sudō and murder him.

The nuances of science and science fiction establish an entertaining framework through which ghostly matters are somehow facilitated. It could be said that *The Secret of the Telegian* presents some rather modern concerns, considering how the horror is spread through a teleport machine. Sudō differs from the H-Man in that without the machine he is nothing but an ordinary, resentful human being. In addition, the issue of Japanese war responsibility and the transformation of hegemonic masculinity is never far behind.

Similar to *The Secret of the Telegian*, *The Human Vapor* starts out as a detective thriller. A bank in downtown Tokyo is robbed, but the perpetrator is nowhere to be seen. A quick-paced chase follows, but the police are at their wit's end when he vanishes into thin air. After the second robbery everything points to the Kasuga residence. The Kasuga clan is one of the most famous clans of *Noh* actors in Japan—due in a large part to the talents and beauty of Fujichiyo Kasuga, played by Kaori Yachigusa.

Considered a person of interest, Fujichiyo is questioned by Detective Okamoto, played by Tatsuya Mihashi. Although finding no reason to suspect Fujichiyo of any wrongdoing through the questioning, Okamoto maintains close surveillance of her daily routines. To the satisfaction of his suspicions, the stolen money is found at the Kasuga residence and Fujichiyo is arrested.

At this point, the film moves from the realm of detective stories to that of the fantastic. Angered by the unfair arrest of Fujichiyo, the real culprit, Mizuno, played by Yoshio Tsuchiya materializes in front of the police and bank representatives. Possessing the ability to not only transform himself into gas, but also to utilize it as a weapon, Mizuno goes on a rampage with his electric blue gas—strangling bank management and prison guards in an effort to free Fujichiyo from her prison. As Fujichiyo is innocent, however, she opts to remain in prison and prove her case through legal means—eventually being released.

Little by little Mizuno's own story is told. Before his transformation he was just a normal library assistant working at a university. He had a dream of becoming a pilot in the Japan Self-Defense Forces, but failed the entrance exam. Feeling bitter and fed up with his life he accepts an offer from researcher Dr. Kyūko Sano, played by Fuyuki Murakami, to become his research assistant in a space development project. Sano promises to enhance Mizuno's body, to build it afresh cell by cell. Accepting the offer, Mizuno is given an injection, after which he sleeps a total of 240 hours. When he wakes up, he has transformed into a human vapor, which comes as a shock to Sano as well, and in a fit of rage, Mizuno kills Sano and discovers how many other victims Sano has sacrificed in order to create his vision of an ultimate human being.

Meanwhile Fujichiyo is planning to use all of her money to hold her final Noh show. It is made clear that after the death of Fujichiyo's father, the Kasuga clan has been suffering from economic stagnation and having a hard time hiring famous stars. Mizuno came to know Fujichiyo from his days as a library assistant, and, mystified by her beauty and poise, he now wants nothing more than to use his new abilities to support her and her love for the art of Noh. The connection between Mizuno and Fujichiyo is revealed in the press, and Fujichiyo's prestigious Noh show is turned into an exhibition that people only attend in order to catch a glimpse of the Human Vapor. The police, in turn, plan on destroying Mizuno after the show, but Fujichiyo beats them to it. After her brilliant final dance she and Mizuno embrace, after which she blows up the whole building, herself and Mizuno included. The scene is reminiscent of the motif of a double suicide, a perfect ending to a story inspired by traditional stage arts in general.—Leena Eerolainen

HIGANJIMA (2009)

DIRECTOR: Tae-Gyun Kim
SCREENPLAY: Tetsuya Oishi, based on manga by Koji Matsumoto
SPECS: 122 minutes; color

Higanjima (Island of Red Spider Lilies) is a horror-thriller film directed by Tae-Gyun Kim (b. 1960). It is based on Koji Matsumoto's popular manga of the same name. The film depicts a young man's quest to find his lost brother on a vampire-populated island.

The film opens with a man running through the woods. He finds an abandoned shack. While he hides, the man laments being deceived into coming to the island by a woman (later revealed to be "Rei"). Two vampires flank him. Suddenly, one vampire is shot twice with arrows, another is crushed. A sword-wielding man (later revealed as Atsushi) enters and informs the frightened man that he is infected. The man dies and, when he awakens as a vampire, is put to rest by Atsushi, played by Dai Watanabe (b. 1984). Outside the shack, a white-haired vampire (later revealed to be Miyabi) taunts the slayer. Atsushi slices through the window grate, but Miyabi, played by Koji Yamamoto (b. 1978), is gone. The blood-soaked credits roll with all the hallmarks of a vampire film: flying bats are silhouetted by a large, full moon. Nonetheless, the dark, looming island distinguishes this film from most in the subgenre.

The film reopens in daylight. Akira, played by Hideo Ishiguro (b. 1989), is introduced. He climbs atop a roof and grabs a puppy he has been protecting from feral dogs. As Akira cares for the puppy, he notices his friend Pon, played by Fumito Moriwaki (b. 1987), has a bandaged hand. Pon is being beaten at home. He will, unfortunately, be a victim throughout the film. Akira soon runs into a large group of young men. The leader challenges him to a fight. Akira dodges his punches with ease. A chase-scene ensues. A mysterious woman pulls Akira into a *rabu hoteru* ("love hotel") for refuge. The next scene shows her showering in silhouette and Akira staring. This woman is Rei, played by Asami Mizukawa (b. 1983). She gives Akira his brother's ID and tells him that his brother Atsushi is safe.

At home, Akira gazes at a newspaper clipping. The headline reads "Couple Still Missing." Atsushi and his girlfriend disappeared over two years ago. Akira reminisces about his kendo matches with Atsushi. In this memory, Atsushi cautions Akira about his unwillingness to be assertive. This becomes a recurring theme in the film. Akira returns to reality when he hears his parents fighting. They struggle with Atsushi's disappearance. The father is an alcoholic and they have lost Akira's college fund. In their mourning for Atsushi, the parents neglect Akira.

The next day, Akira's group spots Rei. She is handing out cash to the gang who chased Akira. Curious, Akira's group follows her to an industrial area. When they collectively look through a window, they find a woman suspended from the ceiling. A man drinks the unidentified woman's blood while Rei placidly watches. The group is caught spying. Ken, played by Tomohisa Yuge (b. 1980), is bitten by the vampire (later revealed as Raiki, played by Motoki Fukami [b. 1980]). As Akira and Raiki fight, Rei runs Raiki through with a forklift. Since there was no transfer of vampire blood into Ken, he is not infected. At this juncture, Rei finally reveals her story: a vampire seized her island. It is her duty to bring human victims to the island. Since it is uncharted, the police cannot help. She reveals that Atsushi is now a vampire slayer. She wants Akira to join him. Akira agrees to assist.

The next day, Akira boards Rei's yacht. Wielding a baseball bat, Ken joins. Akira's other friends soon appear. Ken attempts to deny boarding to the only woman of the group, Yuki, played by Miori Takimoto (b. 1991). Nonetheless, she is adamant (and has a crush on Ken). They arrive at Higanjima after sundown. A reflection of the film's full-title, red spider lilies dot the island. As explained by Rei, the lilies are poisonous by nature and were originally planted on graves to deter scavengers. After a short hike, the group arrives at a small village. They are almost immediately taken hostage.

The next scene shows Rei in Miyabi's room. Raiki emerges from the background. Noticeably disfigured, he threatens Rei but Miyabi claims her as his "plaything." A sex scene follows which culminates in Miyabi drinking Rei's blood while she recalls her mother falling victim to his band of killers.

In the vampire fortress, the group is locked in a cell. A crone draws a circle on the ground and tells Akira's friends to sacrifice one of their own. Kato, played by Masaya Handa (b. 1983), and Nishiyama, played by Osamu Adachi (b. 1987), try to sacrifice Pon for being "good for nothing." Bravely, Ken volunteers himself instead. Yuki tries to accompany him but Ken shoves her away. Ken struggles with the vampires and they unknowingly drop the keys to the cell. Ken is taken to a dank, blood-soaked chamber where he sees befouled instruments and the bodies of other victims. The scene cuts to Akira and friends escaping. Through a grate in the floor, they witness Ken being tortured. Yuki vows to rescue him. The group splits up. All promise to meet at the highest point on the island. When Pon, Kato, and Nishiyama escape the fortress, Pon tells the two young men they betrayed him. He leaves on his own, unable to trust them. Meanwhile, Akira and Yuki fight the vampires and release Ken (whose blood was being drained through surgical tubing). Wearing stolen vampire garb, Ken, Yuki, and Akira escape the compound and run into the woods. There, they find Atsushi.

At daybreak, everyone assembles at the highest peak, except Pon. Atsushi takes the group to an old military facility where they rest. Meanwhile, Pon is lost in the woods. Miyabi's harpy spots him. The film cuts to the group sleeping. Battered and bloody, Pon finds them. Pon informs the group that they are not forgiven and attacks Akira. Pon is infected. Vampires swarm the compound. As Atsushi tries to protect the group, Miyabi watches the scene with delight. In the film's climax, Atsushi temporarily defeats Raiki by severing his arm and Akira must kill Pon but cannot. This grim task is assumed by Atsushi. They flee through tunnels only to be attacked upon emerging. The harpy who tortured Pon kidnaps Yuki. The rest escape.

Later, Atsushi confesses that he damned the once beautiful island two years ago. In a flashback, it is revealed that Higanjima is his girlfriend Ryoko's home. Atsushi takes her to Higanjima to propose marriage. She accepts and they explore the area. Atsushi enters a temple filled with bizarre vampire dolls. Ryoko tells him that she has been instructed not to enter this building. Hearing a voice calling for help, Atsushi unlocks a mysterious-looking vault. Miyabi escapes and immediately drains Ryoko of blood. She dies.

The film cuts to Raiki having a blade-arm installed. Yuki is shown suspended in this chamber. Simultaneously, the group of friends encounters resistance fighters in the woods. Atsushi asks to leave Akira and his friends in their village. Infuriated, Akira requests a session with a master trainer. While he does well in the first session, he fails in the second. Remembering Yuki and Pon, Akira fights with his heart and realizes his preternatural skills. He wishes to rescue Yuki but is told that Atsushi left to fight alone. The film abruptly cuts to a showdown between Raiki and Atsushi. This time, Atsushi cuts off Raiki's sword arm. Raiki flees, but his head is later spotted by Atsushi (apparently, he fell victim to Miyabi's callousness). Atsushi finds Miyabi. Atsushi is attacked by Miyabi's harpy (now revealed to be the crone from the film's beginning). Rei defends Atsushi and then tries to kill Miyabi. She is unsuccessful. Rei and Atsushi pursue Miyabi into the fortress. He awaits them. Yuki is lowered from the ceiling and becomes bait for a gargoyle. Akira swings in and saves her. The entire resistance appears. As the group fights the gargoyle, Miyabi lures Atsushi away. Miyabi is explicit: he wants Atsushi for his "right hand man." Atsushi refuses. Atsushi attempts to destroy Miyabi, but the vampire is simply too strong. Miyabi nearly infects Atsushi but is stopped by Akira. Rigged with explosives by the resistance, the fortress begins collapsing. Rei runs to help Atsushi and Akira as the resistance flees.

Near death, Atsushi is bitten by Miyabi. While in Miyabi's clutch, Atsushi heroically runs his sword through himself and through Miyabi. He instructs Akira to kill the both of them. As Akira readies himself, Miyabi pulls away and the brothers behead him together. Atsushi is infected. He asks Rei to "look after Akira." He thanks Akira, and tells him to confess his true feelings to Yuki. Atsushi disappears in an explosion.

With the island returned to relative normalcy, Akira and his friends depart for home. Aboard Rei's boat, Akira has a vision of Miyama opening his eyes. The island becomes menacing again. The title card appears.—Erica Joan Dymond

Bibliography

Kim, Tae-Gyun. *Higanjima*. Funimation, 2009. Film.

HINO, HIDESHI (1946–)

Hideshi Hino (b. April 19, 1946) is a Japanese manga artist best known for his horror comics. He has also worked as a film director and writer. Hino was born in Manchuria to Japanese immigrant farmers, and with the end of the Second World War and Japan's occupation of Manchuria, his family was forced to flee for their lives. Hino originally considered a career in film, and his first forays into the manga industry were publishing amateur *dōjinshi* works. He made his professional debut in 1967 in *Komu (Com)*, an avant-garde and alternative manga magazine founded by Osamu Tezuka.

Hino's work is dominated by brutal torture and graphic mutilations, although there is frequently a desire (or obsession) in finding the beauty in these horrific acts of torment and destruction. Hino's distinctive artistic style eschews realism in favor of extremely distorted bodily proportions that precariously straddle the line between the cute and the grotesque. Many of Hino's protagonists, somewhat autobiographically, are artists tormented by their pasts and struggling to find ways to integrate violence into their works.

These themes are especially prevalent in one of Hino's best-known manga, *Jigokuhen (Panorama of Hell)*, originally published in 1983. The manga is semi-autobiographical, detailing the story of a disturbed artist who uses his own blood as his medium. Born right as the atomic bomb detonated over Hiroshima, the protagonist recounts the traumas and psychic scars of his past, including brutal abuse and torture inflicted by his family. The story world is hellish, an industrial nightmare choked with executed corpses. The only escape from such a horrific life is death, and *Panorama of Hell*'s artist protagonist (and Hino proxy) is obsessed with this idea.

Hino's 1987 *Gaki Jigoku* (or *Hell Baby*), tells the story of a hideously deformed baby that is abandoned in a garbage dump. Coming back from the dead, the Hell Baby learns to survive within the dump before seeking revenge on her family. Numerous collections of his short stories have been published, including *Jigoku no Komoriuta (Lullabies from Hell)*; the title story is very similar to *Panorama of Hell*, and the other three stories were used as the basis for films in the Theatre of Horror series, described below.

Although horror manga are usually marketed at the shōnen (young boys) and seinen (young men) audiences, some of Hino's work has been aimed at shōjo (young girl) market as well. Originally published in shōjō magazines, this material has appeared outside Japan in several volumes of the *Hino Horror* anthology series, including volumes nine and ten, *Ghost School* and *Death's Reflection*.

In addition to his horror manga, Hino has also worked in J-horror, both as a director and as a writer. His best-known film work involves the controversial Guinea Pig series, for which Hino served as a director, producer, writer, and actor in several productions. The series is infamous for its extremely violent and realistic imagery. The Japanese authorities even questioned the filmmakers, who had to prove that the films did not depict actual murders.

The second film in the series, *Chiniku no Hana* (*Flower of Flesh and Blood*, 1985) was directed by Hino and based on his horror manga. In the film, a man (played by Hino himself) dresses up as a samurai, kidnaps a woman, and brutally dismembers her. Hino also directed *Manhōru no Naka no Ningyo* (*Mermaid in a Manhole*, 1988), the sixth Guinea Pig film to be produced, although it was released fourth. In the film, an artist is exploring the sewers of Okinawa and discovers a mermaid; the sewer environment has made the mermaid sick, and the man takes her home. The mermaid's body is covered in pustules and lacerations, and as her condition worsens and she dies, the artist uses her blood and pus to paint her portrait.

Hino's film credits also include art design work on two productions: *Agi kijin no ikari* (*Agi: Wrath of a Fierce God*, 1984, dir. Kazuyuki Hayakawa) and *Tōkaidō Yotsuya kaidan* (2000, dir. Hideaki Hirano), an OVA adaptation of a famous Japanese ghost story.

A series of six films based on Hino's manga was made in 2004, released abroad as Hino Hideshi's Theatre of Horror. The films were released in two waves. The first three films are *Dead Girl Walking* (dir. Kōji Shiraishi), *Lizard Baby* (dir. Yoshihiro Nakamura), and *The Boy from Hell* (dir. Mari Asato). The last three films are *The Ravaged House: Zōroku's Disease* (dir. Kazuyoshi Kumakiri), *Death Train* (dir. Kazuyuki Sakamoto), and *Occult Detective Club: The Doll Cemetery* (dir. Kiyoshi Yamamoto).—Nicholas Bestor

See also Guinea Pig series

HORRORS OF MALFORMED MEN (1969)

DIRECTOR: Teruo Ishii
SCREENPLAY: Teruo Ishii, Masahiro Kakefuda, based on stories by Edogawa Ranpo
SPECS: 99 minutes; color

Although it was not banned outright, the notorious *Horrors of Malformed Men* (*Edogawa Rampo zenshu: Kyoufu kikei ningen*) has been very difficult to view. It received only limited screenings when it initially premiered. As of this writing Toei, its production company, has never released it on videocassette or DVD in Japan. Adapted from several stories by Edogawa Ranpo (1894–1965), *Horrors* merges horror and detective-mystery thriller genres with exploitation and madness to become a beautiful but grotesque cinematic nightmare experienced during the day.

Director Teruo Ishii's (1924–2005) film begins with an amnesiac man in a cell with a frenzied bevy of semi-clad women at an insane asylum. Played by Teruo Yoshida (b. 1936), he is uncertain of his identity, but believes himself to be sane. After killing a man in self-defense, he escapes from the sanatorium and attempts to trace a lullaby he hears and recognizes from his childhood. But he must flee when a circus performer assisting him is knifed and dies in his arms. While heading to the coast, he discovers that Genzaburo Komoda, a wealthy man whose appearance is identical to his, has just died, and he replaces him by concocting an amazing recovery. Carefully navigating around the man's wife and mistress while attempting to uncover his own roots, he witnesses a series of bizarre events, including the wife's murder. He finally forces his business manager to take him to an island where Jogoro Komoda, Genzaburo's father, has isolated himself for many years to perform research.

The derangements of *Horrors of Malformed Men* completely unfold on this island. Unbeknownst to his family on the mainland, Jogoro had a second son. While on the island, the amnesiac learns that he is actually Hirosuke Hitome, Genzaburo's younger brother. Jogoro, who is physically deformed, had sent Hirosuke to medical school to study surgery. To his horror, Hirosuke discovers that Jogoro wants him to use his training to transmogrify attractive prisoners on the island into grotesqueries to serve hunchbacks and other hideously malformed creatures. Hirosuke also learns that his mother, long believed dead, is instead an old lady chained in a cave, her mad husband's captive, and that he himself, with his father's encouragement, has been engaging in an incestuous relationship with the woman he loves. The unimaginable narrative is unraveled only gradually, through Jogoro's disclosures and the findings of Akechi Kogoro, a master detective often serving as Edogawa Rampo's alter ego in his stories, who has come to the island disguised as a Komoda family servant. These revelations frequently occur within subplots of subplots.

The disturbing island scenes, comprising much of the second half of the film, were shot in the rugged Noto Peninsula, which juts out in the Sea of Japan. Here Tatsumi Hijikata (1928–1986), a founder of the highly stylized Ankoku Butoh, plays a role as delirious as the turbulent water swirling against the rocks on the island's coast. As Hinosuke's father he slithers and swirls in a bestial fashion, uttering gutteral sounds, his eyes popping through his long, decrepit black hair. Jogoro is a freakish force of nature, not merely a deformed human. Hijikata's entire outlaw dance troupe plays supporting roles, initially as demented beings in the insane asylum and later as grizzled denizens on Jogoro's island. The contrast between a straight Teruo Yoshida, an Ishii regular, as Hinosuke, and the delirious Hijikata provides a counterpoint that blends well. The film unfolds slowly, as the confusion of the amnesiac Hinosuke is well reflected in the enigmatic events occurring in Tokyo and the mainland Komoda estate. The savage island unlocks its ghastly secrets only gradually, and they are too macabre to be easily comprehended.

Teruo Ishii was a great admirer of Edogawa Rampo's writings, and made *Horrors* for his fans. Ishii selected elements from several Rampo works. The novella *Strange Tale of Panorama Island* (*Panoramato kidan*) relates a horrific tale of a man who replaces his wealthy double, a college acquaintance, upon learning of the dual's death. He uses the family's money to build an artificial fantasy island, where he murders his wife after she discovers his secret. Rampo's short stories "The Human Chair" (Ningen-Isu), centering upon a man hiding inside a large chair enjoying the warmth of its female occupants, and "The Stroller in the Attic" (Yaneura no sanposha), in which a voyeur concocts crimes while peeking at rooms from the rafters of an attic, advance the subplot of the murdered wife. Noboru Tanaka (1937–2006) adapted these two stories several years later in *Watcher in the Attic* (*Edogawa Rampo ryoki-kan: Yaneura no sanposha*, 1976). "The Twins" (Soseiji), also filmed by Shinya Tsukamoto (b. 1960) as *Gemini* (*Soseiji*, 1999), expresses a disturbing tale of fraternal substitutions. Director Ishii felt he had only limited opportunities to film Rampo works and so chose to mix several stories.

Many Japanese consider Teruo Ishii as the "King of Cult" or "Father of Pinky Violence." Best known in the West for contributions to the *Super Giant/Starman* (*Supa jaiantsu*) children's series from 1957 to 1959, he also directed ten episodes of the *Abashiri Prison* (*Abashiri bangaishi*) series in 1965–1966, transforming Ken Takakura into a superstar as a sympathetic ex-con. Many of his efforts, however, are stylish but sensationalistic B-films, including explorations of gore and cruelty. His Queen Bee (Jo Bachi) pictures, made in 1958–1960, foreshadowed the female *ninkyo yakuza* genre that became popular a decade later. Titles such as *Joy of Torture* (*Toku onna keibatsushi*, 1968) and *Orgies of Edo* (*Zankoku ijo gyakutai*, 1969) require little elaboration. Although he made films in a variety of genres, Ishii retained his interest in Rampo throughout his career, his final work being *Blind Beast vs. Killer Dwarf* (*Moju tai Issun Boshi*, 2001), a digital video adaptation of Rampo works featuring deviant filmmaker Shinya Tsukamoto as detective Akechi Kogoro.

Horrors of Malformed Men was suppressed due to the political incorrectness of its treatment of the handicapped rather than its horrific or erotic elements. *Gemini* director Tsukamoto, an admirer of Teruo Ishii's films, acknowledges watching this rarely projected work at a midnight screening some years ago. It was first shown outside of Japan as part of an Ishii retrospective at the 2003 Udine Far East Film Festival, where it received much acclaim. The retrospective, which introduced the diversity of Ishii's films to the West, was followed by another at the Etrange Festival in Paris in 2005. *Horrors of Malformed Men* was finally released on DVD in the United States in 2007.—Bill Thompson

See also Blind Beast vs. Killer Dwarf; ero guru nansensu genre; Rampo Noir

Bibliography
Ishii, Teruo. *Horrors of Malformed Men*. Synapse Films, 2007. DVD.
Rampo, Edogawa. *The Edogawa Rampo Reader*. Edited and translated by Seth Jacobowitz. Fukuoka, Japan: Kurodahan Press, 2008.
———. *Japanese Tales of Mystery and Imagination*. Translated by James B. Harris. Tokyo and Rutland, VT: Tuttle Books, 1956.
———. *Strange Tale of Panorama Island*. Translated by Elaine Kazu Gilbert. Honolulu: University of Hawaii Press, 2013.

HOUSE (1977)
DIRECTOR: Nobuhiko Obayashi
SCREENPLAY: Chiho Katsura, Chigumi Ōbayashi
SPECS: 88 minutes; color

In the wake of the phenomenal international success of Steven Spielberg's *Jaws* (1975), the renowned blockbuster in which a giant great white shark terrorizes a small island community, motion picture production studios around the globe scrambled to produce the next spectacular monster movie. In Japan, the legendary Toho Studios turned to Nobuhiko Obayashi, an experimental filmmaker and prominent director of television commercials, to develop just such a property. No one, however, could have anticipated that such a commission could have resulted in anything remotely resembling 1977's *House*. Faced with the daunting challenge of crafting an "answer" to *Jaws*, Obayashi not only avoided making a film that could be classified as derivative, but succeeded in creating one of the strangest audiovisual events in cinema history. To this very day, *House* continues to bewilder and beguile generations of moviegoers with its highly imaginative narrative and eclectic, and at times hallucinatory, plot twists and mise-en-scène.

Aware that stale imitation is all-too-frequently the guiding principle behind the creation of the very worst commercial cinema, Obayashi eschewed the conventional practice of relying exclusively on professional screenplay writers to generate a scenario. Instead, he enlisted the assistance of his adolescent daughter, who contributed several flights of fancy as well as a few of her deepest fears. The result was a collection of remarkable images ranging from a human-eating domicile to a piano with a predilection for severing its player's fingers. To these and other outlandish conceits, Obayashi included crucial plot details loosely culled from his memories of having lost many of his childhood friends when Hiroshima, the city in which he was born, was obliterated by the atomic bomb dropped on it by the US military on 6 August 1945. Fittingly, *House*'s frenetic and formally daring collisions of pop culture iconography, bold stylistic flourishes, and audacious revisions of kaidan motifs, reflects this unique combination of disparate visions. Although verging at times on the incomprehensible, *House*'s narrative presents viewers with the adventure of a young girl named Oshari ("Gorgeous") (played by Kimiko Ikegami) who, disenchanted by her father's decision to remarry years after her mother's death, takes six friends to visit an aunt that, we soon discover, is a very troubled ghost with a very strange ghost cat (*bakeneko*).

The aunt's residence, from which the film derives its title, is a supernatural funhouse filled with interconnected rooms and an array of furnishings that soon evidence a voracious appetite for young girls. Seemingly everyday objects possess uncanny and, in many cases, deadly attributes. A refrigerator serves as a supernatural portal; seemingly innocuous furnishings and household items, from mirrors and lighting fixtures to musical instruments and jars, are imbued with menace. In Obayashi's twisted universe, virtually anything can turn lethal in a heartbeat, tearing apart or outright consuming the unsuspecting. Thus, for all of its fairy tale trappings, *House* was decidedly not a film aimed at children. Teenagers and young adults, however, responded enthusiastically to the motion picture's attractive young cast, imaginative set pieces, vibrant color scheme, and quirky, cheerful score. Toho Studios' executives, however, did not share the younger audiences' zeal and, in response to extensive negative reviews, eventually pulled *House* from theaters.

While *House* was more favorably received commercially than critically in Japan upon its release, reviewers in foreign markets were far more receptive of the film's playful take on the horror genre and its over-the-top mélange of special effects, creative editing, hand-drawn animation, and impressionistic art design. What's more, like the Spielberg film that provided the initial inspiration for its production, *House* became a prime example of what has come to be known as an "expanded" or "transmedia" text. Creatively deploying his knowledge of marketing and promotion, a strategy informed by his years of experience in television advertising, Obayashi accompanied *House*'s production cycle and theatrical release with a plethora of related materials and projects. These included collectible promotional cards, an official soundtrack album, assorted manga, and radio dramas inspired by the film's outlandish action. Over the successive decades, *House*'s legend continued to grow, eventually attaining the status of a "cult classic" on par with other campy, genre-bending exercises like Jim Sharman's *The Rocky Horror Picture Show* (1975), David Lynch's *Eraserhead* (1977), and Sam Raimi's *The Evil Dead* (1981) and *The Evil Dead II* (1987). With beautiful DVD and Blu-ray editions of *House* now included within the catalogues of premiere home video distributors like The Criterion Collection and the UK's Masters of Cinema label, Obayashi's idiosyncratic masterpiece of bubblegum-pop-horror is now a staple in the home video collections of cinephiles devoted not only to groundbreaking works of Japanese cinema, but to the strangest motion pictures the film world has to offer.—Jay McRoy

THE HUMAN VAPOR (1960)
Director: Inoshirō Honda
Screenplay: Takeshi Kimura
Specs: 81 minutes; color

The third and final film of Toho's "Weird Science Fiction Cinema" trilogy (tetralogy, if one includes *Matango*, aka *Attack of the Mushroom People* [1963] in the series), *The Human Vapor*, the Japanese title of which translates as "Gas man number one," starts out, like its predecessor *The Secret of the Telegian* (1960), as a crime thriller–science fiction hybrid, but eventually turns into a surprisingly stirring variation on *Phantom of the Opera* with an intriguingly authentic Japanese flavor. It is a genuinely unique blend of cinematic genres and sensibilities usually considered worlds apart, held together by a sincere screenplay, excellent performances, and imaginative but solid direction by Inoshirō Honda.

The film opens with a shrewd montage of a bank heist from the perpetrator's POV, including an initially befuddling shot of a vault door opening seemingly by itself. Detective Okamoto, played by Mihashi Tatsuya (1923–2004), perhaps best known to Euro-American viewers as Toshirō Mifune's hot-headed brother-in-law in Akira Kurosawa's *The Bad Sleep Well* (1960), along with his spunky but savvy reporter-girlfriend Kyoko, played by Keiko Sata, investigate a series of strange bank holdup cases, wherein the culprit seems to disappear into thin air along with his loot. Finally, Okamoto manages to pursue the robber on the run in a speeding car, only to find the latter overturned and empty near a country road. In a nearby mansion, he sneaks a look at a woman garbed in a kimono performing a traditional dance dressed as a *hannya* (female demon). When the dancer removes the demon mask, he is struck by her ethereal beauty.

Okamoto and Kyoko, after several investigating trips, learn that the dancer, Fujichiyo Kasuga, played by Yachigusa Kaoru (b. 1931), is the disgraced successor to a theater troupe suffering from financial problems and power struggles, and that she seems to have found a wealthy sponsor who promised to bankroll her comeback production titled "The Demon of Love." Okamoto is convinced that Fujichiyo's mysterious sponsor is behind the bank heists. When the marked bills turn up from the dancer's debt payments, the police arrest her, prompting the bank robber to make his public appearance. To the police's chagrin, he not only can slip through the metal bars of a vault (in a scene that must surely have influenced an almost identical one in *Terminator: Judgment Day*) but also is invulnerable to bullets, bombs, or anything they can throw at him.

Despite its convoluted plot (the movie tries to set up a few too many red herrings involving the Gas Man's identity, resulting in some unnecessary confusions), *The Human Vapor* proves a gripping mystery-drama garnished with an unusually sophisticated, adult flavor. Unlike most of the Toho special-effects showcases, this title is strongly character driven: we are drawn into the tragic romance between Fujichiyo and the "Gas Man," played by Yoshio Tsuchiya (b. 1927). Neither is the one-dimensional cypher some viewers associate with films of this type.

Yachigusa, classically beautiful, initially expresses horror at the Gas Man's murderous antics, yet is gradually won over by his sincere declaration of devotion and love. However, there is also a hint of romantic fatalism in her character, reminiscent of the female protagonists of early modern Japanese classics who would choose a double suicide as a consummation of their romance rather than, say, eking out a living as fugitives from the law. Equally wonderful is Tsuchiya's presentation of the Gas Man, Mizuno: this might possibly be the best performance ever given by this super-veteran of Japanese special-effects films. Mizuno is a soft-spoken, unassuming librarian with no political or social-class axe to grind: the hints of megalomania or madness are there, but impressively subtle. He is really convincing as a super-human mutant who believes he is not only unstoppable but also un-killable, and thus privileged to stand up for the happiness of someone he truly loves, until of course other scientists attempt to prove him wrong. The arc of his character is genuinely tragic: screenwriter Takeshi Kimura emphasizes the evilness of human experiment that turned him into a gas creature, by having the scientist cop to the fact that "many before you have sacrificed themselves in the name of scientific progress." Yet the Gas Man snuffs out the lives of the meddling policemen or bank guards in an almost casual manner, as if in the gaseous state he is incapable of imagining the pain and fear of other human beings.

The original Japanese cut of *The Human Vapor* ends in an extended special-effects sequence that in my opinion diminishes the emotional power of the climactic exchange between Fujichiyo and the Gas Man. Interestingly, the US import version, aside from adding a voice-over narration by the Gas Man character and shuffling the order of events to tell the story from Mizuno's POV (thus almost eliminating the mystery angle of the first half of the original cut), reedits the final sequence so that the Gas Man's fate is either considerably worse than that shown in the Japanese cut, or, depending on one's interpretation (or level of cynicism), left purposefully vague for a possible sequel.—Kyu Hyun Kim

• I •

ICHI THE KILLER (2001)

DIRECTOR: Takashi Miike
SCREENPLAY: Sakichi Sato
SPECS: 129 minutes; color

Ichi the Killer is a dreamlike horror/crime thriller set in the midst of a Yakuza gang war. Directed by Takashi Miike (b. 1960), the acclaimed director of other films such as *One Missed Call* (2003), *13 Assassins* (2011), and *Hostel* (2006), the film is based upon the manga by writer Hideo Yamamoto (b. 1968).

The film follows three primary characters through several betrayals and cover-ups: the title character Ichi, played by Nao Ōmori (b. 1972), Jijii, played by Shin'ya Tsukamoto (b. 1960), Ichi's handler, and a heavily scarred Yakuza member named Kakihara, played by Tadanobu Asano (b. 1973). The film opens with the assassination of Anjo, Kakihara's immediate superior, a vicious Yakuza crime boss of considerable repute. Shortly after Anjo is killed, a cleanup crew led by Jijii arrives to remove all evidence of the crime as well as to steal the money that Anjo had with him, the sum total of the gang's fortune. While in the process of cleaning the apartment Jijii reveals that it was Ichi who was behind the graphic assassination.

The remaining Yakuza gang assembles to discuss Anjo's disappearance, and several of them believe that he has fled with the money and a prostitute, but Kakihara, his sadomasochistic enforcer believes that he has been kidnapped and vows to find the people responsible.

Kakihara begins his investigation in a nightclub where Anjo's girlfriend "Karen," played by Paulyn Sun (b. 1974) works, and he informs her that Anjo has disappeared with a woman and a large sum of money. Kakihara also notices Jijii and the cleanup crew in the nightclub, in a meeting perhaps orchestrated by Jijii. The crew is recognized by Kakihara, who is surprised to see them, as he had believed that they were out of town. Jijii promises to Kakihara to let him know if he hears anything of Anjo, but also subtly suggests that the disappearance might be attributed to another Yakuza member, Suzuki, played by Susumu Terajima (b. 1963).

After talking to Jijii, Kakihara seeks out Suzuki, believing that he kidnapped Anjo in order to steal the gang's money. As a result Kakihara tortures and interrogates Suzuki by stripping him naked and suspending him from meat hooks before pouring boiling oil upon his body. After the torture Suzuki still will not reveal any information, and even Kakihara comes to believe that he is innocent of any wrongdoing. Unbeknownst to Kakihara and the other gang members the torture is being watched via camera by Jijii and the other members of the cleanup crew.

Because of his mistaken accusation of Suzuki and the Funaki gang, Kakihara performs a variation of *seppuku* (traditional ritual suicide) by cutting off the end of his tongue and presenting it to Suzuki's boss Funaki by means of an apology. Kakihara's grisly apology is not deemed enough by the Yakuza syndicate however, and they consequently cast both Kakihara and the Anjo gang out of the syndicate. Being ostracized from the syndicate does not faze Kakihara however, and he remains focused upon avenging Anjo, whom he now believes to be dead rather than simply missing.

Kakihara's premonition is confirmed when he and other Anjo members raid a hotel room and discover a member of the cleanup crew. The latter is high on heroin and confesses to cleaning up the scene of Anjo's assassination. He also admits to being a former member of the Yakuza and having facial reconstruction surgery to disguise his appearance. While Ichi and the other cleanup members escape the same fate, the captured member reveals that Kakihara is Ichi's next target within the syndicate.

It is then revealed that Suzuki is behind the threat on Kakihara's life, having called Jijii and his crew to put a price on Kakihara. Jijii's role in the series of events begins to crystallize as it becomes clearer that Jijii is secretly pitting the Yakuza gangs against one another to extract a personal profit as well as to undermine the power of the syndicate.

The narrative returns back to Ichi, an awkward youth who is being coerced or trained to kill the Yakuza by Jijii, and who incites highly emotional, sexualized, and violent urges from within Ichi by hypnotizing him and feeding him false memories. Throughout the film Ichi is haunted by these false memories, and particularly by the memory of his witnessing his childhood teacher being raped by a group of fellow students who bullied him. Ichi's relationship to his past is further antagonized by frequent flashbacks such as his reflexively murdering a prostitute he frequented, shortly after killing a pimp who is about to beat her. Jijii harnesses Ichi's emotional and often violent outbursts to serve his own purposes but at times Ichi acts freely as well.

One such instance occurs when Ichi is riding home on his bicycle when he encounters three young boys bullying a fourth, Takeshi. Unbeknownst to Ichi, Takeshi is the son of "Kaneko," played by Hiroyuki Tanaka (b. 1964) a disgraced police officer who is now one of Kakihara's gang members. The image of the bullying triggers a memory within Ichi of being bullied and he reacts by physically attacking one of the boys, before riding off into the night.

Jijii then provokes Ichi into killing several Anjo gang members by telling him that they are "bad guys" like the ones that raped his teacher. Ichi carries out this mission and the room is soon covered in blood and gore; however, upon leaving Takeshi sees Ichi and thanks him for helping him against the bullies. Shortly thereafter, Kaneko, Takeshi's father, is able to repay his debt by protecting Ichi from an aggressive man working in a brothel Ichi solicits. Ichi and Kaneko then share a meal together, and Ichi causes Kaneko to recall how a member of the Anjo gang too once saved him.

Meanwhile, Kakihara, frustrated by the slow pace of his hunt for Ichi, calls upon a pair of corrupt policemen to assist him, the twins "Jirō" and "Saburō," both played by Suzuki Matsuo (b. 1962). Together the brothers, with Kakihara, go to Myu-Myu, a prostitute that Ryu Long, another member of Jijii's clean-up crew, frequents. The brothers begin by torturing Myu-Myu, but when this fails Saburō, who possesses the animalistic ability to track by scent, sniffs her and begins to chase after Ryu. When the twins discover Ryu, he flees and manages to escape them; however, he runs straight into Kakihara, who does capture him. All three men torture Ryu, looking for a way to find either Ichi or Jijii.

While Kakihara and the twins have been chasing Ryu, Jijii has been working to turn Ichi into an even stronger assassin using Karen. Jijii convinces Karen, who was Anjo's girlfriend, to seduce Ichi by pretending to be the teacher whose rape haunts his memory. Karen's advances and inconsistent story confuse the fragile Ichi, who, in a violent fit, kills her. Jijii then instructs Ichi to kill Kakihara, and travels to the Anjo stronghold himself.

Once at the complex Jijii calls Kakihara to inform him that Ichi is on his way to kill him, but he is spotted by an Anjo gang member, whom he subsequently kills. Toward the end of the film Ichi chases Kakihara to the roof of the building and is followed by Kaneko and his son, Takeshi. All of them confront one another upon the rooftop and eventually Kaneko shoots Ichi's leg causing Ichi's reflexes to engage as they had earlier when the prostitute confronted him, and he kills Kaneko. Killing Kaneko causes Ichi to break down and fall upon the ground weeping and asking for forgiveness, and Takeshi rushes forward to attack the groveling Ichi.

Kakihara watches the entire event unfold and looks at Ichi with disappointment when he realizes that Ichi will not fight him, and sticks steel skewers into his ears. After Kakihara sticks the skewers in his ears the film becomes less clear and open to interpretation. The film depicts Kakihara having his head sliced open by Ichi and then falling from the building, but paradoxically Jijii is also seen examining the dead body and finds it unscathed leading some to think that Kakihara imagines Ichi killing him before throwing himself from the rooftop. Precisely what happens and why is left unclear, and the final scenes wherein Kakihara is depicted sitting in a bath tub, and Jijii's corpse is left hanging from a tree do not serve to undo this ambiguity.

The film came under heavy criticism due to several graphic scenes, such as the interrogation of Suzuki and the rape scenes mentioned above, as well as the general level of gore and violence found throughout. This criticism was parodied at the 2001 Toronto Film Festival where vomit bags were passed out to viewers during the film's screening as part of the Midnight Madness Program. However, the gore also led to the film being banned in three countries: Norway, Malaysia, and Germany.—Josh Dawson

See also Miike, Takashi; One Missed Call films

Bibliography
Miike, Takashi dir. *Ichi the Killer*. Media Blasters, 2001. Film.

INFECTION (2004)
DIRECTOR: Masayuki Ochiai
SCREENPLAY: Masayuki Ochiai, Ryoichi Kimizuka
SPECS: 98 minutes; color

Infection, known as *Kansen* in Japanese, is a 2004 horror film written and directed by Masayuki Ochiai. It is based on a story by Ryōichi Kimizuku and stars Koichi Satō, Masanobu Takashima, Kaho Minami, Yōko Maki, Tae Kimura, and

Shiro Sano. The film tells the story of a group of doctors and nurses who find themselves succumbing to an unprecedented infectious disease that is brought into the ward by an unidentified patient. *Infection* was released in Japan and the United States as part of the J-Horror Theater series that was organized by famed horror film producer Takashige Ichise.

As an ambulance races to deliver a critically ill patient to the nearest hospital, doctors Akiba, played by Kochi Satō, and Uozumi, played by Masanobu Takashima, discuss the troubling conditions of the rural central hospital at which they work. With the perpetual problem of understaffing, dwindling medical supplies, unpaid salaries, and a board of directors who won't return phone calls, the hospital is in dire straits. Overhearing the radio transmission of the ambulance operator, they ignore the request for an ER response having already decided not to take any more patients until a staffing solution can be found. When the ambulance arrives at the hospital, Dr. Akiba tells them that they cannot accept the patient, and an argument ensues before it is cut short by the arrival of Nurse Tachibana, played by Tae Kimura, who informs Akiba that a burn patient in room three has fallen out of bed and is in cardiac arrest.

Akiba tells the ambulance crew to take their patient elsewhere and rushes to room three. There he is met by Uozumi and the head nurse Shiozaki, played by Kaho Minami, and nurses Kirino, played by Yōko Maki, and Tachibana. In the confusion of their lifesaving efforts, Akiba mistakenly calls for a medical injection that proves fatal to the patient, an act that sends the hospital staff into a panic over how to proceed. Although Dr. Akiba is at first willing to accept the consequences of his actions, Dr. Uozumi argues that they must cover up the incident to preserve the integrity and reputation of the hospital, thereby protecting their patients and securing their jobs. Having decided to proceed with the cover-up, the doctors and nurses return to their duties only to discover that the patient with the mysterious ailment has been left in their receiving room by the ambulance staff and that their troubles are far from over.

Infection is a notable example of a film that incorporates a variety of horror tropes into its storyline—in particular those related to the subgenres of the epidemic horror and the rundown hospital horror film. As with many examples of these subgenres, the unfolding of the film's narrative is tightly confined in terms of time and space—occurring over the course of a single day and night within the boundaries of the hospital setting. As the infection spreads inexorably from patient to caregivers, the victims cannot escape the long night shift, the hospital itself, or the infection now running rampant within its walls. Though it plays with the conventions of the classic modern-day infectious-disease horror film that are found in such films as *Rabid* (1977), *Warning Sign* (1985), and *Cabin Fever* (2002), *Infection* does not rely solely on such conventions and instead blends its modern elements with traditional Japanese horror concepts.

For much of its runtime, *Infection* functions as if it is a film whose focus is the exploration of body horror inflicted by disease. However, as the story progresses it becomes clear that while the film's victims believe themselves to be suffering from a deadly viral infection, they are in fact experiencing an elaborate psychic illusion after having been cursed by the vengeful spirit of the hospital patient they accidentally killed. The curse of psychic illusion that results in self-harm is a storytelling device that is deployed in the famous Kabuki play *Tōkaidō Yotsuya kaidan*, as well as the 1959 film version directed by Nobuo Nakagawa and other horror stories. In this sense, *Infection* bridges the gap between traditional horror literature and the fears of contemporary society, as the everyday, relatable problems of the protagonists lead inevitability to lethal karmic backlash, and the story turns to questions of the human cost of economic austerity and the importance of doing the right thing no matter the social consequences.

Infection has received mainly positive reviews. Critics have praised it for its frightening and oppressive atmosphere, unsettling setting, and reliance on viewer imagination to supply some of the film's most horrifying elements, while lamenting its slow pace, somewhat disconnected plot elements, and confusing final act.—Sara L. Sumpter

Bibliography

Ochiai, Masayuki, dir. *Infection*. Lionsgate Films, 2005. DVD.

IREZUMI (1966)

DIRECTOR: Yasuzo Masumura
SCREENPLAY: Kaneto Shindō
SPECS: 86 minutes; color

Released in 1966, *Irezumi* is an intimate, erotic, and mysterious film directed by Yasuzo Masumura, and based upon a novel written by Junichirō Tanizaki. The film tells the story of an obsession between lustful men, a vengeful beautiful woman, and an evil tattoo. Seikichi (Gaku Yamamoto) is a mysterious tattoo artist who draws a monstrous spider on the back of a beautiful geisha named Ōtsuya (Ayako Wakao). After Seikichi marks the back of Ōtsuya she becomes a murderess, avenging the treatment she received from the man who betrayed her—apparently killing her beloved Shinsuke (Akio Hasegawa) and selling her as a prostitute. The revenge of Ōtsuya consists in the assassination of every man who shared her bed as a client. The evil spirit of the spider tattoo compels her to commit the crimes of murder.

Masumura's film entails elements of the classic horror films made in the 1950s and 1960s by great directors such as Kaneto Shindo's *Kuroneko* (1968) and *Onibaba* (1964), Kenji Mizoguchi's *Ugetsu Monogatari* (1953), or Masaki Kobayashi's *Kaidan* (1964). Ōtsuya is an evil woman closely related to spirit folktales that involve vengeful and beautiful women with lustful men. In postwar Japan fantasy films became a perfect canvas to show the complexes of a defeated Japan. Masumura uses this ghostly attractive woman from Japanese folktales as an evil entity who seeks men's destruction in a revengeful mission. Women in fantasy literature or in cinema are divine and wickedly powerful due to their ability to seduce men, yet at the same time, they remain oppressed, even in death, by a patriarchal society. The dangerous woman represents both a construct of male desire and an object of his eternal fear. Ōtsuya is both feared and desired.

In postwar fantasy cinema, such as *Irezumi* or *Onibaba*, women seem to be the *other*, even demonic. Women no longer offer any sort of refuge; mothers and wives were seen as emasculators or an unpleasant reminder of male powerlessness. They signify the despoiled Japan, violated both by the foreign conqueror and by the weakness of Japanese men.—Nieves Moreno Redondo and Fernando Ortiz-Moya

IRIE, TAKAKO

Takako Irie (1911–1995) is one of the most important actresses of Japanese cinema before and after the Second World War. She was born in Tokyo as Hideko Higashibōjō into a wealthy, aristocratic, and politically influential family. At the age of eleven she lost her father, a fact that drastically changed the life of the Higashibōjō family. After graduating in 1927 from an art school in Tokyo she moved to Kyoto to reunite with her elder brother, Yasunaga Higashibōjō, who had been working for the Nikkatsu Studios in Kyoto as an actor, scriptwriter, and film director since 1924. As a scriptwriter he was working with Tomu Uchida and Kenji Mizoguchi, and as a film director he made twenty-four films before he died in 1944. His two most famous films were *Kekkon Higeki* (1929) and *Asakusa Hika* (1932), known as *Asakusa Elegy* in English.

Irie started to perform as a stage actress in Elan Vital Theatre in Kyoto, but soon, the same year of her arrival, she joined the Nikkatsu Studios as a promising film star. The Nikkatsu Studios, the oldest film company in Japan, was the most prestigious studio in Japan in the 1920s. Its samurai films, modern social dramas, sometimes leftist works, and romantic stories were a huge success all over the country. When the Kantō Earthquake of 1923 struck Tokyo, all of the movie industry located in the city and its surroundings was devastated. The Nikkatsu Studio in Kyoto was the only studio that was saved at that time, and so all the cinema companies gathered in the old city until the industry in Tokyo was reconstructed.

Irie made her first debut as a film actress at the age of sixteen in the film *Kechinbo chōja*, directed by Tomu Uchida in 1927, after Uchida saw her at the Elan Vital Theatre. The following year she made eleven silent films, one of them with Kenji Mizoguchi and two of them with Minoru Murata. Her realistic acting style and Westernized fashion look afforded her, in a rather short period of time, significant leading roles in a huge number of silent film masterpieces. From 1927 until her first talkie, *Ganraikō*, in 1934 directed by Shigeyoshi Suzuki, she worked in fifty-seven films. Irie is well known in this period of prewar cinema as a tragic heroine, as in Shigeyoshi Mizoguchi's *Taki no shiraito* (1933) known as *The Water Magician* in English. Irie plays the role of Tomo Mizushima, an independent and beautiful water magician woman working in a circus who sacrifices herself in order to provide economic support to the man she loves—a tragic love story that represents the work of Irie before the war, when strong women were fighting against social inequality in modern Japan.

Irie became a major Nikkatsu star very quickly; however, with the advent of the talkies when she was only twenty-one, she and her brother started their own film production company in 1932, Irie Productions. From 1932 to 1937 Irie produced sixteen films and played the leading roles in several films for Kinema Shinkō, such as *The Water Magician* (Kenji Mizoguchi, 1933); for Nikkatsu Studios, such as *Hakui no kajin* (Yutaka Abe, 1936); or for Toho Studios, such as *A Woman's Sorrows* (Mikio Naruse, 1937). At the height of her popularity, Takako dissolved the company and she and her brother moved together to Tokyo to work for Toho Studios.

She continued working during the Second World War, but the 1940s and 1950s were a difficult time for her. The leading roles she played before the war were decreasing; she lost her three elder brothers during the war and became seriously ill in 1950. When she recovered from her illness she started to work again, but no leading roles were offered to her.

Irie started playing many supporting roles in postwar Japanese cinema; no longer a romantic film star, rather, she reinvented her career. After her recovery she signed with Daiei Studios and started to work in a very popular genre in which Daiei was specializing known as *kaidan eiga*, or ghost stories. Her first debut in horror cinema was a remake from a prewar film about a demon cat woman directed in 1953 by Ryōhei Arai, titled *Kaidan Saga Yashiki*. Her realistic and terrifying performance was a huge success and Irie soon became the queen of *kaidan*. During the 1950s she played in almost thirty films as a demon cat woman or *bakeneko eiga*. The most significant was *Kaidan Saga Yashiki*, but audiences would also recall Irie's performances in *Kaibyō Arima goten* (Ryōhei Arai, 1953) and *Kaibyō yonaki numa* (Shin Sakai, 1957). Despite this success she all but left show business in 1959 and opened a bar in the Ginza district of Tokyo. After her retirement she appeared in two TV series and three films, one of them Akira Kurosawa's *Sanjuro* (1962). One of her most remarkable last performances was in 1983 with Ken Uehara, another classic actor from the silent era, in the science fiction film *The Girl Who Leapt through Time* (Nobuhiko Obayashi).

Irie died in Tokyo in 1995 due to pneumonia at the age of eighty-three. She performed in more than one hundred sixty films: horror, social drama, historic, and romantic films. She started her career as a *Modan Gāru* (modern girl) actress in the late twenties to become an independent producer in the 1930s, and a *bakeneko* actress in postwar Japan. Her daughter Wakaba Irie, born in 1943, became a film and television actress after her mother's retirement.—Nieves Moreno Redondo and Fernando Ortiz-Moya

ITŌ, JUNJI (1963–)

Junji Itō (b. 31 July 1963) is a Japanese manga artist specializing in horror comics. He was born in Gifu. Before breaking into the manga industry, Itō worked as a dental technician, a job he retired from in 1990 to focus on his manga career. His work tends toward body horror, with characters undergoing grotesque and painful transformations, usually without any clear cause. Itō identifies Kazuo Umezu as one of his biggest inspirations and cites Hideshi Hino and H. P. Lovecraft as other major influences.

Itō's manga are extremely gruesome, with many of his characters suffering gory dismemberments or otherworldly mutations. Hair is a prominent motif in Itō's work, becoming monstrous and murderous and acting on its own accord. Itō often explores characters who are slowly being driven mad by compulsion, drawn to horrific ends by unseen and unknowable forces. His work can also, however, be darkly comedic, with his transformations often taking ludicrous (albeit macabre) forms: a man in *Uzumaki* transforms into a giant snail, while the protagonists of *Gyo* must escape from a shark on mechanic legs battering down their door.

Itō's first published manga series is *Tomie*, a long-running series that focuses on an immortal high school girl named Tomie. She has the power to make all men fall in love with her, which inevitably leads to obsessive and violent behaviors. Although she can be killed (and frequently is, due to the jealous rages she inspires), Tomie possesses a remarkable regenerative capacity. Not only will she recover from any damage she suffers, but when dismembered the separate pieces produce individual Tomies.

In its first year of publication, *Tomie* won the Umezu Kazuo Award, named after and judged by Umezu Kazuo. Itō has identified Umezu as his favorite manga artist and one of his biggest influences; in 2014, he wrote an autobiographical manga "Umezu Sensei and Me," about his childhood adoration of Umezu's manga and his star-struck experiences with Umezu.

Tomie has been adapted, between 1999 and 2011, into nine films: *Tomie* (1999, dir. Ataru Oikawa), *Tomie: Another Face* (1999, dir. Toshirō Inomata), *Tomie: Replay* (2000, dir. Fujirō Mitsuishi), *Tomie: Re-birth* (2001, dir. Takashi Shimizu), *Tomie: Forbidden Fruit* (2002, dir. Shun Nakahara), *Tomie: Beginning* (2005, dir. Ataru Oikawa), *Tomie: Revenge* (2005, Ataru Oikawa), *Tomie vs. Tomie* (2007, dir. Tomohiro Kubo), and *Tomie: Unlimited* (2011, dir. Noboru Iguchi).

Uzumaki (*Spiral*), written between 1998 and 1999, details the curse that has befallen a fictional Japanese town, Kurōzu-cho (Black vortex town). The citizens of Kurōzu-cho are tormented by spirals; some are driven mad by obsessive fixations on spiral shapes, others find their bodies contorted into horrific spiral forms. One of the manga's main characters, Kirie, finds her hair curling into shapes that hypnotize other citizens. Eventually the town is destroyed, revealing the ruins of an ancient city dominated by spiral motifs. No explanation for the curse is ever discovered, and it is assumed that the cycle will continue onward indefinitely.

Uzumaki was adapted into a 2000 film, directed by the Ukrainian-born Higuchinsky (born Akihiro Higuchi). The film adapts several of the episodes of the manga, although the ending, which was written before the manga had completed its run, does not feature the ancient city of Itō's manga. The manga also inspired two video games, both published on the Bandai WonderSwan, *Uzumaki: Denshi kaiki hen* (*Spiral: Power Vision Strange Edition*) and *Uzumaki: Noroi shimyurēshon* (*Spiral: Curse Simulation*), both released in 2000.

In Itō's *Gyo* (*Fish*), published in 2001 and 2002, half-machine fish monsters invade Japan, releasing an overwhelming and infectious stench. The fish are the result of biological warfare prototypes from World War II; the machines used metal legs to move virus-infected hosts around to spread the deadly odor. The ship carrying the prototypes was sunk during the war, and the machines grafted themselves onto marine life. The grotesque sea life, walking on spider-like metal legs, attack Japan, and begin transforming humans into similar monstrosities. In 2012, a sixty-minute original video animation based on the manga, directed by Takayuki Hirao, was released.

Itō's short manga stories have been collected in several anthology series, including the sixteen-volume *Itō Junji kyōfu manga korekushon* (*Itō Junji Horror Manga Collection*) and the ten-volume *Kyōfu hakubatsukan* (*Horror Museum*).

The first two volumes of both anthologies collect the *Tomie* stories. Alongside the *Tomie* collections, the third volumes of each series, *Nikuiro no kai* (*Flesh-Colored Horror*) and *Yaneura no nagai kami* (*The Long Hair in the Attic*), have been published in English. In addition to the *Tomie* films, several of Itō's other manga have been adapted into films or television dramas, including *Senritsu no senritsu* (*The Fearsome Melody*, 1992, dir. Takumi Kimizuga), *Nagai yume* (*Long Dream*, 2000, dir. Higuchinsky), *Kakashi* (*Scarecrow*, 2001, dir. Norio Tsuruta), *Umeku haisuikan* (*The Groaning Drain*, 2004, dir. Ataru Oikawa), and *Tomio* (2004), directed by Itō himself.—Nicholas Bestor

IZUMIYA, SHIGERU (1948–)

Shigeru Izumiya is a well-known Japanese folk musician, actor, director, and *tarento* (or talent, an individual considered to be a bankable star). Izumiya was born on 11 May 1948 in Aomori Prefecture, but was raised and educated in Tokyo. Although Izumiya is rumored to have dropped out of high school, and to have taken up folk music based solely on the fact that his electric guitar was destroyed in a fire, Izumiya's long and multifaceted artistic career has made him an easily recognized face on the Japanese pop culture scene.

Izumiya's career began in the 1970s, where he emerged as a folk musician; his musical career and genre, which has led to his involvement in a number of films and television shows, has been defined as part of the counterculture of 1970s and 1980s Japan, and earned him the reputation as being a "protest" musician. In 1975 Shigeru became a founding member of the label For Life Records. His musical career has heavily influenced his acting and film career, and has connected him to projects in which he plays multiple on- and off-screen roles.

Beginning in the late 1970s, Shigeru's career shifted more into acting, and his early years saw him tied to a number of breakthrough movies and directors, including horror films and directors who would go on to create horror cinema. In 1979, Izumiya played the lead role of Genji in Shohei Imamura's *Enjanaika*—a film that focused on the lower class and the political and social turmoil that led up to the Meiji Restoration's start in 1868. Izumiya's career in horror cinema is largely influenced by the cyberpunk and punk subgenre; even working with Sōgo Ishii (Gakuryū Ishii, b. 1957) on a number of projects. As an actor, Izumiya played roles in *Kōkō dai panikku* (*Panic in High School*, 1976), and *Bakuretsu toshi* (*Burst City*, 1982), and provided the music for *Kuruizaki sandā rōdo* (*Crazy Thunder Road*, 1980), which won a Blue Ribbon for design and art direction. Since then, Izumiya's acting career has included numerous television and film appearances, including a role in *Gojira: Fainaru uōzu* (Godzilla: Final Wars, 2004), and providing the voice for the tanuki *Gonta* in Hayao Miyazaki's environmental fantasy epic *Heisei tanuki gassen pompoko* (*Pom Poko*, 1994).

After working on the musical score for *Crazy Thunder Road* and working on *Burst City*, Izumiya turned to his own writing and directorial pursuits. In 1982 he released *The Harlem Valentine Day* (credited as writer, producer, director, and composer), a sci-fi thriller. Following this experience, Shigeru went on to work on *Desu pawuda (Death Powder*, 1986) a movie considered to be the precursor to cyberpunk and experimental horror films in Japan. Death Powder's avant-garde narrative, punk-rock soundtrack, and experimental directorial choices were entirely guided by Izumiya, who wrote the screenplay based on his own original concept, controlled and contributed to the musical selections of the movie with tracks such as "Scar People" (1986), and served as producer. Additionally, Izumiya starred in *Death Powder* as Harima, a man who is the first to be affected by the titular death powder and to succumb to the android Guernica.

Shigeru Izumiya's acting career has been largely shaped by the fact that he is typically cast as the "heavy-handed" figure, or the yakuza type; many of his credits include small or recurring roles on television dramas. Izumiya also often appears on panel and talk shows and has hosted a variety of programs as a result of his popularity as a musician, artist, and an actor.

Aside from his role in shaping the course of Japanese cyberpunk horror films, Izumiya has also contributed to a variety of charitable events, largely in support of disaster relief, despite his reputation as a renegade, antiestablishment folk musician. For example, following the 1993 Hokkaido Earthquake, he donated all royalties from his song "Naze, kono jidai ni?" (Why in this era?) to the UNICEF Japan fund for disaster and victim relief. Additionally, after the Nagasaki Mt. Fugen eruption in 1994 he participated in relief concerts and victim spotlight specials. Most recently he also joined with other Japanese artists and musicians to help show support and provide aid for those affected by the Tohoku Earthquake in 2011.

Shigeru Izumiya's career continues to flourish, as he explores his musical, acting, and creative talents. In 2009 he provided the theme for visionary animation director Mamoru Oishii's *Miyamoto Musashi: Sōken ni haseru yume* (*Miyamoto Musashi: The Dream of the Last Samurai*, 2009), an animated film following the life of the legendary Japanese figure. Izumiya continues to be a face seen regularly in the pop culture circles.—Megan Negrych

See also Death Powder

• J •

JIGOKU (1960)
DIRECTOR: Nobuo Nakagawa
SCREENPLAY: Nobuo Nakagawa, Ichirō Miyagawa
SPECS: 101 minutes; color

As long as we have conceived of evil, its punishment and an underworld, we have sought to represent these torments in art. Dating from the late twelfth to thirteenth centuries, for example, are several vivid illustrations that would prove of historical importance to modern filmic representations. Executed with subtle lines and embellished with a variety of dark, rich colors that simultaneously re-create an air of oppression and a sense of transcendental peacefulness, these include *The Hungry Ghosts Scroll* (Gaki Zōshi), the *Hell Scroll* (Jigoku Zōshi) and the *Extermination of Evil* (Hekijae). Each horizontal handscroll depicts the belief that "crimes" committed in this life cause people to be reborn into one of the realms of suffering, among them the eight greater hells and the sixteen lesser hells. It is within this visual tradition, at least in part, that the film *Jigoku* (1960, Hell, aka *The Sinners of Hell*), directed by Nobuo Nakagawa (1905–1984), arose. Just as shockingly disturbing and outrageous as it is poetic, it stars Utako Mitsuya (1936–2004) and Shigeru Amachi (1931–1985). The film was not expected to be well received, given the reputation of Shintoho Studio for churning out low-budget gore films, but the director and the crew went to extraordinary lengths to set this film apart from other horror films of the period.

The story, meant primarily to provide a frame from which to hang a series of creepy set designs, concerns a young theology student, Shirō Shimizu, who flees the scene of a hit-and-run accident. He is plagued with such an overwhelming sense of guilt that his courtship of Yukiko suffers. She is, coincidentally, the daughter of a professor who lectures on Buddhist concepts of Hell. The first half of the film sets the stage for the descent into a bleak, increasingly horrific and expressionistic Hell, littered with sickly blue and red light where lovers struggle among a field of jagged glass shards, the damned run across fields of wriggling hands and feet, and many of those condemned to eternal suffering have their heads and wrists shackled to boards the shape of coffin lids. Shirō himself enters Hell and is sentenced to the Eight Realms of Hell by "Lord Enma" for his sins.

In detailed and graphic scenes of the region, Nakagawa offers a vision of an underworld of torture and degradation: as Shirō runs through each level, for example, he encounters each of his acquaintances, who suffer, in gruesome fashion, a variety of punishments, from being boiled and burned alive, dismembered and flayed, or cut apart and beaten by ogres, only to be revived to suffer anew. While caught in a vortex of damned souls, he finds his baby daughter, left helplessly rotating on the Buddhist wheel of life. Lord Enma gives him a single chance to save her, but he cannot. The moment, precisely nine o'clock, represents the time when all of his friends and family had passed. In a final scene, Yukiko can be seen standing erect and smiling in peaceful light. As she and others call to Shirō, lotus petals suggesting a newfound emotional and moral purity, fall all around.

With its overreliance on graphic images of torture and torment in Hell, *Jigoku* is notable for separating itself from other Japanese horror films of the era such as the anthology horror *Kwaidan* (1964, *Kaidan*) or *Onibaba* (1964). A monumental achievement in the genre, in large part because of its striking departure from traditional Japanese ghost stories, the film shocked—and continues to do so—the larger landscape of contemporary world horror cinema. The remake, also entitled *Jigoku* (1970) was directed by acclaimed Nikkatsu Roman porno director Tatsumi Kuashiro (1927–1995) for Toei Studio. In what has become a cult classic, it was once more remade under the title of *Japanese Hell* (1999), by Teruo Ishii (1924–2005), the Japanese master of all things perverted and taboo.—James Wren

Bibliography

Hearn, Lafcadio. *Kwaidan: Stories and Studies of Strange Things*. Tokyo: Tuttle Publishing, 2005.
Nakagawa, Nobuo, dir. *Jigoku*. Criterion Collection, 2006. DVD.
Sharp, Jasper. *Behind the Pink Curtain: The Complete History of Japanese Sex Cinema*. Guildford, UK: FAB Press, 2008.

JISSŌJI, AKIO (1937–2006)

Akio Jissōji is one of the most distinctive visual artists in the field of Japanese horror-fantasy-SF cinema and TV. He is famous for bringing an almost avant-garde, expressionist sensibility to children's shows, in particular several key episodes of the original *Ultraman* (1966) and *Ultra Seven* (1967), working closely with the special-effects team under the supervision of Eiji Tsuburaya (1901–1970). Less well known are a series of visually striking horror, SF, and dramatic feature films he has made over his roller coaster ride of a career.

Born in 1937 in Yotsuya, Tokyo, Jissōji grew up in Tsingtao, China, and was repatriated along with his family to Japan after 1945. A French Literature major at Waseda University, he initially sought a career in diplomatic service, following in the footsteps of his father, but as a college student he was bitten by the "movie bug." He belonged to the Waseda cinema club (he was one of the few who could read and translate French-language essays in *Cahier du Cinema*, according to recollections of his friends). He joined Radio Tokyo in 1959 and soon branched off into the burgeoning field of TV direction. Jissōji's experimental approach soon clashed with the producers: he broke many conventions of early TV drama, such as substituting a flagrantly "fake" studio background for a location shoot, or showing a long take of actors eating food without any meaningful dialogue. However, his unconventional, almost surrealistic style was in fact welcomed by Tsuburaya and his team, who wanted a director whose imaginative power had the capacity to visualize something as strange (or ridiculous) as a 150-foot-tall space alien with a pair of glowing headlight eyes and a sleek, silver-and-red body design fighting monsters as large as himself.

Jissōji brought his inimitable personal touches to the episodes of *Ultraman* he directed, including the genuinely disturbing "My Home Is Earth" (originally aired on 18 December 1966), in which the mummy-like hideous monster "Jamira" is revealed to be a mutated Earthman left to die by his team of space explorers on a planet with no water, and *Ultra Seven*, including the unforgettably and incongruously beautiful episode "The Targeted Town" (19 November 1967), about an alien menace planting madness-inducing drugs in cigarettes smoked by denizens of an ordinary Japanese town. While the station brass continued to be irritated with Jissōji's "crazy" directional style, the latter not surprisingly gained a sizable fandom, who spoke of the "Jissōji magical touch."

In 1968 and 1969, Jissōji directed four episodes of *The Mystery File* (1968–1969), an SF-tinged contemporary horror series, well received and subsequently endowed with a cult-classic status. In between these episodes, he also debuted as a feature film director with *When the Dusk Approaches* (1968), a dark drama about four students who play a dangerous psychological game involving suicide by gas poisoning, based on a screenplay by Nagisa Ōshima. He continued to direct a series of challenging, erotically charged art-house films, often produced by ATG, the premier independent film company of 1960s and 1970s Japan, culminating in *Asaki yumemishi* (1974).

In the 1980s and 1990s, he kept working, mainly for TV and commercials as well as soft-core erotic films and occasional feature assignments. Notable among his works from this period are *Tokyo: The Last Megalopolis* (1988), a star-studded major production from Toho with an H. R. Giger–designed Buddhist demon making a climactic appearance, and two adaptations of Edogawa Ranpo's voyeuristic classic mysteries, *A Watcher in the Attic* (1992) and *Murder on D Street* (1998), with a heavy emphasis on decadent sexuality. His innovative spirit and eye for beauty, often conjoined to the grotesque, did not fail him in the new millennium, as evidenced by the segment he directed, "The Mirror Hell," in the anthology *Rampo Noir* (2005), a freewheeling adaptation of Edogawa's impressionistic short story, with a new quasi–science fictional wrinkle to the story that is vintage Jissōji.

To many SF-horror fans' sorrow, Jissōji died in 2006 due to stomach cancer. He remained active until the end of his life, and one can only imagine the kind of distinctive and visually striking Japanese horror films he might have continued to make into 2010s, including the results of planned collaboration with the mystery writer Natsuhiko Kyōkoku.—Kyu Hyun Kim

JOYŪ-REI (1996)

DIRECTOR: Hideo Nakata
SCREENPLAY: Hiroshi Takahashi
SPECS: 74 minutes; color

Joyū-rei (*Don't Look Up*), is a 1996 horror film directed by Hideo Nakata from a screenplay by Hiroshi Takahashi. It is based on a story by Hideo Nakata. It stars Yūrei Yanagi, Yasuyo Shirashima, Kei Ishibashi, Ren Oosugi, Takanori Kikuchi, and Dan Li. The film follows the course of an ill-fated movie production, whose cast and crew are menaced by the malevolent spirit of an actress that haunts the studio they are shooting in.

During preproduction for a proposed period film, the director and crew film a test sequence involving the film's two main characters, Hitomi Kurokawa, played by Yasuyo Shirashima and Saori Murakami, played by Kei Ishibashi.

Later, the film crew and studio executives view the test footage in a private screening room, only to discover that it has been recorded over older film footage that has bled through their scenes. The old footage, of another period production, shows a woman holding a conversation with a man, intercut with scenes of a young boy climbing up the stairs of a dilapidated house. Close-ups of the woman reveal the figure of another woman standing behind her, laughing maniacally. Later, the film's director, Toshio Murai, played by Yūrei Yanagi, goes over the footage with the assistance of the film's cinematographer, played by Ren Oosugi, to determine how it got there. Struck with an inexplicable sense of déjà vu, Murai takes possession of the damaged footage and examines it carefully, telling his assistant, played by Takanori Kikuchi, that he saw the footage once before when he was a child. He states that though he cannot remember the story clearly, he was deeply frightened by it. He asks his assistant to do some research on the footage, the actors appearing in it, and when and where it was broadcast.

Given the go-ahead by the studio, the film begins production on a tight schedule. Murai and Hitomi, the lead actress, begin to have feelings for each other, while Saori, the novice supporting actress, spends her free time exploring the studio. Murai and other members of the cast and crew begin to catch glimpses of a woman walking around the rafters of the studio set. At the same time, they experience repeated malfunctions with the camera equipment. When a tragic accident strikes the set, however, Murai determines that the spirit's ill will is focused on his main actress, Hitomi—a realization that leads him to set off on a race against time to unravel the mystery and save the woman he loves.

Joyū-rei is the first feature film production of Hideo Nakata, best known for his work on the internationally successful Ring franchise. It predates *Ring* by two years and also marks the second collaboration between Nakata and screenwriter Hiroshi Takahashi, who would write the screenplay for *Ring*. As a precursor, though not a prequel, to *Ring*, *Joyū-rei* makes use of several narrative and visual elements that would also be employed in the later film. Though both films deal with the traditional story of a vengeful spirit, the inclusion of this iconography in *Ring* is particularly notable in its application to source material that does not rely on such traditional elements. Where the *Ring* novel presents the curse of a restless spirit as a biological terror, the *Ring* film presents it as a supernatural one, thereby altering a modern treatment of horror into a historical treatment in synch with—rather than a subversion of—traditional Japanese horror motifs.

These traditional horror motifs are strongly present in *Joyū-rei*. Though the spirit's motivations are never fully understood, by the characters or by the audience, it is strongly implied that her curse has not only survived through attachment to a specific location, but also has spread itself through the medium of film—a theme that is a cornerstone of the *Ring* story. Furthermore, when the spirit appears, she is always shown as a woman with long, black hair dressed in white—horror iconography that was first codified in the Edo period (1615–1868) and that is explicitly contrasted with the depiction of the living actresses working on the present-day film production. And perhaps most significantly, as with *Ring*, the peril that the main character faces in *Joyū-rei* stems from a failure to understand what it is that the spirit truly wants. While in *Ring* there is a character that remains alive to ultimately solve that mystery, in *Joyū-rei* it is left unexplained.

Joyū-rei, though well-received by film industry professionals, was not a great success in theaters, and it has received extremely limited worldwide distribution. It has never been released on DVD in the United States, although a remake of the film—directed by Fruit Chan and starring Rachael Murphy, Reshad Strik, and Eli Roth—was made in 2009 and released direct-to-DVD in 2010.—Sara Sumpter

See also Ringu

Bibliography
Nakata, Hideo, dir. *Joyū-rei*. Bandai Visual, 2010. DVD.

JU-ON films

The Ju-on franchise is a popular horror film series that details the creation, enactment, and spread of a curse that—engendered by an act of extreme violence—reaches out to all who come into contact with it to destroy their lives. Films in the series have been produced since 1998. The franchise includes short films *4444444444* and *Katasumi* (both of which were released in 1998), made-for-television movies *Ju-on: The Curse* and *Ju-on: The Curse 2* (both released in 2000), and theatrical releases *Ju-on: The Grudge* (2002) and *Ju-on: The Grudge 2* (2003). There are also three American remakes—*The Grudge* (2004), *The Grudge 2* (2006), and *The Grudge 3* (2009), as well as a series of spin-off films—*Ju-on: White Ghost* (2009), *Ju-on: Black Ghost* (also 2009), and *Ju-on: The Beginning of the End* (2014)—in the franchise catalog.

The original short films, made-for-television movies, and theatrical releases were all written and directed by Takashi Shimizu, while the first two American remakes were directed by Shimizu from a screenplay adapted by Stephen Susco. The third American remake was directed by Toby Wilkins from a script by Brad Keene, and neither Shimizu nor Susco were involved in the production. *Ju-on: White Ghost*, written and directed by Ryuta Miyake, and *Ju-on: Black Ghost*, written and directed by Mari Asato, were coproduced by Shimizu and Takashige Ichise for the tenth anniversary of the Ju-on franchise and released together as a double feature, while *Ju-on: The Beginning of the End* was directed by Masayuki Ochiai from a script by Ochiai and Ichise. Over the years, several well-known Japanese actors have been involved in the franchise, including—but not limited to—Yūrei Yanagi, Yumi Yoshiyuki, Chiaki Kuriyama, Tomohiro Kaku, Taro Suwa, Denden, Megumi Okina, Misaki Ito, Misa Uehara, Kanji Tsuda, Noriko Sakai, Chiharu Niiyama, Kei Horie, and Ryo Ishibashi. Takako Fuji and Takashi Matsuyama, who portray the wife and husband whose violent altercation forms the basis for the series' supernatural curse, appear in all of the feature-length films—both Japanese and American—directed by Shimizu, while three separate actors have portrayed their young son over the course of the series.

Over dinner after a long day at work, schoolteacher Shunsuke Kobayashi, played by Yūrei Yanagi, expresses his concern about a student, Toshio Saeki, played by Ryōta Koyama, who has failed to come to class for several days and whose parents have not contacted the school. He notes that the boy's mother, Kayako, played by Takako Fuji, was a college classmate although he has never met the father and asks his pregnant wife, Manami, played by Yue, if she remembers Kayako. Manami, however, only remembers that there was something strange about her. The next day, after Toshio has once again failed to come to class, Kobayashi resolves to go to his house and see what the matter is. When no one answers the doorbell or responds to his call, he walks around the side of the house and finds Toshio looking despondently out of the bathroom window into the garden. Toshio responds listlessly to Kobayashi's questions and, when asked about his parents, collapses on the floor—leading Kobayashi to enter the house and look after him.

Eventually, Kobayashi is able to get Toshio to tell him that his parents have gone out shopping together, but Kobayashi remains confused and unsettled by the situation. The house is in a state of violent disorder, and Toshio himself has recent injuries that have been patched up with a first aid kit, still situated on the living room floor. After Toshio once more falls silent, Kobayashi explores the downstairs rooms of the house, trying to get a sense of what might have happened, but when he returns to the living room he finds Toshio gone. Looking for him upstairs, Kobayashi hears the sound of voices coming from a back bedroom—Toshio speaking to his mother and his mother responding to his many questions. However, Kobayashi finds only Toshio when he opens the door. Thinking he heard Kayako speaking somewhere behind him, Kobayshi explores the other rooms on the upstairs floor.

In the main bedroom Kobayashi finds Kayako's diary and reads it, discovering that she had been desperately in love with him since their college days. Unnerved by the revelations of the diary, Kobayashi is about to leave when he notices a swarm of flies buzzing around the closet. Taking a closer look, he discovers Kayako's beaten and bloody body hidden in the attic. In a panic, he grabs Toshio and attempts to flee, but before he can escape the house the powerful curse reaches out to claim him. He receives a phone call from Kayako's husband, informing him that his wife is dead, and—collapsing in the hall—is found and killed by Kayako, as Toshio looks on. Later, a new family moves into the Saeki house and becomes subject to the curse, and then another, and then another as the malevolent ill will that lingers there gradually spreads.

None of the first six films in the Ju-on series are remakes. Instead, each film is a collection of interrelated stories—presented as nonchronologically ordered vignettes—that follow the effects of the curse as it radiates forward in time and space, claiming the lives of more and more people. The first two short films constitute prequels to the first two made-for-television movies (although the events that they portray take place well after the death of Kobayashi), while the theatrical releases act as sequels. With the exception of *Ju-on: The Curse 2*, which begins with the final two vignettes of the first made-for-television movie, each film contains entirely original content that references, but does not rehash, previous entries in the film franchise. Similarly, the American remakes function more like best-of anthologies, taking pieces from each of the films and weaving them into a new, though familiar, framework, before taking the story in a different direction, while the first two Japanese spinoffs deal with entirely different stories altogether. Only the most recent installment of the franchise, Masayuki Ochiai's *Ju-on: The Beginning of the End*, which reboots the story of the Saeki family with an entirely new cast, could be said to be a true remake.

At the heart of the Ju-on series is a classic narrative motif that has its roots in early Japanese myths, legends, and folktales: vengeful spirits who cannot rest but instead kill both those who have wronged them and all others that happen across their path. References to the spiritually polluting nature of death and the ability of malignant curses to linger when someone has died violently or in the grip of powerful emotions, such as a great anger or a debilitating despair appear in Japan's earliest extant historical texts. Moreover, the volatile irrationality of the dead can be seen in Japan's early mythological tales, while the notion that those men and women who have died in the midst of strong emotions become dangerous vengeful spirits can be found in Japanese legends and literature alike. Though stories of dangerous vengeful spirits are found in literary collections as early as the eighth century, it was the ghost story boom of the Edo period (1615–1868), with its many literary collections, Kabuki plays, and *ukiyo-e* prints, that led to a codification of the story tropes and visual iconography found in the Ju-on franchise and other J-horror films of the late 1990s and early 2000s—most notably *Ring* (1998) and *Dark Water* (2002).

The primary antagonist of the Ju-on franchise is the ghost of Kayako, a young housewife brutally murdered by her husband in a jealous rage and a figure with strong ties to the history of Japanese horror. The ghost of the resentful woman who takes revenge on those who have wronged her is a standard character in Japanese ghost stories and folktales. Though in many early examples of the genre the women often died while bearing enmity for having been abandoned by their husbands—usually to marry a younger, richer woman and/or pursue a better life in the capital—later examples of the trope began to incorporate more overt acts of violence, with husbands or potential families-in-law conspiring to attack or murder the women to get them out of the way. This trope, prevalent in Japanese literature, also made its way into Japanese cinema—with notable examples of the abandoned woman in "The Black Hair" segment of Masaki Kobayashi's *Kwaidan* (1964) and the murdered woman in Nobuo Nakagawa's *Tōkaidō Yotsuya kaidan* (1959), both of which were based on much earlier tales.

The desire to abandon was not the only motivating factor in tales about violence against women, however. In one of the Edo period's most famous stories, *Banchō sarayashiki* (The plate mansion), the woman is murdered because she refuses the amorous advances of her employer. Kayako's death fits within this category. Unlike the vengeful spirits of *Kwaidan* and *Tōkaidō Yotsuya kaidan*, Kayako's husband, Takeo, does not kill her out of a capricious desire to be rid of her but while in the midst of a possessive jealous rage. Nor is Kayako his only victim. Takeo also kills their elementary-school age son, Toshio, and—as is ultimately revealed over the course of the film series—Toshio's cat.

In the Ju-on films, Toshio's death and his cat's are merged. Toshio rarely speaks, but he often cries and yowls like a cat when the films' protagonists are not looking. This is a nod to the *bakeneko* (monster cat) theme that is another staple of Japanese horror stories, and whose origins can also be found in early folktale collections. The incorporation of this motif is not merely a nod to traditional tales, however. It is also a nod to earlier J-horror films. Toshio is possessed by the soul of his cat, who takes revenge on his behalf in much the same way that cats are shown to take human form and seek revenge on behalf of murdered human spirits in such films as *Ghost Cat of Arima Palace* (1953), *The Ghost-Cat Cursed Wall* (1958), *Kuroneko* (1968), and many others—several of which are based on Edo-period Kabuki plays and ghost stories.

Just as the vengeful spirits of the Ju-on franchise owe their narrative framework to earlier tales and films, they owe their visual representation to said works as well. Kayako is consistently depicted with visual elements that have been found in Edo-period ghost prints and Kabuki plays and in modern horror films. The iconography of the traditional Japanese ghost, or *yūrei*, includes long, unkempt, black hair, limp hands, and no feet. They wear white, undecorated kimonos and are often depicted with an unhealthy pallor—an effect that was achieved through the application of blue makeup in Kabuki theater. These elements are in sharp contrast to the representation of living women in the Edo period, who are depicted with elaborate, upswept hairstyles and often shown clasping fans or parasols in their hands. These women wear polychromic kimonos with complex and symbolic designs, and in many cases their feet are displayed peeking out from beneath their clothes—a motif that was perceived as risqué. Kayako, like the ghosts of Edo-period prints and plays, is always shown with long, unbound, black hair, and in many scenes her hair is the first thing that becomes visible to her victims. She wears a white dress, has a starkly unhealthy pallor, and is generally depicted crawling or limping—a characteristic that echoes the legless quality of traditional ghosts.

The reliance on traditional ghost story elements was a deliberate choice on the part of writer-director Takashi Shimizu, who has stated that his primary goal with these films was to create something that he personally found scary. As a child, Shimizu was an avid fan of classic ghost stories, but when he began watching horror films he found most of them startling rather than genuinely frightening on a psychological level. Thus, the Ju-on films constitute an attempt to craft a fundamentally frightening horror story that was both original and familiar to Japanese audiences. For Shimizu, the familiarity of the traditional ghost story themes and imagery that are incorporated into the Ju-on narrative is a crucial component of its fear factor, as nothing is more frightening to the Japanese audience than a random encounter with a vengeful spirit whose wrath cannot be escaped.

Though the randomness of the curse is a defining characteristic of the Japanese film series, all the instances of arbitrary violence were removed from the first American remake. This was done against Shimizu's wishes on the grounds that an American audience would not accept randomness as an explanation for violence. As a result, while the original series featured a number of victims who had never set foot in the house but nevertheless had the misfortune to cross paths with Kayako or Toshio while they were on the hunt for someone else, in the first American remake only the people who actually entered the house were subject to the curse. Additionally, in the original story Kayako was presented as a victim of unpredictable circumstances, whose tragic love for Kobayashi had an essentially rational basis. By contrast, in the American remake she was given a backstory that indicated she was dangerously unbalanced even before her death.

The Ju-on series has proved to be a wildly popular and enduring franchise. Though individual entries have sometimes been poorly reviewed, the series as a whole is considered one of the landmarks of, and writer-director Takashi Shimizu an important and innovative figure in, the J-horror film genre. Of the films in the franchise catalog, *Ju-on: The Curse* and *Ju-on: The Grudge* have been the most highly rated. Sam Raimi, whose production company Ghost House Pictures produced the American remakes, has called *Ju-on: The Grudge* a master class on horror scares, suspense, and the development of a creepy atmosphere. Though the made-for-television movies have not been released in the United States, the short films *4444444444* and *Katasumi* were included on the unrated director's cut edition of *The Grudge* DVD release, and the theatrical films have both been released on DVD by *Lionsgate Films*.—Sara Sumpter

See also 4444444444; Shimizu, Takashi

Bibliography

Asato, Mari, and Ryūta Miyake, dirs. *Ju-on: White Ghost/Black Ghost*. Well Go USA, 2011. DVD.

Ochiai, Masayuki, dir. *Ju-on: The Beginning of the End*. NBC Universal Entertainment Japan, 2014. DVD.

Shimizu, Takashi, dir. *Ju-on: The Curse*. Toei Video Company, 2000. DVD.

———. *Ju-on: The Curse 2*. Toei Video Company, 2000. DVD.

———. *Ju-on: The Grudge*. Lionsgate, 2004. DVD.

———. *The Grudge*. Sony Pictures Home Entertainment, 2005. DVD.

———. *The Grudge* (Unrated Extended Director's Cut). Sony Pictures Home Entertainment, 2005. DVD.

———. *Ju-on: The Grudge 2*. Lionsgate, 2006. DVD.

———. *The Grudge 2*. Sony Pictures Home Entertainment, 2007. DVD.

———. *The Grudge 2* (Unrated Extended Director's Cut). Sony Pictures Home Entertainment, 2007. DVD.

Wilkins, Toby, dir. *The Grudge 3*. Sony Pictures Home Entertainment, 2009. DVD.

JU-ON: THE BEGINNING OF THE END (2014)

DIRECTOR: Masayuki Ochiai

SCREENPLAY: Masayuki Ochiai, Takashige Ichise

SPECS: 91 minutes; color

The success of *Sadako 3D* (2012), directed by Tsutomu Hanabusa, rejuvenated a franchise that had been dormant since the Norio Tsuruta film *Ring 0: Birthday* (2000)—opening the door for a number of other genre reboots. Aside from two shorter stand-alone features released to mark the tenth anniversary of the franchise, the last Japanese installment in the Ju-on series was the 2003 *Ju-on: The Grudge 2*. Series creator Takashi Shimizu directed the first two US remakes, but left before the release of *The Grudge 3* (2009), which was helmed by British director Toby Wilkins. In 2013 it was announced that producer Takashige Ichise, who has been involved with the series since the first V-Cinema installments, was working on a new Ju-on movie, with *Parasite Eve* (1997) director Masayuki Ochiai overseeing the project, cowritten by Ichise and Ochiai.

The film begins with police and social workers breaking into a house and discovering the body of Toshio Saeki, played by Kai Kobayashi, a young boy who has been dead for several days. Adding to the suspense and mystery, Toshio's parents are also missing.

On a parallel storyline, Yui, played by Nozomi Sasaki, is a young substitute teacher who has just been offered her first permanent teaching post. Concerned that one of her pupils, Toshio, has been absent for several days, Yui goes to his house, an action that brings her into contact with the evil that resides there.

Sensing that something is wrong with her, Yui's boyfriend begins investigating the house and the events that occurred there. A group of teenage girls are also drawn into the matter when they decide to check out the rumors that the place may be haunted. Only one of them believes the stories, but all four of them fall victim to the curse.

Like the earlier episodes in the series, *Ju-on: The Beginning of the End* is centered around a single house where a number of murders were committed, leapfrogging back and forth through time in an ever-widening web around the house. Although maintaining the same approach, the script reworks the story, keeping certain elements but altering others and introducing new ideas. Even when he's referencing scenes from the earlier films, Ochiai handles the material very differently, preferring to shoot in well-lit areas, a marked contrast to the gloomy interiors used by Takashi Shimizu. He is also a more energetic director, drawing stronger and more mobile performances from his cast and favoring sharper, quicker camera movements. This is not necessarily a superior approach, but it's clear that Ochiai is trying to put his own stamp upon the film rather than attempting to reproduce the same feel as Shimizu's films.

Ochiai does have at least one advantage over his predecessor: he is not limited by the same financial considerations. Shimizu did his best to overcome the obvious low budgets that were available to him, and for the most part he succeeded. However, when making *Ju-on: The Beginning of the End*, Ochiai clearly had access to the kind of budget that Shimizu did not have. This is most apparent in the special effects, which are (even allowing for technological differences) far superior to those seen in any of the Japanese Ju-on films. The most obvious example appears when Ochiai restages the memorably unpleasant death and mutilation of Asumi Miwa from the very first V-Cinema installment. Hampered by poor computer-generated imagery, this scene was never quite as effective as it could have been, but here it is enlarged upon and supported by excellent special effects, giving it the kind of impact it deserves. These differences, combined with Ochiai's own personalized take on the material, ensure that *Ju-on: The Beginning of the End* becomes a new and original chapter in the series, as opposed to a would-be Shimizu Takashi film.

Ochiai is a stalwart of the Japanese horror scene, having started his career in the early 1990s working on the popular long-running TV franchise Tales of the Unusual. His debut feature, *Parasite Eve*, an adaptation of the bestselling Sena Hideaki novel, was a box office success and prefigured the arrival of later sci-fi/horror hits such as *Spiral* (1998) and *Another Heaven* (2000). After directing *Infection* (2004) as part of the Takashige Ichise J-Horror Theatre project, Ochiai made his international debut with *Shutter* (2008), the Japanese-American remake of the 2004 Thai hit of the same name. As well as handling the Ju-on reboot, he also directed the first new installment of the successful Haunted School franchise in fifteen years, *Haunted School: Curse of the Word Spirit* (2014).—Jim Harper

JU-REI: THE UNCANNY (2004)
DIRECTOR: Koji Shiraishi
SCREENPLAY: Naoyuki Yokota
SPECS: 76 minutes; color

Ju-rei: The Uncanny, also known as *Ju-rei 2: Kuro Jurei*, is a 2004 supernatural horror film in the subgenre of *kaidan* stories. *Ju-rei: The Uncanny* tells the story of a malicious spirit through a series of vignettes, labeled "chapters," which are structured in reverse chronological order. Following other successful films in the *kaidan* subgenre, the subject matter and anachronistic structure is similar to that of the 2000 film *Ju-on: The Curse*. *Ju-Rei: The Uncanny* was preceded by *Ju-Rei: The Movie*, released one year earlier, which features stories about ghosts told through vignettes but without the interconnectedness of *the Uncanny*.

Ju-rei: The Uncanny is the first feature film credit for Koji Shiraishi, who went on to direct other genre films such as *Shirome* (2010), *Occult* (2009), and *Noroi: The Curse* (2005), which was written by Yokota and features a malicious *kaidan*. These three all employ the "found footage" style of hand-held, first-person camera perspective. Though *Ju-rei: The Uncanny* is shot in a more traditional manner, it utilizes video instead of film and certain scenes contain hand-held, moving shots similar to that of a "found footage" style. Naoyuki Yokota and Shiraishi also collaborated on the 2007 film, *A Slit-Mouthed Woman* (also referred to as *Carved*).

The film begins with chapter 10, in which a group of girls in an urban setting practice synchronized dance moves. After one girl sees a dark figure, they discuss rumors about *the* dark figure. Clicking and croaking sounds accompany the revelation of the figure, which pulls one girl out of the frame. The scene cuts to black when the figure's white face is revealed.

Moving backward chronologically, chapter 9 introduces Noriko Maeda, played by Chinatsu Wakatsuki, whose family and friends are at the center of the story. By showing the end of the story first, the plot is not propelled in a typical linear fashion, but rather bits of information are given during each segment that fill in blanks caused by the preceding vignettes. For instance, Noriko is trying to talk to, but unable to hear, her father on the phone. He is not seen until a later segment (earlier in the linear story). Another character is alluded to when Noriko erases her note on the refrigerator: "I'll be at Rie's."

Eerie elements are introduced as Noriko searches the house for her mother and brother, such as a figure seen at the window and at the top of the stairs and Noriko hearing only a growl when she answers a phone call from her friend Hitomi, played by Eriko Ichinohe. Many shots of Noriko's search through the house are handheld and similar to the "found-footage" style of Shiraishi's subsequent films. Slowly, Noriko investigates each room, finally finding Hitomi in the bathroom. The chapter ends when Hitomi's body falls back toward the camera, her eyes wide and her mouth open in an exaggerated "O." Hearing the same clicking noises from the previous chapter, Noriko is grabbed and pulled off-screen.

Chapter 8 introduces Noriko's father, Kazushige, played by Ichiro Ogura, and continues the previous chapter's confinement of action to one location, this time in a hotel. Kazushige has the phone conversation with his daughter as referenced in the previous chapter. He is disturbed later by visions of black ink smudges spreading across a fax and complains to the front desk of noises coming from the adjoining room. After being told that no one is staying in the room next to his, two dark-haired, white-faced figures crawl up the side of his bed.

Chapters 7 and 6 focus on Noriko's friend Rie, played by Miku Ueno. While in her apartment, Rie is clearly upset by a news story about a woman and child found dead in Tokyo and turns off the television quickly. While they are alluded to here briefly, the woman and child are the focus of the final "prologue" segment of the film. Unseen by visiting Noriko, Rie is frightened by ghosts in her apartment. Her visions occur again in chapter 6 when she is at work. Chapter 7 ends with Rie hiding in bed underneath the covers and then pulling them back to reveal a ghost inches from her face. Chapter 6, as the other segments, finishes with a startling revelation when a ghost boy, who appears in a pile of dark hair, grabs Rie's boss, a hairstylist.

Chapter 5 continues to introduce bits of the back-story and introduces Noriko's young brother Junya, played by Kenji Shiyo. Waiting for his mother after school, Junya's teacher tells him of strange, ghostly occurrences. The ghostly climax at the end of this chapter does not happen with a quick visual cut, as seen in other chapters, but rather with a long, wide shot of a stairwell. Junya comes down and then up the stairs, clicking noises are heard, and his body falls to the floor. The shot holds, lights flickering, to reveal a dark figure that disappears.

The reason for Junya's long wait at school is explained in the next chapter. The shortest of the vignettes, Chapter 4 has Junya's mother "Mayuko," played by Hiromi Senno, exiting a hospital and getting into her car where a ghost quickly grabs her. This chapter includes a new occurrence, absent from all other chapters, of static covering the screen and the changing of the image to black and white. In Chapter 3, ghosts terrorize Noriko and Junya's grandmother in the hospital during Mayuko's visit. This segment features a strong contrast between long, wide, static images and dynamic, hand-held shots. The ghost, unseen by Mayuko, darts toward the grandmother to end the scene.

Chapters 2 and 1 explain what happened to Noriko and Rie's friend Hitomi when the friends went to the cinema earlier in the day. After watching a movie about a "cursed video," Hitomi faints and is taken to Noriko's house. Chapter 1 then reveals that Hitomi spoke to a young girl in the theater who told her of the "black-shadowed person" coming to kill her. Turning, Hitomi sees the ghostly figure crawling on the theater floor toward her. In addition to influence of other *kaidan* films, this sequence evidences another similarity *Ju-rei: The Uncanny* shares with other horror films of its era: technology—in this case, a movie—as a transmitter for a curse or corruption.

The final segment, "Prologue," functions as a denouement by explaining the origins of the "black-shadowed person." The news story Rie saw in chapter 7 is at the root. The missing woman, Michiko, Kazumi Nagashio, is seen via a POV shot from her hiding child. Her husband is discussing divorce, but she responds by saying, "the black-shadowed person is coming." Michiko reaches for a glass bowl and beats her husband to death with it. Accompanied by heavy breathing and the now familiar clicking sounds, the final ghost reveal of the film is of a dark shape covering the small opening of the child's bedroom door to plunge the frame into darkness. A deep voice croaks, "You will die." The tying of this violent act to a malignant spirit is a theme similar to other *kaidan* films such as *Ju-on: The Grudge* (2002).—Jeffrey Bullins

JUNK (1999)

DIRECTOR: Atsushi Muroga
SCREENPLAY: Atsushi Muroga
SPECS: 83 minutes; color

Junk, known in Japan as *Junk Shiryogari*, is the title of the 1999 survival horror film written and directed by Atsushi Muroga. The film drops small-time hoods, yakuza thugs, and a scientist into a secret US military facility in Okinawa where zombies suddenly run rampant. Very much a film of its time, *Junk* combines disreputable genres to limited effect.

According to the storyline, two American scientists are experimenting on a young, dead Japanese woman, injecting her with a neon green substance called "DNX"—a chemical they hope will reanimate her lifeless body. It does. The woman's eyes pop open and she rises to take a bite out of the neck of her attendants. In a hospital on the island, Dr. Nakata, played by Yuji Kishimoto (b. 1970) is seeing patients when two US soldiers approach him with a call to action, reporting to the military base.

Elsewhere in Okinawa, another young woman, Saki, played by Kaori Shimamura (b. 1971), is awaiting the rest of her posse in a getaway car. While they execute a jewelry heist, she negotiates for the sale of a dream car. The robbery goes poorly, one of the thieves is stabbed in the foot, and they all make a quick getaway with Saki driving.

When the thieves are ready to deliver the goods to the yakuza, they agree to meet in a warehouse that just happens to be the military base where the reanimation experiments were conducted. They stumble upon the wandering ghouls and must fight their way out, only to be greeted by the yakuza, led by Ramone, played by Tate Gouta (b. 1962). Ramone, as would be expected, has no intention of paying for the stolen jewels and would have killed the remaining crew if not for the intervention of a zombified thief. Saki and Akira, played by Osamu Ehara (b. 1966) make a run for it through the warehouse.

Switching scenes, the soldiers wanted Dr. Nakata because of his involvement with the original experiment on DNX. They blackmail him to encourage his participation in covering up the accident, and he agrees to initiate a remote self-destruct sequence via a computer link. However, the reanimated woman from the film's first scene interrupts the sequence and sends back a message that reads "I love you." Nakata decides he has to tend to matters at the warehouse personally and boards a helicopter flying toward chaos.

Akira and Saki run around shooting shuffling zombies in search of Ramone, who, by the time they find him, is already one of the undead. Nakata and his partner kill their share of zombies while in search of the super-zombie who dismantled a self-destruct sequence. Akira then manages to escape to the getaway van, leaving Saki, whom he believes to be dead. Akira eventually finds Nakata and they team up to survive. It turns out, unsurprisingly, that the super-zombie Nakata is looking for just happens to be his dead wife Kyoko, played by Miwa. He prepares to kill her, but it isn't that simple—she is, after all, a super-zombie. As a super-zombie, no matter how many times Nakata and Saki kill her, Kyoko bounces back, turning into a white-haired ghost figure—at one point they even cut off her legs to no avail. Eventually, Kyoko kills Nakata, but Saki gets the better of her with help from Akira, who returns to provide aid in Saki's final quest to destroy the warehouse.

Junk portends escapist fun targeted at horror fans interested in gore and the modern crime films of Hong Kong–based auteurs made popular worldwide in the early 1990s by the critical success of Tarantino's *Reservoir Dogs*, a film that referenced the work of Hong Kong director Ringo Lam. Muroga is hardly the only young director to follow this theme while it was hot; indeed, he had already crafted similar work in his 1995 heist film *Score*. *Junk* replicates the heist gone wrong situation from that film and adds more gruesome foes.

Muroga made his reputation by working cheap, making *Score* in the Philippines for under $30,000 and *Junk* too appears to be made as inexpensively. The zombie makeup is poorly done, the movie was filmed on Super 16 mm, and there is no real set design to speak of. The George Romero ethos of working cheaply has proven to produce brilliance with a talented team; however, Muroga lacked such assistance.

More forgiving critics give Muroga credit for considering the plight of the people of Okinawa, who have dealt with problems stemming from having a military base on their island for decades. In a twist of social commentary, it appears seemingly true that no matter what the natives do to interfere, the US military bases will remain on the island, as in the film where the base commander promises to continue the DNX experiments. In the end, Muroga seems more interested in paying homage to the final shots of Tarantino's *From Dusk Till Dawn*, when Saki looks back with concern as the warehouse exudes black smoke into the skies above Okinawa.—Mark N. Mays

Bibliography

Muroga, Atsushi, dir. *Junk*. Japan Home Video, 2001. DVD.
——. *Score*. Shochiku-Fuji Company, 1995. DVD.
Tarantino, Quentin, dir. *From Dusk Till Dawn*. Miramax, 1994. DVD.
——. *Reservoir Dogs*. Miramax, 1992. DVD.

• K •

KAGERŌ-ZA (1981)
DIRECTOR: Seijun Suzuki
SCREENPLAY: Yōzō Tanaka
SPECS: 139 minutes; color

Maverick filmmaker Seijun Suzuki (b. 1923) is best known as a B-movie director who was fired from the Nikkatsu Studio in 1968. Although many university students and the Japanese counterculture considered him a visionary, Nikkatsu considered his films, primarily yakuza and action genre works assigned to him by the studio, to be incoherent visual stylizations that did not make money. Blacklisted by all the film studios, he worked primarily on commercials and television productions and as an actor during the 1970s. Suzuki began collaboration with producer Genjiro Arato (b. 1948) in 1980, creating what has become known as his Taisho Roman trilogy, consisting of *Zigeunerweisen* (*Tsigoineruwaizen*, 1980), *Kagero-za* (*Heat Haze Theatre*, 1981), and *Yumeji* (1991). All three are set in the liberal Taisho era (the mentally afflicted Emperor Yoshihito, posthumously named Taisho, reigned between 1912 and 1926). Independently produced and thus not restrained by studio strictures, they allowed Suzuki to experiment more freely with his stylistic innovations. Leisurely paced and nonlinear, these surrealistic works expand the boundaries of ghost stories into dreams or dreamlike universes, and may be even more enigmatic than the contentious films that caused his Nikkatsu discharge.

With the success of *Zigeunerweisen*, Suzuki was able to follow up with *Kagero-za*. Whereas *Zigeunerweisen* includes several dreamlike sequences, *Kagero-za* flows more loosely, as if it were a dream itself. It is set in 1926 in Taisho Tokyo with Shungo Matsuzaki, played by action star Yusaku Matsuda (1949–1989), searching for a lost love letter from a married woman. He is a playwright of Shinpa melodrama, Japan's first effort to emulate the realism of Western theater, and a dandy who is supported by wealthy hedonist Tamawaki, played by Katsuo Nakamura (b. 1938). As he looks for the letter, a mysterious woman, played by Michiyo Okusu (b. 1946), who was Aochi's sensuous wife in *Zigeunerweisen*, asks him to escort her to the hospital so she can visit a friend who may be dying. She is carrying flowers she gathered in a cemetery, an act she claims represents her compassion. She is afraid of an old woman who, in the rising vapor near the hospital, sells bladder cherries containing women's souls. (The bladder cherry is also called a Chinese lantern; its fruit is covered by a paper-like substance resembling a paper lantern. The seeds are often used to guide the souls of the dead in Japan.) The woman has Mitsuzaki's letter with her flowers, but she instead gives him a cherry, representing her soul. Matsuzaki narrates to an intrigued Tamawaki how he met the woman two more times, once as she pushes a vulgar old woman on some stairs, then washes her hair in the waters of a shrine because the old woman's hand had touched the hair. The final time they meet she seduces him after he crosses a river to reach her, and he becomes obsessed with her. Upon parting, she tells him that they will die as lovers the next time they meet.

When Matsuzaki goes on a walk in the morning following a drinking bout with Tamawaki, he meets Ine, Tamawaki's wife, the woman who had been hospitalized. She resembles the illusive temptress from the past. Matsuzaki learns that Ine had died shortly before his encounter with her upon visiting Tamawaki.

The conundrum intensifies from this point. Matsuzaki discovers that Tamawaki actually had two wives, Irene and Shinako. Tamawaki met Irene while in Germany. When they returned to Japan, he attempted to restyle her as Japanese by changing her name to Ine, dyeing her blond hair black, and covering her blue eyes with darkened lenses. Meanwhile, Matsuzaki receives a letter from a woman, presumably his enchantress, inviting him to rendezvous in Kanazawa. He runs into Tamawaki on the Kanazawa-bound train, who tells Matsuzaki he is heading there to witness a lovers' suicide. Matsuzaki fears that the woman of his desires is Tamawaki's other wife Shinako, and that he may be heading toward an uncanny destruction, orchestrated by his patron.

Matsuzaki continues to pursue his eternal woman in this alluring enchantress. His romanticized notions are shattered when Tamawaki tells him that Shinako would be willing to commit a double suicide out of pride but not for love. When he finally meets Shinako, she tells him that she had written the dangerous letter in her dreams, but someone else must have sent it. Later, enticed by the erotic embrace of two powerful enchantresses, his everyday world is further overtaken by a megacosm of fantasy. Seemingly trapped in the web of sorceresses who may be or may not be ghosts but are having intercourse with the living, he manages to survive, tainted and disoriented.

Kagero-za transforms elements from several theatrical traditions. Matsuzaki is a Shinpa playwright, attempting to fuse a new reality into an evolving society, yet he becomes bound up in the realms of the irrational and the supernatural. His universe becomes conjoined to those of Kabuki and Noh. Water and water imagery continually link the real world with that of the supernatural. In traveling to Kanazawa, Matsuzaki embarks upon what may be a *michiyuki*, a traditional lover's journey in Kabuki. He then becomes fearful and loses interest in her. Shinako is later forced to complain to Ine that Ine even took her lover. A children's Kabuki reproduces a number of Kabuki elements, but director Suzuki's wry humor changes them to parody. The Kabuki scenes trace the relationships between *Kagero-za*'s main characters while Shinako, Tamawaki, and Matsuzaki sit in the audience. Shinako can only acknowledge to the play's masked author that she is well informed; out of Shinako's sight, the author reveals herself to be the old lady Shinako had pushed down the stairs. Matsuzaki then attempts to shoot one of the little actresses. Upon leaving the theater early, he ironically complains that there is too much reality within the stylized play for him.

Irene/Ine serves as a doppelgänger (double) in *Kagero-za*. Her hair and eyes appear to be dark during the day, but are transformed to blonde and blue in the moonlight. In Kanazaka Matsuzaki witnesses her glide blonde-haired over the river waters in a boat with the black-haired Shinako, the old and the new wives closely resembling each other. Tamawaki parodies her to entertain Matsuzaki by donning a blond wig and a kimono, looking absolutely depraved with his black mustache. When Matsuzaki informs Ine that she can't be alive because he had witnessed her funeral, she readily replies that she had noticed him from her casket.

This kinetic film is based on a story by Gothic storyteller Kyoka Izumi (1873–1939), who is best known for his depictions of ghosts and other supernatural entities attempting to infringe prosaic realms. This obsessive and eccentric writer, heavily influenced by his Edo upbringing and his mother's early death, often presents archetypal beauties that both seduce and extricate weaker men. His fictive and idiosyncratic tales contain innuendos reaching toward issues of modernity. Like Hyakken, author of *Zigeunerweisen*, Kyoka was rediscovered by the Japanese during the 1970s. *Demon Pond* (*Yashagaike*) is his best-known work in the West. His free-flowing, stylistic depiction of the fantastic fit well with Suzuki's chaotic vision.

Following *Zigeunerweisen*'s success, producer Genjiro Arato decided to exhibit *Kagero-za* in a similar fashion, screening it in Cinema Placet's inflatable tent. Katsuo Nakamura, who played the rifle-toting Tamawaki, received several Best Supporting Actor awards from several Japanese sources, including the Japanese Academy Award and the film journal *Kinema Junpo*. The film also finished high on *Kinema Junpo*'s annual critics' poll. It was presented at several international film festivals, including a sidebar at the Berlin Festival. As Seijun Suzuki's works continue to become better known, it has gained further recognition at Suzuki festivals.—Bill Thompson

See also Yumeji; Zigeunerweisen

Bibliography

Cornyetz, Nina. *Dangerous Women, Deadly Words: Phallic Fantasy and Modernity in Three Japanese Writers*. Stanford, CA: Stanford University Press, 1999.

Izumi, Kyoka. *Japanese Gothic Tales*. Translated by Charles Shiro Inouye. Honolulu: University of Hawaii Press, 1996.

Suzuki, Seijun. *Kagero-za*. Kino Video/KimStim, 1993. DVD.

KAIDAN KASANE-GA-FUCHI (1957)

DIRECTOR: Nobuo Nakagawa
SCREENPLAY: Kōhan Kawauchi
SPECS: 66 minutes; black and white

Kaidan Kasane-ga-fuchi (lit. The ghosts of Kasane swamp) is a 1957 black-and-white film by Nobuo Nakagawa (1905–1984). Nakagawa directed this film for the Shintōhō studios, which, from the mid-1950s until its bankruptcy in 1961, released many popular horror and *ero guro* movies under the producer Mitsugu Okura.

The film was originally based on a ghost story titled *Shinkei Kasanegafuchi*, written by the *rakugo* storytelling artist San'yūtei Enchō in 1859, which centers around a narrative of karmic retribution. Among the many film adaptations of this material is a 1926 version by the well-known director Kenji Mizoguchi, titled *Kyōren no onna shisho* (*The Passion of a Woman Teacher*), which, like most prewar Japanese horror films, is now considered lost. The same holds true for an adaptation by Shigeru Mokudō that featured the great horror film star of the prewar period Sumiko Suzuki (1904–1985) in the leading role. Hideo Nakata, director of *Ringu*, directed the most recent version in 2007, titled *Kaidan*, an interpretation of the material inspired in many ways by the classic ghost films of the 1950s.

Kaidan Kasane-ga-fuchi was the first film Nakagawa Nobuo realized for Shintōhō's annual horror program, which was scheduled in summer around the Japanese Bon festival (a festival to honor one's ancestors' spirits) and ensured outstanding commercial success on account of its popularity as a "chilling" pastime against the summer heat. The story's point of departure is a cruel murder that occurs during the winter of 1774 in the village of Hanyū in Shimōsa. The samurai Fukami slays the blind masseur Sōetsu, because Fukami is not able to repay the considerable amount of money he owes the masseur. Though Fukami arranges for the disposal of the body in the Kasane swamp, he cannot escape his guilt. Ghostly apparitions first drive him to kill his wife and, afterward, lure him into the moor, where he eventually drowns.

Twenty years later, Fukami's son Shinkichi, played by Takashi Wada (b. 1929) lives as a servant in a rich merchant's household in Edo and gets along well with the daughter of the house, O-Hisa, played by Noriko Kitazawa (b. 1938). O-Hisa's shamisen teacher, O-Rui, played by Katsuko Wakasugi (b. 1926)—who, as it later turns out, is none other than the daughter of the murdered Sōetsu— seduces the younger Shinkichi. He is thrown out of the merchant's house as a result of the affair and must seek refuge with his mistress.

Their happiness, however, is short lived, as O-Rui accidentally injures her face with the plectrum of her shamisen. The wound inflames, quickly develops into an ugly abscess that covers an entire half of her face, and she becomes so ill that she is almost completely bed-ridden. Her pupils cease to visit her, with the exception of O-Hisa, who, O-Rui suspects, only visits because of her infatuation with Shinkichi. Shinkichi is then tormented by O-Rui's burning jealousy, and the treacherous, masterless samurai Omura, played by Tetsuro Tamba (1922–2006) pushes him into planning a secret escape with O-Hisa, who is soon to be married off against her will by her stepmother. O-Rui disturbs a meeting between O-Hisa and Shinkichi, rushing at them with a short sword, but in struggling with her lover, O-Rui falls down the stairs and her condition worsens. After her servant finally tells her that Shinkichi wants to leave her and, moreover, that he is the son of her father's murderer, O-Rui dies in great anger and distress. Upon learning of O-Rui's death, Shinkichi and O-Hisa escape together. On their way, they meet a strange figure who leads them into the Kasane swamp, where O-Hisa suddenly takes O-Rui's shape. Shinkichi, who thinks he is attacking O-Rui's ghost, accidentally kills O-Hisa with a sickle he finds in the swamp. Shortly afterward, Shinkichi himself is killed by Omura, who had been after the couple's money all along. Shortly after the murder, O-Rui's ghost appears. Omura frantically tries to attack her with his sword, but eventually stumbles into the moor, where Sōetsu's ghost emerges and finally drowns him. In *Kaidan Kasane-ga-fuchi*, thus, the curse of the murdered Sōetsu extends over two generations and the children cannot escape the karmic retribution brought about by their fathers.

In *Kaidan Kasane-ga-fuchi,* Nakagawa developed many stylistic devices, which were to reappear in his 1959 masterpiece, *Tōkaidō Yotsuya kaidan,* such as the slow, tense sequence that first reveals the deformed face of O-Rui through its reflection in water and fully captures the cognitive process of recognition. Nakagawa works with carefully arranged sequence shots and uses gruesome masks, double exposure, and clever cuts to create effective ghostly apparitions. Composer Chūmei Watanabe (b. 1925) arranged classical Japanese music with Western orchestral music and jazz elements for the score of the film.—Elisabeth Scherer

See also Nakagawa, Nobuo; Okura, Mitsugu; Suzuki, Sumiko; *Tōkaidō Yotsuya kaidan*

Bibliography

Nakagawa, Nobuo, dir. *Kaidan Kasane-ga-fuchi.* Shintōhō, 1957. Film.
Suzuki, Kensuke. *Jigoku de yōi hai! Nakagawa Nobuo. Kaidan kyōfu eiga no gōka.* Tokyo: Waizu Shuppan, 2000.

KAKASHI (2001)

DIRECTOR: Norio Tsuruta
SCREENPLAY: Norio Tsuruta, Satoru Tamaki, Ryuta Mitaku, Osamu Murakami
SPECS: 86 minutes; color

Few authors have been as heavily associated with the post-*Ring* Japanese horror boom as manga artist Itō Junji. Having written the original source novels for the Ring series and the Hideo Nakata film, *Dark Water* (2002), Itō's works have been adapted into nearly two dozen movies and multiple television episodes. One of his most famous works, the cycle of stories about the beautiful and notoriously indestructible teenager Tomie, has been turned into a long-running franchise comprising nine films, thus far. His stories have been tackled by a number of prominent directors, including Takashi Shimizu, Ryūta Miyake, Ataru Oikawa, and Norio Tsuruta, who turned two of Itō's short manga stories into the film *Kakashi* (*Scarecrow*).

According to the storyline, Kaoru, played by Maho Nomami, undertakes a search for her brother who has suddenly disappeared from his flat. Coincidentally finding a number of letters from her old schoolmate Izumi, played by Kō Shibasaki, she begins to reconstruct a series of puzzling events. Suspecting that her brother might have gone to visit her, Kaoru drives to Izumi's home in an isolated village called Kozukata. Izumi's father tells her that his daughter died some time ago and that Kaoru's brother has never been there. Not believing his story, particularly the details of Izumi's death, Kaoru takes advantage of the fact that her car has broken down to stay in Kozukata and dig some more. As well as being incredibly suspicious of outsiders, the villagers are preparing for an important festival, the details of which are kept carefully hidden.

Like the successes of the Ataru Oikawa movies known as *Higurashi no naku koro ni* and *Forbidden Siren,* directed by Yukihiko Tsutsumi, *Kakashi* belongs to a strain of contemporary horror that taps into the fear and distrust the urban Japanese feel for countryside life and their rural cousins. Cell phones don't work properly, the locals are surly and superstitious, and the old-timers still gather to swap unpleasant stories and poke their fingers at the newcomers. A key and recurring feature in the film is its rural religious practices. Unlike the warm and reassuring Buddhist traditions of home altars and funerary lanterns, the practices of rural Japan are perceived as belonging to darker and more primal traditions, often involving sacrifice and the propitiation of ancient deities. In *Kakashi* this is represented by the difference between the usual rites intended to thank the spirits of the *kakashi* for watching over the crops and what the villagers of Kozukata are trying to do: bringing the spirits of the dead back to life to inhabit the *kakashi*.

A slow-burning, deliberate film, *Kakashi* takes time to establish its scenario before moving the plot elements forward. For almost an hour Tsuruta concentrates on documenting the pervasive weirdness of Kozukata and its inhabitants (their refusal to engage with outsiders, their seeming obsession with straw), as well as Kaoru's increasingly fragile mental state, exemplified by her terrifying dreams about Izumi that prefigure later events in the film. Although sometimes effective, these elements cannot hide the fact that very little actually happens in the first half of the film.

Kakashi's greatest assets are the scarecrows themselves. At a time when the majority of its contemporaries were employing ghosts based on *Ring*'s Sadako (pale female phantoms in white with long, dark hair), Tsuruta's *kakashi* are an unusual, original variation on the traditional "vengeful spirits" that have dominated Japanese horror cinema since its inception. Like many artificial representations of human beings (dolls, mannequins), in the right context these scarecrows can be extremely unsettling. This culminates in two key scenes where the *kakashi* come to life. In the first, a young girl is killed by her father—not entirely accidentally. With the memory of her demise still fresh, the first thing the new *kakashi* does is turn upon her father, a moment heavily reminiscent of a similar scene in George A. Romero's *Night of the Living Dead* (1968). Even more effective is Izumi's revival. As a possible suicide, Izumi has no desire to return to a world that caused her nothing but pain. Instead of running straight into her mother's waiting arms, Izumi snaps her neck like a twig.

Aside from the pacing issues, critics may note that *Kakashi*'s only serious misstep involves the climax of the film, which seems influenced by Stephen King's novel *Pet Sematary* (and the 1989 movie adaptation). Like the main character in the novel, Kaoru takes the opportunity to bring a loved one (her brother) back to life, despite knowing that the process makes the returnees thoroughly evil.—Jim Harper

See also Itō, Junji

KAKURENBO: HIDE AND SEEK (2005)
DIRECTOR: Shūhei Morita
SCREENPLAY: Shiro Kuro, Shūhei Morita
SPECS: 25 minutes; color

Kakurenbo: Hide and Seek is a 2005 short animated supernatural horror/suspense film written and directed by Shūhei Morita with production by YamatoWorks. It is notable for its thematic structure and cell-shaded animation. The plot follows eight youths who, despite a recent rash of missing children, play a nighttime game of *otokoyo* (hide-and-seek) in an abandoned section of Tokyo while wearing fox masks. They are soon terrorized by a series of demons as the fate of the missing children is revealed. The film received high praise upon its release, including a number of awards and nominations.

The story begins with three friends, Noshiga (voiced by Rei Naito, b. 1961), Tachiji (Mika Ishibashi), and Suku (Akiko Kobayashi, b. 1979), talking about the mysterious disappearances of children within the city. An unknown girl's voice interrupts them with eerie laughter and telling about a version of hide-and-seek played at night. The next scene shows the three friends following a series of signs to locate Otokoyo Square, where the game initiates. After introducing Hikora (Junko Takeuchi, b. 1972), whose sister is one of the missing children, the eight disperse in smaller groups, with the friends staying together as they explore underground tunnels. A sudden shaking in the tunnel leads them to argue over the potential cause; Noshiga spots a statue in the dark that startles him into anger and he throws a stick at it. After the crew leaves the statue appears to come to life.

Exhausted and hungry, Noshiga sits down to complain, and his companions offer to go searching for food. Alone, he grows sleepy and starts to nod off, then is awakened by a sound from deeper in the tunnel. His friends return as he wonders about the cause and they alert Noshiga to the sound's origin: the statue from earlier is revealed as an actual demon. The boys run, but Tachiji is knocked unconscious when Noshiga inadvertently slams into him. He revives some time later, feeling that the demon is nearby. As he turns around, the demon is briefly shown to assault the boy.

A pair of mute twins, Inmu and Yanku, is shown running from a third, cart-based demon, which crashes through walls in pursuit, but they escape. The camera then follows another pair, Hikora and Yaimao (Makoto Ueki, b. 1977), who discover a poster illustrating four types of demons, with a fifth resembling a fox in the center. A third member of their party glances out the window and watches as Noshiga and Suku run from a four-legged demon, just barely escaping down an alleyway. Back in the tunnel network, the pair searches for a hiding place. Noshiga climbs into a trashcan, forcing Suku to run for a doorway. Suku screams and Noshiga peers out to look, allowing the first demon to spot him. Noshiga scrambles to escape, blacks out, and the scene changes again.

Returning to the twins, who are still on the run, we see that they have armed themselves with a stone and hockey stick, with which they attack the demon as the screen wipes to Hikora and Yaimao who, with their mysterious female companion, have stumbled across an open courtyard where a spider-like demon chases them. Yaimao sacrifices himself to buy time for the others. The girl is then revealed to be in league with the demons, which emerge on all sides, surrounding Hikora. He yells Yaimao's name and runs at the spider-demon as the screen fades to black. Hikora wakes up to hear the voice of his missing sister, Sorincha (Masami Suzuki, b. 1972), counting to ten as if playing hide-and-seek. Sorincha's body then morphs into the fox demon from the poster and explains that the town is lit by the energy of the missing children. Hikora then sees the bodies of the other players strapped into an electrical device. The demon tells him that he has won the game and is now "it." The final scene shows a new group of children running to hide as Hikora counts to ten.

The film was released in 2005 to critical acclaim, including the Best Short award at the Fantasia Film Festival; nominated for Best Film at the Seoul Comics and Animation Festival; and named a Notable Entry at the Tokyo International Anime Fair. It explores themes of lost innocence and the dangers of industrial urbanization. The use of traditional motifs, such as a timeless children's game and fox masks, is contrasted against the backdrop of a postindustrial environment, thereby highlighting the pathos of tradition and nature surrendering to urbanization.—Jared Miracle

Bibliography

Morita, Shuhei, dir. *Kakurenbo: Hide and Seek*. YamatoWorks, 2005. Film.

KANASHIMI NO BERADONNA (1973)

DIRECTOR: Eiichi Yamamoto
SCREENPLAY: Yoshiyuki Fukuda, Eiichi Yamamoto
SPECS: 93 minutes; color

After the success achieved with the animated TV series *Astro Boy*, Ōsamu Tezuka went on to explore new media territories. Tezuka wanted to reach an adult audience, and to accomplish this ambition he came up with a series of feature-length films targeting mostly male audiences. This was the point of departure for the erotic trilogy called Animerama, produced by Mushi Productions, which had been formed by Tezuka in 1961. One of the six members of the original team, Eiichi Yamamoto, was chosen to take charge of the first installment, *A Thousand and One Nights* (1969), whereas the second part, *Cleopatra* (1970), was codirected by Tezuka himself and Yamamoto. By the time Mushi Productions was planning the last episode of *Animerama*, Tezuka had left the studio in order to dedicate himself to his new manga career. Thus, Eiichi Yamamoto was put in charge of the closing chapter: *Kanashimi no Beradonna* (1973). Although the result was a beautiful hand-drawn masterpiece of animation, the film was a commercial flop and the final blow to a company in its death throes—indeed, Mushi Productions would declare bankruptcy that year.

In addition to its erotic approach, the Animerama series shared another narrative point in common, since the plots are vaguely based on literary sources and historical events. In this particular case, the film was loosely inspired by *Satanism and Witchcraft: A Study in Mediaeval Superstition*, originally entitled *La sorcière* (The witch), a classic written in 1862 by the historian Jules Michelet. The story follows "Jeanne," an attractive and virginal young woman raped on the very day of her wedding. Set in medieval times, the movie narrates how the people around her drag Jeanne down to Hell. Immediately after the first bloody—even gory—rape, a phallic demon offers Jeanne power in exchange for sexual intercourse, leading to the second aggression to her body. With each betrayal and sexual assault, the young woman gradually loses her innocence and gains power. She becomes an outcast who lives free in the forest but, paradoxically, she ends up helping those who hunted her down, and ordinary people begin to venerate her. The powerful, obscure Catholic feudal lord Baron, afraid of her power, condemns her to be burned at the stake. However, she proves immortal, because she represents all women subjugated to the patriarchal world.

In *Kanashimi no Beradonna*, Eiichi Yamamoto seems to make a statement about the situation of women in a male-dominated society. Even though the story is set in the distant Middle Ages, the filmmaker points out women's situation purely as objects of desire, forced to become toys in the capricious hands of selfish men. If the film can be interpreted at first glance as a road to perdition, in the end Jeanne gains independence. Freed from men and religious oppression, she is able to develop her will and sexuality without remorse. In this sense, the director's closing argument is encouraging, conveying the notion that as history unfolds, so do women's rights and their position in society.

If the final installment is greatly appealing in a narrative sense, its visual execution is absolutely inspiring, audacious, and alluring. Yamamoto's gamble on experimental animation achieves a chef d'oeuvre in which every frame is a work of art. The combined work of the versatile artist and illustrator Kuni Fukai and the animation director Gisaburō Sugii was vital in crafting such incredible animation. The budget was so limited, however, that the film was labeled by the prestigious scholar Tsugata Nobuyuki as "inanimate animation." Although one has to remark on the stillness of the images, Yamamoto took advantage of this budgetary setback. Throughout *Kanashimi no Beradonna*, the still images can be read in three directions: from the bottom up when Jeanne receives the divine blessing from God; from right to left when the narration stays with earthly matters; and from top to bottom when she embraces evil. This horizontal choice of reading, as in Japanese reading, is particularly significant if one bears in mind that all of the artistic work takes Western painting as its primary source. This decision, in addition to the presence of Kuni Fukai, is the single apparent link to Japanese painting tradition, to the ancient picture scrolls known as *emakimono*. The rest of the references are connected to a long, heterogeneous list of Western artists inclusive of Edvard Munch, Gustav Klimt, Aubrey Beardsley, and Marc Chagall.—Laura Montero Plata

KENPEI TO YŪREI (1958)
DIRECTOR: Nobuo Nakagawa
SCREENPLAY: Yoshihiro Ishikawa
SPECS: 75 minutes; black and white

During wartime, handsome but serpentine MP Lieutenant Namishima, played by Shigeru Amachi, sets his eyes on Akiko, played by Naoko Kubo, a beautiful young wife of Corporal Tazawa, played by Shōji Nakayama. Namishima frames Tazawa so that the latter appears to be a traitor who has sold key military secrets to the enemies, when in fact he himself is in cahoots with a shady Chinese spy. Tazawa, maintaining his innocence, is executed by the firing squad, and Namishima forcibly imposes himself on the inconsolable Akiko, driving Tazawa's mother, played by Fumiko Miyata, to death in the process. However, he is unaware of the presence of Tazawa's twin brother, also played by Nakayama, who, along with Akiko, follow him to Wuhan, China, where Namishima, now promoted, is enjoying the decadent life of a double agent. Neither does he realize that Tazawa's vengeful spirit is about to rudely intrude into his waking life.

Kenpei to yūrei, is a 1958 low-budget, but surprisingly colorful production. This delirious ghostly horror-war-espionage genre hybrid, was conceived by

Shin-Toho producer Mitsugi Ōkura as a quick follow-up to *Kenpei to barabara shibijin* (The military policeman and the dismembered beauty, 1957) directed by Namiki Kyōtarō, an unexpected hit also starring Amachi and Nakayama. Despite its superbly exploitative title, the 1957 film was a straightforward murder mystery with northeast China serving as an "exotic" background. It is claimed that it was producer Ōkura, a former silent film narrator with the known preference for the "erotic and grotesque," who insisted on inserting supernatural elements into another straightforward mystery. Yet it is Nobuo Nakagawa, one of the great journeyman directors of 1950s and 1960s Japanese cinema and best known among the Anglophone viewership for the indescribable *Jigoku* (1960), who transforms this hastily produced follow-up from a lukewarm potboiler into a stunning exercise in expressionist cinema.

Nakagawa was conversant in a variety of genres—comedies, period dramas, gangster action, and of course, horror—and capable of putting together fast-paced programmers with impressive technical sophistication under trying conditions. *Kenpei to yūrei* suffers from threadbare resources, but Nakagawa's direction is ahead of its time in many ways: witness the 1960s American TV–like fast pan of the camera, among other dazzling sleights of hand he displays. It is true that the film's *chinoiserie*-draped, international espionage shenanigans are cheaply done and at times distract the viewers from the ghost story. Fortunately, in the crucial moments Nakagawa dials up the scare quotient with marvelous vistas of crucified bodies, a coffin overflowing with seawater, and a disembodied hand greeting the horrified perpetrator. Shigeru Amachi makes for a conniving but strangely sympathetic villain and Yōko Mihara in the rather non-PC role of a Chinese-agent femme fatale is memorable as well.—Kyu Hyun Kim

KILLERS (2014)
DIRECTOR: Kimo Stamboel and Timo Tjahjanto
SCREENPLAY: Timo Tjahjanto
SPECS: 137 minutes (126 minutes, censored); color

The first in a line of international coproductions from Nikkatsu, Japan's oldest studio, *Killers* (2014) is the result of a collaboration with the Indonesian Guerilla Merah Films. The film was directed by the Mo Brothers, executive produced by Welsh action film director Gareth Huw Evans of *The Raid: Redemption* (2011), *The Raid 2* (2015), and *The Raid 3* (announced), and produced by Yoshinori Chiba. Shooting took place in Indonesia as well as Japan, and premiered at the 2014 Sundance Film Festival preceding its release in each country, and followed by a festival run at Nippon Connection in Frankfurt, JAPAN CUTS in New York, and Fantasia International Film Festival in Montreal. The Japanese and international version of the film includes violence and nudity, which have been removed from the Indonesian version. Kimo Stamboel and Timo Tjahjanto, known as the "the Mo Brothers," although they are not related save for their similar first names, collaborated on several shorts and omnibus horror films before their feature debut with *Macabre* (2009). *Killers* marks their second full-length film, with a story and screenplay by Tjahjanto and Takuji Ushiyama, starring Japanese actor Kazuki Kitamura as the cold and mysterious wealthy killer Shuhei Nomura and

Indonesian rapper and actor Oka Antara as honest Jakarta journalist Bayu Aditya at the end of his rope, in addition to Rin Takanashi as Hisae Kawahara, one of Nomura's potential victims; Luna Maya as Bayu's estranged wife, Dina; and Epy Kusnandar as Mei Kurokawa.

Intercutting between Tokyo and Jakarta, the production's transnational scope enhances its plot of an eerily handsome and quietly deranged serial killer, Nomura, who anonymously uploads videos to the Internet of himself killing women lured to his torture chamber home. Bayu, whose career and personal life have been significantly damaged by the corrupt politician he sought to expose, encounters these videos online and is disturbed yet absorbed by their violent content. Nomura befriends Hisae, a young florist raising her younger autistic brother, Soichi; however, his fascination with her appears to be deeper than that for his victims' flesh and mortality, instead linked to his own sister and parentless adolescence. After a brush with death in which Bayu defends himself against thieves, he uploads his own rough cell phone video of the brutal affair, capturing the bloody moment of his victim's death, just like Nomura. Nomura, sensing a protégé or competitor, seeks out Bayu online and nurtures his emerging blood thirst in cat-and-mouse laptop text and video chats, while Bayu begins to consider the possibilities of vigilante justice. When his wife, Dina, and young daughter, Elly, played by Ersya Aurelia, begin to move on in their lives without him, Bayu's obsession with Dharma, played by Ray Sahetapy—the politician who wronged him—only grows, and he begins to exact revenge on his seedy associates. Nomura's actions grow more reckless as well, giving Soichi a taser to attack his bullies, and contracting a prostitute and murdering her pimp in the restroom of a nightclub. As Bayu is increasingly shocked by his own ruthless actions and their grotesque results, Hisae comes closer to unmasking Nomura, who soon travels to Indonesia to force Bayu's transformation into a killer like him in an operatic and homoerotically charged climax. This Indonesian-Japanese horror-thriller focuses on the dark side of life, however, only as a flip-side of the hunger for power and control in everyday contemporary existence, sex, and the consumption of violent images.

The stylization of the film's exceedingly violent torture scenes, inventive action sequences, and sickly comic flourishes are humanized by Antara's emotionally open performance and continuously relatable transformation as the upright Bayu, and enlivened by Kitamura's equally physical turn as the placid serial killer Nomura. Kitamura's role came as the actor entered his mid-forties, adding inventive and brave performances in *Killers*, Yoshitaka Yamaguchi's *Neko Samurai* (2014), and Dave Boyle's *Man from Reno* (2014) to an already eclectic filmography. Channeling Seijun Suzuki's *Branded to Kill* (1967) via Johnnie To's *Fulltime Killer* (2001), and Mary Harron and Bret Easton Ellis's *American Psycho* (2000), the idea of Nomura's being a wealthy expat returned to Tokyo from the United States after the financial crisis deepens a provocative commentary within the film, suggesting via the killers' erotic attraction to violent media images the violence that undergirds political life under globalization.—Joel Neville Anderson

KOTOKO (2011)

DIRECTOR: Shin'ya Tsukamoto
SCREENPLAY: Shin'ya Tsukamoto
SPECS: 91 minutes; color

Shin'ya Tsukamoto's (b. 1960) *Kotoko* is a film about a broken mind. It tells a story of Kotoko, played by Okinawa-born Japanese pop singer Cocco (b. 1977). Kotoko is a young single mother, who does everything in her power to keep her infant son Daijirō safe. However, it seems that the real threat for her son's well-being is Kotoko herself.

The film starts by introducing the daily life of Kotoko. She has a ring on her finger, but as she states, it's only to keep off men; she has everything she could possibly want in her son. However, it soon becomes apparent that Kotoko is unable to control her life and behavior—leaving her son exposed to her madness. For example, she suffers from double vision, which makes it extremely difficult to get through the day. In one instance, a random encounter with a stranger makes her lash out because, instead of one approaching person, Kotoko often witnesses two—the one indifferent, the other with malevolent intentions. She cannot decipher between real and hallucinatory and is thus certain that someone is there to harm her son. The only thing that helps to keep her sanity is singing, which Kotoko is often seen doing.

Eventually Kotoko's tiring life comes to a halt when she becomes unable to care for Daijirō anymore. She is suspected of having beaten him while suffering from a nervous breakdown, and Daijirō is taken away from her to stay with Kotoko's sister. Kotoko is left all alone, and her self-harming only intensifies. Somewhere between delusion and reality she cuts herself, falling deeper and deeper into the dark pit created by her absolute loneliness and isolation from the world.

One day Kotoko encounters a man, Tanaka, played by Tsukamoto himself, who falls in love with her singing. The two start to date. At first it seems this could be the happiness both Kotoko and Tanaka are looking for, but little by little Tanaka's mental instability becomes apparent. The two of them beat and cut each other in a passionate sadomasochistic frenzy; nonetheless, they become engaged to be married. Cohabitation, however, does not seem to suit Tanaka, who silently disappears one day. Kotoko's hope of retrieving her son from her sister's care diminishes, as she falls deeper and deeper into the abyss of her own mind. Finally there is nothing but pure psychological pain.

Audience reception of *Kotoko* was diverse. Some stated it was all too unpleasant and that there was no way they would want to get immersed in a delusional audiovisual text in which Kotoko's psychological frenzy correlates with the horror of the spectator. The feeling in the film is utterly claustrophobic and marks thus Kotoko's view of the world, which has gotten smaller and smaller due to her sickness. Tsukamoto's use of a handheld camera is continuous with the unstable mental workings of Kotoko herself. While threat is often coded as coming from "outside" in works of horror, in *Kotoko* Tanaka becomes merely a vehicle toward an even greater fall. What is ultimately threatening is the complete destruction of Kotoko's psyche and in that the iconic character of the Japanese mother. Tsukamoto also highlights a clear contradiction between the anxious surroundings of the urban and the leisurely atmosphere of the countryside, in which Kotoko's sister and her family, together with Daijirō, live.

The film ends in a pure Tsukamoto-esque visual fantasy. When Kotoko's mind finally snaps, she is in a playroom for children., and the toys come alive with pure magic, creating an extraordinary scene that is both horrifying in what it implies and beautiful in its real manifestation. Tsukamoto stays true to his roots in theater and does not use any exaggerated computer graphics in creating his psychological hell on Earth. Instead the mood is created using tangible props that are both childlike and handmade. But this is exactly what Kotoko finally becomes: a mere child inside her womanly body.

Kotoko is a one-woman show, with Tsukamoto's character only acting as a catalyst. The physical pain they cause each other is a form of Tsukamoto's existential agony: life is to be felt through pain. And as long as there is pain, there is life. Kotoko had its premiere at the Sixty-Eighth Venice International Film Festival—with which Tsukamoto has had a long and colorful history—in 2012 and won the award for a best film in the Orizzonti section.—Leena Eerolainen

KUCHISAKE ONNA (2007)

DIRECTOR: Kōji Shiraishi
SCREENPLAY: Naoyuki Yokota, Kōji Shiraishi
SPECS: 90 minutes; color

Kuchisake Onna (2007), known as The Slit-Mouthed Woman in English, is a horror film directed by Kōji Shiraishi (b. 1973). In the film, a rumor of a strange woman with her mouth cut wider at each end, Kuchisake Onna, spreads in a small town, scaring many children. One day the rumor becomes real and children go missing. Two teachers gather information and attempt to rescue the missing children, while also revealing a secret about the birth of Kuchisake Onna. The story of Kuchisake Onna is based on a popular urban legend of the late 1970s that frightened school children nationwide and became a recognized moral panic.

The story is set in an imaginary suburban town named Shizukawa in Kanagawa prefecture. A rumor that Kuchisake Onna has come back to the town and that she kidnaps children begins to spread by word of mouth, frightening the elementary school children. According to the rumor, when a boy was playing alone in Shizukawa East Park, a tall woman with long hair wearing a white mask appeared and asked the boy, "Am I pretty?" The woman then took off her mask, revealing her mouth slit all the way up to her ears, and took the boy to her hideout to slit his mouth with scissors.

The adults do not take it seriously at first, but one day the rumor becomes real when a group of Shizukawa Elementary School students try to investigate the credibility of the rumor. Just as the rumor says, when the clock strikes 5 PM, a strange tall woman in a coat with a white mask appears and takes away one of the boys. This incident frightens the small quiet town, including a teacher, Kyōko Yamashita, played by Eriko Satō (b. 1981), and her students at Shizukawa Elementary School. Although the teachers and the parents try to protect their students, Yamashita is helpless when Kuchisake Onna appears and kidnaps one of her students, Mika Sasaki, played by Rie Kuwana (b. 1993). Yamashita feels responsible and begins her own investigation to rescue the kidnapped child, together with her colleague, Noboru Matsuzaki, played by Haruhiko Katō (b. 1975).

The original rumor of Kuchisake Onna used in the film is based on an urban legend that was so popular that it even became somewhat of a panic in 1979. The details of the rumor varied by region, but generally the story went as follows: a tall woman with long black hair in a trench coat wearing a large white mask would walk up and ask a person, "Am I pretty?" (*"Watashi, kirei?"*). If the person replied "Yes," the woman would take off her mask and reveal her mouth widely slit all the way up to her ears, asking, "Even with this?" And she would slit the person's mouth and/or stab the person to death with a sickle.

The details differed by region; in some places the woman was in a red trench coat, and had a kitchen knife or a pair of scissors. The reasons the woman had the slit mouth also varied, from the congenital to the acquired, including an accident during plastic surgery, a car accident, physical abuse by her sister, and her own self-mutilation. The woman was believed to run faster than police on a motorcycle, so no one could get away from her. It was believed that there were a few ways to slow her down, including giving her hard candy—her favorite—or shouting aloud, "pomade, pomade, pomade," as she detested scented hair ointment. Another way to escape was to reply "Kind of" or "So-so" when she asked if she was pretty.

This rumor of Kuchisake Onna spread nationwide through word of mouth and media, frightening school children. As a result, at some schools the students walked home in groups and newsletters were distributed to help calm their fear of Kuchisake Onna. By the late 1970s, the rumor seemed to have all but disappeared.

The film *Kuchisake Onna* revitalized this phenomenon from 1979 and also created her hideous birth story for the contemporary audience. As Yamashita and Matsuzaki continue their investigation, they begin to suspect that the woman may actually be his mother, who disappeared about thirty years ago when the original rumor of the Kuchisake Onna woman began to circulate. Matsuzaki hears the voice, "Am I pretty?" inside his head whenever the Kuchisake Onna appears to kidnap a child, and one day they finally succeed in saving a child by stabbing the Kuchisake Onna to death. A few seconds later, however, the dead body transforms into the mother of another child, proving the Kuchisake Onna's immortality and ability to possess. After putting pieces of Matsuzaki's childhood memories and information from their students together, they finally arrive at a deserted house with a red roof, believed to be the Kuchisake Onna's hideout, which is the house where Matsuzaki and his missing siblings grew up. The two go into the abandoned house to save the missing students and face the Kuchisake Onna and her hideous secrets.

As the story progresses, not only does the film reveal the secret concerning the birth of the Kuchisake Onna, but also the abusive mother-and-child relationships of the other characters: Mika Sasaki, the kidnapped student, was physically and verbally abused by her mother, Mayumi Sasaki, played by Chiharu Kawai (b. 1973), ever since they lost Mika's father in a car accident. The teacher, Yamashita, is divorced due to her abusive parenting of her daughter and has been temporarily suspended from seeing her. Her colleague, Matsuzaki, grew up being abused by her mother, Taeko Matsuzaki, played by Miki Mizuno (b. 1974), who has been missing for thirty years.

These sub-stories illustrate a theme of an abusive mother in the absence of the father, as well as the struggles of the mother and child. The revivals of the immortal Kuchisake Onna also suggest a horrible cycle of child abuse and domestic violence that can carry over to the next generation. By incorporating the story of abusive characters with the Kuchisake Onna figure, the film offers social commentary on existing contemporary issues families face. Indeed, perhaps the storyline suggests that just as the tale of the Kuchisake Onna is horrifying, it can be equally horrifying in real life when a person who is supposed to be a guardian turns abusive and harmful to the children.

The film received positive reviews for its special-effects makeup used for the slit-mouth and its interesting attempt to unravel the famous urban legend. The Kuchisake Onna boom continued with *Kuchisake Onna 2* (2008), directed by Kōtarō Terauchi, as the sequel, and *Kuchisake Onna 0: Beginning* (2008), by Kazuto Kojima, as the prequel. Neither of these titles, however, is directly related to the original *Kuchisake Onna*.—Yoko Inagi

See also Shiraishi, Kōji

Bibliography

Shiraishi, Kōji, dir. *Kuchisake Onna*. Tornado Film, 2007. DVD.

Takano, Seiji. "Toshi Densetsu no Rinri to Jūjutsu" [Ethics and occult arts of urban legends]. *Nishi Nihon Shūkyō Gaku Zasshi* 22 (2000): 80–93.

KUMASHIRO, TATSUMI (1927–1995)

Tatsumi Kumashiro was one of 1970s Japan's most prolific and successful directors, remembered best for his Nureta series of soft-core pornographic films produced for Nikkatsu. A lifelong scholar of Western film and literature, Kumashiro was never content to produce simple skin flicks, imbuing his films with beautiful cinematography, complex characters, and pointed critiques of what he considered to be draconian censorship laws. Kumashiro and the *Roman poruno* films that gave him his big break muddied the distinction between porn and high art and added two decades of life to a dying studio giant.

Kumashiro was born 24 April 1927 in Saga. He was enrolled in medical school throughout World War II but as soon as hostilities ceased dropped out to study English literature at Waseda University with the intention of becoming a novelist. He would later take a position as an assistant director at Shochiku in 1952, and he took the same position at Nikkatsu in 1955.

After working as an assistant on four films throughout the 1960s, Kumashiro was finally offered a chance to direct a film of his own, an adaptation of Tanaka Komimasa's novel *Front Row Life*. Even this early effort is full of Kumashiro's personal tropes, most notably in the camerawork and the film's subject matter. *Front Row Life* was well received by critics but performed poorly at the box office, leading Nikkatsu to demote him again to an assistant. Kumashiro married leading lady Tōnoka Hatsue, but the marriage quickly folded.

By 1971, Nikkatsu's golden age was long over, and the struggling studio made the decision to produce soft-core pornography exclusively in order to remain profitable. Nikkatsu's studio heads aimed to dominate the genre with larger budgets and higher standards of production than had been enjoyed by the pink cinema (*pinku eiga*) of the 1960s. Nikkatsu's new priorities alienated the studio's stable of established talent, leading to a mass exodus of directors and performers. Due largely to this vacuum, Kumashiro was once again given a chance to direct his own film. *Wet Lips* (*Nureta kuchibiru*) was released in early 1972 and became a sizable hit. Kumashiro was already forty-four years old.

The director followed up later that year with *Ichijo's Wet Lust* (*Nureta yokujo*). Starring the notorious performer Sayuri Ichijo as a fictionalized version of herself, the film covers the stripper's daily interactions with her boyfriend, manager, and rival—all while retaining Nikkatsu's designated quota of one sex scene per quarter hour. The film was a massive success, scoring Kumashiro *Kinema Junpo*'s honors for Best Screenplay and Best Director. In a retrospective published in 1999, *Kinema Junpo* marked *Ichijo* number thirty-one on its list of the best Japanese films of all time.

Ichijo was the first of ten films Kumashiro would complete before the end of 1974, firmly cementing his reputation as the king of *Roman poruno*. His success at Nikkatsu earned him greater production budgets and offers from other studios to create more mainstream films like 1975's *Light of Africa* (*Africa no hikari*) or a 1979 remake of Nobuo Nakagawa's *Jigoku*. Kumashiro's films grew darker and more complex throughout the 1970s. This period is best characterized by his 1979 film *A Woman with Red Hair* (*Akai kami no onna*), Kumashiro's most claustrophobic film and arguably one of his best.

Nikkatsu released its final *Roman poruno* in 1988, after a successful seventeen-year run with Kumashiro at the helm. The rise of home video and the market for hardcore pornography it enabled proved too great an adversary for studio-funded soft-core films. The company declared bankruptcy in 1993.

Kumashiro continued to produce films throughout the 1980s, but his output slowed considerably after he suffered a collapsed lung in 1983. His final two projects were filmed while Kumashiro wore an oxygen mask. One of those films, *Like a Rolling Stone* (*Bo no kanashimi*), became the respected auteur's last great masterpiece, earning him Best Director honors at the Hochi Film Awards and awards for Best Director and Best Film at the Blue Ribbon Awards. Kumashiro died 24 February 1995.

Kumashiro is virtually unknown in the West, though he has received some attention in the European festival circuit and at least one retrospective at the Japan Society in New York City. The boundary between pornography and the mainstream has always been somewhat porous in Japanese cinema. The films produced by Kumashiro and his contemporaries actively reflected this. His films therefore struggled to find a place among Western audiences, for whom pornography and drama are distinctly separate genres, divided by gaps of both artistry and respectability. Even when his films were screened abroad (a number of his films have been shown at Cannes), audiences mocked the heavily censored love scenes.

Japanese obscenity laws demand that genitalia be fogged out in any situation, sexual or otherwise. For a porn director like Kumashiro, dealing with these constraints was a daily frustration, and a number of his films deal with issues of censorship. At least two of these, *World of Geisha* (*Yojo-han fusuma no urabari*) and *Woods Are Wet* (*Onna jigoku: Mori wa nureta*), both filmed in 1973, were produced in direct response to Kumashiro's friend and colleague Seiichiro Yamaguchi's indictment for obscenity for his film *Koi no karyūdo: Rabu hantā* (1972). Yamaguchi was later acquitted; his was the only obscenity trial for decades until Suwa Yuuji was convicted in 2004. Kumashiro himself only experienced minor pressure from authorities. His resistance to censorship operated entirely within the bounds of the law: When a scene required censorship, Kumashiro would cover the offending image with an unnecessarily large black bar, obscuring obscenity even as he drew all attention to it. The infamous nude leapfrog scene at the climax of *Lovers Are Wet* (*Koibito-tachi wa nureta*) is a prime example. For the scene, Kumashiro actually scratched away the surface of the film, hiding the actors' genitals but leaving bright, thrashing starbursts in their place.

Kumashiro was fond of long takes and handheld cameras. With a handheld, he could maneuver around the tiny sets his budgets afforded him, filming the action from a multitude of angles and imbuing his scenery with an illusory depth and space. Being able to work with limited resources was part of the *Roman poruno* experience, but no one was better at it than Kumashiro. An area of production in which Kumashiro most explicitly explored the avant-garde was editing. Kumashiro deployed innumerable inserts and jump cuts to disorient the viewer and disrupt any sense of temporality. Stock footage of real-world exteriors and landmarks spliced in between scenes helped build up each film's universe.

Kumashiro's films tended to focus on singular moments in time; thus, backstory was often eliminated as a way to situate the audience directly in the story's action. As a replacement for missing backstory and as a way to quickly flesh out and differentiate his characters, Kumashiro relied on what came to be called the Kumashiro gymnastics. Each character was often given some sort of unusual quirk or mannerism: raising one's leg during orgasm, perhaps, or tapping one's head on the wall. This style of characterization has drawn favorable comparisons to that of French director Robert Bresson.

Kumashiro's films, being pornography, are obviously explorations of the complex relationships between the sexes, but ultimately Kumashiro's artistry overcomes limitations of the genre. The sex scenes in his films are sometimes comical and frequently disturbing. If Kumashiro even intended the sex to be arousing to the viewer, it appears to have been a secondary concern. The sex in these films serves to connect the characters and demonstrate their idiosyncrasies, driving them forward and pushing them into conflict. Kumashiro found working in pornography the freest avenue of expression to explore the issues he wanted to explore. But Kumashiro, constrained by audience expectations and studio contracts, was still a pornographer, and so his films remain largely unrecognized outside his home country.

Western audiences, either morally opposed to porn or at the very least trained to avoid discussing it publicly, are not well acclimated to the style of filmmaking Kumashiro exemplified. Porn in the Western world is often equated with the exploitation of women. Some viewers are likely troubled by Kumashiro's depiction of his female characters, which can at times seem mean-spirited and exploitative. However, properly contextualized, it becomes clear that Kumashiro often seeks to illuminate gender disparities and draw attention to sexual double standards. This is most readily apparent in *Ichijo's Wet Lust*. The real-life Sayuri Ichijo wrestled with Japan's courts for her right to perform; her most famous act, wherein a member of the audience is allowed to inspect her vagina with a magnifying glass, was not allowed to be shown in the film. Kumashiro's film functions as an exploration of Ichijo's right to express herself freely. In the police scenes,

Kumashiro pointedly demonstrates that it is the women who always draw punishment for obscenity, never the men who pay for or otherwise enable the performance. Kumashiro's other films deal with similar issues. They are challenging films made even more so by virtue of pornography's unsavory reputation among most audiences. Kumashiro's films defy those genre conventions, transforming pornography into serious film and making a case for porn to be considered a legitimate variety of artistic expression.—Boleyn Key

KURONEKO (1968)
DIRECTOR: Kaneto Shindo
SCREENPLAY: Naoyuki Yokota and Kōji Shiraishi
SPECS: 90 minutes; color

The *bakeneko* or "ghost cat" films form a whole subgenre of Japanese horror cinema that enjoyed a vogue in the 1950s but gradually trickled away and hasn't reemerged in any substantial form since. Kaneto Shindo's *Kuroneko* (*Yabu no naka no kuroneko*, 1968) is the most critically acclaimed of these films, and its hard-to-surpass skillfulness may have been one of the nails in the genre's coffin. *Kuroneko* stands out from other *bakeneko* films as a tragic folktale that nonetheless embodies both the artistic expressionism and the social consciousness associated with the late 1960s.

The opening scene is one of shocking realism: first a long-shot of a band of roving samurai swarming across a rural setting in complete silence, then dramatic close-ups as they methodically loot a house, rape the two women living there, and burn what's left to the ground. At this point, a black cat licks the blood of the dead women, and the brutal reality of war gives way to a dreamlike chiaroscuro fairytale, as roles reverse and we see the same two women, now ghosts, trap and murder a well-dressed samurai. At times more of a Noh-style dance performance, *Kuroneko* evokes the ethereal grace of a well-told ghost story. The simple, allegorical plot is prevented from being dull or predictable thanks to a captivating visual style, including vividly white figures seemingly cut out of a thick surrounding darkness, composite images that frame the action with claustrophobic bamboo, and a ghost house designed as though it were a theater stage.

Due to the presence of undead vampiric cat women, *Kuroneko* falls into the horror genre more overtly than its acclaimed predecessor *Onibaba* (1964), but in many ways it is the twin of director Shindo Kaneto's earlier film. As in *Onibaba*, the setting is Japan's war-torn feudal past, in which Otawa Nobuko (who married Shindo in 1977) plays a mother living with the wife of her son, who has been forced to abandon his family and join the fighting. Also as in *Onibaba*, the women become a predatory team who set traps for wandering samurai, though the narrative context for this framework is very different for each film. A more thematic similarity is the way in which erotic desire is set against society at large, trapping the characters in a destructive downward spiral with no shortage of Freudian undertones. In terms of style, just as the tall swaying grass of *Onibaba* became an otherworldy, marginal space that visually dominated the film and its protagonists, so too does the bamboo of *Kuroneko* perform a similar function. Also present in both films is repetitive, drum-heavy music that escalates the tension between characters while reminding us of the unseen but ongoing warfare that has determined their troubled relationships. The key way in which *Kuroneko* moves away from its predecessor is its foregrounding of dramatic tragedy, social critique, and performance.

The stage-like house in the bamboo grove, very reminiscent of the classic *Ugetsu Monogatari*'s (1953) ghost house, is itself almost the star of the film. When first we see it, the still house is framed by a panning shot of bamboo, a surreal image that distances the house from the world around it. Within the house, the mise-en-scène is constantly in a state of flux: as the characters move around, subtle changes to the set create a world moving along a spectrum between a grand noble's residence, a dilapidated ruin, and the outside grove of shifting bamboo. When the first victim of the cat women is seated in the house, his speech about the glories of war is subverted by the slow panning image of bamboo that appears behind him—the instability of the house visually undermines the samurai's self-assured justification of what he sees as a noble war. In another example, we see the mother leaving the room, and, by keeping the shot fixed on her slow disappearance into darkness, the camera implies that the house extends into other, unseen places, a sort of underworld for its inhabitants. In this dark space, we see the women grieving with each other, moving from spot to spot, and always being lit by a bright, theatrical light when they fall still. The obvious artifice of the lighting contributes to the image of an unstable, potentially transformative setting.

Far from a flight into pure fantasy, this in-between world is a reflection of the social conflicts in the film's narrative. "Mother! Monster!" cries the returned son as he confronts his dead mother, torn by his familial love and his duty as a samurai to slay monstrous beings, just as his family is torn by their duty to "an evil god" to kill all samurai that they encounter as well as their own love for a son and husband. Paralleling the pressures of the elite, brutal samurai class and the will of an evil god may seem like unsubtle moralizing, but when *Kuroneko* was made it would have been more natural for its audience to associate the ceremony-obsessed, authoritarian, and war-mongering samurai of the film with Japan's struggle in the Second World War, grounding the fable more firmly and urgently in modern-day life. Aesthetically speaking, the conflict between desire and duty gives birth to the unstable identities of the film's three protagonists, while the resulting anguish they feel is embodied in the dance-like struggles, erotic and violent, between them.—Seán Hudson

See also Onibaba; Shindō, Kaneto

Bibliography
Shindo Kaneto, dir. *Kuroneko*. Kindai Eiga Kyokai, 1968. Film.

KUROSAWA, KIYOSHI (1955–)
Born on 19 July 1955, in the port city of Kobe, Japan, Kiyoshi Kurosawa is a Japanese film director and screenwriter. Under the guidance of noted film critic and scholar of French literature, Shigehiko Hasumi (b. 1936), at Rikkyo University in Tokyo, he had initially begun making 8 mm films while still a student. In the 1980s, he began directing commercially, working on pink films and low-budget

direct-to-video productions, in particular with highly formulaic yakuza action films. In the early 1990s, Kurosawa won a scholarship to study filmmaking in the United States with the Sundance Institute. His work as prodigious as he is prolific, he is best known for his many contributions to the genre of Japanese horror, in particular an intense focus on the juxtaposition of the *individual* with its *social context*. In nearly all of his later horror films, the narrative trajectory boils down to the (bizarre) manner in which a main character's individuality or personal morality is shaped in highly unexpected ways through strange, even horrific circumstances.

As a young filmmaker associated with Nikkatsu Kabushikigaisha, the oldest major movie studio in Japan and best known for its film and television productions, Kurosawa belonged to a production organization called the Director's Company, founded in 1982. There he was offered a chance with Million Film Studio to direct a pink film, in this instance a brand of sex-oriented film called *roman poruno*, or romantic porn. The result was *Kandagawa Pervert War* (1983), remembered less for its lascivious sexual content, perhaps, than its inventive directorial devices, playful mannerisms, and in-joke allusions to American western films. He undertook a second film, *College Girl: Shameful Seminar* (1983), but the studio canceled its release, ostensibly because of its sore lack of erotic appeal. Not to be defeated, Kurosawa purchased the footage with the financial assistance of outside backers and revamped it as *The Excitement of the Do-Re-Mi-Fa Girl* (1985).

Several years later, he would undertake the horror film *Sweet Home* (1989), produced by Jūzō Itami (1933–1997). It was released simultaneously with a video game of the same title. The film is of a rather straightforward slasher variety with, of course, a Japanese slant, reflecting as it were, Kurosawa's interest in psychological horror.

Kurosawa first achieved international acclaim with his 1997 crime thriller film *Cure*. As a police detective tries to uncover the secret behind a series of gruesome murders all committed in the same manner by different people who have no memory of what they have done, a larger gruesome story unfolds in what critics would recognize as part thriller, part horror with a distinct Gothic tinge.

That same year, he experimented with the yakuza suspense thriller by filming two works back-to-back, *Serpent's Path* (1998) and *Eyes of the Spider* (1998). While both built upon the same premise, a father's revenge for the murder of his child, each developed entirely different storylines.

In 1999, he directed several films, among them *License to Live* and *Barren Illusions*. He followed these with his "semi-sequel" to *Cure*, the detective film *Charisma*. While it opens to an all-too-familiar pattern of an overworked, rumpled, and unfocused police officer's napping while on a case, it quickly unfolds as a visually compelling, multi-layered, and insightful film on radicalism, individuality, and balance by which Kurosawa is able to explore matters of conscience, spiritual longing, and personal disharmony through the manifestation of a metaphoric environmental malady. In the end, as conflicting ideologies struggle between natural and created order, an oppressive, alienating, and ominous wasteland of irreconcilable and consuming intolerance emerges to take control.

In 2000, Kurosawa adapted the 1964 British novel *Séance on a Wet Afternoon* by Mark McShane (b. 1930) to the small screen. His version, *Séance*, premiering on Kansai TV, is illustrative of his artistic preference for deep space (shots whose on-camera space recedes very far back in the frame) and for architectural frames within frames that lend themselves easily to the ambiguities of horror film and action-packed thrillers alike.

Shortly thereafter, he returned to filming for the big screen. His horror film *Pulse* (2001) was screened as part of the section Un Certain Regard at the 2001 Cannes Film Festival. The movie was well received critically and quickly found a cult following. From the opening shot of the single vessel, adrift on a vast, turbulent ocean, Kurosawa sets into motion a pervasive sense of foreboding and unnaturalness with his use of predominantly medium shots, dark interiors, diffused tonal lighting, shadows, and delayed focus shifts. Distorted shots and green-hued images in juxtaposition with the anonymous woman's suicide leap from the roof of an industrial complex or a disorienting evening commute on an empty train, for example, ground the film as a socially relevant allegory on the dichotomy of human interaction and the self-induced alienation inherent in contemporary urban existence.

Over the next several years, Kurosawa would release *Bright Future* (2003) and the digital feature black comedy, *Doppelgänger* (2003), as well as his big screen return with another love story, *Loft* (2005), and his mystery-cum-horror film, *Retribution* (2006), followed in the next year. He culminated this era in his career with the release of the middle-class family drama, *Tokyo Sonata* (2008), a film that went on to be named the Best Film at the Third Asian Film Awards and received the Prix Un Certain Regard at the 2008 Cannes Film Festival.

After a five-year hiatus from the big screen, Kurosawa returned to lackluster reviews with the quasi-scientific psycho-fantasy drama *Real* (2013), a film that focuses on a single image, a childhood drawing of a giant plesiosaur. His *Seventh Code* (2013), however, would prove redemptive for him, as he was named Best Director at the Eighth Rome Film Festival later that year. His romantic drama, *Journey to the Shore* (2015), screened in the Un Certain Regard section at the 2015 Cannes Film Festival, once more brought him the award for Best Director.

However much Kiyoshi Kurosawa might engage with issues of environmental critique—his choice of locations suggests a decided preference for urban blight and decaying open spaces, abandoned buildings—his films nonetheless occupy two extremes: the quotidian materials of mass culture and esoteric, erudite abstraction. He credits his mentor Shigehiko Hasumi with having introduced him to the complexities of Alfred Hitchcock (1899–1980) and Yasujirō Ozu (1903–1963). He has also an affinity for American film directors, the likes of Don Siegel (1912–1991), Sam Peckinpah (1925–1984), Robert Aldrich (1918–1983), Richard Fleischer (1916–2006), and Tobe Hooper (b. 1943).—James A. Wren

Bibliography

Andrew, Dudley, ed. *Opening Bazin*. London: Oxford University Press, 2011.

Blair, Gavin J. "Japanese Director Kiyoshi Kurosawa 'Very Surprised' about Two Wins at Rome Film Fest." *Hollywood Reporter*, 18 November 2013.

Hoover, Travis Mackenzie. "J-Horror Mash-Up: Kiyoshi Kurosawa's Retribution." *Slant Magazine*, 6 December 2006.

Ma, Kevin. "Kurosawa Kiyoshi Takes Journey to the Shore." *Film Business Asia*, 20 June 2014.

Oumano, Elena. *Cinema Today: A Conversation with Thirty-Nine Filmmakers from Around the World*. New Brunswick, NJ: Rutgers University Press, 2011.

Palmer, Tim. "The Rules of the World: Japanese Ecocinema and Kiyoshi Kurosawa." In *Framing the World: Explorations in Ecocriticism and Film*, edited by Paula Willoquet-Maricondi, 209–24. Charlottesville: University of Virginia Press, 2010.

Richie, Donald. *A Hundred Years of Japanese Film: A Concise History*. Tokyo: Kodansha International, 2001.

Tesse, Jean-Philippe. "Critique: *Loft* by Kiyoshi Kurosawa." *Cahiers du Cinema*, January 2007.

White, Jerry. *The Films of Kiyoshi Kurosawa: Master of Fear*. Berkeley, CA: Stone Bridge Press, 2007.

KWAIDAN (1964)

DIRECTOR: Masaki Kobayashi
SCREENPLAY: Yōko Mizuki
SPECS: 183 minutes; color

The Japanese portmanteau film *Kwaidan* (1964) was directed by Masaki Kobayashi (1916–1996), taking its plot lines from *Kwaidan: Stories and Studies of Strange Things* (1904), a collection of Japanese folktales compiled by Lafcadio Hearn (1850–1904). The film is an assemblage of four separate and unrelated stories. Hearn, in fact, made a conscious choice to retain Setsu's Izumo dialect, a choice that the director continued. Well received by a movie-going audience and film critics alike, it was awarded the Special Jury Prize at the 1965 Cannes Film Festival and received an Academy Award nomination for Best Foreign Language Film.

The first tale, "The Black Hair," focuses on an impoverished swordsman living in Kyoto. Discontented with his lot in life, he divorces his wife, a weaver, to marry the daughter of a wealthy land-owning family. With his new wife in tow, he assumes the post of district governor. The marriage, however, is anything but blissful. His confrontations with a wife who is as callous as she is shallow make him grow to regret leaving his devoted first wife behind. Ultimately, the second wife withdraws to her marriage chambers in indignation, and he refuses to follow. Intending to return home and reconcile with his first wife, he tells his second wife that it was his foolish youth and being impoverished that made him marry her to obtain greater social status and wealth. Admitting his folly, he informs her that their marriage is over, thereby freeing her to return to her family.

He, too, returns to his first home and finds that his wife is quite understanding about his reasons for the initial divorce, and they reunite. Before going to bed, he promises that he will remain forever by her side. The following morning, he wakes to find next to him the rotted corpse that was once his wife. He tries to escape, only to fall beneath the floor. The final image is of a man disheveled and balding, unable to do anything but remain faithful to his promise never to abandon her again.

The second sequence, "The Woman of the Snow," is based on a particular tale of the *onnayuki*, perhaps the best-known of the many *yōkai*, or strange apparitions, said to wander around Japan. Set in Musashi Province, the tale unwinds as Minokichi, a woodcutter, and his elder, Mosaku, seek refuge in the hut of a fisherman during a snowstorm. As he wakes, he sees that his companion has been killed by a beautiful apparition, who eventually spares his life provided, of course, that he never speak of the matter again.

True to his word, he departs and on the road home he meets a beautiful young woman, Yuki, who looks suspiciously like the ghost who had killed Mosaku. He takes her with him back home, where she meets his approving mother. They soon fall in love and live happily together for the next ten years, during which time she bears him three healthy children. Yet in spite of the lapse of time, she seems never to age.

Then, one night during a snowstorm, Minokichi suggests that her appearance reminds him of the spirit he had earlier encountered, and thus, he begins to relate the details of that night at the fisherman's hut. She reveals herself to him, reminding him that he has broken his word. She does not, however, kill him but instead, she departs with a warning that should he fail to care for his children she would return and fulfill her threats against him. Minokichi remains behind with the children, heartbroken.

The following tale, "Hōichi the Earless," recounts a moment in the life of a *biwa hoshi*, or blind musician who wanders the countryside. He is a master at recounting episodes from the medieval epic *The Tale of the Heike*, in particular the Battle of Nan-no-ura, fought between the Taira and Minamoto clans during the last years of the Genpei War (1180–1185). One day, he is summoned to sing for a royal family. Friends and priests alike express their uneasiness and a growing concern that he may be before a hall of ghosts. To protect him, a priest and his acolyte pen the text of The Heart Sutra on his body, and they instruct him to go outside and sit perfectly still, as if in meditation.

The final tale, "In a Cup of Tea," relates a moment when a writer anticipates a visit from his publisher. As he waits, he begins to see unknown faces as they appear in his cup of tea.

A common thread to each of these reiterations is the vengeance of ghosts. And while we find a similar motif repeated in the supernatural psychological horror film *Ringu* (1998), directed by Nakata Hideo (b. 1961), and the *Ju-on* films, directed by Takashi Shimizu (b. 1972), it is important that one be able to distinguish between those nuanced tales from the distant past and contemporary, at times simplistic and overt stories of urban ghosts said to haunt the Japanese landscape.—James A. Wren

Bibliography

Hearn, Lafcadio. *Kwaidan: Stories and Studies of Strange Things*. Tokyo: Tuttle Publishing, 2005.
Shimizu, Takashi, dir. *Ju-On: The Curse*. Toei, 2000. Film.
Kobayashi, Masaki, dir. *Kwaidan*. Toho, 1964. Film.
Nakata, Hideo, dir. *Ringu*. Toho, 1998. Film.
The Heart Sutra. Translated by Red Pine. New York: Counterpoint, 2005.

KYŌFU (2010)

DIRECTOR: Hiroshi Takahashi
SCREENPLAY: Hiroshi Takahashi
SPECS: 94 minutes; color

One of the six films developed and produced in the first decade of the twenty-first century by Takashige Ichise (b. 1961), known in some circles as "Father of J-Horror," and distributed by the major studio Toho, *Kyōfu* (also known as *The Sylvian Experiments*) came out in 2010 as the J-horror boom was winding down. With screens overpopulated by long-haired, faceless girl ghosts and sequels, offshoots and imitators of *Ring* and *Ju-on* and their series, *Kyōfu* thus never received the proper credit it deserved.

Written and directed by Hiroshi Takahashi (b. 1959), a veteran screenwriter who struck it big with the Hideo Nakata (b. 1961) version of *Ring* (1998) and *Ju-on* (2003), *Kyōfu* distinguishes itself from other popular J-horror titles, by harkening back to the fascination with scientific breakthrough and forbidden knowledge typically found in the early twentieth-century Japanese SF. In this way, it is perhaps more resonant with the contemporary cinematic variations of H. P. Lovecraft, such as Stuart Gordon's *Dreams in the Witch House* (2005) or the omnibus film *Necronomicon* (1993) than with a typical J-horror, although its slow-burn, creeping atmosphere of anxiety is the kind often associated with the latter label.

The movie opens with a cryptic but uneasy scene in which two young children, Kaori (Mina Fujii, b. 1988) and Miyuki (Yuri Nakamura, aka Yu-ri Seong, b. 1982), sneak a peek at their parents watching a documentary film on a human experiment conducted by the Japanese military on the Chinese and Russian subjects during wartime. Apparently, one or more of the experimental subjects succeeded in opening a portal to another dimension, with disastrous results. Two decades later, Kaori learns that her sister Miyuki has committed suicide, but she continues to feel the latter's "presence" in her life. It turns out, Miyuki was a member of a voluntary group-suicide website, and she, along with other members, have been brought into a secret laboratory run by the sister's mother, Dr. Ota (Nagisa Katahira, b. 1959), determined to continue the wartime experiments. In a faithfully Lovecraftian fashion, just what lies beneath the glowing portal is never clearly shown, although director Takahashi does succeed in suggesting some formless, all-devouring horror that threatens to spill into our world, at least until the climax in which less-than-convincing computer-generated imagery effects intervene. He also pulls off the radical reality-shift plot twist at the end, although the impatient or inattentive viewers might still remain confused as the end credits roll.

In addition to its unusually cerebral content, *The Sylvian Experiments* boasts an interesting cast. The attractive Mina Fujii is fine as the distressed lead actress, but the film really belongs to Yuri Nakamura, (also seen in such mainstream films as *Like Father, Like Son* [2013] and *Genome Hazard* [2014]), whose restrained, creepy portrayal of the otherworldly Miyuki drives the narrative and grounds it emotionally. The dark history of wartime human experiments by the Japanese military in Northeast China (Manchuria) is a fertile ground for developing SF-horror hybrid films, among which *Kyōfu* should be counted as a moderate success.—Kyu Hyun Kim

See also Ju-on films; *Ringu*

Bibliography

Takahashi Hiroshi, dir. *The Sylvian Experiments* [*Kyōfu*]. Cell/Entertainment Farm/Geneon Entertainment/Oz Company/Tokyo Theater K. K., 2010. Film.

• L •

THE LIVING SKELETON (1968)
DIRECTOR: Hiroki Matsuno
SCREENPLAY: Kobayashi Kyūzō, Kikuma Shimoiizaka
SPECS: 81 minutes; black and white

Shochiku, founded in 1895 as a specialist in theater production, has maintained its well-deserved reputation not only as a custodian of the artistic, drama-oriented aspects of Japanese filmmaking (represented by the works of such titans as Kenji Mizoguchi, Yasujirō Ozu, and Hideki Kobayashi) but also as an innovator in cinematic medium: Shochiku was the first film studio to release a full-fledged talkie in Japan (*Madame and the Wife*, 1931) and also Japan's first color film (*Carmen Comes Home*, 1951). Yet, curiously Shochiku expressed little interest in the special effects–laden SF-fantasy genre, producing only a handful of these films in the 1960s, leaving the field to Toho (and to a lesser extent, Daiei). Moreover, it is widely acknowledged that the qualities of these films are uneven, to say the least. The studio's sole foray into giant monster territory, *X from Outer Space* (*Uchū dai-kaijū Girara*, 1967), is regarded by some connoisseurs as the worst *kaijū eiga* ever made in Japan, a reputation that any film would surely find it impossible to live up to. The best known to the Euro-American viewers among them is probably *Goke, Body Snatcher from Hell* (*Kyūketsuki Gokemidoro*, 1968), an openly nihilistic alien-invasion saga that annoyingly received a boost on the stateside cult film recognition meter due to its key scene being "referenced" by Quentin Tarantino in *Kill Bill*.

The Living Skeleton is a late entry and perhaps the most obscure among the Shochiku's special effects–oriented genre films, filmed in black and white (at a time when color had become the dominant format). The film opens with a violent and desperate sequence in which a group of marauding pirates takes over a cargo ship, *Ryūō Maru*, and massacre its captain and crew. Yoriko, played by Kikko Matsuoka (b. 1947), the beautiful wife of the ship's on-board doctor, is one of the victims. Three years later, Yoriko's twin sister Saeko, entrusted to the care of Catholic priest Akashi, played by Masumi Okada (1935–2006), while scuba-diving, runs into a group of skeletons chained together and sunk at the bottom of the ocean. Her boyfriend Mochizuki, played by Yasunori Irikawa (1939–2011), brushes their experience off as an illusion, but Saeko is convinced that the skeletons were real, and senses that her sister is dead as well. Soon they are seeing *Ryūō Maru* floating in the stormy sea, and Saeko is possessed by Yoriko's vengeful spirit, who seeks revenge against the pirates, now living as wealthy local notables.

The Living Skeleton was allegedly chopped into the current version by the producers, against the opposition of its screenwriter, Kobayashi Kyūzō (1935–2006, well known for a political mystery *August without the Emperor* [1978]), which goes some way to explaining the considerable incoherence and lack of sufficient exposition in the plot. As compensation, director Hiroki Matsuno keeps the pace brisk and whips up dollops of Gothic atmosphere. Fortunately, exotic beauty Matsuoka is very effective in the dual role, and her stalking and killing of the villains are mostly well done, including a "What's the matter, cat got your tongue?" sequence set in a shower stall. Yet the film is obviously hampered by its low budget as well as technical limitations. The underwater skeletons, making their appearance in the film's first major "boo!" moment, are so fake looking that they are goofy rather than scary: the miniature photography of the ghost ship is okay, but its interiors lack the kind of detail and creative touches that one is used to seeing in comparable Toho productions. The gory finale involving flesh-dissolving chemicals (the screenplay—or, if Kobayashi's recollection is to be believed, a senselessly truncated version on display here—suddenly decides to add a medical-horror angle concerning the Japanese wartime experiment in biological warfare) is conceptually interesting but its cutback from superimposition of animated "wounds" on still photos to what appear to be wax dummies smoking and fizzing is less than convincing.

While obviously not an A-rank horror classic in any way, *The Living Skeleton* is, goofiness and all, quite entertaining and provides a handful of impressive set pieces, grounded by Matsuoka's sympathetic performance. The film languished in obscurity for many years outside Japan despite its moderate cult following in the country. Criterion Collection in 2012 rectified this problem by releasing *X from Outer Space*, *Goke*, the insect-mutation SF *Genocide* (1968), and the title in question in a box set christened "When Horror Came to Shochiku." Neither *The Living Skeleton* nor the film's original Japanese title (which translates as "Bloodsucking skeleton ship") is really accurate: No skeleton comes alive and no character, ghost or otherwise, sucks blood, unless one takes into account Yoriko's zombie husband chortling, "I need fresh meat and blood!" during the logic-challenged climax.—Kyu Hyun Kim

LOFT (2005)

DIRECTOR: Kiyoshi Kurosawa
SCREENPLAY: Kiyoshi Kurosawa
SPECS: 115 minutes; color

Perhaps more than any film by director Kiyoshi Kurosawa (b. 1955), *Loft*—alternately titled as *Shi no otome* (Maiden of death)—reveals the director's attempts to work within the horror genre, and particularly the J-horror genre, while revitalizing its conventions at the same time.

One of Kurosawa's lesser-known films, *Loft* tells the story of an award-winning romance novelist, Reiko Haruna, played by Miki Nakatani (star of the film *Rasen* from 1998), who moves to a secluded house to finish work on a book. Inevitably, strange things happen at her new abode: Reiko begins to cough up mud, as if possessed by some unseen force; she encounters a mysterious anthropologist, Minoru Yoshioka, played by Etsushi Toyokawa, moving the mummified remains of a young woman found in a nearby swamp; and she witnesses a strange long-haired woman roaming the nearby forest. In one particular eerie scene, Reiko spots the girl dripping wet at the end of a pier extending out over a pond near the house—a not-so-subtle reference to the predominance of "dead wet girls" in Japanese horror films like *Ringu* (1998).

Reiko feels eerily connected to both the mummy and long-haired woman. She discovers that the woman was also a writer who lived in the house while finishing her own novel and that they share the same editor, a man named Kijima, played by Hidetoshi Nishijima, who encouraged the woman to move into the house before she went missing. She also discovers the draft of a romance novel that the missing writer left behind and decides to revise the work as her own. The mud that Reiko continues to cough up, moreover, links her to both the mummy, which has been buried in the muck of the swamp for hundreds of years, and the missing writer, whose body, we later learn, rests on the bottom of the murky pond.

Confirming Reiko's and the audience's suspicions, it is revealed that the missing writer was murdered by Kijima. Just as he is about to kill Reiko too, however, Kijima is apprehended by the authorities, who show up at Reiko's house. With the mystery solved, Reiko and Minoru recognize their mutual attraction and go to the pier to plan their future. As they stand together over the pond, however, a gear contraption anchored to the pier suddenly begins to turn, raising the body of the dead girl out of the pond while pulling Minoru into the water to his death. In the last shot of the film, Reiko stands in shock as the decomposing body of the girl hangs above her suspended in the air.

Despite its use of J-horror trappings, *Loft*, like many of Kurosawa's films, does not evoke fear in the same way that horror audiences may be conditioned to experience it. *Loft* lacks the visual unity and narrative momentum that creates the tension often expected in the horror experience. Indeed, Kurosawa suggests that he is not interested in creating cohesive stories in his films, often shifting the responsibility to the viewer to make sense of the visuals in his works. This is because "true horror," for Kurosawa, should evoke terrifying experiences that resist the narrative and visual order that have become a part of the horror genre. *Loft* captures the disorienting effects of true horror through a fragmented editing style. Jump cuts link scenes and images in ways that are not clear, and the lack of eye-line matching, Kurosawa admits, disrupts continuity in many of the scenes in the film.

Along with a fragmented visual and narrative style, *Loft*, like much of Kurosawa's work, reproduces the defamiliarizing experience of horror by drawing attention to the things outside the field of vision. For this reason, characters often move about behind translucent screens, or leave the confines of the frame altogether, drawing the viewer's imagination to the things that they cannot see and creating the sense of ambiguity and mystery that Kurosawa identifies with horror. Through the narrative and visual disorder of *Loft*, then, Kurosawa refines the conventional view of horror, highlighting the mystery of a world not captured within the confines of the camera frame.—Marc Yamada

· M ·

MAKAI TENSHŌ (1981)
DIRECTOR: Kinji Fukasaku
SCREENPLAY: Kinji Fukasaku, Tatsuo Nogami
SPECS: 122 minutes; color

Makai Tenshō (literally, "Resurrection from the demon realm"), often translated as *Samurai Reincarnation* in English, refers to several cinematic adaptations of a 1967 novel of the same name written by Futarō Yamada (1922–2001). The most popular of these adaptations was a 1981 horror film, directed by Kinji Fukasaku (1930–2003). The film centers on the leader of an Edo-period uprising in Japan and his attempt to overthrow the Tokugawa shogunate. The only one capable of defeating him is one of Japan's most legendary samurai. A work of historical fiction, the film (as well as the original novel) takes place after the Shimabara rebellion of 1637–1638, reconstructing the lives of several historical personages in the process. The film was critically acclaimed in Japan and won two Japanese Academy Awards.

The film tells the story of Shirō Tokisada Amakusa (ca. 1621–1638), the historical Christian leader of a group of peasants who openly revolted in 1637 as a result of heavy taxes and the Tokugawa persecution of Christians. This revolt—known today as the Shimabara Rebellion—failed, and as a result, Amakusa was beheaded and his company of Christians were all slaughtered. This is where the historical background ends. The film opens on a Noh play being performed in post-rebellion Shimabara, just outside where Amakusa and his men still lie slaughtered, impaled, and beheaded. Thunder sounds as the eyes in Amakusa's disembodied head open. Lightning strikes the area and the Tokugawa soldiers viewing the play are killed instantly. The performer alone rises, revealing himself as a resurrected Amakusa, portrayed by Kenji Sawada (b. 1948).

Amakusa laments that God has forsaken him and his people, refusing to aid them in their plight. He then renounces God and sells his soul to the powers of darkness, swearing vengeance on the shogunate that brutally slaughtered his Christian compatriots. Granted the power to reanimate the dead, he begins to amass an army of resurrected followers, coaxing them into joining him by appealing to their earthly laments and grudges. At his side are the spurned Christian Gracia Hosokawa (1562–1600), the legendary swordsman Musashi Miyamoto (ca. 1584–1645), the Buddhist warrior-monk Hōshin Inshun, and the Iga ninja Kirimaru. Standing in Amakusa's path of vengeance is a single man: the renowned samurai Jūbei Mitsuyoshi Yagyū (1607–1650), played by Sonny Chiba (b. 1939).

Amakusa's plot unfolds slowly, first targeting Nobutsuna Matsudaira (1596–1662), the man who historically subdued the Christian rebels at Shimabara. As Hosokawa seduces the Tokugawa shogun, Ietsuna (1641–1680), Amakusa strangles Matsudaira with a rope of hair harvested from the female Shimabara corpses.

191

Amakusa's actions catch the attention of Jūbei's father, Munenori Yagyū (1571–1646), the shogun's own sword instructor. Inshun battles with him, but they both lose; Inshun is slain, and Munenori succumbs to sickness. The dying swordsman laments that his failing health prevented him from testing his son Jūbei at swordplay. Amakusa arrives, telling Munenori that this wish can still be granted. Blinded by his own wants like the others, Munenori accepts Amakusa's offer and is resurrected as a demon.

Jūbei—absent for nearly the entire first half of the film—arrives and discovers what has happened to his father. Rather than fight, he retreats and visits the stigmatized blacksmith Muramasa. Jūbei requests from him a sword capable of killing Amakusa and his demonic entourage. Kirimaru also begins to fall for a woman named Omitsu and laments having accepted Amakusa's offer. He begs Jūbei to kill him, but the latter refuses. Eventually, the blade that Jūbei commissioned is finished at the cost of Muramasa's life.

In the meantime, Amakusa has cursed all the crops harvested on the shogun's lands, throwing the peasants into chaotic uproar against the shogunate. He eventually incites them, rallying them to take up arms against the shogun himself. Hosokawa has also beguiled Ietsuna into sniping at his own people with a bow, believing them to be deer. In the uproar created by the peasants, Kirimaru attempts to flee with Omitsu, but Amakusa intervenes. Kirimaru defies his master and is killed as a result. Kirimaru's body is brought to Jūbei, who promises vengeance. Miyamoto also appears, challenging Jūbei to a duel. The two legends cross swords and Miyamoto is cut down.

The Edo government is in chaos; peasants plague them from outside, and Hosokawa and Munenori slay the Tokugawa men from within. In the chaos, the castle catches fire, becoming a truly hellish scene. Ietsuna is killed as Hosokawa plunges with him into the flames. It is only then that Jūbei appears on the scene, face to face with his father, Munenori. The two clash amid the conflagration and Munenori is slain.

Amakusa appears, offering Jūbei eternal life as a demon. Jūbei refuses and the two fight. Amakusa is eventually beheaded, but not killed. He exclaims that as long as humans exist in the world, he shall return again. Amakusa then vanishes, leaving Jūbei alone in the inferno.

As expected from Yamada, *Makai Tenshō* is filled with swordplay, murder, and sexuality. While the gore in Fukasaku's film adaptation is not intense, violence lurks around every corner—several are sliced or stabbed to death, others are strangled, or burned. Between Amakusa's vengeance and Jūbei's vow to defeat him, numerous lives are lost. Fukasaku also explores the sexual realm of the novel, largely through the character of Hosokawa. She entrances the shogun, Ietsuna, enslaving him with enough lust for her body that he forgoes his responsibilities as shogun. Elements of *ero guro nansensu* can be seen throughout the film.

Three other cinematic adaptions of *Makai Tenshō* exist: a two-part 1996 direct-to-video version, directed by Kazumasa Shirai, a 1997 animated version, directed by Yasunori Urata, and a 2003 film directed by Hideyuki Hirayama (b. 1950). Each of these was adapted from the same novel, yet they each portray the source material differently. The secondary scenes included in each adapta-

tion also tend to vary drastically, flavoring each film in its own individual way.
—Joseph P. Elacqua

See also ero guro nansensu genre

Bibliography
Fukasaku Kinji, dir. *Makai Tenshō: Samurai Reincarnation*. Kadokawa Haruki Jimusho, 1981. Film.
Hirayama, Hideyuki, dir. *Samurai Resurrection*. Kadokawa Shoten, 2003. Film.
Shirai, Kazumasa, dir. *Reborn from Hell: Samurai Armageddon*. GAGA, 1996. Film.
———. *Reborn from Hell II: Jubei's Revenge*. GAGA, 1996. Film.
Urata, Yasunori, dir. *Ninja Resurrection*. Phoenix Entertainment, 1997. TV miniseries

MAREBITO (2004)
DIRECTOR: Takashi Shimizu
SCREENPLAY: Chiaki Konaka
SPECS: 92 minutes; color

Marebito is a 2004 horror film directed by Takashi Shimizu from a screenplay by Chiaki Konaka. It stars Shin'ya Tsukamoto, Kazuhiro Nakahara, and Tomomi Miyashita. The film focuses on the life of a freelance cinematographer named Takuyoshi Masuoka, played by Shin'ya Tsukamoto, who spends the majority of his time wandering around Tokyo, shooting city scenes in the hopes of capturing something strange on film. Filmed between the completion of 2003's *Ju-on: The Grudge 2* and the start of production for 2004's *The Grudge*, the film represents a significant departure from the narrative and aesthetic horror style that director Takashi Shimizu is most known for.

Masuoka is a down-on-his-luck freelance cameraman working in Tokyo. Fascinated by the relationship between the lens and the human eye, Masuoka spends his free time filming different neighborhoods in Tokyo and obsessively watching the footage in an attempt to capture the realities of urban life. One day, as he is passing through a subway station, Masuoka captures footage of a gruesome suicide: with a look of unbridled fear on his face, a frenzied man named Mr. Kuroki, played by Kazuhiro Nakahara takes his own life by stabbing himself in the eye. Masuoka, after watching and re-watching the footage, becomes convinced that the man killed himself over something he had seen—something more terrible than could possibly be imagined. He decides to track down this unspeakable thing in the hopes of experiencing the same level of terror for himself.

In the tunnels under Tokyo, the ghost of Mr. Kuroki meets Masuoka. Mr. Kuroki explains that all urban areas of the world have tunnels that lead to "Agartha"—the capital of the subterranean realm within the hollow earth. He also warns Masuoka to be careful of the "Deros," violent creatures that roam the underworld. However, he disappears when Masuoka mentions his suicide, leaving Masuoka to discover a vast underground network of monumental cliffs alone. When Masuoka finds what appears to be a young girl, played by Tomomi Miyashita, lying naked and chained in a shallow cave, he names her "F" and takes her home with the intention of studying her. His studies prove inconclusive, however, and in the process of observing F his own grip on reality slowly but steadily begins to slip.

The screenplay for *Marebito* was adapted by author Chiaki Konaka from his novel of the same name, and it extensively references elements of nineteenth-century "lost continent" and "hollow Earth" theories, early twentieth-century pulp horror narratives, and traditional Japanese folklore. Though there are explicit references to Lovecraftian concepts, most notably to the author's 1936 novella *At the Mountains of Madness*, the film draws primarily from the writings of Richard Sharpe Shaver, whose 1945 essay "A Warning to Future Man" (published by *Amazing Stories* as "I Remember Lemuria!") about a subterranean realm of the hollow Earth, informs much of the characters', and consequently the audience's understanding of the film's setting and principal dangers.

While the writings of Richard Shaver are a major influence on the visual and narrative tone of the film, *Marebito* is also strongly influenced by traditional Japanese beliefs about the supernatural beings from which the film takes its title. In folklore, *Marebito* has a somewhat broad definition. Most commonly the term refers to traveling gods who visit villages from far-off other worlds. However, it can also be used to apply to any being—human or otherwise—who comes from a space that lies outside the social, political, or spiritual realm of the community. The concept of that which lies "outside" is one of *Marebito*'s most primary themes, and it underpins Masuoka's question to find an unknown terror. For as Masuoka states, he is seeking an unknown terror because the horrors of his world, whether real or imagined, are fundamentally known—that is to say, they come from the inside—and are therefore meaningless. It is this very desire to know the unknown, to go beyond the boundaries, and to find out what lies outside, that ultimately blurs the line between Masuoka and the so-called *marebito* that he has brought back with him.

Marebito has received mixed-to-positive reviews. While some critics have argued that the film's methodical pace and lack of traditional horror elements diminish its affective impact, others have praised it for its embrace of atypical horror elements and high level of historical and cultural literacy. Following its debut in Tokyo, *Marebito* was screened at the Seattle International Film Festival.—Sara L. Sumpter

See also Shimizu, Takashi

Bibliography
Shimizu, Takashi, dir. *Marebito*. Kino Lorber Films, 2006. DVD.

MATANGO (1963)
DIRECTOR: Ishirō Honda
SCREENPLAY: Takeshi Kimura
SPECS: 89 minutes; color

Matango is a 1963 *tokusatsu* (special effects) horror film directed by Ishirō Honda (1911–1993) with special effects directed by Eiji Tsuburaya (1901–1970). The film's English title has been given variously as *Attack of the Mushroom People*, *Curse of the Mushroom People*, and *Fungus of Terror*.

The main story is introduced through an outer frame narrative from the perspective of a man held in a psychiatric ward. He tells the story of being marooned on a strange, deserted island with a small group of people after their yacht was wrecked in a storm. The members of the group include the narrator, a professor named Kenji Murai, played by Akira Kubo (b. 1936); the singer Mami Sekiguchi, played by Kumi Mizuno (b. 1937); the skipper Naoyuki Sakuta, played by Hiroshi Koizumi (b. 1926); the skipper's assistant Senzō Koyama, played by Kenji Sahara (b. 1932); the writer Etsurō Yoshida, played by Hiroshi Tachikawa (b. 1931); the yacht's owner Masafumi Kasai, played by Yoshio Tsuchiya (b. 1927); and the student Akiko Sōma, played by Miki Yashiro (b. 1943). As they begin to explore the island, they find it to be rife with an unfamiliar type of mushroom. They discover a decrepit shipwreck, which is also overrun on the inside with a damp fungus. They find no bodies of the ship's former crew. The ship has a meager supply of rations on board, so they clean the interior and use it as a makeshift shelter. From the equipment on board they infer that the ship must have been a research vessel looking into some sort of incident involving radioactivity. They also find a log that includes an ominous proscription against eating the native mushrooms.

At first the stranded group tries to survive off the discovered rations, but the food quickly dwindles. The relations between the group members grow tense, and quarrels break out among them, driven by hunger, jealousy, and sexual tension. Eventually Yoshida gives in to his urges and starts to eat the island's mushrooms. As a result, he descends into madness, which sets off a chain of violent events that leave Koyama dead and shatter any remaining sense of solidarity among the other group members. Mami sides with Yoshida, and the two are sent away in exile; Sakuta disappears after repairing the yacht, and it is later revealed that he died at sea in a failed escape attempt; and then Mami returns to the ship and convinces Kasai to come with her into the forest, where he begins to eat the mushrooms, too. At this point it is fully revealed to the viewer that the mushrooms turn those who eat them into the "mushroom people" of the film's English title—a fate to which Yoshida has already succumbed.

This leaves Murai and Akiko as the two remaining members of the group still at the shipwreck. The mushroom people lead a raid on them, however, and succeed in kidnapping Akiko, who ultimately gives in to the temptation and eats the mushrooms, as well. Unable to save Akiko, Murai manages to escape on the yacht, which has drifted back to the island, and he is rescued and brought safely back to Japan. Returning to the outer frame narrative in the psychiatric ward, Murai turns to face the camera in a final reveal: his face is covered with a fungal growth, and in the last scene of the film it is made clear that he, too, indulged in the mushrooms.

As has been noted by previous commentators, the tone of Matango is remarkably dark for a tokusatsu film, and it succeeds as a sophisticated examination of what happens when social bonds break down in dire circumstances. The gradual dissolution of the camaraderie between the group members, and the outbursts of power struggles fueled by lust and selfishness, are in a sense the true sources of the horror in the film. Matango is particularly amenable to allegorical and metaphorical interpretations, wherein the group becomes a microcosm for Japanese society, for example, and the anti-nuclear themes, prominent throughout many tokusatsu films of the 1950s and 1960s, are made explicit with the original research purpose of the shipwrecked vessel.

The screenplay of *Matango* is an adaptation of William Hope Hodgson's (1877–1918) short story "The Voice in the Night," which was first published in the November 1907 edition of *Blue Book Magazine*. Hodgson's story had been translated under the title "Yami no koe" by Kazuo Ōkado (1909–1974) in the August 1961 "special issue" of *S-F magajin* (which may be rendered as *Sci-Fi Magazine* in English), historically one of Japan's most important venues for the publication of science fiction as well as weird fiction and other subcultural genres. This Japanese translation was then adapted for the screen by Masami Fukushima (1929–1976), *S-F magajin*'s editor and a science fiction writer, and, in a more limited capacity, by one of the preeminent figures in Japanese science fiction, Shin'ichi Hoshi (1926–1997).

The final screenplay of *Matango* diverges from Hodgson's story in some important ways. For one thing, the nature of the outer frame narrative is different. Hodgson's story is told from the perspective of a sailor who comes across one of the "mushroom people" in the middle of the Pacific Ocean; apparently starving, the mysterious individual calls out and begs for food under the cover of darkness. The narrator and his companion grant them some rations, and coax out of the shadowy figure the story of how he and his fiancée were marooned on a strange, mushroomed island and have already begun to turn into mushroom people themselves. There is no yachting group in Hodgson's story, then, and no Murai figure who survives long enough to make it back to civilization. Accordingly, the changing dynamics of the interpersonal relations of the group that are such a central element of *Matango*'s plot are absent from Hodgson's original, wherein man and woman, in apparent harmony, become a doomed, inverse image of Adam and Eve as they gradually turn inhuman among the fungal freaks that populate the island. As the original's publication date should make clear, the use of radioactivity as a backdrop to the plot is also absent from Hodgson's story.

Hodgson is a pivotal figure in the evolution of the English-language weird tale in the sense that his works form an intermediate step between the Late Gothic flourishes of the 1890s, epitomized by Bram Stoker's (1847–1912) *Dracula* (1897), and the scientifically informed cosmic horror of the 1920s, epitomized by the work of H. P. Lovecraft (1890–1937). In this regard, *Matango* does retain a central characteristic of Hodgson's work that comes to the fore in "The Voice in the Night"—that is, an interest in the relationship between human civilization and the natural world. For Hodgson, the sea often becomes the site of the boundary between these two worlds. The theme, which is retained to great effect in *Matango*, of humans becoming other (vegetable or fungal) life forms, and the exploration of the mushy, smeared line between human civilization and the fruity world of flora, suggest the applicability of an "ecogothic" or even ecocritical approach to both the original story and the film adaptation, and ultimately highlight the way that *Matango* uses the horror genre to speak to anxieties about the limitations of humanity's ability to rationally comprehend its relationship with the world around it.—Peter Bernard

MEATBALL MACHINE (2005)

DIRECTOR: Yudai Yamaguchi, Jun'ichi Yamamoto
SCREENPLAY: Jun'ya Katō
SPECS: 90 minutes; color

Directed by Yudai Yamaguchi (b. 1971) and Jun'ichi Yamamoto (b. 1972, whose original idea and 1999 film of the same name was the source of inspiration), *Meatball Machine* is a 2005 horror science fiction film that combines cyberpunk, gore, and body horror. Two lonely and shy people find comfort in each other only to be torn apart, becoming hosts to parasitic creatures that use their bodies for gory battles to the death.

The film opens with a man about to hang himself, interrupted and attacked by a tentacled creature. He has now become an armored, mindless cyborg that fights another of his kind. As they fight, a mysterious and masked interloper, played by Toru Tezuka (b. 1962), does away with them both, as a young bandaged woman with a throbbing wound lurks in the darkness.

The next day, a young man, Yoji, played by Issei Takahashi (b. 1980), makes his way into work at a machine shop and sees something strange sink into a murky river. He is a quiet type and does not join in his coworkers' bawdy talk of women and debauchery. Instead, he eats lunch alone, watching a young woman, Sachiko, played by Aoba Kawai (b. 1981), across the way, as she hangs laundry out to dry. She is the object of his desire, and he thinks of her that evening as he masturbates. He is almost discovered by his nosey neighbor Doi, played by Shoichiro Masumoto (b. 1969), who asks to borrow money, promising to pay him back later.

The strange thing Yoji sees in the river is a tentacled creature, emerging and taking up residence in a curious little boy, and then a motorist after he runs the boy down. At work, Yoji must endure his vulgar coworkers as they make crude comments about Sachiko. Yoji later heads to a porn theater where he is harassed by an aggressive transvestite and beaten up. Lying in a heap of garbage, he narrowly misses being infested by a creature that was earlier wounded by the mysterious masked man. Yoji takes it home, and after examining it, brings it to work to see if he can open the rock hard armor with industrial tools, which fail to make a dent in it.

Doi makes good on his offer to pay Yoji back and takes him out for dinner. When he finds out Yoji is a virgin, he takes him to a prostitute, but Yoji cannot go through with it, and on his way home he catches his creepy coworker, Tanaka, played by Kenichi Kawasaki, attempting to rape Sachiko. Yoji steps in and is beaten up, but they are able to chase Tanaka away. Sachiko helps Yoji home and cleans his wounds. After an awkward kiss, she reveals that she is ashamed of scarring she suffered at the hands of her abusive father. She tells Yoji she wants to fall in love but feels she can't because of emotional and physical abuse. As they talk, the creature stirs in Yoji's closet and graphically attacks Sachiko, taking over her body. Yoji is horrified and tries to help but is once again beaten down as the parasitic monster does its work. Doi stops by and is gutted by the new, horrific Sachiko, who attacks Yoji and escapes into the night.

The mysterious man finds Yoji and takes him to his hideout, where he reveals that the creatures are parasites attracted to, and fueled by, negative thoughts. He has no idea where they come from, but they take over the hosts' bodies encapsulated in silver spheres and create weapons from their organs in order to battle each other, leaving the winner to eat the loser parasite. He tells Yoji there is no way to save Sachiko, and even though he has rescued his daughter Michino, played by Ayano Yamamoto (b. 1986), the wounded woman with him, she is still infested with a parasite. He goes to the cyborg battles so he can harvest parasites to feed her; and also breeds a mutation of the parasites to keep her alive. He plans to infect Yoji to provide more food for her. Yoji is helpless as the man wounds him and leaves him to be infected; however Yoji musters up enough strength fight total infestation. He is left with most of his former self intact, but encased in a biomechanical cyborg body. After killing the mystery man, Yoji escapes, fueled by his last memory of Sachiko, determined to save her from her cyborg fate. He finds her in the midst of torturing Tanaka, her would-be rapist, and what ensues is an almost twenty-minute drawn out, blood-soaked battle between the doomed lovers with endless over-the-top bio-weapons as Yoji tries in vain to regain the Sachiko he remembers.

Yoji finally grants Sachiko's final wish and kills her, squashing her mortally wounded parasite in its sphere. Michino appears, taking off her bandage to reveal the throbbing wound in her own sphere and crushes it as her final swan song. In a voice-over during the final moments of the film, Yoji says he can only preserve the memory of Sachiko since he couldn't save her, and in order to do so he must detonate the bomb he has created in his biomechanical body to defy the parasite within.

After Yoji self-destructs, we are introduced to two of the parasites, which are actually aliens. They reveal that are they are using humans as hosts for their games, and notice that humans are resilient beyond comprehension. Because of this, Yoji and Sachiko become prototypes for the next level of games, as the previous "necroborgs" prohibited emotional drive. The new models will be more powerful because of their emotional bond, and the code name for this game is Meatball Machine.

This schlocky and violent film combines many themes including doomed love, industrialization, alienation, self-sacrifice, and a sense of powerlessness in modern society, covered by a thick layer of practical gore effects, buckets of blood, and dark humor. There is plenty of sexual and pseudo-sexual imagery with rape, masturbation, and humans violated by the parasites, implying society's subconscious fear of an all-consuming industrialization and losing one's autonomy. Yoji and Sachiko transform into machines despite their resistance, playing loosely within a cyberpunk vein of a technologically advanced world that bastardizes the natural.

Inspired by *Tetsuo: The Iron Man* (1989, dir. Shi'ya Tsukamoto), *Meatball Machine* is most noted for the "necroborg" design by Keita Ameimya (b. 1959) and practical gore special effects by Yoshihiro Nishimura (b. 1967), who went on to create his own short entitled *Meatball Machine: Reject of Death.*—Carolyn Mauricette

See also Tetsuo: The Iron Man

Bibliography
Balmain, Colette. "Techno-Horror and Urban Alienation." In *Introduction to Japanese Horror Film*. Edinburgh: Edinburgh University Press, 2008.
Nishimura, Yoshihiro, dir. *Meatball Machine: Reject of Death*. King Record Co., 2007. Film.
Yamaguchi, Yudai, and Jun'ichi Yamamoto, dirs. *Meatball Machine*. King Records Co., 2005. Film.
Yamaguchi, Yukihiko, prod. *Maximum Meatball Machine*. Pants Productions, 2005. Featurette.

MIIKE, TAKASHI (1960–)

Born on 24 August 1960, in Yao City (a postwar development in Osaka Prefecture, on the border with Nara), an area inhabited largely by the working class and immigrants, Takashi Miike was himself the son of a welder and a seamstress. He graduated from Yokohama Hōsō Eiga Senmon Gakkō (Yokohama Vocational School of Broadcast and Film), a post-secondary institution founded by noted director and two-time winner of the Palme d'Or, Shohei Imamura (1926–2006), who as dean offered his guidance to those in attendance. Building upon shots of graphic and lurid bloodshed and sexual perversion alike, Miike's work can best be characterized by depictions of life hidden away from, lying just beyond the mainstream Japanese experience, with frequent reliance upon the activities of a disenfranchised criminal element, especially yakuza, or the marginalized immigrant populations often overlooked as they set about their daily lives in the hustle and bustle of Japanese urban centers. In most instances, his characterizations, marked by their overt cartoonish manner, reflect both his dark sense of humor and an insistence on challenging the boundaries of Japanese censors at every turn. As prolific as he is prodigious, more often than not his films are less accessible than most, targeting art house audiences and fans of extreme cinema. He has directed over ninety theatrical, video, and small-screen productions, and his unrelenting imagery, challenging and offending the Japanese censors, has garnered him international notoriety—so much so that he commands a strong cult following outside of Japan.

Miike's first films were for the small screen, followed shortly thereafter by several direct-to-video V-cinema releases. The latter provide him with unprecedented creative freedom certainly, but the format by its very nature circumvents the redolent eye of current censorship, in turn allowing greater risks with content and images used. These early endeavors, limited by the media itself, were released in rapid succession in the early nineties. They include the made-for-television *Shissō Feraari 250 GTO/Rasuto ran: Ai to uragiri no hyaku-oku en* (1991), *Toppū! Minipato tai—Aikyacchi Jankushon* (1991), and *Redi hantā: Koroshi no pureryūdo* (1991), as well as *A Human Murder Weapon* (1992), *Bodyguard Kiba* (1993,) and *Shinjuku Outlaw* (1994), all of which went largely unnoticed. He did, however, find a modicum of critical attention with his film, *The Third Gangster* (1995).

The release of the first of what would become the "Black Society Trilogy," *Shinjuku Triad Society* (1995), however, helped him find an audience. His extreme style and recurring themes already apparent, its commercial success bolstered studio support for his work, thereby allowing him the freedom to work with a larger budget. The other films comprising the trilogy, *Rainy Dog* (1997) and *Ley Lines* (1999), proved equally as lucrative as the first.

With *Audition* (1999), a psychological horror-romance based on the novel by Ryū Murakami (b. 1952) of the same title, Miike found his stride as a filmmaker. Following a screening at the 1999 Vancouver International Film Festival, where it received critical attention, it was released in Japan on 3 March 2000. Audiences quickly took notice, as well, and over time, the work has earned him the respect of diehard enthusiasts.

In 2001, the ultra-violent film, *Ichi the Killer*, was released amid much controversy. An adaptation from a popular manga by Yamamoto Hideo (b. 1968) of a sadomasochistic yakuza-enforcer by the same name, the extreme violence (e.g., slicing a man in half from head to groin, severing another's face, which then slides down a nearby wall) was initially exploited by the media and promoters alike. During its international premiere at the Toronto International Film Festival in 2001, for example, the audience received along with their tickets a "barf bag," emblazoned with the logo of the film. Its further reception was less enthusiastic. Citing the nature of its misogynistic violence, the British Board of Film Classification refused its release in Britain without significant editing; Hong Kong censors demanded that a full fifteen minutes of footage be cut. While it was banned outright in several countries because of its graphic depictions of sexual depravity, perverse cruelty, and violence, it was released in the US market uncut but, as a result, unrated.

That same year, Miike directed the surreal and farcical musical-comedy-horror, *The Happiness of the Katakuris* (2001), based loosely on the South Korean feature film *The Quiet Family*, directed by Kim Jee-woon. Miike returns to the overtly comic and cartoonish as he makes extensive use of claymation sequences, as well as musical and dance numbers, a karaoke-style sing-along, and dream sequences. The film received a Special Jury Prize for Miike at the 2004 Festival International du Film Fantastique de Gérardmer (Gérardmer, France). Several mainstream and commercial titles followed soon after.

The children's fantasy drama, *The Great Yokai War* (2005), moves beyond the well-known *yokai* of Japanese folklore (e.g., *kappa*) to introduce other such spiritual elements found to occupy everything in the world around us. These spirits conspire against humanity to seek revenge as they fashion Cyborg-beings from the fusion of human beings with discarded junk. A Great Goblin and a magical sword add to the action and suspense and go far to hold the interests of Miike's intended audience.

The direct-to-video production of gothic-inspired *Demon Pond* (2005), adapted from the Kabuki drama penned by Izumi Kyōka (1873–1939), recalls a mystical and tragic tale of the small mountain village close to the devil lake that, nonetheless, suffers both from drought and water shortage and a fear of the local dragon.

That same year, Miike was invited to direct, alongside acclaimed filmmakers of horror the likes of Italian director Dario Argento (b. 1940), American writer and director John Carpenter (b. 1948) and Tobe Hooper (b. 1943), an episode of the Masters of Horror anthology series. When the American cable network Showtime acquired the rights to the series, Miike's episode, *Imprint* was deemed by executives to be "the most disturbing film . . .ever seen" and was canceled.

Miike then turned his hand to his particular rendering of the Spaghetti Western. In his *Sukiyaki Western Django* (2007) a "nameless" gunman arrives to assist a prostitute's revenge against warring gangs. It premiered at the Venice Film Festival on 5 September 2007, and was released ten days later in Japan. With *13 Assassins* (2010) Miike teams up with Nobuyasu Kita (b. 1960), renowned cinematographer and master of light and frame.

International competitions and subsequent awards have since become a matter of course. Competing at the 2011 Cannes Film Festival was his *Hara-Kiri:*

Death of a Samurai, a melodramatic 3-D remake of the 1962 *Harakiri*, originally directed by Masaki Kobayashi (1916–1996). Academy-award winning composer Ryuichi Sakamoto (b. 1952) penned the original score. With *Lesson of Evil* (2012) released shortly thereafter, a beguiling high school teacher is revealed to be a psychopathic killer. *Shield of Straw*, a revenge-thriller, received a nomination for the Palme d'Or at the 2013 Cannes Film Festival. Benefiting in no small part from the "play-within-a play" structure, *Over Your Dead Body* (2014) builds upon the traditional Kabuki themes of love and lust, vengeance and death but, as Miike renders them, in such a manner as to distort, even eliminate the lines between reality and fantasy in order to accentuation the imminent horror of the moment.

With a renewed emphasis in pop culture, Miike released *As the Gods Will* (2014), his action-packed adaptation of the popular *Kamisama ni Iu Toori* (2013–present), originally written by Muneyuki Kaneshiro and illustrated by Akeji Fujimura. As a popular and charismatic high school teacher is revealed to be a psychopathic teacher from hell, heads explode and roll here and there, blood and gore abound, and adolescents are forced into a perversion of children's games where they can do no more than laugh and cry—and eventually die.

As a master of exploitation to affect, Miike continues to prove himself a leading director of horror films in contemporary Japan. However outrageous the blending of genres with the yakuza-cum-vampire action-fantasy, *Yakuza Apocalypse* (2015), shot at Nikkatsu Studios, he promises ever more grandeur and further excess with the much-anticipated 2016 release of *Terra Formars* based upon the 2011 manga written by Yū Sasuga (b. 1988) and illustrated by Tachibana Kenichi (b. 1977). Behind an ambitious plan to terraform Mars lurks ravage and decay, as the process is set into motion with the unleashing of mold and cockroaches. And precisely because he is known for churning out an average of three films a year since the early 1990s, audiences can expect the outrage to continue unabated for some time to come.—James A. Wren

Bibliography

Black, Art. "Takashi Miike Revisited." *Asian Cult Cinema* 38 (2003): 12–17.

Gerow, Aaron. "The Homelessness of Style and the Problems of Studying Miike Takashi." *Canadian Journal of Film Studies* 18, no. 1 (2009): 24–43.

Hoad, Phil. "Takashi Miike: Why I Am Bringing Japanese Classics Back to Life." *Guardian*, 5 May 2005.

"Izo: Takashi Miike's History Lesson." *Asian Cinema* 16, no. 2 (2005): 85–109.

Kehr, Dave. "Horror Film Made for Showtime Will Not Be Shown." *New York Times*, 19 January 2006.

Mes, Tom. *Agitator: The Cinema of Takashi Miike*. Godalming, UK: FAB Press, 2003.

Williams, Tony. "Takashi Miike's Cinema of Outrage." *cineACTION* 64 (2004): 54–62.

MIZUKI, SHIGERU (1922–)

Shigeru Mizuki (b. 8 March 1922, born Shigeru Mura) is a prominent Japanese manga artist. Mizuki comes from the rural community of Sakaiminato in Tottori Prefecture (most sources identify Sakaiminato as his birthplace, although other sources reveal he was born while his family was visiting Osaka). In 1942, he was drafted into the Imperial Japanese Army, serving his time during the Second World War stationed on New Britain Island in Papua New Guinea. During the war, he contracted malaria, lost his left arm in an Allied bombing, and was held as a prisoner of war in Rabaul. Understandably disillusioned by his time in the military, Mizuki strongly considered staying in Papua New Guinea and only returned to Japan reluctantly after the war. Before breaking into manga, Mizuki worked as a movie theater manager and a kamishibai artist.

Growing up in Sakaiminato, Mizuki was exposed from a young age to local folklore. In 1977, he released an autobiographical memoir, *Nonnonbā to ore* (Granny Nonnon and me), which recounted his experiences in Sakaiminato, where his neighbor Nonnonbā filled his head with local ghost stories. Many of these stories dealt with *yōkai*, a category of traditional Japanese spirits and monsters. Yōkai is a broad term, and they take many forms. Many are monster-like figures, like the child-sized amphibious *kappa*, the ogre- or demon-like *oni*, and the long-nosed *tengu*. Some are conventional animals, like *kitsune* (foxes) and *tanuki* (raccoon dogs), which are believed to have magical abilities. Other yōkai were originally humans, but were transformed into monstrous or grotesque forms, often because of extreme emotions.

Mizuki, throughout his career, has positioned himself as an expert on yōkai, and his yōkai-themed manga have done much to popularize these aspects of Japanese folklore. Mizuki's work, generally aimed at young children, has been extremely popular for the last five decades.

Mizuki's most famous creation is *GeGeGe no Kitarō* (Spooky Kitarō), originally titled *Hakaba no Kitarō* (Kitarō of the graveyard). The series stars a young yōkai boy named Kitarō, who is missing his left eye (although his distinctive hairstyle generally covers this). He is accompanied by Medami-Oyaji ("Eyeball-Father"), the reincarnation of his dead father, whose body is now an eyeball atop a tiny human-like body. Together with other yōkai (both from Japanese folklore and others created by Mizuki), Kitarō and his father work to maintain the peace between the worlds of the humans and the yōkai. First adapted into an anime in 1968, the series has been broadcast on television in five different iterations. Alongside several anime films, the franchise also produced two live-action films, both directed by Katsuhide Motoki and with Eiji Wentz in the title role: 2007's *GeGeGe no Kitarō* and 2008's *GeGeGe no Kitarō: Sennen noroi uta* (*Kitarō and the Millennium Curse*).

Mizuki's work with yōkai extends beyond the GeGeGe no Kitarō franchise. He also works as a chronicler and collector of Japanese ghost stories, and has published numerous encyclopedia of yōkai throughout his career, including *Mizuki Shigeru no Nihon Yōkai Meguri* (Mizuki Shigeru's ghosts and demons). In his hometown of Sakaiminato, one can find Mizuki Shigeru Road, a tourist attraction featuring over one hundred bronze statues of Mizuki's creations, and the Mizuki Shigeru Kinenkan (Memorial Hall), so named despite Mizuki being still alive.

Mizuki appears as the Great Yōkai Elder in *Yōkai daisensō* (*The Great Yōkai War*), Miike Takashi's 2005 film. Miike's film shares a name with a storyline from *GeGeGe no Kitarō*, although it is an adaptation of Aramata Hiroshi's novel of the same name. Katō Yasunori, the main character of Aramata's *Teito mono-*

gatari (Tales of the imperial capital) series, is the film's antagonist. Like his most famous creation, Kitarō, Mizuki's character is interested in brokering peace between humans and yōkai; near the end of *Yōkai Daisensō*, the Great Yōkai Elder muses that "War is meaningless. You only get hungry."

Although Mizuki is best known for his horror manga and yōkai research, he has also earned great acclaim for his non-horror work, much of which is nonfiction focused on World War II. One acclaimed example is *Sōin Gyokusai Seyo* ([Let us all die honorably], released in the United States as *Onward to Our Noble Deaths*). The manga, written in 1973, details Mizuki's experiences during the war in Papua New Guinea. He has also published a manga biography of Adolf Hitler, as well as *Komikku Shōwa-shi* ("A Comics History of the Shōwa Era"), an eight-volume history of the period of Japanese history spanning the reign of Emperor Shōwa (Hirohito), from December 25, 1926 to January 7, 1989.—Nicholas Bestor

MOKUDŌ, SHIGERU (1901–1983)

Shigeru Mokudō was an actor and film director who became Japan's most prolific creator of horror movies, or *kaiki eiga*, during the latter half of the 1930s, with at least half-a-dozen such pictures to his credit between 1937 and 1940. Dismissed by critics of the day as unimaginative B-cinema, Mokudō's work in the genre remains largely forgotten despite its seminal role in establishing the look and sound of talkie-era Japanese *kaiki eiga*. Like earlier silent adaptations of *kaidan* ghost stories and *bakeneko* cat tales, Mokudō's horror films borrow much from Japan's traditional theater arts. At the same time, they demonstrate a keen awareness of the atmospheric cinematography of German Expressionism, as well as the effective use of sound pioneered in Universal Studio's monster movies earlier in the decade. Adapting these techniques to domestic *kaiki eiga*, Mokudō crafted what might be deemed the first true horror movies in Japanese cinema history, neither straight adaptations of Kabuki theater nor pale imitations of Hollywood horror but a hybrid style that would set the pattern for Japanese horror films for the next thirty years.

Born in what is now the Sumida ward of Tokyo, Mokudō first found success in the movies as a child actor, appearing in various Nikkatsu productions from the age of twelve, occasionally as an *oyama*, a female impersonator. When Nikkatsu's Tokyo studio was destroyed in the Great Kantō Earthquake of 1923, Mokudō, like most of the Japanese film industry, relocated to Kyoto, where he continued to work for Nikkatsu as an actor in their *gendai geki*, or "contemporary drama" unit. Often appearing in the films of director Kenji Mizoguchi, Mokudō dabbled in screenwriting and apprenticed under Mizoguchi as an assistant director, finally transferring to Nikkatsu's directorial division in 1927. He would go on to direct over thirty pictures for the studio, most of them *gendai geki* dramas, before abruptly leaving the company in 1932.

Following a four-year hiatus from filmmaking, Mokudō joined the Shinkō Kyoto studio in 1936. Unlike the larger, wealthier Nikkatsu, Shinkō was a comparatively minor B-studio specializing in *jidai geki* period pictures and ninja films that amused young matinee audiences, but lacked the critical respect of the *gendai geki* Mokudō was used to making. In 1937 Shinkō put Mokudō to work on *Saga kaibyōden* (The legend of the Saga ghost cat), the studio's first attempt at a *bakeneko* or "ghost cat" picture, one of the staples of the domestic *kaiki* genre of filmmaking that had been perennially popular during the 1910s and 1920s, but had experienced a lull in production in more recent years. The film starred Sumiko Suzuki (1904–1985), a onetime vamp actress who had frequently played ghosts and monsters onscreen in the silent era, and her star appeal made *Saga kaibyōden* a breakout hit for the studio, despite mostly negative reviews. Mokudō and Suzuki became Shinkō's go-to pair for horror, and the duo would spend the next several years crafting multiple variations on the *bakeneko* formula, as well as adaptations of other traditional ghost stories like *Yotsuya kaidan* (1937) and *Kaidan kyōren onna shishō* (Passion of a jealous teacher, 1938), a variation on the Kasane Swamp legend.

Only a few minutes of footage from *Kaidan kyōren onna shishō* still exist, and most of Mokudō's *kaiki* pictures are completely lost. Movie reviews from journals like *Kinema Junpō* and *Eiga Hyōron* wrote them off as uninspired exercises in crass entertainment at the time of their release, but the director's two surviving horror pictures, *Arima neko* (The cat of Arima, 1937) and *Kaidan oshidori chō* (Kaidan: The mandarin duck curtain, 1938), afford a glimpse of his talent for the genre, as well as demonstrate the pioneering influence his work had on postwar Japanese horror films of the 1950s and 1960s. *Arima neko* contains few *kaiki* flourishes before the climax, in which Sumiko Suzuki's character lends her physical form to the spirit of the titular cat monster, and even these final ten minutes are dominated by a *tachimawari* fight sequence between Suzuki and an army of spear-wielding maidens, which perhaps owes more to samurai action films than the horror genre. Nonetheless, isolated moments show that Mokudō and his crew were aware of working in an emerging transnational aesthetic of horror filmmaking. A memorable shot of Suzuki as the *bakeneko*, her enchanting eyes glittering as she slowly slinks towards her victim straight-on into the camera before sinking her fangs into the poor woman's throat, resonates strongly with Bela Lugosi's iconic performance as Count Dracula. Suspenseful and slowly paced, this brief, quiet moment of creepy horror becomes all the more effective for being placed amid the frantic action of the *tachimawari* battle.

Kaidan oshidori chō weaves the ghostly, horrific elements more evenly throughout its story, and despite a damning review in *Kinema Junpō* accusing the film of wanton sadism, here Mokudō expertly marshals the formal techniques of his craft in the service of horror. Suzuki Sumiko stars as an innocent woman facially disfigured and ultimately murdered by a callously cruel matron, only to return from the grave to seek her bloody revenge. Mokudō withholds the reveal of Suzuki's facial scarring for maximum suspense, concealing the actress in a dark room with carefully placed shadows that simultaneously recall similar staging in both the Kabuki theater's *kaidan* ghost plays as well as German Expressionist works like *The Cabinet of Dr. Caligari* (1920) and Hollywood derivatives like *The Cat and the Canary* (1927). *Kaidan oshidori chō* also makes use of sound in ways now taken for granted in classic horror, punctuating shots of Suzuki lurking in the shadows with the sounds of howling wind and a temple bell tolling in the distance, rather like the storms and church bells that figure in many Western vampire and werewolf pictures. Perhaps the film's most effective moment of horror, however, occurs near the climax, as Suzuki's ghost completes its vendetta. Mokudō's cutting increases pace rapidly, mirroring the mounting panic of the human victims of Suzuki's wrath and the otherworldly assault of vengeful spirits who appear and disappear at will. In one swift two-shot vignette, the matron's henchwomen are disposing of the body of yet another of their mistress's victims, when they suddenly drop the corpse amid exclamations of horror. The film cuts to a point-of-view shot from the women's perspective, which for a brief instant consists of an empty frame, into which Suzuki's ghostly visage suddenly flies up into the shot from the bottom of the frame in extreme close-up. Universal's monster movies of the 1930s rarely produced anything as terrifically startling.

By 1940 increasingly strict government censorship had effectively transformed the Japanese film industry into a wartime propaganda machine, forcing the studios to cease production of ghost cat films and *kaidan* adaptations, which were deemed too frivolous for a nation at war. Mokudō, who by this time had been professionally pegged as a *"kaidan* director," retired from the film world for good in 1941. However, when horror returned to Japanese movie screens in the mid-1950s, it plainly owed much to his pioneering influence. Daiei remade many of his prewar *bakeneko* pictures, and apart from replacing Sumiko Suzuki with Takako Irie (1911–1995), faithfully replicated works like *Arima neko*. Director Nakagawa Nobuo's horror films produced at the Shintōhō studio around the same time garnered rare praise for the genre from the critics, who commended his use of lighting, montage, and mise-en-scène in pictures like *Tōkaidō Yotsuya kaidan* (1959), but Nakagawa's work employs many of the same techniques seen in *Kaidan oshidori chō* twenty years earlier. Like Nakagawa, Mokudō would probably have preferred to be remembered for his work on *gendai geki* dramas, but it is his precious few surviving examples of *kaiki eiga* that mark his lasting contribution to the history of Japanese cinema.—Michael Crandol

See also Nakagawa, Nobuo; Suzuki, Sumiko

MOON CHILD (2003)

DIRECTOR: Takahisa Zeze
SCREENPLAY: Takahisa Zeze, Kishū Izuchi
SPECS: 120 minutes; color

Moon Child is a 2003 action film directed by Takahisa Zeze from a screenplay by Zeze and Kishū Izuchi. It is based on a story by pop star Gackt. It stars Gackt, HYDE, Leehom Wang, Zeny Kwok, Tarō Yamamoto, and Susumu Terajima. The film follows the adventures of a group of orphans living on the streets of the fictional East Asian nation of "Mallepa," who are befriended, and subsequently taken in, by a vampire named Kei, played by HYDE.

In the year 2000, as the vampire Kei and his maker, Luka, played by Etsushi Toyokawa, observe the New Year's Eve celebrations in Tokyo, Luka informs Kei that he is tired after so many centuries of life and has decided to die. Kei begs Luka not to leave him alone, but Luka insists that Kei go on by himself. Years later, in 2014, Kei meets a band of Japanese orphans, who have been living by their wits on the streets of the multiethnic "Special Economic Zone of Mallepa," when their youngest member, Sho, played by Gackt, attempts to rob him. After defending the children from a Chinese gangster seeking revenge for an earlier scam, Kei takes them in. Sho; his older brother Shinji, played by Susumu Terajima; and their friend Toshi, played by Tarō Yamamoto grow up in a life of crime, keeping the secret of Kei's vampirism.

One evening years later, they meet Son, played by Leehom Wang—a young man who has come to take revenge on the men who raped his sister, Yi-che, played by Zeny Kwok—in the middle of a heist. Kei and Sho, now working as partners along with Toshi, help Son to get his revenge, and the two groups become friends. As they spend an idyllic summer together both Kei and Sho come to have feelings for Yi-che, but the good times are not to last. As Kei begins to feel more and more out of place among his human friends, the crime syndicate that they have been stealing from comes after them. Toshi is killed, Kei is exposed and flees, and Sho is left to form his own rival crime syndicate. When Son eventually joins forces with the Chinese against Sho's fledgling gang, the two friends find themselves on diverging paths that will ultimately bring them to a deadly confrontation.

Moon Child is part of a vast conceptual art project created by the Japanese pop star Gackt. Known as the "Moon Saga," the concept piece involves a series of musical albums (*MOON*, *Crescent*, and *Diabolos*) and highly theatrical concert tour productions (*Waning Moon*, *Waxing Moon*, and *The Sixth Day/Seventh Night*), as well as a two-part musical stage play (*Secrets of Yoshitsune I & II*) that all work together to tell the origin story of a group of vampire-like beings who first came into existence during the 1500s. Spanning centuries, the "Moon Saga" has unfolded out of chronological order over the course of more than a decade, and, according to Gackt, the fragments of the story are meant to be pieced together by the audience like a jigsaw puzzle. *Moon Child*, which was released in between the releases of related albums *MOON* and *Crescent*, relates the final chapter of the epic, which follows the story's characters in the present day and near future. As such, it is less concerned with the engagement of traditional horror themes and more concerned with operating within the conceptual framework established by Gackt.

At the heart of the film, and the "Moon Saga" itself, is a question about the nature of existence—specifically, what makes existence both worthwhile as well as a hardship? For Gackt, the characters are driven constantly by the conflicting impulses of their own inclinations and the inclinations they adopt through contact with other people—the different moons who shed light on their existential paths. Sho's personal existential conflict derives from his desire to stop along the path and not progress. Unable to let go of the ephemeral moments of happiness that have passed, he is unwilling to move on from the good times spent with his friends, and this unwillingness prevents them all from attaining a similar measure of happiness again. This theme of the futility in holding on to that which has passed, which is a primary topic of the "Moon Saga" as a whole, is a fundamental principle of Buddhism and a persistent motif in Japanese literature.

Moon Child performed well at the Japanese box office and was well received by fans of Gackt. It has received mixed reviews from critics, who cite the film's confusing chronology, abrupt shifts in tone, and lack of a cohesive plot as major stumbling blocks. After its release in Japan, *Moon Child* was screened at the

Cannes International Film Festival and the Philadelphia Film Festival.—Sara L. Sumpter

Bibliography
Zeze, Takahisa, dir. *Moon Child*. TLA Releasing, 2004. DVD.

MOROHOSHI, DAIJIRŌ (1949–)

Daijirō Morohoshi (b. 1949) is a Japanese graphic novelist with a cult following. Morohoshi creates stories by blending his imagination with real historical events, myths, and folklores. Together with surreal narratives, his unique drawing style adds an uncanny mood to his works. Japanese readers may sense a connection with an East Asian literary genre called *denkimono*, which refers to oddities and the supernatural, whereas English-speaking readers may notice an influence of Lovecraft's Cthulhu Mythos in some of Morohoshi's works. Although Morohoshi lacks a mass appeal, quite a few Japanese manga artists have paid homage to this reclusive creator. In recent years, some of his works have been adapted into films and television dramas, which attract a younger audience to Morohoshi's works.

In 1970, Morohoshi made his professional debut with *Junko Kyōkatsu* (Junko blackmail) in an influential comic magazine, *COM*, which was published by Osamu Tezuka's publishing firm Mushi Pro-shōji. This is a gloomy drama of a former stripper, whose ex-lover came back asking for reconciliation. In 1974, Morohoshi began the *Yōkai Hunter* series in *Shōne Jump Weekly*. This series revolves around a mysterious archeologist, Rējirō Hieda, who conducts fieldwork across Japan to solve mysteries behind history and folklore. Although it was terminated only after five episodes, this early letdown did not stop him from creating new stories. In 1973, *Fuan no ritsuzō* (A sinister specter), a story of a bizarre experience of a businessman, was included in the prestigious *Best Japanese Science Fiction Anthology*. The following year, *Sēbutsutoshi* (Bio-city), which touches upon the interface between human bodies and machines, won the seventh Tezuka Award, and also was included to the *1974 Best Japanese Science Fiction Anthology*. After a number of short stories in various comic magazines, *Ankoku-shinwa* was serialized in *Shōen Jump Weekly* in 1976. *Ankoku-shinwa*, again heavily drawing on the ancient Japanese history, illustrates the protagonist Takeshi's quest to become the universal king. The follow-up series, *Kōshi Ankokuden* (The dark history of Confucius), features Confucius and the Buddha in a return to the genesis of Japan. Finally Morohoshi's first commercial break came when *Seiyū Yōenden* (Journey to the West: Monster Monkey's commentary), an adaptation of Chinese fantasy novel *Journey to the West*, appeared in *Super Action Monthly* in 1983. This series is arguably the most popular among Morohoshi's works, and new episodes continue to be added in different magazines with intervals.

In an interview, Morohoshi named Osamu Tezuka as his inspiration. For other sources of inspiration, he refers to Greek mythology and English adventure novels, such as *Treasure Island*, rather than horror and mystery novels, which he started reading only after becoming a professional graphic artist. Although Morohoshi's drawing style is rather awkward and not as flawless and sophisticated as that of another *denkimono* manga artist, Yukinobu Hoshino (b. 1951), it somehow suits his surreal narratives. Even Tezuka was said to take special notice of his unusual drawing style.

Although Morohoshi's works appeal to a limited number of manga enthusiasts, his works continue to influence fellow manga artists and filmmakers alike. For example, Hayao Miyazaki is said to have acknowledged some influence from Morohoshi. In an essay, Miyazaki refers to Morohoshi's works as excellent examples of portraying people without any moral judgment. In addition to Miyazaki, other prominent manga artists, such as Moto Hagio, Ryōko Yamagishi, Rumiko Takahashi, and Hisashi Eguchi, have paid homage to Morohoshi.

Recent years saw a surge of interest in Morohoshi's works in Japan. Some of his works were adapted into live action films, such as *Yōkai hantā: Hiruko* (1991), *Kidan* (2005), and *Kabeotoko* (2007). The film adaptation of *Yumemiru kikai* (*The Dreaming Machine*) was to be directed by Satoshi Kon, but Kon's untimely death in 2010 halted the production of the film. In 2008, *Shiori and Shimiko* (1995–) won an excellence award at the Japanese Agency for Cultural Affairs' Japan Media Arts Festival, and in 2014, *Uriko Hime no yoru*, *Cinderella no asa* (Princess Uriko's night, Cinderella's morning) won an Encouragement Prize from Minister of Education, Culture, Sports, Science and Technology. As a result, this highly reclusive graphic artist gained a new audience.—Senjo Nakai

See also Tsukamoto, Shin'ya

Bibliography

Daijiro, Morohoshi. "A Sinister Spectre." In *Kaiki: Uncanny Tales from Japan (Volume 3): Tales of the Metropolis*, edited by Masao Higashi. Fukuoka: Kurodahan Press, 2012.

Hayakawa, Wataru, dir. *Kabe-otoko* [*The Wall Man*]. Tornado Film, 2007. Film.

Hayao, Miyazaki. *Shuppatsuten 1979–1996* [The point of departure: From 1979 to 1996]. Tokyo: Studio Ghibli, 1996.

Komatsu, Takashi, dir. *Kidan* [*Inferno*]. Xanadeux, 2005. Film.

Morohoshi Daijiro: Ikai to zokuse no hazama kara [Morohoshi Daijiro: Between the otherworld to world]. Tokyo: Kawade Shobō Shinsha, 2011.

Nobunaga, Minami. *Gendai-manga no Bōkenshatachi* [Challengers of modern manga]. Tokyo: NTT, 2008.

Tsukamoto, Shinya, dir. *Yōkai hantā: Hiruko* [*Hiruko the Goblin*]. Shochiku-Fuji 1991. Film.

· N ·

NAKAGAWA, NOBUO (1905–1984)

Nobuo Nakagawa was a film director best known for his *Kaidan*, or ghostly horror films. He was born in Kyoto, where his parents were working for a local *ryokan*, a Japanese traditional inn. He was sent to study at a commercial school in Hyōgo prefecture, but after graduating he first tried to become a novelist. For this aim, Nakagawa published his writings in a *dōjinshi*, a self-published fan magazine, but he soon gave up on this dream. Instead, he sought to enter the film industry.

Nakagawa was soon hired by Makino Productions, a studio established by Shōzō Makino—considered the "father of Japanese cinema"—after a piece he wrote on the differences between stories and screenplays was published by Japan's leading film journal, *Kinema Junpō*. At Makino Productions, Nakagawa was mainly an assistant to other directors, but he also wrote several screenplays that were filmed by the studio. In addition, until Makino Productions' bankruptcy, Nakagawa continued to publish his ideas about filming techniques in *Kinema Junpō*. In 1934, Nakagawa was hired by the newly established Ichikawa Utaemon Productions, where he directed for the first time. His directorial debut, *Sword of the God of War*, a silent *jidaigeki* (period drama)—based on his own original script—was released during his first year at the company.

Nakagawa went on to direct some two-dozen films within a variety of genres for several different studios, including a few musical comedies starring the famous singing comedian Enoken (1904–1970), for the Tōhō studio in Tokyo. After the colonization of large parts of China by Japan's Imperial Army, Nakagawa followed the war overseas to direct documentary films. His reputation as a master director of mainly low-budget horror films, therefore, stems from a later chapter in his career.

Nakagawa returned to fiction filmmaking after the war, as a director at Shintōhō Studios, with a new film starring Enoken. For several years after, he directed films pertaining to many genres, such as crime (*Lynch*, 1949), romance (*Kiss at Moonrise*, 1950), melodrama, (*Wandering Journey*, 1951), period drama (*Sunset over Mount Fuji*, 1952), and thriller (*Dandy Sashichi Detective Story: Six Famous Beauties*, 1956). Gradually, however Nakagawa directed more and more horror films—a genre he then worked on almost exclusively. Such films Nakagawa directed ranged from ghost and vampire themes like *The Ghost of Kasane Swamp* (1957) and *The Woman Vampire* (1958), to classic Kabuki adaptations like *Tōkaidō Yotsuya kaidan* (1959). Additionally, Nakagawa also added a personal exploration of the mythological underworld (*Hell*, 1960), as well as his swan song, an artistic horror film (*The Living Koheiji*, 1982).

Given the staggering number of films Nakagawa has directed, nearly one hundred over a period of several decades, among which are dozens pertaining to the horror genre, it is difficult to single out cinematic style and themes as characteristic of his entire oeuvre. However, some common tropes are nevertheless visible in many of Nakagawa's films, such as preference for camera movement with relatively long takes over fast editing. Moreover, and in contrast to his emphasis on cinematic techniques, his horror films tend to have some impressions of theatrical performances, particularly that of the Kabuki theater, with elaborated sets and stage-like interiors, as well as exaggerated makeup and acting. In terms of their narratives, in many of Nakagawa's horror films, despite the frequent appearances of ghosts, living dead, human beings in animal forms, and possessed individuals, a consistent psychological force seem to be more dominant in motivating characters and carrying the plot. Often, leading characters in Nakagawa's horror films are tormented by feelings of guilt and remorse after committing a crime against, or an injustice to, a person close to them, a relative, a lover, or a family member. Many times these are committed for material interests, such as wealth or social mobility. Negative actions by the protagonist then usually lead to the death of those betrayed, either directly, by the hands of the protagonist, or as an indirect result of those actions, but in nearly all cases, death comes in overtly cruel and gruesome ways. Soon after their death, the victims reappear, mostly deformed and covered with blood, but usually it is not clear whether it is only the protagonists' hallucinations caused by guilt or whether these are real supernatural beings. However, repentance and forgiveness are never possible, and the punishment upon the sinful protagonists, who desperately seek relief for their suffering souls, is eventually found only in suicide.—Rea Amit

NEO TOKYO (1987)

DIRECTOR: Yoshiaki Kawajiri, Rintaro, Katsuhiro Ōtomo
SCREENPLAY: Rintaro, Yoshiaki Kawajiri, Katsuhiro Ōtomo
SPECS: 50 minutes; color

In 1987 three animators collaborated to give shape to an ambitious project called *Neo Tokyo*. Under the leadership of the veteran animator and filmmaker Rintarō, two young artists, Yoshiaki Kawajiri and Katsuhiro Ōtomo, created an omnibus film whose central theme was a nightmarish vision. The three animators had worked together on *Harmagedon* in 1983 and they had a common interest in anime despite the fact that their artistic universes were remarkably different.

Adapting short stories by Taku Mayumura, featured in his novel *Meikyū monogatari*, Rintarō himself and Masao Maruyama—former producers and cofounders of Madhouse—produced the anthological film. The proposal was divided into three separated segments, and created and designed by three unique artists. Rintarō was responsible for the opening and ending of the film with *Labyrinth Labyrinthos*, a single chapter divided into two parts that was inspired by the English literary classic *Alice's Adventures in Wonderland*. As audiences walk with Chihiro to the other side of the mirror, they witness an eclectic, chilling journey to an impossible town populated by all kinds of bizarre creatures. In order to convey the nightmarish atmosphere, Rintarō combines surrealism, expressionism, and even video game aesthetics. The use of intertitles and the dark chromatic palette filled with cold tones—reds and blacks—leave no doubt as to his visual heritage from expressionist classic silent film, notably *Nosferatu* by F. W. Murnau. In addition, *Labyrinth Labyrinthos* is similar to two other omnibus films in which Katsuhiro Ōtomo was involved:

Robot Carnival (1987) and *Short Peace* (2013). On the one hand, Rintarō seems to link his opening with Ōtomo's in *Robot Carnival*, made the same year only few months earlier, returning to the topic of a diabolic parade in town. In the other, along with Kōji Morimoto's introductory chapter for *Short Peace*, it also includes the game *Mādadayo* (the Japanese version for hide-and-seek), helping to create the uneasy atmosphere experienced by both female protagonists. In the latter case, the reference is a clear homage to *Neo Tokyo*, making associations with almost all the anthology films in which Ōtomo had worked.

Yoshiaki Kawajiri moved away from the style of Rintarō, his mentor, and established his characteristic style within *Running Man*. The plot revolves around Zack Hugh, a racing driver who has won the lethal Death Circus race for the last ten years. A journalist approaches him and discovers his dark and terrifying secret: he has telekinetic abilities that allow him to interfere with electronic devices. The driver, unable to stop his interactions with his car, ends up merging with the machine, dying on the track and beginning a horrifying, eternal race in the afterlife. At this point, a connection can be seen with Ōtomo's *Akira* (1988) given that, like Tetsuo in that film, Hugh is incapable of controlling his powers. In addition, the depiction of the cars in the race as points of light was perfected by Ōtomo at the beginning of his masterpiece.

As Kawajiri himself has recognized, in this segment he used his cinematographic style: a taste for setting his world in the shadows; limited and functional animation; monochromatic backgrounds; limited facial expressions; a fixed camera and prolonged shots in order to create a sense of speed. Moreover, he used his almost omnipresent narrative dichotomy between a human world and an underworld inhabited by demons or semi-demons, albeit declining in *Running Man* to introduce sexual references —another of his main leitmotivs.

The third story, *Construction Cancellation Order*, is an allegory of human technological dependence. The audience here faces another futuristic nightmare, although this time the starting point is set in a political science fiction scenario. Katsuhiro Ōtomo wisely blends humor and tragedy in his plot about a white-collar worker sent to South Africa to deal with a robot revolution that threatens to put his company out of business. The reiteration of the same situation with slight narrative differences and the ironic use of classical music provide the right tone and allow the filmmaker to make a brutal critique of bureaucratic inertia and the blind obedience of contemporary societies. Terror is also portrayed repeatedly, even if the classic elements of horror appearing throughout *Neo Tokyo* are usually reinforced using different scales of red shades. Ōtomo uses his tale to develop one of his favorite topics: the inability of human beings to adapt to the frenetic technological race. In this sense, the gigantic organic machine connected to every single robot through a sort of umbilical cord is a prefiguration of *Akira*.—Laura Montero Plata

NERAWARETA GAKUEN films

Nerawareta Gakuen (1981)
DIRECTOR: Nobuhiko Ōbayashi
SCREENPLAY: Taku Mayumura (novel)
SPECS: 90 minutes; color

Nerawareta Gakuen (1997)
DIRECTOR: Atsushi Shimizu
SCREENPLAY: Shimako Sato, Atsushi Shimizu
SPECS: 80 minutes; color

Nerawareta Gakuen (2012)
DIRECTOR: Ryosuke Nakamura
SCREENPLAY: Ryosuke Nakamura, Yuko Naito
SPECS: 110 minutes; color

Taku Mayumura is an outstanding and prolific Japanese science fiction writer who made his debut in the early sixties. He gained solid fame as a popular novelist and the audiovisual industry became interested in his work, first in television and then rapidly in the film sector, too. In 1974, his *Maboroshi no Pen Friend* came to life as a *dorama* or TV drama on the NHK Japanese national public broadcasting channel. However, the most popular story in his vast array of literary texts is without doubt *Nerawareta gakuen*, a title that could be translated into English as "The targeted school." Written in 1973, it was first presented as a *dorama* in 1977 and was broadcast on NHK as *Mirai kara no chōsen*. Four years later, in 1981, the filmmaker Nobuhiko Ōbayashi shot the first cinematographic version of the novel, also titled *Nerawareta Gakuen*. Moreover, the next three TV versions released in 1982 (Fuji TV), 1987 (Fuji TV), and 1997 (TV Tokyo) shared the same name. In addition to all of these productions, a second movie directed by Atsushi Shimizu, *Nerawareta Gakuen (The Messiah from the Future)*, was released in 1997. Despite its popularity, it wasn't until fifteen years later before the last adaptation was made into a full-length film. For the first time, the remake was made as an animation.

The story narrates the everyday life of a teenager with hidden psychic powers who gets caught in a battle with alien forces that are taking control of the local school. Despite the similarities in the general storytelling, each version has its own distinctive features; the only element in common between them seems to be the character of Kōji Seki. For instance, if one compares Ōbayashi's version with the one by the anime director Ryōsuke Nakamura, the role played by the stars is completely different. In the 1981 film, the main character is a young girl named "Yuka Mitamura," whereas in the most recent work the lead role is that of "Kōji," although he shares this position with three other adolescents (Natsuki, Kahori, and Kyōgoku). In this way, the character with special powers changes gender. Thus, here we have an interesting shift in the retelling of the film genre, since the original story was related to a magical female teenager. This change could be one of the reasons behind the introduction of several sexual references, missing in the first film. Moreover, Ōbayashi's adaptation is simpler in its narrative development: a prototypical battle between good and evil. Its low budget didn't help to create the supernatural sequences smoothly, the result being a cult B movie with a kitsch eighties look. Meanwhile, Nakamura is more interested in showing the problems related to the process of maturing through adolescence. Hence, his script—in collaboration with Yūko Naito—presents a complex universe in which every action hides plausible reasons. The horror is put aside and the film becomes a melancholic portrayal of difficult human relationships. In this sense, this version has been widely compared to the cinema of Makoto Shinkai, one of the more prominent filmmakers in current Japanese animation. Indeed, it is true that *Nerawareta Gakuen* uses an extremely similar character design, art direction, and sensitivity. The film has gorgeous backgrounds surrounded by cherry blossom petals reminiscent of those seen in Shinkai's cinematographic work, and the leitmotiv revolves around badly timed loves, leaving the audience asking for a less confusing solution to the narrative conflict. Unfortunately, the cryptic screenplay moves away from the simplicity of Shinkai's world. The anime focuses on existential digressions, concentrating its attention on unanswered questions about freedom, love, destruction, moral responsibility, and history. Ryōsuke Nakamura uses different strategies to incorporate this philosophical discourse, primarily by using a long discussion about William Shakespeare's drama *A Midsummer Night's Dream* and the subplot about the lack of interpersonal communication in current society due to the use of new technologies, especially mobile phones. As a consequence, and despite his methods, the mission of this half-alien, half-human Ryōsuke is precisely to revive communications among mankind, and to connect past and future to preserve humanity. Moreover, the idea is much more appealing than the one introduced in the first cinematographic version of Nobuhiko Ōbayashi, even if in both cases the ending may bring with it some bitterness.

In a nutshell, the first *Nerawareta Gakuen* could be classified among the popular *tokusatsu* fantasy-horror genre of the eighties, with its easy-going narration, whereas the animated film produced by Sunrise plunges into metaphysical disquisitions backed by refined artwork.—Laura Montero Plata

NIGHTMARE DETECTIVE (2006)

DIRECTOR: Shin'ya Tsukamoto
SCREENPLAY: Shin'ya Tsukamoto, Hisakatsu Kuroki
SPECS: 106 minutes; color

Nightmare Detective (*Akumu tantei*, 2006) is a fast-paced and gory thriller that follows a police investigation into a series of apparent suicides in which the victims are linked by a mysterious phone call and a violent dream prior to death. To solve the case, the police turn to a reluctant recluse gifted/cursed with the power to enter people's dreams. The expressionistic telling of this story seeks to unite a pulpy, comic-book style with somber introspection on death, dreams, and desires, and as such *Nightmare Detective* is primarily noteworthy as an interesting hodge-podge of influences and aesthetics, as well as something of a turning point in the career of creator Shin'ya Tsukamoto.

Tsukamoto is an important figure in Japanese cinema—while his work is rooted in an expressive and often avant-garde style, it has flirted with and even been co-opted into the mainstream. While Tsukamoto is habitually (and patronizingly) referred to in the West as "Japan's answer to" David Cronenberg or David Lynch, he has a distinctive yet flexible style that is firmly his own. Perhaps his personal involvement beyond the directorial role in his films contributes to their image as personal visions: in *Nightmare Detective*, Tsukamoto is also credited as a script-writer, cinematographer, editor, producer, production designer, and to top it off he plays the villain (and is the most convincing of the actors to boot). Though many of his films can be said to exist between art house aesthetics and mainstream audience expectations, *Nightmare Detective* apparently aims to bridge the two. Arguably more than in any other Tsukamoto film, *Nightmare Detective* appeals to a wider audience by pairing expressive elements with conventional techniques. For example, the casting of J-pop idol Hitomi and film star Matsuda Ryuhei as the leading characters ensured a larger and more varied audience, in terms of age and gender, than one would expect on the release of a Tsukamoto film. Then there's the familiar story-telling: the first part of the film follows a stereotypical police-procedural narrative interspersed with tense scenes of supernatural horror as people fall victim to their dreams.

Nonetheless, we can see the interplay of different styles from the very start. After the viewer is introduced to the eponymous hero in a surreal dream sequence, the title-screen appears accompanied by cheesy "cool-guy" music straight from a 1990s police drama, reinforced by classic shots of the whirling lights of a busy highway. The camera then lingers on a girl on her phone sitting by the side of the hectic road, and as she discusses suicide the image slowly cross-fades between various close-ups of her body, a technique that pulls us out of the narrative and gently guides our attention to the tactile body on the screen. This return to an art house aesthetic effectively contrasts with what has come before, much as it is also troubling in its objectification of the soon-to-be murdered girl: although the effect is used throughout the film to signal a distancing from reality, none of the male victims are subjected to this relentless slithering over their flesh by the camera. Perhaps a male gaze can be said to be one of the more unfortunate familiar stylistic devices, of which there are many, incorporated into *Nightmare Detective*'s milieu. Shaky cameras, yellow tonal pallets, and de-saturated colors are some of the many effects that appear haphazardly throughout the film, denying a cohesive visual style but also refusing to resonate between each other or even as stand-alone moments of experimentation, eclipsed as they are by the high-speed narrative.

Although Tsukamoto's works are easily misunderstood as Japanese counterparts to Western films, in *Nightmare Detective* the similarities with other films are too strong to be ignored. Not that this is a necessarily negative thing: for example, while the point-of-view camera as invisible monster is a general horror trope, perhaps it hasn't been used as extensively and successfully as it is in *Nightmare Detective* since Sam Raimi's *The Evil Dead* films (1981, 1987). Meanwhile, the plot borrows heavily from *Cure* (*Kyua*, 1997) and *Nightmare on Elm Street* (1984), even including a protracted "don't fall asleep!" scene in which the protagonist inevitably drifts off. In terms of tone, the drudging police procedure following a trail of creatively brutalized victims through a relentlessly gloomy world is evocative of *Se7en* (1995). There are some rather unique and well-executed touches: for instance, the policewoman's character is haunted by a ghost in a black and red dress that eventually reveals itself as a facet of the policewoman's self she wishes to repress: a self that wants to scream hysterically at the sight of blood, and even to take its own life. Then again, the visualization of these internal struggles within dreams is reminiscent of Kon Satoshi's anime

Paprika (2006), another palpable strand in *Nightmare Detective*'s disjointed tapestry of ideas.—Seán Hudson

See also Nightmare Detective 2

Bibliography

Rucka, Nicholas. "Nightmare Detective." *Midnight Eye*. Accessed January 19, 2015. www.midnighteye.com/reviews/nightmare-detective/
Tsukamoto, Shinya, dir. *Nightmare Detective*. Movie-Eye Entertainment Inc., 2006. Film.

NIGHTMARE DETECTIVE 2 (2008)

DIRECTOR: Shin'ya Tsukamoto
SCREENPLAY: Hisakatsu Kuroki and Shin'ya Tsukamoto
SPECS: 102 minutes; color

A film with a title like *Nightmare Detective 2* (*Akumu tantei 2*, 2008) suggests the campy, creepy, crime-solving suspense that, while undercut by somber existential musings, was a major feature of the first film in this series. However, director Shin'ya Tsukamoto returns to his troubled detective with a new style that transforms many of the themes and visual motifs of the first film into something far more introspective, scary, and emotionally compelling. Made at a time when the J-horror boom spawned by *Ringu* (1996) had all but shrunk to all-too-easily parodied tropes, *Nightmare Detective 2* was surprising proof that many of these undoubtedly overused elements (advancing females with faces obscured by long hair, vengeful schoolgirls, and tense elevator journeys to name a few) could still be re-created in an imaginative and absorbing manner—in this case to illustrate a vision of profound grief and torturous human connection. Interestingly, this vision is almost an antithesis to the image of horror championed by J-horror giant Kurosawa Kiyoshi, which is one of lost identities and alienated disconnection.

Nightmare Detective 2 begins a new case for "Kagenuma Kyoichi," played by Matsuda Ryuhei, a psychic detective who can enter people's dreams, in which a girl who has bullied one of her schoolmates is disturbed by a recurring nightmare, and so goes to Kagenuma for help. Reluctant at first, Kagenuma becomes involved in the case as he finds similarities between what's happening to the girl and his own traumatic past. The focus on Kagenuma's past and his relationship with his mother shows us that Tsukamoto (who once again makes the film his own by involving himself in the directing, scriptwriting, editing, and cinematography) clearly wanted to continue the character development of the rather two-dimensional angst-ridden detective he had created in his 2006 film. In doing so, the focus shifts further away from a plot-driven narrative and closer to an introspective, psychological exposition. It is telling that this shift in focus is accompanied by one of genre: while *Nightmare Detective* is a thriller and battle of wills between heroes and a monster, *Nightmare Detective 2* is a ghost story, and relies less on aggressive gore and more on slow tension building to achieve its affective impact. In the first film dreams are primarily spatial, a danger zone where characters are constantly being chased. In the sequel, however, dreams are primarily temporal, images that give birth to past events and hold the threat of resurfacing traumas. Rather than being hunted by a monster, the protagonists are threatened by a haunting—a simple difference which nonetheless radically changes the aesthetic between the two films.

While the often unsteady camera and the seemingly haphazard use of color filters of the first film are repeated to a lesser degree here, the acting and special effects are greatly improved on. Indeed, the latter are especially noteworthy given the tendency of computer-generated imagery to detract from many horror films by rendering the otherwise unknowable object of fear into a visible form—a form that may well come to be a laughable artifact of an older technology just a few years after a film's release. The computer-generated imagery of *Nightmare Detective 2* may eventually fall into this trap as well, but its chances of enduring are stronger thanks to a mix of striking images and concealing camerawork. For example, at a moment of great tension within the dream of protagonist Mashiro Yukie (an impressive performance by then-newcomer Miura Yui), Kagenuma suddenly emerges from her body to take her place in the dream narrative, physically clawing his way out of her skin as she slumps to the floor like a discarded shell. This image is convincing not only because of its preceding build-up of tension, but also because the camera focuses on Mashiro's horrified face rather than Kagenuma's emerging and triumphant one: the camera asks the viewer to empathize with the body that is suddenly transformed into the discarded skin of another, making the image one of vulnerability and bodily instability rather than a simple shock—in other words, strange images are used to draw the viewer in rather than repulse and push them away. A more overt example is the cave-like hole with rippling, breathing walls that appears in an unsettlingly bright and idyllic forest scene, tearing through sky and trees alike. For all the disparate strangeness of many of the film's more surreal images, they work together to communicate an overall sense of the interconnected layering and depths of bodies and images.

Nonetheless, what is most notable about *Nightmare Detective 2* is less its experimental imagery and more its bravery in returning to the school-girl ghost stories that were the foundation of the J-horror movement but had stagnated and been done to death (excuse the pun) by the time of this film's release. In a scene reminiscent of *Ju-on: The Grudge* (2002) and its countless offspring, Mashiro is being haunted by something (either a ghost or her own inner demons; as in many superior horror films the distinction is ambiguous) in her apartment, and begins flipping through a magazine as if to distract herself from reality. As she moves faster and faster through the pages, the camera cuts between her increasingly anxious face and a slow zoom on the turning pages, practically convincing the viewer that at any moment something terrible will reveal itself in or behind the magazine itself. When nothing does, we are left to marvel that somehow a simple magazine could have been made terrifying through innovative cinematography alone. There are various other examples of the refreshing of J-horror in *Nightmare Detective 2*, such as a stereotypical "crawling woman" moment of terror being suddenly interrupted by a remarkably touching scene in which Kagenuma's mother cooks him a hamburger. This freshness will no doubt appeal to fans of the subgenre's original boom.—Seán Hudson

See also Nightmare Detective

Bibliography
Tsukamoto, Shin'ya, dir. *Nightmare Detective 2*. Movie-Eye Entertainment Inc., 2008. Film.

NIJI OTOKO (1949)

DIRECTOR: Kyohiko Ushihara
SCREENPLAY: Hajime Takaiwa
SPECS: 81 minutes; black and white

Released in 1949, *Niji otoko* was directed by Kyohiko Ushihara (1897–1985). The film is based on Kikuo Tsunoda's (b. 1906) unique detective story of the same name. The film belongs to a series of "Daiei thrillers" that include various mystery and horror stories based on the works of famous Japanese suspense authors, such as Edogawa Rampo. *Niji otoko*, although a crime story, explicitly uses horror genre conventions in creating a claustrophobic chamber drama around a family murder mystery. Ushihara makes use of all the genre classics—thunderstorms, a death mediated by phone, erratic shock editing, and bright lighting strikes—in creating highly dynamic scenes of danger.

The story begins when newspaper reporter Mimi Torikai and her boyfriend of the same profession, Ryōsuke Akiishi, find out that Mimi's old classmate Yurie is suspected of a recent countryside murder. Mimi and Ryōsuke arrive at Yurie's, only to be faced with a seemingly supernatural case of murders. Yurie tries to convince them that the murders are committed by a mystical creature, "Niji Otoko" (Rainbow Man). A legend tells that anyone who sees Niji Otoko undergoes a kind of transformation himself. Soon it becomes apparent that Yurie's family, the Mayas, seem to be plagued with the curse of the Rainbow Man. One after another they die screaming "Niji Otoko! Niji Otoko!" The first victim whose death is shown in a manner influenced by horror is Yurie's grandmother.

Mimi and Ryōsuke become immersed in the strange cycle of deaths with Detective Okabe as their help. They start interviewing and interrogating the various members of the Maya clan, all of whom seem to have something to hide. As the story unfolds, the patriarch of the family, renowned scientist Ryūzō Maya, only received his PhD degree after stealing his friend's work at the university, and Yurie's brother Katsuto, an aspiring painter, tends to paint erotic, grotesque, and violent pictures of his mother's death. The paintings show the exact ways in which Yurie's mother is finally killed. As the characters are killed off, it is often Yurie who is found somewhere near the corpses with a knife in her hands. But eventually she, too, becomes a victim of an attack. It is only then revealed that she was pregnant; the baby is lost in the attack. All the while there is one more relative, creepy and confident Toyohiko, lurking in the background together with the Rainbow Man.

As the film concludes, it is revealed that it is not a supernatural belief, character, or legend that is killing the members of the clan. Instead there is a killer who uses mescaline in first poisoning his victims and only then stabbing them. The apparition of a rainbow is due to this poisoning, a mere drug-induced hallucinatory trip. In this way *Niji Otoko* ceases to be a supernatural horror film and moves into the realm of a detective thriller. Finally Toyohiko is found guilty of all the murders, but even this is not enough. He is actually Hachirō—presumed dead—who has been masquerading as Toyohiko. Thus it is not Hachirō but Toyohiko, who was the very first victim found in the countryside. Hachirō vows that all the murders were committed in the name of love for Yurie.

The story of *Niji Otoko* is also interesting because the copy was lost for years, until a version of it was eventually found and released as a laser disc in

1992. In this case, *Niji Otoko* marketed itself as "part-color," two years before the first official color film made in Japan. It seems that the original color parts—which were lost from the discovered copy—were just random colors on screen rather than any comprehensive part of the film *per se*. Nonetheless, these four scenes—altogether 11 seconds—were enough to conjure up an image of a rainbow, a crucial part of the story. In the current version the "rainbow scenes" are made to resemble the original, based on interviews of the original staff.—Leena Eerolainen

NORIKO'S DINNER TABLE (2005)
DIRECTOR: Sion Sono
SCREENPLAY: Sion Sono
SPECS: 159 minutes; color

In *Noriko's Dinner Table* (*Noriko no shokutaku*, 2005), prolific director Sion Sono returns audiences to the oblique (pop-)cultural and philosophical terrain he introduced them to in his cult film sensation *Suicide Circle* (*Jisatsu sākuru*, 2001). *Noriko's Dinner Table*, however, is neither a prequel nor a sequel to *Suicide Circle*, although the graphic mass suicides that helped make Sono's 2001 film so memorable are revisited within the course of *Noriko's Dinner Table*'s 159-minute running time. Rather, the action in *Noriko's Dinner Table* parallels that in *Suicide Circle*, providing viewers with a variation on several of *Suicide Circle*'s themes. Although we learn more about the machinations and motivations that ultimately resulted in *Suicide Circle*'s most spectacular set pieces, *Noriko's Dinner Table*'s primary concerns constellate around a single specific question posed repeatedly during its predecessor's narrative: "Are you connected to yourself?"

Loosely based on his 2002 novel *Suicide Circle: The Complete Edition* (*Jisatsu sākuru: Kanzeban*), *Noriko's Dinner Table* adopts a literary/novelistic structure. Divided into four chapters, each named after one of the film's central protagonists, *Noriko's Dinner Table* tells the story of seventeen-year-old Noriko Shimabara, played by Kazue Fukiishi, who, living at home with her mother, Taeko; her sister, Yuka; and her father, Tetsuo, feels woefully unfulfilled. Forbidden by her father from going to Tokyo to pursue her education, Noriko views her daily life as a veil of hypocrisy and illusion. She sees her family as imitating contentment and togetherness while repressing their individual dissatisfactions and estrangements. Finding solace through the virtual companionship she experiences during her repeated visits to Haikyo.com (a website whose domain name translates literally as "ruins"), Noriko soon leaves home and travels to Tokyo to meet up with "Ueno Station 54," a charismatic young woman named Kumiko, played by Tsugumi. Kumiko, Noriko discovers, operates a business that allows lonely people to rent "family" in order to ease the despair they feel within an increasingly atomistic culture. However, Kumiko's strange occupation is soon revealed to be merely one facet of a complex organization (I.C. Corp) that in many ways resembles a cult whose members elect to disavow their previously established identities and, instead, seek ultimate liberation through embracing emptiness and perpetually reinventing themselves based upon the needs of their desperate, emotionally wounded clientele. Under Kumiko's tutelage, Noriko renames herself Mitsuko, and it is not long before Noriko's sister, Yuka, fearing that Noriko's recent disappearance may be related to a series of mass suicides, sets out to find her sister. Once in Tokyo, Yuka also falls under Kumiko's spell, changing her name to Yoko. Finally, reeling from his daughters' disappearances and his wife's suicidal despair, Tetsuo uses his skills as an investigative reporter to track down the members of his broken family. This quest results in a series of graphically violent conflicts that Sion Sono renders in visceral details that are every bit as grisly and unsettling as anything in 2001's *Suicide Circle*.

Noriko's Dinner Table can be classified as a "horror film," but to reduce it to one specific genre would be to underestimate the dramatic power arising from the work's ability to exceed the parameters of a particular *kind of* film (e.g., "horror"). As a provocative permutation of the family melodrama, *Noriko's Dinner Table* explores shifting generational perspectives and their impacts upon familial bonds. Similarly, as a work in which detection and the process of infiltrating secretive organizations factor significantly into the building of tension, Sono's film could likewise be categorized as a thriller. Several of the implicit social critiques in *Suicide Circle* are also detectable in *Noriko's Dinner Table*: from peer pressure and suicide, to the isolating inertia of social media and the idolization of idealized female beauty within a culture of cuteness (*kawaii*). However, these issues pale in comparison to the larger, existential concerns that inform Sono's film.

Through her transformation from Noriko to Mitsuko (and then back to Noriko), as well as through her jettisoning of her disingenuous family unit for a collective of individuals who embrace artifice in order to provide desperate customers with fleeting moments of imaginary intimacy, Noriko essentially trades one model of inauthenticity for another. Whether going through the motions as a dutiful daughter in the patriarchal household into which she was born, or through impersonating a doting daughter for a pretend father, Noriko's performance of a "self" for the benefit of others' expectations begs the question: "Are you connected to yourself?" Indeed, this question could be posed to each of the film's major characters. Whether simulating idealized domestic roles or disavowing autonomy in the hopes of attaining liberation through emptiness, each of the characters who gather with Noriko around the film's multiple dinner tables (that familiar symbol of unity) struggles to alleviate their existential suffering. However, as Noriko eventually learns, it is only through a sincere personal engagement with the world one encounters that genuine relationships become possible.—Jay McRoy

NOROI (2005)
DIRECTOR: Kōji Shiraishi
SCREENPLAY: Kōji Shiraishi, Naoyuki Yokota
SPECS: 115 minutes; color

Noroi, known in English as *Noroi: The Curse*, is a slow-building "found-footage" horror film directed by Kōji Shiraishi (b. 1973) released in 2005. *Noroi* weaves together a complex story of curses, demons, and the forgotten with strong attention paid to atmospheric tension and the slow-building narrative in order to pursue a more subtle and highly effective horror experience. Presented to audiences as a documentary, the film opens and closes without ever rolling actor/crew credits.

Noroi's plot revolves around the disappearance of renowned supernatural investigator, Masafumi Kobayashi (Jin Muraki), and the footage taken by his cameraman, Hisashi Miyajima (as himself), concerning the final paranormal investigation prior to his vanishing, beginning in 2002 and ending in 2004. The film begins with Kobayashi's investigation of a neighbor's complaints of strange sounds emanating from the home of Junko Ishii (Tomono Kuga); while investigating, he makes note of the fact that there are many dead pigeons, and the video footage captures a strange little boy standing in the window, followed by strange sounds later identified by an "audio expert" as belonging to multiple infants.

Over the course of two years following this initial incident, Kobayashi amasses a group of individuals who have been affected from seemingly unconnected paranormal events: Kana Yano (Rio Kanno), a young clairvoyant/psychic who has been haunted by a strange pattern of knots and a featureless mask with large black eyes after appearing on a television broadcast about children with strange abilities; Marika Matsumoto (as herself), an actress who has been plagued by strange occurrences since appearing on an amateur ghost hunter show and hearing someone call her name at an abandoned Shinto shrine; and psychic Mitsuo Hori (Satoru Jitsunashi), a reclusive hermit wearing a tinfoil hat who warns others of pigeons and ectoplasmic worms that only he has the ability to see.

Shiraishi's slow narrative buildup creates a complex weaving of character interactions that serve as Kobayashi's map as he attempts to find out the truth behind the seemingly unconnected individuals and their paranormal concerns. The sense of increasing unease is crucial in the pacing of the plot and in forming the character motivations and relationships so that the audience forgets that they are suspending their disbelief, and become invested in the depth of the story. While Shiraishi has never stated whether or not he based the narrative for *Noroi* on a particular case, the premise of the film ties tightly to the issue of fading local traditions and beliefs in small villages in Japan, which are in danger of being forgotten due to urbanization, expansion, and an aging population.

The tension is further raised when Kana Yano goes missing, and her parents inform Kobayashi that Hori, who had told them he knew where the girl had gone, visited them. Hori leaves Kobayashi with the strange name "Kagutaba," and a drawing, which Hori is certain will lead Kobayashi to Kana. Shortly after this, Marika begins to exhibit strange nocturnal behaviors, including the voicing of strange sounds, sleepwalking, and using any rope-like object to create knotted, noose-like patterns. After filming Marika for a night, Kobayashi is surprised to find a voice clearly saying "Kagutaba," with no source.

With Hori's drawing and Kagutaba as clues, Kobayashi is surprised to find himself led to the town of Shimokage, where an esoteric Shinto sect is connected to Kagutaba. More perplexing yet, Kobayashi finds himself once more on the trail of Junko Ishii, who had once lived in Shimokage and played the role of Kagutaba in a religious ceremony, before having a delirious breakdown. On the path of Junko, Kobayashi also finds out that she had been a nurse in Tokyo, in charge of disposing the fetuses of late-stage abortion procedures.

As everything begins to weave tightly together, Marika and Hori become more and more affected by their experiences, and it is believed that Kana is in danger. In an effort to break the curse and free Kana from the worms, Kobayashi, Hori, and Marika journey to Shimokage to re-create the ritual performed there in the past. Shiraishi's mounting atmospheric tension is capped off by a shaky cam rush through the area to find Kana, who ultimately does not survive her experience, and dies with Junko in what appears to have been a sacrificial rite cut short; in what Kobayashi believes is a stroke of luck, the small boy he had seen two years before in Junko's house is still alive, and he leaves Shimokage behind.

Shiraishi closes the film with Miyajima receiving a video parcel from Kobayashi after his disappearance; as the camera films from the ground near a prone Kobayashi, the audience watches the small boy taken from the house, Kobayashi's wife self-immolates, and Kagutaba is released on the unsuspecting world thanks to Kobayashi, Marika, and Hori's attempts to stop the curse.

Shiraishi challenges the audience to question what they have seen, and pushes them further into a more psychological J-horror experience when compared to some of his later, more graphic cinematic ventures. Utilizing Japan's rich supernatural and cultural history, Shiraishi's *Noroi* received favorable reviews from critics, audiences, and fans of the J-horror genre.—Megan Negrych

See also Ju-rei: The Uncanny; Kuchisake Onna; Occult; Shiraishi, Kōji

Bibliography
Shiraishi, Kōji, dir. *Noroi*. Xanadeux Company, 2005. Film.

• O •

OBAYASHI, NOBUHIKO (1938–)

House (*Hausu*), Nobuhiko Obayashi's (b. 1938) pop-culture horror film, not only was his first theatrical feature and a surprise hit in Japan in 1977, but was also responsible for engendering his international recognition as a cult film maker upon its discovery in the West more than three decades later. It is an absurdist tale of a house possessed by a sexually repressed spirit. Psychedelically tongue-in-cheek rather than terror inducing, it transformed Obayashi's career from a creator of avant-garde films and outlandish commercials to one of offbeat features for commercial cinemas.

Born in Onomichi, in Hiroshima Province, Obayashi lost a number of friends to the atomic bomb. He made experimental Super 8 and 16 mm films while in college, then moved to Tokyo to further pursue his passion. Together with Takahiko Iimura and Donald Richie, he helped found Film Independent, an experimental film collective, in 1964. His *The Man Who Ate* won the jury prize at the 1963 Belgian International Experimental Film Festival. Other early works, like the 1968 *Emotion*, which he estimates was screened at 60 percent of Japan's colleges, used experimental techniques and editing strategies, including stop action, collage, and pixilation fused with mad visual and stylistic innovations. *Emotion* incorporates dark irony with several film genres, including the American western, to create an irreverent vampire film with quotes from Roger Vadim's 1960 *Et mourir de plaisir* (*Blood and Roses*). As avant-garde performances became increasingly popular in Tokyo, Obayashi took part in various group shows (Yoko Ono was another frequent participant), including one held in a hall in Shinjuku that was attended by a producer from Dentsu, Japan's largest advertising company. The producer invited the directors of the short films to create commercials incorporating their experimental techniques. Excited at the prospect of being able to use professional equipment, Obayashi was the only group member to accept this offer, and he went on to make over two thousand commercials. His acclaimed ads featured such international stars as Charles Bronson, Kirk Douglas, Sophia Loren, Catherine Deneuve, and Ringo Starr.

With the Japanese film industry facing a box office crisis in the mid-1970s, Toho invited Obayashi to script a horror film. *House*, the result, was greenlighted by Toho. Two years later, after all of Toho's in-house directors turned *House* down, Obayashi was hired to direct it. This was particularly eventful since Obayashi had not served the mandatory multiyear apprenticeship demanded by Japanese studios at that time. The film's seven attractive but ill-fated virginal schoolgirls were played by young models that Obayashi had met while shooting commercials. His experimental cinematic techniques were primarily extensions of those used in his earlier films and commercials. He turned down the opportunity to work with Toho's renowned special effects department, believing their efforts would make his film appear too realistic. Obayashi instead chose to create fantasy-like effects and imagery such as schmaltzy but beautiful sunsets and sweet music that he felt evoked a sensation of delight within the context of the fantasy. Coming from the Hiroshima area, he also references the war through the emotional state of the aunt who owns the mansion. As the story goes, years later she's still awaiting her fiancé's return from the war; this is the event that leads to the haunting of the house. Obayashi also depicts the aunt's wedding dress, lovely but unworn, beautiful like cotton candy, then cuts immediately to footage of the bomb.

Much of *House* resonates throughout Obayashi's later features. He frequently incorporates the aesthetics and experimental cinematic techniques from *House* and his earlier works into them. Several of the later films are adolescent fantasies concerned with dislocations of time and/or space. *The Girl Who Leapt through Time* (*Toki o kakeru shojo*, 1983) centers on a precocious teenager with the ability to time travel. In *The Aimed School* (*Nerawareta Gakuen*, 1981; also titled *School in the Crosshairs*) another high school girl discovers that she possesses special psychic powers, and must duel with a boy with similar abilities attempting to tyrannize their school. In *The Drifting Classroom* (*Hyoryu kyoshitsu*, 1987) a school is transported to another dimension during a hurricane, and the students must survive pestilence and loneliness while earth is devastated. *Exchange Students* (*Tenkosei*, 1982, later remade by Obayashi in 2007) concerns Kazuo, a boy just entering puberty, and Kazumi, a ninth-grade girl, who inadvertently exchange bodies. Kazuo, just entering the stage in which he is curious about girls' bodies, now finds himself possessing one.

The Discarnates (*Ijin-tachi to no natsu*, 1988) is a different type of ghost/horror film. Harada is a recently divorced and lonely television scriptwriter who lost his parents when he was twelve. His life changes when he finds himself in the Asakusa district of Tokyo as it was when he was a boy. He meets his parents, who are the same age as when they died, then begins to interact with them to fill a missing void in his life. Harada now feels able to freely enter into a relationship with a woman possessing a mysterious background. But he suddenly finds himself rapidly aging. In this haunting story of acceptance of the past Obayashi wonderfully re-creates the Asakusa of the 1950s.

Obayashi directed a variety of films during his prolific career. *Beijing Watermelon* (*Pekinteki suita*, 1989) sensitively portrays a greengrocer who comes to sympathize with Chinese students in Japan. The heartfelt *I Want to Hear the Wind's Song* (*Kaze no uta ga kikitai*, 1998), based on a true story, centers on a deaf couple as they struggle to overcome their disabilities. His 1998 *Sada* recounts the life of Abe Sada, also depicted in Nagisa Oshima's (1932–2013) 1976 *In the Realm of the Senses* (*Ai no corrida*). Obayashi portrays fourteen-year-old Sada as a victim of rape, her adolescence ruined. Obayashi also set two trilogies in his native Onomichi, and has also incorporated antiwar themes into several works.

Only a few of Obayashi's works have been presented at film festivals. Among them, *Sada* won the FIPRESCI (International Film Critics) Prize at the Berlin International Film Festival. *The Discarnates* was presented at the Moscow Film Festival, and *Beijing Watermelon* played at New Directors/New Films in New York. In 2009 he was awarded the distinguished Order of the Rising Sun from the Japanese government for his film career.

Obayashi's works are belatedly being discovered in the West due to the late release of *House*. They have only won a few awards in Japan, but are often popular with audiences, particularly teenage girls who enjoy his youth fantasies. One category in which they have received recognition in Japan is that of Best Female Newcomer, for which several actresses in his films centered on adolescents have been honored by various award-granting agencies. Even though he now works closer to the mainstream, his works continue to retain their edginess.—Bill Thompson

See also The Discarnates; House

Bibliography

Criterion Films. *Constructing a "House."* DVD extra with *House.*
Obayashi, Nobuhiko. *The Discarnates.* 35 mm.
———. *Emotion.* Criterion Films. DVD extra with *House.*
———. *House.* Criterion Films. DVD.
Roquet, Paul. "Nobuhiku Obayashi: Vagabond of Time." Accessed 25 May 2015. http://www.mid nighteye.com/features/nobuhiko-obayashi-vagabond-of-time/.

OCCULT (2009)

DIRECTOR: Kōji Shiraishi
SCREENPLAY: Kōji Shiraishi
SPECS: 110 minutes; color

Occult (Okaruto) is an investigative mockumentary/POV horror film that blends a realistic style with mystical, Lovecraftian content. The film is written and directed by Kōji Shiraishi and was released in 2009.

Occult follows the enquiries of several filmmakers as they investigate the motivations and the implications of a spree killer's random stabbings and eventual disappearance at Myogasaki, a Japanese sightseeing tourist attraction. During the stabbings, the spree killer, Ken Matsuki, engraves a mystical mark onto the side of a tourist named Shohei. Through a series of interviews with Shohei, the documentary team discovers that Shohei has been having mystical and paranormal experiences such as telekinesis and visions of UFOs and ghosts—all of which are presumably linked to the spree killer. When Koji (the director of the documentary team) follows Shohei to capture these experiences on film, the UFOs and ghosts become more prevalent—and Koji begins seeing the apparitions around Shohei as well. Eventually, Koji becomes an accomplice of Shohei's plan to fulfill a mystical purpose, to kill hundreds of innocent people through a suicide bombing at the busy Shibuya Train Station, freeing the victims to become part of "another dimension." Koji helps Shohei prepare for his post-death destiny and captures the experience on film. Shohei carries a video camera on his suicide mission so that he can capture the "other dimension." Years later, Koji, who survives the explosion, is sent a mysterious random film; Koji recognizes that the film has been sent by Shohei from the afterlife dimension—revealing that Shohei is in hell.

Using POV style (a style similar to *Cannibal Holocaust* [1980] and *The Blair Witch Project* [1999]), Kōji Shiraishi weaves a strong sense of realism into *Occult*. The first half of the film is formal investigative journalism, albeit fictional. The documentary crew, along with the audience of *Occult*, is trying to piece together the evidence to solve the mystery of the Myogasaki stabbings. Additionally, *Occult*'s primary plot points are loosely based on acts of real-life terrorism. For example, the Myogasaki stabbings that begin and spark the events of the film are loosely based on the phenomenon of random spree killings and stabbings in Japan (sixty-seven multiple stabbing rampages between 1998 and 2007)—the worst being the Akihabara Massacre, a spree stabbing where seven people were killed, which occurred just a year before *Occult* was released. Furthermore, the Shibuya train station bombing scene in *Occult* also mimics realistic international suicide bombing scenarios.

In juxtaposition to the realism, *Occult* weaves a tapestry of mystical elements that certainly explore the "occult" in the most fundamental meaning of the word: "not disclosed, secret, communicated only to the initiated." *Occult* specifically touches on transcendent motivations of the spree killers: dreams, symbology, ghosts, UFOs, and Lovecraftian mythos. The presence of Lovecraftian lore builds throughout the film. The blend of alien "out of space" elements (e.g., UFOs), motivations by a higher power, and even a notable scene where Shohei's head briefly becomes a knot of tentacles (i.e., Cthulhu), lead to this film being often labeled as Japanese Lovecraftian horror.

Various critics recognize a dark sense of humor that pervades *Occult*. This irreverence mixed with the irony of the final "hell" scene, rhetorically undercuts the severity of the film. While critics generally acknowledge *Occult*'s well-crafted story, critics also lambaste the poor computer-generated special effects that detract from the realism of the film. Scenes such as Shohei's head transforming into tentacles and the final hell sequence are notably artificial; the final hell sequence can be seen as cartoonish in its hallucinogenic depiction. These poor special effects can be attributed to the small budget of the film.

Kōji Shiraishi plays himself in *Occult* as the director of the documentary team and one of the central characters of the film. Shiraishi considers *Occult* to be his most personal work and he has remarked that it was the first time in his independent filmmaking career that he was given complete artistic freedom. Shiraishi has proceeded to make horror films as *Shirome* (2010) and *Cult* (2013), which are similar to *Occult*'s mockumentary/POV-style.

Occult premiered at the Yubari International Fantastic Film Festival in February 2009 and was released in Japan in March 2009. The 110-minute film, also known as *The Unidentified*, is produced and distributed by Creative Axa Co. Ltd. and Image Rings.—Gavin F. Hurley

OIKAWA, ATARU (1957–)

Ataru Oikawa (b. 1957) is one of the leading directors in low-budget horror scenario films, made famous after his first production, *Tomie*, in 1999. He is a rather prolific artist, directing thirty-four works in total, counting films, original videos, television, and Internet series. Oikawa is also a well-known screenwriter—having written thirty-six pieces in total—and producer, for which he counts the celebrated 1990 production, *Gattubi—Bokura wa kono natsu nekutai wo suru*.

Working for Magazine House Ltd., Oikawa joined as editor in 1982, initiating his transition to cinema as a screenwriter in the 1988 horror film *Door*, directed by Takahashi Banmei. In 1990, he debuted as a director and wrote the script for a youth drama, *Okutopāsu āmī Shibuya de aitai* (Octopus army: I want to meet in Shibuya). Since this debut, Oikawa has worked as a screenwriter and director within the film industry, as well as in television dramas, Internet films, and original videos. Despite his reputation as a horror cinema director, especially for his works *Tomie* and the Shrill Cries series, he has actually made major contributions to almost all genres including romance (*Kissho Tennyo*, 2007 and *Lover's Kiss*, 2003); erotic genre (*Menotto*, 2005); sci-fi (*Einstein Girl*, 2005 and *Cutie Girl: Bishōjo bowler kiki ippatsu*, 2003); action (*Tokyo yoru bōdō: Kenka no hanamichi—Tokyo bangai hen*, 1998); drama (*Okutopāsu āmī Shibuya de aitai*,1988, *Nihonsei shōnen*, 1995, and *Samurai Girl 21*, 2001); comedy (*Fight Girls*, 2003); as well as action (*Tamagawa shōjo sensō*, 2001).

In his first script (*Door*, 1988), Oikawa created a suspense-thriller about the fear that exists in everyday life. The film is an original story inspired by a day he himself lost his cell phone and experienced visions of what would happen if a stranger found it and decided to act in unpredictable ways. The plot revolves around an ordinary thirty-year-old businessman named Akira who loses his cell phone and the bizarre incidents that unfold as he recovers it.

In the following year, along with Kiyoshi Kurosawa, Oikawa scripted *Abunai hanashi: Mugen monogatari*. The project was a Japanese anthology film with three different stories by Izutsu Kazuyuki, Kiyoshi Kurosawa, and Banmei Takahashi. Oikawa and Kurosawa's story, *Yatsura wa konya mo yattekita*, was a horror story thriller about a writer working under the stress generated by two strangers that threaten him at his home.

After ten years experimenting with several genres in original videos and cinema, in 1999 he returned to the horror genre, writing the script and directing the first installment of *Tomie*, followed later by *Tomie: Beginning* (2005) and *Tomie: Revenge* (2005). Of the nine *Tomie* films, Oikawa dealt with three considered to be an adaptation of Junji Ito's horror manga. *Tomie*, a cult manga, features different stories about a beautiful high school student named "Tomie," portrayed as an antagonist of males, and the recipient of their anger. Finding herself bullied and killed by male rage, her death engenders a series of reincarnations—a new Tomie from every part of her body. Exploring issues of feminism and the overarching powers of a patriarchal Japanese society, Oikawa's Tomie struck a chord with a variety of audiences that saw Tomie as both a monster produced by major gender disparities, as well as a heroine of justice that takes revenge on those that take advantage of such inequalities.

In 2004 Oikawa wrote the script of *Tōkyō densetsu: Ugomeku machi no kyōki* (Tokyo Psycho) based on the *otaku* serial killer, Miyazaki Tsutomu, who murdered four young girls in Tokyo between 1988 and 1989. The plot revolves around intense instances of stalking and terror—themes in which Oikawa is considered to be at his best. Although set in the seemingly everyday hustle and bustle of Tokyo, the architectural and environmental backdrop created by Oikawa is one of isolation and emptiness. Throughout the film, Oikawa develops what appears to be social commentary about *otaku*, or disconnected and isolated youth depicting them as individuals that appear trapped between tradition and modernity where their stalking that leads to murder is somehow tied to environmental factors.

In 2004 Oikawa directed and wrote *Umeku haisuikan*, considered to be an adaptation of *The Groaning Drain*—a horror story from the Junji Ito manga *Museum of Terror*. In part, taking up the vilified *otaku* theme once again, Oikawa tells the story of two beautiful sisters that conspire to thwart the advances of a stalking *otaku*. In a peculiar, if not surreal, storyline, a drainpipe through which the characters hear sounds, comes alive to swallow the cast one by one.

In 2007, Oikawa directed and wrote the script of *1303 go shitsu*, also known as *Apartment 1303*, based on a novel by Kei Oishi—celebrated author of *Ju-on*. The film is a complicated mix of suicides and ghostly interactions. Critics have noted that this Oikawa piece explores notions of patriarchy, Japanese feminism, and the tension between traditional Japanese family models and those of the Western nuclear family. Despite what seemed to be new thematic territory for Oikawa, the film received relatively positive reviews.

Considered to be one of today's most talented writers, directors, and producers of Japanese horror films, Ataru Oikawa continues to introduce new and complex features that draw upon the eerie nuances of all things strange and uncanny. His record of output and persistence is telling of his work ethic. Indeed, in the three-year period between 2008 and 2011 alone, Oikawa generated four films, including *9 plus 1*, adapted the 7th Expansion's visual novel *Higurashi no naku koro ni* into two films *Higurashi no naku koro ni* (2008) and *Higurashi no naku koro ni: Chikai* (2009), as well as wrote and directed *Shōjo sensō* (2011). As such a celebrated artist in his field, Oikawa's work is becoming increasingly important to students of Japanese film in general and its horror genre in particular.—Sabrina Vaquerizo González

Bibliography

Balmain, Colette. "Inside the Well of Loneliness: Towards a Definition of the Japanese Horror Film." *Electronic Journal of Contemporary Japanese Studies* 2 (May 2006). Accessed 30 December 2014. http://www.japanesestudies.org.uk/discussionpapers/2006/Balmain.html.

———. *Introduction to Japanese Horror Film*. Edinburgh: Edinburgh University Press, 2008.

Hong Kong–Asia Film Financing Forum. "Door." *HAF.org*. 2009. Accessed 28 December 2014. http://www.haf.org.hk/haf/pdf/project09/se7.pdf.

OKURA, MITSUGU (1899–1978)

Mitsugu Okura was a *benshi*, theater owner, and film studio executive. As the head of the Shintōhō studio during the latter half of the 1950s, Okura produced several of the finest examples of classic Japanese horror cinema or *kaiki eiga*. During the 1960s Okura founded his own studio, Okura Films, where he continued to produce horror and other low-budget exploitation pictures, helping pioneer the *pinku* genre of mainstream soft-core erotic film.

Okura got his start in the film industry at the age of thirteen as a *benshi*, the live, in-house narrators of silent cinema in Japan. Unlike other early cinemas, silent Japanese film made sparing use of inter-titles, relying on the (often improvised) verbal explanations of the *benshi* for narrative clarity. A good *benshi* had to possess a flair for the theatrical and a strong sense of showmanship, and the young Okura proved one of the more successful at his craft. He also gained a keen appreciation of the necessity of giving the audience what they wanted, a business philosophy that would also characterize his later role as a producer of horror movies and other lurid but popular genres of film.

From working-class roots, by the age of twenty-five Okura had amassed a small fortune via his successful *benshi* career, and in 1924 he used it to purchase a chain of thirty-six underperforming theaters, personally undertaking their management. Having learned the value of thrift from his poor upbringing and the importance of pandering to the tastes of a mass audience from his time as a *benshi*, Okura quickly turned the fortunes of his new venture around. He later did the same for the struggling Nikkatsu theater chains, and soon became known in the Japanese film world as a miracle worker who could turn losses into profits.

Okura's reputation brought the board members of Shintōhō calling in 1955 with an offer to take over management of the studio. Originally founded in 1949 by defectors from Tōhō as a studio by and for artists, Shintōhō had produced award-winning films like Kenji Mizoguchi's *Life of Oharu* (*Saikaku ichidai onna*, 1952), but by the middle of the decade it was dangerously in the red. Given absolute authority over the studio, Okura took Shintōhō in a completely different direction, slashing budgets and shooting schedules, refusing to hire big-name directors and stars, and focusing exclusively on the production of popular genre pictures. Recalling the prewar box office successes of traditional *kaidan* ghost story adaptations, Okura made horror films a top priority. When the studio released its first version of *Yotsuya kaidan* during the summer Obon festival of the dead in 1956, its financial success vindicated Okura's faith in the disreputable genre. Much to the chagrin of the studio's creative staff, which preferred to work on more critically respectable projects, Okura mandated the production of at least two horror films each year in time for Obon to be released as a "monster cavalcade" (*obake daikai*) double feature.

Nobuo Nakagawa (1905–1984), who by 1957 was Shintōhō's senior director, reluctantly found himself in charge of many such pictures, Okura wanting his top talent on the job. Between 1957 and 1960 Nakagawa and art director Haruyasu Kurosawa collaborated on several innovative horror projects for Okura, including the first color *bakeneko* (ghost cat) movie, *Mansion of the Ghost Cat* (*Bōrei kaibyō yashiki*, 1958), Japan's first Western-style vampire movie, *Lady Vampire* (*Onna kyūketsuki*, 1959), and what are widely considered Nakagawa's two masterpieces, *Tōkaidō Yotsuya kaidan* (1959) and *Jigoku* (1960). Rather like the contemporaneous Hammer horror films, Nakagawa and Kurosawa's shocking, full-color displays of blood and violence helped cement Shintōhō's reputation as a producer of seedy, lurid exploitation films, but they also brought the genre of *kaiki eiga* unprecedented positive critical acclaim. Long-running film magazine *Kinema Junpō*, typically dismissive of domestic horror films as poorly produced trash, praised Nakagawa's work in the genre for bringing genuine scares and psychological depth to the genre. While *Jigoku* was a pet project Nakagawa pitched to Okura, the director freely admitted in later years he created his other horror classics only at Okura's insistence.

Horror was of course not the only exploitation genre Okura put the studio into the business of making. In 1956 *Revenge of the Pearl Queen* (*Ona shinju-ō no fukushū*) rocked the Japanese film scene with its "all-nude" scenes of busty actress Michiko Maeda, and inaugurated a series of Shintōhō skin flicks about *ama*, Japan's female pearl divers. Seeking to combine two of his most profitable genres, Okura produced the horror/bathing beauty hybrids *Diving Girls in a Haunted House* (*Ama no bakemono yashiki*, 1959) and *Diving Girl's Ghost* (*Kaidan ama yūrei*, 1960). Of *Diving Girls in a Haunted House, Kinema Junpō* proclaimed, "It stinks, but the title is some kind of genius." Shintōhō's scandalous skin flicks were matched in reputation by rumors of Okura's own illicit affairs with the studio's contract actresses, which reportedly resulted in the creation of one of the studio's final horror classics, *Vampire Bride* (*Hanayome kyūketsuma*, 1960). According to industry gossip, actress Junko Ikeuchi refused Okura's advances, and as punishment was forced to perform the titular role in *Vampire Bride*, a hideous, hair-covered monster that was a far cry from the sexy female vampire the film's title might suggest.

Scandals with actresses, a criminal investigation into claims of embezzlement, and the revelation that he had discreetly sold the studio's second lot to a subcontracted studio all conspired to force Okura's resignation from Shintōhō near the end of 1960. Although his Midas Touch had initially turned the studio's struggling fortunes around, by the time he left the company Shintōhō had fallen back into the red. Unlike the other major studios, Shintōhō owned none of its own theaters, and despite Okura's best efforts to produce cheap but entertaining crowd pleasers, was unable to secure enough distribution to remain viable. Less than a year after Okura left, Shintōhō filed for bankruptcy. Okura went on to found his own studio, Okura Films, in 1962, where he would spend the remainder of his career producing horror movies and skin flicks on minuscule budgets that made his B-grade Shintōhō pictures look downright lavish by comparison. *Pinku eiga* soft-core pornography eventually became the studio's stock-in-trade, and Okura Films never managed to duplicate the critical success of the *kaidan* classics Nobuo Nakagawa and Haruyasu Kurosawa created under Okura's orders at Shintōhō.

Mitsugu Okura's reputation in Japanese film history remains rather ignominious, remembered mainly as the man who turned Shintōhō from a haven for film artists into a factory for cheap exploitation pictures. For the development of the horror genre in Japan, however, Okura's importance is hard to overstate. While other studios limited horror film production to program pictures hastily completed between prestige projects, Okura made his horror movies A-list efforts, using the latest technological innovations like widescreen and color, and assigning top talent like Nakagawa and Kurosawa to bring them to spectacular life onscreen. Without his intervention, classic Japanese horror cinema would look very different indeed.—Michael Crandol

See also The Bloody Sword of the 99th Virgin; The Ghost of Chibusa Enoki; Jigoku; Nakagawa, Nobuo; *Vampire Bride*

ONE MISSED CALL films

One Missed Call (2003)
DIRECTOR: Takashi Miike
SCREENPLAY: Minako Daira
SPECS: 112 minutes; color

One Missed Call 2 (2005)
DIRECTOR: Renpei Tsukamoto
SCREENPLAY: Minako Daira
SPECS: 105 minutes; color

One Missed Call: Final (2006)
DIRECTOR: Manabu Aso
SCREENPLAY: Minako Daira, Jiro Shin
SPECS: 109 minutes; color

One Missed Call (*Chakushin ari*) (2003) is the first in a trilogy of films involving a series of disappearances and murders surrounding mysterious cell phone calls, and would go on to inspire an American-made spin-off. The first film was directed by Takashi Miike (b. 1960), who is also known for *Ichi the Killer* (2001) and *Hostel* (2006) among several other film projects.

The film begins with Yumi Nakamura, played by Ko Shibasaki (b. 1981) a university student out at dinner with her friends. Yumi leaves dinner with her friend Yoko Okazaki, who receives a strange missed call from her own mobile number; the caller leaves a voicemail that contains Yumi's voice exclaiming "it's beginning to rain" followed by a scream. The message is even more confusing in that the date on it is two days in the future. The girls ignore the voicemail, but two days later at the exact time of the message Yoko dies while on the phone with Yumi and her last words are those they had heard in the message.

Yumi hears other students discussing the phenomenon of the phone calls and attempts to save another student, Kenji Kawai, who had also received a voicemail but initially doesn't believe the stories. Yumi succeeds in scaring him into believing in the curse, but before he can react, he is dragged to his death in an elevator shaft.

A friend of Yumi's, Natsumi Konishi, played by Kazue Fukiishi (b. 1982), also receives the call while staying with Yumi, and is pressured by a journalist to have an exorcism performed on her on live TV. The exorcism is to take place at the precise moment Natsumi is to die, following the phone call; however, it fails when Natsumi is twisted to death by an unseen force. After dying, a small candy is found in her mouth like the other victims.

Yumi also meets Hiroshi Yamashita, played by Shin'ichi Tsutsumi (b. 1964), a detective who has been investigating the cell phone cases since his sister died in what he believes to be the first case. In reading his sister's journal, Hiroshi and Yumi uncover the story of Marie Mizunuma, played by Mariko Tsutsui (b. 1962), a mother whose children Hiroshi's sister took special care over, believing that Marie had been abusing them. The connection to the killings is made more concrete when the pair discover that one of Marie's children, Mimiko, died from an asthma attack, and the sound of an asthma pump was heard at Kenji's death.

Following Natsumi's death Yumi receives a phone call and decides to pursue the investigation of Marie by going to the burned hospital where she was last seen. They find Marie's body in the hospital and in the confrontation Hiroshi is forced out of the room.

Hiroshi continues to investigate and discovers a video camera that Marie had placed to watch her children while she was away, and the tape shows that it was not Marie that abused her children, but rather Mimiko, who attacked her sister Nanako and provided her candy to remain silent. In the last confrontation Mimiko cuts Nanako's hand, which prompts Marie to leave Mimiko alone while she takes Nanako to the hospital—while alone Mimiko dies by succumbing to an asthma attack. After making this discovery Hisoshi goes to tell Yumi, but instead finds her already possessed by Mimiko, and proceeds to stab him. The film ends with Hiroshi waking up in the hospital with Yumi standing with him holding a knife and giving him a small red candy to eat—the same candy found in the others' mouths.

Taking place a year after the events of the first film *One Missed Call 2* (*Chakushin ari 2*) is directed by Renpei Tsukamoto (b. 1963) and tells the story of Kyoko Okudera, played by Rie Kogure (b. 1984) and Naoto Sakurai, played by Hisashi Yoshizaawa (b. 1978) a young couple who become linked to the continued cell phone curse from the original film.

Kyoko, a teacher, is convinced by her coworker, Madoka Uchiyama, to take a night off from studying to visit her boyfriend, Naoto, at the restaurant where he is working. While they are at the restaurant, the owner, Mr. Wang, answers his daughter Mei-Feng's cell phone and discovers it is her voice on the other end, shortly before she arrives carrying groceries.

As the restaurant closes, Mei-Feng exchanges numbers with Kyoko and Madoka, after she gets a new cell phone. Naoto is in the kitchen looking for Mr. Wang so he can go home when Madoka receives a phone call from a ring tone the girls recognize from Natsumi's television death in the first film. Shortly thereafter Naoto discovers Mr. Wang dead in the kitchen.

The police are alerted and detective Motomiya questions Naoto about whether or not there was a candy in Mr. Wang's mouth when his body was found. Naoto lies about the involvement of cell phones to Motomiya, but reveals the truth to another detective, Takako Nozoe, played by Asaka Seto (b. 1976).

Meanwhile Kyoko and Madoka are talking via video on their cell phones and Kyoko spots a disturbing figure behind Madoka, which she seems unable to see. Kyoko panics and throws her phone, ending the call and rushing with Naoto to Madoka's apartment. There they find Madoka, killed and contorted in her shower. Kyoko's cell phone then receives the same call that Mr. Wang and Madoka had along with a picture of her behind a chain-link fence.

Detective Motomiya decides to perform an autopsy on all the victims to see if there are any clues, while Takako, Naoto, and Kyoko investigate Mimiko's past more closely. While visiting Mimiko's grandmother, they learn that Mimiko was conceived when her mother was raped by an individual with severe mental illness. Mimiko's grandfather catches this man, stabs him to death, then flees to his native Taiwan. Takako pursues this lead and seeks out Mimiko's grandfather, but finds him dead. Motomiya then discovers that all the victims have coal dust in their stomachs, consistent with a mine near where Mimiko's grandfather lived, and Takako informs him that the murders began in Taiwan long before Mimiko had died.

Kyoko and Naoto are tormented by strange events around their apartment and decide to follow Takako to Taiwan to solve the mystery. The three of them meet and decide to head to the mining town where the coal originally came from, which, while once prosperous and populated, has since been reduced to a single elderly woman named Shu-mei Gao. Gao tells Takako, Kyoko, and Naoto the story of Li Li, a child who was bullied by others until one day she started to foresee the deaths of town members, watching them die off one by one. Before they were all dead however, they sewed her mouth shut to stop her from speaking and sealed her within the coal mine. Takako's estranged husband then calls Takako to reveal that he also received the phone call, and hadn't told her hoping she would drop the case.

The trio splits up to look for an alternative entrance to the coal mine after finding the main one blocked. Locating a second entrance, Takako enters the mine, but faints when she encounters Mimiko's ghost. In the mine Kyoko opens a sack and Madoka crawls out and attacks her; she escapes Madoka only to be trapped in a different area with Mimiko's ghost. Mimiko attacks Naoto but he manages to free Kyoko by answering her phone, and sacrifices himself in the process.

Kyoko wakes up in a hospital bed with Takako waiting beside her, but then Takako receives a phone call informing her that detective Motomiya is dead, having died in a car crash. The death is off-putting in that it occurred prior to the phone conversation Takako had with him in which he cleared Mimiko of the murders. After this phone call Takako rushes to Yuting's apartment only to find his body, and a videotape showing herself as the murderer. The film ends with Takako pulling a red candy from her mouth and smiling at the camera.

One Missed Call: Final (*Chakushin ari final*) the third and final film in the series was directed by Manabu Aso (b. 1964) and expands from the series' previous reliance upon cell phones and instead incorporates computer technologies as well.

The film opens with a girl in high school, Asuka Matsuda, played by Maki Horikita (b. 1988) discovering her close friend "PAM" in an attempted suicide. Asuka saves PAM, who, however, lies unconscious recovering in a hospital. As the rest of the high school class has left Japan for Seoul, South Korea, on an extensive field trip, Asuka, grieving for her friend and looking to take revenge on the apparent bullies who were responsible for her attempted suicide, opens a class photo on her computer and initiates the cell phone curse from the first two films.

Asuka proceeds to have the students killed one by one, selecting them from the class photo. After being selected, the students receive a phone call with the message that death can be avoided by forwarding it to a friend. This prompts many of the students to forward the message, but at the cost of their friends and even teachers' lives.

Emiri Kusama, played by Meisa Kuroki (b. 1988), Asuka's only friend, confides in her boyfriend that Asuka is actually PAM, PAM being the shortened form of "SPAM" the nickname the bullies gave Asuka. It is then revealed that the force behind the phone calls is none other than "Mimiko" from the other previous films disguised as Asuka who remains in a coma.

Realizing that Mimiko's power comes from Asuka's computer Emiri and her boyfriend work to spread the word of the curse to flood the computer's inbox with e-mails and somehow shut it down. The real Asuka comes home from the hospital during this process, and talks to Emiri through video-chat, having been awakened when Emiri apologizes to her for not having stopped the bullies. In the middle of this conversation, Mimiko transports the two girls back to their school where Asuka is haunted by students who died from her curse.

The film ends with Emiri offering herself as Mimiko's final victim, Mimiko presenting her with a red candy, but at that exact moment the flood of e-mails comes through and causes Asuka's computer to explode with Mimiko inside. Emiri's boyfriend takes her phone from her and answers Mimiko's final call, dying for her. The final scene shows Emiri, who has lost her voice, and Asuka walking along the beach, fulfilling a promise they had made before Asuka's bullying began.—Josh Dawson

Bibliography

Aso, Manabu dir. *One Missed Call: Final*. Toho Company, 2006. Film.
Miike, Takashi dir. *One Missed Call*. Kadokawa Eiga K.K., 2004. Film.
Tsukamoto, Renpei dir. *One Missed Call 2*. Toho Company, 2005. Film.

ONIBABA (1964)

DIRECTOR: Kaneto Shindō
SCREENPLAY: Kaneto Shindō
SPECS: 103 minutes; black and white

Kaneto Shindō's *Onibaba* marked a change of course for the director on its release in 1964, following over a decade of melodrama and social conscience movies, or "tendency films." Though *Onibaba* can be seen as the director's horror debut, it incorporates several themes that run consistently throughout much of Shindō's directorial and scriptwriting work, including a focus on class struggle and the inner lives and desires of women, a strong antinuclear agenda, and the juxtaposition of youth and sexual power with waste, decay, and death. Shindō's change of genre was popular with both audiences and critics; *Onibaba* won several awards including the Grand Prix at the Panama Film Festival, Best Supporting Actress for Jitsuko Yoshimura, and Best Cinematography for Kiyomi Kuroda at the Blue Ribbon Awards in 1964.

Nobuko Otowa (1925–1994), lifelong collaborator and eventual wife of the director, is a constant presence in his work. Playing against a star persona based on youth, beauty, innocence, and suffering, Otowa's titular "demon hag" is an older peasant woman bent on avenging rather than capitulating to her suffering. Her son has joined one of the many factions fighting in a civil war, leaving Otowa's unnamed "hag" living with her daughter-in-law (Jitsuko Yoshimura) in a makeshift hut. The two use a nearby pit to trap and kill passing samurai, stripping the bodies and selling their armor and weaponry for food. When a neighbor returns from the war with the news that Otowa's son is dead, and seduces the daughter-in-law, Otowa's hag fears for her own survival if the girl leaves her. She poses as a demon, using a *han'nya* mask taken from a dead samurai, to scare the girl into leaving her new lover, but when the mask fuses to her face she must confess her scheme to her daughter-in-law. The two try to dislodge the mask, but find that the damage it has done to Otowa's face has turned her into the demon hag of the title.

The hag is constructed as a horror from the opening shot, a bird's eye view of the two women stripping the corpses of two samurai. A crab pattern on Otowa's kimono invites comparison of the women's livelihoods with those of the scavenging crustaceans. Later indoor shots employ oddly drawn makeup and high-key lighting angled upward, emphasizing the eerie qualities of Otowa's face and body to create a monstrous and threatening appearance. The scars left when the mask is torn away strongly resemble the keloid scars of the *hibakusha*, or atomic exposure victim. Shindō had made several films dealing with atomic exposure in the years after the end of the Allied occupation in 1952 (*Genbaku no Ko* [*Children of Hiroshima*], 1952; *Daigo Fukuryū Maru* [*Lucky Dragon Number 5*], 1959) and is said to have modeled Otowa's disfigured face on his research into the scars left by exposure to atomic bombs.

Unlike the individual atom bomb victim, however, the hag is positioned as both victim and antagonist, as Shindō uses the tropes of the horror genre to problematize the simplistic "victim complex" espoused by many films of the 1950s. The victim complex refers to a popular understanding of Japan's Fifteen Years War in East Asia and subsequent entry into the Second World War as the result of decisions made by an imperial government that deceived its citizens into supporting the war effort. Shindō had addressed popular debates around the victim complex in many previous films; *Onibaba* crafts a cinematic representation of the victim complex by articulating Otowa's character as an excessive or monstrous mother, counterbalancing the suffering mothers of the *hahamono*, or "mother film," which tended toward supporting and repeating ideas of Japanese victimhood.

The monstrous protagonist of *Onibaba* is the victim of class as much as gender violence, depicting war responsibility as intertwined between ruling classes and lower classes, and between victims and victimizers, to complicate the idea of a "demon" or total evil, defined against humanity or pure good. The intertwining of victim and victimizer is reflected in Otowa's character, who channels the cinematic conventions of both the mother and the "A-bomb maiden" as bodily testament to the destructive force of atomic warfare. Otowa's characterization subverts both cinematic norms in that she is neither the weak mother of the *hahamono* nor the beautiful *hibakusha* "maiden"; instead, her active role in the violence perpetrated onscreen problematizes the common cinematic trope of the feminine as locus of innocence.—Jennifer Coates

Bibliography

Desser, David. *Eros Plus Massacre: An Introduction to the Japanese New Wave Cinema*. Bloomington: Indiana University Press, 1988.

Lowenstein, Adam. "Allegorizing Hiroshima: Shindo Kaneto's *Onibaba* as Trauma Text." In *Trauma and Cinema: Cross-Cultural Explorations*, edited by E. Ann Kaplan and Ban Wang, 145–62. Aberdeen: Hong Kong University Press, 2004.

McDonald, Keiko I. *Reading a Japanese Film: Cinema in Context*. Honolulu: University of Hawai'i Press, 2006.

Shindō, Kaneto, dir. *Onibaba*. Kindai Eiga Kyōkai and Tokyo Eiga Company/Tōhō, 1964. Film.

ONMYŌJI (2001)

DIRECTOR: Yōjirō Takita
SCREENPLAY: Baku Yumemakura
SPECS: 112 minutes; color

Onmyōji (literally, The master of yin-yang in English), is a 2001 film directed by Yōjirō Takita (b. 1955). It is heavily based on the popular novel series of the same name authored by Baku Yumemakura (b. 1951), but is not a cinematic adaptation of any one book in the series. The series takes its title from figures called *onmyōji*, who were employed by the early Japanese court in order to regulate calendars, chart and interpret astronomical portents, perform rituals, and sometimes even exorcise demons. Their tasks were often performed through the interpretation or manipulation of the Chinese forces of yin and yang, hence their names. Onmyōji in the series are heavily romanticized, portrayed similarly to wizards or magicians, although they played a much more bureaucratic role in Japanese history.

The 2001 film centers on two historical figures: Abe no Seimei (ca. 921–1005), the most celebrated of Japan's onmyōji, and Minamoto no Hiromasa (918–980), a love-struck court noble and musician. The former is portrayed by kyōgen actor Mansai Nomura II (b. 1966), and the latter by Hideaki Itō (b. 1975). Hiromasa visits Seimei early in the film in order to enlist his aid as an onmyōji, and the two develop a unique partnership. As they delve together into the darkness that slowly envelops the capital of Heian, Seimei and Hiromasa interact similarly to Sherlock Holmes and Dr. Watson, respectively. Often, it is Seimei who seems to understand all of the world's happenings, and it is Hiromasa who must have them all explained. They are joined by a supporting character, Mitsumushi, played by pop singer Eriko Imai (b. 1983). Mitsumushi is one of several *shikigami*—magical servants—controlled by Seimei. Together, their main rival is the head onmyōji, Dōson, played by Hiroyuki Sanada (b. 1960). Not a historical figure, Dōson is heavily based upon the historical Seimei's mythical rival, Ashiya Dōman.

The film opens with a flashback to the founding of the Heian capital in 794 and the simultaneous pacification of the vengeful spirit of Prince Sawara (ca. 750–785). Some one hundred fifty years later, spirits and demons appear frequently, unsettling all in the capital. One noble, Fujiwara no Kaneie (929–990), is plagued by a visitation of a ghost carrying a large melon. The following day, the melon is attached to a pine tree in his gardens. In response, Kaneie sends Hiromasa to visit Seimei and obtain his advice. Upon entering Seimei's villa, Hiromasa learns of Seimei's vast capabilities—among them, hearing voices from afar and the manipulation of *shikigami*. This climaxes when Seimei returns to Kaneie, and determines that the melon is cursed. He whispers a spell over the melon and cuts it open, revealing a snake inside. Hiromasa and Seimei allow the snake to live, following it to a rotting corpse in the river—a woman that Kaneie spurned who then committed suicide.

Peace in the capital is fleeting, as political machinations reach their height. When a new prince is born, the minister Fujiwara no Morosuke (909–960) loses the opportunity for his grandson to become emperor. He spurns his daughter,

Sukehime—a woman with whom Hiromasa has become smitten—and makes a bargain with Dōson, the head court onmyōji. Dōson curses the young prince in an attempt to eliminate him and restore Morosuke's grandson's claim to the throne. With few other options, Hiromasa visits Seimei and again requests his assistance.

Seimei first enlists the aid of a mysterious woman named Aone, who has lived more than one hundred fifty years. When Seimei successfully exorcises Dōson's demon, Aone's body is used to contain it. He then draws it out to defeat it, but Hiromasa lets it escape. Morosuke calls for Seimei's arrest, but fails to stop him. During the conflict, Aone is wounded, but she reveals that she has been cursed with eternal life.

Undeterred, Dōson sends a woman to kill the emperor. Once again, Seimei's skills are employed to save his life. When the demon arrives, it is revealed that it is actually Sukehime being controlled by Dōson. When his plan is almost foiled, Dōson transforms Sukehime into a *namanari* demon. Hiromasa's feelings for Sukehime restore her consciousness and she uses his sword to open her own throat out of love for him.

The magical contest between Seimei and Dōson rises to an apex when Dōson realizes he is no longer on equal ground with Seimei. He offers his body to the vengeful Prince Sawara, who uses it to take revenge on the Japanese court. Through Dōson, Sawara summons an army of undead spirits who possess the army and thereby ravage the capital. While Seimei seeks to restore the seal on Prince Sawara, Hiromasa engages Dōson and fails.

When Seimei arrives at the capital, Aone calls out to the spirit of Prince Sawara within Dōson, whom she loved dearly back when she was young. She reasons with him, allowing both of their spirits to finally sleep together in tranquility. Dōson, once again too weak to defeat Seimei, refuses to concede. He engages Seimei in one last fight, during which he seems to deal the killing stroke to Seimei. It is quickly revealed that he has been actually fighting a *shikigami* that resembles Seimei and the real Seimei has actually been casting a spell to seal away Dōson's powers in the background. Finally defeated, Dōson states that he will be watching Seimei from the afterlife. He commits suicide, smiling at Seimei one final time. With Dōson's death, the capital is saved and peace has been regained. Seimei and Hiromasa discuss the results of their adventure and the film ends.

The film includes a fair amount of gore: several soldiers lose limbs, many are slashed or stabbed to death, and at least three characters commit suicide. Blood is equally plentiful as a ritual constituent in one of Dōson's powerful spells.

Rather than political machinations or sorcery, *Onmyōji* has much to say about humanity itself. One of the most important themes running through the film is actually that of love. Viewers experience the love of good friends (Seimei and Hiromasa), the ephemerality of love (Hiromasa and Sukehime, Kaneie and his spurned lover), the immortality of love (Sawara and Aone), and the utter lack of love (Dōson). Seimei himself states that the human heart can turn itself into a demon or a Buddha.

The fourth-highest-earning Japanese production of 2001, the film was a commercial success, grossing over 3 billion yen in revenue. It won two Japanese

Academy Awards, a Blue Ribbon Award, and a Mainichi Film Concourse Award among others. In conjunction with its American distribution on DVD, the film received a limited theatrical release at four theaters in the United States.

In 2003, Yōjirō Takita directed a sequel, *Onmyōji II*. Aside from these two films, the visual portion of the Onmyōji franchise also took the form of a 2001 ten-episode drama series directed by Masaaki Odagiri and starring pop music star Gorō Inagaki (b. 1973) as Seimei.—Joseph P. Elacqua

See also Onmyōji II

Bibliography

Odagiri, Masaaki, dir. *Onmyōji*. NHK, 2001. Series.
Takita, Yōjirō, dir. *Onmyōji*. Kadokawa Shoten, 2001. Film.
———. *Onmyōji II*. Kadokawa Shoten, 2003. Film.

ONMYŌJI II (2003)

DIRECTOR: Yōjirō Takita
SCREENPLAY: Itaru Ira, Yōjirō Takita, Baku Yumemakura
SPECS: 112 minutes; color

Onmyōji II is a 2003 sequel film to *Onmyōji* (literally, The master of yin-yang), directed by Yōjirō Takita (b. 1955). Like its predecessor, *Onmyōji II* is heavily based on the popular novel series of the same name authored by Baku Yumemakura (b. 1951). This film contains a unique story of its own, not to be found in the novels.

Mansai Nomura II (b. 1966) and Hideaki Itō (b. 1975) reprise their roles as the legendary onmyōji Abe no Seimei (ca. 921–1005) and the love-struck court noble Minamoto no Hiromasa (918–980) respectively. Having become good friends in the first film, Hiromasa again enlists Seimei's help to save the capital of Heian from its supernatural troubles. As in the first film, their relationship is much akin to that of Sherlock Holmes and Dr. Watson—Seimei always seems to possess some key knowledge outside of the viewer's purview, and it is to Hiromasa that he explains these phenomena. As before, they are joined by Mitsumushi, Seimei's magical assistant, played by Eriko Imai (b. 1983).

Seimei, Hiromasa, and Mitsumushi are joined by two new supporting characters: the so-called "tomboy princess," Himiko, who has the power to heal simple wounds, and a mysterious biwa player named Susa. They are played by Kyōko Fukada (b. 1982) and Hayato Ichihara (b. 1987), respectively. Seimei's main foil in this film is Genkaku, a magic-wielding peasant with a long-lasting grudge of vengeance against the Japanese aristocracy. He is portrayed by Kiichi Nakai (b. 1961).

The film begins with a courtier having his leg ripped off and being thrown out of his carriage by a demon in the darkness. It is the fourth such attack, though a different body part (previously shoulder, nose, and mouth) is targeted each time. Complicating the issue, Himiko—with whom Hiromasa is infatuated—seems to sleepwalk without memory on the nights that the demon has attacked. One night, Hiromasa hears Susa playing and joins with his flute. The two musicians quickly become friends as Hiromasa learns the melody from Susa by ear. As their joined melody resounds, Himiko begins to sleepwalk.

The following day, Seimei is called to investigate a sword called Ame no Murakumo that has been moving on its own within the treasury. The sword "cried out" eighteen years prior and the capital remained at peace, but the emperor orders Seimei to investigate anyway. As Seimei investigates, the emperor's ministers ask Genkaku to come to the capital and use his power to replace Seimei.

A Shinto priestess is killed the following night, her eye gouged out. The "demon" (revealed to the audience as Susa) escapes the capital's soldiers in the night as Himiko sleepwalks closer to his location. The two find themselves on opposite sides of a wall, through which her power assuages the demonic force controlling him. When Seimei investigates the next morning, Genkaku arrives to meet him. Seimei reveals that it was not an authentic demon that killed the priestess.

Susa awakens under Himiko's watch and they introduce themselves to each other. Shortly thereafter, Hiromasa arrives to play the melody that Susa taught him. He is pleasantly surprised to see Susa already present, and the two decide to play the song in unison. Himiko becomes entranced, feeling some kind of nostalgia. As the song's pace heightens, a pain tears through Susa's shoulder. Himiko removes a flap of his clothing and sees a pulsating mark resembling a four-headed dragon. Immediately, she is subject to the same pain, grabbing her own shoulder. Susa flees Himiko's residence in fear.

Himiko's father visits Seimei regarding the demon. He reveals that eighteen years ago, when the sword cried out, the soldiers of the capital had raided a village in Izumo—the same place from which the Ame no Murakumo sword originated. It was there that he discovered Himiko and her talent for healing. Rather than killing her, he chose to raise her as his daughter.

While attempting to determine who will be attacked next, Seimei teaches Hiromasa that the sword is said to seal away eight basic human desires. These eight are related to a legendary eight-headed dragon called Yamata no Orochi, from whose body the sword is said to have been born. Together, they determine that there will be two more victims and who the next will be. Mitsumushi steals a lock of his hair, which Seimei uses to set a trap.

A possessed Susa takes the bait and is trapped. Hiromasa recognizes Susa and accidentally frees the boy, who attacks Seimei. Hiromasa's flute calms Susa, who flees. Later, Himiko wakes from her bed, clutching her shoulder. Susa arrives, begging her to flee the capital, as he is the "demon" everyone is chasing. In response, Himiko visits Seimei, revealing that her shoulder bears a mark similar to Susa's. Upon applying a spell, Seimei releases her memories of Izumo and the image of a four-headed dragon appears in the sky. Meanwhile, Genkaku—revealed to be Susa's father—forces Susa to tear out the shoulder of the seventh victim, leaving one final victim: Himiko.

Seimei and Himiko journey to Izumo where it is revealed that she and Susa are siblings, and Genkaku is also her father. After his village was destroyed, Genkaku made an oath with the gods that his son should be reborn as the savage deity Susanoo, a deity that would destroy his opponents and rule the land. However, in return the god demanded the young Himiko—herself a reincarnation of the Shintō sun goddess Amaterasu, sister to Susanoo—as the final sacrifice.

Susa and Genkaku also arrive at Izumo to finish their task. While the latter seals Seimei in a magical prison, Himiko allows Susa to take her life. In doing so, the sun eclipses and Susa's shoulder mark grows four extra "heads." While Seimei and Hiromasa tend to Himiko, Susa and Genkaku arrive at the capital, beginning their onslaught. Susa takes the sword Ame no Murakumo from its resting place, and uses it to unleash his full power as the raging god Susanoo.

Himiko's death mirrors the Shintō myth of Amaterasu hiding in a cave and casting the world in darkness. Seimei and Hiromasa travel to the place where it is enshrined, the onmyōji now impersonating the trickster goddess that drew Amaterasu out of the cave. Seimei's dance reveals the place in which Amaterasu has hidden herself. Then, Susanoo and Genkaku arrive to challenge the heroes. Susanoo is paralyzed by Hiromasa's flute, so Genkaku steals the sword and attacks Seimei. During the fight, Amaterasu is revived; she restores Susa and they return to heaven as light returns to the world again.

Like the original, this film is firmly situated within the realm of mythology and legend, but does not spend quite as much time explaining these influences as its predecessor. Some of the mythological background regarding Amaterasu and Susanoo is left unexplored, though nearly all Japanese viewers are more than familiar with these myths. While the film can easily be enjoyed without knowledge of these myths, they are easily found in English translation.—Joseph P. Elacqua

See also Onmyōji

Bibliography

Takita, Yōjirō, dir. *Onmyōji*. Kadokawa Shoten, 2001. Film.
———. *Onmyōji II*. Kadokawa Shoten, 2003. Film.

ORGAN (1996)

DIRECTOR: Kei Fujiwara
SCREENPLAY: Kei Fujiwara
SPECS: 110 minutes; color

Organ, or *Orugan* in Japanese, is a 1996 Japanese avant-garde body-horror film directed by Kei Fujiwara (b. 1957) which chronicles two undercover cops, Numata and Tosaka, who become involved in an underground ring of organ thieves—thieves that are harvesting body parts collected by biology teacher Saeki and his malevolent sister Yoko. Fujiwara, who is noted for her role in Shinya Tsukamoto's (b. 1960) 1989 film *Tetsuo: The Iron Man*, also plays the role of the one-eyed Yoko in the film. The film has gained a cult following for its fantastic imagery and excessive gore in the tradition of the body-horror genre and specifically the work of Tsukamoto and director David Cronenberg (b. 1943), of which the film makes reference to.

The storyline in *Organ* is played out through multiple plotlines that revolve around an organ-stealing syndicate run by deranged biology teacher Saeki, played by Kimihiko Hasegawa, and his evil sister, Yoko, played by Fujiwara herself. In the first storyline, cops Numata, played by Kenji Nasa, and Tosaka, played by Takao Komoto, are working undercover and plan to break up Saeki's attempt to harvest the organs of a man that is still alive. Tosaka blows the cover of both cops when he frantically orders Saeki to place the dying man's organs back in his body so that he can be saved. Gunfire is exchanged and Tosaka is captured by the syndicate, while Numata is knocked out. Numata is able to escape, but after his botched attempt to bring down the syndicate, he spirals into a crazed obsession with finding his partner. This leads Numata to be removed from police duty and he wanders the streets attempting to seek out a lead for where Tosaka might be located. Tosaka's brother, who is also a police officer, is attempting to find the organ thieves a well, and like Numata, he is on a personal manhunt to locate his brother's whereabouts.

While Tosaka's brother and Numata desperately search for Tosaka, Saeki, who harvests organs by night, also has a job at an all-girls school where he teaches biology, having a particular fascination with butterflies. Saeki murders young girls by performing grisly experiments on their innards once they come to his office for private tutoring. In a particularly fantastical scene that demonstrates Fujiwara's skill with bodily special effects, Saeki imagines that the young student he is in the process of killing emerges from a cocoon as a butterfly-human hybrid, covered in a thick placenta-like substance. Saeki is also secretly keeping Tosaka alive in his lab in which he injects him with certain drugs. Tosaka's limbs have been removed and his body is also covered in various plants. While Tosaka's plant-covered body is beginning to rot away, Saeki's body is also mysteriously rotting from a self-induced bodily experiment and is covered in large sections of decaying flesh from which pus and blood occasionally spurt from. It is not clear why Saeki has caused his own demise, but it is suggested that it is the result of a traumatic event that occurred when he was a child. Through a flashback, it is learned that Saeki and Yoko were violently attacked by their mother, who bit off Saeki's genitals and blinded Yoko in one eye. In response, Saeki and Yoko were forced to kill their own mother.

The bloody conclusion of the film ties together the various subplots of *Organ*. Tosaka's brother is on the heels of the organ thieves when he is jumped in a bar by members of the yakuza the organ thieves have been working with. He is beaten up but is able to escape. Meanwhile, other members of the yakuza, who have grown tired of the unwanted attention that Yoko and Saeki's activities have brought upon the syndicate, trap Yoko in a tunnel and attempt to kill her. She is able to defend herself, however, and violently kills all of her attackers.

At the all-girls school, Saeki, whose flesh continues to rot away, is confronted by a female teacher who constantly accuses him of being a pervert. She rips open his shirt and sees his rotting flesh, which prompts her to cut into it with a knife, releasing blood and pus from the wound. This sexually arouses her and in the most disturbing sequence of the film, Saeki and the teacher engage in sex in which both of their bodies are covered in blood and pus.

Numata finally finds Saeki's office and begins to stab Saeki's dying body, acting out his revenge for what Saeki has done to Tosaka. In the film's final confrontation, Tosaka's brother and Yoko also enter the school simultaneously and after a bloody struggle, Yoko shoots Tosaka's brother dead. As Numata continues to stab Saeki, the body of the blood-covered teacher that was presumably dead after Saeki had visibly removed her organs, springs up and pushes Numata through a window. At this time, it is also revealed that an older gentleman that Numata had questioned at the beginning of the film, who also appears to be working for the syndicate, is the father of Yoko and Saeki. The old man attempts to reason with Yoko and Saeki in hopes of putting an end to their rampage, but Yoko violently stabs him to death. In the final scene, Numata who survived his fall is introduced to what is left of Tosaka's body in a hospital room. Tosaka, who is barely alive and is missing his limbs, is covered in rotting flesh and pus. Tosaka is able to remove his breathing tube to ask Numata "Why me . . . and not you?"

Although Fujiwara's *Organ* received generally negative reviews from critics, it has gained a cult following among fans of the J-gore subgenre for its fantastical special effects and grotesque, often surreal imagery. Its grotesque body transformations draw influence from Tsukamoto's *Tetsuo: The Iron Man* whose protagonist turns into a walking pile of metal parts from the inside out. The film also draws upon the traditions of the body-horror genre in a Cronenbergian sense, specifically with Saeki's grotesque transformation as his body continues to rot, which is reminiscent of David Cronenberg's 1986 film *The Fly*, where the main protagonist mistakenly transforms himself into a mutated, insect-like creature.—Edwin Lohmeyer

See also Fujiwara, Kei; *Tetsuo: The Iron Man*

Bibliography
Fujiwara, Kei, dir. *Organ*. Organ Vital, 1996. Film.

OTOGIRISO (2001)
DIRECTOR: Ten Shimoyama
SCREENPLAY: Goro Nakajima, Takenori Sentō
SPECS: 110 minutes; color

Otogiriso (English title *St. John's Wort*) began with a video game of the same name. Director Ten Shimoyama and screenwriter Goro Nakajima use a number of graphic effects to enforce the film's main theme, the difficulty of deciding what is real.

Otogiriso begins with the blurred and garish, out-of-focus glowing figures of a young girl, a house, chains, candles, dolls, as well as other things that may well be torture paraphernalia. The camera then pulls back to show the audience that they're looking into a video game. "It's not there yet," agree the developers, two young men, Kohei and Shinichi, and the young woman artist, Toko. They change the scene; we see two shadowy figures on the screen and one says, "Mother don't leave me!"

Another girl, Nami, enters the trio's office. Nami is also an artist. Nami's mother died when she was born and her father gave her up to relatives when she was two or three. The gamer trio is using the outline of her life as the basis for their game. Nami's late father was a famous painter, Kaizawa Soichi, and she has just inherited a large old house. She asks Kohei, with whom she was once romantically involved, to go with her to investigate the house. He agrees and takes his camera, hoping to be able to capture more video ideas.

Even in these preliminary, establishing scenes, director Shimoyama uses altered-state videography and disorienting cuts to blur the distinction between the "real" world and the video game world. When the caretaker for the mansion Nami has inherited greets her, for example, the scene shifts to a graphic-and-text representation, so we do not see his face nor hear his voice. The grounds of the mansion are covered in St. John's wort. This plant can be used as an antidepressant, but in large doses can induce psychosis. The aunt who raised Nami also told her that in old poems the plant was used as a symbol of revenge. The presence of the plant surrounding the mansion acts as a sinister, if almost subliminal, element.

As Nami and Kohei begin to explore, video sources, points of view, and color palettes begin to proliferate and separate. We see actions from the conventional camera-as-watcher point of view, in various computer graphics–inflected forms, through at least three levels of color saturation, as well as from the oblique angles of black and white surveillance camera feeds. All of these carry their own suggestions about who is in the mansion, and what is happening.

Nami and Kohei look at some of her father's paintings, which are disturbing in a Francis Bacon–like manner. Kohei, who hadn't known that Soichi was her father, is a fan and identifies one large painting as *Woman with Eyes of Flame*, a "rumored but never seen" masterpiece. To Nami it looks unfinished.

Kohei and Nami, in movies paralleling the video game format, enter one room after another and try to puzzle out what the contents mean: one room is a bedroom with a dingy bathroom and an old music box with a photo of twins—Nami and another girl named Naomi. Nami has never before heard of her twin. There are more rooms, containing such items as a crossbow and, in her father's hidden studio, more paintings and a sketchbook splattered with blood. There are many suggestions that Nami's father used to capture and torture children, and paint them as they suffered.

Kohei feeds his videos back to the gamer's technical center, and Toko creates a map of the house, pinpointing where the caretaker has a hidden surveillance room. Nami wants to interrogate the caretaker because, she says, "I don't know who I am or what I am!"

Nami's twin turns out to be a disturbed boy, dressed as a girl. It is he who had been his father's model for all the paintings—paintings that also include sprigs of St. John's wort somewhere in them.

A horrific final scene ends with Nami and Kohei amid the St. John's wort, watching the mansion burn. A sudden last surprise pushes the narrative out of Nami's "real" story back into the video game construction level. This confusion is compounded when the trio compliments her on her last surprise and she says, "I didn't do that last part!"

If viewers want to come to the more comforting conclusion that it was all a video game, Shimoyama's film will allow them to do so. But a genuine engagement with *Otogiriso* will leave the viewer with unsettling questions about the nature of reality and illusion, memory and identity, and doubt in our ability to decide anything with genuine certainty.—William Bamberger

ŌTOMO, KATSUHIRO (1954–)

Acclaimed *mangaka* and filmmaker Katsuhiro Ōtomo was largely responsible for the aesthetic revival in anime during the 1980s and 1990s. Ōtomo made his professional debut in 1973 in *Action* magazine with *Gun Report*, adapting Prosper Mérimée's *Mateo Falcone* into manga. Ōtomo's first major work was *Fireball* (1979), in which he introduced some of his main topics: futuristic dystopias, psychic abilities, organic interaction between technology and humans, and massive destruction as result of technological experimentation. He continued this horrific narrative path with *Domu: A Child's Dream* (1980–1981), a deadly fight between a psychic little girl and a capricious, selfish old man. These are remarkable pieces, but without a doubt his greatest manga masterpiece is *Akira* (1982–1990), serialized in the prestigious *Young Magazine*.

Around this time, Ōtomo was invited by the acclaimed animator Rintarō to become part of the team of *Harmagedon* (1983) as a character designer, along with Kōji Morimoto and Yoshiaki Kawajiri, when he and his colleagues felt very disappointed about the lack of opportunities in the Japanese animation industry. At this stage, Ōtomo began to combine his graphic work with his desire to become a film director. He had begun to flirt with cinema in 1982, shooting and writing the 16 mm short film called *Freedom for Us*. However, his true debut as a filmmaker came in 1987 with two omnibus films: *Robot Carnival* and *Neo Tokyo*, in which Ōtomo explores his central interests: humor, catastrophic human-technology relationships, and dystopias.

These works enabled the creator of *Akira* to be reunited with animator colleagues such as Kawajiri, Rintarō, Morimoto, Hiroyuki Kitakubo, and Takashi Nakamura, who would continue to work in anime in the 1990s and beyond. The idea of *Robot Carnival* came from Ōtomo himself, inspired by the first episode of Ōsamu Tezuka's *Astroboy*. After the animated trials, he decided to adapt *Akira* to the big screen. The ambitious project caused a revolution in anime and achieved unprecedented international recognition for the Japanese animation industry. From a narrative point of view, this was the first truly complex anime, with density and strong characters. From a technical perspective, Ōtomo challenged the traditional commercial animation that had been created to date; he refused the constraints of limited animation and made a commitment to hyperrealism by introducing extremely detailed backgrounds, lip-synching, and a palette of 327 individual colors.

In terms of the plot, *Akira* crystallized the thematic concerns of the author and his preferences for cyberpunk narrative. Military malpractice is the eye of the storm, with an organization willing to experiment on human subjects in a catastrophic post-nuclear Neo Tokyo. The human-machine interaction developed in Ōtomo's previous works goes a step further, creating a single, terrifying entity able to destroy everything in its path. In this sense, his contribution to *Roujin Z* (1991) as screenwriter, directed by his friend Hiroyuki Kitakubo, takes the same stance, harshly criticizing the Japanese health care system by depicting a futuristic military experiment with defenseless, dependant elders. Also in 1991, Ōtomo filmed his first live-action movie, *World Apartment Horror*, based on an original plan from a young Satoshi Kon.

In 1995, Ōtomo collaborated in his third anthology film with Kon, Morimoto, and Tensai Okamura. The beautiful nightmare named *Memories* recovered short stories written by Ōtomo and published under the same title. Ōtomo focused again on military activities intruding in everyday life with two contributions:

as a writer for the *Stink Bomb* segment and as director for *Cannon Fodder*. The merger of three very different visual styles in combination with a fluid, heterogeneous sense of narration made this work one of the greatest achievements of Katsuhiro Ōtomo's professional career.

Filmmaker, producer, screenwriter, designer, and innovator, this renowned visionary has succeeded in accomplishing personal projects and sponsoring future promises in the industry. At the end of the 1990s, he supported the cinematographic debut of Satoshi Kon with *Perfect Blue* (1997) and Hirotsugu Kawasaki with *Spriggan* (1998). In 2001, he made a screen adaptation of Ōsamu Tezuka's *Metropolis*, a manga inspired by Fritz Lang's film, under the orders of his old friend Rintarō as director. Three years later, he released his long-awaited *Steamboy* (2004), a retro-futuristic film set in the Victorian era that took nine years to complete. Among his recent works, we can highlight the live-action supernatural *Mushi-shi* (2006) and the fourth and last omnibus film in which he has been involved: *Short Peace* (2013).—Laura Montero Plata

· P ·

PINK FILMS

While nudity would remain a taboo on the big screen until the 1960s, the end of World War II signaled the emergence of an erotic sensibility in Japanese cinema. From the mid-1950s, with the graphic releases from Shintōhō Film Company and the explicit dialogue of violence and promiscuity inscribing all matters *taiyozoku* (the so-called "Sun Tribe," the Japanese equivalent of the French term *nouvelle vague*), among them *Crazed Fruit* (1956), directed by Kō Nakahira (1926–1978), a heretofore unprecedented frankness of all things sexual made itself felt. The term *pinku eiga*, first coined in 1963 by journalist and educational philosopher Minoru Murai (b. 1922), referred initially to any work with nudity and, sometime later, as a broad cinematic term to categorize a wide variety of works with adult content. In the early years, these films were known either as *erodakushon eiga* ("eroduction films") or *sanbyakuman eiga* ("three-million-yen-films"), and overt displays of nudity and sex first appeared in the controversial and popular independent production, now recognized as the original pink film, *Flesh Market* (1962), directed by Satoru Kobayashi (1930–2001). It was well received, at least from the standpoint of audiences, for its uncanny engagement with not only genital close-ups but also the complexities inherent in representations of gender and the human mind.

Following this release, productions of pink film quickly fell into the rigidly formulaic and, as such, adhered to traditional approaches to filmmaking. As a rule, they are shot on 16 mm or 35 mm film, edited on flatbeds with analogue sound design, and, when released, appear in triple-bills, given that each film is approximately one hour in duration. Likewise, their content is dictated by a required minimum quota of sex scenes that must occur no more than ten minutes apart; they are further restricted by time, with no more than one week allowed to shoot the entire work, and by finances, with minuscule budgets allotted in most instances.

But it would be a grave mistake to equate the genre with so-called pornographic sex films (including the Western notion of "stage" films), as many non-Japanese, by applying a rigid moral imperative, have done. Such dismissive assessments could not be further from the truth.

The first wave of pink films, from 1962 to 1971, occurred contemporaneously with US sexploitation film genres, in particular the "nudie-cuties" and "roughies." As provocative as he was innovative, the director Tsuji Takechi (1912–1988) almost immediately introduced a new set of rules for content, reflecting his lofty literary and artistic aspirations and incorporating politically sensitive subject matter with what others might have seen as "hardcore" performances. He compensated for legal restriction on public nudity and the so-called "no-hair laws" by introducing "fogging," in which the prohibited images are hidden in production by a mosaic ("pixilated") overlay. His *Daydream* (1964), for example, made extensive use of a big budget to enhance its production value. With its highly publicized release, the film quickly proved a public relations nightmare for the Japanese government, who deemed it as a national embarrassment at the very time when the world was meant to be focused on the Tokyo Olympic Games. The release of *Black Snow* (1965), however, only escalated matters. The police stepped in and confiscated all copies of the film under Article 175 of the Criminal Code of Japan, forbidding the production and distribution of "obscene" or morally corrupt materials (taken in part from the Chinese moral dictate *wu fa wu tian*, "no hair, no heaven"). The director was summarily arrested, and his subsequent high-profile trial, reconfigured as a larger question, whether the film was "art or obscenity" (*geijitsu ka, waisetsu ka*), ostensibly pitted the Japanese intellectual elite against the state. Film directors Nagisa Oshima (1932–2013) and Seijun Suzuki (b. 1923), as well as celebrity authors Yukio Mishima (1925–1970) and Kobo Abe (1924–1993) readily testified in Takechi's defense. His subsequent win and the publicity surrounding the trial only helped bring about a boom in the production of pink films.

In point of fact, Takechi's first film, *A Night in Japan: Woman, Woman, Woman Story* (1963), was by definition a sex-documentary focused on the place of women in nightlife and included a nude Noh performance, strippers, and geisha. Likewise, *Gate of Flesh* (1964) directed by Seijun Suzuki, was recognized not as "pink" but as "sexploitation," becoming the first mainstream film to contain nudity, as well as sex, foul language, and violent beatings and torture. Similar works, including *Story of Heresy in the Meiji Era* (1968), with its emphasis on phallic worship, and *Tokyo Bathhouse* (1968), featuring some thirty sex-film stars in cameo appearances, also fall outside of the purview of pink-styled film. Takechi's remake of *Daydream* (1981) is largely recognized as the first theatrical hardcore pornographic film in Japan.

Early pink films were mainly independent, low-budget productions filmed at Nihon Cinema and World Eiga, as well as at the larger Shintōhō and Nikkatsu Studios, and were shown at their own chain of specialty theaters. In 1965, the director Kōji Wakamatsu (1936–2012) opened Wakamatsu Studio after having departed the staff at Nikkatsu. His independent works are critically respected and concerned with sex and extreme violence mixed with political messages. His most controversial early films dealing with misogyny and sadism are *The Embryo Hunts in Secret* (1966), *Violated Angles* (1967), and *Go, Go Second Time Virgin* (1969). The same year as Wakamatsu became independent, directors Kan Mukai (1937–2008) and Giichi Nishihara (1929–2009) established their own production companies, Mukai Productions and Aoi Eiga, respectively.

Pink films coming out of these studios run the gamut, including comedies, romantic dramas, exploitation movies, and horror, and since the mid-1960s, they comprise the biggest Japanese film genre. By the late 1970s, their production, including Roman porno ("romance pornography") accounted for more than 70 percent of yearly film production. Furthermore, attesting to artistry and popular interest in the subject, since 1971 at least one or two such works have been chosen among the ten best films of the year by Japanese critics. Doubtless, men and women alike have been attracted by the form, so much so that Roman porno holds a significant place in contemporary Japanese culture, where pink films represent less a specific genre than an ongoing—evolving—cycle of specialization. These "fetishes" include, among others, S&M, drama, High School Girl, Live Action, and Vampire Flicks, in addition to comedy, fantasy, and adventure films.

The second wave of pink film, 1971–1982, is perhaps best characterized as Nikkatsu Roman porn. Certainly, the first reason for its arrival is economic: a boom led to an increase in disposable income for luxury goods, including televisions, as well as an invasion of popular American films, to which Japanese films began losing audience. The second follows from that loss: with major film studios struggling for survival, Nikkatsu chair Takashi Itamochi (b. 1930) made the decision in 1971 to shift high production values and professional talent away from action films toward the pink film genre with *Apartment Wife: Affair in the Afternoon* (1971), directed by Nishimura Shōgorō (b. 1930). This single work proved so popular with Japanese audiences that it spurred some twenty sequels over the next seven years. Thus, Nikkatsu gave its Roman porn directors considerable artistic and financial freedom in creating their films, provided of course they included at least four nude or sex scenes per hour. Making a virtue of necessity, Tatsumi Kumashiro (1927–1995) directed an unprecedented number of financial and critical hits, including *Ichijo's Wet Desire* (1972) and *Woman with Red Hair* (1979). Noboru Tanaka (1937–2006) directed *A Woman Called Sada Abe* (1975). The subgenre of S&M films began in earnest with *Flower and Snake* (1974) and *Wife to Be Sacrificed* (1974), both directed by Masaru Konuma (b. 1937). These films regained a lion's share of the market until the early 1980s, when ownership of VCRs first became widespread. AV ("adult video," with its focus on private viewership) soon followed. As early as 1982 the AVs had already attained an approximately equal share of the adult entertainment market with erotic films. By 1988, Nikkatsu conceded defeat and closed it production facilities, following its release of *Bed Partner* (1988), directed by Daisuke Gotō (b. 1957).

In 1980, the Zoom-Up Film Festival began handing out its Pink Film Awards. They continued this practice for the next fifteen years.

Those directors of pink films remaining in the genre—Mamoru Watanabe (1931–2013), Genji Nakamura (b. 1947), and Banmei Takahashi (b. 1949)—shifted their focus once more to concentrate on technical finesse and narrative content. Watanabe directed *Virgin Rope Makeover*. Nakamura directed one of the first widely distributed, well-received films with a homosexual theme, *Legend of the Big Penis: Beautiful Mystery* (1983). Takahashi directed *New Love in Tokyo* (1994), the first Japanese theatrical film to display genitals. The style of their works have earned them a place among other widely acclaimed "art cinema."

Another prominent cult director of this era, Kazuo Komizu (1946), built a reputation on his very popular "splatter-eros" films, bridging the genres of horror and erotica. Notable among his works is *Entrails of a Virgin*, in which a group of photographers and their models engage in S&M while attending a retreat in the forest. They are murdered one by one by a filth-covered "demon" and his unnaturally large penis. Hardly surprising that most of the sex scenes are fogged.

The third wave of pink film is dominated by "sexploitation," or grind house films, an unsettling mix of comedy and torture referred to as "pinky violence." In the Jyoshi Kou market, beginning in 1971, the focus shifted to films in series—among them the Sensational Line, the Abnormal Line, and the Shameless

Line, launched with *Girl Boss* (1972) and *Terrifying Girls' High School* (1973), both directed by Norifumi Suzuki (1933–2014). The women-in-prison series Sasori, directed by Shun'ya Itō (b. 1937), included *Female Convict #701: Scorpion* (1972). Toei also introduced "nunsploitation" films as a subgenre imported from Italy, with the critically acclaimed *School of the Holy Beast* (1974), also directed by Suzuki. *Criminal Women: Killing Melody* (1973) is also significant, if for no other reason than that their themes would be echoed and revived in films such as *Kill Bill* (2003) and *Kill Bill II* (2004), directed by maverick American Quentin Tarantino (b. 1963).

The period since 2000 has witnessed a significant growth in the pink film, characterized by individualistic styles and a keen sense of foreboding and introspection, indicative of the insecurity of Japan's post-bubble generation. Toshiya Ueno (1963) suggested just these characteristics with the release of his *Keep on Masturbating: Non-Stop Pleasure* (1994), which won the "Best Film" award at the Pink Grand Prix. *The Glamorous Life of Sachiko Hanai* (2003) directed by Meike Mitsuru (b. 1969), made an impression in international film festivals and garnered critical acclaim. Other works worthy of remark include sci-fi pink *RoboGeisha* (2009), splatter film *Helldriver* (2010), and the gangster noir *Gun Woman* (2014). But what is perhaps far more impressive, the genre itself provided a fertile ground from which a number of award-winning filmmakers and their films were later launched. Readily apparent among those receiving international acclaim are the romantic drama *Shall We Dance* (1996), written and directed by Masayuki Suo (b. 1956); the horror-thriller cult film *Cure* (1997), directed by Kiyoshi Kurosawa (b. 1955); and *Departures* (2008), for which Yōjirō Takita (b. 1955) received the 2009 Academy Award for Best Foreign Film.—James A. Wren

Bibliography

Allison, Anne. *Permitted and Prohibited Desires: Mothers, Comics, and Censorship in Japan.* Berkeley: University of California Press, 2000.

Anderson, Joseph, and Richie, Donald. *The Japanese Film: Art and Industry.* Princeton, NJ: Princeton University Press, 1982.

Bornoff, Nicholas. "Bye-Bye Pink Cinema, Hello Adult Video." In *Pink Samurai: An Erotic Exploration of Japanese Society: The Pursuit and Politics of Sex in Japan.* London: HarperCollins, 1994.

Boyreau, Jacques. *Sexytime: The Post-Porn Rise of the Pornoisseur.* Seattle, WA: Fantagraphics, 2012.

Connell, Ryann. "Japan's Former Pink Princess Trades Raunchy Scenes for Rural Canteen." *Mainichi Shimbun* 2 March 2006.

Desser, David. *Eros Plus Massacre: An Introduction to the Japanese New Wave Cinema.* Bloomington: Indiana University Press, 1988.

Fentone, Steve. "A Rip of the Flesh: The Japanese 'Pink Film' Cycle." *She* 2, no. 11 (1998): 5.

Hayashi, Sharon. "The Fantastic Trajectory of Pink Art Cinema from Stalin to Bush." In *Global Art Cinemas: New Theories and Histories*, edited by Rosalind Galt and Karl Schoonover, 48–61. London: Oxford University Press, 2010.

Hirano, Kyoko. "Japan." In *World Cinema since 1945*, edited by William Luhr, 412. New York: The Ungar Publishing Company, 1987.

Hunter, Jack. *Tokyo Grindhouse Volume One: Pinky Violence Bad Girl Cinema.* N.p. Glitter Books, 2012.

Johnson, William. "A New View of Porn: The Films of Tatsumi Kumashiro." *Film Quarterly* 57, no. 1 (Fall 2003).

Macias, Patrick. "Nikkatsu's Roman Porno." In *TokyoScope: The Japanese Cult Film Companion*, 187. San Francisco, CA: Cadence Books, 2001.

Park, Soo-mee. "Erotic Film Fest Pushes the Envelope in Korea: Pink Film Festival Celebrates Japanese Erotic Satire." *Hollywood Reporter*, 3 November 2008.

Richie, Donald. *A Hundred Years of Japanese Film: A Concise History*. Tokyo: Kodansha International, 2001.

———. "The Japanese Eroduction." In *A Lateral View: Essays on Culture and Style in Contemporary Japan*, 156–69. Berkeley, CA: Stone Bridge Press, 1987.

Sato, Tadao. *Currents in Japanese Cinema*. Translated. and edited by Gregory Barrett, 212–13. Tokyo: Kodansha, 1987.

Schilling, Mark. *No Borders, No Limits: Nikkatsu Action Cinema (Cinema Classics)*. Guildford, UK: Fab Press, 2007.

Sharp, Jasper. *Behind the Pink Curtain: The Complete History of Japanese Sex Cinema*. Guildford, UK: FAB Press, 2008.

Sharp, Jasper. "Pink Thrills: Japanese Sex Movies Go Global." *Japan Times* 4 December (2008).

Thompson, Bill. "Jitsuroko [sic] Abe Sada." In *Magill's Survey of Cinema: Foreign Language Films, Volume 4*, edited by Frank N. Magill, 1568–73. Englewood Cliffs, NJ: Salem Press, 1985.

Weisser, Thomas, and Weisser, Yuko Mihara. *Japanese Cinema Encyclopedia: The Sex Films*. Miami, FL: Vital Books (Asian Cult Cinema Publications), 1998.

P.O.V.: A CURSED FILM (2012)
DIRECTOR: Norio Tsuruta
SCREENPLAY: Norio Tsuruta
SPECS: 92 minutes; color

The Japanese fascination with "found-footage" films—called *shinrei no bideo*, or ghost videos—predates both *The Blair Witch Project* (1999) and Hideo Nakata's *Ring* (1998), but the subsequent wave of international found-footage films and *faux*-documentaries—including *Cloverfield* (2008), the Spanish [Rec] movies, and the lucrative Paranormal Activity franchise—revived Japanese interest in the subgenre. Toshikazu Nagae directed a special Japan-only installment of the latter series, entitled *Paranormal Activity: Tokyo Night* (2010), while Kōji Shiraishi has made a number of superior *faux*-documentaries, beginning with *The Curse* (2006), arguably the best in its field. *P.O.V.: A Cursed Film* (2012) is Norio Tsuruta's contribution to the subgenre.

Although he has yet to score a hit on the level of *Ring* (1998) or the *Ju-on* films, Norio Tsuruta occupies an important position in the world of contemporary Japanese horror. Not only did his early V-cinema films play a key role in preparing the way for the Japanese horror boom that began with *Ring*, but he has also crafted a number of well-made, efficiently scary movies, including *Ring 0: Birthday* (2000), *Kakashi* (2001), and *Orochi: Blood* (2008).

After a somewhat superfluous message warning the viewer not to show the film to anyone else, *P.O.V.* begins as a behind-the-scenes featurette about teenage talk show host Mirai (Mirai Shida) and her guest of the day, actress Haruna (Haruna Kawaguchi). They start by showing clips of "ghost videos" sent in by the fans, but are slightly disturbed to find one that seems real, depicting a ghostly hand pushing open a door. Fear begins to set in when Haruna realizes that these clips are ones she filmed a few years ago, in an effort to capture her school's supposed ghosts on film. Unfortunately, while her original footage failed to record anything supernatural, it now depicts a disembodied hand, a shower that turns itself on, and a ghostly face at an upstairs window. Believing herself to be cursed for trying to film ghosts, Haruna starts to panic. Accompanied by their manager, the director, and a skeptical teacher, the two girls head to Haruna's old school to try and find the source of the supernatural manifestations.

With just a handful of characters and two primary locations, *P.O.V.* is a lean, economical film that wastes little time. Tsuruta sets up simple and effective scares that might not be entirely original (ghostly images reflected in windows, for example) but work well because he's taken the time to set up realistic, believable characters. Mirai and Haruna are just nice kids, desperately trying to find a way out of this situation, but the adults are another thing entirely. Tachibana the director views the events taking place in terms of great footage and a hit movie, even if it's putting the girls' lives in danger. Haruna's manager has valuable information about what's happening, but his own agenda prevents him from doing anything to help out. The teacher is just as selfish, stubbornly refusing to accept that anything unusual is happening. Her primary ambition is using the girls to dispel the growing rumors about the haunted school. Her skeptical façade comes to look increasingly ridiculous as paranoia and fear take over, and she ends up hysterically accusing everyone of being part of a grand conspiracy to make her look stupid. These tensions add a welcome extra dimension to what is otherwise a fairly straightforward story.

Instead of staying with a streamlined seventy-five-minute running time, Tsuruta adds a lengthy final act that takes place outside the "found-footage" framework. Aside from serving no narrative purpose (the rest of the film is essentially self-contained), this final act is almost entirely drawn from Kōji Suzuki's 1995 novel *Spiral* and Jōji Iida's 1998 film adaptation. It seems likely that this addition was intended to compete with Tsutomu Hanbusa's reboot of the Ring franchise, *Sadako 3D* (2012), but it's an unnecessary addition to an otherwise well-constructed, effective horror film.—Jim Harper

PRAY (2005)

DIRECTOR: Yuichi Sato
SCREENPLAY: Tomoko Ogawa
SPECS: 77 minutes; color

Pray is a 2005 horror film directed by Yuichi Sato and written by Tomoko Ogawa. The film stars Tetsuji Tamayama and Asami Mizukawa as a pair of would-be kidnappers who wind up abducting a girl who, her parents claim, is already dead. A clever ghost story, this film succeeds in large part thanks to the way it subverts the clichéd figure of the ghostly little girl by revealing that the little girl's spirit is far more benevolent than she first appears. It is the living who ultimately harm Mitsuru the most.

Pray begins in the wake of the kidnapping of a little girl named Ai Shinohara, by Mitsuru and his girlfriend Maki. They break into Mitsuru's old elementary school in Hiroshima Prefecture and call the girl's parents to demand a ransom of 50 million yen. However, Ai's parents deliver some shocking news to Mitsuru and Maki: their daughter has actually been dead for exactly a year.

After Ai wakes up and disappears, the kidnappers split up to search for her. Meanwhile, Ai's parents visit a spiritualist to consult with her about their daughter. They reveal that their daughter's body was never found and that they hope that she might finally grant them closure. The spiritualist tells them that while Ai is most certainly dead, she can be found at "Fukuyama Elementary."

Ai reveals herself to Mitsuru and follows him back to Maki. He finds some craft materials and sets her up in an old classroom. Mitsuru and Maki's interactions become increasingly heated, and during one of their arguments, Ai disappears once again. While they search for her, they are startled by a loud moaning reverberating through the school. Mitsuru traces the noise back to the audio room, where his friends Yasuda, Shima, and Yuki are waiting.

While Yasuda and Mitsuru talk, Maki screams out, claiming to have seen someone else stalking the halls. Mitsuru calms her down and goes outside to look for Ai again. He finds her by the playground and they take turns on the slide. When she disappears again, Yasuda accuses Mitsuru of letting her go, and finally confesses that he and Maki invented the dead girl story as part of a plan to betray Mitsuru and take his cut of the ransom. Mitsuru confronts Maki, but they are interrupted when Yuki discovers Shima murdered, his hand severed and left near the body.

A stunned Mitsuru follows a series of noises to the girls' restroom, where he discovers the body of the real Ai, a teenager, rotting in one of the stalls. Yasuda confesses to an affair with her, but swears her death was a suicide and that he had nothing to do with it. The group decides to murder the little girl and escape while they still can. Mitsuru finds her and lets her go, while the ghost of the real Ai appears and murders Yuki.

Yasuda attacks with a knife when he realizes the girl has escaped. Mitsuru gets the upper hand, but Maki appears behind him and dashes his head with a fire extinguisher. Ai's ghost appears and lures Yasuda into breaking his own neck. Avenged, she vanishes. Maki goes to finish off Mitsuru, but the little girl distracts her and she slips on the fire extinguisher, stabbing herself. The little girl kneels by Mitsuru's side and reveals that the spirit of Mitsuru's sister Megumi, whose death he has always felt responsible for, possesses her. She absolves him of his guilt and stays with him while he dies.

The film juggles a number of flashbacks and subplots, yet delivers an ending that disrupts *Pray*'s otherwise steady pace. It's never fully explained, however, why the group of kidnappers and accomplices need so much money so quickly, despite one character briefly mentioning that the money might be intended for a drug deal. Nonetheless, this vague addition leaves a substantial amount of room to focus squarely on the Fukuyama Elementary setting and all of its eerie architecture.

The film's sets, which seem to have been set up in an actual abandoned school, are appropriately moody, offering Mitsuru plenty of dark corners in which to perch with his leather jacket and Marlboros. The only area where the production really comes up short is with its gore effects, which are less than stellar; this is forgivable, however, since *Pray* is more of suspense film than a slasher, relying on atmosphere instead of jump-scares and arterial spray.—Boleyn Key

PREMONITION (2004)
DIRECTOR: Norio Tsuruta
SCREENPLAY: Noboru Takagi, Norio Tsuruta
SPECS: 95 minutes; color

Produced by Takashige Ichise (b. 1961) and backed by the major studio Toho, *Premonition* was released on the same day and paired with *Infection* (2004), as a part of the campaign to promote what Ichise and the production team designated as "J-horror." The motion picture starts with the protagonist, Hideki Satomi (popular TV actor Hiroshi Mikami), driving in a car with his wife, Ayaka (singer Noriko Sakai), and young daughter. While trying to make a phone call in a telephone box, a drifting piece of newspaper happens to catch his eye. To his disbelief, the article on the newspaper "reports" the death of his daughter. When she dies in a freak accident as foretold by the newspaper, his marriage unravels. Several years later, now a high school teacher, Hideki runs into a mysterious student who seems to predict the exact date and manner of her death. Realizing that the newspaper that foretells a person's death is not a figment of his imagination but a real artifact, he, with the help of his ex-wife, Ayaka, tries to pin down the origins of the alleged "Fear News."

Premonition is directed by Norio Tsuruta (b. 1960), who started out as a software developer and a promoter but pioneered TV and direct-to-video projects that laid out the groundwork for the success of J-horror in the early 2000s, including *Scary Stories from School* (*Gakko kaidan*, 1999) and the True Ghosts series (*Shinrei I–IV*, 1996–1999). Tsuruta is claimed by some to be the filmmaker who has perfected the now-familiar J-horror style. His approach is partly based on the strategy of turning less-than-desirable material conditions of a direct-to-video production into strengths. Typical is his use of low-resolution video, such as amateurishly recorded VHS tapes or CCTV footage, to heighten the "creepy" qualities of the ghostly imagery, not unlike the way contemporary low-budget horror films attempt to scare the viewers through manipulation of various types of "found footage."

Ironically, in the case of *Premonition*, the plot's emphasis on a print medium as the source of horror vitiates the effectiveness of Tsuruta's minimalist approach. The idea of the supernatural newspaper is based on Tsunoda Jirō's (b. 1936) extremely popular comic series *Fear Newspaper* (*Kyōfu shinbun*, 1973–1975), in which a junior high school student, Rei Kigata, is possessed by an evil spirit who calls himself "Poltergeist." Kigata is delivered a copy of *Fear Newspaper* every day, endowing him with the ability to predict misfortunes and deaths that will befall others, but also eating away at his life force, eventually killing him. Kigata makes an appearance in *Premonition* (played as an old man by Kei Yamamoto, b. 1940) but is poorly integrated into the plot and his presence would mean little to the viewers not familiar with the original comic series.

In the end, *Premonition* fails to rise above the fray in terms of what we expect from a typical "J-horror" production, even in terms of existential dread, the kind that slowly creeps up your spine, that its sister film, *Infection*, successfully cultivates. The best aspect of the film remains its genuinely disturbing electronic-ambience score provided by the ultra-talented Kenji Kawai (1957, *Ring* [1998], *Ghost in the Shell* [1995]).—Kyu Hyun Kim

See also Infection; Shimizu, Takashi

Bibliography

Tsuruta, Norio, dir. *Premonition* (*Yogen*), Fellah Pictures-Nikkatsu-Toho-Geneon Entertainment-Oz Company-TBS, 2004. Film.

PUELLA MAGI MADOKA MAGICA: THE MOVIE films

Puella Magi Madoka Magica: The Movie—Beginnings (2012)
DIRECTOR: Yukihiro Miyamoto, Akiyuki Shinbo
SCREENPLAY: Gen Urobuchi
SPECS: 130 minutes; color

Puella Magi Madoka Magica: The Movie—Eternal (2012)
DIRECTOR: Yukihiro Miyamoto, Akiyuki Shinbo
SCREENPLAY: Gen Urobuchi
SPECS: 109 minutes; color

Puella Magi Madoka Magica: The Movie—Rebellion (2013)
DIRECTOR: Yukihiro Miyamoto, Akiyuki Shinbo
SCREENPLAY: Gen Urobuchi
SPECS: 116 minutes; color

Puella Magi Madoka Magica: The Movie is a series of three interlinked films titled *Beginnings, Eternal,* and *Rebellion,* based on a 2011 anime. Produced by animation house Shaft and Aniplex, the films offer a dark twist on the normally bright and cheerful "magical girl" genre. Intended by director Akiyuki Shinbo (b. 1961) and writer Gen Urobuchi (b. 1972) as a deconstruction of the genre, *Madoka Magica* examines the emotional stress and despair that a life of danger places upon a group of young girls fighting powerful witches. The first two movies in the trilogy retell the events chronicled in the original anime, with the third film serving as a conclusion. The films were financially successful at the Japanese box office and enjoyed limited runs in the United States. In the tradition of most successful anime franchises, Puella Magi Madoka Magica spawned a line of toys, figures, and collectibles that remain popular.

The story centers on middle school student Madoka Kaname. Madoka lives a happy, quiet life until the day she and her friend Miki Sayaka encounter a rabbit-like alien named Kyubey who offers them a single wish. In exchange they must agree to become magical girls and battle against witches. On the same day, Madoka meets Homura Akemi, a mysterious new transfer student who is intent on ensuring Madoka does not accept Kyubey's offer. Sayaka opts to sign a contract to heal an injured boy she loves, but quickly discovers the life of a magical girl is a far cry from what she imagined or Kyubey intimated. The twist in the plot comes when the girls discover the secret that has been hidden from them: all magical girls either die or eventually succumb to despair and become witches.

Kyubey and his race of Incubators are only interested in the energy released by a magical girl's emotions to offset entropy in the universe, an unhappy cycle they are only too willing to perpetuate. Kyubey is particularly interested in Madoka, who inexplicably possesses an enormous amount of energy.

Homura resets time, revealing her origin as a sickly girl who befriended Madoka, only to watch her die in battle against the most powerful witch of all. Homura has been living through different timelines in a futile quest to save Madoka, each attempt ending in failure. Ultimately, Madoka, imbued with the energy of multiple incarnations Homura has accidentally instilled in her by replaying the same month over and over, rewrites reality and prevents magical girls from becoming witches at the cost of their mortal existence.

In *Rebellion*, Homura discovers she has been living in an artificial world for an indeterminate amount of time. Her investigation leads her to discover that the alien Incubators have trapped her soul in order to observe and control Madoka in their relentless bid for energy sources. As a final twist, Homura reveals her love for Madoka has become dark and obsessive, replacing the despair that normally would have destroyed her. Calling herself a demon, she rewrites reality to her own wishes, usurping Madoka's power and returning the major characters to lives as normal girls in order to fulfill her now possessive goals—saving Madoka and taking a major role in her life.

The horror in Puella Magi Madoka Magica does not come from the witches and battles, but from the realization of the characters that they are doomed to either die in battle or be reborn as the very witches they have fought, all under the watchful eye of an emotionless and amoral Kyubey. The world of Madoka is one of young girls trapped in an uncaring universe and a grim inescapable cycle engineered by inhuman aliens who cannot understand their suffering, yet insist it is for a greater good. The witches are highly abstracted, and even the deaths of major characters are handled relatively bloodlessly and without gore, keeping a perversely colorful and bright tone throughout the film at odds with the dark content. Even the original promise of salvation of the series is undermined in the last moments of *Rebellion.*

Dealing with multiple timelines and condensing a twelve-episode series into two films, the storyline is dense, with the final film impenetrable unless all three are watched in sequence. Yet Puella Magi Madoka Magica: The Movie is a stellar example of anime's narrative potential. The designs and traditional animation are spectacular, the script is clever and incorporates allusions to Faust, and the witch sequences take their cues from modern artists such as Paul Klee.—Daniel Fandino

Bibliography
Shinbo, Akiyuki, dir. Puella Magi Madoka Magica: The Movie. Aniplex, 2012–2013. Film series.

PULSE (2001)
DIRECTOR: Kiyoshi Kurosawa
SCREENPLAY: Kiyoshi Kurosawa
SPECS: 118 minutes; color

In the 1950s and 1960s, the cheap efforts of B-grade horror moviemakers prepared a chutney of half erotic, half horror films that ultimately produced laughter in place of fear among the audience, whereas directors in the 1970s and 1980s fooled their audiences with a blending of blood and violence, and named it horror. Perhaps the first serious effort to save the horror cult was made by Kiyoshi Kurosawa. Long considered a preserver of the horror cult, demonstrated through his 1997 breakthrough film *Cure*, Kurosawa seems to have maintained on-screen horror in its raw form.

Pulse (2001), written and directed by Kurosawa, is a 118-minute long film. In *Pulse*, Kurosawa demonstrates how horror movies can be cast as works of art, employing traditional tools of a filmmaker, such as cinematography, editing, lighting, composition, and sound over artificial special effects. More significantly, he includes rich themes with highly effective storytelling.

In *Pulse*, the plot features two parallel storylines divided along the experiences of two separate characters: a young woman named Michi, played by Kimko Aso, and a young man named Ryosuke, played by Haruhiko Katō. Set in the city of Tokyo, ghosts invade the world of the living through the Internet, generating strange, chilling, and mysterious events that unfold in tandem with the two characters' lives. The relationship between these two characters, however, is rather vague, as it is only near the end of the film when the two characters meet.

The story speeds up when a young Internet user commits suicide. Michi and her coworkers have been trying to get in touch with Taguchi, played by Kenji Mizuhashi, as he has been working on a computer disk they desperately need. As they have not heard from him in over a week, Michi visits Taguchi's apartment and tries to talk to him, to no avail. To the shock of Michi and her coworkers, Taguchi then hangs himself in another room. Suspecting the suicide is associated with Taguchi's interaction with the computer hardware, they open the disk, in which they're able to view a scene closely resembling Taguchi peering into his own computer. Zooming in further they discover it's actually a series of images, embedded within themselves—a "Droste Effect" of Taguchi and his computer.

Scenes later, although appearing without real explanation, fragments of Tokyo dissolve or disappear mysteriously. Additionally there are incidents when ghosts attack Michi's friends, and doors with red tape begin to blanket the whole city.

Along the second storyline, Ryosuke has recently signed up for a new Internet service provider. His computer starts functioning by itself and showing him disturbing images of people in dark rooms. He discusses this incident with his friend Harue, played by Koyuki Katō, who advises Ryosuke to print out such images. To his surprise, however the computer does not follow Ryosuke's command, and starts showing him a video of a man with a plastic bag on his head, standing in a room with the phrase "HELP ME" written all over the walls. Soon, Harue begins to behave strangely and she disappears.

Soon ghosts start appearing everywhere, and people start vanishing. Evacuations of Tokyo begin, and alas, Ryosuke meets Michi. Finally, in between apocalyptic scenes, they find a ship ready to depart from Tokyo.

Pulse has become a treatise on contemporary isolation and miscommunication among young Internet users. Some critics contend that the message of this film is rather simple: the dead enter the world of the living, and influence their lives so much that they start questioning the relevance of life.—Amitabh Vikram Dwivedi

• R •

RAMPO NOIR (2005)

DIRECTOR: Akio Jissōji, Atsushi Kaneko, Hisayasu Satō, Suguru Takeuchi
SCREENPLAY: Atsushi Kaneko, Akio Satsukawa, Suguru Takeuchi, Shirō Yumeno
SPECS: 134 minutes; color

So who is Rampo? Taro Hirai (1894–1965) selected Edogawa Rampo as his nom de plume, a Japanese representation of the name Edgar Allan Poe. He meticulously chose characters meaning "faltering drunkenly along the Edo River," the river suggestive of Tokyo's low town, to write his name. So acclaimed were his works that the Edogawa Rampo Prize for promising crime fiction writers was named in his honor and has been awarded annually since 1955 by the Mystery Writers of Japan. Considered the father of contemporary detective and horror fiction in Japan, Rampo created macabre works that often pushed psychological boundaries toward madness. His eccentric characters and bizarre plots were hallmarks of *ero guro nansensu* (erotic grotesque nonsense) popular in late Taisho and early Showa Japan. Fictional detective Kogoro Akechi, his alter ego and frequent protagonist, uses deductive logic to solve singular crimes much like Sherlock Holmes, another key influence on Rampo, although the Japanese master's tales, often featuring subplots within subplots, are considerably more sinister.

The 2005 *Rampo Noir* (*Rampo jigoku*, literally "Rampo hell") consists of four dark cinematic adaptations of Rampo works centered upon erotic and grotesque relationships, each by a different director. All include celebrated actor Tadanobu Asano (b. 1973), who received the 2005 Mainichi Film Concours Best Actor Award. Running only six and a half minutes, "Mars Canal" ("Kasei no Unga") is the initial episode and the first film made by pop music video and advertising director Suguro Takeuchi (b. 1962). At times silent, the evocative images of this free-flowing work feature a naked Asano sprinting through a desolate wilderness coupled with images of his violent relationship with a woman. He finally collapses upon reaching a reflecting pool of water, gazing into it as if entering a feverish trip into the imagination or into hell, setting the table for the forthcoming episodes. Much of Rampo's "Mars Canal" also featured an avant-garde stream of consciousness narrative; in his conclusion, dropped by Takeuchi, the man wakes up and realizes this has just been a dream.

Veteran filmmaker Akio Jissōji (1937–2006) directed "Mirror Hell" ("Kagami Jigoku"), the second episode. He is known both for children's programs, in particular *Ultraman*, and highly charged works often centering upon erotic and sadomasochistic relationships. A great admirer of Rampo, he has made two other Rampo adaptations.

In "Mirror Hell" detective Kogoro Akechi must solve a mystery in which he encounters a narcissistic mirror maker meditating upon his work and three women who meet untimely deaths through strange phenomena. Their faces are disfigured by microwave-like radiation through vibrations that occur as they are looking through mirrors. Although both Rampo's tale of madness and Jissōji's episode conclude with the insane artisan's efforts to seal himself inside a sphere with a mirrored interior to merge with its *kami* (god), Jissōji has otherwise re-written the work, adding the murders and incorporating Rampo's favorite detective (played by Asano). A stylish work set in traditional Kamakura, it is replete with elegant compositions of ornate mirrors, often arranged to capture multiple kaleidoscopic reflections of the same image.

The harrowing third episode of *Rampo Noir*, "The Caterpillar" ("Imo-mushi"), was directed by Hisayasu Satō (b. 1959). Satō is best known for his gore-fest *Splatter: Naked Blood* (*Megyaku: Naked Blood*, 1996). Rampo's original short story concerns Lieutenant Sunaga, a soldier who returns from the war with his limbs severed, his face grotesquely distorted, and his hearing gone. Although his hometown villagers regard him as a war god, they ignore him except during ceremonial occasions. His shocked wife initially attends him proudly, but after three years is worn out and psychologically distraught. Satō retains the concept of the soldier as little more than an unrecognizable torso. On the surface Sunaga's wife, played by Hanae Kan (b. 1990), appears to be an ideal spouse supporting her husband in the cinematic episode. However, Satō's Sunaga returned home relatively unscathed. His wife then amputated him to prevent her "little butterfly" from leaving her, and uses him for further sadomasochistic grotesqueries. Asano plays only a minor Akechi role in a tag-on to the end of this sequence. "The Caterpillar" was the only Rampo story to be initially censored, although *The Mystery of Rampo* (*Rampo*, 1994), another omnibus film based on Rampo narratives, improperly infers that another work was banned instead. Director Koji Wakamatsu (1936–2012) created an altogether different feature-length interpretation of *Caterpillar* in 2010, for which Shinobu Terajimu (b. 1973) won the Best Actress Award at the Berlin Film Festival.

"Crawling Bugs" ("Mushi"), the final episode, was Atsushi Kaneko's (b. 1966) initial cinematic offering; he is best known as the manga artist who created *Bambi and Her Pink Gun* and *Soil*. This kitschy episode is a dark black comedy concerning a mysophobic (obsessively fearing germs and contamination) chauffeur (Asano) consumed with the illusion of love. Infatuated by the worldly starlet he taxis around, the fixated driver attempts to protect her body's purity to ill-fated results. Incorporating supersaturated colors and a hallucinogenic garden of artificial flowers and trees, the set for the chauffeur's home and his overstepping of boundaries approaches surrealism.

Rampo Noir, made in 2005 when the J-horror craze was ebbing, dispenses with that genre's supernatural elements. Using elements initially grounded in this world, all four directors modify and expand upon Rampo's original works while focusing upon their own obsessions. Rampo's fantastic tales have been filmed numerous times, frequently serving as fodder for directors' reinterpretations. Among many other Rampo adaptations are Noboru Tanaka's *Stroller in the Attic* (*Edogawa Rampo ryoki-kan: Yaneura no sanposha*, 1976), which was later filmed by Akio Jissōji in 1992; Teruo Ishii's *Horrors of Malformed Men* (*Kyofu kikei ningen: Edogawa Rampo zenshu*, 1969); Shin'ya Tsukamoto's *Gemini* (*Soseiji*, 1999);

Yasuzo Masumura's *Blind Beast* (*Moju*, 1969) and his *Black Lizard* (*Kurotokage*, 1968); Tai Kato's *Beast in the Shadows* (*Edogawa Rampo no inju, 1977*); Kōji Wakamatsu's *Caterpillar* (*Imomushi*, 2010); and Kazuyoshi Okuyama's *The Mystery of Rampo* (*Rampo*, 1994).—Bill Thompson

See also Blind Beast vs. Killer Dwarf; ero guru nansensu genre; *Horrors of Malformed Men*; Jissōji, Akio

Bibliography

Rampo, Edogawa. *Japanese Tales of Mystery and Imagination*, translated by James B. Harris. Tokyo and Rutland, VT: Tuttle Books, 1956.

———. *The Edogawa Rampo Reader*. Edited and translated by Seth Jacobowitz. Fukuoka, Japan: Kurodahan Press, 2008.

Takeuchi, Suguro, Akio Jissoji, Hisuyasu Sato, and Atsushi Kaneko. *Rampo Noir*. Kadokawa Video, 2005. DVD.

RASEN (1998)

DIRECTOR: Jōji Iida
SCREENPLAY: Jōji Iida
SPECS: 97 minutes; color

Based on a 1995 Suzuki Kōji novel of the same name, the horror film *Rasen*, directed by Jōji Iida, debuted in 1998 alongside *Ringu* as a double-billed feature sequel. Although *Ringu* received critical acclaim, *Rasen* was largely considered a failure and is now virtually thought to be the forgotten sequel to *Ringu*, replaced by *Ringu 2*.

Rasen tells the story of a young pathologist named Mitsuo Andō, played by Kōichi Satō, and his tireless investigation of the death of his longtime friend, Ryūji Takayama, played by Hiroyuki Sanada. Given the opportunity to conduct the autopsy, Andō discovers several mysteries, inclusive of an ulcer in Takayama's throat, traces of a smallpox-like virus, and a sliver of paper containing a series of numbers in his intestinal tract—numbers that are later revealed to be a code left for Andō by Takayama.

In addition to the enigmas of Ryūji's death, the deaths of Ryūji's ex-wife Reiko Asakawa, played by Nanako Matsushima, and son Yōichi Asakawa, not physically appearing in *Rasen*, establish a murder mystery of sorts, leaving Andō to reconstruct the unexplained deaths and put the memory of his friends to rest. Assisting Andō along the way is Ryūji's girlfriend, Mai Takano, played by Miki Takatani, the only survivor and carry-over character from the *Ringu* film. In a somewhat predictable fashion, Andō and Takano engage in a brief but intimate love affair. Consistent with the theme threading through all Ringu-related films, the transmission of a curse takes place through the viewing of a videotape—Andō procures and watches the cursed videotape, infecting himself.

Seeking to escape his own plight—the death of his young son—and take advantage of an opportunity to outdo his smarter former friend Ryūji, Mitsuo spends the night with Mai, not only allowing the virus a biological means of propagation, but also impregnating Mai with what will become the reincarnation of Sadako, the murdered girl from *Ring*, now a vengeful spirit, in the guise of Mai.

Ryūji—having always been endowed with a power to see the future of other people—knew about Sadako's plan to come back to life using Mai as the conduit.

Through a combination of artificial insemination and DNA replication methods being researched and perfected at Mitsuo's laboratory, both Ryūji and Mitsuo's son, Takanori, are brought back to life via a hastened maturation process. Mitsuo has sold off humanity by assisting Sadako in her ultimate goal—the infection of as many people as possible and the propagation of her vengeance. Though Mitsuo has destroyed any remaining cursed videotapes, Mai and Ryūji have plans to help Sadako's will propagate further through the novelization of Asakawa Reiko's diary, which will infect its readers with Sadako's virulent curse.

Themes of familial dissolution, paternal protection, and the haunting, exponentially multiplying social repercussions of such alterations in society's genetic makeup characterize the film, as they do most of Suzuki Kōji's writing and related works. The three fathers of the film are all guilty of committing acts that kill the family and thrust their lives into chaos: Ikuma Heihachiroh regrets the birth of his daughter, Sadako; Ryūji has little to do with his son's life after his divorce from Reiko; and Mitsuo lives in a constant state of remorse for the death of his son—a state of purgatory as is reflected in the chaotic, transitory state of his home and the routine of reaching for the scalpel after every nightmare, but being unable to commit the act. *Rasen* portrays all of these characters as being incapable of holding together their families. Each attempts his own resolution: Heihachiroh bludgeons his daughter and throws her still-living body down a well, seen reenacted in *Rasen*; Ryūji absolves himself of fatherhood by choosing not to bring his recently deceased son back to life; and Mitsuo clones his son and lifts his burden of feeling responsible for Takanori's death, but only by assuring the deaths of countless unnamed others as the result of reincarnating Sadako.

The clearly defined boundaries created through *Rasen*'s attempts to establish a scientific, mathematical, and logical exactitude within the narrative conflict with the emotional and atmospheric *Ringu*, converting what was an existential and ethereal problem into one that can be rationalized through scientific inquiry. Within the incompatibility of this transition occur some losses of narrative consistency, thus alienating viewers of *Ringu*. For instance, how are we to reconcile the Ryūji in *Ringu*, who spent the entire film attempting to find a way to lift Sadako's curse with that in *Rasen*, who is now an agent working toward the propagation of the same curse? The result of this schism is that *Rasen* becomes more science fiction than horror, more an exercise in pondering the intersection between technology and human morality than an exploration of what is fundamentally unknowable.

Rasen failed to attain the popularity and cult following of its predecessor and was disavowed as a sequel. *Ringu 2* (1999) took its place.—Jason Christopher Jones

REINCARNATION (2005)

DIRECTOR: Takashi Shimizu
SCREENPLAY: Takashi Shimizu, Masaki Adachi
SPECS: 96 minutes; color

Reincarnation, known as *Rinne* in Japanese, is a 2005 horror film directed by Takashi Shimizu from a screenplay by Shimizu and Masaki Adachi. It stars Yūka, Karina Nose, Kippei Shiina, Tetta Sugimoto, Shun Oguri, Marika Matsumoto, Mao Sasaki, and Atsushi Haruta and features a cameo by the well-known horror film director Kiyoshi Kurosawa, who was a mentor of Shimizu's. *Reincarnation* was released in Japan and the United States as part of the J-Horror Theater Series that was spearheaded by famed horror film producer Takashige Ichise.

In Tokyo, fledgling actress Nagisa Sugiura (Yūka) attends an audition for director Ikuo Matsumura's (Kippei Shiina) new film, *Memories*, which is based on the true story of a professor (Atsushi Haruta) who—thirty-five years ago—murdered eleven people, including his two children, at an isolated resort hotel. Convinced that she has not made a good showing, and feeling uncomfortable over the fact that the director would not stop glaring at her during the audition, Nagisa tells her agent (Tetta Sugimoto) that she is sure that nothing will come of it. On her way home from the audition, Nagisa repeatedly catches glimpses of a sickly little girl (Mao Sasaki) in a yellow dress, clutching a large doll and staring at her. The feeling of being watched by the little girl continues even at home, where she is later contacted by her agent and told that she has been cast in the film. When Nagisa learns that the entire cast and crew will travel to the site of the mass murder, she confesses to her agent that she has a bad feeling about the situation and wants to back out of the production. Her agent convinces her to stay with the project, and she joins the production at the Ono Kanko Hotel, where strange visions continue to plague her.

In the meantime, a young college student named Yayoi Kinoshita (Karina Nose) has begun to have dreams about the hotel—a place she has dreamed about since childhood although she has never been there. Her boyfriend (Shun Oguri) puts her in touch with another student, named Yuka Morita (Marika Matsumoto), who claims to have been one of the eleven murder victims in a past life. Yuka suggests that the dreams are memories from a past life experience and shows Yayoi how to do research into her own past lives before disappearing under mysterious circumstances. Suspecting that she, too, has a connection to the horrific events at the Ono Kanko Hotel, Yayoi sets off on a quest to determine what happened and how she was involved—a quest that will lead her to cross paths with Nagisa under terrifying and perilous circumstances, as the ties that bind the two women together cinch more and more tightly closed.

Though *Reincarnation* owes much of its narrative structure, thematic content, and atmosphere to earlier films in the J-horror catalogue, the film has been noted—as has 2004's *Marebito*—as a deviation by director Takashi Shimizu away from the horror tropes that dominated his Ju-on franchise and that made him a household name in the horror industry in both Japan and the United States. While *Marebito* involves an almost total rejection of those tropes, *Reincarnation* presents the audience with an evolution of them. The film features concepts and images that are reminiscent of the J-horror scene of the late 1990s and early 2000s in an adapted and subverted form. The story involves the ever-present vengeful spirit that is the staple of the genre, but the visual characteristics of the spirits who appear are not restricted to the iconography that was utilized extensively by Shimizu in his Ju-on franchise and by other directors working in the genre during the same time period.

Reincarnation received mainly positive reviews. Critics praised its production value and attention to atmosphere, noting that the film relies more on the development of psychological dread than a sequence of interconnected jump scares. They have also cited the film's tightly plotted storyline, inclusion of newly evolved horror concepts, and generally strong performances as elements that make *Reincarnation* an example of the J-horror genre at its best. The film debuted at the Tokyo International Film Festival in 2005 and was given a short theatrical release in the United States the following year as part of the first annual After Dark Horrorfest (also known as 8 Films to Die For).—Sara L. Sumpter

See also: Ju-on films; *Marebito*; Shimizu, Takashi

Bibliography
Shimizu, Takashi, dir. *Reincarnation*. Lionsgate Films, 2007. DVD.

RESIDENT EVIL: DAMNATION (2012)
DIRECTOR: Makoto Kamiya
SCREENPLAY: Shotaro Suga
SPECS: 100 minutes; color

Resident Evil: Damnation is a 2012 action-horror, computer-animated feature, released as a joint venture between Sony Pictures and video game company Capcom, and based on a highly successful video game series. Directed by Makoto Kamiya (b. 1965), and known under the original title of *Biohazard Damnation* in Japan, the film sees game protagonist "Leon Kennedy," voiced by Matthew Mercer, searching for bio-organic weapons in a fictional Eastern European country. Unlike the American live-action Resident Evil adaptations, the storyline of *Damnation* remains firmly ensconced in the video game universe. The film follows the same overall plot lines and utilizes the same character designs, voice actors, and style as recent entries in the game series. Focusing on action yet still containing blood, gore, and horrific imagery, the film was produced by game industry veteran Hiroyuki Kobayashi (b. 1972), who worked on several of the Resident Evil games and oversaw the previous animated installment, 2008's *Resident Evil: Degeneration*.

Playing like a feature-length version of a Resident Evil game, *Damnation* centers on American agent Leon Kennedy, who appeared in *Degeneration* and in Resident Evil games 2, 4, and 6. Kennedy enters the Eastern Slav Republic to investigate the potential use of engineered biological weapons called BOWs in an ongoing civil war. Driven by a personal desire to stop their spread due to his previous encounters with the monstrous bio-weapons, Leon ignores orders to abort his mission given soon after his arrival. Leon meets with his contact, and is promptly attacked by a Licker BOW. The contact is killed, and Leon is spared but captured by rebel fighters. While being held by the rebels, Leon learns they are infected by "Plagas," a parasite that places the host into a zombie-like state. An attack by the government gives Leon the chance to escape, and he finds the Plaga has spread among the population of the city. A rebel named "Buddy," voiced by Dave Wittenberg, injects himself with a dominant Plaga organism that allows for control of the previously uncontrollable BOWs to continue the fight for independence.

As Leon deals with the rebels, mercenary Ada Wong, voiced by Courtenay Taylor, passes herself off as a UN weapons inspector to Eastern Slav president Svetlana Belikova, voiced by Wendee Lee. When her ruse is uncovered, Belikova fights her to a standstill, but Ada is still captured. She easily escapes and meets with Leon in the basement of the presidential palace. Ada shows Leon a chamber where dominant Plagas are being grown, the reason for her presence in the country. Moments later, Belikova and a contingent of soldiers arrive. Buddy appears in command of a group of Lickers, who slaughter the government troops. To kill Leon, Buddy, and the Lickers, President Belikova releases her own massive BOWs called Tyrants. Leon and Buddy manage to escape the basement and use a tank to successfully kill one Tyrant. The armored vehicle is incapacitated just as another pair of Tyrants appears. The two are saved at the last moment by appearance of warplanes as the United States and Russia intervene in the crisis. Leon shoots Buddy in the spine to prevent the Plaga parasite from taking complete control of him. In light of the intervention, President Belikova resigns. In the final scenes, Buddy is shown to have survived, Leon discusses the events of the previous days with another agent, and Ada entertains an offer from her shadowy employer for a sample of the dominant Plaga she managed to steal.

The plot of *Damnation* is convoluted, yet the viewing experience improves with an understanding of the creatures, motivations, and backstories within the overall narrative of the game world. Veteran anime writer Shotaro Suga (b. 1972) keeps the story similar in tone to the games, and director Kamiya doesn't take many cinematic chances, allowing the action to unfold in styles that evoke the sequences found in the games as well. The CG animation is well done and in sync with the CG used for Resident Evil 6, and is coupled with solid voice acting. True to its video game roots and mindful of its potential audience, *Damnation* was available for download through the Playstation Network, Xbox Live, and other outlets before a DVD was released. For viewers unfamiliar with Resident Evil, much of the detail may be lost, but fans of the survival horror franchise would certainly be rewarded by the appearance of familiar characters.—Daniel Fandino

Bibliography
Kamiya, Makoto, dir. *Resident Evil: Damnation*. Sony, 2012. Film.

RETRIBUTION (2006)
DIRECTOR: Kiyoshi Kurosawa
SCREENPLAY: Kiyoshi Kurosawa
SPECS: 105 minutes; color

Originally commissioned to be part of J-horror producer Ichise Takashige's "J-Horror Theatre" series of films, *Retribution* (or *The Scream*, were the title translated semantically rather than based on mysterious marketing criteria) is something of a "greatest hits" film from horror genius Kiyoshi Kurosawa, as it showcases a great deal of themes and stylistic motifs from his previous work. However, it gradually takes on its own style to become something of an essay on Kurosawa's usual concerns: identity, trauma, apocalypse, and rebirth.

As in Kurosawa's seminal *Cure* (1997), the plot focuses on a detective (again played by the expertly brooding Koji Yakusho) struggling to understand the connection between a string of murders committed by otherwise ordinary citizens. Yoshioka, as he is called in *Retribution*, is troubled by evidence linking the crimes despite the fact that the murderers are all apparently unconnected people who have their own personal motives for killing. More troubling still is the recurring evidence that seems to implicate the detective himself as a suspect—which is stressful enough without the addition of a screaming ghost in a red dress that has begun to haunt him.

Despite this thrilling setup, the pace is slow, the shots are long, and the muted color palette helps create a Tokyo gray and oppressive. The setting is crucial: the film unfolds in an industrial bay area that, we are told, is constantly changing as more land is pulled up from the sea. Although Kurosawa films usually eschew symbolism to highlight the formal composition of the mise-en-scène, this land is clearly allegorical, with frequent earthquakes threatening to tear apart Yoshioka's sanity—in one scene reminiscent of Roman Polanski's claustrophobic-apartment horror films, an enormous crack opens in the wall, creating a threshold for the ghost to crawl through. More generally, the marginal, metamorphosing, and dead-looking world between the city and the sea expresses the existence of the humans who live there—only the ghost, in her vibrant red dress, stands out as an active, ironically vital force. The murderers themselves act without passion, methodically removing an everyday source of frustration (a delinquent son, a self-centered boyfriend, etc.) almost as though killing were part of a daily routine. The undramatic motives are embodied by undramatic shots that keep the violence at a spatial and psychological distance from the viewer. Mainstream cinematic cues that prepare us for moments of high drama—such as close-ups, tense music, fast cutting between characters—are shocking in their absence. As a product of the desolate landscape, it is not the transgression but the mundanity of murder that provokes horror in us.

The other agent of horror is, of course, the ghost. The ghost's liminal presence is filmed using a variety of creative techniques, including theatrical spotlighting against a distant wall, the flatness of the image trapping the woman's body on a two-dimensional plane from which she can break free with a few terrifying steps toward the camera. In a reworking of a dance-like scene from Kurosawa's gripping yet parodic Loft (in which the confused male protagonist is also called Yoshioka), the ghost puts her hands on the detective's shoulders, and slowly forces him to the floor. This moment of touch and physicality is affecting in its transgressive boundary-crossing—the spiritual becomes physical, and the feminine becomes masculine as the ghost moves from an ethereal, abstract embodiment of the hero's troubled mind to the concrete image of a woman's body overpowering a man's. In this vein, the film's images of both the ghost and the socially and physically disintegrating world can be seen as an exercise in capturing in-betweeness on film, not to mention an opportunity to explore the director's usual philosophical concerns.

As well as the ideas recycled from his previous work, the ghost's distinctive red clothing brings with it something of the atmosphere of Don't Look Now (1973), another influence that Kurosawa uses to thread together the patchwork body of Retribution. At certain points the dress seems to take on a life of its own: Yoshioka is frightened by it in the morgue, and when the ghost flies through the sky her body disappears, leaving just a fluttering redness receding into the clouds. The vibrancy of the dress complements the film's interest in identities that lack a human core, as seen in the murderous actions that can't be traced back to an individual's psychology. If the film's supernatural aggression is more present in a red dress than a stable monstrous identity, then it is a red dress that can be worn by anyone—a recurring image that manifests itself across Kurosawa's oeuvre is that a monster is not a type of being, but a role that is open to anyone to perform. Hence the tension as Yoshioka uncovers more clues that seem to reveal an unknown dark side to his character, while at the same time we see him discovering more about the ghost's tragic past—the difference between hero and villain, monster and victim is shown to be unstable and, therefore, the film's manifested source of unease.—Seán Hudson

See also Cure; Kurosawa, Kiyoshi; Loft

Bibliography
Kurosawa, Kiyoshi, dir. *Retribution*. Avex Entertainment, 2006. Film.

RING 0: BIRTHDAY (2000)

DIRECTOR: Norio Tsuruta
SCREENPLAY: Hiroshi Takahashi
SPECS: 99 minutes; color/black and white

Some novels manage to encapsulate the essence of what they have to say in the first sentence alone; *Ring 0: Birthday* (*Ringu Zero: Basudei*, 2000) achieves something similar with its impressively allusive title-screen. As we hear the story of a young Sadako being the sole survivor of a group of children swept out to sea, the camera pans toward an ocean until the whole screen is filled with waves. The faint sound of children crying for help can be heard as the waves darken, mimicking the powerful opening image of *Ring* (*Ringu*, 1998): black waves that dissolve into a television static. Rather than transform the ominous sea into modern technology, *Ring 0: Birthday*'s version of this image has the black waves circumscribed by a circle that becomes an iris, channeling the iconic image of Sadako's well as seen from its depths. Finally, the single eye becomes decentered in the frame, reconfiguring *Ring*'s climactic moment of horror: in its notorious finale, the viewer is shocked by the unexpected close-up of one of Sadako's eyes, glaring viciously between matted strands of black hair. Far from mere repetition, this early intertextual moment indicates that *Ring 0: Birthday* has a specific agenda for its iconic source material, as we shall see.

The title-screen's montage of three key images from *Ring* not only functions as an homage, but also shows a progression in two senses. Firstly, we see a chronological progression of images that move from the very beginning of *Ring* to its end, showing that *Ring 0: Birthday* represents a new chapter in the story. Secondly, and more importantly, the eye of Sadako that we see is anything but monstrous: with a dilating pupil and a quivering eyelid, it's an image of vulnerability and perhaps fear, appropriate if Sadako can still hear the shouts of her drowning classmates as we the viewers can. What's more, the circumscribed ocean evokes the idea of a turbulent world behind and within the eye, or the "I": Sadako has been embodied here as a complex, psychologically motivated human rather than the object of terror viewers are familiar with. In the space of an impressive twenty seconds, then, *Ring 0: Birthday* viscerally communicates that it will both develop and depart from the style, themes, and story of its influential predecessors. The eye that revealed her as demonically inhuman is reappropriated to figure Sadako as emotionally human—for an audience familiar with *Ring*, this well-executed opening will be especially affecting.

The idea of reappropriation is especially relevant for this example of that staple of horror franchises, the prequel or origin story. That Norio Tsuruta, the man whose *Scary True Stories* (*Honto ni atta kowai hanashi*, 1991) were highly stylistically formative for the J-horror boom of the 1990s, was asked to direct this particular film has a certain poetic justice to it, whether intentional or not. As *Ring* was the film that kick-started the movement that came to be known as J-horror, it feels fitting that the origin story of *Ring* is helmed by the originator of its aesthetic. Nonetheless, the resulting film intentionally strays far from the J-Horror model, so far that it almost wanders out of the realm of horror entirely.

In this film, to make human means to move from horror to drama. Sadako (as portrayed by Nakama Yukie) is an actor; she's in love; she's ostracized by the other members of her troupe; and she's doomed from the start by her unpredictable supernatural powers. The final, stilted stagger toward her victims seems more like an obligatory trope, worn out and unoriginal, though it is quickly succeeded by the film's true climax: an emotional and social betrayal more brutal and shocking than the previous ones we've seen Sadako suffer, and one that firmly cements her status as a tragic victim. Although the chill of seeing her increasingly trapped and abused is horrifying, her inescapable interment evokes an emotion (pity) far removed from the tense dread we experience when we see the protagonists of Nakata Hideo's *Ring* films standing at the bottom of the same well.

There exists a further contextual point of interest regarding Tsuruta's reappropriation of Sadako. The most successful Japanese *kaidan eiga*, or ghost story films, have drawn on the Japanese tradition of presenting female ghosts as avengers of injustices suffered during life. Thus, the "monsters" are also victims, transmitters of an evil action rather than an evil being—this model is apparent from *Yotsuya kaidan* (first filmed in 1912) to *Ju-on: The Grudge* (2002), with notable exceptions. *Ring* is one such exception, as the presence of Sadako appears to be mostly demonic—that she was thrown down a well is ultimately taken to be further proof of her relentless evil rather than as a reason to feel sorry for her. In contrast, *Ring 0: Birthday* all-too-firmly hammers home the image of Sadako as a victim, thereby bringing the *Ring* saga full circle not only by returning to the overarching narrative's past, but also by situating that narrative in a more traditional ghost story framework (although the final product probably owes more in its execution to *Carrie* [1976] and its ilk).—Seán Hudson

See also Ringu; Ringu 2

Bibliography
Tsuruta, Norio, dir. *Ring 0: Birthday*. Toho, 2000. Film.

RINGU (1998)
DIRECTOR: Hideo Nakata
SCREENPLAY: Kōji Suzuki
SPECS: 96 minutes; black and white/color

Ringu (1998), directed by Hideo Nakata, is an adaptation of the novel by the same name, written by Kōji Suzuki, which was based on a traditional Japanese ghost story known as *Banchō sarayashiki* (*The Dish Mansion at Banchō*). The movie and its sequel *Rasen* (*Spiral*) were released in Japanese cinemas simultaneously in 1998 and became commercial successes. With a budget of 1.2 million US dollars, *The Ring* generated some 13 million dollars at the box office, making it a financial success as well. Considered one of the most outstanding and internationally well-known Japanese horror film productions, *Ringu*'s popularity would go on to inspire several other remakes and theme adaptations within other national cinema industries, inclusive of *The Ring Virus* (1999) in Korea, or *The Ring* (2002) in the United States.

Ringu begins by introducing two female teenagers, Masami (Hitomi Satō) and Tomoko (Yūko Takeuchi), discussing an urban legend associated with a videotape and its power to kill anyone that views its contents within seven days of watching it. As Tomoko viewed the videotape a week prior, she becomes the first victim of its wrath, dying in front of Masami, and establishing a pattern of other similar deaths throughout the film.

Reiko Asakawa (Nanako Matsushima), a reporter investigating the videotape and the pervasive popularity of its urban legend lore, learns of Tomoko's recent death. While Masami is under observation in a mental hospital, Reiko discovers that the teenagers visited Izu, the province from which the videotape is believed to have originated. Traveling to Izu to trace the girls' footsteps, she locates the cabin where they stayed during their visit and happens upon the ominous videotape. Reiko then views the videotape's content. Both intrigued and disturbed by its bizarre images, she watches it through to its conclusion, at which time she receives an anonymous phone call with a voice uttering the words "seven days."

Fearing that her fate is sealed and tied to the next seven days, Reiko seeks the help of her ex-husband and fellow reporter, Ryūji Takayama (Hiroyuki Sanada). After taking a photograph of Reiko, Ryūji discovers that the image of her face is blurred. Captivated by the whole milieu of events associated with the videotape, Ryūji's curiosity consumes him, and he too decides to view its contents.

In an attempt to further analyze the videotape, Reiko creates a copy of the footage, stumbling upon a hidden message that states, "frolic in brine, goblins be thine"—articulated in an Izu dialect spoken on the island of Ōshima. Unbeknownst to Reiko, her son, Yoichi (Rikiya Ōtaka), also views the videotape, explaining that the late Tomoko told him to do so.

With the seven-day time frame closing, Reiko and Ryūji set sail for Ōshima island in search of answers about the videotape, as well as following-up on a lead associated with the life of the psychic Shizuko Yamamura—a mysterious figure who had committed suicide after being accused of faking her supernatural powers. Believing that the videotape was created by Yamamura's daughter, Sadako (Rie Inō)—who also possesses supernatural powers—Reiko and Ryūji infer that it is Sadako's vengeful spirit that is orchestrating these murders. Reiko and Ryūji reason that they need to search for the body of Sadako, in the hope of appeasing her spirit and putting her tormented soul to rest.

Returning home the next day, Ryūji finds that his television mysteriously switches itself to the image of a well, from out of which Sadako is crawling. Ryūji is then killed by some kind of shock and subsequent cardiac arrest. Learning of his death, Reiko desperately searches for a way to save her son from a similar fate.

Ringu has become one of the most well-known film productions in Japan, generating enormous interest in the Japanese horror genre around the world. In addition to *Ringu*'s many movie adaptations both within Japan and abroad, the use of Sadako-like imagery and other tropes associated with digital technology as instruments of murder are commonly found among other horror and suspense films—an indication of *Ringu*'s impact on the film industry at large.—Frank Jacob

Bibliography

Goldberg, Ruth. "Demons in the Family: Tracking the Japanese 'Uncanny Mother Film' from *A Page of Madness* to *Ringu*." In *Planks of Reason: Essays on the Horror Film*, edited by Barry Keith Grant and Christopher Sharrett, 370–85. Lanham, MD: Scarecrow Press, 2004.

Martin, Daniel. "Japan's 'Blair Witch': Restraint, Maturity, and Generic Canons in the British Critical Reception of 'Ring.'" *Cinema Journal* 48, no. 3 (2009): 35–51.

Meikle, Denis. *The Ring Companion*. London: Titan Books, 2005.

Tateishi, Reimi. "The Japanese Horror Film Series: Ring and Eko Eko Azarak." In *Fear without Frontiers: Horror Cinema across the Globe*, edited by Steven Jay Schneider, 284–96. London: FAB Press, 2003.

Wee, Valerie. "Visual Aesthetics and Ways of Seeing: Comparing 'Ringu' and 'The Ring.'" *Cinema Journal* 50, no. 2 (2011): 41–60.

RINGU 2 (1999)

DIRECTOR: Hideo Nakata
SCREENPLAY: Hiroshi Takahashi
SPECS: 95 minutes; color

Ringu 2 (1999) is a follow up to the popular and successful *Ringu* (1998), both of which would go on to inspire North American spinoffs. The film was directed by Hideo Nakata (b. 1961), who also directed *Dark Water* (2002) and *Ringu*. The plot of *Ringu 2* follows immediately from that of the first and is based upon the novel written by Kōji Suzuki (b. 1957), which was then adapted for the screen by Hiroshi Takahashi (b. 1965). The film details the continued struggle between those who view a mysterious VHS tape and Sadako Yamamura, a child with powerful psychic abilities who was shunned by her father.

The film begins with Takaishi Yamamura (Yoichi Numata, b. 1924), Sadako's uncle, coming to a morgue to inspect her body, which was recovered by Reiko Asakawa (Nanako Matsushima, b. 1973) and her ex-husband, Ryuji Takayama, from a well in the first film. Takaishi refuses to look upon the corpse and notices a length of hair moving underneath the gurney where the body lies, prompting his swift departure.

Elsewhere, Mai Takano (Miki Nakatani, b. 1976) searches for more information regarding the sudden death of her professor, Ryuji Takayama, which occurred in the first film. While pursuing this information Mai encounters Okazaki (Yūrei Yanagi, b. 1963) a reporter at the same news station that Reiko once worked at, who is continuing to investigate the mysterious tapes that precipitated Reiko's disappearance and Ryuji's death.

Mai and Okazaki travel to Reiko's apartment where they find a charred video tape in the bathtub, and receive a phone call meant for Reiko claiming that

Reiko's father, Koichi Asakawa (Katsumi Muramatsu, b. 1939) has been found dead. At the Koichi home, they find a note telling Reiko not to worry, that the tape has been destroyed.

The two investigators then part ways to search for clues on their own. Okazaki, searching for someone who has the tape, uses his professional connections to track down and interview Kanae Sawaguchi, a student who, it is later revealed, has seen the tape, and claims to have several friends who possess it and show it to one another out of fear. At the end of the interview, Okazaki offers to buy a tape from Sawaguchi, before leaving with Mai to investigate another lead, Masami Kurahashi, who is a friend of Tomoko Oishi's, the original victim, and was a witness to her death.

Kurahashi is now in a mental hospital and refuses to leave her room due to a fear of the TV in the common room. Mai and Okazaki then meet with Dr. Kawajiri to discuss Kurahashi and he reveals himself to be a friend of Ryuji's and a believer in the tape's powers.

Mai warns Okazaki to stop the story about the tape. She finds Reiko and her son, Yoichi, who have been in hiding since the first series of deaths. Yoichi has become a mute, and Reiko asks Mai to go and speak to Dr. Kawajiri on behalf of her and her son. When Mai arrives, Dr. Kawajiri is conducting an experiment on Kurahashi to solve the issue of the tape, which he believes is a case of energy transfer. The experiment fails, and during the chaos of an energy surge Mai destroys the tape they are using.

Under pressure from the police, and discovering that Sawaguchi has also died after viewing the tape, Mai reveals where Reiko and Yoichi are hiding, and they are taken into questioning. At the police station, Yoichi reveals his own psychic powers and flees with his mother, but Reiko is struck and killed by a car in the process. Mai and Yoichi travel to Izu to track down Yamamura, who has taken Sadako's remains and dumped them into the sea. Dr. Kawajiri follows them there, and together they decide to use Yoichi's psychic powers to remove Sadako's curse. Yamamura and Dr. Kawajiri both die during the experiment when Sadako's coffin reappears in the pool they opted to use to channel the psychic power; Mai and Yoichi black out. They awaken in a well with Ryuji, who takes Yoichi's "fear," and they proceed to climb out using a rope but are pursued by Sadako. When they emerge from the well they find themselves in the pool from the experiment that took Yamamura and Kawajiri's lives.

The film ends with Okazaki in the hospital overcome by his involvement in Sawaguchi's death, and Sawaguchi's ghost standing over him laughing.—Josh Dawson

See also Dark Water; Ringu

Bibliography
Nakata, Hideo dir. *Ringu 2*. Toho Company, 1999. Film.

THE RING VIRUS (1999)
Director: Dong-bin Kim
Screenplay: Dong-bin Kim
Specs: 108 minutes; color/black and white

The Ring Virus is a 1999 South Korean horror film that was adapted mostly from Koji Suzuki's 1991 novel, *Ringu*. The Japanese film adaptation had been released in 1998—but not in South Korea. Long-standing tensions over language and cultural autonomy on the part of both nations made it illegal to bring *Ringu* to South Korea. After the Pacific War and until 2004, South Korea had restricted the import of all Japanese cultural products. Although this ban was slowly lifted beginning in 1998, the wildly popular *Ringu* could not at first be imported to and distributed in South Korea. Rather, the film could enter the country legitimately only as a remake; thus *Ring Virus* was born out of political necessity married to cultural expediency.

Ring Virus was of "mixed race." Omega Project, a Japanese company that had helped produce *Ringu*, helped finance *Ring Virus* with AFDF Korea and Hanmac Films. However, the South Korean producers reportedly never actually paid for the remake rights, so *Ring Virus* still constituted an illegal enterprise. It is considered a significant, coproduced, Japanese-Korean transcultural product.

Dong-bin Kim is credited as director and screenwriter, using Hideo Nakata's adaptation. *Ring Virus* runs 108 minutes, 13 minutes longer than the original, and follows the novel's plot closely yet re-creating some of the Japanese film's shots faithfully.

In the book and in each film adaptation, the protagonist is a journalist whose curiosity about a cursed video that brings promised death to viewers in exactly seven days entraps him in an endless cycle of murder. In each version, the journalist shares a past with an eccentric genius who agrees, skeptically, to assist in an investigation of the deaths and, ultimately, the dark secret behind an indecipherable, yet otherwise innocuous videotape. The duo unravels a bizarre case involving rape and murder and their cover-up, along with a curse that lingers in a spell transmitted through the videotape. Unable to break the spell, to which the journalist's child has also succumbed, they must find a way to mitigate or control its power, if at all possible.

Ring Virus differs significantly from the book in that the latter's journalist protagonist was a man named Kazuyuki Asakawa, whereas the South Korean movie features a female journalist named Hong Sun-Joo (Eun-Kyung Shin). She partners with a coroner friend, Choi-Yul (Jin-Yeong Jeong), who investigated one of the earlier, mysterious deaths. In the novel, Asagawa's partner is an old friend: an odd-duck, but genius college philosophy professor, Ryuji, who has more than a lay knowledge of medicine.

Ring Virus follows Suzuki's novel more closely, however, than does the Japanese film. Sun-Joo and Choi find that the videotape was created by a long-missing psychic named Park Eun-Suh (Doona Bae; in the novel and Japanese film, the character is named Sadako), an illegitimate hermaphrodite. Eun-Suh possesses powers of telekinesis, which she uses to exact revenge against society after she is raped and left for dead at the bottom of a well.

As in the book, *Ring Virus* includes the tape's important beginning and concluding messages (roughly, "Watch till the end, you will be eaten by the lost" and "Whoever watches this will die in a week").

Some reviewers have criticized *Ring Virus* for its slower pace than either the Japanese or American versions, but in that way, its plot is like the book's:

more detail than horror. For example, attention and time are devoted in each to how Choi/Ryuji analyzes the tape, categorizing segments into categories of realism and abstraction. Choi deduces that the dark, blurry edges of the realistic scenes represent a human's-eye view, and the intervening instances of darkness represent the eye's blinks. Choi is further able to conclude by the number of eye blinks per minute, that a woman, Eun-Suh, created the video telekinetically through her own eyes and the images in her mind.

The South Korean version, like Suzuki's novel, is more graphic than either the Japanese or later American (*The Ring*, 2002, 115 minutes) film adaptations. The book and *Ring Virus* both address Eun-Suh's hermaphroditism plainly, revealing that she has both male and female genitalia; vulva and testicles, but no penis. Her rape and murder—by her half-brother, with whom she becomes romantically involved until he discovers her secret—are also included in the book and in *Ring Virus*.—Kimiko Akita and Rick Kenney

• S •

SADAKO 3D (2012)

DIRECTOR: Tsutomu Hanabusa
SCREENPLAY: Yoshinobu Fujioka, Tsutomu Hanabusa
SPECS: 96 minutes; color

Sadako 3D is a 2012 entry into the popular Ring franchise, in which the legend of Sadako is, quite literally, resurrected. The film is set thirteen years after the original *Ring* and is based on the novels by Koji Suzuki (b. 1957) and directed by Tsutomu Hanabusa (b. 1968). *Sadako 3D* updates the *Ring* legend with the curse now being spread through the Internet via mobile phones, laptops, and PCs, and linked to the real-life Japanese video sharing website *Nico Nico Douga*. The film is notable for its innovative cross-platform marketing, which included Shibuya's scramble crossing being flooded with "Sadakos," and "Sadako" throwing the first pitch at a Tokyo Dome baseball game.

The film opens with a man throwing a body into a well. The well already holds a number of other dead women, all with the same long dark hair and a white dress. Back at his apartment, the man laughs maniacally, frantically writing on the wall before setting up his mobile phone and preparing to live stream on *Nico Nico Douga*. He opens the stream with the words "Let's get started."

Shortly afterward, a spur of suicides has piqued the interest of Detective Koiso, played by Ryōsei Tayama (b. 1951), and his partner, Nakamura. The latest victim was watching a video and purposefully walked out in front of a truck. Meanwhile, in teacher Akane's (Satomi Ishihara, b. 1986) class a girl named Noriko is searching for a rumored "cursed video" on her phone, but can only find dead links that take her to an "Error 404" page. Akane confiscates and turns off Noriko's phone, but is suspicious when it later turns itself back on.

At home, Akane's boyfriend, Takanori, played by Kōji Seto (b. 1988), and his friend Enoki are also searching for the video. Enoki explains that the video was a *Nico Nico Douga* live broadcast in which a man committed suicide. He has heard that "If you watch it you die." That same night Noriko gives up searching and walks away from her phone, but a video begins to play, with a male voice saying "let's get started." Suddenly, a hand comes from the screen and throws her out of the window, still clutching her mobile phone. A voice says "you're not the one."

Further investigating the suicides, Nakamura confirms that the five people who watched the live broadcast are all dead, having committed suicide at the same time. The two detectives discover that the video was created by an artist named Kashiwada (Yusuke Yamamoto, b. 1988). They travel to his apartment and learn that Kashiwada committed suicide after receiving heavy online criticism.

Risa is in the school library investigating the video that she believes killed her friend Noriko. After reaching an "Error 404" screen the video begins to play. Kashiwada says the familiar "let's get started'" and talks about how he will take his revenge, through resurrecting "S." He is then choked by an invisible force and falls to the floor dead. A long braid of hair emerges from the screen and grabs Risa, but Akane saves her. The computer screen shatters and a voice says to Akane "you are the one." It is revealed through flashbacks that Akane has telekinetic powers, and as a child she saved her school from an attack but was branded an outsider as a result.

Later, at home, the video begins playing on Takanori's computer, but using her telekinetic powers Akane shatters the screen. The pair run out into the street, and multiple Sadakos appear to emerge from video screens. A giant Sadako emerges from a video truck and drags Takanori into the screen.

Following Noriko's suicide, Detective Koiso returns to Kashiwada's room and reveals the hidden writing on the walls. He learns that Kashiwada planned to find a vessel to resurrect Sadako, whose thoughts remain in the well. He killed multiple women in this search but when that did not work he created the video so that Sadako could find her host.

Believing she can save Takanori, Akane travels with Nakamura to Sadako's childhood home. However, Nakamura is killed by a "failed version of Sadako," which emerges from the well. Akane fends off a number of the creatures before being dragged into a mobile phone showing the "Error 404" page. Having been transported to the roof, Sadako now holds Akane by the throat and tells her once more, "You're the one." Akane trades her life for Takanori's and is possessed by Sadako. Now lying on the floor of the room where Akane was snatched, Takanori hears Akane's screams coming from the mobile phone. He picks up a rock and smashes the phone, effectively freeing Akane as she falls through the roof covered in hair, but still alive.

After the credits, Kashiwada's video begins to play again but with the revised line, "Now let's get started again."—Aimee Richmond

See also Rasen; Ring 0: Birthday; Ringu; Ringu 2, The Ring Virus

Bibliography

Hanabusa, Tsutomo, dir. *Sadako 3D*. Kadokawa Pictures, 2012. DVD.
Hanabusa, Tsutomo, dir. *Sadako 2 3D*. Kadokawa, 2013. Film.
Nakata, Hideo, dir. *Ring*. Ace Pictures, 1998. DVD.

SAIMIN (1999)

DIRECTOR: Masayuki Ochiai
SCREENPLAY: Masayuki Ochiai, Yasushi Fukuda
SPECS: 110 minutes; color

Saimin, a 1999 film by Masayuki Ochiai also known as *The Hypnotist* for US DVD release, is an adaptation of the novel *Saimin* by Keisuke Matsuoka (b. 1968), telling the tale of three bizarre suicides.

Detective Sakurai, Ken Utsui (1931–2014) is alerted to a suicide at a wedding. The groom, an unlikely candidate for self-destruction, has strangled himself with his tie. At the coroner's examination, Sakurai finds that there are two more strange deaths: a seventy-three-year-old man who jumped out of a high-rise window, and an athlete that ran herself so hard she broke both legs and died from the trauma. All the victims spoke of a green monkey before they died, so the detective assumes this is a drug and the deaths are drug related; however, no narcotics are found in the victims.

Dr. Saga, played by Goro Inagaki (b. 1973), a psychologist that specializes in hypnosis, demonstrates the basics of the mental state; according to him, the hypnotist is the only one who can control his subject based on trust. In contrast to this clinical representation, Jissoji, played by Takeshi Masu (b. 1955), is a television sensationalist, abusing the power of hypnosis for his own amusement and preying on his attractive young subjects. Jissoji is approached one evening by a meek young woman, Yuka Irie, played by Miho Kanno (b. 1977), who begs him to help her because she is chased by the green monkey. He is annoyed and cruel with her at first, but when she suddenly declares that she is an alien, he realizes that she is under a hypnotic spell, which seems perfect for his own twisted pleasure.

Detective Sakurai sees Dr. Saga at the police station teaching a seminar, and later that day, they both end up at the same bar, where Sakurai waxes philosophical about the motives of criminals and the illogical deaths that have just happened. The young doctor suggests that maybe these deaths were caused by hypnosis, and as they discuss this, they fail to notice Yuka appearing on Jissoji's TV show, talking about her alien identity. Sakurai and Saga become a team and, along with Sakurai's assistant Mitsui, played by Yuki Watanabe (b. 1981), continue to investigate as more deaths occur. They devise a theory that the hypnotist uses triggers to remotely set his subjects off to commit suicide. Later, Saga illustrates the potential of hypnosis to the detective by putting him under. He remembers his betrayal of a childhood friend, finally understanding how memories are unlocked.

Mitsui finds out more information on Yuka. She was a temporary employee at a bank, and had to be hospitalized due to anorexia. When the team visits the hospital, they find out from a nurse that Yuka used to hear voices at night. That voice belonged to a social worker known as "Rat," who hypnotized Yuka for his perverse pleasures. When Sakurai asks the nurse whether she thought Jissoji and Rat are the same person, she couldn't be sure.

Yuka escapes Jissoji for a little while and Dr. Saga follows her to a seedy bar, where he witnesses what he believes to be symptoms of dissociative identity disorder. Yuka has become the sensual Reiko, and she takes the doctor back to her apartment where she reveals that she knows of Yuka but has never seen her. Reiko seduces the doctor, and in the morning, becomes the timid Yuka again. Saga apologizes for sleeping with her, vowing to help and protect her. She speaks of the ocean to him, and they fall under a spell. Meanwhile, Sakurai realizes that Jissoji is not the killer because he has been electrocuted on a billboard.

Yuka is brought in for a police interview where the chief and his cronies dispute Dr. Saga's theory of hypnosis and Yuka's other personalities. He brings out Reiko to prove her multiple personalities, but they soon find out there is one more entity inside her that is evil and powerful. She mesmerizes them and escapes. As the team reviews the interview video, Sakurai gets a call from the real killer, telling him to be ready for "The New World." Sakurai realizes that he is referring to Dvorak's symphony, which he received tickets to, and the police mobilize to the concert hall. Unfortunately, the police who attended Yuka's interview now respond to unknown triggers, and a police officer and the chief both kill themselves gruesomely. Mitsui realizes the trigger is the clang of metal, and that there is a clash of cymbals in the fourth movement of the symphony, so they rush to alert Sakurai, who awaits the killer there. Mitsui drops her keys, and is put under, nearly killing herself and Dr. Saga. He manages to rush to the hall, and almost succeeds in saving Sakurai, but a triangle's chime puts Sakurai into a spell where he remembers the betrayal of his friend and kills himself over the guilt.

The police find Rat's apartment, covered with pictures of Yuka. Rat is hooked up to wires and television monitors, and is noticeably near death. Dr. Saga questions him about Yuka, and Rat tells him that through hypnosis he unleashed something terrible from Yuka. Then he dies, and Saga goes back to the station where he finds the evil Yuka. She tries to put Saga under a suicidal spell by clanging a pipe, telling him she is here to teach humans what they really are—machines—and those that don't love their children must be punished, implying past abuse. They struggle and she falls out of a window, but Saga catches her. He vows to love and protect her, and she tells him that she loves him, which is another hypnosis trigger for him to see what she calls his "ugly soul." She falls to her death, and he tries to follow, but is saved.

Three days later, Saga has nightmares of evil Yuka and tries to drown himself by drinking water after remembering the talk of the ocean with her. Yuka has programmed him with her limitless control even after her death. In the final scene, a uniformed officer who has been obsessed with a billboard of a girl that looks like Yuka, drops his hat and walks away as the camera closes in on her eyes.

This film draws on many influences, including film noir, serial killers, and classic possession films, to create a fairly unique and somewhat disjointed psychological thriller. There also appears to be some social commentary on the subliminal and exploitive nature of societal messages, the disconnect and suppression of our emotions, and the notions of suicide in Japanese culture. *Saimin* took third place for Best Asian Film at the Fantasia Film Festival in 1999, and Best Lighting Award at the Mainichi Film Concours in 2000.—Carolyn Mauricette

See also Infection

Bibliography
Ochiai, Masayuki, dir., *Hypnosis*. Toho, 1999. Film.

SAYONARA JUPITER (1984)
DIRECTOR: Koji Hashimoto, Sakyo Komatsu
SCREENPLAY: Sakyo Komatsu
SPECS: 130 minutes; color

Sayonara Jupiter (also known as *Bye Bye Jupiter*, 1984) is either one of the Holy Grails among the Japanese *tokusatsu* (special effects) films or an excellent example for illustrating why Japan, with its bountiful financial resources (at least in the early 1980s) and technological acumen, was totally unable to come up with something like *Star Wars*. A head-spinning combination of an extremely sincere (and, for the most part, well thought-out) science fictional premise and its ideas; impressive, if dated, special effects; a bizarre, sixties-style plot of peace-niks vs. space capitalists; ridiculous performances (mostly by barely professional non-Japanese actors); and, finally, the kind of dour, lugubrious attitude more appropriate for a wartime propaganda film than an SF epic, *Jupiter* is sometimes unintentionally hilarious, although it certainly has its moments.

The film's SF pedigree is in fact not to be trifled with: it is directed by Koji Hashimoto (1936–2005), veteran assistant director for many of Toho's prestigious and expensive projects and the eventual director of the 1984 *Godzilla*, and written by Sakyo Komatsu (1931–2011), one of Japan's most celebrated SF writers and author of the mega-seller *Japan Sinks*. They try hard to infuse adult contents and serious SF themes into a basically juvenile space-adventure story but are unable to purge the sense of incongruity and even silliness from the proceedings. A zero-gravity sex scene between the film's hero, Dr. Honda (Miura Tomokazu) and heroine, Maria (Diane d'Angely) is simply laughable. Non-Japanese characters such as Senator Shadllic (Andrew Hughes in a role allegedly intended for Orson Wells) might as well be howling at the moon for all the sense their dialogue makes. If all that is not enough, how about a hippie songwriter with his pet dolphin, also named Jupiter? Thankfully the dolphin does not actually pop up on screen and sing a tune about peace in the solar system.

But amid all this groan-inducing silliness and the puffed-up air of self-importance are hints of a good science fiction film. Certainly, Komatsu had done his best to cinematically illustrate the idea of "solarization"—that is, turning the gas giant planet Jupiter into a second sun, thus allowing humankind to terraform its satellites and the outer planets in the solar system (the idea also prominently featured in Arthur C. Clarke's *2010*). Indeed, *Jupiter* sports more than a few interesting details that anticipate other science fiction literature and films, including a distinctively cetacean alien ship, a variant of which was featured later in *Star Trek: The Voyage Home* (1986).

The premise of exploring the mysterious alien intelligence ensconced in Jupiter's cold, stormy atmosphere and the dilemma faced by the Earth explorers of whether to destroy alien forms of life encountered on Jupiter in order to create an energy resource would have sufficed to sustain a two-hour-plus film. Unfortunately, Komatsu and his collaborators decided to go for a safer route and introduce a wandering black hole that just *happens* to approach the solar system at the very opportune moment when the explorers are trying to solarize Jupiter. This plot turn has the expected effect of reducing the last third of the film to a ponderous, unexciting action film, with laser guns blasting, race-against-time suspense building (which it actually doesn't, as post-1960s Japanese blockbusters seem *singularly* incapable of generating cinematic suspense of this kind), and heroes making noble sacrifices to save the Earth against that pesky black hole. The lovers are reunited in death, the grumpy Shadllic relents and pays respects to their monument, and everybody at the controls dabs his or her eyes with handkerchiefs.

As for the special effects, yes, we can tell that the spaceships are miniature models strung up on wires and hurtled through a black star-field backdrop, and nothing here approaches the eye-opening sense of wonder generated by similar effects in *Star Wars*, but they are high-quality for the time period, and occasionally impressive in their design and execution. The artificially induced flood that reveals alien landscape paintings in the Martian arctic region is a case in point: the sequence demonstrates how modulation of slow-motion photography combined with the exquisitely scaled miniature landscape can create a believable illusion of massive tons of water roaring down toward the viewers. While not an underappreciated gem by a long shot, *Sayonara Jupiter* will please fans of Japanese genre cinema, and it remains an interesting curio for open-minded casual viewers.

Discotek's Region 1 DVD, released in 2007 and still in print as of June 2015, is probably the best way to access this film worldwide (Geneon Entertainments Japanese Region 2 DVD, already prohibitively expensive, has long been out of print). The DVD includes an introductory essay written by Komatsu translated into English and Yuko Weisser's recollection of a regional theater production of *Sayonara Jupiter*, reconceived as a burlesque comedy with chatty and rambunctious yakuza molls taking a group tour to the big planet, illustrated by rare still photos from the theater performance.—Kyu Hyun Kim

See also War in Space

Bibliography

Hashimoto, Kōji, dir. *Sayonara Jupiter* [*Sayonara Jupitā*]. Toho Entertainment, 1984. Film.

SCHOOLGIRL APOCALYPSE (2011)

DIRECTOR: John Cairns
SCREENPLAY: John Cairns
SPECS: 86 minutes; color

Schoolgirl Apocalypse is the debut film of American writer/director John Cairns. This is a nontraditional zombie horror movie; it is a coming-of-age story set in rural Japan, where teenager Sakura Ishizuka discovers her inner resilience and strength during a zombie outbreak affecting only males. Told between live-action and animated dream/hallucination sequences, using her bow and arrow, Sakura learns to survive and defend herself from both the zombies and a female sociopath while finding solace in dreams set in her English textbook starring a boy named Billy. When she finds the real-life Billy, she begins a journey to save him, which results in saving herself and the world as she restores the men to their previous selves.

The film begins as Sakura meets her friend Rinko and Rinko's little brother on their way to school. While in school, the boys and men begin bleeding from their ears. Rinko notices something is wrong when a boy in her archery club shoots an arrow at her and her teacher only stares at her with bleeding ears. She notices more strange behavior on her way home as a policeman pets a building and a woman silently warns her away. When she arrives home, she has an argument with her mother and doesn't mention the strange behavior. Her father arrives home and immediately attacks her and her mother. Sakura's mother manages to kill her father before dying. Now alone, Sakura packs a bag with her phone and English textbook, and grabs her bow and arrow. She makes her way toward Rinko's house while talking to her on the phone and hears Rinko being attacked. She finds Rinko injured from wounds sustained by Rinko's little brother. He and other males quickly descend on the injured girl and Sakura runs away in shock, watching from the woods as the men tear apart her friend.

Sakura hides in a large pipe from a construction site where she tries to focus on her English textbook. She only leaves the security of the pipe to scavenge through the grocery bag of a dead female bicyclist. A van breaks down on the road and the woman driver coaxes Sakura out, informing her that only men are attacking. The woman, Atsuko, tries to convince Sakura that they should work together to survive. Atsuko offers Sakura food and talks about the importance of having more than just a survival plan. Atsuko is taking her son to the sea, convinced that will help him, and shows Sakura that there is a piercing sound coming from the radio and electronic devices that makes men worse. Sakura had plans to travel to her grandmother's, but using Atsuko's binoculars she sees that the village is abandoned. Sakura runs away with Atsuko's backpack.

In the backpack, Sakura finds canned food, a map with a compass, a flashlight, and a first aid kit. She goes to sleep and has her first hallucination dream in which she talks to a character in her English textbook, Billy. He tells her that he can help her, insisting she is stronger than she believes. She shoots arrows at the kite he is flying and when she wakes up, she is holding her bow and sees that the arrows are in a sign on a wall nearby. A young woman, Aoi, with strange sores on her arm shows Sakura photographs she has taken of her. Aoi riffles through Sakura's bag and attacks Sakura when she tries to stop her, knocking Sakura out.

Sakura has a hallucination in which Billy tells her that Aoi is worse than the men and that she kidnapped him. He needs to go to the sea and tells Sakura that she is strong. He asks Sakura to help him as he falls beneath the water in the dream. She dives after him, swimming toward a pulsing light, and wakes up. Sakura collects her bow and arrow and starts after Aoi. She sees Aoi leaving a building and starts exploring it. She finds her things there and finds a room reminiscent of the setting where she swam to search for Billy in her dream. In the room, she finds a woman in a white lab coat chained up with her eyes bandaged, who tells her to help the boy. She finds a boy that looks like Billy; he nods when she asks if it's him. Sakura puts him in a wheelchair, frees the scientist, and they are trying to escape when Aoi returns and starts to attack Sakura. Sakura shoots her with an arrow but the scientist knocks Sakura out while waving around a chair. When Sakura wakes up, she has a sore on her arm similar to Aoi's and finds the scientist beating the tied up Aoi. Sakura stops the scientist and Aoi escapes. The scientist tells Sakura that she had been trying to get the boy to the sea when Aoi captured them. Sakura hears a car horn and runs outside to shut it off, seeing approaching men. She begins to run away but comes back to protect Billy and the scientist. She leads the zombies away from the others and uses her bow and arrow to kill them. They then begin their trip to the sea, followed by Aoi.

The scientist tells Sakura about her own hallucinations, explaining that she ripped out her own eyes to avoid seeing her dead brother's mangled face. She was working in a lab when some people found the boy on the shore and brought him in. Then the men started going crazy, attacking the women. The scientist was escaping when she found the boy with a woman who told her to get him back to the sea. She tells Sakura that there must be a connection between the piercing sound coming from electronic devices, the hallucinations, and the men attacking. Sakura has another hallucination in which she is walking with Billy on the shore near a pier and he tells her, "She knew we were coming." The rays of the sun become tentacles, frightening Sakura as Billy smiles happily. Sakura wakes up and finds the scientist dead.

Sakura and Billy continue toward the sea when Sakura sees Aoi following them. They get to the sea by the time Aoi has almost caught up to them. Sakura sees the pier from her dream and sits down next to Billy. The bodies of dead men are lying along the shore line and more men are walking toward the shore when a pulse comes from the horizon. It knocks Sakura and Aoi back, hurting them but killing most of the men. The sore on Sakura's arm is getting worse and when Billy puts his hand on her arm, she grabs a rock and bashes his head, shattering it. She enters into another dream where Billy tells Sakura that they can be together. He puts his hands on her and when she wakes up, she finds an alien creature in the shell of Billy, using tentacles to eat from her arm. Understanding the origin of the hallucinations, she retrieves her bow and arrow and shoots the creature dead. She carries its body to the sea and drops it into the water. Aoi slowly joins her, no longer homicidal, and they warily watch the men approach but they are confused rather than violent. Aoi laughs but Sakura just walks away.

Cairns grew up in New Orleans, Louisiana, moving to Japan in the late 1990s. Rino Higa plays Sakura in one of her first film roles and Mai Tsujimoto plays Aoi. Yuki'e Kitō produced the movie for the Lantis KK production studio. It premiered at the Bucheon International Fantastic Film Festival in 2011 and was screened at the Foreign Correspondence Club of Japan. It premiered in Europe and North America in 2012 at the Japan Filmfest Hamburg in Germany and the Fantasia Film Festival in Montreal, Canada. It received mostly positive reviews from critics and mixed reviews from audiences for its nontraditional approach to a zombie film, use of setting, and coming of age theme.—Paula S. Kiser

SCREAM QUEEN FILMFEST TOKYO

While anywhere in the world women have a prominent position in horror films in terms of female characters on screen, the horror genre is often considered to be a male-dominated domain, especially with regard to the overwhelming number of male directors, producers, and others in filmmaking roles. This is also the case of Japanese cinema, where the representation of women in the horror genre has expanded from classical *yūrei* stories, such as *Ugetsu monogatari* and the many adaptations of *Tokaido Yotsuya kaidan*, to more contemporary elaborations of victims in the Guinea Pig series and other gore-slasher films. Most of these female characters in Japanese cinema often embody—and sometimes even challenge—the historical/male anxieties concerning female sexuality, motherhood, and changing gender roles created by Japanese male filmmakers. Curiously, the few women making horror films in Japan such as Kei Fujiwara, Mari Asato, or Shimako Satō, are not usually labeled as "female directors." This can be interpreted as an indication that the filmmaker's gender is an irrelevant matter for producers and audiences in the horror film world, but also as evidence of the invisibility of women behind the camera in the horror genre. The Scream Queen Filmfest Tokyo, an event established to promote the visibility and professional advancement of females in the J-horror industry, could be considered a response to this latter interpretation.

Launched in 2013, the Scream Queen Filmfest Tokyo showcases horror and dark fantasy shorts directed by women from around the world, presenting itself under the slogan *kawaii, kedo, kowai*, which plays with the words *kawaii* (cute, often applied to and/or used by women) and *kowai* (scary) combining gender and genre in the expression "cute but scary." It is held annually during the last week of October, anticipating the scary celebrations of Halloween, at the Uplink Factory in Shibuya—a renowned cultural space for independent and experimental art. In each of the past editions, the festival has featured roughly twenty-five short films grouped in two-hour programs, followed by question-and-answer sessions with international and Japanese guests. Together with this, beyond the screening room, the festival typically offers special events about genre-related topics such as horror makeup sessions, fantasy art exhibitions, and even horror-themed food and drink services.

In recent years, most of the short films came from outside of Japan (mainly from Canada, Australia, the United States, and the UK, but also from a variety of Asian and Spanish-speaking countries such as South Korea, Hong Kong, Indonesia, Taiwan, Mexico, Spain, and Uruguay. However, a remarkable number of Japanese women filmmakers have also attended the festival and screened their works from within the horror genre. For example, newcomer directors such as Maya Katō and Mari Okada have presented their shorts, as well as such rising stars within the animation fields as Toshiko Hata and Naoka Kōno. Indeed, indicative of this new wave of Japanese artists is the work of Kayoko Asakura, whose short-film, *Hide and Seek*, premiered at the 2013 event. Along with these new names, some more established directors, like filmmaking veteran Mari Asato, have also participated in the event.

The Japanese female producer Mai Nakanishi is the mastermind behind the planning and organization of the festival. Having studied and worked in North America as a horror film producer, Nakanishi has experienced firsthand what it means to be a successful female in the J-horror industry. Indeed, in 2014, she collaborated in the American horror anthology, *ABC of the Death 2*, taking over productions under the direction of Japanese male filmmakers Soichi Umezawa and Hajime Ōhata.

The festival is also linked to the American horror scene through the now defunct Viscera Film Festival, an annual horror film festival for women filmmakers that was initially held online, and later in Los Angeles, which generously supported the first edition of Scream Queen Filmfest Tokyo. To encourage women to explore and represent horror stories in films, Nakanishi's festival participates in global initiatives such as "Women in Horror Month" every February, as well as a more local dimension bringing the Scream Queen Filmfest experience to different cities throughout Japan such as Nagoya and Matsumoto.—Alejandra Armendáriz Hernández

SÉANCE (2000)

DIRECTOR: Kiyoshi Kurosawa
SCREENPLAY: Kiyoshi Kurosawa, Mark McShane
SPECS: 118 minutes; color

Kiyoshi Kurosawa (b. 1955) has worked in several genres, and is especially known for reconceiving the Japanese horror film by incorporating unsettling elements of the supernatural into the ordinary, delineating the commonplace with surprising depth of character. Among such works, perhaps none focus as intently upon the notion of "ordinariness" as strongly as his disturbing 2000 Séance (Kourei), in which a sound-effects engineer and his psychic wife are consumed by unintended consequences in their efforts to aid a kidnapped little girl.

Sato, who works with sound effects and recordings, is a well-respected, easygoing technician dedicated to his work. He is portrayed by Koji Yakusho (b. 1956), a frequent Kurosawa star who has received international acclaim through *Shall We Dance?* (*Shall We Dansu?*, 1996), *Unagi* (*The Eel*, 1997), and other works. His wife, Junko, played by Jun Fubuki (b. 1952), is a psychic who has received only limited recognition for her special skills. These abilities are demonstrated in *Séance*'s opening sequence. While awaiting Hayasaka, a talented student of psychology with a special interest in parapsychological phenomena, she is aware of a presence appearing behind her as she examines a makeup box that had belonged to the observing entity. Junko's breath is visible as she exhales, a sign of a supernatural encounter.

At home Junko consoles a client while Sato unwinds. A nearby table quivers, causing pens and popcorn and loose cigarettes to move slightly as Junko invites the spirit to a séance. Such activity is presented as an unremarkable part of Sato and Junko's everyday lives. After dinner Junko tells her husband that she needs a change and is getting part-time waitressing work. Her sensory abilities continue to operate at the restaurant the next day, as she detects the presence of a visitant lingering near an overworked businessman whose papers are spread over the table. Feeling stressed by it, she takes a break, not responding when it rises in back of her.

Junko desires recognition for both herself and her field. Instead, her facility works against her in the outside world, creating tensions that disturb her in the restaurant, and she quits this job the following day. She sees an opportunity for change when the police ask her to help locate a missing child. Unbeknownst to either Sato or herself, Yoko, the child, has escaped her abductor, and hides in Sato's equipment box while he is recording sounds in the woods. Sato then locks the box and tosses it into his trunk, where it sits in the garage. Junko senses Yoko's presence at home. When she and Sato locate the unconscious Yoko, the medium schemes to achieve greater preeminence by hiding Yoko elsewhere, then informing the authorities where to look. But the plan goes terribly wrong when the weak girl dies, and they instead bury her body in the woods.

The child's apparition appears to them, first while Junko is doing housework, later in front of Sato when he is working outside their house. Director Kurosawa notes in interviews that Japanese ghosts are relatively passive, but that their presence induces tremendous guilt on the offending party. The normally collected Sato attempts to beat the apparition, subsequently imploring it to castigate only him and not his wife. He then sees a doppelgänger (double of himself) expressionlessly watching him work in his yard. Earlier in the film, Hayasaka, the psychology student, had discussed the concept of the doppelgänger with his advisor, hypothesizing that it was an out-of-body projection, often serving as an omen of death. Sato instead confronts his double, dousing him with gasoline and defiantly setting him on fire.

Sato even has a Shinto priest purify his house. When the curate completes his task and tells him he believes the evil has dissipated, Sato asks him for advice concerning what he should do next. The priest responds that peace will be granted to those who live modest lives, and that he should not fear being ordinary. Sato answers that no couple is more ordinary than his wife and himself, but that he simply cannot accept fate. As they part, he asks the holy man if hell exists. The response is that it does if one thinks it so; otherwise, it does not, but he himself doesn't know.

Sometime later Junko is cleaning the bedroom where the couple kept the child, and discovers the little girl's yellow hairpiece nestled on the floor in back of the bed. Meanwhile the police locate Yoko's body. The coroner is confused because the girl's body is too fresh, and she must have died after her kidnapper was arrested. When the detectives question Junko, she performs a false séance, unaware of their discovery. She finally breaks down, clutching the hairpiece, when told that the body has been located.

Junko is presented as someone with talents but is not able to perform ordinary tasks such as waitressing. While many can sympathize and identify with her for her desire for recognition, in her attempt to achieve appreciation, she puts aside the urgent needs of the child and deceptively pushes beyond her actual capabilities. She thus loses all the credibility she has strived for throughout her lifetime. Although not intending to do harm, her actions appear to be illogical, desperate expressions.

Kiyoshi Kurosawa often incorporates images and sounds to heighten the viewer's emotions and fears. As Junko speaks with Hayasaka concerning the circumstances of his late grandmother's death in *Séance*'s initial sequence, she moves in front of an open window in a medium shot. Dynamic leaves suddenly flutter audibly in a tree outside the window directly behind her for just a few seconds to uncannily augment their conversation. In another scene, while Junko folds clothes in her kitchen, a door leading to the garage where the girl is trapped inside the box is preternaturally illuminated then darkened several times, presumably due to the sun and clouds. The small stairway between the kitchen and the garage door later becomes identified with Yoko. While supposedly unconscious in bed upstairs, the girl appears eerily crawling up these steps, her head bent down and covered by her long dark hair. She then faints again. Later, when she returns as a ghostly presence she is first seen here.

Hair can also be subliminally associated with other phantasms as well. The face of the apparition in the restaurant appears featureless, also draped by long black hair. Junko is the only living adult depicted with long hair, which similarly streams over her face while she performs séances. Likewise, Kurosawa focuses on sounds to enhance the atmosphere, not simply those that Sato records, but often through mysterious noises, some drawn from nature, rather than music.

Séance was based on *Séance on a Wet Afternoon* by British author Mark Mc-Shane, a novel also filmed by Bryan Forbes, but Kurosawa substantially changed McShane's work. Originally made for Japanese television, it was shot in 16 mm then blown up to 35 mm. It received several international awards, including the FIPRESCI Prize at the Un Certain Regard section of the 2001 Cannes Film Festival and the Critic's Prize at the Fantasia International Film Festival in Montreal in 2001. It was also nominated for the Woosuk Award at the Jeonju (Korea) Film Festival later that year. *Séance* helped cement Kiyoshi Kurosawa's reputation as a master of horror.—Bill Thompson

See also Cure; Doppelgänger; Kurosawa, Kiyoshi; Pulse; Retribution

Bibliography

D., Chris (Chris Desjardins). *Outlaw Masters of Japanese Film*. London, New York: I.B. Taurus, 2005.
Kurosawa, Kiyoshi, dir. *Séance*. HomeVision, 2005. DVD.
White, Jerry. *The Films of Kiyoshi Kurosawa: Master of Fear*. Berkeley: Stone Bridge Press, 2007.

THE SECRET OF THE TELEGIAN (1960)

Director: Jun Fukuda
Screenplay: Shinichi Sekizawa
Specs: 85 minutes; color

Also known as *The Transmitted Man* or *The Telegraphed Man*, among other alternative titles, *The Secret of the Telegian* (1960) is Toho's follow-up to *The H-Man* (1958) in the "Weird Science Fiction Cinema" franchise. For this entry, *The H-Man*'s director, Ishirō Honda, mired in the production of a relatively large-scale SF film *Battle in Outer Space* (1959), yielded his directorial seat to his longtime assistant director Jun Fukuda (1923–2000). The premise was possibly derived from a short story titled "A Teleported Beauty," written by the well-known Japanese SF writer Jūsa Unno.

The atmospheric opening sequence sets up a locked-room murder mystery. A middle-aged man is stabbed to death by a military bayonet inside the carnival attraction, "Cave of the Demons." The detective assigned to the case, Okazaki, played by Yoshio Tsuchiya (b. 1927), and the meddling but light-footed journalist Kirioka, played by Kōji Tsuruta (1924–1987), quickly realize that the culprit could not have escaped without being seen. Kirioka picks up what looks like a coil for refrigerating equipment, and Okazaki recovers an old Army dog tag, which turns out to belong to one Corporal Sudo, played by Tadao Nakamaru (1933–2009). Getting help from Akiko, played by Yumi Shirakawa (b. 1936), the daughter of the refrigerating machine shop owner who had supplied parts to Sudo and his scientist-employer, Dr. Niki, played by Takamaru Sasaki (1898–1986), Kirioka and Okazaki learn that Sudo has been using Dr. Niki's wartime research regarding electronic teleportation of matter over long distance, to take revenge on a group of former superiors who had absconded with a secret stash of the Imperial Army and left him for dead in the process.

Above all, *The Secret of the Telegian* is certainly entertaining. The reveal of Sudo as a teleported man caught between being a crackling electronic hologram and a flesh-and-blood person, accompanied by appropriately shiver-inducing music and sound effects, is incredibly effective. Nakamaru, usually stuck in the secondary role of a policeman or minor villain until this film, gives a subtle but powerful performance as a cool villain who is nonetheless a victim of the injustices of the Pacific War, invoking audience sympathy. The teleportation machine itself is a well-designed prop, a glowing stack of fluorescent rings encased in clear plastic, anticipating the antiseptic glamour and inhuman efficiency of such high-tech devices of terror seen in David Cronenberg's *The Fly* (1986) and other later SF films. The terror of gradual atomic disintegration, suggested through minimalist but efficient burn-like makeup on Sudo's face as he goes through multiple rounds of teleportation against Dr. Niki's advice, is conveyed well, culminating in the thrilling climax involving a somewhat deus-ex-machina-like earthquake.

The film did not receive a proper DVD release, even in Japan, until quite recently, unlike other titles in the Toho stable of 1960s classics. One of the reasons may be that *The Secret of the Telegian* includes an eyebrow-raising sequence about halfway into the film, in which the cops visit a cabaret run by one of Sudo's archenemies. It turns out that the cabaret is not only managed by a Korean (referred to euphemistically as a "third-country citizen" [*sankokunin*]) but is also organized on the theme of nostalgia for the wartime past. The cabaret's name is "Daihonei" (The General Headquarters), all serving girls are attired in sexed-up naval uniforms, waiters wear the army uniform, the menus are called "Military Rations," hard liquors are called "Missiles" or "Fire-bombs," and so on. Of course, this nostalgic flavor does not prevent the sequence from throwing in a semi-naked dancer body-painted in gold (four years ahead of *Goldfinger* [1964]) dancing provocatively. Why a Toho SF film about human teleportation featured such a contrasting theme sequence is unclear, but it does not seem to have been intended as an overt political statement (the ultra-kitschy quality of the whole sequence may well have been intended by the filmmakers). Combined with the movie's main theme, indictment of the Japanese military technology developed during the Pacific War, this sequence points to a sense of ambivalence on the part of Japanese genre filmmakers toward the wartime memory, the terrible war already becoming a "past" experience, only fifteen years following Japan's defeat.—Kyu Hyun Kim

See also The H-Man; The Human Vapor

SHIKOKU (1999)
DIRECTOR: Shunichi Nagasaki
SCREENPLAY: Takenori Sento, Kunimi Manda
SPECS: 100 minutes; color

Shikoku (1999), the Japanese character for which translates as "The country of the dead," rather than "The four provinces," which is the correct spelling for the Japanese island of Shikoku, is actually set and filmed on location at Kōchi Prefecture on the island. Famous for beef and the Tosa fighting dogs, Shikoku, especially Kōchi, happens to be one of the birthplaces of democratic thought and political parties in late nineteenth-century Japan. It is also a geographically striking region, with dense vegetation, some of it jungle.

Based on the 1996 novel written by the controversial horror-fantasy writer Masako Bandō (1958–2014), a Kōchi native, the film draws upon local myths and religious practices, especially the belief that a spiritually powerful medium could open a portal into the world of the dead, following pilgrimages to the eighty-eight sacred places in the island. "Hinako" (Yui Natsukawa, b. 1968), returns to her hometown in Kōchi after almost a decade. She is reunited with her high school friend Akisawa (Michitaka Tsutsui, b. 1971) but is shocked when she is told Akisawa's former sweetheart Sayori (the erstwhile teenage star Chiaki Kuriyama, b. 1984, well-known stateside due to her appearance in *Kill Bill* vol. 1 [2003]) died at the age of sixteen. She later learns that Sayori's death had something to do with a religious ritual gone horribly wrong, and the girl's medium mother, Teruko (Toshie Negishi, b. 1954), insane with grief, had actually completed her pilgrimage to the eighty-eight sacred sites and is preparing the final rite to bring Sayori back from the dead. Hinako and Akisawa learn that the portal, once opened, could spill out the dead into the living world, and they attempt to stop Teruko. But they are too late, and Sayori comes back from the murky depth of black water, not a day aged from her sixteen-year-old self.

Directed by Shun'ichi Nagasaki (b. 1956)—who was responsible for psychological dramas such as the Sundance-screened *Seducer* (1989) and the Japanese remake (2005) of the Korean masterpiece *Christmas in August* (1998)—*Shikoku* is rather subdued as a horror film, although the scene in which Sayori is resurrected and other scenes depicting supernatural events are suitably atmospheric. The effectiveness of the film depends much on the excellent performances of the leads. Natsukawa expresses her character's not-quite-requited romantic feelings toward Akisawa with subtlety and compassion. Kuriyama, too, is uncommonly good in a physically demanding role, articulating confusion, sorrow, and resentment at having been brought back into a world into which she was not able to naturally grow up. The finale embraces the romantic cliché of a *Romeo and Juliet*, rather than the rite of exorcism that would have restored the rational order, confirming the film's identity as a romantic fantasy under the guise of a horror film.—Kyu Hyun Kim

Bibliography
Nagasaki, Shun'ichi, dir. *Shikoku*. Toho, 1999. Film.

SHIMIZU, TAKASHI (1972–)

The market for horror films is highly unpredictable. Very few producers undertake projects to fund horror movies, as this genre is not as popular as others in mainstream cinema, such as drama, romantic-comedy, thriller, and action. The professional career of the writer and director Takashi Shimizu (b. 1972) started as a maker of two three-minute pieces for the series titled *Gakoo no kaidan G* (*Haunted School G* in English). Shimizu, a young and rather inexperienced director, was hired to work on the made-for-television series.

In his first piece, titled *4444444444*, a high school student receives a phone call from the number 4444444444. When the boy replies to the phone, he hears nothing except a cat meowing. The boy also sees a ghostly boy with blood oozing from his mouth. Actually, the number 4, *shi*, which is a homonym for "death," is an inauspicious number in Japan—a subtle, yet traditional convention that Shimizu incorporated for its eerie appeal.

In the second segment, called *Katasumi* (In a corner), two high school girls go to feed their rabbit. One cuts her finger and the other goes to get a bandage. When she returns, she finds her friend and the rabbit have been killed—and a ghostly woman is crawling toward her.

In February 1998, Takashi released the straight-to-video films *Ju-on* and *Ju-on II*. Like *Ringu*, *Ju-on* also became an underground hit, blending two approaches: US aesthetic trappings and visual and narrative metaphors associated with Japanese culture. Realizing the profit potential, the production houses moved forward in generating a theoretical remake. *Ju-on*, was then released in theaters in 2002 as *Ju-on: The Grudge* followed by release of *Ju-on: The Grudge II* in January 2003—both of which received substantial acclaim.

Although Shimizu is heavily influenced by such US horror cinema hits as *A Nightmare on Elm Street* and *Friday the 13th*, he commonly incorporates Japanese features in his films—capitalizing on the rich spiritual and superstitious traditions of the *kaidan* lore. Shimizu's movies are often said to rely upon atmosphere, as opposed to depending solely upon plot, narratives, and characters.

In general, Shimizu has achieved a fair amount of success through his work and has gone on to develop a respectable career in both the Japanese and North American film industries. Indeed, Sam Raimi, an American film producer, invited Shimizu for an American remake of the Ju-on film series. The remake script was written by Stephen Susco and directed by Shimizu and was later released as *The Grudge*. During this remake, Shimizu directed *Marebito* (2004)—in just eight days—then went on to film two others, titled *White Ghost/Black Ghost*, released on the tenth anniversary of the Ju-on series. Shimizu also directed a Hollywood movie titled *7500*, starring Ryan Kwanten, shot in 2010 and released in 2014. Finally, Shimizu also tried his hand at 3-D films with his *Senritsu meikyû 3D* (*The Shock Labyrinth*) released in 2009 and *Rabitto horâ 3D* (*Tormented*) in 2011.—Amitabh Vikram Dwivedi

See also 4444444444

Bibliography

McRoy, J. *Japanese Horror Cinema*. Edinburgh: Edinburgh University Press, 2006.
Naughton, J., and A. Smith. *Movies: A Crash Course*. New York: Watson-Guptill Publications, 1998.
Schneider, S. J. *Fear without Frontiers: Horror Cinema across the Globe*. Godalming, UK: FAB, 2003.

SHINDŌ, KANETO (1912–2012)

Kaneto Shindō's life spans a century of Japanese cinema; his work covers most of the major film genres in many different filmmaking roles and incorporates key themes and moments in Japan's modern history. Born in Hiroshima in 1912, Shindō began his career as a film developer at Shinko Kinema in Kyoto in 1934. He became interested in scriptwriting after reading several discarded scripts left around the developing department, reading as he dried rolls of film. When the company moved to Tokyo in 1935, Shindō took the place of a colleague who stayed behind in Kyoto and joined the art department under Mizutani Hiroshi.

He began to write film scripts, earning four months' salary for a script that was never made.

In the late 1930s, Shindō became an assistant to director Kenji Mizoguchi, who gave him advice on his scriptwriting and invited him to move to Koa Film, a Shōchiku subsidiary, in 1942. Moving to Shōchiku's main studios in 1943, Shindō's career was interrupted by the war when he was conscripted as an army cleaner. On his return, he secured a scriptwriter's position at Shōchiku, where he worked on award-winning melodramas such as *Anjō ke no butōkai* (*The Ball at the Anjo House*, 1947), directed by Kōzaburō Yoshimura.

Despite this success, Shindō was unhappy at Shōchiku, as was his collaborator, director Kōzaburō Yoshimura. The two formed an independent production company in 1950 called Kindai Eiga Kyōkai, and Shindō made his directorial debut with the autobiographical *Aisai monogatari* (*Story of a Beloved Wife*) in 1951. Nobuko Otowa, who took the role of the wife and would become Shindō's lover, became the foundation of the actor stable Shindō built at Kindai Eiga as he moved from his early melodrama, romance, and social conscience films (known as *keikō eiga* or "tendency films") into the horror genre.

In many senses these early films deal with elements of horror in everyday life; *Genbaku no ko* (*Children of Hiroshima*, 1952) depicts the bombing of Hiroshima in graphic detail, considering it was commissioned by the Teacher's Union of Japan, while *Shukuzu* (1953) focuses on the harsh conditions of life as a geisha. *Daigo Fukuryū Maru* (*Lucky Dragon Number 5*, 1959), an account of the suffering of the fishermen exposed to nuclear fallout after an American test in the Bikini Atoll, returns to the nuclear theme, incorporating the visual style of the *kaiju eiga* or monster genre in the depiction of the horrors at sea. Such serious and often depressing fare was often critically lauded, but struggled at the box office and the new company suffered financial instability until the widespread critical acclaim for *Hadaka no shima* (*Naked Island*) in 1960.

By Shindō's horror debut with *Onibaba* in 1964, the director had developed both a stock cast and a visual language for the depiction of suffering and terror. The film draws on these staples, with the addition of cinematography by Kiyomi Kuroda and a striking score from Hayashi Hikaru. It was a critical and popular success, winning the Grand Prix at the 1964 Panama Film Festival and Blue Ribbon awards for the cinematography and supporting actress. Shindō's next three films *Akutō* (1965), *Honnō* (*Lost Sex*, 1966), and *Sei no kigen* (*Libido* 1967) dealt with sexuality and nuclear issues, but continued the eerie tone of *Onibaba*, as did his script for *Manji* (dir. Masumura Yasuzō, 1964). He returned to the horror genre with *Kuroneko* in 1968, winning the Mainichi awards for Best Actress for Otowa and Best Cinematography for Kiyomi Kuroda.

Shindō Kaneto directed more than forty-five films in his lifetime, and contributed to many more as scriptwriter, art director, and collaborator. He was awarded the Person of Cultural Merit Award in 1998, the Golden St. George at the Twenty-First Moscow International Film Festival in 1999, the Order of Culture in 2002, and the Japan Academy Lifetime Award in 2003. His legacy has reinvigorated the local film scene in Hiroshima; a website dedicated to "100 years of Shindō Kaneto" celebrates his efforts to tell the world about postwar life in Hiroshima, supported by Hiroshima Prefecture, the City of Hiroshima, the Hiroshima

City of the Future Foundation, Hiroshima Chamber of Commerce and Industry, and several other municipal bodies. Shindō also contributed to scholarship on Japanese film studies, publishing several manuscripts on his mentor, Mizoguchi Kenji, a biography of the actor Tonoyama Taiji, and accounts of his own script-writing and filmmaking career, as well as his experience of old age. While many scholars struggle to analyze Shindō's output due to its diversity and ever-changing style, his impact on Japanese cinema is undeniable.—Jennifer Coates

Bibliography

Anon. "100 Years of Kaneto Shindō." Accessed 5 January 2015. http://hyakunennokiseki.web.fc2.com/en_about.html.

Hirano, Kyoko. "Shindō Kaneto." *Film Reference*. Accessed 5 January 2015. http://www.filmreference.com/Directors-Sc-St/Shindō-Kaneto.html.

Shindō, Kaneto. *11 sai no ryugi*. Edited by Nagase, Hiroko. Tokyo: PHP Kenkyūsho, 2012.

Shindō, Kaneto, dir. *Aisai monogatari*. Kindai Eiga Kyōkai, 1951. Film.

SHIRAISHI, KŌJI (1973–)

From the mid-1990s onward, Japanese horror has been dominated by Hideo Nakata, Kiyoshi Kurosawa, Takashi Shimizu, and Norio Tsuruta. Since their ascendancy, there have been few new contenders. Veterans like Takashi Miike, Shūsuke Kaneko, and Yukihiko Tsutsumi have directed occasional horror films—some of them excellent—but have no allegiance to the genre as a whole, while comparative newcomers like Yoshihiro Nakamura will take on horror projects as a way to further their fledgling careers, but quickly move on to other pastures. The only new director of the past decade to have built up a consistent career making horror movies is Kōji Shiraishi, who has since become one of the mainstays of contemporary Japanese horror.

Although his first project—an uninspired hybrid of *Ju-on: The Grudge* (2002) and *Memento* (2001) released in the United States as *Ju-rei: The Uncanny*—did not bode well for the young director, Shiraishi found himself in good company with the next one, a V-cinema anthology known internationally as *Dark Tales of Japan*. He was one of two newcomers that contributed (the other being Yoshihiro Nakamura), as well as heavyweights Takashi Shimizu, Norio Tsuruta, and Masayuki Ochiai. To his credit, Shiraishi's segment is one of the best.

More importantly it brought Shiraishi into contact with Takashige Ichise, who produced his next film, the fake documentary *The Curse* (2005). Purporting to be an account of the final investigation undertaken by a journalist who has since disappeared, *The Curse* covers a lot of ground in its 115-minute running time, from TV shows about psychic schoolchildren to bizarre rural cults and mass suicides. Fully conversant with reality TV and the Japanese fascination with the supernatural, the film's pseudo-veracity is reinforced by a string of plausible cameos, including historian and horror novelist Hiroshi Aramata, popular TV host and former AV star Ai Iijima, and comedy duo The Ungirls. Compelling, grotesque, and genuinely scary, *The Curse* is among the best of its kind.

Shiraishi has returned to the field a number of times, with diminishing results. *Occult* (2009) begins as an investigation into a spree killing at a Japanese tourist resort, but changes direction halfway through when it becomes clear that one of the victims is building up to his own act of mass murder. The film is consistently engaging and often chilling but is undercut by a humorous ending. *Shirome* (2010) is one of Shiraishi's best, with real-life pop idols Momoiro Clover recruited as ghost-hunters exploring the legend of "Shirome," a deity who grants wishes to the pure of heart but drags the impure down to hell. Unaware that it's all an elaborate practical joke, the girls are suitably terrified when things start to happen, with Shiraishi ramping up the tension mercilessly. *Cult* (2013), the director's second attempt at this process, is far less successful, thanks to a mundane premise and poor effects. When these films are viewed together, it becomes clear that Shiraishi has a tendency to repeat himself; the unconscious scribbling in *The Curse* also shows up in *Occult*, for example.

Away from the found-footage/fake documentary niche, Shiraishi has been less prolific. His first feature film after *The Curse* was *Carved: The Slit-Mouthed Woman* (2007), a film based on the popular Japanese urban legend of the *kuchi-sake-onna* ("slit-mouthed woman"), a mutilated ghost who stalks her prey with a surgical mask and a large pair of scissors. In *Carved*, she is the vengeful spirit of an abusive parent whose child was forced to kill her in self-defense after the deaths of his siblings. With a sensitive issue at its core and several scenes of cruelty to children, *Carved* is hardly light viewing, which explains its low-key release outside Japan. Rushed into production following a sudden revival in the legend's popularity, the film was preceded by an AV ("adult video," the Japanese term for hardcore pornography) version and followed by a sequel and a prequel. Shiraishi returned to urban legends for the V-cinema releases *Teke Teke* and *Teke Teke 2* (both 2009), efficiently scary films about a legless vengeful spirit who chops her victims in half.

Shiraishi joined the ranks of notorious Japanese directors in 2009, when his film *Grotesque* (2009) was refused a certificate from the British Board of Film Classification (the BBFC), effectively banning it from screening or release within the United Kingdom. The film in question is an unpleasant example of "torture porn," the subgenre that flourished in the wake of *Saw* (2004) and *Hostel* (2005). Despite these problems, Shiraishi continues to be one of the more interesting directors working in the contemporary Japanese horror scene.—Jim Harper

SHIROME (2010)

DIRECTOR: Kōji Shiraishi
SCREENPLAY: Kōji Shiraishi
SPECS: 83 minutes; color

Shirome is a 2010 Japanese horror film directed by Kōji Shiraishi (b. 1973). The action of this film is preceded by a text describing the "urban legend" of Shirome. Shirome is a spirit that resides in an empty school building and grants wishes. Inside the building there is a butterfly painted on the wall. The legend says that if someone stands in front of it, calls out to Shirome three times, and makes a serious wish, Shirome will grant that wish. However, if someone enters the building to mock or if a wish is made insincerely, Shirome will appear with huge white glaring eyes (*Shirome* translates as "White eyes") and drag the mocker straight to hell.

Shirome is, in part, a mock "found-footage" style film, stating that it is made up of footage from a cable television show that was not broadcast because the content was too controversial. The action proper begins with an in-progress performance by Momoiro Clover, a female idol group, energetically singing and dancing in a rehearsal studio. Momoiro Clover is a genuine Japanese singing group (who have since added a "Z" to their name) that film and television director Kōji Shiraishi builds his film around. Shiraishi plays himself within the film, which is structured as an informal documentary about filming the group's visit to Shirome for a "survival entertainment" television program where celebrities investigate haunted houses and other supernatural sites. The group is very emotive, whimpering, and falling to their knees as they listen.

A teller of ghostly tales is brought into the studio to talk with the panicky girls. He tells them there are a number of walls in the area with mysterious butterfly paintings. He also adds details about those who were not sincere and sure of their wish and so taken by Shirome. Some went missing, some died accidentally, and some committed suicide. The storyteller falls to the floor and vomits.

The film stops here, and when it begins again Shiraishi is explaining the schedule for the group's visit to Shirome. The group sings and dances through another song, then agree on a group wish to make to Shirome. They will wish to perform on a famous singing competition show. Sitting in a brightly lit, gleaming room the director asks the girls if they would sell their souls to the devil to achieve their wish. They all say they would.

The group has a sleep-over on the floor of the rehearsal studio. One girl says she feels like they are being watched. They wave to the camera and turn it off, but a night-vision style shot soon appears—with the static interference that marks the found-footage horror genre. One girl sits up, looks around, and the tape ends. On the bus the next day they sing songs about how to be cute and have soft cheeks, and songs about their perky personalities. Then one of the girls says she heard a sound like footsteps the night before, and saw white eyes on the ceiling. Another says she saw the same thing.

They are blindfolded and taken to the school building. The girls begin whimpering again, but their desire to be on the television show is stronger than their fears. Shiraishi introduces a psychic and an exorcist to help them prepare. They all go into the school, where the storyteller joins them. The exorcist warns them against trying to use Shirome for television ratings. The storyteller becomes possessed and has to be taken away.

The girls all have videos cameras and enter the building; they are perky and confident again. The spirit makes noise; the girls sing to buoy their spirits. They find Shirome's schoolroom. The psychic tries to get them to leave, but they press on, occasionally breaking into song. Inside the dark classroom they find the butterfly on the wall. They have a CD player and dance and sing their wish, then address the butterfly directly. There is a great deal of clatter from an unknown source, a loud groaning, and a strange figure is seen looming over the girls. Once again the film is interrupted.

The film resumes with the girls performing on the television show. As they perform, their boy fans at the edge of the stage appear to sicken. The director's voice says they may have been cursed. He again asks them if they would sell their souls and they all say yes. The girls collapse and a ghostly figure descends over them. The narration then says that Momoiro Clover's popularity is ever increasing. The film ends.

While *Shirome* belongs to the horror film genre, it seems aimed directly at pre-adolescent and very young teen viewers.—William Bamberger

SHIRŌ, SANO (1955–)

Born in Yamanashi Prefecture on 4 March 1955, Sano Shirō lived in Tokyo and Matsue, Shimane, as a child, but returned to Tokyo when he entered art school. During this time, he joined several theatrical troupes, among them the Jōkyō Gekijō, founded by Japanese dramatist Jurō Kara (b. 1940). While his first starring role was in the film *To Sleep So as to Dream* (1986, Yume Miruyoni Nemuritai) under the direction of newcomer Hayashi Kaizō (b. 1957), it would be some years later before he found his artistic niche as a young, aloof, and perverted business-man. Once he landed such a role as the psychologically deviant Fuyuhiko in the television drama *I Have Always Loved You* (1992), he attracted critical note and, almost immediately, a particular cult following. The series is made up of thirteen episodes.

The storyline of this drama appears at first to be straightforward. A decade earlier, finding herself caught in an unbalanced love triangle of a sort, Miwa's friend committed suicide. The suicide caused the entire town to put the blame on the couple. The action begins as Miwa and Yosuke happen to meet again. Though the love between them still exists, the reality makes their being together impossible. Miwa is getting married soon, and Yosuke has then established a new relationship with Ritsuko. Unfortunately, Miwa's marriage proves a failure, and yet she seems unable to resolve her situation. Over the course of the series, the underlying psychological suspense becomes increasingly complicated, as she begins to reflect on her previous commitment to Yosuke. As she does, she once more sets into motion a series of unfortunate events that brings harm to those she loves.

Shirō has also appeared in such films as *Tokyo: The Megalopolis* (1988), a *tokusatsu* (a term that applies to any live-action film or television drama featuring considerable use of special effects) historical fantasy/science fiction epic film directed by Jissoji Akio (1937–2006); *Four Days of Snow and Blood* (1989); *Violent Cop* (1989), directed by Takeshi Kitano (b. 1947); *Evil Dead Trap 2* (1991), directed by Izō Hashimoto (b. 1954); *Evil Dead Trap 3: Broken Love Killer* (1993), directed by Toshiharu Ikeda (1954–2010); *Uneasy Encounters* (1994), directed by Makoto Wada (b. 1972); *Godzilla Millenium* (1999), directed by Takao Okawara (1949); *The Princess Blade* (2001), directed by video-game designer Shinsuke Sato (1970); *Godzilla Mothra, and King Ghidorah: Giant Monsters All-Out* (2001), directed by Shuske Kaneko (b. 1955); *Godzilla: Final Wars* (2004), directed by Ryuhei Kitamura (b. 1969); *Infection* (2004), directed by Masayuki Ochiai (b. 1958); *Ah! House Collapses!* (2004), directed by Naoki Kubo and Ito Terry (1949); *The Great Yokai War* (2005), directed by Takashi Miike (b. 1960); *Waiting in the Dark* (2006), directed by Daisuke Tengan (b. 1959); *Persona* (2008); and *Nobody to Watch Over Me* (2009), directed by Ryōichi Kimizuka (b. 1958).

Additionally, with the film *Karaoke* (1999) and the television series *Tales of Terror* (2003), for example, Shirō established himself early in his career as a nononsense director with an acute sense for detail.—James A. Wren

Bibliography

Clements, Jonathan, and Makoto Tamamuro. *The Dorama Encyclopedia: A Guide to Japanese TV Drama since 1953*. Berkeley, CA: Stone Bridge Press, 2003.
Jissoji, Akio, dir. *Tokyo: The Last Megalopolis*. Toho, 1988. Film.
Ochiai, Masayuki, dir. *Infection*. Toho, 2004. Film.
Okawara, Takao, dir. *Godzilla 2000*. Toho, 1999. Film.
Sato, Shinsuke, dir. *Princess Blade*. GAGA, 2001. Film.

SONO, SION (1961–)

Born in Aichi Prefecture in 1961, the writer/director Sion Sono started his career as a poet at the age of seventeen. The IPA fellowship helped him to choose a career as a film director. Sono's films often narrate the tales of socially marginalized youths, typically teenagers and young adults. These subjects are commonly portrayed as indulging in criminal activities or as victims of sexual abuse, extortion, and murder. Most of the scenes in his films contain blood and graphic violence that resonate with various anime and *pinku eiga* themes couched in the Japanese film industry.

As early as his years as a student, Sono found success in making shorts on Super 8 film. In the late 1980s and 1990s, he succeeded in making and starring in his debut feature film titled *Bicycle Sighs* (*Jitensha toiki*). Released in 1990, *Bicycle Sighs*—a feature-length film shot in 16 mm—received worldwide acclaim and helped to establish his career as a cult director. A tale of two underachievers, *Bicycle Sighs* tells the story of Shiro and Keita and how they survive in perfectionist Japan. In addition to directing, Sono also cowrote and starred in the film.

Sono's second feature film *The Room* (*Heya*), released in 1992, is a tale of a serial killer who is in search of a room. With the assistance of a real estate agent this serial killer protagonist succeeds in locating a room in a bleak and isolated district in the outskirts of Tokyo—perfect for his ominous ventures. The film was well received and honored with Sundance Film Festival's Special Jury Prize. This film was also featured in forty-nine other film festivals, including the Rotterdam Film Festival and the Berlin Film Festival.

In 2002, Sono wrote and directed *Suicide Circle*. The film features the eerie tale of a seemingly unrelated wave of suicides among schoolgirls. Strikingly strange and unusual, *Suicide Circle* went on to win the Jury Prize for the "Most Ground-Breaking Film" at the Fantasia Film Festival—perhaps attributable to the way in which Sono indirectly addressed contemporary notions of youth suicides in Japan.

Similar to his style of direction displayed in *Bicycle Sighs*, in 2005 he wrote and directed *Into a Dream* (*Yume no naka e*), about the life of a theater group member searching through his past to find the individual that infected him with a sexually transmitted disease.

Shortly after *Into a Dream*, Sono went onto write and direct his 2005 release titled *Noriko's Dinner Table*. The film tells the story of an investigation of the suicides of fifty-four schoolgirls and is a prequel to his *Suicide Circle. Noriko's Dinner Table* was featured in twelve different film festivals across the globe. For this film, Sono received a Don Quixote Award and a Special Mention at the Karlovy Vary Film Festival for his superb direction.

Later in 2005, Sono wrote, directed, composed, and cinematographed *Strange Circus (Kimyo na sakasu)*. A horror drama, *Strange Circus* tells the story of bizarre incest-laden relationships between a father and daughter and the subsequent jealous rampages such relationships generate—in particular the vengeful actions of the mother, who unleashes her wrath upon her young victimized daughter after watching her be violated by the father. As the film contains all the components of sexual and familial taboos, Sono is squarely within his element.

Sono's 2008 release, titled *Love Exposure (Ai no mukidashi)*, deals with the themes of lust, love, family, and the art of "upskirt photography." Despite the length of the film—even its shortened version is four hours long—*Love Exposure* received many awards in various film festivals, including the Caligari Film Award.

In addition to *Love Exposure* and adding to what has been dubbed his "Trilogy of Hate," Sono directed two films in quick succession, titled *Cold Fish* (2010) and *Guilty of Romance* (2011). *Cold Fish* is a story of a tropical fish store owner whose family and life are taken over by a mad and power-hungry sociopath set on extorting labor and money. Premiered in the Sixty-Seventh Venice International Film Festival, this movie received the best screenplay award in Fantastic Fest 2010.—Amitabh Vikram Dwivedi

Bibliography

Balmain, C. *Introduction to Japanese Horror Film*. Edinburgh: Edinburgh University Press, 2008.

Harper, J. *Flowers from Hell: The Modern Japanese Horror Film*. Hereford, UK: Noir, 2008.

McRoy, J. *Japanese Horror Cinema*. Honolulu: University of Hawaii Press, 2005.

McRoy, J. *Nightmare Japan: Contemporary Japanese Horror Cinema*. Amsterdam: Rodopi, 2008.

SŌSEIJI (1999)

DIRECTOR: Shin'ya Tsukamoto
SCREENPLAY: Shin'ya Tsukamoto
SPECS: 84 minutes; color

This 1999 psychological horror/thriller, also known as *Gemini*, moves at a different pace for director Shin'ya Tsukamoto (b. 1960), who also directed *Tetsuo: The Iron Man* and *Tokyo Fist*, among others. Here, Tsukamoto adapted famed mystery writer Edogawa Rampo's (1894–1965) short story "Sōseiji: Aru shikeishū ga kyokaishi ni uchiaketa hanashi" ("The Twins: A Condemned Criminal's Confession to a Priest"), about twin brothers and how their different lives intersect causing death, heartbreak, and mayhem.

Set in the Meiji period, the film opens with an animal carcass being eaten by filthy rats and maggots, which is immediately juxtaposed with a clean waiting room filled with eager patients. The awaiting patients are there to see Yukio Daitokuji (Masahiro Motoki, b. 1965), a celebrated doctor and war hero in the village. He lives an affluent life with his wife, Rin (Ryō, b. 1973); his parents; and ample servants for his home and practice. Even though Yukio and Rin are quite happy, Yukio's mother (Shiho Fujimura, b. 1939) has never completely accepted Rin, who is an amnesiac. Yukio also keeps the way he met Rin a secret; he had found her by a river naked and traumatized by a fire, which was what prompted the loss of her memory.

During dinner one evening, Yukio feels torn between helping patients he deems useless and putting them out of their misery. His father (Yasutaka Tsutsui, b. 1934) reminds him that God is the only one in charge of dispatching lives. Yukio also mentions a sense of melancholy and a shadowy figure in the house that makes him very uneasy, but his father slyly assures him that all of that is nonsense. The next day, a mysterious stench invades the house and they search for the cause, and later, Rin hears noises in the night only to find her father-in-law gruesomely murdered.

Yukio's mother is devastated and thinks Rin is responsible for the murder, but after drinking late into the night, she asks for forgiveness. Still acting strangely, she sees a shadowy figure in the darkness, and is frozen in terror as a man who is the spitting image of Yukio covered in dirt, rags, and fur does a demonic dance and cartwheels through the house, revealing a snake-like birthmark on his leg. She clutches at her chest, and having a weak heart, dies from the sight.

After having the house searched by the police, Yukio is disturbed by the two deaths and unsettled by his own image. That night, a woman from the slums brings her sick baby for help, and at the same time, the mayor has had a drunken accident. Yukio decides to help the mayor and has the mother and child swept away, fearing the plague they may carry. Later, Rin argues with Yukio because she feels he made a choice based on class and his disgust for the poor and sick. He expresses a wish that the slums be burned down with the inhabitants and cruelly reminds her that she is validated by him because she doesn't know who she is.

The following morning, finding himself alone, Yukio hears a noise in the garden. He is attacked and thrown down an old well by his doppelgänger. This double is none other than Yukio's twin brother, Sutekichi (also played by Motoki), who has the same mannerisms as Yukio. He closes the office for a spell, sanitizing the area in case of plague and letting the staff take a short holiday. Sutekichi had been put adrift on the river after birth because of an imperfection: a snake-like birthmark. He was found by a street performer and raised in the slums, making his living by stealing and dancing with the street troupe. Growing up poor because of his family's elitist vanity, he is filled with hate and gets his revenge by killing his parents and taking over Yukio's life. Rin's secret past is also revealed: She was Sutekichi's lover, and they were wild and ruthless together. Rin has been hiding her identity under the guise of an amnesiac. She is unaware that Sutekichi is now masquerading as Yukio until she has a dream reliving their renegade life. It is then that she starts to suspect the differences in the imposter Yukio's behavior, but Sutekichi maintains his role and makes her think she is unstable.

Sutekichi keeps Yukio alive, regularly throwing food down the well while threatening to harm Yukio's patients and taunting him about bedding his wife. Finally, Yukio pleads for death, so Sutekichi tells him to kill himself and throws a knife down the well. Yukio uses the knife to climb out of the well, and covered in filth and rags, fights Sutekichi, finally strangling him. This violent act leaves Yukio distraught, as he has become the very thing he loathed. Meanwhile Rin returns to the river and is about to surrender to the frosty waters because she is remorseful about deceiving Yukio, when she hears him call her name. He now looks like Sutekichi.

Nine months later, Rin gives birth to twins, presumably the spawn of Sutekichi, one with a snake birthmark on his leg. They start the cycle once more by sending the marked child down the river, and he is discovered by a slum dweller. Yukio's life seems normal again, but he is a changed man. One day he follows a dirty child to the slums where we see smoke rising from the makeshift buildings as fires smolder.

Tsukamoto adds his signature commentary on transformations to Rampo's short story about a brother's greed, making it a complex period horror piece about class, corruption, and duality. It is different from his usual frenetic bloodbaths, being more of a haunting family melodrama punctuated by the tension-building score of Tsukamoto's longtime composer collaborator, Chu Isikawa. Although Tsukamoto is known for doing mainly independent film, the Toho-commissioned *Sōseiji* was well received, and with star power like the ex-boy-band member turned award-winning actor, Motoki, it went on to win three international film festival awards (Catalonian International Film Festival, 2000, Pusan International Film Festival, 1999, and Neuchatel International Fantasy Film Festival, 2000). This deep-seated social commentary about appearances and the evils of privilege is still lauded as a brilliant and artful departure from Tsukamoto's more violent fare.—Carolyn Mauricette

See also: *Tetsuo: The Iron Man*; Tsukamoto, Shin'ya

Bibliography

Mes, Tom, and Jasper Sharp. "Shinya Tsukamoto." In *The Midnight Eye Guide to New Japanese Film*, 143–57. Berkeley, CA: Stone Bridge Press, 2005.
Rampo, Edogawa. "The Twins (A Condemned Criminal's Confession to a Priest)." In *Japanese Tales of Mystery and Imagination*. Translated by James B. Harris, 135–51. Tokyo and Rutland, VT: Tuttle Publishing, 2012.
Tsukamoto, Shin'ya, dir. *Sōseiji* (*Twins*). Sedic International Inc., Marubeni, 1999. DVD.

SPLATTER: NAKED BLOOD (1996)

DIRECTOR: Hisayasu Satō
SCREENPLAY: Taketoshi Watari
SPECS: 76 minutes; color

With fifty-eight features to his name since 1985, Hisayasu Satō has emerged as one of Japanese cinema's most prolific directors. He is also one of its most daring visual artists, frequently deploying low-budget, guerilla filmmaking tactics to tell stories that range in genre from darkly themed soft-core erotica, or "pink films" (*pinku eiga*), to works of science fiction and horror. It is to these latter genres that 1996's *Splatter: Naked Blood* most explicitly conforms, though it is not without sequences designed to titillate audiences by capitalizing on cinema's role as a voyeuristic medium capable of arousing our senses even as it confronts our sensibilities.

In *Splatter: Naked Blood*, Eiji, a seventeen-year-old genius with a predilection for science, invents a painkiller that causes the human brain to construe pain as pleasure. Eiji sees his invention, which his christens Myson, as an attempt to continue his late father's quest to use science's potential to help humanity transcend its physical and philosophical limitations. Desperate for human test subjects, Eiji slips his elixir into an intravenous contraceptive that his mother, an established scientist, subsequently administers to three young women. These unwitting test subjects include: a woman obsessed with physical beauty, a woman for whom eating is the greatest pleasure, and Mikami, a woman who hasn't slept since the "shock" of the onset of her menses "blocked" her "sleep cycle." Eiji chronicles Myson's impact by surreptitiously videotaping the three women as they go about their daily activities. Nothing, however, can prepare him for what he witnesses through his camera's viewfinder. The woman for whom beauty equals pleasure pierces her body with a seemingly endless array of sharp objects, eventually transforming herself into a human pincushion. In a series of equally unsettling scenes, the woman for whom eating is "joy" literally consumes herself through graphically rendered acts of auto-cannibalism.

When Mikami catches Eiji spying on her with his video camera, she experiences her disdain for his voyeurism as romantic arousal. She brings Eiji into her private world by showing him her "sleeping installation," a virtual reality unit that, attached to a cactus (which Mikami feels is the most "peaceful" of plants), allows her to experience a dreamlike state by showing her the "scenery" of her heart. As the narrative builds toward its climax, Mikami murders her fellow test subjects and then slices a gaping vaginal-shaped wound in Eiji's mother's stomach. Finally, after a cyber-enhanced sexual encounter with Eiji, Mikami injects the young scientist with Myson before cutting his throat. In the film's final sequence, set several years after Eiji's death, we see Mikami and her young son—also named Eiji—traveling throughout the countryside and spraying the air with a substance that might be Myson. Before driving off on a motorcycle equipped with a canister and spraying tube, she tells her son: "I think I'll go west today. It hasn't spread there yet." Her child, in a moment of direct address, meets our gaze and says: "The dream has not ended yet."

Akin to works by filmmakers ranging from Canada's David Cronenberg and France's Gaspar Noe to Japan's Shinji Tsukamoto and Yoshihiro Nishimura, Hisayasu Satō's *Splatter: Naked Blood* can perhaps best be described as an example of "body horror" in that it uses the traumatized human form as a means of exploring a nexus of cultural and political concerns. For example, through explicit scenes of self-mutilation and murder, as well as by having an intravenous contraceptive delivered by a female scientist (Eiji's mother) serve as the carrier for Eiji's paternally inspired analgesic, Myson (the very name of which is suggestive of patriarchal power/lineage), Satō explores dominant gender codes by depicting female desire and the masculine attempt to control such passions as potentially dangerous or destructive. Similarly, in overtly confrontational sequences like the infamous self-cannibalization scene, during which the young woman for whom eating is the greatest of pleasures uses a knife and fork to devour her own vulva, Sato inventively challenges Japanese censorship regulations. By blatantly displaying that which can't be shown legally in Japanese cinema (human genitalia) through the removal of the "obscene" object from its traditional context, Sato at once shocks his audience and begs them to confront the very logics that inform such prohibitions. Lastly, both Eiji's video camera and the virtual reality device through which his sexual encounter with Mikami is filtered function as metaphors for the ways that technology mediates and conditions many of our most intimate human relations.—Jay McRoy

STACY (2001)

DIRECTOR: Naoyuki Tomomatsu
SCREENPLAY: Chisato Ōgawara
SPECS: 76 minutes; color

Stacy, also known as Stacy: Attack of the School Girl Zombies and known as Stacii in Japan, is the title of director Naoyuki Tomomatsu's darkly comic adaptation of rock musician Kenji Otsuki's graphic novel. The film, released in 2001 explores an alternate reality where a virus has infected every girl between the ages of 15 and 17, turning them into flesh-eating zombies. Tomomatsu shot the film on digital video, which gives the appropriately garish special effects a cartoonish appearance.

The world is stunned by the disease that is killing young high-school-aged women, a disease of unknown origin and no cure on the horizon, that the world has nicknamed "Stacies." Tomomatsu uses a narrator to inform the viewer of the history of the disease. The first sign of the fatal illness is a state of euphoria called "Near Death Happiness" (NDH) that causes the victim to act giddy. The victims die soon afterward and are then reanimated into bloodthirsty zombies whose skin turns glowing blue because of a substance called "Butterfly Twinkle Powder." The disease has been infecting victims for ten years worldwide at the movie's opening scene. The "Romero Rekill Special Unit" is the governmental agency charged with disposing of the reanimated bodies. It is illegal for anyone other than a family member to perform a rekill.

A group of puppeteers, including Shibukawa (Toshinori Omi, b. 1965) and Matsui (Makoto Sakamoto, b. 1977), watch a recruitment video for the Romero troops while they work. As they discuss the possibility of conscription for military service, Tomomatsu intercuts shots of a zombie schoolgirl's body riddled by bullets with the dance of a lifeless puppet. As Shibukawa's coworkers leave for home, one comments that no one cares about puppet shows anymore, a notion that disturbs Shibukawa.

Matsui decides his fate lies with the military, leaving Shibukawa alone with the dolls. A girl appears in the studio, introducing herself as Eiko, soon to become a Stacy. She's decided that Shibukawa should be the person who will perform her rekill.

Matsui is assigned to a squad led by Captain Sunaga (Shungiku Uchida, b. 1959). She orders Matsui to protect the movie's mad scientist, Dr. Inugami (author Yasutaka Tsutsui, b. 1934), while his fellow new recruit Arita (Yamazaki Katsuyuki, b. 1976) is given the task of becoming Sunaga's sex toy. In fact, Arita has joined the military to find his lost love, Momo, and perform the rekill.

Next, Tomomatsu introduces the "Drew Illegal Killing Unit," a trio of young girls led by Nozomi (Chibana Hayashi, b. 1982). In Tokyo, potential Stacies are picking handsome young gigolos to perform their rekilling (like the men of Host Clubs), and these three girls have decided to promote themselves as rekillers for hire to raise the money to pay the most popular choice for rekilling.

Throughout the film's scenes featuring the Romero troops, one trooper constantly mentions a series of murders of teenage girls that happened before the onset of the disease. He wonders how the other men, most too young to recall, could be so indifferent to the carnage they witness daily. In his angst, he draws his weapon on the team. But before any shots can be fired, Eiko appears with her NDH-powered optimism and quells the anger with a thank you. She tells the men that it's alright to cry over the Stacies, and they cry buckets of tears.

The film meanders before allowing all the disparate elements to coalesce. Matsui, disturbed by the zombie experiments, starts to believe the girls are being manipulated by a godlike, amoral "puppet master" via the Twinkle powder and decides to set them free. Chaos ensues. His fellow soldiers are killed, except for Arita, who finds his love, Momo, and runs off with her. The Drew unit appears at the facility to execute a contract kill, but end up battling, and losing to, the Romero troops who have been following them. One of the Romero squad is the man responsible for the serial killing referenced earlier, and as the Drew unit lies dead, they reanimate as Stacies to absolve him of his crime.

After the chaos, we return to Eiko and Shibukawa. He's completely enamored of her now in her last hours as a human, and can fulfill her wish to be the person to rekill her. He has decided to turn her story into a play, and we learn in the bizarre epilogue that the play has become the bible of a new world. Stacies are now integrated into society and have relationships and children, and those children usher in a new world.

The "moe" phenomenon in Japanese culture may be helpful in understanding what can be a confusing and convoluted plot. "Moe" can be thought of as a depiction of female characters in fictional works who are young; attractive; and, above all, demure and devoted to a male figure. Whenever Eiko appears on screen alone, she's filmed in soft focus (as soft as digital could get in 2000), sometimes accompanied by a glow, always accompanied by a plaintive piano score.

Hayao Miyazaki discussed the subject in an interview with author/film-maker Ryū Murakami in 1988, stating, "Now, there are too many people who shamelessly depict (such heroines) as if they just want (such girls) as pets, and things are escalating more and more."

Miyazaki's comments predated the popular use of "Moe" as slang, but his description explains *Stacy* as well as anything could. The colliding storylines, zombie film references, and *Robocop*-like satire obscures Tomomatsu's exploration of theme. However, he does drop a few clues. The men, mostly middle aged but all older than most of the women in *Stacy*, interact with the girls as objects, whether Dr. Inugami is performing experiments on their body parts or Tomomatsu is comparing them to dolls. They may be protective of the girls, unreasonably so in Arita's case, but still end up destroying them.

The Drew unit represents a different type of character from Eiko and her hapless peers. The girls took their name after American actress Drew Barrymore, ostensibly in her *Charlie's Angels* guise as a tough, but sweet crime fighter. Nozomi has dyed her hair blonde to resemble Barrymore, while one of the other girls cosplays as Chun-Li from the *Street Fighter II* game. They are trying to exercise agency in their own death while the Romero troops are out to stop them. When they fail in their attempt, they too become posthumous cheerleaders for the male figures who (re)murder them.

Dr. Inugami discovers that the Twinkle powder activates when the Stacies are nearby someone they love. A test subject glows when a picture of her and her boyfriend is on the dissection table, and Momo turns into a blue moon when Arita appears in front of her. The parodic and satirical elements in the film would suggest that Tomomatsu finds "moe" ridiculous. However, the twenty minutes he spends with Eiko, the epitome of moe subservience, at the end of the film suggests that the pink cinema director may be as susceptible to moe charms as anyone.—Mark N. Mays

Bibliography

Henwood-Greer, Eric (ed.). "Why Heroines in Miyazaki Works: A Collection of Short Excerpts." Trans. by Ryoko Toyama. Nausicaa.net. http://www.nausicaa.net/miyazaki/interviews/heroines .html

McG, dir. *Charlie's Angels*. Columbia Pictures Corporation, 2000. Film.

Tomomatsu, Naoyuki, dir. *Stacy*. GAGA, 2001. Film.

Verhooven, Paul, dir. *Robocop*. Orion Pictures, 1987. Film.

STRANGE CIRCUS (2005)

DIRECTOR: Shion Sono
SCREENPLAY: Shion Sono
SPECS: 108 minutes; color

Strange Circus, known as *Kimyō na sākasu* in Japanese, is a 2005 horror-drama film written and directed by Sion Sono (b. 1961). The film tells the story of a young suicidal girl, her jealous mother, and her sex-crazed, depraved father who works as the principal at her school. The viewer is invited into the family's home as a series of tragic events unfold, including incest, rape, physical abuse, and murder, which are graphically depicted and interspersed between scenes of a macabre circus freak show. Only later is it revealed that these events are apparently the fictional content of a book being written by a famous author, but appearances are not what they seem. The film received a positive reception both at home and abroad with screenings and awards won at several international film festivals.

The film follows the highly dysfunctional family of a schoolgirl named Mitsuko, played by Rie Kuwana (b. 1993) and Mai Takahashi (b. 1984). Mitsuko's life takes a tragic turn when, drawn by unfamiliar sounds, she inadvertently peeks into her parents' room while they are copulating. As a consequence, her father, Gozo, played by Hiroshi Oguchi (b. 1950), places Mitsuko in a cello case in which he has cut out a peephole and forces her to watch as he engages in aggressive sex with his wife, Sayuri, played by Masumi Miyazaki (b. 1968). Gozo then begins to alternate between them, placing Sayuri in the cello case, forcing his wife to watch as he rapes their daughter.

Sayuri becomes jealous and incensed over these events, displacing her anger onto Mitsuko, taking every opportunity to berate and violently beat Mitsuko whenever Gozo is not home. When one of Sayuri's earrings goes missing, a fight erupts between her and Mitsuko resulting in Sayuri's death after a spill down the stairs. From this point forward Mitsuko completely takes the place of her mother, continually being raped by Gozo. No longer able to endure the abuse, and further depressed by her falling grades, Mitsuko unsuccessfully attempts suicide by jumping from the school rooftop, resulting in paralysis and reliance upon the use of a wheelchair.

The film's plot takes a major twist when it is revealed that the unfolding drama is actually part of a fictional novel being written by a famous author named Taeko, also played by Masumi Miyazaki. Taeko, like Mitsuko, just so happens to use a wheelchair. Adding to the bizarre similarities between them, Taeko has a "pet" that she keeps hidden in a cello case, feeding it by furiously packing food into a peephole in the case.

Taeko befriends one of the publisher's new staff members, a timid, sexually ambiguous character named Yuji, played by Issei Ishida (b. 1974). Yuji is obsessed with Taeko, asking her directly whether her book is based on her own life, which Taeko denies. The film cuts to a scene of Yuji's bedroom, covered with pictures and news clippings of Taeko, along with another scene of his visit to a support group for people who have mutilated their bodies, revealing his mutilation to the group, but not the audience.

Yuji kidnaps Taeko's "pet" and demands that Taeko meet him at her childhood home. She is met there by Yuji who forces Taeko to acknowledge her past as the abusive, negligent mother she once was. Yuji leads Taeko to her conjugal room whereupon he exposes his chest, bearing the scars where his breasts once were. He recounts to Taeko how he changed his identity from that of Mitsuko to Yuji, taking a job with the publisher in order to get close to her after being placed in protective care during his youth. All the while, Yuji repeatedly and violently kicks Taeko's "pet," his own father, Gozo, who is chained to the bed groaning, bloodied, and rendered a stump by dismemberment. The film culminates in a murderous act of revenge as Yuji takes a chainsaw to both of his parents.

Akin to many of Sono's horror films, *Strange Circus* does not shy away from scenes of realistically vivid sexual acts and barbaric brutality. The sex scenes are tailored after those of aggressive hard-core pornography. Scenes such as those of Mitsuko walking through a blood-soaked hallway, stabbing herself in the legs, and repeatedly kicking her father in the finale are replete with stomach-turning gore and sickening, lifelike sound effects.

The film has received overwhelmingly positive reviews. It won the Reader Jury of the "Berliner Zeitung" award at the Berlin International Film Festival, Best Feature Film at the Fantasia Film Festival, and was chosen as an Official Selection at the Tokyo International Fantasia Film Festival.—Emil Marmol

See also ero guro nansensu genre

Bibliography
Sono, Sion, dir. *Strange Circus*. Sedic International, 2005. Film.

SUICIDE CIRCLE (2001)
DIRECTOR: Shion Sono
SCREENPLAY: Shion Sono
SPECS: 99 minutes; color

Since the dawn of the twenty-first century, Shion Sono has emerged as one of Japanese cinema's most original and provocative directors. His breakthrough feature, *Suicide Circle* (*Jisatsu saakuru*, 2001), introduces viewers to a striking vision of a contemporary Japan plagued by a series of spectacular yet baffling mass suicides. In the film's memorable opening sequence, dozens of schoolgirls join hands on a crowded subway platform before leaping to their deaths beneath the squealing wheels of speeding train. Such an introduction may lead spectators to assume that the remainder of the motion picture will be unremittingly bleak. However, by contrasting moments like these with peppy, brightly lit music video clips featuring a cheerful yet potentially malevolent prepubescent pop group called Dessert, Sono advances a darkly humorous and biting critique of an image-obsessed culture informed by rampant consumerism, socially alienating communications technologies, and a pervasive if ultimately transitory culture of "cuteness," or *kawaisa*. At the same time, Sono infuses his narrative with an intriguing existentialist consideration of what it means to live authentically in a world in which despite—or, perhaps, because of—the proliferation of social media, the quality of one's relationship to his/her fellow human beings still depends upon the extent to which one is "connected to oneself."

Suicide Circle's plot is complex, requiring viewers to both acknowledge and embrace their role as active participants in the cinematic experience. Throughout the work's relatively modest and often deliriously paced ninety-nine-minute running time, audiences encounter strategically placed digressions, frustrating "red herrings," and an assortment of tropes culled from an array of genres that range from splatter films and police procedurals to family melodramas and high-camp exercises in cinematic excess. In the process, *Suicide Circle*'s narrative follows the exploits of four central protagonists: Kuroda, a seasoned homicide detective and the patriarch of a quietly dysfunctional family; Shibusawa, a young officer who assists Kuroda in his investigation; "The Bat," a female *otaku* who divides her life between the virtual expanses of cyberspace and the physical confines of her dimly lit bedroom; and Mitsuko, a young woman struggling to make sense of her life in the days and weeks following her boyfriend's suicidal plunge from the window of a tall building. As the film progresses, each of these characters pursues a series of leads, several of which culminate in sequences that vacillate between the sanguine and the surreal.

For instance, in one of the film's stranger storylines, a gang of glam rockers led by a flamboyant and androgynous chanteur named Genesis, kidnaps "The Bat" and her best friend, eventually raping and murdering them in an abandoned bowling alley. Detective Kuroda, obsessed with discovering the common thread behind the increasingly frequent suicides, blows his brains out after failing to prevent his own family from taking their lives. His demise, in turn, motivates Shibusawa to redouble his efforts to stem the rising tide of self-slaughter. In the process, he strives to protect Mitsuko, whose own investigation into the reasons behind her boyfriend's death leads to her discovery of an underground collective of children dedicated to transforming Japan with the apparent assistance of the pop idols, Dessert. Rejecting the escalating solipsism inherent within the contemporary cultural climate, these children seemingly encourage Dessert's many fans either to take their own lives as part of the increasingly fashionable suicide trend, or, if possible, to reject the inertia of such destructive pop culture preoc-cupations in favor of engaging in the kind of serious introspection that will make it possible for them to forge meaningful "connections" with others.

Much of *Suicide Circle*'s action is inflected with a darkly satirical tone, and like most satirists, Shion Sono uses his art to entertain his audience while also encouraging them to scrutinize the social and cultural logics of the world in which they live. In a 2008 "round table" discussion in the pages of *Rue Morgue*, a popular Canadian magazine dedicated primarily to horror film and television, Sono remarks that because of this socially critical approach he does not consider *Suicide Circle* to be a horror film. He understands, however, why so many people classify it as such, going so far as to claim that "Japan itself is horror," and thus all motion pictures that endeavor to "describe contemporary Japan" could be consid-ered "horror movies." This sentiment is particularly instructive, especially if one reads *Suicide Circle* as critiquing the impact of a rampant consumerist ideology that privileges image over substance, while also noting how the proliferation of emerging communication technologies ironically enhances rather than alleviates social alienation. In Japan, as in much of the developed world, cell phones, com-puters, video game consoles, and televisions have become ubiquitous. As the new millennium progresses, this profusion of technology, as well as the allure of new gadgets and images, shows no sign of abating. Nor, importantly, does the para-doxical phenomenon of embracing innovation as a means of defining oneself as both *apart from* and as *a part of* a larger, collective identity without which one's adoption of a particular "style" would have little to no meaning.

The almost viral appeal of suicide in Sono's film functions as an allegory for the increasingly expansive yet ultimately destructive impact of a cultural logic predicated upon defining oneself through fads and fashion. Eager to resist the world forged by previous generations while simultaneously struggling to find their place in a hyper-mediated society before they've even managed to under-stand who they are as individuals, the young men and women in *Suicide Circle* form impromptu "suicide clubs" to which death is the ultimate price of admis-sion. When, for example, one of Detective Kuroda's fellow officers suggests that the series of suicides is merely a fad that will wane in time, Kuroda responds by sternly warning his men: "Not a word about a suicide club or kids will be dying all over Japan." Indeed, by never resolving the ultimate mystery at the heart of *Suicide Circle*'s narrative, Sono's film further critiques a culture fueled by the appeal of spectacle rather than a valuation of substance or meaning discovered through critical self-reflection. For Sono, such an approach to interpersonal rela-tionships is all too familiar in a postmodern mediascape driven by sound bytes, pop idolatry, and the transience of commercial products.

By purposefully denying audiences the conventional pleasures and satisfac-tions that more traditional modes of narrative closure provide, Sono's film mir-rors the way that more and more people encounter the world: "I thought that [such an approach] depicts the current state of Japan or the world. Incidents such as 9/11 and the Japanese cult Aum's attacks were reported as sensational news. However, no explanations about why the incidents happened, who was responsible for the acts, or why they engaged in acts of terrorism were provided. I intentionally made [the film] hard to understand in order to express this." In this sense, *Suicide Circle* explores how popular media and emerging modes of technological mediation, though promising greater communication and access to knowledge, ultimately facilitate—or risk enabling—an ahistorical approach to understanding one's national culture that is, in itself, a destructive/suicidal posture.

The most conspicuous social edifice collapsing in *Suicide Circle* is the family unit. In fact, depictions of shattered families and the theme of generational alienation permeate all four of the film's major narrative threads, and even in the montage sequences depicting the rapid spread of suicides across Japan, typical family gatherings like dinners and birthday parties become frenzied sites of graphic self-slaughter. Such moments underscore the extent to which individual feelings of disconnection and purposelessness translate to interpersonal discord rendered all the more palpable and poignant when couched in rituals performed for the sake of maintaining appearance rather than fostering fellowship. This motif of the dissolution of traditional familial bonds, coupled with narratives in which characters desperately attempt to forge alternative, if ultimately equally destructive, "familial" relationships permeate Sono's filmography, from *Noriko's Dinner Table* (2005) and *Love Exposure* (2008) to *Strange Circus* (2005) and *Cold Fish* (2010). This is not to suggest that Sono's cinematic vision is irredeemably pessimistic. If one can "connect" with oneself, the potential to create meaningful human interactions and interpersonal relationships remains. Perhaps no detail in *Suicide Circle* better illustrates this than the grotesque and unsettling spiraling chains of flesh found at the locations of the grisliest mass suicides. While these bloody wheels comprised of precisely sewn rectangles of skin may wind inward to a nothingness at their centers, they also curve outward toward the possibility of infinite connections that need not conform to the destructive cycles that came before. The future, Sono suggests, is in our hands. As the lyrics sung by the pop sirens Dessert remind us, it is always possible to "find life again."—Jay McRoy

Bibliography
Mes, Tom, Jay McRoy, and Sion Sono. "Underage Rage in Japan." *Rue Morgue Magazine*, June 2008.

THE SUICIDE MANUAL (2003)
DIRECTOR: Osamu Fukutani
SCREENPLAY: Hiroshi Kanno, Osamu Fukutani
SPECS: 86 minutes; color

The 2003 horror film, *The Suicide Manual,* directed by Osamu Fukutani (b. 1967), opens in an alley at night. Through a window one can see a burning brazier, a man lying next to some spilled pills, and other bodies. A title card comes up, informing us that the briquettes were used by a group attempting to commit suicide by carbon monoxide poisoning.

At a television station a cameraman-producer and his boss debate the approach to take in a story about the suicides. The cameraman-producer, "Yu," wants to try to examine the psychology of those who are committing suicide. His boss wants a simple documentary about "trendy" group suicide.

Yu and Rie, a woman who is his assistant, take their equipment and conduct some on-the-street interviews. The people interviewed are not very interested in the subject. Rie suggests they go to the site. When Yu declines to go she teases him, telling him that he is afraid of being possessed by an evil spirit. At the apartment, they encounter a young girl named Nanami, who had planned to commit suicide with the others. When a woman named Ricky, who she thought would join their group didn't appear, Nanami left to look for her.

Ricky is well known on suicide bulletin board sites, and teaches others about the freedom and right to die. Nanami calls her a "goddess." Nanami loans Yu *The Suicide Manual*, the DVD that Ricky had sent her. Nanami wants to commit suicide because the other students at her school hate her and make a fool of her. She believes that if she kills herself she will be able to return as a spirit and exact revenge.

Yu plays the DVD. Ricky presents various ways of committing suicide, commenting on them as she does. She calls hanging "a work of art," and the taking of pills is presented as a very reasonable and thorough method. In talking about jumping off a building she is very precise about the number of stories necessary to ensure success. These alternatives are presented in beautifully shot and visually striking images. The DVD also features images of what Ricky calls the "ultimate" suicide machine, an iron frame into which the aspiring suicide is locked, and when it is self-activated, a number of sharp blades pierce the restrained body.

Yu and Rei meet Nanami on the roof of the television station building the next day to return the video. She stands on the ledge and tells them the view reminds her that "life is nothing much." Nanami later calls to say that she has spoken to Ricky and is going to throw herself off the top of the television studio building. They return just in time to see her jump.

Yu's boss berates him for not capturing Nanami's suicide on tape. "How irritating," his boss says. He tells the depressed Yu that he is just like the people in the suicide groups, not really alive. The difference, his boss says, is that he doesn't have the courage to kill himself.

Yu goes online to try to contact Ricky and writes that he is serious about committing suicide. Rie reads his posts, and instead of trying to dissuade Yu she says that because she has already peaked professionally, she, too, wants to die. They meet with a small suicide group, a man and two women. Yu asks for their reasons. "Don't be a wet blanket," the man in the group says to Yu. He has potassium cyanide and asks, "Shall we die now?" The man kills himself, but the girls ask Yu for a ride. The girls drug him and when he awakens they are dead, their bodies up in a tree.

Yu disintegrates further and begins hallucinating. He and Rie plan to cut their throats; Rie goes through with it, but Yu cannot. She later appears to him as an apparition, telling him that he was heartless not to go through with it with her; she tries to tempt him to kill himself. Yu runs off into a forest and loses consciousness. When he awakens he's in the ultimate suicide machine. A shadowy female figure stands nearby with a video camera. Yu triggers the machine and dies.

In 1993 Japanese author Wataru Tsurumi published *The Complete Manual of Suicide*, a book detailing ways in which people might kill themselves. Amid the controversy surrounding the book he said that he had written it to try to discourage suicide and that he never wanted anyone to end their life. This book appears to have been the inspiration for the film, and a similar disclaimer appears during the film's opening moments.—William Bamberger

SUZUKI, KOJI (1957–)

Koji Suzuki is considered "the Stephen King of Japan" and is best known for his 1991 *Ringu*, which was adapted by Hideo Nakata into a film by the same name in 1998. Suzuki's book has been adapted into seven Japanese films and their sequels, as well as a Korean adaptation (*Ring Virus*, 1999) and an American version (*The Ring*, 2002). *Ringu* was published in English in 2003. "Floating Water," a short story from his critically acclaimed 1996 collection, *Dark Water*, was also adapted in 2002 by Nakata into a film, *Honogurai mizu no soko kara* (From the bottom of dark water), which was in turn adapted into and released as a Hollywood feature film, *Dark Water*, in 2005.

Suzuki was born on 13 May 1957 in Hamamatsu, southwest of Tokyo, and majored in French at Keio University. After graduating, he worked for a while as a *juku* (cram) teacher, helping Japanese students prepare for school entrance exams. In 1990, his first work, *Rakuen* (*Paradise*) won the Japanese Fantasy Novel Award. He began writing *Ringu* while a stay-at-home father—unusual in Japan—taking care of his elder daughter, then two years old, while his wife taught Japanese history. He has said *Ringu* was inspired by his love for his two daughters; the protagonist, Asakawa Kazuyuki, fights supernatural evil to save the life of his wife and his daughter. *Rasen* (*Spiral*), his 1996 sequel to *Ringu*, won the Yoshikawa Eiji Young Writer Award.

Asked in a 2003 interview what he thought of the Japanese horror film, Suzuki said he thought it "necessary for human beings to be sensitive for fear. It's a very necessary instinct for existence. If there is no sense of terror or fear, you won't live long. An original instinct." Suzuki said that he did not believe in evil, but rather considered himself "very much an optimist" and therefore "not so interested in the concept of evil." He conceded, however, that "for a novel, it is necessary to have evil. . . . If there is no dark, there is no contrast, and it doesn't highlight what you are trying to show. Dark and light."

In contrast to his writing of horror novels—which he now eschews—and based on his experience as primary caregiver for his daughters, Suzuki has written extensively (including *Fusei no tanjo*, *Kazoku no kizuna*, and *Papa-ism*) and critically about traditional fatherhood in Japan, where "salarymen" are commonly absent fathers. He addressed the Japanese Diet (Parliament) on the subject. Suzuki has written a children's book, *Namida* (*Tears*), and translated *The Little Sod Diaries* into Japanese. In 2009, he teamed with Hayashi Paper Corporation to have his latest horror novella, *Drop*, the story of an evil spirit that inhabits a toilet bowl, printed on toilet paper.—Kimiko Akita and Rick Kenney

SUZUKI, SUMIKO (1904–1985)

Sumiko Suzuki was an actress famous for her many appearances in classic Japanese horror films or *kaiki eiga* of the 1920s and 1930s. Japan's first genuine horror movie star, Suzuki was dubbed the *"bakeneko* (ghost cat) actress" for her signature performances of the traditional cat monster onscreen. She has been somewhat misleadingly referred to in English as "Japan's first scream queen," although Suzuki most often played the monster, not its victim, making her place in Japanese pop culture history more analogous to Bela Lugosi and Boris Karloff than Fay Wray.

Born in Tokyo in 1904, Suzuki began acting at the age of fifteen, making her feature film debut with a supporting role in Hollywood-trained director Thomas Kurihara's *Lust of the White Serpent* (*Jasei no in*, 1921). Based on Ueda Akinari's story from *Ugetsu monogatari* about a white snake which transforms into a beautiful woman and seduces a hapless human lover, the film was in some respects a prototypical *kaiki eiga*, foreshadowing Suzuki's future career in horror. However, she would first find fame as a *yōfu* or "vamp" actress, appearing as the romantic foil/antagonist opposite the heroic samurai leads of numerous B-grade period action films during the latter half of the 1920s. Actresses were a relatively new phenomenon in Japanese cinema at the time; previously female roles were most often played onscreen by *oyama*, female impersonators, in the tradition of the Kabuki theater. The novelty of seeing a beautiful woman holding her own in combat against the macho male heroes of *jidai geki* period films created a vogue for vamps, and Sumiko Suzuki's large, coquettish eyes coupled with her onscreen physicality made her one of the most popular.

Toward the end of the 1920s the B-studios began casting vamp actresses as ghosts and monsters in adaptations of famous Edo-period (1600–1868) *kaidan* or "ghost stories." These roles typically called for a beauty-to-beast transformation about halfway through the story, as the archetypal suffering heroines of *kaidan* return from the grave as hideous ghosts or *bakeneko* cat monsters to seek revenge on their oppressors. Alternately beautiful and dangerous, feminine and fearsome, roles like the ghost of Oiwa in *Yotsuya kaidan* represented an externalization of the same ambiguity that made the vamps popular with audiences. Suzuki appeared as Oiwa three times between 1927 and 1931, as well as playing other famous ghosts like Okiku in *Isetsu Banchō sarayashiki* (1929).

Following the transition to sound and a lull in horror film production in Japan during the early 1930s, Suzuki found herself under contract to Shinkō, the studio that would become the home of Japanese horror in the years leading up to World War II. Already at the ripe old age of 32 in 1936, Suzuki was beginning to lose the role of the beautiful lead to younger actresses, but when Shinkō decided to make its first talkie *bakeneko* picture, *Saga kaibyōden* (The legend of the Saga ghost cat) for release in early 1937, Suzuki was offered the chance to reprise her monstrous beauty-to-beast performances from a decade before. Despite a chilly critical reception, the film proved a hit with audiences and ignited a horror boom among the minor studios. Deeming Suzuki's star persona a key ingredient to Shinkō's success, the other studios sought to cast well-known actresses in their own horror productions, but it was Sumiko Suzuki who would prove the biggest box office draw in prewar Japanese horror films and become forever known as the *"bakeneko* actress."

Although she reprised her role as Oiwa for Shinkō in yet another version of *Yotsuya kaidan* (1937) and appeared as a sympathetic ghost just as often as a ferocious cat monster, it was her portrayals of the *bakeneko* in Shinkō productions like *Arima neko* (The cat of Arima, 1937), *Kaibyō akakabe Daimyojin* (The ghost cat in the red wall, 1938), and *Yamabuki neko* (The yellow rose cat, 1940) that made her into an icon. Most of these films do not survive, but reviews and promotional images show that Suzuki's makeup as the *bakeneko* was fairly restrained. Whereas her successor in the 1950s, Irie Takako (1911–1995), sported comparatively elaborate, grotesque cat makeup, Suzuki was able to sell the part mainly through her performance, often with only disheveled hair and bloodstained lips to suggest her monstrous feline nature. In *Arima neko* Suzuki conveys the otherworldly monstrosity of the *bakeneko* with her large, penetrating eyes and wire-assisted feats of superhuman agility, features reminiscent of her earlier vamp performances that allow her natural beauty and physical appeal to shine through even while portraying a non-human monster. Ironically, in her only horror film to have screened outside of Japan, 1938's *The Ghost Cat and the Mysterious Shamisen* (*Kaibyō nazo no shamisen*), Suzuki takes a break from her usual *bakeneko* roles, appearing instead as the villainous human target of the cat spirit's wrath.

At the height of her popularity Suzuki took her *bakeneko* act to the stage, performing the same roles she had appeared in on-screen for live audiences. She even traveled to the United States in 1940 to appear in an imported *bakeneko* play on Broadway, just before the outbreak of war between Japan and America. Upon returning to her home country, Suzuki quit the movie business to focus on her stage tours. When the Daiei studio revived the *bakeneko* genre in the early 1950s, another aging silver screen beauty, Irie Takako, inherited the mantle of "the *bakeneko* actress." Suzuki would, however, come out of retirement to play the ghost cat on film one last time, in Tōei's *Ghost Cat and the Clockwork Ceiling* (*Kaibyō karakuri tenjō*, 1958). Following this final curtain call, Suzuki retired from acting altogether and spent her remaining years in Nagoya, where she died in 1985.—Michael Crandol

See also bakeneko; Ghost Cat of Arima Palace; Irie, Takako

SWEET HOME (1989)
DIRECTOR: Kiyoshi Kurosawa
SCREENPLAY: Kiyoshi Kurosawa
SPECS: 100 minutes; color

Sweet Home is a 1989 take on the haunted house story. Ably directed by Kiyoshi Kurosawa (b. 1955) and featuring effects work by Dick Smith (b. 1922), the film chronicles the supernatural events that engulf the members of a small team investigating an old mansion. In search of frescos painted by a renowned artist, the group accidentally awakens a malevolent spirit. *Sweet Home* was released alongside a video game adaptation that is regarded as one of the first entries in the survival horror genre. The game inspired the highly successful Resident Evil franchise, which in turn led to an American-made series of films.

The story of *Sweet Home* revolves around a film crew as they search the abandoned home of artist Ichiro Mamiya for lost artworks. Ostensibly led by Kazuo Hoshio, played by Shingo Yamashiro (b. 1938), the crew comprises producer Akiko Hayakawa, portrayed by Nobuko Miyamoto (b. 1945), reporter Asuka, and cameraman Ryo Taguchi. Along for the trip is Kazuo's daughter Emi, played by idol singer Nokko (b. 1963). The crew is allowed to search the house by local authorities, who are aware something supernatural lurks inside. After discovering a series of disturbing frescos, Asuka is seemingly possessed and unearths a small coffin with the body of a child inside. Emi is chased out of the house by a dark force, and while Kazuo and Akiko go to retrieve her, Asuka and Ryo are attacked by malignant shadows. Ryo's lower body is incinerated by the shadows, and the terrified Asuka kills him as he crawls after her. A falling pole arm then kills Asuka. Before the rest of the team can escape the house, Emi is taken by the shadows.

The history of the house, and the tragedy that befell the Mamiya family, are revealed by quirky gas station attendant Kenichi Yamamura, portrayed by producer Juzo Itami (b. 1933). The young son of Ichiro and Fujin Mamiya was accidentally killed after he wandered into the mansion's furnace to play. Driven to madness by his death, Lady Mamiya began murdering local children to give her son playmates in the afterlife. When confronted by enraged townspeople, she committed suicide in the furnace. The film crew disturbed her angry spirit, the only thing keeping the living darkness and shadows inhabiting the house in check.

Kenichi dies in a failed attempt to rescue Emi. Kazuo also tries to save his daughter but is trapped by the house. Akiko realizes that the core of Lady Mamiya's rage and strength is her attachment to her lost child. Akiko takes the coffin, dons Emi's deceased mother's clothing, and confronts Lady Mamiya in the basement. As Akiko fends off a monstrous Lady Mamiya, Emi offers the body of the dead child to the ghost. Mother and son reunited, the spirits of both shed their horrific forms and ascend upward as radiant white figures. Akiko and Emi leave the house, finding Kazuo bewildered but still alive.

Director Kurosawa, who later helmed *Pulse* and *Cure*, brings a solid vision to *Sweet Home*. While the plot is reminiscent of other haunted house stories, an emphasis on the mother-child relationship lends the production additional narrative weight. Kurosawa makes the most of the haunted house setting with effective use of color, light, and shadows, particularly in scenes where the characters are menaced by shadowy tendrils and figures on the walls. Academy Award winning American artist Dick Smith was brought in to handle makeup and special effects, resulting in impressive visuals and a memorable final encounter with Lady Mamiya. However, Kurosawa's original work was altered by subsequent edits and reshoots carried out by Itami, who continued to tinker with the film after production.

Sweet Home's lasting influence on modern popular culture lies in its collaboration with the video game industry. An adaptation of the film was developed by Capcom for the Family Computer (Nintendo Entertainment System in the United States) and both the game and film were released simultaneously in Japan. The *Sweet Home* game became highly influential on the development of the original Resident Evil game, which was originally intended as a *Sweet Home* remake. Kurosawa's involvement with the game offers new interpretations of the film, such as clues within the game that suggest Ichiro Mamiya and Kenichi Yamamura are the same person. This form of trans-media narrative continues to be a feature in many Japanese productions.—Daniel Fandino

Bibliography

Kurosawa, Kiyoshi, dir. *Sweet Home*. Toho, 1989. Film.

• T •

TALES OF TERROR FROM TOKYO

Like many countries, Japan has a thriving made-for-TV horror scene. For the successful post-*Ring* horror movie, a short-lived TV series is as essential as the song that plays over the end credits of the film, and the list of hits that have spawned follow-up series includes Hideo Nakata's *Ring* (1998), Jōji Iida's *Spiral* (1998) and *Another Heaven* (2000), Masayuki Ochiai's *Hypnosis* (1999), Takashi Miike's *One Missed Call* (2004), and the Eko Eko Azarak film series. Iida himself has been a key figure in Japanese TV horror, having created *Night Head*, a supernatural drama about two friends with psychic abilities and one of the most popular television shows of the 1990s. Not many of these productions have been seen in the West, but one of the few TV series that has received an English-language release is *Kaidan shin mimibukuro*, or *Tales of Terror from Tokyo*, based on a series of books written by Hirokatsu Kihara and Ichirō Nakayama.

In its original form, *Tales of Terror from Tokyo* had a simple core concept: horrific or weird stories, each one only five minutes in length. The directors chosen ranged from established genre heavyweights like *Ring* scriptwriter Hiroshi Takahashi, Takashi Shimizu, and Norio Tsuruta, all veterans of the horror anthology scene, to first-time directors and music video specialists trying to make their way into the mainstream (as well as a couple of segments handled by Kihara and Nakayama, the original authors). The list of directors contains a great many figures who would later become prominent or noteworthy within the Japanese horror scene, including Yūdai Yamaguchi (*Meatball Machine*), Noboru Iguchi (*Machine Girl*), Kei Horie (*The Locker*), and Mari Asato (*Bilocation, Fatal Frame*).

The five-minute format does not allow for much character development or complex stories, but some of the directors manage to produce interesting results within that framework, although many are content to simply rely on the standard urban legends and spooky stories; "The School Excursion" repeats the old superstition about the last stall on the left in the girls' toilet, for example. Keisuke Toyoshima's "The Visitor" manages to create a high level of tension from a simple story about a young girl who suspects that there is something malevolent waiting outside her front door. In Ryūta Miyake's "The Train," two girls sit in a friend's flat complaining about the noise from the nearby railway line, only to be reminded that the apartment overlooks a river, with no line nearby. Then there is the unsettling "The Garden," directed by Hiroshi Takahashi, about a woman haunted by the ghosts of the children she fed to whatever it is she keeps in a cage at the bottom of the garden. Although it relies on child actors, Norio Tsuruta's "Let's Play" works surprisingly well. A young girl likes playing with her new friend upstairs, but doesn't realize that the girl has been trapped in that empty apartment for years, and needs to find a replacement before she can leave.

Occasionally directors were allowed to handle longer stories: Akio Yoshida turned in the atmospheric two-part tale "Examination Room #3," about a boy who takes his sexually reluctant girlfriend to an abandoned hospital in the (somewhat ludicrous) hope that the experience will put her "in the mood." Ironically enough, she becomes possessed by the ghost of a nymphomaniac who was once a resident of the hospital; horrified, the boyfriend flees. Years later he meets the girl again, only to discover that she still returns to the hospital to relive the experience. In contrast, Yūdai Yamaguchi's three-part "Please Don't" name-checks *The Legend of Hell House* (1973) and prefigures the popularity of "found-footage" films, but wastes the opportunity on a mild spoof.

The original TV series ran for three years, but like the *Haunted School* franchise it produced a number of spin-offs, including several made-for-TV specials and several theatrical films. The first of these, *Tales from Tokyo: The Movie* (2004), retained the anthology format but dispensed with the obligatory five-minute limit: some segments are five minutes long, but others stretch to ten, fifteen, or twenty minutes. Although many sources claim that the movie was constructed from the segments of the TV series, it actually consists of entirely new material, most of it shot by directors already associated with the franchise. The film opens with Akio Yoshida's "The Night Watchman," a twenty-minute episode that is one of the most interesting tales in the movie. On the surface, it's a fairly mundane *Ju-on*-style ghost story about a succession of night watchmen plagued by the unquiet spirits that reside in the abandoned building they're supposed to be guarding. The manifestations are largely routine, but what matters are the reactions of the one guard who's been working in the building for months. Unlike his terrified coworkers, this guard blithely states that "it's all in the mind" and gets on with the job. Even when the ghosts are literally everywhere, he still maintains that it's all psychological, much to the frustration of his superiors (including guest star Naoto Takenaka), who begin to suspect that there may be something wrong with the man.

Much of the film is on the same level as the TV series, but it does boast one surprisingly effective episode, "Line of Sight," directed by Keisuke Toyoshima. During a class project a high school student films herself talking about her ambitions and inadvertently picks up what she assumes is just a reflection or a blur. However, her classmates are convinced it's a supernatural image, and the unhappy, withdrawn girl soon finds herself a celebrity at the school. Unfortunately, the more her footage gets replayed, the clearer (and more sinister) the image seems to become. Despite only having ten minutes to work with, Toyoshima presents a well-defined character and a clearly progressing story that succeeds in drawing the viewer in.

The second theatrical movie, *Tales of Terror: Haunted Apartment*, was released in 2005 and directed by Akio Yoshida, one of the mainstays of the franchise. Unlike the other releases, *Haunted Apartment* abandoned the anthology format in favor of a traditional feature film about a teenage girl moving into a new apartment that has a few quirks, to say the least. When her mother dies in an accident, Aimi Yamato and her father are forced to look for a smaller place to live. They soon find a suitable apartment and move in, assisted by their enthusiastic new neighbors, who also tell them that there are a series of special rules for new tenants to observe: always be home by midnight; don't mention the name of the landlord's daughter; and most sinister of all, you can't move out unless you're the oldest tenant in the building. Even then, you can only go if you manage to bring a new tenant in. That explains why the building's geriatric manager (played by Isao Yatsu, from *Forbidden Siren*) was so excited when they agreed to move in. These "rules" are certainly bizarre, but they don't explain why Aimi keeps seeing the pale shade of a girl in a sailor suit uniform everywhere, from the balcony to her own bedroom.

Moving into a haunted apartment is a common device in Japanese horror, from the Ju-on series to Hideo Nakata's *Dark Water* (2002) and *The Complex* (2013). Typically the setting is an old, cramped, and off-color apartment that easily generates a sense of claustrophobia and paranoia, something Yoshida taps into easily. He's less comfortable with the more humorous aspects of Mutsuki Watanabe's script, which occasionally threaten to tip *Haunted Apartment* into black comedy territory. These elements become even more incongruous when the final twist is played out; it's a surprising twist, but also a deeply serious one that casts everything seen so far in a new light. It also destabilizes the film badly, removing much of the entertainment value.

Yoshida returned to the series in 2009 to direct one of a pair of made-for-TV specials, each following a single story but not extended to full feature length. The second was handled by Keisuke Toyoshima, the man responsible for many of the best episodes of the original TV series. This was followed a year later by another made-for-TV special that resurrected the short-episode anthology format, while a further theatrical feature was released in 2012, consisting of four tales, all directed by Noboru Iguchi. None of these later installments have been released in the West, but English-language home video releases of the earlier works have maintained an interest in the franchise.—Jim Harper

TALES OF THE UNUSUAL (2000)

DIRECTOR: Mamoru Hoshi, Masayuki Ochiai, Hisao Ogura, Masayuki Suzuki
SCREENPLAY: Tomoko Aizawa, Ryōichi Kimizuka, Masayuki Ochiai, Katsuhide Suzuki, Motoki Nakamura
SPECS: 126 minutes; color

The 2000 film release titled *Tales of the Unusual* was directed by several directors: Mamoru Hoshi, Masayuki Ochiai, Hisao Ogura, and Masayuki Suzuki. The film presents four stories, only one of which can truly be termed a horror story. The film opens on a small group standing in a train station looking out at a pouring rain. To relieve the boredom one of them tells four tales, each prompted by the words or actions of the others. The film's anthology-style format, and the mysterious man in dark glasses and a suit, played by well-known Japanese television actor Tamori, who tells the tales, has prompted comparisons with the American television series *The Twilight Zone* (1959–1964), created and hosted by Rod Serling. (A closer parallel, however, would be Serling's follow-up series, *Night Gallery*, which featured an anthology format.) *Tales of the Unusual* is, in fact, based on a popular Japanese television show.

The film shifts away from the train station when the man in the dark glasses looks at one young man's video camera and begins telling the first of his tales. This is the horror story, "One Snowy Night." The film shifts from the train station to the sight of an airplane propeller flying straight into the viewer's eyes. A two-engine prop plane crashes in a snowy landscape. One woman's ankle is badly injured but the others all appear to be in remarkably good health. They leave the shattered plane in hopes of finding better shelter. The injured woman, Mari, falls behind and she is finally left in a pit dug in the snow with a lid over it in hopes that she will survive until they find help. She is screaming after them as they leave her.

The group finds an empty hut and manages to start a fire. Two of them, a man and a woman who is Mari's friend, return to try to save Mari. They find that she has tried to dig herself out. Only her head is showing above the snow, and she is still alive. When the man tries to dig her out his shovel pierces her chest and blood flows into the snow. The man runs back to the hut in horror, but Mari's friend remains. Mari's hand reaches out and tries to grab her; she is still not quite dead. The friend runs away, leaving Mari staring at the shovel the man left behind.

Back at the hut the survivors try to sleep, taking turns keeping watch. Mari's friend is on watch and as she drops off a blurry figure passes through the frame. At the next watch change one of the men is found dead, marks on his neck. Later, another man lights a cigarette and in the glow of his lighter sees a figure. A hand reaches around from behind his head and he dies. The remaining survivors, a man and Mari's friend, turn on a night-vision video camera and sit where it can tape them. When Mari's friend awakens the last man is dead, a hatchet in his back. She runs back the videotape and sees the recording of a woman, her face not visible, killing the man. She throws off her blanket and we see that she is wearing the killer's dress. Her fingers now look like Mari's fingers when Mari reached out to grab her. A hand seizes her from behind; it is a rescue worker.

The camera pulls back to show the woman in the snow, surrounded by dead bodies. Mari is still frozen in the snow. There is no hut in sight, only the murdered bodies of the survivors. The last shot of the story is of the video camera, its screen showing a ghostly female figure walking in the snow.

The second tale, "Samurai Cellular" is prompted by a man obsessively speaking into a cell phone. This tale is a farce, complete with comic music and pratfalls. The story begins with an archeological expedition recovering a long-buried cell phone. The scene then shifts to eighteenth-century Japan. The leader of a samurai clan, "Oishi," is more interested in sex than in war and is a bit of a coward. He comes upon a ringing cell phone in the middle of a dirt path. He accidentally activates it and the voice on the other end tells him he is calling from three hundred years in the future. The caller has read that Oishi was a great samurai warrior who led his clan bravely and the call is to check up on the truth of this tale.

After a number of comic episodes involving the artifact from the future, Oishi is overheard by his clan, bragging into the phone about what a great warrior he is and how he is now going into battle. Those who overhear are inspired and prepare for the fight. When the moment comes to set out, Oishi marches forward with the phone to his ear, in conversation with the future. He then drops it into the snow and goes off to fulfill his historical role.

The last scene of this tale is of a modern twenty-something sitting in an enormous hall of callers, all doing the same kind of historical verification by cell phone. A bin full of corroded cell phones passes through the shot.

A young guitarist's checkerboard pattern shirt inspires the storyteller to tell the third tale, "Chess." A chess master, Akira Kato, loses a game against a super computer called Super Blue. The story cuts to a scene in a run-down street, littered with papers showing the chess champion's defeat. He is living on the street, still wearing his contestant's badge.

A mysterious rich man has him brought to his office to play a chess match. The champion plays without looking at the board; he looks out the window at the city below instead. The visuals and emotions are exaggerated during this encounter: the sight of a chessboard makes him ill, sounds of actual combat are superimposed; when he looks out the window, checkerboard patterns are everywhere in the streets and squares. Then when a piece is taken in the game, a man is killed in the corresponding position on the square below. It becomes difficult to know if anything is real: he becomes the king in the chess game and the wife he lost because of his chess obsession is the queen; he is in a car and it only moves diagonally, like a bishop. He decides what is real is that his wife is bound and gagged on a giant chessboard and will be killed if he cannot win the game. He moves to try to protect her and he is stabbed. In the end it has all been a psychological game, staged by his wife and friends to try to restore his confidence and have him return to playing chess.

In the final tale, "Marriage Simulation," a young man and woman, Yuichi and Haru, meet outside a movie theater. It is raining and neither has an umbrella. A poster behind them announces that the film is *Montparnasse*; the poster shows people walking under umbrellas. He invites her to attend the film, to pass the time until the rain stops. The film cuts to a wedding chapel—the pair are planning their wedding. As part of the wedding package they tape comments to one another to be viewed on their tenth anniversary.

The chapel also offers a "Marriage Simulation" service. Technicians explain the procedure. The instructions include a touch of self-mockery: "It's not like a movie, where the plot is decided from the start. According to your emotional reactions, both the development and result may change." They are attached to the simulator machine, a virtual reality device that projects the prediction to their brains, both visually and auditorily. Their story follows an arc of initial enthusiasm, growing disappointment, frustration, and tears. Detaching themselves from the simulator, they decide not to marry after all.

Later, their recorded "tenth anniversary" statements are mailed back to them. Through what appears to be a mix-up, they each receive the statement recorded by the other. Viewing these heart-felt recordings they decide they still have feelings for one another, and they reunite. At this point they awaken and discover that the entire sequence of events—including their previous, illusory, awakening—has been part of the simulation, showing them that whatever might happen they belong together.

In the last moments of *Tales of the Unusual* the film returns once again to the train station. The rain has stopped and all of the passengers except the mysterious storyteller depart. The rain begins again—the mysterious man's attitude suggests that he has stopped the rain and started it again—and more refugees from the downpour begin to gather in the station. It appears likely that more tales are to come.—William Bamberger

TAMAMI: THE BABY'S CURSE (2008)

DIRECTOR: Yudai Yamaguchi
SCREENPLAY: Hirotoshi Kobayashi
SPECS: 100 minutes; color

The J-horror boom of the late 1990s and early 2000s saw the popularization (and US remaking) of several films featuring demonic children. There was the *Ring* series (the demonic Sadako and her famous one-eyed death glare), *The Grudge* (a pale, hollow-eyed little boy), *Dark Water* (the drowned little girl-ghost with vengeful tendencies), and *One Missed Call* (vengeful spirit of a dead child and a guilty mother). With the exception, perhaps, of *The Grudge*, all of these films presented audiences with a dilemma: the monsters in question were terrifying, but they were also childlike and pitiful. Themes of maternal guilt ran through all of them, with often not-so-subtle critiques of motherly failings and the breakdown of the family unit.

Released in 2008, *Tamami: The Baby's Curse* (*Akanbo shōjo*) has echoes of all of these films. There's a guilty mother, a vengeful child-spirit determined to destroy those she feels have wronged her, a body count, and ultimately a moment in which we're expected to feel sympathy—or at least pity—for the monster. Where previous J-horror films of this type provided detailed origin stories for their monsters, though, *Tamami* leaves viewers in the dark. We're never certain why baby Tamami rages, whether she's a real baby, a ghost, or demon, or even why she was abandoned in the first place.

Tamami opens in a rainstorm straight out of Frankenstein, with blindingly white lightning and loud crashes of thunder. We are in the car with the teenage Yoko Nanjo (Nako Mizusawa) and her guardian from an orphanage (Keisuke Horibe). Yoko has just learned that she is not in fact an orphan—she is the long-lost daughter of the wealthy Nanjo family and is being driven to their secluded mansion.

Tamami seems to borrow heavily from *Rebecca*—there's an imposing mansion, a cool and unwelcoming housekeeper, a new family member trying to fit in, and a bunch of people who seem to know more than they're letting on. Something is clearly wrong in the house. Strange laughter comes from within the walls. Yoko's mother (Atsuko Asano) seems disturbed and carries a teddy bear around with her, talking to it as if it were a child.

We eventually learn that Yoko had a sister, Tamami, who died (or perhaps didn't) when she was a baby. It is Tamami's laughter that Yoko is hearing throughout the house. The second half of the film shifts abruptly from atmospheric chills to over-the-top violence and gore, with the murderous Tamami killing or maiming almost every member of the cast in increasingly creative ways.

Tamami leaves viewers with a lot of perplexing questions. If the film is indeed set only a decade or so after World War II, why do all of the characters seem to be dressed in contemporary fashions? Why was the infant Tamami left behind at the hospital—was it simply because she was deformed? Or did her father actually kill her and lie about it? What is the creature that now terrorizes the gothic mansion where the story takes place—is it a ghost? Or is it the real Tamami, who was perhaps always a demon/changeling and never a "child"?

Tamami was directed by Yudai Yamaguchi, whose previous credits include the splatter flicks *Meatball Machine* (2005) and *Battlefield Baseball* (2003). *Tamami* frequently has the feel of a wacky splatter film, though it alternates between genuinely shocking death scenes (a tower room full of medieval weaponry gets put to good use) and unbridled goofiness (a not-so-convincing Tamami bounces off walls and attacks people by biting them in the neck). Nako Mizusawa gives an affecting performance as daughter Yoko, and Atsuko Asano projects real torment as the mother consumed by grief. Ultimately, we even come to feel pity for the demonic Tamami, whose only line, uttered near the end of the film, is "I'm sorry."

Though it's not as polished or tonally consistent as similar films like *The Ring* and *Dark Water*, *Tamami* does contain an interesting mix of cheap shocks, disturbing violence, and poignancy. Its unanswered questions are a bit frustrating, but there are interesting hints throughout the film of what actually happened, leaving viewers to draw their own conclusions. Minus the scenes of dismemberment and sudden attacks by a sharp-toothed, monster baby, *Tamami* is basically the story of an orphan who is reunited with her family only to lose them all over again.—Lindsay Nelson

TEITO MONOGATARI GAIDEN (1995)
DIRECTOR: Izo Hashimoto
SCREENPLAY: Rika Yamagami
SPECS: 103 minutes; color

Teito monogatari gaiden ("The tale of the imperial capital: Side story"), directed by Izo Hashimoto (b. 1954), is a 1995 sequel to the film *Tokyo: The Last Megalopolis* (as well as its anime counterpart, *Doomed Megalopolis*). Like its better-known precursors, *Teito Monogatari Gaiden* is based on a side novel in the Teito Monogatari series written by Hiroshi Aramata (b. 1947).

Teito monogatari gaiden is notably more grim and violent than its predecessors. It also contains a far greater emphasis on sexuality. These darker elements might be attributed to director Rintarō's anime adaptation of *Doomed Megalopolis*—itself featuring darker elements than its predecessor, Akio Jissōji's 1988 film, *Tokyo: The Last Megalopolis*.

Unlike its cinematic predecessors, *Teito monogatari gaiden* does not focus on Katō Yasunori and his goal to awaken the spirit of the ancient warlord Taira no Masakado (d. 940) and destroy Tokyo. Instead, this film centers on Junya Yanase (portrayed by Nishimura Kazuhiko, b. 1966), a male nurse who becomes obsessed with the lore behind Katō and Masakado. Yanase works at a mental hospital conspicuously located nearby Masakado's gravesite, but he is no ordinary medical professional.

The film opens with a scene of his other obsession: he is engaging in sexual relations with a woman. When she stops him from going any further, Yanase attempts to strangle her with the sheets and then with his own hands. She puts up a fight, and he drags her by the hair to the window, bashing her head against its frame until she is close to death. He throws her on the bed and has his way with her, during which she takes her last breath and passes.

The next scene introduces two principal characters: a homeless woman (played by Kazuko Shirakawa, b. 1947) scavenging through garbage, and a drunk younger woman named Michiyo (played by Sawa Suzuki, b. 1972) in heels and a nice dress, attempting to walk down the street. Following her is a strange blob-like creature. Neither woman is introduced until later in the film.

One man's steps echo through the mental hospital into a common room. Although the man looks like Katō, it is actually Yanase impersonating him. He goes to one man—Junichi Narutaki (played by Hatsuo Yamaya, b. 1933), a friend of the Tatsumiya family from the original film—unsuccessfully attempting to trigger his fears. When Yanase begins to strangle Narutaki, the other patients attack Yanase and help to free Narutaki. Yanase's supervisor watches the incident via camera.

That night, Yanase is driving and spots Michiyo. She approaches his car, using her reflection in his window to put on new lipstick and he picks her up. The scene shifts to the two of them having sex. He attempts to strangle her, but he stops quickly when she does not resist him—he lets her live. Later, she finds a Noh mask that he is working on that he has named "Katō."

Narutaki and his fellow patients attempt to stop Katō's influence from within, but it seems to be all part of their delusion. Narutaki holds items in his hands—such as a feng shui compass—that aren't really there. Regardless, he and the inmates attempt to set up a magical barrier against Katō in the hospital courtyard. In doing so, Narutaki notices the homeless woman from before, revealing her identity as Keiko Tatsumiya (née Mekata), the shrine maiden who defeated Katō in the first film. He begs her to help him in the fight against Katō. It is then that she first meets Yanase, from whom she senses a dark aura. Keiko later sees Yanase with Michiyo, and she panics. She travels to a secluded area and begins chanting a spell. In the meantime, Yanase sees Michiyo feeding the strange blob-like creature that followed her back in the beginning.

Shortly thereafter, Yanase picks up a new girl off the street, unknowingly observed by Michiyo. When Yanase pulls up to the mental hospital the next day, Keiko observes him dragging the new girl's dead body into the hospital. Inside, he places the body in a secluded pool of muck, floating in which is at least one other female corpse. When Keiko enters, Yanase's victims writhe to life before her.

Michiyo takes Yanase to the Ōzawa Therapy center, run by her father. There, sexual deviants give in to their desires as a form of therapy. When Michiyo joins the crowd, she is embraced, to Yanase's increasing disgust. In the meantime, Keiko returns to her seclusion, calling a host of spirits to her presence. The scene quickly juxtaposes between Michiyo and Keiko, portraying them both as the center of an orgiastic event. Yanase draws Michiyo from the scene and they witness Keiko. While the film depicts Keiko at the center of an orgy, she is actually purifying the spirits of the dead in the area—including Yanase's two victims in the hospital pool.

Back at the hospital courtyard, Yanase kicks down the invisible barrier that Narutaki and his fellow patients have set up. It is left to the audience to decide whether or not Yanase is becoming part of the delusion, or if Narutaki and his comrades are actually sane. As Yanase's obsession with Katō comes to a head, Narutaki pleads again for Keiko to help them, but she refuses, even after realizing that it is Yanase channeling Katō's spirit to the present. She refuses to believe, thinking that this is simply Narutaki's delusion and instead wants to flee Tokyo with him. When he adamantly refuses, she cleans herself up. Donning her shrine priestess garb, she performs a ritual to empower a katana against Katō's influence.

Meanwhile, at the hospital, with Michiyo's assistance, Yanase performs a masked one-man show for the mental patients. He performs the role of Masakado and uses a large doll strapped to his back to portray Katō. However, once the latter is introduced, its eyes fill with light. The doll—possessed by Katō's undying anger—begins to control Yanase. Keiko appears, challenging him with her spiritually imbued katana. However, utilizing Katō's power, Yanase easily disarms her, forcing her to flee with Michiyo. As Yanase systematically kills all of the patients—including Narutaki—the hospital director is calmly watching Yanase on the monitors, receiving oral sex from one of the nurses.

Michiyo returns to the Ōzawa center, where her father lies dead. Yanase arrives behind her. The Katō doll is not with him. A few moments pass before it is clear that Yanase is now directly possessed by Katō. Suddenly, the bloblike creature that had been following Michiyo attacks Yanase, affixing itself to his face. Keiko arrives on the scene, chanting a spell. The creature disappears and Yanase collapses, finally free of Katō's curse. Hurt in the aftermath, Keiko reveals that Michiyo is of the Tatsumiya clan—members of Masakado's direct bloodline—and that Katō's plan was to use Michiyo's spirit to reawaken Masakado and destroy Tokyo. Before passing away, Keiko also states that the creature was a magical servant tasked with protecting her.

Police sirens sound and the newly exorcised Yanase becomes hysterical; while no longer possessed, he is still a murderer. He and Michiyo flee, taking refuge in an abandoned bowling alley. As Michiyo laments her father's death, he embraces her and they have sex once again. Directly afterward, they are attacked by the spirits of the girls that Yanase murdered, who take Michiyo away.

Yanase returns to the hospital pool to find the corpses of the women he killed missing, but the corpses of the patients and staff members he slaughtered under Katō's control are still intact. Several police officers come out from hiding and arrest Yanase for his crimes. As they are placing him into the police car, he bolts and escapes their grasp, hands still cuffed. The car ignition starts and the vehicle explodes, killing all but the police chief and Yanase. Watching from an upper hospital window is the hospital director, holding Yanase's Katō doll—the eyes of which still emit light.

Yanase stabs himself in the stomach, but does not die immediately. He escapes and the detective follows. Yanase finds his way to a theater where Michiyo—now possessed by the spirit of Masakado—attempts to kill him. The bloblike creature immediately attacks Michiyo. It inexplicably explodes, seeming to free her from being possessed. As Yanase and Michiyo leave, Yanase's Katō doll is seen sitting in the front row.

The two flee underground, where Yanase's wounds catch up with him. The two embrace in sexual union one last time. Meanwhile, the hospital director emerges from the theater, acting as if possessed. He states that the Katō doll's role is over and decapitates it. Further, he announces that he is neither god nor Masakado—he is himself. As the director and the injured police chief each attempt to track down Michiyo, she pleads to Masakado for help. Under Masakado's influence, the director and the police chief inadvertently kill each other, after which Michiyo passes away in Yanase's arms, leaving him to bleed out alone.

Darker and more sexualized than any other cinematic entry in the franchise, *Teito monogatari gaiden* seems like an exploitation film at its core, inexplicably attached to the Teito Monogatari franchise. However, in truth, it seems to demonstrate a full coupling of the film franchise with the *ero guro nansensu* genre. While no less complicated than any of its predecessors, the film creates a unique juxtaposition regarding the perception of reality. While Narutaki and the other patients are seemingly the ones that are hallucinating, it becomes clear that Yanase and the hospital director are the ones who have truly gone insane.

Unlike the other films in the franchise, *Teito monogatari gaiden* was not successful in Japan, and various reasons have emerged to explain this. First, Yasunori Katō (played in all three previous films by Kyūsaku Shimada, b. 1955)—the central character and main antagonist of the entire franchise—does not actually appear. This, however, did not stop the film staff from using Shimada's likeness in promotional materials for the film, suggesting that he would appear. Its release through V-cinema (rather than via Toho, like its predecessors) has also been viewed as evidence that a respectable company rejected the film, likely due to its darker and less savory content. However, it may instead have been a necessary move due to the fewer mandated restrictions and greater freedoms allowed for content appearing in V-cinema releases.—Joseph Elacqua

See also ero guro nansensu genre

Bibliography
Hashimoto, Izo, dir. *Teito monogatari gaiden*. V-Cinema, 1995. Film.

TEKETEKE and *TEKETEKE 2* (2009)
DIRECTOR: Kōji Shiraishi
SCREENPLAY: Takeki Akimoto
SPECS: *Teketeke*: 70 minutes; color
    Teketeke 2: 73 minutes; color

Toshi densetsu—urban legends about paranormal creatures and their attacks on innocent victims, traditionally passed by word of mouth—are so popular in Japan as to appear with some frequency in movies, anime, and manga alike, suggesting their endurance in the common imagination. As "cautionary tales," they incorporate to varying degrees moral prohibitions, warning children especially not to bully others, not to walk home late at night, or not to talk to strangers. The case of the *teketeke* arose from talk of a ghost of a young schoolgirl, said to have fallen on a railway line and to have been cut in half by the oncoming train. Now an *onroyō*, or vengeful spirit, she carries a scythe and travels on either her hands or elbows, or by dragging her upper torso behind her, making the scratching sound that is mimicked in the onomatopoeia "teketeke" (the English equivalent of which is "clack clack"). According to the legend, if she encounters anyone at night, she will slice that person in half at the torso, mirroring her own disfigurement. Building upon the supernatural premise to express the horror of the demonic, the films *Teketeke* (2009) and its sequel *Teketeke 2* (2009), both directed by Kōji Shiraishi (b. 1973), take their horrific plots from these legends.

In *Teketeke*, a young girl learns of the urban legend of *teketeke* after her friend is killed in a gruesome way. The legend tells of a female ghost that has no legs. When she visits the spot where her friend died, she makes contact with the now-vindictive, rancorous, unforgiving spirit. She manages to escape, but the legend suggests that she will die in three days and now she has to dig deeper to uncover those secrets buried in the tale, for only they can save her.

The sequel, *Teketeke 2*, however, is little more than the continuation of the tale. Interesting to note, the main figure in the legend is also known as "bata-bata" (again, mimicking the sound she makes as she runs on her elbows). Closely related is the tale of another girl, "Reiko Kashima," who died on the train tracks and lost her legs. Her name is a truncation of the term *kamen shinin ma*, or "mask of a dead-person demon." She is said to haunt bathroom stalls and will ask the occupant where her legs are. An incorrect answer results in the legs being ripped off. In order to remain safe, the victim must respond that her legs are at the Meishin Railway and answer that Reiko had shared this information. Sometimes, however, the apparition will pose a trick question, "What is my name?" To answer with "Kashima Reiko" in this instance will result in her attacking. The correct answer instead must be "Kamen Shinin Ma."

Filmic reiterations similar to the *Teketeke* series are quite numerous, including *Hanako of the Toilet* (1998), directed by Yukihiko Tsutsumi (b. 1955); *Otoshimono* (2006), directed by Takeshi Furusawa (b. 1972); *The Slit-Mouthed Woman* (2007), directed by Kōji Shiraishi; as well as the animated short, *Hanako-san* (2014), written and directed by American, Dan Tabor.—James A. Wren

Bibliography

Ballaster, Ros. *Fables of the East: 1662–1785*. London: Oxford University Press, 2005.

Freeman, Richard. *The Great Yokai Encylopaedia: The A–Z of Japanese Monsters*. Bideford, UK: CFZ Press, 2010.

Hearn, Lafcadio. *Kwaidan: Stories and Studies of Strange Things*. Tokyo: Tuttle Publishing, 2005.

Shiraishi, Kōji, dir. *Teketeke*. Art Port, 2009. Film.

———. *Teketeke 2*. Art Port, 2009. Film.

Yoda, H., and M. Alt. *Yokai Attack! The Japanese Monster Survival Guide*. Tokyo: Kodansha International, 2008.

TEN NIGHTS OF DREAMS (2007)

DIRECTOR: Akio Jissoji, Kon Ichikawa, Takashi Shimizu, Atsushi Shimizu, Keisuke Toyoshima, Matsuo Suzuki, Yoshitaka Amano and Masaaki Kawahara, Nobuhiro Yamashita, Miwa Nishikawa, Yūdai Yamaguchi

SCREENPLAY: Kenichiro Nagao, Miwa Nishikawa, Yūdai Yamaguchi, Junya Katō, Matsuo Suzuki, Keisuke Toyoshima, Shin'ichi Inotsume, Kokuji Yanagi, Kuze Teruhiko

SPECS: 100 minutes; color/black and white

Ten Nights of Dreams, or *Yume Juuya* in Japanese, is a 2008 film adaptation of Natsume Soseki's (b. 1867) collection of ten short horror stories published in 1908, in which each of the ten stories corresponds to one dream. One hundred years after the publication of the tales, the film aims to solve the mystery behind Soseki's riddle. The dreams are filmed by different directors, who each use their own style and interpret each story in their own way. Each dream is set in a different location and time; nonetheless, despite the differences, the film's ten segments share an oneiric atmosphere.

"The First Night, Love," directed by Akio Jissoji (b. 1937), tells the story of a writer staying at an inn and his relationship with the maid who takes care of him. After her death, he has to wait for one hundred years until she returns to him in an act of love.

"The Second Night, Anguish," directed by Kon Ichikawa (b. 1915), tells the story of a samurai who is unable to achieve enlightenment through meditation. The impossibility of reaching enlightenment drives the samurai to attempt suicide, an act that he is equally unable to achieve, leading to his anguish.

"The Third Night, Son," directed by Takashi Shimizu (b. 1972) tells the story as if Soseki were the dreamer. A man is walking in the woods carrying a blind child on his back. Then, the child conveys to the dreamer that he, the dreamer, killed him. The dreamer suddenly remembers that he is a killer, that he killed himself when he was thirteen.

In "The Fourth Night, Nostalgia," directed by Atsushi Shimizu (b. 1964), a grown-up Soseki travels to a mysterious and semi-abandoned town, where he encounters the town children. However, they are long-ago missing children, and they walk into the sea, leaving Soseki alone.

"The Fifth Night, Fear," directed by Keisuke Toyoshima (b. 1971), tells the story of a woman who tries to fall in love, but is stopped by a monster chasing her.

"The Sixth Night, Passion," directed by Matsuo Suzuki (b. 1962), is an encounter with a sculptor who performs a dance as his carving technique in front of an eclectic audience. The final sculpture is embedded inside the trunk of a tree and is revealed after two hammer hits.

"The Seventh Night, Loneliness," directed by Yoshitaka Amano (b. 1952) and Masaaki Kawahara, is the only animated segment of the film and also the only one in English in the original version. During an intergalactic journey, a lonely man finally decides to kill himself after meditating deeply about the meaning of life itself and his own existence.

In "The Eighth Night, Imagine," directed by Nobuhiro Yamashita (b. 1976), Soseki appears again, struggling to write his next story. In this process, images of his real life and his imagination are intertwined to portray his creative process.

"The Ninth Night, Family Love," directed by Miwa Nishikawa (b. 1974), tells the story of a woman who desperately prays for the safe return of her husband, who is on the war front. Yet, he died long ago.

"The Tenth Night, Egoism," directed by Yūdai Yamaguchi (b. 1971) tells the story of Shotaro, the best-looking man of the city. He thinks that "unattractive" women have no right to live, and therefore, he kills them. One day, he meets the beautiful Yoshino, who is secretly planning to avenge all those murdered women.

The film is a surreal collection of shorts that mix fantasy and horror in a reinterpretation of Soseki's tales. The overall collection of shorts works effectively to portray the world of dreams and nightmares through the different

directional styles. Many of the dreams are creepy and terrifying; others are odd
with a humorous twist; and still others conjure up anxiety. The shorts represent a good approximation to the world of horror and mystery that can occur
nightly.—Fernando Ortiz-Moya and Nieves Moreno Redondo

TETSUO films

Tetsuo: The Iron Man (1989)
DIRECTOR: Shin'ya Tsukamoto
SCREENPLAY: Shin'ya Tsukamoto
SPECS: 67 minutes; black and white

Tetsuo II: Body Hammer (1992)
DIRECTOR: Shin'ya Tsukamoto
SCREENPLAY: Shin'ya Tsukamoto
SPECS: 83 minutes; color

Tetsuo: The Bullet Man (2009)
DIRECTOR: Shin'ya Tsukamoto
SCREENPLAY: Shin'ya Tsukamoto
SPECS: 71 minutes; color

The cyberpunk Tetsuo franchise of films, already cult classics melding science
fiction with horror, is comprised of three works. Directed by Shin'ya Tsukamoto
(b. 1960) and filmed in black and white, the original low-budget film *Tetsuo:
The Iron Man* (1989) was an overwhelming financial success, leading to the less-
successful production of *Tetsuo II: Body Hammer* (1992). *Tetsuo: The Bullet Man*
(2009) followed almost two decades later and played to the next generation of fans.
Taken together, they bolstered Tsukamoto's recognition internationally, resulting in superstardom and in what can only be called a worldwide cult following.

Falling precariously between modern-day nightmare and techno-fetishist
science-fiction fantasy, *Tetsuo: The Iron Man*, often compared in hindsight to
the surrealist works of American director David Lynch (b. 1946) and with the
body horror—some say, venereal horror—films of Canadian David Cronenberg
(b. 1943), brings together as a hybrid explosive violence, bizarre imagery and
black humor into a cinematic horror experience of extraordinary proportions.
It was Tsukamoto's first movie to be shot on 16 mm, all of his previous work
having been filmed with Super 8 cameras. It opens as "the man" (or "Metal
Fetish") cuts a massive gash in his leg and thrusts a large threaded steel rod
into his wound. The injury fails to heal, and once he sees the maggots festering
in the wound, he grows agitated, lets out a blood-curdling scream, and runs
out into the street, where he is hit by a car driven by a Japanese businessman.
The businessman and his girlfriend collect the body and dump it into a ravine.
In a flashback, it is revealed that their actions led to inflamed passions and
sexual intercourse. But Metal Fetish has his revenge, as the body of his killer
begins to undergo a metamorphosis until he is changed into a walking pile of
scrap metal.

Notable among the graphic and disturbing episodes that run throughout the film are several highly stylized chase scenes alongside similar recurrent meta-morphoses (a demure office worker devolves into a wild metal-infected woman), as well as a terrifying dream sequence alongside yet another metamorphosis (the girlfriend, transformed into an exotic dancer with a snake-like metal probe, terrorizes and rapes the businessman) and the moments thereafter when, waking from this dream, the businessman and his girlfriend have sex at his apartment and then eat ravenously, erotically. In these instances, images of violence combine with decay and death, resulting in a sexual awakening induced by the intercalating worlds of desire and death as a singular act that defines personal and social identities alike. This morbid and decadent sense of beauty, in fact, equates violence and death with the only aesthetic experiences available. Similar to the relationship in Samuel Beckett's *Waiting for Godot*, where Didi and Gogo's discussion of hanging themselves produces orgasm, in these images we see the symbolic joining of the remains of life with death, the union of which validates sexual longing and culminates in sexual release.

It is at this point that the businessman suddenly discovers his penis has mutated into a gargantuan power drill. He begins to fight with his girlfriend, as the terror increases so, too, does he acquire more and more metal on his body. Neither able to prevail nor resist further, she impales herself on his drill and dies.

Helpless to do anything, the businessman, now the Iron Man, is visited by the Metal Fetishist, who emerges from his dead girlfriend's corpse to show him a vision of a "New World" of nothing save scrap metal. He goes so far as to turn cats into grotesque metal creatures. As Iron Man flees, he is followed by Metal Fetish into an abandoned building. A final battle ensues, and the film ends as Iron Man struggles to merge with the Fetish into a two-headed metal monster. They agree to turn the whole world into metal and rust it, scattering it into the dust of the universe as they proclaim, "Our love can put an end to this fucking world. Let's Go!" As the duo charges through the streets as a twisted fusion of men and accumulated metal, what emerges is largely phallic in form. Reflecting the revolutionary nature of Tsukamoto's approach to the genre, the film ends not as a narrative of events but in a single moment of participation with the words "GAME OVER."

Tetsuo II is less a sequel per se than a bigger-budget reworking of *Tetsuo: The Iron Man*, utilizing similar themes and ideas to the earlier film. In this case, after his son is kidnapped by a gang of violent thugs, a Japanese salary man succumbs to his rage and his body transforms into a lethal weapon, something of a cyber-kinetic gun of a sort. And while it was not so well received as its predecessor, it did win the Critic's Award at the Third Yubari International Fantastic Film Festival in February, 1992. Likewise, for his efforts, Tsukamoto earned a number of awards and accolades, among them a Silver Raven in Brussels, the 1992 Fanta-sporto International Fantasy Film Special Jury Award, and a nomination for Director's Prize at the Sitges-Catalonian International Film Festival that same year.

Following a hiatus of some two decades, in 2009, Tsukamoto returned to the subject storyline with *Tetsuo: The Bullet Man*. His first effort entirely filmed in English premiered as part of the 2009 Venice Film Festival and later in the United States with the Tribeca Film Festival. In this particular telling, "Anthony," the son of an American father and a Japanese mother, now deceased, lives and works in Tokyo. Following the death of his own son, who is run down and killed by Yatsu, Anthony begins his transformation into metal. He discovers a secret room where files and papers have been stored away detailing the Tetsuo Project. His father had recorded the process by which individuals might be turned into androids.

Anthony's father then calls him to explain everything: Anthony's mother had grown disillusioned with the outcome of the Tetsuo Project, having envisioned a process whereby she might help give disabled and infirm people new bodies. As she realized that she was dying, she insisted that she become a Tetsuo android, thereby allowing the American scientist to have a child. At this point, it becomes obvious that Anthony and his own son are also a part of the Tetsuo Project.

Yatsu realizes that the only way he will find peace is to be shot by the father of the boy he killed. As Anthony's rage explodes onto the scene, he transforms into a gigantic metallic beast with a cannon in his center. Rather than kill Yatsu, however, Anthony instead consumes him in an act that once more returns him to human form. In a flash-forward some five years later, he walks into the street and is harassed by a group of young thugs who attempt to intimidate him. He restrains himself and his anger, however, and he walks away, with newfound calm and confidence as the closing credits of the film roll. All the while, we hear an original song track entitled "Theme for Tetsuo: The Bullet Man," performed by the industrial rock band, Nine Inch Nails.—James A. Wren

Bibliography

Balmain, Colette. *Introduction to Japanese Horror Film*. Edinburgh: Edinburgh University Press, 2008.

Jacoby, Alexander, and Donald Richie. *A Critical Handbook of Japanese Film Directors: From the Silent Era to the Present Day*. Berkeley, CA: Stone Bridge Press, 2008.

Mes, Tom, Jasper Sharp, and Hideo Nakata. *The Midnight Eye Guide to New Japanese Film*. Berkeley, CA: Stone Bridge Press, 2004.

Phillips, Alistar, and Julian Stringer. *Japanese Cinema: Texts and Contexts*. London: Routledge, 2007.

Richards, Andy. *Asian Horror*. Harpenden, UK: Kamera Books, 2010.

Standish, Isolde. *A New History of Japanese Cinema: A Century of Narrative Film*. London: Bloomsbury Academic, 2006.

TŌKAIDŌ YOTSUYA KAIDAN (1959)

DIRECTOR: Nobuo Nakagawa
SCREENPLAY: Masayoshi Ōnuki, Yoshihiro Ishikawa
SPECS: 76 minutes; color

Nobuo Nakagawa's 1959 film is based on the popular Kabuki play of the same name, written in 1825 by Tsuruya Nanboku. Since its first performance, the story has entranced audiences, first as the play, then in the *ukiyo-e* woodblock print form, before being made into two short films in 1913 and 1915. Feature-length interpretations followed in 1923 and 1928, but the militarization of the 1930s oriented film content toward nationalistic and patriotic themes. The horror genre was revitalized in the early postwar period in a trend hailed by Tadao Satō as a return to the Edo-period (1603–1867) appreciation of "erotic grotesque nonsensu" stories, or *ero guro nansensu*. The Edo era Yotsuya tale played a large part in this horror revival; several remakes followed Kinoshita Keisuke's critically acclaimed *Yotsuya kaidan* of 1949. Nakagawa came to the story fresh from a series of successful horror films including *Kaii Utsunomiya tenjō* (*Ghost of Hanging in Utsunomiya*, 1956), *Kaidan kasane ga fuchi* (*The Depths*, 1957), and *Bōrei kaibyō yashiki* (*Black Cat Mansion*, 1958). Though Daiei released a version of the tale in the same month (*Yotsuya kaidan*, dir. Kenji Misumi), Nakagawa's adaptation for Shintōhō was the starrier and more successful film.

The story follows Iemon Tamiya (Shigeru Amachi), an itinerant samurai who becomes increasingly violent in attempting to improve his fortunes. Falling for the bourgeois Oiwa (Katsuko Wakasugi), he fails to persuade her father to permit their marriage and kills him and his retainer in violent frustration. Lamp carrier Naosuke (Emi Shuntaro) witnesses the murders and offers to help cover up the crime in exchange for an escalating series of favors. Shortly after their marriage, reduced to a life of poverty as a fan maker, Iemon grows frustrated by his life with his wife and young son and falls for a wealthy local woman named Oume (Junko Ikeuchi). He plans to poison Oiwa after framing her as an adulteress and to kill Takuetsu, the masseuse he has posed as her lover. However, the poison only disfigures Oiwa's face, causing her to stab herself with a razor after threatening Takuetsu. Iemon kills the masseuse and nails the two to a screen door to perpetuate the adultery story, before throwing their bodies in the river.

On the night of Iemon's wedding to Oume, the ghosts of Oiwa and Takuetsu return and trick Iemon into killing Oume and her parents. While Oiwa appears to Iemon in her disfigured form, becoming increasingly green-tinged and decomposed, she appears to her sister, Osode, and the son of their father's murdered retainer, in her previous uninjured form, leading them to Iemon and revealing his crimes. The two avenge her death, forcing Iemon to confess before killing him by the river where he had dumped Oiwa's body. While the storyline of *Tōkaidō Yotsuya kaidan* is centered on the "hungry ghost" motif, in which a dead person is unable to pass into the spirit world while unfinished business remains in the human realm, the final scene of Nakagawa's version implies that Oiwa has attained peace. Silhouetted against the moon and evening mist, her face is once again free of scarring and she holds her baby son. Her white kimono and loose hair conform to the costume of the *yurei*, or female ghost, as she floats and fades into the darkness.

Stylistically, Nakagawa's film references both the visual codes of *ukiyo-e* ghost images and the Kabuki stage. The first half of the film is mainly composed of long shots; in the widescreen format common to Shintōhō and Tōhō studio productions of the late 1950s, these long shots are reminiscent of Kabuki theater as is the bright coloring and prolific use of the color red. The scene in which Iemon first meets Oume illustrates this stylistic motif; the action takes place behind a slatted screen with two wide red panels at either side. The actors move swiftly across this space in straight lateral bursts reminiscent of the movements of Kabuki actors. Shintōhō further stressed the Kabuki connection by distributing the film during summer; horror Kabuki plays were traditionally performed in the summer months as the "chills" of fear felt by the audience were thought to counteract the heat of the summer weather.

Tōkaidō Yotsuya kaidan looks forward as well as back; the neon color palette of the fantasy scenes in which Iemon imagines himself tortured by terrifying bloody images of Oiwa and Takuetsu anticipates the tones of Nakagawa's celebrated *Jigoku* (*Hell*, 1960), as does the characterization of Naosuke. Goading Iemon into ever more reckless and violent acts, Naosuke's characterization is the forerunner to Numata Yōichi's Tamura in the later film, who ruins his friend's life by involving him in ever darker deeds. In 1959, *Tōkaidō Yotsuya kaidan* hinted at the future of the Japanese horror genre, driven to constant innovation by the imminent decline in cinema attendance, and at the same time positioned the genre within its long domestic historical context.—Jennifer Coates

Bibliography

Izawa, Jun. "Yotsuya kaidan." In *Nihon eiga sakuhin zenshū: Kinema Junpō zōkan 11.20-gō*. Tokyo: Kinema Junpōsha, 1973.

Misumi, Kenji, dir. *Yotsuya kaidan*. Daiei, 1959. Film.

Nakagawa, Nobuo, dir. *Bōrei kaibyōyashiki*. Shintōhō, 1958. Film.

———. *Kaidan kasane ga fuchi*. Shintōhō, 1957. Film.

———. *Kaii Utsunomiya tenjō*. Shintōhō, 1956. Film.

———. *Jigoku*. Shinōhō, 1960. Film.

———. *Tōkaidō Yotsuya kaidan*. Shintōhō, 1959. Film.

Satō, Tadao. "Kiki to mosaku." In *Kōza nihon eiga, vol.6: Nihon eiga no mosaku*, edited by Imamura, Shōhei et al., 2–75. Tokyo: Iwanami Shoten, 1987.

Yasuda, Sumio. "Yotsuya Kaidan." *Eiga Hyōron* 6, no. 9 (September 1949): 19–20.

TOKYO BABYLON 1999 (1993)

Director: Jōji Iida
Screenplay: Ōkawa Nanase
Specs: 63 minutes; color

Tokyo Babylon 1999 is a thriller directed in 1993 by Jōji Iida. The script was written by Ōkawa Nanase (b. 1967), the director and author of the all-female manga artist group known as CLAMP. The film itself serves primarily as a bridge between two of CLAMP's best-known manga series: *Tokyo Babylon* (1990–1993) and *X* (1992–). The film's plot is heavily adapted from "Call," the plot arc represented in the third volume of the *Tokyo Babylon* manga.

The film opens on three teenage schoolgirls, one—Megumi—in tears. Her friends take her to the apartment of a man named Tomokichi Kanayama, where four other girls have already gathered and are discussing the arts of the *onmyōji* (masters of yin-yang) of Japan's past—diviners with a talent for manipulating the forces of nature. Upon arriving, Megumi becomes hysterical, bemoaning that she was harshly reprimanded by one of her teachers, Mr. Tanaka. Unmoved, Kanayama explains that all of their hearts have been wounded somehow, and tells them that they are all "special." He goes on to describe that the capital of Tokyo is also special; regardless of how many are killed in natural disasters, it remains the capital. In doing so, he implies that the schoolgirls can each stand strong against those who hurt them. Standing outside Kanayama's apartment is a man dressed in a black suit and dark shades.

The next scene opens on an exorcism. The protagonist of the series, the modern young onmyōji Subaru Sumeragi (played by Toshihide Tonesaku, b. 1972), attempts to expel a ghost from a young girl. The exorcism is successful, but before departing, the demon taunts Sumeragi, stating that the intense hatred burning in his heart is causing his powers to weaken.

Outside Kanayama's apartment, the mysterious man removes his shades, revealing a glass right eye. This man is the series' antagonist, Seishirō Sakurazuka, portrayed by Wataru Shihōdō (b. 1962). Like Sumeragi, Sakurazuka is an onmyōji, but his powers are used for assassination. The two onmyōji were once great friends until events occurring in the *Tokyo Babylon* manga destroyed that bond. In recent years, Sumeragi has been chasing Sakurazuka with the intent to kill him, but has not yet managed to do so.

Sakurazuka breaks the barrier protecting Kanayama's apartment and appears inside. Realizing he is a threat, Kanayama begins a spell, but Sakurazuka tightens his throat. The assassin tells Kanayama that the maliciousness of his own spells has summoned maggots to eat his flesh. Kanayama lifts his shirt, sees the maggots burrowing into his flesh, and screams. Meanwhile, things have gotten worse for Megumi, who flees to Kanayama's apartment for refuge. She discovers his corpse as well as a box sealed with a talisman. Opening it, she discovers a book of onmyōji curses, which she steals.

Sumeragi meets with his assistant, Shūhei Amano (played by Shigemitsu Ogi, b. 1961), who informs him of Kanayama's murder. He reminds Sumeragi that Kanayama had learned his spells from the Sumeragi family and then disappeared for twelve years. The detective states that it was Sakurazuka who killed him. Investigating the apartment, Sumeragi discovers the talisman and the empty box it once sealed.

The seven girls have met to discuss the book, especially regarding a death curse detailed therein. Ultimately, the book becomes their means to extract vengeance on their enemies. Tanaka is chosen to test the spell's powers. The girls review his acts, judge him guilty, and then begin the curse. Amano and Sumeragi review the corpse, the latter easily determining the cause.

In the wake of Tanaka's death, Megumi has second thoughts, but the others largely take it upon themselves to punish those who do evil. One of the girls admits to having been raped by three men and rolls her sleeve above her forearm, scarred from a suicide attempt. The girls perform the ritual again.

Amano and Sumeragi investigate the deaths of the girl's three rapists. Sumeragi concludes not only that it is the same curse, but also that the curse is being used by amateurs. This curse contains too much power for a job this easy; a professional onmyōji would know that extra power would backlash upon its caster. Sumeragi senses a strange energy at the crime scene and finds all seven girls among the crowd there. Upon confronting one, the girls flee, one of them deciding that he should be their next target. A red wormlike creature slithers by one of the girls' feet. They are also targeted by hallucinations.

Returning to his apartment, Sumeragi finds Haruka waiting for him. When she leaves, Sumeragi finds himself face-to-face with Sakurazuka. The assassin explains that Kanayama brought the emotionally wounded girls in order to complete the spell. He had killed Kanayama to bring an end to it, though the girls are continuing his legacy. Sakurazuka leaves, stating that he will spare the girls for a while longer, and that their unfinished business must wait for another time.

A sick Megumi is visited at school by Sumeragi. He discovers a red leech-like creature at the base of her neck and tears it away. It is the same type of creature that ate away at Kanayama—a wormlike insect summoned as part of the backlash for powerful spells. Sumeragi exorcises the evil influence from Megumi so that the backlash will no longer affect her. When the girls call her cell phone, Sumeragi attempts to stop them over the phone and they target him with a spell, which he reflects back upon them. The backlash causes them to hallucinate and vomit.

Sumeragi finds the other six girls and tries to dissuade them from cursing others to death. However, the girls consider their acts justified. One of the girls has lost consciousness completely, and the others blame Sumeragi for it. The five remaining girls chant the curse against him, but he does not deflect it for fear of further harming the girls. Their magic violently repels the onmyōji from the room and he loses consciousness.

Sakurazuka arrives, examining Sumeragi's wounds. The assassin praises him, stating that he hasn't changed at all. Sakurazuka then turns on the girls, stating that it is power—not justice—that determines how the world functions. With one hand, he causes them to drop to the floor, gasping for air. When Sakurazuka raises his hand to strike again, a now-conscious Sumeragi demands that he stop. The young onmyōji affirms that he will protect the girls from their deaths at Sakurazuka's hands.

Sumeragi asks if the assassin honestly feels no pain or remorse, having killed so many people. He cannot forget about the death of his sister Hokuto at Sakurazuka's hands, several years prior. Sumeragi's emotions finally reach their breaking point and the two onmyōji begin to fight for the first time in years. Both are wounded, but before the battle can continue, Haruka's voice begs that they stop. But Sumeragi hears the voice as his sister Hokuto's. Possessing Haruka's body, Hokuto begs her brother not to use his powers out of hatred. Sakurazuka thanks his rival and calmly exits, knowing that their decisive battle is fated for a future meeting.

Sumeragi carries Haruka outside, with the other girls following. He remarks to Amano that they have wandered off the correct path and simply need to be shown the right way again. Sumeragi acknowledges that in this case, he is exactly like them.

The film opens the door for CLAMP's still unfinished manga series, *X*, during which Sumeragi and Sakurazuka have several other encounters, and finally meet their ultimate destinies.

The importance of *Tokyo Babylon 1999* lies in the fact that it is the first live-action film to be based on a CLAMP work. Despite international acclaim for the two manga series that it connects, *Tokyo Babylon 1999* did not receive any major awards. It was released only in Japan, and only on VHS, making it a rare find today.—Joseph Elacqua

See also Onmyōji.

Bibliography

Clamp. *Tokyo Babylon.* 18.5 vols. Tokyo: Kadokawa Shoten, 1992–2002. Manga.

Clamp. *X.* 7 vols. Tokyo: Shinshōkan, 1990–1993. Manga.

Iida Jōji, dir. *Tokyo Babylon 1999.* PDS, 1993. Film.

TOKYO GORE POLICE (2008)

DIRECTOR: Yoshihiro Nishimura
SCREENPLAY: Yoshihiro Nishimura, Maki Mizui, Kengo Kaji
SPECS: 110 minutes; color

Tokyo Gore Police is a 2008 comedy-action-horror film helmed by director and noted special-effects artist Yoshihiro Nishimura (b. 1967). A joint Japanese-American production, the film was shot in only two weeks. Structured in a series of set pieces, *Tokyo Gore Police* keeps up a frenetic pace of violence and disturbing imagery built around a tale of betrayal and revenge. True to the word *gore* in the title, the action is rife with gleeful decapitations, fountains of blood, and severed body parts.

In an alternate Japan, a privatized police force is facing a rash of crimes committed by engineers, criminals who have the ability to transform an injury into a deadly weapon. At the head of the anti-engineer squad is Ruka, played by Eihi Shiina (b. 1976), a young woman fostered by the police commissioner general after her patrolman father was murdered at an anti-privatization rally years before. Quiet, withdrawn, and prone to cutting herself, Ruka has been trained since childhood by the commissioner, played by Shun Sugata (b. 1955), to be the ultimate weapon against engineers. While on the hunt for the mysterious creator of the engineers, a figure known as the "Key Man," portrayed by Itsuji Itao (b. 1963), Ruka is captured and a key-shaped organic tumor is inserted into her scarred arm, turning her into an engineer.

Ruka follows a series of clues to an abandoned apartment where the Key Man waits. He reveals her father was assassinated on the orders of the police commissioner, as Ruka's father was the driving force behind the movement to prevent privatization. The Key Man's father was the assassin, an ex-police sniper forced to perform the killing to support his family. The Key Man's father was betrayed and shot by the commissioner, fueling the Key Man's rage. Rebuffing his offer to join forces in order to take revenge, Ruka cleaves the Key Man in half with her katana and goes to confront her foster father.

While Ruka is pursuing her leads, a policeman who was transformed into an engineer assaults the station, goading the commissioner into declaring an all-out war against the engineers. His orders translate into indiscriminate violence on the streets, as police officers devolve into brutal killers, murdering civilians and executing anyone suspected of being an engineer. Ruka, now armed with the knowledge of the corruption at the heart of the police force, turns against her former teammates, but not before her only friend is drawn and quartered by renegade cops. As she slaughters the policemen responsible, Ruka is shot in the hand and eye, wounds that are quickly replaced by a snakelike claw arm and a cybernetic eye. Augmented by the engineer weapons, she battles her way to the station and confronts her foster father with his deception. Ruka engages the commissioner in a duel, climaxing with his decapitation. The film ends with a revived Key Man and his schoolgirl accomplice walking away after a commercial announces the privatization of Japan's armed forces.

Nishimura was tapped to direct the film after working on 2008's *Machine Girl*, and he chose to remake his 1995 independent film *Anatomia Extinction*. His special-effects background and splatter sensibilities resonate throughout

Tokyo Gore Police. From an early shot of a man's head exploding to an image of Tokyo Tower silhouetted against a colossal Mount Fuji, *Tokyo Gore Police* makes no excuses about being unabashedly cartoonish, bloody, and over the top. Ruka uses a bazooka to rocket jump to the top of a building, police wear neo-samurai armor, a chain gun fires severed hands, breasts spew flesh-dissolving acid, and a hyperactive dispatcher gives Ruka her orders and provides exposition for the audience. The action sequences and the police uniforms echo sentai shows, as Ruka's fellow officers transform from her costumed allies into an army of murderous minions. Taking a page from *RoboCop*, Nishimura fleshes out his strange alternate Japan with bizarre commercials touting fashion razors for self-mutilation and public service announcements warning against ritual suicide. Of particular shock horror note is a scene where a police officer enters a grotesque club to bid on the services of mutated companions.

Nishimura revisited the blood-soaked world of *Tokyo Gore Police* in 2009 with an equally outlandish short sequel entitled *63 Minutes After*, and collaborated again with Eihi Shiina in his second major directorial outing, 2010's *Helldriver*.—Daniel Fandino

Bibliography

Nishimura, Yoshihiro, dir. *Tokyo Gore Police*, Nikkatsu, 2008. Film.

TOKYO GORE SCHOOL (2009)

DIRECTOR: Yōhei Fukuda
SCREENPLAY: Yōhei Fukuda, Kiyoshi Yamamoto
SPECS: 109 minutes; color

Tokyo Gore School, known in Japanese as *Gakkō ura saito*, is a 2009 Japanese horror-thriller film directed by Yōhei Fukuda. The film revolves around a large group of students that engage in an online game played via cell phones through which they fight each other, often to the death, in order to protect their darkest personal secrets, as information is made public once an opponent captures another's phone. Depending on their fighting skills and ability to be defeated, students are worth point values that are also awarded to a victor once another student is beaten. As per the sadistic rules of the game, points earned through the assault and theft of a fellow student's phone can be used by the victor to delete their own personal secrets, in turn protecting their privacy. Contrary to Fukuda's cinematographic work on Kōji Shiraishi's (b. 1973) 2009 sadistic splatter-horror film *Grotesque*, *Tokyo Gore School* is restrained in its extreme violence and arterial splatter, with only a few scenes that depict graphic gore. Fukuda's film draws influence from director Kinji Fukasaku's (b. 1930) successful 2000 action thriller *Battle Royale* in which the Japanese government under the "Battle Royale" legislature, forces a group of students to fight to the death in which the last student standing remains victorious.

Tokyo Gore School revolves around the popular class president of the high school Hayato Fujiwara, played by Yusuke Yamada (b. 1987), who lives by the creed that life is divided into winners and losers, and that the strong will prevail against the weak. After a suicide attempt in which a student, Shinichi Sanada, leaps from a building in response to being bullied by a band of delinquent youths led by Kenji Todoroki, played by Shunya Shiraishi (b. 1990), Fujiwara is suddenly chased across the city by several unknown students who attempt to assault him. Fujiwara is able to escape and after subduing and subsequently interrogating an attacking student named Masashi Kajima, played by Shoichi Matsuda (b. 1986), finds out that he is unwillingly a contestant in the popular mobile game. Fujiwara decides that in order to protect his darkest secrets he must fight the game's other players and crown himself as winner. He begins to collect points by defeating several opponents and uses them to erase some of his personal secrets per the rules of the game. Fujiwara soon saves a female student, Chiori Kinoshita, played by Nako Mizusawa (b. 1993), from assault by an opponent and befriends her as she reminds him of an individual from his past named Yoko.

As Fujiwara and Chiori navigate the school grounds avoiding potential assaulters, they are confronted by a countermovement of weaker "nerds," who have banded together so as to defend themselves from the game's opponents based on the principle of "strength by numbers." The counter group is led by Shinichiro Kamiya, played by Shinwa Kataoka (b. 1985), who uses a bus that consistently drives him and his fellow students around so as to avoid danger. It is soon revealed that Kamiya is the son of the Minister of Education and it is suspected that his father is controlling the game. Fujiwara soon parts from both the counter group of nerds and Chiori, as he feels that their weak-willed nature will threaten his odds of winning the game. In the meantime, Kamiya and his fellow students are captured by Todoroki and his henchmen, who begin to torture them, even going as far as to viciously beat a student's head in with a metal rod. Fujiwara soon reunites with Chiori and selfishly decides that he must defeat Todoroki even if it means using Chiori as a decoy and placing her in harm's way. In an old storage building, Todoroki and Fujiwara confront each other and face off in an epic fight, in which Fujiwara stabs Todoroki in the neck, which splatters blood upon Fujiwara's face. With his new points earned from defeating Todoroki, Fujiwara attempts to delete the entirety of his secrets from the game database only to discover that he is one point short and decides to take Chiori's phone in a final effort to win. Before he can betray Chiori, she sneaks up on Fujiwara and stabs a knife through his hand. She then reveals that in junior high, Fujiwara had attempted to intercede and stop the bullying of her deceased sister, Yoko, which in turned caused Fujiwara to become bullied by the very girl he attempted to defend. In his frustration and angst, Fujiwara took revenge. Yoko is often mentioned by Fujiwara as a mysterious figure from his past through the film. Chiori reveals Fujiwara's dark secret in that he raped Yoko, which caused her to commit suicide in front of him by slitting her own wrists. Chiori had used the game as a means to carry out her own revenge against Fujiwara. Once Fujiwara sees that he has lost the game, he leaps from a window to his own death as opposed to having to live with the guilt of his atrocities committed against Yoko. As Fujiwara slowly dies, Chiori reveals to him via his cell phone that his darkest secret stored by the game was in actuality that he had defecated in his pants in elementary school. At the conclusion of the film, a series of interviews once again suggest that the Minister of Education created the game as part of his School Justice Bill as a way to eliminate delinquent students by pitting them against each other.

Tokyo Gore School, although restrained in its gore and splatter compared to Fukuda's somewhat popular hack and slash approach taken by his bikini-wearing girls that fight zombie hoards in his 2008 *Chanbara Beauty* or his cinematographic work in Kōji Shiraishi's *Grotesque*, does express its carnage through the lens of the prominent social issue of cyberbullying within Japanese society. This theme of bullying within the Japanese school system is taken up by Fukuda once more in his 2010 film *X-Game*, in which students are forced by hooded figures to torture each other through a series of sadistic events.—Edwin Lohmeyer

See also Battle Royale

Bibliography

Fukuda, Yōhei, dir. *Tokyo Gore School*. JollyRoger, 2009. Film

TOKYO: THE LAST MEGALOPOLIS (1988)

DIRECTOR: Akio Jissōji
SCREENPLAY: Kaizo Hayashi
SPECS: 135 minutes; color

Tokyo: The Last Megalopolis is a 1988 epic film directed by Akio Jissōji (1937–2006). Its original title, *Teito Monogatari* (The tale of the imperial capital) is the name of the novel upon which it is based. The original novel, authored by Hiroshi Aramata (b. 1947), is presently twelve volumes long. Epic in size and scope, the novel includes a host of characters—both fictional and historical—and ultimately presents a detailed history of Tokyo, covering nearly the entire twentieth century.

The 1988 narrative-heavy film adaptation is based on the first four volumes of the novel, but presents its source material in an interesting manner. Rather than altering and adapting the original narrative to fit a two-hour time frame, the film lavishes much of its time and detail on the most central scenes of the novel. As a result, these scenes are presented in a largely disjointed manner. This allows the film to maintain most of the major narrative elements, but also causes it to rely heavily on the viewers' familiarity with the original novel.

Lacking a true protagonist, the film focuses largely on the novel's main antagonist: a powerful sorcerer (i.e., an *onmyōji*, or "master of yin-yang") named Yasunori Katō, portrayed by Kyūsaku Shimada (b. 1955). Katō's main ambition is to level the capital of Tokyo by awakening the spirit of Taira no Masakado (d. 940), an ancient rebel who almost succeeded in overthrowing the Japanese central government. Nearly one millennium later, Katō seeks to fulfill Masakado's vengeance. Katō's machinations focus on the Tatsumiya family—the modern direct descendants of Masakado. With help from the onmyōji Yasumasa Hirai, the Tatsumiyas and others attempt to stop Katō from destroying the city.

The year is 1912. The film opens on a conversation between Hirai, portrayed by Mikijiro Hira, and Eiichi Shibusawa (1840–1931), portrayed by Shintarō Katsu (1931–1997). An industrialist and economist who introduced Western capitalism to Japan, Shibusawa seeks to transform Tokyo into the perfect city. Having learned that a mass of spiritual energy is building up at the site of Masakado's grave in Tokyo, Hirai begs Shibusawa to consider geomantic and other magical means as well.

The film then cuts to a fair attended by Yōichiro Tatsumiya, played by Junichi Ishida (b. 1954), and his sister Yukari, portrayed by Haruka Sugata. Eventually, they encounter the villainous Katō, who intends to kidnap Yukari. She takes refuge inside a temple, guarded by Hirai and a number of onmyōji, who chant Buddhist sutras in defense. Outside the temple, Katō's assistant, the Chinese witch Feng Hong, releases magical talismans that transform into ravens and attack the temple guards. Katō's powers overcome Hirai and he escapes with Yukari. At a hidden stronghold, Katō and Hong magically manipulate Yukari until Masakado's spirit begins to speak through her. He warns the two to leave his grave alone. Hirai's magic interrupts Katō, who flees, leaving Yukari behind, still a slave to his magic.

In the meantime, Keiko Mekata (portrayed by Mieko Harada, b. 1958), a shrine maiden, is tasked with stopping Masakado from rising. Shibusawa also holds a meeting regarding the development of a new Tokyo, attended by Hirai.

Hirai then focuses his power on removing Katō's curse from Yukari. He exorcises Katō's influence, which takes the form of a worm-like creature that Yukari vomits up. Hirai reveals that Yukari is pregnant, inferring that Katō is the father. He states that Katō must have targeted Yukari because she is a female of Masakado's bloodline. Katō's goal is to utilize Yukari as a spiritual medium to awaken the spirit of Masakado. Katō's power combined with Masakado's would easily destroy all of Tokyo.

Privately, Hirai performs a ritual to divine the date on which Katō will destroy the city. He sits before an open scroll that illustrates the deities of the zodiac. Vigorously stabbing himself in the stomach, Hirai's blood flows down the scroll, pooling at the figure indicating 1922. As Hirai is bleeding out, Katō appears, insulting Hirai's technique. He presses his boot to Hirai's back, pushing more blood from the wound. The blood flows and pools at the final figure in the scroll, revealing that Katō will actually destroy the city in 1923.

The film cuts to 1923—eleven years later—revealing that Katō now plans to destroy the city with a giant earthquake that will send an enormous amount of spiritual energy to Masakado's grave, awakening him. Now in the Chinese city of Dalian, Katō holds a ceremony to send a great amount of spiritual energy to Tokyo through the ground. In 1923, two new characters come into the spotlight: Shigemaru Kuroda, a master of feng shui (Chinese geomancy) that aids in the fight against Katō, and Yukiko Tatsumiya, Yukari's daughter and Katō's new target.

When Katō returns to revive Masakado, he must face spells that Hirai had passed down to his comrades: among them, their friend Junichi Narutaki, portrayed by Shirō Sano (b. 1955), and the author Rohan Kōda (1867–1947), portrayed by Kōji Takahashi (b. 1935). Katō's power is too great, however, and he quickly dispels the magic barriers keeping him from Masakado's grave. The following day, September 1, the Great Kantō Earthquake devastates Tokyo, causing unprecedented destruction. Yet the spirit of Masakado does not awaken; the city—though severely damaged—has not yet been annihilated.

In the wake of the earthquake, many new developments begin. The industrialist Torahiko Terada (1878–1935) and the businessman Noritsugu Hayakawa
(1881–1942) join forces to establish an underground railway. Keiko takes up Hirai's mantle and becomes the main spiritual force against Katō.

The film cuts to 1927, at which point smaller scenes are strung together
with little continuity. We see, for example, that Yukari's brother Yōichirō has
married Keiko. The team working on the underground railway continues their
work, only to find it infested with Katō's demons. A new character, author and
fortune-teller Izumi Kyōka (1873–1939), divines that Keiko possesses the great
power of Avalokiteśvara, the bodhisattva of compassion.

On Yukiko's birthday, she is kidnapped by Katō in Ginza. Keiko pursues
Katō, who reveals that if Yukari could not awaken Masakado, then surely his
child will. Despite Keiko's prowess, Katō escapes with Yukiko. Later, taking
refuge in an abandoned temple, Katō transports Yukiko to Masakado's grave in
order to awaken his spirit.

In the meantime, Terada seeks out the help of the biologist Makoto Nishimura
(1883–1956)—played by his real-life son, Kō Nishimura (1923–1997)—and his artificial robot Gakutensoku to clear the underground tunnels of Katō's demons.
Gakutensoku is able to clear more of a path for them, but the demons eventually
deactivate him. Nishimura engages the machine's self-destruct mechanism to
destroy the demons.

Keiko and Shigemaru discover Katō's location and travel there to stop him.
They are greeted by an animated statue of an asura (an Indian demigod) with a
weapon in each of its many hands. Shigemaru tells Keiko to go ahead. In the
meantime, Yukari, Yōichirō, and Kōda travel to Masakado's gravesite to rescue
Yukiko. They are too late, however, as Masakado begins to awaken.

Keiko finally comes face-to-face with Katō, who has not completely succeeded in awakening Masakado. Keiko reveals that Katō is not Yukiko's biological father. While not expressly stated in the film, it is implied (and explicitly
stated elsewhere) that Yukiko is a result of the incestuous union of Yukari and
her brother Yōichirō, the latter being the oldest male descendant of Masakado.
Keiko and Katō duel with spells and magic.

Meanwhile, Yōichirō offers himself to the awakening Masakado as a substitute for his daughter. He and Yukiko are both swallowed into the gravesite to
keep Masakado from rising again. His plans foiled again, Katō falls to the ground
convulsing, blood dripping from his mouth. He rises once again and is the target
of Keiko's dagger. He drives her dagger into his body, urging Keiko to hate him,
for her hatred will fuel his return. Shortly thereafter, Yukiko and her parents
awaken unharmed on the temple grounds.

In the wake of Katō's defeat, Tokyo is bustling with people, becoming more
modern and flourishing more than ever. The film cuts to the shrine seen at the
beginning, again full of joy and festivity. One of Izumi's tarot cards is taken
by the wind, and kneeling upon the ground to retrieve it, he notices that it is
the Devil card. A man—possibly Katō—brushes past him, but as soon as Izumi
stands, the man is gone, lost in the crowds. The credits roll, followed by a warning: "Yasunori Katō will return."

Despite the disconnected nature of the film, it does narrate a truly epic tale about the inhabitants of Tokyo and their fight against Katō. The fight between good and evil is not the only dichotomy portrayed in the film. Also prominent is the juxtaposition between magic (symbolized by Katō and the other onmyōji) and modernity (symbolized by the various historical figures that transform Tokyo into a civilized metropolis). While the power of magic is rather strong throughout the film, those times are changing; Tokyo is slowly but surely abandoning its superstitious ways and embracing instead modern technological innovations and Western culture.

The film was a commercial success, making about 1.79 billion yen at the box office against its original 800 million yen budget. It won an award at the Eighteenth Takasaki Film Festival and received two Japanese Academy Award nominations. The film also boasts a 150-meter-long open set of Showa-period Ginza that featured some three thousand extras and cost roughly 300 million yen. The larger demons appearing throughout the film were designed by famed creature designer H. R. Giger, though more than ten people competed to be able to design Katō's smaller demons (which, themselves took more than fifty people to operate).

The film also served to boost the careers of a number of figures involved in the Japanese horror film scene, primarily that of Takashige Ichise (b. 1961), who would later produce the film's sequel, *Tokyo: The Last War*, as well as franchises familiar to Western viewership such as *Ringu* and *Ju-on*. Shimada's portrayal of Katō was deemed so iconic that he went on to reprise his role in the sequel and the animated adaptation. Katō also rose to great heights as an archetype villain in Japan. He is sometimes referred to as the "Japanese Dracula" and his iconic image has influenced that of otherwise unrelated characters in modern Japanese pop culture (for example, M. Bison/Vega of the *Street Fighter* video game franchise and General Wazikashi of the *Riki-ō* manga series, among others).

The film's clear success in Japan paved the way for a direct sequel, *Tokyo: The Last War* (1989), an animated adaptation, *Doomed Megalopolis* (1991), a spin-off film, *Teito Monogatari Gaiden* (1995), and finally a film based on its spin-off series, *Tokyo Dragon* (1997). *Tokyo: The Last Megalopolis*—alongside the original novel—is also widely credited as the beginning of an "onmyōji boom" in modern Japanese media. This boom led to a number of other onmyōji-related films, such as *Tokyo Babylon 1999* (1993), *Onmyōji* (2001), and *Onmyōji II* (2003).

Complementing its popularity in Japan, *Tokyo: The Last Megalopolis* was well praised and it received positive reviews in Europe (released in 1995). Despite this, North American reception is often mixed-to-negative. A major contributing factor is that the film did not see a North American release until 1998, ten years after its Japanese release. As such, it was often unfavorably compared to the animated *Doomed Megalopolis* (released in North America in 1995). Most of the negative reception focuses on the film's convoluted plot and the large number of characters. These difficult elements were noted by European viewers, but were not taken to be problematic. Positive North American reviews are plentiful, but they are often mired in a sea of negative ones, the latter being largely ignorant of the epic scope of its source.—Joseph P. Elacqua

See also Doomed Megalopolis; Onmyōji, Shirō, Sano; *Teito Monogatari Gaiden*

Bibliography
Jissōji, Akio, dir. *Tokyo: The Last Megalopolis.* Takashige Ichise, 1988. Film.

TOKYO ZOMBIE (2005)
DIRECTOR: Sakichi Sato
SCREENPLAY: Sakichi Sato
SPECS: 103 minutes; color

Tokyo Zombie, known as *Tokyo zonbi* in Japanese, is Sakichi Sato's 2005 satirical adaptation of Yusaku Hanakuma's 1999 graphic novel about two dim-witted factory workers trying to survive a zombie apocalypse.

Fujio, played by Tadanobu Asano, and Mitsuo, played by Sho Aikawa, are working in a fire extinguisher factory, which happens to be nearby a makeshift public trash dump nicknamed "Black Fuji," we're told by the young girl narrator. Black Fuji is a popular dumping ground for unwanted pornography and general trash, but mostly dead bodies. Mitsuo, a jujitsu expert, spends his days attempting to instruct the younger Fujio in the manly martial art. When their officious supervisor catches them slacking, he doles out corporeal punishment to Mitsuo, and Fujio stops him by bashing his boss in the head with a fire extinguisher. They are attempting to bury the body and their crime in Black Fuji when Fujio notices his old junior high school teacher dumping the body of a dead, pants-less young boy. Fujio flashes back to the memory of being beaten by the lascivious instructor and can't resist taking the opportunity for some revenge. The teacher is left unconscious and pants-less himself, and is startled by the appearance of the film's first zombie.

Through a comedy of many errors, the pair succumb to the realization that Tokyo is slowly being decimated by a zombie horde, a process memorably explained in a cameo appearance by the idiosyncratic Kazuo Umezu, renowned manga artist and television commentator, playing himself.

The pair decide to travel north, surmising that "zombies would not travel to the north." Mitsuo, who has convinced himself he has stomach cancer when he really has a peptic ulcer, is determined to get Fujio to Russia, the manliest of nations, where Fujio can continue his training ostensibly without having to bother with zombies.

When the immature Fujio fails to scavenge for supplies to Mitsuo's satisfaction, Mitsuo forces a return trip to a nearby *conbini* (convenience store). There they find Yoko (Eriko Okuda), a rough-hewn young woman trying to escape a zombie horde while carrying a cash register. Micho saves her life, but suffers a zombie bite in the process. He decides he's done for anyway, and leaps from the delivery van into the river. Fujio attacks Yoko out of grief and a marked inability to express himself in few other ways. While they grapple, a thief obsessed with Calpis (a Japanese soft drink) runs off with the van, as well as Fujio's cache of Calpis, leaving Fujio with Yoko and a bag containing Mitsuo's old jujitsu gi.

The narrator returns to tell us that five years have passed and Tokyo has fallen. The fall is illustrated by stylized animation while the narrator informs us that the rich have built a sanctuary where survivors are enslaved and killed when they are no longer useful. Only slaves that fight successfully in a gladiator-style arena have a chance at a decent life. Fujio is one of those gladiators.

The first battle takes place in a dreary metal box with a gaggle of tackily dressed middle-aged women cheering as men battle zombies. Fujio dispenses of his foe in one punch for which he is roundly booed. His fight doesn't provide the stress-relieving entertainment these women crave. He's the villain in these fights, but he doesn't care, he is simply trying to survive.

The passage of time has changed Fujio's situation, yet he remains the same. He stayed with Yoko and brought her to this slave sanctuary. They have a daughter, Fumiyo, who doesn't speak, just watches her parents snipe at each other, mostly over Fujio's obsession with the shrine he made to his fallen mentor. Fujio still craves the macho lessons in jujitsu he received from Mitsuo, and the time they spent together.

The fight promoters have set up Fujio to fight an unbelievably talented grappling zombie in order to appease those women who find Fujio to be a bore. Fujio finds that his jujitsu talents are lacking compared to the onslaught of the undead martial artist. He manages to survive the battle, but his ego doesn't. He swears off fighting, which enrages Yoko, because that's the only way they have to make money to eat. After he receives another thrashing, from Yoko this time, Fujio swears he's going to make it to Russia, leaving Yoko and Fumiyo alone.

Fujio's escape is thwarted, and it's back to the arena for the slave. The fight promoter saved his life by promising his betters that Fujio would fight the ultimate fighting zombie. That zombie turns out to be Mitsuo. A stunned Fujio tries to reason with Mitsuo at first, and appears to get through to him until Mitsuo throws him in a leg lock.

Meanwhile, the Calpis-obsessed thief reappears on a roof across from the sanctuary. He has learned that there are cases of the beverage stashed away inside, so he and some other ruffians attack the stronghold, blowing the gates wide open.

Mitsuo continues to battle Fujio but Fujio can't get the upper hand. Mitsuo, clearly lucid and not a zombie, starts to tease Fujio about his childhood molestation experience, which causes Fujio to go berserk, pummeling his mentor's skull. A comically deformed Mitsuo passes on some manly advice to Fujio before passing out. It turns out that Mitsuo was, in fact, bitten by a zombie wearing dentures. Still, his chronic hypochondria leads him to believe he's a zombie and he tries to act accordingly.

The ruffians break into the arena and cause havoc, and Fujio recognizes the Calpis thief. He's very apologetic for a thief and offers Fujio his motorcycle with side car as a peace offering. Fujio takes the bike back to his family. Fumiyo finally speaks—she is the story's narrator after all—and they ride off out of the compound, now overrun by both zombies and thugs. And Mitsuo is chasing after them.

Tokyo Zombie is a broad, slapstick, gross-out comedy that plays the apocalypse for laughs. It does briefly bother with theme, but it is primarily a comic character study.

The zombies that crawl from Black Fuji are the detritus of Japanese society, the waste that the wasteful throw away, and that which ultimately destroys the place. Sato, who wrote and directed this adaptation, casts this thought aside while allowing Asano and Aikawa time to show off their physical comedy skills and deadpan delivery. Asano, in an Afro wig, plays Fujio as burying the pain of his abuse deeply, and he is blissfully unaware, more interested in chips and Calpis and jujitsu than anything else. Aikawa plays his character straight as well, very serious, dispensing his philosophy on jujitsu's ability to turn boys into men as if it were profound. His hypochondria is merely a plot device that allows the men to reunite and allows Fujio his epiphany: the realization that he has the power to create his own persona, with or without Mitsuo or jujitsu.

Sato, who wrote the screenplay for Takashi Miike's *Ichi the Killer*, does return to social commentary with the presentation of the sanctuary. The inhabitants, led by Umezu himself (now Prince Umezu), are a gross lot of older, wealthy citizens still preying on those less fortunate. Sato does not forget that the story suggests they started all this by dumping their secrets on Black Fuji, and gives them a suitable comeuppance in the end.

The dissolution of Japanese society seemed to be on the minds of many filmmakers around Takashi's age, like Sion Sono and Hideaki Anno, who spent a lot of film stock trying to find answers. Sato hasn't come to a much different conclusion; the older generation mucked things up royally so following their lead isn't going to solve anything. The kids have to learn from us mavericks, they're saying, and forge their own path, just like Fujio.—Mark N. Mays

Bibliography

Sato, Sakichi, dir. *Tokyo Zombie*. 2005, Toshiba Entertainment. Film.
Takashi, Miike, dir. *Ichi the Killer*. Prénom H Co. Ltd., 2001. Film.

TORMENTED (2011)

DIRECTOR: Takashi Shimizu
SCREENPLAY: Sōtarō Hayashi
SPECS: 83 minutes; color

Known as *Rabbito Horā 3D* (*Rabbit Horror 3D*) in Japan, *Tormented* is a 2011 horror film directed by Takashi Shimizu (b. 1972). Although not named as a sequel, the film includes several crossover elements with Shimizu's 2009 film *The Shock Labyrinth 3D*, and is regarded as a companion piece. *Tormented* premiered at the Sixty-Eighth Venice International Film Festival in 2011.

Much of the film takes place through dream sequences and flashbacks, through which the traumatic past of the central character, Kiriko, played by Hikari Mitsushima (b. 1985), is revealed. The film frequently blurs the boundaries between genuine and imagined realities. There are, for example many references to *Alice in Wonderland*, and many parallels between Kiriko's experiences and the *Little Mermaid* book that her father is illustrating. The film fits into the subgenre of a "puzzle film," leaving the viewer questioning what is real, and lending itself to reevaluation upon second viewing.

The film tells the story of Kiriko and her younger half-brother Daigo, played by Takeru Shibuya (b. 2000). The pair live with their father Kōhei (Teruyuki Kagawa, b. 1965), who makes a living designing and illustrating pop-up books. Both siblings are plagued by trauma. Kiriko works in the school library and has not spoken for a decade, since the death of her mother from an unexplained illness. Daigo, whose mother, Kyoko, died before he was born, drops out of school following an incident in which he kills a sick rabbit and is labeled by his classmates as a "rabbit killer." Kiriko homeschools Daigo, and their father largely leaves them to their own devices. He doesn't speak to Daigo or acknowledge his impending birthday, for which Kiriko is preparing to give him a pressed flower, as she does every year.

Shortly before Daigo's tenth birthday, Kiriko takes him to the cinema to watch *The Shock Labyrinth 3D*. As Daigo reaches for a 3-D rabbit doll projected from the screen it appears to materialize and he takes it home. Following this incident Daigo becomes haunted by someone in a rabbit suit. In his dreams the rabbit suit leads him into a theme park, and the pair ride on a carousel. In what appears to be another dream the rabbit pulls Daigo into the same closet where his father was previously looking at old photos. Kiriko awakes to Daigo's screams to find him locked in the closet. In another experience, Daigo is pulled through the mattress of his bed by the rabbit; this time Kiriko follows him and they go to an abandoned hospital. Daigo's mother, Kyoko, is inside the rabbit costume. Kiriko tells her father, "Kyoko is coming. I saw her. Daigo too."

Rather than the haunting of Daigo, the puzzle comes to be what the rabbit represents to Kiriko. The film begins to unravel the past of when Kiriko first met Kyoko, playing out the sense of threat that a child can encounter at the replacement of a biological parent. The person in the rabbit suit takes young Kiriko on the carousel, with Kyoko once more revealed to be in the costume. Kyoko gives Kiriko a toy rabbit and then there is a horrible accident. Kiriko walks away holding a baby and Kyoko is dead. Kiriko awakens to find herself holding the rabbit toy.

Having burned the toy rabbit, Kiriko and Daigo return to the cinema where it all began. However, this time Daigo is sucked into the screen and carried off by the person in the rabbit costume. The next scene shows Kiriko in a mental hospital, being told that Daigo doesn't exist and died before he was born. Kiriko notes that hallucinations of Daigo are taking over her life, and that he is set on coming into this world to haunt her father.

To protect her father, Kiriko goes to the hospital where Kyoko was taken, only to hear her father talking to Daigo. Daigo tells Kiriko that she can't erase him and that she created him that day on the carousel. Mirroring the story of the mermaid, Kiriko is given the opportunity to stab Daigo, but unlike the mermaid, she takes the opportunity, only to be stabbed herself. Daigo then pushes Kiriko over the spiral staircase and drops the toy rabbit after her. She appears to dissolve into foam but in reality lands on the floor dead. The toy rabbit crawls off the screen. Kiriko's father, who was sitting outside the hospital all along, leaves hand in hand with Daigo.—Aimee Richmond

See also Shimizu, Takashi

Bibliography

Shimizu, Takashi, dir. *The Shock Labyrinth 3D*. Asmik Ace Entertainment, 2009. DVD.
Shimizu, Takashi, dir. *Tormented*. Phantom Film, 2011. Film.

TSUBURAYA PRODUCTIONS

Tsuburaya Productions Co., Ltd. is a Japanese film production company, founded in 1963 by Eiji Tsuburaya (1901–1970). The company, originally founded as a laboratory, specialized in visual effects, and has produced numerous films and television shows, its most well known being the *Ultraman* series. Today, the company has expanded its business from film production to character merchandising, licensing, and event planning, serving both national and international customers.

The founder of Tsuburaya Productions, Eiji Tsuburaya, was a leading visual effects film director who established unique film genres: *tokusatsu* (special effects) and *kaijū* (monstrous creature) films. *Tokusatsu* films typically use a detailed miniature diorama set in the studio, and film crews, for instance, explode and destroy the miniature city or create storms and shipwreck a vessel in the miniature sea. This was done to shoot realistic and dynamic scenes at lower cost. In *tokusatsu-kaijū* films, actors in life-sized *kaijū* and superhero costumes perform action scenes on the miniature set. Utilizing these techniques, Tsuburaya supervised numerous *tokusatsu* films as a special visual effects director, including *Godzilla* (1954), *Mothra* (1961), *King Ghidora* (1964), and *Ultraman* (1967). For the viewers living in the age of high economic growth (1954–1973), in his early *kaijū* films, Tsuburaya attempted to raise social and environmental issues, such as pollution and the destruction of nature, and describe the irrationality and the sadness in life through the defeated. In the era before the computer-generated imagery became a major technique for visual effects, Tsuburaya pursued realistic, appealing shots on his handmade *tokusatsu* miniature set. Not only did he establish unique film genres, but he also helped the Japanese film industries to develop and flourish with his innovative techniques.

Long before *Godzilla* and other *kaijū* series were born, Eiji Tsuburaya directed numerous *tokusatsu* movies on various subjects, from drama and fantasy to wars. During World War II, the imperial government ordered Tsuburaya to produce war films to whip up the war spirit of the nation. Tsuburaya had no choice but to direct several *tokusatsu* war films with Tōhō Studios, which later led to his purge from Tōhō. After the war, under the ruling of the US General Headquarters, public officials and people in certain private sectors were purged from their positions, because they were considered to have engaged in patriotic work during the war.

Upon the resignation from Tōhō, Tsuburaya established Tsuburaya Special Visual Effects Laboratory (Tsuburaya Tokugi Kenkyūjo) in 1948 at his home in Soshigaya, Tokyo, which was the origin of Tsuburaya Productions today. The laboratory was moved inside of Tōhō Studios in 1950, and was incorporated as Tsuburaya Special Visual Effects Productions (Tsuburaya Tokugi Production) in 1963. The company was renamed as Tsuburaya Productions in 1968.

Tsuburaya Productions' first *tokusatsu-kaijū* films, *Ultraman* (1967) and *Ultra Seven* (1968) were major successes. This led to the birth of a long-running television series titled, *Ultra Series*, which has continued to create new *Ultraman* and other *kaijū* stories to this day. Today, the company continues to produce other films and television shows, as well as other services including merchandising, licensing, and event planning.

While Tsuburaya Productions is most known for its *Ultraman* and *tokusatsu-kaijū* films, the company also produced horror and suspense films and television series targeted for adult viewers. In his early days, the founder, Eiji Tsuburaya, utilized his visual effects techniques not only in the *kaijū* films, but also in horror and mystery films. First Tsuburaya filmed *Tōmei Ningen Arawaru* (*Invisible Man Appears*) in 1949 at Daiei Studios, and then *Tōmei Ningen* in 1954 at Tōhō Studios. Then he filmed a horror series, the Henshin Ningen series, at Tōhō Studios, including *Bijo to ekitai ningen* (*The H-Man*) in 1958, *Densō ningen* (*The Secret of the Telegian*) in 1960, *Gasu ningen dai-ichi gō* (*The Human Vapor*) in 1960, and *Matango* (1963), an extra episode. Tsuburaya also supervised visual effects in two *kaijū*-horror films coproduced by Japanese and US film productions: *Frankenstein versus Subterranean Monster Baragon* (1965) and *Frankenstein's Monsters: Sanda versus Gaira* (1966).

With this experience, Tsuburaya produced a *tokusatsu* television series for adult viewers titled *Kaiki daisakusen* (*Operation: Mystery!*) in 1968, where SRI: Science Research Institute resolves mysterious and terrifying cases utilizing scientific methods. Tsuburaya Productions produced the sequels to this original series in 2007 and 2013. Another popular horror television series was produced in 1973 under the title *Kyōfu gekijō umbalance* (Horror theatre, unbalance) in 1973. This series was again targeting the adult viewers and dealt with terrors in real life, such as absurdity, grudge, and envy lurking in people.

Since the founding of the company, the Tsuburaya family controlled the management of Tsuburaya Productions, as well as other subsidiary Tsuburaya group companies, Tsuburaya Enterprises (1968–2008) and Tsuburaya Music. Despite the success with its *Ultraman* series and merchandise business featuring *Ultraman*'s characters and the *kaijū*, the company continued to operate in the red. Deaths and scandals in the family brought changes in power several times. After the forced dismissal of the sixth president, Hideaki Tsuburaya (b. 1959), approved by his own cousin, Kazuo Tsuburaya (b. 1961), the fourth and eighth president, the Tsuburaya family entirely withdrew from the management in 2007. The company's years of deficit operations, as well as the family members' differences in management strategies are believed to have been what caused the withdrawal of the family from managing the company.—Yoko Inagi

See also Frankenstein versus Subterranean Monster Baragon; Frankenstein's Monsters: Sanda vs. Gaira; Godzilla; The H-Man; Henshin Ningen films; *The Human Vapor; Matango; The Secret of the Telegian*

Bibliography
Ragone, August. *Eiji Tsuburaya: Master of Monster: Defending the Earth with Ultraman, Godzilla, and Friends in the Golden Age of Japanese Science Fiction Film*. San Francisco: Chronicle Books, 2007.
Tsuburaya, Hideaki. *Ultraman ga naiteiru: Tsuburaya pro no shippai*. Tokyo: Kōdansha, 2013.
Tsuburaya Eiji no eizō sekai. Ed. Shingo Yamamoto. Tokyo: Jitsugyō no Nihonsha, 1983.

TSUKAMOTO, SHIN'YA (1960–)
While he may not be as closely associated with J-horror as Hideo Nakata, Kiyoshi Kurosawa, or Takashi Shimizu, director Shin'ya Tsukamoto surely stands with

those other capable filmmakers, since the majority of his films can be classified as horror to some extent. Since he claims light and darkness as major themes in his work, he seems particularly suited for the Manichaean horror genre. Tsukamoto's rapid cutting and propensity to experiment in his work have also established him as one of the more significant formalist filmmakers in contemporary cinema. His genre work, working primarily in horror and "cyberpunk" science fiction, has also helped forge his status as a cult director, but one critically renowned.

Born 1 January 1960 in Tokyo's Shibuya ward, Tsukamoto made a few feature-length films as a teenager (some longer than any in his "official" filmography, which are marked by their brevity), but became disillusioned and gave up making films from 1979 to 1986, working instead in experimental, underground theater, while also making commercials, following his time studying art at Nihon University. Even the name of Tsukamoto's production company, Kaijyu Theater, reflects his influences. His two early science-fiction shorts, *The Phantom of Regular Size* (1986) and *The Adventure of Denchu Kozo* (1987), having originated from his stage plays, achieved some notoriety at film festivals and on television. But their primary legacies were as trial runs, as they are thematically similar to the film that launched Tsukamoto into the international scene, *Tetsuo, the Iron Man* (1989).

Tetsuo also set in motion one of the most dominant themes in Tsukamoto's oeuvre: transformation. When *Tetsuo* won "Best Film" at Fantafestival in Rome (despite playing without subtitles), its success at a foreign film festival also revived interest in the moribund Japanese film industry of the late-1980s, heralding the arrival of a younger generation of Japanese directors, those born in the late 1950s to early 1960s (Kiyoshi Kurosawa, Takashi Miike, Nakata). A union of metal and flesh in its play on the enduring Tsukamoto theme of man in conflict with the Tokyo metropolis, *Tetsuo* was the cinematic equivalent of industrial music. Its popularity and themes also meant that Tsukamoto would thereafter be labeled a "cyberpunk" director, even though he rarely returned to the form, as *Tetsuo* resembled his shorts more than his later features. The film's theme of metal led to the decision to shoot in black and white, which Tsukamoto has returned to for *Bullet Ballet* (1998) and the blue-tinted *A Snake in June* (2002), in addition to his effective use of monochromatic sequences in the *Tetsuo* sequels, *Vital* (2004), and *Nightmare Detective* (2006).

The sequel, *Tetsuo II: The Body Hammer* (1992), was more polished and in color (although still retaining a bluish monochromatic palette for much of the film), but lacked the inventiveness of its predecessor. Still, this sequel is saturated with experimental elements just as bizarre, experimental, and disturbing, if not as innovative, as its predecessor. Quentin Tarantino was so impressed with the first two *Tetsuo* films that there were initial plans for an American sequel that Tsukamoto would direct and Tarantino produce. Although these plans did not materialize, in 2009 a second sequel would finally arrive, *Tetsuo: The Bullet Man*, which, interestingly enough, was still shot in English.

The 1990s were bookended by two studio horror films: *Hiruko the Goblin* (1991) and *Gemini* (1999). *Hiruko the Goblin* marked quite a departure from *Tetsuo*, but Tsukamoto was attracted to the ability to create the various creatures for the film that recalled his fondness for the *kaiju* genre. Overall, *Hiruko* is more conventional in style (especially following on the heels of *Tetsuo*) but its tale of unexplained decapitations, goblins, and a school built at the gates of hell keep it offbeat, if uninspired. *Gemini* was an attempt at period horror based on mystery writer Edogawa Rampo, although Tsukamoto used the original story more as a point of departure for his screenplay.

His first film of the twenty-first century, *A Snake in June*, was his first film to foreground eroticism since *Tetsuo*, although not a horror film. After the focus on the (female) body in *A Snake of June*, Tsukamoto wanted to dig deeper—inside the human body—for his next film, *Vital*. This horror/thriller drama tackles the theme of dissection in a non-exploitative fashion, involving a medical student (Tadanobu Asano, one of the few major international stars in a Tsukamoto film) who suffers from amnesia after an automobile accident that also killed his girlfriend. His memories return to him however, when he coincidentally dissects her body during the semester. Although many of Tsukamoto's horror films cross several generic lines, *Haze* (2005) was a return to pure horror, one of the most brutal depictions of a hell and surely one of the most claustrophobic settings, as its bewildered protagonist crawls through a concrete labyrinth. A precursor to later films such as *127 Hours* (2010) and *Buried* (2011), the film exists in two versions, a fifty-minute version and one that is half as long.

Tsukamoto continued with the horror genre for his two *Nightmare Detective* films. In the first, what seems like double-suicide pacts over phones is something even more sinister and grisly, and a criminal investigation team must employ the titular detective (played by Ryuhei Matsuda) to help them solve the case. Matsuda returned for *Nightmare Detective 2* (2008), but the sequel seemed more akin to Nakata's *kwaidan* than its gory, blood-spattered predecessor, while also deviating from one of Tsukamoto's most dominant themes: the relationship between the Tokyo megalopolis and humanity. Tsukamoto continued his interest in horror with *Kotoko* (2011), which did not see the same extent of international distribution as Tsukamoto's other works. He followed it with a 2014 adaptation of Shohei Ooka's disturbing World War II novel *Nobi* (English title: *Fires on the Plain*), previously adapted by Kon Ichikawa in 1959. Although technically a war film, Ooka's tale is quite horrific, particularly in its depictions of cannibalism. Some critics accused Tsukamoto's gory adaptation of going even further, privileging the harrowing elements over the novel's antiwar message. Overall, the film was not received as well as another major non-horror film in his oeuvre, the 1995 boxing film *Tokyo Fist*, which touches on horror if one counts the Grand Guignol–inspired splatter elements both inside and outside of the ring, particularly in how Tsukamoto links pugilism with body modification.

With the exception of Robert Rodriguez, Tsukamoto has few contemporary rivals in his versatility, in that he has always worn many hats as a filmmaker, acting as director, writer, producer, editor, cinematographer, actor, and production designer/art director on almost all of his films. But Tsukamoto does Rodriguez one better, in that the former acts in (almost) all of his films, even performing the lead in *Tokyo Fist*, *Bullet Ballet*, *Haze*, and *Fires on the Plain*, and the lead villain in the *Tetsuo* films, *A Snake of June*, and *Nightmare Detective*. Because he did not come up through the ranks as an assistant director, he also enjoys seeing how other directors work by acting for them, with several memorable appearances in films like *Ichi the Killer* (2001) and *Blind Beast vs. Killer Dwarf* (2001), while also supporting his projects to a great extent by lending his voice to dozens of television and radio commercials over his career.

Furthermore, Tsukamoto has remained fiercely independent in his filmmaking practices, and even when directing a studio project (such as *Hiruko the Goblin* or *Gemini*), Tsukamoto makes the projects his own, cementing his legacy as one of the most uncompromising directors in Japan today. Tsukamoto's influence can be noticed in filmmakers from Miike (*Full Metal Yazuka*) to Yoshihiro Nishimura (*Tokyo Gore Police*). Throughout his career, Tsukamoto has established himself as not only one of the most transgressive filmmakers in Japan, but indeed the world.— Zachary Thomas Ingle

Bibliography

Mes, Tom. *Iron Man: The Cinema of Shinya Tsukamoto*. Surrey, England, UK: FAB Press, 2005.

Mes, Tom, and Jasper Sharp. *The Midnight Eye Guide to New Japanese Film*. Berkeley, CA: Stone Bridge Press, 2005.

· U ·

UGETSU MONOGATARI (1953)

DIRECTOR: Kenji Mizoguchi
SCREENPLAY: Yoshikata Yoda, Matsutarō Kawaguchi
SPECS: 96 minutes; black and white

Ugetsu monogatari (Tales of moonlight and rain), internationally released under the title *Ugetsu*, is a 1953 black-and-white film by Kenji Mizoguchi (1898–1956), which cannot be directly attributed to the horror genre, but contains supernatural elements and is characterized by an uncanny atmosphere. The film is based on a collection of stories by Akinari Ueda (1734–1809) and its aesthetics draw on classical Japanese arts. *Ugetsu monogatari* tells the story of a simple potter who leaves his family to do business in the city, where he falls into the clutches of a ghostly woman who eventually entangles him in an erotic adventure. *Ugetsu monogatari* won the "Silver Lion" award at the Venice Film Festival in 1953 and is considered one of the first Japanese films to gain broad recognition internationally.

The film is set during the Azuchi-Momoyama period (1573–1603), an era known for its many military conflicts that led to the political unification of Japan. Accompanied by his sister and her husband, the potter Genjurō, played by Masayuki Mori (1911–1973), leaves his wife, Miyagi, played by Kinuyo Tanaka (1909–1977), and their son, Gen'ichi, in their home village to sell his goods in the city. There, a strange and aristocratically dressed young woman, Machiko Kyō, (b. 1924) appears at his stall and asks him to deliver pottery to her palace.

Once there, the young woman, whose name is Wakasa, entertains and flatters him. Later, her elderly servant tells Genjurō what fate has determined for him: he shall marry Wakasa and swear eternal love to her. Genjurō is overwhelmed by the young woman's beauty, follows her will, and enjoys the seemingly carefree life of the palace. Already, it seems that he has been weakened, become totally submissive, and lost his own will. While Genjurō is joyfully leading a luxurious life with Wakasa, his wife Miyagi, who had taken refuge in the mountains after a raid on the village, is robbed and killed by two famished soldiers.

The supernatural forces at work in Wakasa's palace are first indicated by the singing voice of her dead father that can be heard when Wakasa dances. Genjurō receives an even clearer warning when he is sent to go shopping in the city: a monk tells him to return home to his wife and child. Wakasa, so the monk says, is a ghost and Genjurō is already on the verge of death.

Back at the palace, Wakasa and her servant discover characters with Buddhist content on Genjurō's body, apparently the work of the monk. Following this shock, they reveal their truly uncanny nature. According to the servant, the noble lady had died in the turmoil of war, before she could experience the joys of love. Thus, she returned to Earth to find happiness. The women beg Genjurō to come with them, but he draws his sword and strikes wildly at the air. When he wakes up in the morning, as though from a nightmare, Genjurō realizes that the Kutsuki Palace was, in reality, just a heap of ruins. He returns to his village, where he has a brief encounter with his late wife Miyagi's peaceful ghost, before he resumes leading a simple life and taking care of his son.

Ugetsu monogatari owes a good deal of its distinctive atmosphere to numerous resources borrowed from classical Nōh theater. The film's music, the mask-like makeup of Wakasa, her magnificent costumes, and the construction of her palace are all drawn from Nōh staging. Additionally, Mizoguchi also staged the love affair between Genjurō and Wakasa in an elaborate sequence, whose mise-en-scène and camera work reminds one of Japanese scroll paintings (*emakimono*). Some shots are reminiscent of Japanese ink paintings in their composition and contrast, no doubt due to the fact that the cinematographer Kazuo Miyagawa had studied this traditional art for fourteen years. Director Mizoguchi succeeded in making the uncanny felt without resorting to direct representations of the supernatural or special effects. Fear in *Ugetsu monogatari* hangs like a fine mist over each scene. This is especially evident in the lavish nature photography and the eerie architecture of Wakasa's lonely palace.

With her unconcealed eroticism, Wakasa can be seen as a prototype for Japanese femme fatale figures of this period, which are usually not living beings. The female ghost is a representation of female desire, and its positioning outside human society allows for addressing an issue that would otherwise be considered outrageous. Unbridled female eroticism is thus indeed taken up as a subject, but with a skeptical attitude manifest in the representation of women's sexuality as being eventually destructive to men. The woman is banished by the monk, who appears here as a kind of agent of patriarchal reality, into nonexistence, while the man concludes his amorous episode, in which he abandoned his dominance and lustfully devoted himself entirely to the passions of a woman, seeing it as nothing more than a short escapist phase.—Elisabeth Scherer

Bibliography

Ima-Izumi, Yoko. "A Land Where Femmes Fatales Fear to Tread: Eroticism and Japanese Cinema." *Japan Review* 10 (1998): 123–50.

Mizoguchi, Kenji, dir. *Ugetsu onogatari*. Daiei, 1953. Film.

Ueda, Akinari. *Ugetsu Monogatari: Tales of Moonlight and Rain*. Edited and translated by Leon M. Zolbrod. London: Routledge, 2011.

Yomota, Inuhiko, ed. *Eiga kantoku Mizoguchi Kenji*. Tokyo: Shin'yo-sha, 1999.

UMEZU, KAZUO (1936–)

Kazuo Umezu (b. 1936) is a Japanese manga artist best known for his horror comics as well as his "Makato-chan" character. Umezu was born in Kōya-chō, Wakayama Prefecture. He began drawing manga while still in school and made his professional debut in 1955 with *Mori no kyodai* (Siblings of the forest), an adaptation of the Grimm fairy tale *Hansel and Gretel*. Some of his early work was written under the pen name Kazuo Yamaji. Umezu retired from illustrating in 1995 due to tendonitis, though he continues to appear as a *tarento* (celebrity personality) on Japanese television.

One of Umezu's most famous horror manga is *Hyōryū kyōshitsu* (*The Drifting Classroom*), published between 1972 and 1974. A Japanese elementary school is mysteriously transported forward in time to a postapocalyptic wasteland. After one of the teachers goes insane and murders most of the adults, the children are left to fend for themselves in a world ravaged by environmental disasters, devastating diseases, and deadly monsters. The series received the Shōgakukan Manga Award in 1974, and has been adapted three times: first, as a Japanese live-action film, directed by Nobuhiko Ōbayashi, in 1987; later, as an American live-action film called *Drifting School*, directed by Jun'ichi Mimura, in 1995; and finally, as a Japanese television drama series called *Long Love Letter: Drifting Classroom*, in 2002.

The main character of *Nekome kozō* (*Cat-Eyed Boy*), published between 1967 and 1968, is an outcast nekomata, a cat-like yōkai (a broad category of monsters in Japanese folklore). Rejected by yōkai society because of his near-human appearance, the Cat-Eyed Boy travels alone, encountering monstrous and horrific events wherever he goes. *Cat-Eyed Boy* was adapted into a half-hour anime, directed by Keinosuke Tsuchiya in 1976, and again as a live-action film, directed by Noboru Iguchi, in 2006.

Umezu's long career has produced a huge number of manga. *Orochi* (aka *Orochi: Blood*) was published in 1969 and 1970, and adapted into a live-action film, directed by Norio Tsuruta, in 2007. *Senrei* ("Baptism," aka *Baptism of Blood*) is a shōjō (young girl) manga published between 1974 and 1976. *Kami no hidari te akuma no migi te* (*God's Left Hand, Devil's Right Hand*) was published between 1986 and 1989 and adapted into a film, directed by Shūsuke Kaneko, in 2006.

A series of television adaptations, known as *Umezu Kazuo kyōfu gekijō* (*Umezu Kazuo's Horror Theater*), were produced in 2005 for the fiftieth anniversary of Umezu's career. Six films were made: *Mushi tachi no ie* (*Bug's House*, dir. Kiyoshi Kurosawa); *Zesshoku* (*Ambrosia*, dir. Tadafumi Itō); *Negai* (*The Wish*, dir. Atsushi Shimizu); *Madara no shōjō* (*The Harlequin Girl*, dir. Noboru Iguchi); *Purezento* (*Present*, dir. Yūdai Yamaguchi); and *Death Make* (dir. Taichi).

In 2014, Umezu made his directorial debut with *Mazā* (*Mother*), an autobiographical film starring Kabuki actor Ainosuke Kataoka as Umezu. In the film, an editor is working on a book about Umezu's life and begins probing into his relationship with his recently deceased mother, Ichie. As she delves into their lives, she soon discovers that Ichie has come back as a vengeful ghost and is killing off her family.

Although Umezu is primarily associated with horror manga, his long career has featured diverse subject matters and themes. His most famous creation is Makoto-chan, the title character in a series of gag manga that originally ran from 1976 to 1981 with a follow-up series published in 1988 and 1989. The series, which relies heavily on puerile humor, stars Makoto Sawada, a kindergarten boy who almost always has snot running down his face. Makoto-chan's catchphrase is "Gwashi!," which is paired with a hand sign of pressing the middle and pinky fingers to the palm; Umezu often uses this as his own signature gesture. An anime film based on Makoto-chan, directed by Tsutomu Shibuyama, was released in 1980.

Another significant non-horror work is his manga adaptation of *Ultraman*, a long-running *tokusatsu* (special effects) franchise. The original television show in the series aired in 1966 and 1967; while the show was on the air, Umezu wrote a manga based on the character. Even within this context, Umezu's style and sensibilities are apparent. The monsters and aliens that Ultraman battles are illustrated in extreme detail, given more grotesque forms than the television series could afford.

Fans often use affectionate nicknames for Umezu, including both "Umezz" and "Kazz." He is also well known for a red-and-white horizontal stripes motif. When Kataoka portrayed the author in *Mother*, he was costumed in Umezu's signature long-sleeved red-and-white shirts, and when Umezu constructed a house in the Kichijōji neighborhood of Musashino, it was painted in his garish style. He is widely acclaimed as one of the foremost figures in horror manga, and in 1986, an Umezu Kazuo Award was established and judged by Umezu, awarded in recognition of promising and upcoming horror artists.—Nicholas Bestor

UZUMAKI (2000)

DIRECTOR: Higuchinsky
SCREENPLAY: Kengo Kaji, Chika Yasuo, Takao Nitta
SPECS: 90 minutes; black and white

Uzumaki is a 2000 horror film directed by Higuchinsky (b. 1969), based on a manga by Junji Ito (b. 1963). Also known under the English title *Spiral*, the film follows the increasingly disturbing events that befall a small town slowly being corrupted by the titular uzumaki, malignant spirals capable of twisting both minds and bodies. Structured into four acts, each roughly corresponding to a story arc in the manga, *Uzumaki* is marked by imaginative visuals, quirky directing, and a novel concept set within the confines of a small mountain town.

The normal life of schoolgirl Kirie Goshima, played by Eriko Hatsune (b. 1982), is shattered when she witnesses her boyfriend's father, Toshio, obsessively recording the spirals of a snail's shell, the first sign something is amiss in the small town of Kurozu-cho. Her boyfriend, Shuichi, portrayed by Fhi Fan (b. 1980), is more aware of something dangerous and supernatural at work, having sensed a disquieting presence since childhood. Soon the entire town is in the grip of spiral-related madness and horrifying transformations. Popular girl Kyoko's hair grows into unusual spiral curls, fellow students begin a slimy change into human-sized snails, and Toshio dies in an attempt to commune with the spiral by jamming himself into a washing machine. At his wake, Shuichi's mother, Yukie, sees the smoke from Toshio's cremation form his face in the sky as it joins a sickly green cloud hanging over the town.

When a hospitalized Yukie, now terrified of spirals, commits suicide after a ghostly Toshio informs her of the spiral shape of her cochlea, Kirie and Shuichi agree it is time to flee the doomed town. As they rush to Kirie's house to save her father, Shuichi is caught at last by the malevolent force infecting the town, his body twisting itself into a spiral and dying in Kirie's arms. As she mourns, he jerks back to life, crawling after her as his body continues to change and calling for her to join with the spiral. The final moments of the film look at the denizens of the town, destroyed by the power of the spiral. Kyoko's emaciated corpse is trapped by her own hair wrapped around a utility pole, the spiral locks now towering over her, flailing at the green-black skies like monstrous tentacles. A hapless news crew sent to cover the strange phenomena lies dead by the roadside, their remains transformed into snails, while Shuichi's twisted dead body is shown on the floor of Kirie's father's workshop. Only the absence of Kirie's body and a final voice-over hints at her survival.

Despite the horror roots of the film, Higuchinsky imbues *Uzumaki* with a sense of playfulness through the use of unusual camera angles, lingering point-of-view shots, and odd musical cues. The stylistic choices add a degree of humor to the film, at times undercutting the tension, before the film settles into a grim, serious tone. The depiction of the deaths in the film are effectively managed, with most being a variation on the image of a spiral. Toshio dies twisted in a washing machine, Kirie's obsessive admirer is struck by a car and his body is wrapped around the axle, and the impact of the driver's head on the windshield leaves a spiral crack punctuated by a severed eyeball in the center. Equally clever is the subtle use of digital effects to create spirals throughout the film, spinning and vanishing on the corners of buildings and walls at the edges of the screen. A reliance on green filters gives *Uzumaki* an otherworldly feel, while also evoking the original green coloring found in sections of the manga.

The nature of the sinister spirals in *Uzumaki* is never clearly defined, though the film hints at some ancient evil within the town lake. Whether the uzumaki is a malignant supernatural force or some form of cosmic, elemental concept capable of warping reality, the power that destroys Kurozu-cho is a Lovecraftian unknown, beyond the ability of the characters to understand, much less defeat. As is often the case in adaptations of manga, Uzumaki takes liberties with the source material. The *Uzumaki* manga was still ongoing at the time of filming, so Ito's intended resolution was unavailable. The majority of the film is covered in the first two sections, adapting stories from the manga, which builds up a suitable sense of unease and impending disaster. The film then opts to quickly hurtle toward a conclusion, wrapping up events in a series of stills in the final three-minute segment.—Daniel Fandino

Bibliography

Higuchinsky, dir. *Uzumaki*. Nikkatsu, 2000. Film.

<h1 style="text-align:center">• V •</h1>

VAMPIRE BRIDE (1960)

DIRECTOR: Kyōtarō Namiki
SCREENPLAY: Kyōtarō Namiki
SPECS: 80 minutes; black and white

Vampire Bride (*Hanayome kyūketsuma*) is a 1960 Shintōhō horror film directed by Kyōtarō Namiki (1902–2001). Having had financial success with their period ghost story adaptations like *Yotsuya kaidan* (1956) and *The Ghost Story of Kasane's Swamp* (*Kaidan Kasane ga fuchi*, 1957), Shintōhō began experimenting with contemporarily set horror films that often owed a more obvious debt to the Universal Studios' horror movies of the 1930s. *Vampire Bride* continues the trend established by the previous year's release, *Lady Vampire* (*Onna kyūketsuki*) of liberally mixing Hollywood vampire and werewolf iconography with Japanese cultural and narrative motifs. Despite the curiously fascinating results, the film remains most famous for the rumors that studio boss Mitsugu Okura (1899–1978) forced lead actress Junko Ikeuchi (1933–2010) to play the title monster as punishment for spurning his lecherous advances.

Ikeuchi stars as Fujiko Shirai, a beautiful ballet student struggling to support her bedridden mother. The envy of her classmates Eiko, played by Reiko Seto, Kiyoko, played by Hiroko Amakusa, and Satoe, played by Yasuko Mita, Fujiko draws the romantic attention of two newspaper reporters, Sadao, played by Tatsuo Terashima and Motoyasu, played by Keiji Takamiya, much to the ire of the other girls. After a movie studio scouts her to become their next leading lady, Fujiko believes her mother's financial troubles are over, and her happiness increases when Sadao proposes marriage. Eiko, Kiyoko, and Satoe's jealousy now boiling over, the three rivals conspire to murder Fujiko during a beach excursion, pushing her over a cliff while picking wildflowers. Fujiko survives the fall but suffers serious facial scarring on the left side of her face. Her movie career dashed, debt collectors seize the family's belongings. Fujiko's despondent mother commits suicide, leaving behind a cryptic note for her daughter with instructions to seek her great-grandmother, Okoto Kageyama, played by Satsuki Fujie.

Journeying to the remote countryside, Fujiko locates her relative, an ancient witch residing in a mountain cave. Okoto, who has been waiting several hundred years for the Kageyama descendent to arrive, insists she seek revenge on Eiko, Kiyoko, and Satoe. The old witch then performs an arcane rite in an attempt to restore Fujiko's beauty, but when the young woman awakens to find the facial disfigurement has only gotten worse, she stabs herself in despair. Okoto undertakes a second rite to restore Fujiko to life, slitting her own wrist and having Fujiko drink her blood. Fujiko wakes, her facial scarring now healed, but she soon transforms into a hideous, hair-covered beast with a thirst for blood. Afterward Sadao, who has been searching for his fiancée, meets Okoto's mute, hunchbacked servant, who leads him to a grave marked "Shirai Fujiko."

Time passes. Eiko marries Motoyasu; Satoe is now engaged to Sadao, and Kiyoko will also soon wed. The sudden arrival in Tokyo of beauty pageant winner Kageyama Sayoko, who bears an uncanny resemblance to Fujiko, sends the three women into a nervous panic that their old rival has come back to have her revenge. Meanwhile Motoyasu follows Sayoko home, accusing her of being Fujiko and professing he still loves her right before trying to rape her. Sayoko transforms into the blood-drinking beast and tears Motoyasu apart, then stalks and kills Eiko. She next visits Kiyoko on her wedding night in the magical guise of her new husband, changing into her monstrous form and mauling her to death on the nuptial bed.

Satoe, now convinced that Sayoko is indeed Fujiko and responsible for the murders of Eiko and Kiyoko, confesses their crime to Sadao. Convinced of her remorsefulness, Sadao forgives her, and they agree to proceed with plans for marriage. Sayoko, who has been stalking Satoe as the vampire beast, overhears their conversation and relents, vowing to spare her final victim. However, her monstrous urges overwhelm her on the couple's wedding day, killing Satoe before being fatally shot by the wedding guests. The wounded creature staggers into the woods and dies, reverting to the beautiful form of Fujiko. Sadao finds the body and carries her remains back to civilization as the film closes.

As the synopsis above makes clear, the titular "vampire" of *Vampire Bride* is not a bride at all, but a monster that preys on brides, much as the vampire in Shintōhō's *Lady Vampire* is in fact a male vampire that stalks beautiful women. Since the films' titles actually describe the vampires' culinary preferences rather than the vampires themselves, "Bride Vampire" might be a more accurate, if awkward, rendering of the Japanese. Ikeuchi's repulsive, hair-covered monster is certainly a far cry from Hammer's sexy *Brides of Dracula*, released the same year as *Vampire Bride*, and English-speaking audiences expecting a seductive succubus in a low-cut gown will be disappointed.

The film owes more to Universal's Wolf Man series starring Lon Chaney Jr. than Hammer's lascivious Dracula series, featuring several striking transformation scenes in which the beautiful Ikeuchi gradually devolves into a hairy, fanged monster via a series of cuts and dissolves. In terms of narrative, however, traditional Japanese *kaidan* ghost stories of karmic revenge provided the main source of inspiration. Unlike Western vampires and werewolves preying upon innocent victims, Fujiko, like the female ghosts of classic Edo-period (1600–1868) *kaidan*, is the victim herself. Her facial disfigurement at the hands of her three treacherous classmates deliberately recalls similar injuries suffered by Oiwa in *Yotsuya kaidan* and Orui in *The Ghost Story of Kasane's Swamp*, as does her subsequent death and monstrous resurrection to seek vengeance on her oppressors.

Ikeuchi's facial-scar makeup is no more grotesque than what other actresses like Irie Takako and Wakasugi Katsuko wore in many similar *kaidan* productions. Yet the added monstrosity of Ikeuchi's hairy, werewolf-like transformation sequences—a decidedly unflattering and masculine image for a young female starlet—helped perpetuate the rumor that the role was a sort of public shaming orchestrated by Shintōhō head Mitsugu Okura. Infamous for having affairs with the studio's actresses, Okura was reportedly infuriated by Ikeuchi's decision to marry and leave the studio, and when her marriage failed and she asked for her old job back, starring in *Vampire Bride* was the price she had to pay. Whatever the truth of the matter, the result was one of Shintōhō's weirdest and most indelible horror films.—Michael Crandol

See also Okura, Mitsugu

Bibliography
Namiki Kyōtarō, dir. *Vampire Bride*. Shintōhō, 1960. Film.

VAMPIRE GIRL VS. FRANKENSTEIN GIRL (2009)
DIRECTOR: Yoshihiro Nishimura, Naoyuki Tomomatsu
SCREENPLAY: Naoyuki Tomomatsu
SPECS: 84 minutes; color

Directors Yoshihiro Nishimura (b. 1967) and Naoyuki Tomomatsu (b. 1967) take characters from the manga *Kyūketsu Shōjo tai Shōjo Furanken*, written by Shungiku Uchida (b. 1959), to create an absurd, no-holds barred, and across-the-board offensive comedy about a monstrous high school love triangle.

On Valentine's Day in Japan, girls give boys boxes of chocolates as a sign of affection. In this case, the handsome Jyugon, played by Takumi Saito (b. 1981), is the object of affection of Keiko, played by Eri Otoguro (b. 1982); however, their mean teacher confiscates all the Valentine's tokens. Keiko is a spoiled brat and the daughter of the meek vice principal, played by Kanji Tsuda (b. 1965), who refrains from standing up to the teacher's actions.

After class, Jyugon is stopped by Monami, played by Yukie Kawamura (b. 1986), a transfer student who flies under the radar—rarely noticed and often absent from classes. She offers Jyugon a chocolate that this mean teacher has failed to collect from her because of her evasive nature. He takes and eats the chocolate only to realize it is filled with blood. After a psychedelic episode, he is accosted by Keiko who scolds him for eating a chocolate from Monami, now her rival in a romantic competition for Jyugon's attention.

The film then introduces two student clubs: the "Wrist Cut Club," and the "Dark Girls Club." In the Wrist Cut Club, suicidal girls practice slicing their wrists in preparation for an upcoming competition, while in the latter Dark Girls Club, the members satirize Ganjuro Girls—young women who break the traditional obsession with culturally acceptable white skin by wearing dark and colorful makeup. This group is led by "Afro-Rika," played by Namie Terada, who is obsessed with being the darkest, fastest, and most famous. They serve a larger purpose later in the film.

Jyugon takes himself to the sexy and strange Nurse Midori, played by Sayaka Kametani (b. 1976), where he lies down after feeling ill from the chocolate. He is surprised that Monami is there as well, and she reveals to him that he has actually consumed her blood, is now half vampire, and to be fully turned he must drink her blood one more time. She tempts him with a bloody kiss but is interrupted by an angry Keiko, who accuses Monami of stealing boyfriends and slaps her, letting loose a droplet of Monami's blood.

Scenes later, Keiko's meek father is a ruse for his insane, mad scientist alter ego, Kenji Furano. In full-on traditional Kabuki costuming, Furano, with the help of Nurse Midori, tries to create life with kidnapped students. He is frustrated because he has not been successful.

Through a series of fast-paced cuts from scene to scene, Monami tells Jyugon about killing creepy older men who prey on young schoolgirls, including the chocolate confiscating teacher, who spied on one of Monami's kills. She tells Jyugon that she wants him to be immortal with her and she will kill him if he doesn't comply. He agrees to become a vampire and as he accepts her bloody kiss, sees in a vision how her mother, played by Eihi Shiina (b. 1976) tried to escape the vampire hunter Francis Xavier, played by Yukihide Benny, but is eventually killed. Monami has gone through the ages alone and wants a companion. Midori finds Monami's blood droplet and tries to mop it up but it has a life of its own. She eventually catches it and brings it to Furano, who feeds it blood, creating a life source for his maniacal experiments.

Keiko catches Monami and Jyugon as they kiss again, and as a fight between the girls ensues once more, Keiko falls to her death. Midori breaks the news to Furano about his daughter, and he decides to experiment on her with screws that have been soaked in Monami's blood, making them writhe with life. Murders start to occur as Nurse Midori runs amok collecting body parts: the winning wrist cutter's arms for their strength in cutting, Afro-Rika's legs for their speed, and the *Ju-on* obsessed Chinese teacher's lungs that can withstand any pollution. The students become enraged, and when they find out about Nurse Midori's actions, they chase her off the school roof to her death.

Monami gets a threatening message on the classroom chalkboard to meet on campus that night because a new and improved Keiko is holding Jyugon captive. Monami arrives to the challenge and the girls exchange insults in yet another fight. This time, however Keiko is a combination of the body parts Nurse Midori collected, and can detach limbs with her trusty power drill to create new weapons against Monami's blood swords. In a peculiar twist, the fight moves to Tokyo Tower.

Ridiculous fights ensue, with flying body parts, gouts of blood spraying, and Keiko morphing into a spider-like monstrosity that is conquered by Monami's lethally animated blood. She saves Jyugon but is weakened by the battle, and gives her magical cloak to Jyugon to save him from a fall. Igor finally appears after his win with Furano and Franken-nurse Midori, and saves Monami from a fatal fall. He hands her over to Jyugon and fades away to dust.

This zany, disjointed, and fast-paced film is signature Nishimura with ridiculous body horror, practical gore effects, and at times offensive parodies of cultural groups. It is interesting to note that Nishimura seems to lack cultural sensitivity with regard to some of the racial representations in the film. His parodies of the Chinese and African characters have deep roots in historical significance, if not blatant racism. First, the African characters seem to be one-dimensional and a knee-jerk response to the 1990s "ganguro" phenomenon. It seems that Nishimura only advances stereotypical notions of the early encounters between the Japanese and Africans during the mid-1800s, as well as current tropes that demonize, defame, and degrade people of color. Not limiting his offensive depictions to Africans only, Nishimura parodies a Chinese teacher, questioning, among other character traits, his intelligence. The relationship between China and Japan has been historically unstable, and it is evident here that Nishimura has no regard for stemming such issues—mocking his Chinese neighbors. Unfortunately, the director, who has also derided Native American, Chinese, and African peoples in his earlier short film *Meatball Machine: Reject or Death*, seems oblivious to the hurtful depictions of other races, and apparently harbors an assumption that the average movie viewer is from one ethnic group and will have an understanding of his attempt at humor.

In an industry where global admiration is sought after and seen as a measure of success, it is puzzling why a filmmaker would risk the possibility of alienating markets all over the world and perhaps suffer monetary loss and censorship. This however was not the case in at least one instance in 2009, when *Vampire Girl vs. Frankenstein Girl* actually won the "Audience Award" at the New York Asian Film Festival. Along with that perplexing win, in North America, Western reviewers soften the huge social faux pas with disclaimers instead of outright criticism, implying a hierarchy of what is acceptable racism in film. Ironically in his film *Helldriver*, he sought to explore themes of segregation and human rights—an indication that he's clearly familiar with the notion of discrimination. Yet, what is evident in this film is that he was both insensitive and divisive in his artistic expressions.—Carolyn Mauricette

See also Audition; Helldriver; Miike, Takashi

Bibliography

"A History of Racism in Fashion: Japan's Ganguro Girls" *Complex*, 12 September 2012. Accessed 10 February 2015. http://ca.complex.com/style/2012/09/a-history-of-racism-in-fashion/japans-ganguro-girls.

Huang, Yanzhong. "China, Japan and the Twenty-One Demands" *Asia Unbound* (blog), 21 January 2015. Accessed 10 February 2015. http://blogs.cfr.org/asia/2015/01/21/china-japan-and-the-twenty-one-demands/.

Liu, Xuexin. "The Hip Hop Impact on Japanese Youth Culture." *Southeast Review of Asian Studies* 27 (2005). Accessed 10 February 2015. http://www.uky.edu/Centers/Asia/SECAAS/Seras/2005/Liu.htm.

Nishimura, Yoshihiro, dir. *Meatball Machine: Reject of Death*. King Record Co., 2007. Film.

Nishimura,Yoshihiro, and Naoyuki Tomomatsu, dirs. *Vampire Girl vs. Frankenstein Girl*. Excellent Films, 2009. Film.

Zurui. "Are Japanese Sambos Better Than American Sambos?" *Black Tokyo* (blog), 22 July 2013. Accessed 10 February 2015. http://www.blacktokyo.com/2013/07/22/are-japanese-sambos-better-than-american-sambos/.

VAMPIRE HUNTER D: BLOODLUST (2000)

DIRECTOR: Yoshiaki Kawajiri
SCREENPLAY: Yoshiaki Kawajiri
SPECS: 103 minutes; color

Violent, moody, and atmospheric, *Vampire Hunter D: Bloodlust* is a 2000 anime film that deftly combines classic vampire gothic horror with science fiction, postapocalyptic, and Western themes. Written and directed by Yoshiaki Karajiri (b. 1950) and produced by *Madhouse*, the film is a sequel to the 1985 movie, *Vampire Hunter D*. Both films are based on the long-running Vampire Hunter D novel series, written by Hideyuki Kikuchi (b. 1949) and illustrated by renowned artist Yoshitake Amano (b. 1952). *Bloodlust* is an adaptation of the third novel in the series, *Demon Deathchase*.

Vampire Hunter D: Bloodlust takes place in a distant future where vampires rule over a postapocalyptic Earth. The power of the vampires is slowly waning, as bounty hunters seeking the rewards for their destruction offered by the human population are constantly challenging these vampires. D, the voice of Hideyuki Tanaka, is a bounty hunter, the product of a union between a vampire and a human mother, with most of the powers of a vampire and without the major weaknesses. D's incredible abilities are also due in part to his lineage, as his father is Dracula, greatest of the vampires. Inhumanly beautiful, armed with a sword, and riding a cybernetic horse, D is respected and feared but remains an outcast, accepted by neither the vampire nor human populations. His only companion is a talkative parasitic demonic face set into his palm and known as "Left Hand," voiced by Michael McShane, which also possesses various magical powers.

When the vampire lord Meyer Link, voiced by John Rafter Lee, kidnaps a young woman named Charlotte, voiced by Emi Shinohara, D is hired by her family to retrieve her, if possible, or to kill her if she has been turned into a vampire. To complicate matters, a second band of bounty hunters is also hired. Among the mercenaries is Leila, voiced by Megumi Hayashibara, who hunts vampires for revenge after the death of her family. After clashes with three super-powered guards, D discovers that Charlotte's kidnapping was staged and that the human and vampire are actually in love. Despite this, D and the other bounty hunters continue to attempt a rescue for their own personal reasons. D and Leila save each other's lives on different occasions as they fight these guards. During a lull in the chase, D quietly agrees to a request from Leila that, whoever dies first, the survivor will place flowers on the other's grave.

Link and Charlotte arrive at the Castle of Chaythe, which is inhabited by the ghost of the vampire Carmila, voiced by Beverley Maeda. D learns the guards were hired by Carmila, not Link, to ensure Charlotte's safe arrival at the castle. Carmila lured Link and Charlotte to her home with the promise of safe passage from Earth in an ancient spaceship. The ghostly vampire shows her true intentions by incapacitating Link and draining Charlotte's blood in a bid to return to life. In separate conflicts, D dispatches Carmila's angry spirit and Link destroys her corrupted mortal body. After a brief battle with a devastated Link, D opts to spare the vampire. As the castle crumbles around them, D and Leila escape while Link boards the spaceship carrying Charlotte's body. The two bounty hunters watch as the old spacecraft lifts off and claws its way to the stars.

Years later, D arrives at Leila's funeral, fulfilling his earlier promise. The funeral is attended by scores of mourners. D tells Leila's granddaughter that Leila was afraid she would die alone and un-mourned. He states he is glad she was wrong and returns to his wanderings.

The 1985 film *Vampire Hunter D* was an original video animation (OVA) with a limited budget. The success of the first installment allowed *Vampire Hunter D: Bloodlust* the higher budget of a theatrical film. The visuals of the sequel seem to better represent the original novel artwork by Amano, who had gained fame since the release of the first film, particularly for his work on the Final Fantasy game series. Uncommon for an anime film, *Bloodlust* was produced with the intention of debuting as an American release. The English version was recorded first and a Japanese dub was released later in 2001. *Bloodlust* enjoyed a limited theatrical release in the United States and continues to have favorable reviews. A video game adaptation preceded the film in 1999.—Daniel Fandino

VERSUS (2000)
DIRECTOR: Ryūhei Kitamura
SCREENPLAY: Ryūhei Kitamura
SPECS: 119 minutes; color

Versus is a 2000 action horror film, directed by Ryūhei Kitamura and based on a screenplay by Kitamura and assistant director Yūdai Yamaguchi. It stars Tak Sakaguchi, Hideo Sakaki, and Chieko Misaka. The film follows the exploits of an unnamed Prisoner KCS2-303, played by Tak Sakaguchi, who has recently escaped a prison convoy and is now on the run in an enchanted forest, and the assortment of characters—police, criminals, and supernatural beings—that are in pursuit of him. After debuting at the Tokyo International Fantastic Film Festival, *Versus* went on to be screened at film festivals around the world, achieving cult status both in Japan and abroad.

In an unnamed forest, a Warring States–period (1467–1603) warrior battles a horde of undead fighters. He slaughters them all before being killed himself by a mendicant priest. As the warrior dies he sees another man waiting to confront the priest. In the present day, two prisoners run through the forest, having just escaped a convoy. They rendezvous with a gang of yakuza, who informs them that they must wait for their boss. When Prisoner KCS2-303 realizes that the gang has kidnapped a young woman, played by Chieko Misaka, he demands that they release her. Upon their refusal to do so, he kills one of the yakuza who promptly returns to life as a zombie—leading everyone to realize that they are in a place where the dead can come back to life. In the confusion, Prisoner KCS2-303 kills the undead yakuza once again and escapes with the young woman into the forest, setting off a series of chases, captures, and escapes that—the characters slowly come to realize—they have all acted out before in previous lives.

Originally envisioned as a sequel to Kitamura's 1997 short film *Down to Hell*, *Versus* quickly morphed into a larger project—ultimately involving over one-hundred-fifty cast and crew members and a shooting schedule that took over seven months. While the premise of an enchanted forest where the dead come back to life was retained as a core idea of film, virtually all other elements of the plot were altered prior to, and in the course of, shooting. Kitamura has described *Versus* as an attempt to produce a Japanese action film that could compete with Hollywood action films in spite of a lack of financial resources. For Kitamura, the Japanese film industry's aversion to making so-called "entertainment movies" was something that he wanted to challenge. Heavily influenced by action and horror films of the 1980s—in particular *The Evil Dead* (1981), *The Terminator* (1984), *Commando* (1985), and *Highlander* (1986)—Kitamura sought to combine the practical effects of 1980s films with the high-production values of more modern films like *The Matrix* (1999) in order to create a sense of "an 80s spirit in a millennium-style film."

Though Kitamura claims that *Versus* is not a horror film, it nevertheless takes much of its tone from classic films in the zombie genre, including George Romero's *Dawn of the Dead* (1978) and Lucio Fulci's *Zombi 2* (1979). Furthermore, the film derives much of its plot and several of its visual elements from classical Japanese tales of horror. The zombies who come to life and pursue the yakuza gangsters are specifically identified as victims of those gangsters. In this way, their conflict is situated within the category of vengeful ghost stories—an idea that is echoed in the costume of the primary female protagonist, who appears throughout the film in a white sweater and black slacks, drawing upon the iconography long used to symbolize the legless, white-robed ghosts of the Edo-period (1615–1868) horror stories, prints and paintings, and Kabuki plays. Moreover, with its central story of reincarnation and karmic ties, *Versus* explores a theme that has defined Japanese classical literature since the Heian period (794–1185).

Versus was well-received by fans of genre films across the world, although it received mixed reviews from Japanese cinema experts. Following its debut in Tokyo, *Versus* was screened at such prestigious festivals as the Fantastic'Arts Film Festival in Gérardmer, France, the Japan Filmfest in Hamburg, Germany, and the Toronto International Film Festival. It has since gone on to become a cult classic, with its popularity resulting in the release of an "Ultimate" cut of the film—a version that features an additional ten minutes of sequences, as well as a revised musical score and fresh special effects, all of which were added in 2004 when the cast and crew reunited to film new material for the special release.—Sara L. Sumpter

Bibliography
Kitamura, Ryūhei, dir. *Versus* (Director's Cut). Tokyo Shock, 2003. DVD.

VIRUS (1980)
DIRECTOR: Kinji Fukasaku
SCREENPLAY: Kōji Takada, Kinji Fukasaku, Gregory Knapp
SPECS: 108 minutes; color

Virus, alternately titled *Day of Resurrection* and known in Japanese as *Fukkatsu no hi*, is a 1980 postapocalyptic horror film. It is based on the novel of the same name written by Sakyo Komatsu. The film is helmed by the award-winning, and critically acclaimed director Kinji Fukasaku (b. 1930). At the time of its making, *Virus* was the most financially ambitious endeavor in Japanese cinematic history. The film chronicles the progression of a genetically engineered virus that lays waste to all of mankind with the exception of a handful of survivors.

The film opens with a man supporting himself with a walking stick wandering a desolate wasteland. The plot begins with a clandestine meeting in East Germany between "Dr. Krause," played by Ken Pogue (b. 1934) and a mysterious man. Dr. Krause is entrusting this man with the transfer of a deadly pathogen to his colleague in Zurich. The pathogen is the "MM88" virus. It is a doomsday virus that amplifies any other virus to fatality. The meeting is cut short by a gun battle. The unnamed man absconds with the virus. He manages to fly off with it only to crash shortly after, releasing the virus.

One month later, a car is seen driving up to the Institute for Biological Research at the University of Maryland. It is there that Colonel Rankin, played by George Touliatos (b. 1929) meets Dr. Meyer, played by Stuart Gillard (b. 1950), to discuss the dangers of the MM88 virus. Colonel Rankin exhorts him to develop a vaccine for MM88. Dr. Meyer says that there is no possible vaccine; he further explains that the virus is extremely pernicious and terrifying. He also accuses Rankin of trying to weaponize the virus. Colonel Rankin confirms this, stating the importance of having an end game weapon against the Soviets and how a vaccine is crucial to the plan. Dr. Meyer storms out of the room in disgust. In fear that he is a threat of becoming a whistleblower Rankin silences Dr. Meyer by having him institutionalized.

The film then cuts to a scene in the White House of "President Richardson," played by Glenn Ford (b. 1916), and his cabinet, watching footage of a virus that started in Italy and is now plaguing Europe and Japan. Demonstrations in the United States show that the situation is not much better at home. The president demands a vaccine be developed. It is revealed to the president that a placebo has been administered to calm the masses but the virus has yet to be identified and no vaccine is forthcoming.

General Garland, played by Henry Silva (b. 1928), enters the room showing the casualties around the globe. There is some speculation that this could be germ warfare. General Garland calls for the activation of the ARS or Automatic Response System for nuclear war. The president doubts the germ warfare theory based on the ubiquity of deaths worldwide. Seeming to confirm his thoughts, the Kremlin calls to say that the Chief of State of the USSR has died of what is coined the "Italian Flu."

The film briefly cuts to a dire scene of a short-staffed Japanese hospital struggling with hordes of patients before cutting back to the White House. President Richardson is taking a private audience with General Garland when Senator Barkley, played by Robert Vaughn (b. 1932), enters and says that they might be able to combat the virus if they look inward to Operation Phoenix. Senator Barkley asks General Garland to elucidate the operation to the president. General Garland claims that it was just a routine theoretical study. Senator Barkley argues that this particular study was biological warfare–focused and that a sample of a virus titled MM88 was lost. Colonel Rankin is called into the Oval Office. Rankin claims that MM88 was not stolen and that it would be a moot point as MM88 was benign and a failure. As proof of Rankin and Garland's deceit, Senator Barkley introduces Dr. Meyer. The doctor, recently released from the mental institution and worse for wear, enters the Oval Office and confirms that the "Italian Flu" is actually the MM88 virus. President Richardson angrily excuses General Garland from his office. A call interrupts the meeting informing the president that his wife has fallen ill. He turns to Dr. Meyer and asks him what is needed to combat this blight.

Another brief snippet shows the ravages of Japan, the country is under martial law. Bodies are being burned in the streets. Back at the Oval Office, the president and Senator Barkley are shown as deathly ill and bemoaning the passing of Dr. Meyer. The president has a revelation that Palmer Station in Antarctica might be the last hope for humanity as most of the world has expired. He holds this belief because the virus cannot propagate in extreme cold. He calls to check on the status of the virus at the facility.

Admiral Conway, played by George Kennedy (b. 1925), answers stating that the virus has not impacted anyone at Palmer Station or any of the other stations in Antarctica. The president sends out a message to all of the international Antarctic bases. He tells them that the world has been "beset by a horrible plague" but that the weather in Antarctica has been a shield for the Antarctic research stations. He beseeches them to work together as an international coalition. The senator dies after hearing the speech which is followed shortly thereafter by the death of President Richardson. General Garland enters the Oval Office and informs the corpse of the president that he is going to activate the ARS, which he then proceeds to arm in the White House bunker.

Back in Antarctica, two representatives of the Japanese Showa Station are shown skiing. Their transport vehicle has broken down and they are going to the nearest research station on their path to a meeting of the newly formed Federal Council of Antarctica at Palmer Station. They reach the Norwegian station whereupon they find a bloodbath. A pregnant member of the station, played by Olivia Hussey (b. 1951), has survived by hiding behind a locked steel door. The woman, Marit, explains that the whole station went mad. A killing spree ensued including her own husband's attempt to take her life. The two Japanese representatives split up. Dr. Yoshizumi, played by Masao Kusakari (b. 1952), remains with Marit. Commander Nakanishi, played by Isao Natsuyagi (b. 1939), continues on to the meeting.

Admiral Conway speaks at the coalition meeting. He is grim in his assessment that the 855 men and 8 women from the research stations are probably the sole survivors of the plague and that they only have two years of supplies. His plan is to subsist on those supplies until the virus dies off so that they can leave Antarctica and repopulate the Earth. "Dr. Borodinov," played by Chris Wiggins (b. 1931), of the Soviet station agrees that this is the best and only option. There is some discord at the meeting which escalates into a brawl. Major Carter, played by Bo Svenson (b. 1941) defuses the chaos by firing his gun and distracting everyone. It is at this point that someone hands Admiral Conway a distress signal sent by a nearby submarine. The submarine is Soviet and wishes to disembark for emergency assistance.

Ensign Smirnov, played by Jan Muszynski (b. 1948), of the submarine and Admiral Conway speak. Smirnov discloses that his crew is sick with the "Italian Flu" and in urgent need of medical attention. Conway regretfully tells Smirnov that he cannot allow them to disembark. Smirnov starts insisting angrily when the transmission is interrupted by Captain McCloud, played by Chuck Connors (b. 1921), of the British submarine HMS *Nereid*. He emphatically tells Smirnov to stay away from the base. When Smirnov refuses, Dr. Bordinov gives his blessing to engage the Soviet vessel.

The two vessels take attack positions. The soviet submarine is quickly sunk. Captain McCloud's crew is invited to disembark, by unanimous vote, because they show no signs of illness. The *Nereid* will do so after doing a final sweep of Japan in search of healthy survivors.

Back at the Norwegian Station, Marit has given birth to a baby girl. Marit and Dr. Yoshizumi have received a proclamation from the Federal Council of Antarctica welcoming the child, named Gry, to the new world.

Back at the Federal Council of Antarctica, one of the remaining eight women has been raped. The council engages in a conversation about how to repopulate the world with 855 men and only eight women. Women have been proclaimed the most valuable resource and are told that they must "accommodate" to more than one man for the survival of the human race.

At the Showa station, Dr. Yamauchi, played by Shin'ichi "Sonny" Chiba (b. 1939), is desperately trying to hail anybody in Japan. The *Nereid* responds to Showa stating that they are on their final pass of Japan and about to launch a surveillance drone. The drone paints a bleak picture of unmitigated devastation. Grief stricken, Dr. Yamauchi runs off into the snow to his death.

The drone takes an air sample from Japan. Dr. Latour, played by Cec Linder (1921–1992), informs Captain McCloud that the sample has tested positive for MM88. The captain insists that the sample be destroyed. Dr. Latour counters that the sample is crucial to developing a vaccine. Captain McCloud allows the doctor to keep the sample in isolation.

Back at Palmer Station, the survivors are celebrating Christmas. Dr. Yoshizumi watches Marit and Gry with sadness. Marit makes an attempt to comfort the doctor. She hands him a pendant that she says is from Gry. The intimacy is interrupted by a young man who has drawn Marit, conceivably by a random lottery, for copulation. As this is a rule, she agrees. Dr. Yoshizumi retreats to his quarters to work on his ongoing seismology report.

The next morning Dr. Yoshizumi explains his findings to the council. Off-shore drilling that started prior to the virus could cause a cataclysmic earthquake equivalent to a nuclear-scale event near Washington, D.C. Upset by the news, Admiral Conway asks Major Carter, an ex-liaison to the Joint Chiefs of Staff, to speak. Carter describes the ARS and how a major earthquake would trigger that system. A Soviet captain explains that once missiles land in the USSR an automatic nuclear retaliation will launch that would include Palmer Station. Admiral Conway suggests that someone needs to disarm the ARS.

A random drawing of cards to choose who will disarm the ARS is cut short when Major Carter volunteers, after which Dr. Yoshizumi decides to aid him in the suicide mission. At first, Major Carter feels that the doctor would be an impediment. Dr. Yoshizumi convinces the major of his mettle by engaging him in a physical altercation.

The council meets to plan the trip. The women and children will be sent out of range of the missiles should the two men be unsuccessful in their mission. Captain Lopez, played by Edward James Olmos (b. 1947) ends the meeting with a soulful serenade while playing the piano. Dr. Yoshizumi goes to his quarters to find Marit waiting for him. They embrace passionately and make love.

Before being escorted to Washington by the *Nereid*, Dr. Latour informs Major Carter and Dr. Yoshizumi that he may have developed a working vaccine. As they face certain death, the men agree to be test subjects for the prospective treatment.

The duo reach Washington, D.C., and rush to disarm the ARS. Washington is a wasteland, riddled with corpses. They frantically reach the White House as small-scale earthquakes start. They encounter a number of obstacles on their path to the ARS console. An explosion claims the major's life. With the earth shaking heavily, Dr. Yoshizumi reaches the console just in time to watch the missiles launch.

Dr. Yoshizumi informs the *Nereid* of his failure and that everyone in the federation should do what they can to survive. He also tells Captain McCloud that, in the very least, the vaccination appears to be effective. This conversation is followed by a montage of exploding nuclear bombs across the globe.

The film flashes forward four years. Dr. Yoshizumi is shown to be the wandering man from the beginning of the film. He is now weather-beaten and alone. He enters a church and stares into the eyes of a fallen statue of Christ. His thoughts go back to his love for Marit. He looks at her gifted pendant longingly.

Back in Antarctica, a small group of dejected survivors plan on finally moving north. Most have lost the will to live. In tattered clothing, Marit sits at the seaside and sees a man approaching from the distance. He flashes a reflection of the pendant and she knows that it is him. Reunited with Marit, Dr. Yoshizumi mutters, "Life is wonderful."

The film was released to little fanfare and a poor critical reception. Despite its unprecedented budget, solid cast, and strong director, the film gained little to no traction and is generally considered to be a box office bomb. Little is known about its earnings and release history. Many iterations of the film have been cut ranging from 108- to 158-minute versions. These variations range from giving the estimable Shin'ichi "Sonny" Chiba more screen time, to a deeper focus on Dr. Yoshizumi and Marit's relationship. There is also a much less negative ending that does not include a nuclear holocaust.—Evan Marmol

Bibliography
Fukasaku, Kinji, dir. *Virus*. Haruki Kadokawa Films, 1980. Film.

VISITOR Q (2001)
DIRECTOR: Takashi Miike
SCREENPLAY: Itaru Ira
SPECS: 84 minutes; color, black and white

Visitor Q, released in 2001 and directed by Takashi Miike, is the sixth and final installment in the "Love Cinema" film series produced by CineRocket. Like the other films in the series, it was shot on digital video, had a modest budget, and received a small theatrical run. *Visitor Q* took only one week to shoot and had a budget of 7 million yen. While the film does not contain traditional horror genre elements such as monsters or supernatural occurrences, it does contain, like many of Miike's other films, extremely violent and sexual images. His follow-up to *Visitor Q*, *Ichi the Killer* (2001) was banned in a number of countries due to graphic violence.

Though Miike's previous film *Audition* (1999) is widely accepted as a horror film, he has mentioned that he does not think of genre when he makes films. However, he did find the realism of the novel *Audition* to be frightening. Similarly, *Visitor Q* maintains a realistic style via documentary-like handheld shots, POV perspective, and diegetic sound. Likewise, many scenes in the film consist of long, unedited takes composed as a wide shot. While this is the style for the majority of the film, scenes that break away from it are highlighted by their stark contrast.

The film begins with text on a black background: "Have you ever done it with your dad?" A shocking question, it sets the tone for a film that contains graphic depictions of aberrant sexual behavior such as incest and necrophilia. In this opening scene, two members of the family at the center of the story are introduced; father Kiyoshi Yamazaki, a news reporter played by Kenichi Endo, and daughter Miki (Fujiko) who has recently become a prostitute. The scene takes place entirely in a hotel room and is predominantly composed of footage from a camcorder held by Kiyoshi, who is filming an interview with Miki for a story about "youth today." These shots are interspersed with still images taken by Miki. After Miki seduces her father into having sex, he is shocked to find that his camera had been on the entire time. Further, he does not have enough money to pay Miki for her services and promises to "give the rest to [her] mother." A preoccupation with the recorded image continues through the entire film and is not dissimilar to other films that use technology as a horror element such as *Ring* (1998) and *One Missed Call* (2003).

Text introduces the next very short scene, "Have you ever been hit on the head?" Kiyoshi is sitting in a train station when a man smoking outside opens a window and hits him in the head with a rock. The next scene has a similarly violent question, "Have you ever hit your mother?" Introduced here are the other two members of the Yamazaki family, mother Keiko, played by Shungiku Uchida, and son Takuya, played by Jun Muto. Takuya violently abuses his mother, whipping her with rug beaters and pushing her through a shoji (a paper screen). After returning to his room and putting on a respirator mask, bullies outside the house torment Takuya by shooting fireworks through his window. Meanwhile, Keiko's dysfunction is exhibited when she retreats to her room to inject heroin.

Kiyoshi finally makes it home, but not before being hit on the head a second time by the stranger, who is seen next having dinner at the Yamazaki home. Though his name is never given, this stranger is the titular "Visitor Q," played by Kazushi Watanabe. Both he and Kiyoshi eat hungrily and pay no mind to Takuya's severe beating of his mother. In a moment of dark humor, Q asks for more ice and Keiko comes tumbling through a shoji, jumps up and immediately serves him. Moments of comedy are peppered throughout the film during sequences of extreme violence or disturbing sexual behavior.

Some information about the visitor is suggested when Q explains to Takuya that he used to live in their house. Meanwhile, unable to sleep, Kiyoshi goes outside to sit in his car and watch video footage of a previous interview he conducted with youth he met on the street. The teenagers abuse and humiliate him by sodomizing him with his microphone. This is graphically depicted and the "scandal" is subsequently referenced by his colleague as a reason for Kiyoshi's denial of work.

The next day, on the way to work, Kiyoshi stops to film Takuya being beat up by bullies. Kiyoshi's obsession with his work is evidenced when he pitches the story of covering his son's bullying himself during a meeting with a colleague, who leaves disgusted. Contrasting with the film's predominant visual style, this scene is preceded by a jarring series of swirling images of the city.

The same day, Keiko, prostituting herself, is in a hotel room with a man who asks her to beat him with a belt. She obliges, but hits him weakly. After she returns home and shoots heroin, she finds Q downstairs. The two embrace, but their interaction turns sexual when Q begins to rub her breasts. She looks down, surprised to find that she is lactating. Takuya walks in and comedically drops his school bag. After this, Keiko is more assertive and responds to Takuya's pelting her with food during dinner by returning with a knife and throwing it at his head. Likewise, she and Q are both uninterested when bullies begin shooting fireworks into the house. Kiyoshi grabs his camera to document the attack, yelling, "How am I supposed to feel? I know my family is being destroyed!"

The next day, Takuya is tied up and humiliated by bullies as Kiyoshi, his colleague, and Q watch. Disgusted, his colleague attempts to leave but she is attacked by Kiyoshi who throws her on the ground, attempts to rape her, and chokes her to death. Q films the entire encounter, and continues to film as they put the body in the trunk, take her home, and discuss chopping her into pieces. Takuya, meanwhile, is tied up and helpless in a ditch.

While Kiyoshi is mapping lines on the corpse, he begins to rub the body and becomes aroused. He explains that he does not care if she is dead and will have sex with her anyway. The scene cuts between a static wide shot and images from the camcorder Kiyoshi is holding. He documents the event and exclaims, "The mysteries of life are amazing!" While humor and necrophilia may seem disparate, comedy is injected into this scene via the evacuation of the corpse's bowels and the onset of rigor mortis that causes Kiyoshi to become stuck inside the body.

Kiyoshi calls to Keiko for help, but she is preoccupied in the kitchen. Wearing a trash bag, she is squirting milk from her breasts as Q watches from under an umbrella. She runs to Kiyoshi, and seeing his condition, then runs to the store to buy oil and vinegar, in which she bathes him, attempting to liberate him from the corpse. This is finally achieved when she injects him with heroin, and a comedic cork popping sound effect accompanies the release.

With Kiyoshi ordering him, Q continues to videotape everything, including the bloody massacre that occurs when bullies show up to the house. Kiyoshi runs outside, hits one boy, and then proceeds to saw into another's head while Keiko plunges a screwdriver into the head of a third bully. Afterward, Kiyoshi and Keiko appear to have a very enjoyable time chopping up the dead bodies. Stylistically different, this scene features exaggerated sound effects and quick cuts.

While his parents are dispatching the bullies, Takuya is lying facedown in the pool of breast milk and vaginal fluids that covers the kitchen floor. He inquires of Q if the visitor came to their house "to destroy it." Without answer, Visitor Q disappears. He is seen next encountering daughter Miki on the street. When she propositions him, he picks up a rock. Glancing at the rock and then at him, the scene cuts to black. The violence is implied when we see Miki arrive at home with a black eye and cuts on her face.

The film culminates with Miki discovering her mother outside in the greenhouse breastfeeding her father. For the first time in the film, lyrical nondiegetic music is heard. Smiling, Miki goes outside to suckle Keiko's other breast. A sense of healing is implied here, as her facial injuries are no longer present. Likewise,

Keiko's scars from Takuya's beatings have faded. This concluding wide shot of the reconvened family is held and finally cuts to black.—Jeffrey Bullins

VITAL (2004)

DIRECTOR: Shin'ya Tsukamoto
SCREENPLAY: Shin'ya Tsukamoto
SPECS: 86 minutes; color

His 2004 film *Vital* (*Vuitaru*) clearly debunks any notions that Shin'ya Tsukamoto (b. 1960) is simply a director of body horror and cyberpunk even though he made only three *Tetsuo* films. A turbulent nightmare is represented by swirling circular images that are followed by thick smoke and a chaotic series of belching foundry chimneys, underexposed and ghost-like, merging together to create a coherent row. Accelerated by jarring, unrhythmical music, *Vital*'s abstract beginning suggests a continuation of *Tetsuo*'s throbbing metal world. Immediately a cut to the close-up of a human face, a camera circling over it while receding, then suggests entry into another universe.

Hiroshi Takigi, played by Tadanobu Asano (b. 1973), gradually opens his eyes. He has been unconscious for some time. Remembering nothing, after an auto accident he cannot even identify his parents, the juxtaposed smoke stacks suggesting his physical awakening. His parents' later conversation reveals his former interest in medicine that has somehow ebbed. As Hiroshi walks dispiritedly through unrecognizable spaces to rehabilitate himself, he eventually discovers a clue to his former identity through a cached collection of medical school textbooks. Enrolling in a medical college despite amnesia, he also moves into a room so barren even its pipes are visible. At school he attracts the attention of Ikumi, the icy top student, performed by a model named Kiki (b. 1978), toward whom he is initially unresponsive. His professors possess considerable knowledge about the body, but can merely ponder notions of the soul and the realm of the unconscious.

As time passes (three years), Hiroshi continues to brood, but remains disconnected from his past. During their dissection semester he and Ikumi are part of the same team. Shocked by the cutting of a cadaver, Ikumi is suddenly unable to function. She mopes, and then attempts to choke herself. In stopping her, Hiroshi suddenly recalls a woman from his past, with whom he played potentially dangerous strangulation games. He then reenacts them with Ikumi. Noticing a blue butterfly tattoo on the arm of the woman in his memory, Hiroshi suddenly bolts to the lab, observes the same tattoo in his dissection corpse, and establishes that the corpse is that of his former girlfriend.

Hiroshi learns from his father that Ryoko Oyama, the girlfriend, played by the classically trained dancer Nami Tsukamoto (b. 1979), was killed in the car crash, dying before he awoke. As Hiroshi obsessively continues the dissection, his mind frequently flashes to scenes with her. Ryoko walks melodically through his room, admiring the realism in some of his drawings, but says, "As for me, I'm not sure if I am real. It's like I'm sleeping and dreaming." Later Ryoko dances using expressive contemporary movements. Hiroshi comes to realize that what he is envisioning may not be fragments of memories from past events but suggestions of something else. When he meets with Ryoko's parents, they are initially disturbed, but eventually reconcile with him to link to their daughter. As they draw closer, her father tells him that he has no recollection of her dancing.

Passionately protecting her body while dissecting it, Hiroshi repulses his team members, and all except Ikumi transfer to other groups. Hiroshi's sketches are extremely thorough and realistic (Tsukamoto has stated that Leonardo da Vinci's anatomy studios served as an inspiration). After four months, the dissection period is completed. As he contemplatively sits in front of Ryoko's coffin before rewrapping the body, his mind flashes to an idyllic Okinawan beach, where she dances lyrically and evocatively. Then she cries, "I didn't want to die." Later they embrace and fall asleep in a lush and vivid tropical forest. Ryoko awakens, gazing lovingly upon him. When Hiroshi wakes, she is no longer there and he is unable to locate her. Then his consciousness returns to the dissection lab.

Ikumi, who once jealously followed Hiroshi to Ryoko's parents' home, comes to realize the extent of Hiroshi's continued involvement with Ryoko. Although disappointed, she accepts Hiroshi's apology, understanding that he is too tied to Ryoko and cannot have a relationship with her. At Ryoko's cremation ceremony Hiroshi's father tells his dissection professor that Hiroshi intends to continue his medical studies. Hiroshi appears to be able to carry on with her spirit near.

Although *Vital* is not a traditional horror film, Ryoko's spiritual dimension is difficult to fully grasp. She is not a ghost living in the realm of the dead, but appears to possess some kind of consciousness. She lost cognition following the accident, awakening for about five hours just before passing away and vehemently insisting that her body be dissected after her death. Following his discussions with Hiroshi, her father grasps that Ryoko is communicating with her boyfriend in the present.

Before the accident she and Hiroshi had played sadomasochistic games with death. In Okinawa she gazes lovingly at him, acknowledging that she is no longer physically in the same world as he is, but desiring to give him a positive sendoff. She dances freely and passionately, now possessing a new freedom, to leave Hiroshi with the fondest of remembrances.

Shin'ya Tsukamoto has incorporated Tokyo as a harsh and artificial urban environment into the theme of all his films. Here he expands his view to consider notions of memory and consciousness. His Tokyo is dark, frequently filled with rain, and as barren as Hiroshi's room. Even though the maverick Tsukamoto does not show blood during dissection scenes, he uses a queasy yellow filter and shots of the room's aging walls to symbolize the city by inducing an atmosphere of squeamishness. Likewise, Hiroshi's barren apartment is featured through a bleak blue filter, pointing to alienation. In contrast, Okinawa is lush and calm, vibrant and vital, pulsating with energy during Ryoko's mesmerizing dance. Starting with *Tetsuo*, Tsukamoto frequently explored body mutations. In *Vital* he instead delves into the interior of the body, linking it with human consciousness and the human spirit.

The first time Tsukamoto filmed outside Tokyo, *Vital* was initially presented at the Orizzonti section of the 2004 Venice Film Festival, where his work has been exhibited regularly since 1998 (his *A Snake in June* [*Rokugatsu no Hebi*] won its Special Jury Prize in 2002), and several other international film festivals including the London and Toronto film festivals and New Directors/New Films in New York. This film marks the first time Tsukamoto filmed outside Tokyo, blending his dreamlike Okinawan scenes with the realism of the dissections, learned by actual observation at a medical school. Filled with unhurried calm and vibrant warmth despite its inherent sadness, its moods and rich ambiguities brace the vulnerabilities of Hiroshi's fractured psyche.—Bill Thompson

See also Kotoko; Nightmare Detective; Nightmare Detective 2; Tetsuo: The Iron Man

Bibliography

Mes, Tom. *Iron Man: The Cinema of Shinya Tsukamoto*. Godalming, UK: FAB Press, 2005.

Muramatsu, Masahiro. *Basic Tsukamoto*. Pathfinder Home Entertainment, 2003. DVD.

Schilling, Mark. "Shinya Tsukamoto Interview." Accessed 10 January 2015. http://japanesemovies .homestead.com/tsukamoto.html.

Tsukamoto, Shin'ya. *Vital*. Tartan Asia Extreme, 2005. DVD.

· W ·

WAR IN SPACE (1977)

DIRECTOR: Jun Fukuda
SCREENPLAY: Shuichi Nagahara, Ryuzo Nakanishi
SPECS: 85 minutes; color

Toho Studio's *War in Space* (1977) is an unabashedly juvenile program that probably holds some kind of international record for the earliest theatrical rip-off of *Star Wars*. It was rushed into production in late 1977 to meet the January 1978 deadline, to compete directly against *Star Wars*, scheduled to open in Japan in the same month. To Toho's credit, they eschewed copying any overt plot element or character from the American mega-hit. For example, there was no R2-D2 stand-in, and although there was a somewhat laughable pseudo-Chewbacca carrying a big Grim Reaper's scythe, it was so far removed from the real Chewbacca that it went relatively unnoticed. Instead, Toho relied on the crack team of largely TV-trained young cast, the stunt expertise of the Japan Action Club, and the abilities of the veterans of the late 1960s–mid-1970s Godzilla franchise, including special-effects supervisor Teruyoshi Nakano (b. 1935) and the veteran helmer Jun Fukuda (1923–2000), to produce quickly and cheaply a reasonably entertaining space opera.

The result is not one of the finest hours of Toho Studio, but for the followers of Japanese popular culture, it presents a great opportunity to watch the 1970s TV stars Kensaku Morita (b. 1949)—also a singer and known to the Japanese as "Moriken"—and Hiroshi Miyauchi (b. 1947), the cult actor with many devoted fans for having played title roles in *Masked Rider V 3* and *Kaiketsu Zubatto*. Also appearing is Yūko Asano (b. 1960), one of the original "idol entertainers," who was only seventeen at the time of filming. Ryō Ikebe (1918–2010), who played a decadent young yakuza in *A Pale Flower* (1964), brings a surprising level of gravitas and poignancy to the role of Gōten's captain.

Working with a slightly bigger budget than was given to the Godzilla films of the mid-1970s, Fukuda and the special-effects team do their best to suggest a large-scale interplanetary warfare with hastily constructed models of UFOs and spaceships, making excellent use of the 2.35:1 widescreen. In a few spots, such as the hilariously underpopulated interior of the enemy spaceship, the film does reveal its expeditious origins. Moreover, the aliens are inexplicably made up to look like Roman soldiers, albeit with green pancake makeup, and their Great Demonic Spacecraft Carrier, "*Daimakan*," seems to fly right out of *Ben Hur* (1959). No doubt the film's enduring cult appeal partly comes from the bizarre, eyebrow-raising designs of the Earth's defense vessel *Gōten* (*Heaven Shaker*) and the *Daimakan*, which traverse the point at which the cool becomes the eye-poppingly ridiculous, and finally just plain weird. Nor is there any point in asking why Commander Hell dresses the captive Jun in black leather hot pants, though that does serve the purpose of revealing her notorious "99 centimeter" legs. By the final battle, the filmmakers freely acknowledge that the whole sequence is nothing more than two admittedly cool-looking (if overtly phallus-shaped) children's toys blasting light and belching smoke at one another. Yet instead of cringing from embarrassment, they valiantly throw themselves into hurling these toy-ships at one another. Their enthusiasm is definitely infectious. Most viewers with appropriately scaled-down levels of expectation will probably find themselves enjoying all this, with silly grins on their faces.

War in Space, like another Japanese *Star Wars* rip-off from the rival studio Toei, *Message from Space* (1978), had been difficult to see outside Japan, despite its reputation as kid-in-a-candy-store entertainment for Japanese special-effects fans, if not as a serious work of art, until Discotek Media released an excellent Region 1 DVD edition in 2006. Unfortunately, since then the company has shut down and the DVD is as of January 2015 out of print. A Region 2 DVD released from Toho has, as usual, no English subtitles.—Kyu Hyun Kim

Bibliography
Fukuda Jun, dir. *War in Space* [*Wakusei daisensō*]. Toho, 1977. Film.

WARNING FROM SPACE (1956)
DIRECTOR: Kōji Shima
SCREENPLAY: Hideo Oguni, Edward Palmer, Gentaro Nakajima, Jay Cipes
SPECS: 87 minutes; color

Warning from Space was the first full-color *tokusatsu* (special-effects) film produced in Japan, directed by Kōji Shima (real name Takehiko Kagoshima, a prolific actor of the 1920s and 1930s) and released by Daiei Studios in 1956. The plot centers around a mysterious race of starfish-shaped aliens called "Pairans" who appear in a space station above the Earth. Inspired by the success of *kaijū* (monster) films like *Gojira*, promotional materials for the movie portrayed the Pairans as gigantic red monsters looming over Tokyo. In fact they stand only as tall as a human in a black starfish suit, and their intent, it turns out, is ultimately benevolent. Avant-garde artist Tarōj Okamoto designed the Pairans, equipped with a single glowing blue eye in the center of their bodies—their influence has been felt through the years in movies, television, and video games. The film itself combines familiar tropes from American science fiction movies like *The Day the Earth Stood Still* and *When Worlds Collide*, while also introducing a number of new notions: a hidden planet on an orbit directly opposite Earth's; and aliens transforming their bodies into human form in order to walk among us, both of which would appear consistently in subsequent Japanese productions.

The Pairans appear almost immediately, but for the first half of the film their mission is unclear. In the English dub they talk in ambiguously menacing terms about humanity and the need to stop its "blundering." In order to do so they set out to contact a trio of scientists (Drs. Isobe, Komura, and Matsuda, played by stalwarts Shōzō Nanbu, Bontarō Miake, and Isao Yamagata, respectively), but when they land on Earth aboard their flying saucers amid a cacophony of radio static, and then loom suddenly out of the shadows, humanity is understandably terrified. In order to more effectively transmit their message, one of the Pairans agrees to take human form, and assumes the shape of popular performer Hikari Aozara, played by Toyomi Karita, whose sudden nightclub scenes are unintentionally hilarious. The Pairan manifests amazing abilities in human form, and the scientists quickly begin to suspect that she may not be of this Earth. In the second half of the film the true villain is revealed: Planet R, a glowing red heavenly body that is on a collision course with Earth. As it accelerates toward our planet the great heat that it emits threatens all life. Cooperation then becomes the theme, both between human and Pairan (though the aliens inexplicably disappear from the film until the final moments) and between the various nations of the world, as they pool their stockpile of nuclear weapons to try and throw Planet R off course. Another villain appears in the form of a mustachioed arms dealer (and scientific skeptic) who kidnaps Dr. Matsuda, just when the world needs him most. Dr. Matsuda has created humanity's last hope: a formula for a substance even more explosive than the hydrogen bomb. But he remains captive, tied to a chair for over a month while the people of Earth await their doom. As Planet R approaches, the sky is bathed in red, animals begin to die, and earthquakes and tidal waves ravage the land amid eerie shots of a deserted Tokyo. Despite the fact that the villain is a planet seen through a telescope—and all that stands between the Earth and total destruction is a trio of aging scientists and an alien woman disguised as a popular nightclub performer—the film manages a kind of apocalyptic intensity that is in some ways more frightening than modern, nail-biting whiz-bang nonsense like *Armageddon* or *Pacific Rim*.

Beneath its veneer of silly effects and bad acting, *Warning from Space* is unusual and compelling, though the message of the film is somewhat muddled: a strange marriage of anti-nuclear politics on the one hand, and a climax that highlights the absolute necessity to use the destructive power of science to save the world on the other. The latter runs somewhat counter to the message brought by the Pairans, who tell the Earthlings that there is only evil in power used destructively. Thematically, *Warning* differs somewhat between the Japanese and English-language versions. In the former, the Pairans choose Japan as the recipient of their anti-nuclear warning because it is the only nation that has suffered the devastation of the bomb, while in the latter it is simply the "best suited." At the end of the film we see the reversal of the devastation wrought by Planet R: small animals and little children alike return to a happy world, their safety ensured by the judicious use of the most destructive superweapon ever created. It is made explicit in the Japanese version, however, that the world has expended its entire nuclear stockpile, leaving humanity to live on in a world free from atom and hydrogen bombs, but the English dub (made in the early 1960s) again excises such explicit antinuclear sentiments. In fact, apart from an evacuation sequence that evokes wartime anxiety, essentially all traces of the psychological and physical damage from the war have been removed from the Japan portrayed in *Warning from Space*. But it is these very thematic peculiarities and contradictions that invest the film with a deeper interest than it may appear, on the surface, to possess.—Daniel F. Joseph

WILD ZERO (1999)

DIRECTOR: Tetsuro Takeuchi
SCREENPLAY: Tetsuro Takeuchi, Satoshi Takagi
SPECS: 98 minutes; color

Wild Zero is a 1999 splatter-gore horror comedy film directed by Tetsuro Takeuchi from a screenplay by Takeuchi and Katsuaki Takemoto. It stars Masashi Endō, Kwancharu Shitichai, Makoto Inamiya, Haruka Nakajo, and Guitar Wolf (Seiji), Drum Wolf (Tōru), and Bass Wolf (Billy) from the band Guitar Wolf—all of whom appear in the film as fictionalized versions of themselves. The film narrates the experiences of a young *Guitar Wolf* fan who fights for love in the midst of an alien zombie invasion with the help of his favorite musicians. Since its Tokyo debut, *Wild Zero* has gone on to become a cult classic with regular screenings at midnight festivals around the world.

While the rockabilly garage-punk band *Guitar Wolf* gives a raucous performance on a night club stage, the band's biggest fan, "Ace," played by Masashi Endō, looks on—enthralled by the power of rock 'n' roll. After the concert, Ace gathers his courage before making his way backstage to approach the owner of the club for a chance to perform. Meanwhile, in a back room, the members of *Guitar Wolf* engage in an argument with a corrupt club owner about who controls the band's musical direction. The heated argument quickly escalates to guns drawn on all sides. Arriving in time to hear the club owner proclaim that rock 'n' roll is dead, Ace bursts in to declare that rock 'n' roll will never die, receiving a punch for his pains and setting off a lethal gun battle. In the chaos, the club owner's finger is shot off and the leader of *Guitar Wolf*, who is also known as "Guitar Wolf," makes Ace his blood brother. He gives Ace a whistle and tells him to blow it if he ever needs any help.

The next day, as Ace is traveling through the countryside on his scooter, he stumbles onto, and inadvertently prevents, an attempted robbery at a remote gas station. Coincidences abound, Ace then meets Tobio, played by Kwancharu Shitichai—a young woman abandoned by her boyfriend and now waiting at the station for a ride. Though the two have an instant attraction to one another, Ace continues on without her, blissfully unaware that a meteorite that causes people to turn into zombies has landed. With the country rapidly descending into a state of emergency, Ace doesn't get far before he runs across a band of zombies who have killed and converted a group of yakuza on their way to a meeting with an arms dealer named Yamazaki, played by Haruka Nakajo. Remembering the young woman he left behind, Ace returns to help Tobio only to the find that the gas station is now overrun with zombies as well. As the two desperately flee to a nearby abandoned warehouse, Ace blows his whistle in the hopes that *Guitar Wolf* can save both him and the woman of his dreams.

In the end, a grand finale of a bloody battle arises between Ace, Tobio, *Guitar Wolf*, and just about everyone else featured in the film. With a gang of misfits, an arms dealer, and the erstwhile gas station robbers, an all or nothing fight ensues to save the world not just from alien invasion and zombification, but from the revenge-bent nightclub owner who remains determined to get *Guitar Wolf*—and Japan itself—under his thumb.

Unlike a majority of horror films being produced in Japan in the late 1990s and early 2000s, *Wild Zero* does not utilize the vengeful spirit trope—a renaissance in which Japanese cinema was popularized by such films as *Ring* (1998), the Ju-on franchise (1998–2003), and *Dark Water* (2002). Instead the film blends elements from a wide array of Western cinematic genres—notably science fiction B-movies of the 1950s, zombie films of the 1960s, and exploitation flicks of the 1970s—with aspects of Japanese yakuza features to produce a film that is generally regarded as an exuberant, if at times silly and somewhat nonsensical, action adventure.

Wild Zero received positive reviews, with critics praising its fast pace, wild antics, goofy gore, and iron-clad commitment to a thoroughly off-the-wall premise. *Wild Zero* had its international debut at the Toronto International Film Festival and has since become a regular feature of the midnight movies circuit. It was released on DVD in the United States by Synapse Films. The US release contains a number of special features, including an interactive drinking game that automatically signals players with a pop-up beer mug icon (or three) anytime one of the game rules is fulfilled.—Sara L. Sumpter

Bibliography
Takeuchi, Tetsuro, dir. *Wild Zero*. Synapse Films, 2003. DVD.

• X •

X-CROSS (2007)

DIRECTOR: Kenta Fukasaku
SCREENPLAY: Tetsuya Oishi
SPECS: 90 minutes; color

X-Cross, known as *XX Ekusu-Kurosu: Makyo densetsu* in Japanese, is a 2007 horror film that incorporates elements of action, thriller, and comedy. It is directed by Kenta Fukasaku (b. 1972), son of legendary filmmaker Kinji Fukasaku, and is based on the hit novel *Sono ketai wa XX de* by Nobuyuki Joko. The film follows two young women in their early twenties as they take a road trip to a relaxing hot spring getaway in a remote village after one of them has a heart-wrenching breakup with her boyfriend. What they do not realize is that the freakish, limping inhabitants of this village have a fetish-like penchant for cutting off the legs of young women. To make matters worse, they are followed there by a deranged, scissor-wielding woman, who is hell-bent on killing one of them for stealing her boyfriend away from her. The audience is kept in suspense throughout the film, guessing as to who has set them up for such an unfortunate journey. The film has enjoyed a positive reception with screenings at film festivals around the world.

The film opens up with Shiyori Mizuno, played by Nao Matsushita (b. 1985), inside one of the retreat's cabins, whereupon she receives a phone call from a frantic Akira Mononobe, played by Nozomu Iwao (b. 1975), who pleads with her to leave before they cut off her legs. In the first of many chronological ellipses, the film rewinds to Shiyori and her friend Aiko Hiuke, a "bad girl," played by Ami Suzuki (b. 1982), driving to the hot springs in Ashikari Village. It is on the road that they first encounter the psychotic scissor-wielding killer Reika, played by Maju Ozawa (b. 1977), nearly running her over accidentally. When they arrive, they are transported by villagers to the resort area by minivan, passing what we find out later are scarecrows of mummified women who are worshipped as goddesses.

Shiyori and Aiko bathe in the hot springs. When Shiyori leaves the spring to go back to the cabin, Aiko makes a suspicious phone call to an unidentified recipient, stating "everything is on schedule." Once back at the cabin, Shiyori finds a ringing mobile phone in the closet. The caller is Mononobe, a professor of folklore at Jonan University. The mobile phone had been left there by Mononobe's sister, who was recently sacrificed by the villagers. He explains that the villagers are descendants of an ancient Japanese sect of loggers that cut off women's left legs to ward off disasters and to prevent them from fleeing while the men worked, and that they also cut the tendons in the legs of their newborns to prevent them from leaving. He further informs her that they then started capturing women travelers and subjecting them to the same fate. The cabin's power is cut, and Shiyori is surrounded by knife and torch wielding villagers. She makes her escape by jumping out of the second-story window. Mononobe implores her not to trust anyone, including Aiko, who brought her there.

Separated, the two women attempt to meet in a bathroom; however, they end up in two different places. During a phone conversation, Shiyori asks Aiko if she can trust her. They are abruptly cut off after Aiko replies, "Listen, Shiyori, the truth is . . ." Shiyori then calls her friend Yayoi, played by Shoko Nakagawa (b. 1985), in order to verify what Mononobe has told her. Yayoi confirms part of what Mononobe has told her, that there is no mention of Ashikari village on the Internet, but suggests she not trust either Mononobe or Aiko. Doubt is cast on Yayoi's own trustworthiness as the camera pans down to a cast on her leg, suggesting she might be one of the villagers.

The film cuts back to the earlier scene where Shiyori has left Aiko in the hot spring by herself. Reika confronts Aiko, and follows her to a large men's bathroom. During the confrontation, Reika removes her black robe to reveal a pink and frilly Lolita garb underneath. Reika tells Aiko that she is going to kill her as revenge for stealing away her boyfriend. Injured by Reika's massive scissors, Aiko fights back and escapes by spraying her in the face with caustic bathroom cleaning fluids.

The film reunites us with Shiyori who has managed to escape from the villagers after being trapped and apprehended in a drainage tunnel. She continues on her way to the location where she has agreed to meet Mononobe. Adding to the suspense, Mononobe continually implores her to trust him. Just as Shiyori is about to be recaptured by the villagers, her ex-boyfriend and the reason for the trip in the first place, Asamiya Keiichi, played by Hiroyuki Ikeuchi (b. 1976), pulls up in a red Porsche and rescues her. While in the car, Yayoi messages Shiyori to tell her that Mononobe could be a villager as there is no record of him at Jonan University.

The film cuts back to Aiko, who is now hiding from Reika in a portable toilet. Still in pursuit, Reika approaches with an absurdly large pair of scissors. Reika knocks the portable toilet over with Aiko still inside. Aiko kicks off the door, which flies into the air in highly exaggerated fashion. The ensuing heavy metal music and slow motion shot of Aiko shaking the toilet water out of her hair, followed by her line, "I'm pissed," signals a humorous turn. Aiko picks up a chainsaw and engages Reika in a battle to the death, which includes multiple reciprocal head-butts. After Reika gains the upper hand, Aiko douses her with flammable liquid, which she then ignites, blowing up Reika in the process with an illogically powerful blast.

Asamiya, while driving away with Shiyori, explains to her that Aiko had engineered their entire breakup and the events that followed. Shiyori phones Aiko to accuse her of knowing about the village secret and calls her a murderer. At the same time as Shiyori notices that Asamiya is driving her back into the village, she receives a call from Mononobe, who tells her he has discovered it was Asamiya who took his sister to the village to be sacrificed. With a sinister look Asamiya slams on the brakes of his car, knocking out Shiyori, who is slammed into the dashboard. Aiko, who until now has had no knowledge of the villagers' dark practices, is phoned by Yayoi, who explains everything to her and pleads that she help Shiyori.

Shiyori wakes up to find herself surrounded by nightmarish, zombie-like villagers and bound to a cross that is lying horizontally. She is hoisted up into a vertical position to have her leg cut off in a ritualistic ceremony presided over by Asamiya. Shiyori will be his "living sacrifice" and will spend the rest of her life with him. Just as Asamiya is swinging the axe toward Shiryori's leg, Aiko shows up to save her. Aiko uses the flash on her phone to stun the villagers and then threatens to use the pictures she has taken to expose the village to the outside world. Aiko cuts Shiyori free, but the villagers regroup and attempt to capture them.

Reika unexpectedly appears, yet again, in her unending quest to dispatch Aiko. However, she needs to get past the villagers in order to complete her task. What follows is an all-out, three way battle with Reika slicing, slashing, and impaling any villager in her path, spraying their blood all over the place. Mononobe finally makes his entrance, arriving in an SUV to rescue Shiyori. As Shiyori and Aiko battle toward Mononobe's vehicle, Reika suddenly traps Aiko beneath her. Shiyori saves Aiko, who is moments away from death, by striking Reika in the back with a club, knocking her into a crowd of villagers. The two quickly jump in the back of the waiting SUV and speed away with the villagers in pursuit. Asamiya makes one final attempt to capture Shiyori by latching on to the back of the vehicle. Shiyori kicks him squarely in the face and he falls clumsily into the other pursuing villagers, ending the chase.

While they are driving toward Tokyo in the light of the breaking dawn, there is a comically goofy exchange between the three about the possibility of romance between Mononobe and Shiyori. The movie ends abruptly when, driving through a tunnel, Reika jumps onto the top of the SUV, and peeks her head menacingly through the rear window.

X-Cross has received generally positive reviews and was considered by many to be an improvement over Kenta Fukasaku's previous films. The film incorporates an inventive and unique nonlinear editing style, allowing the viewer to see events from different perspectives and time frames. It premiered in 2008 at the New York Asian Film Festival and in Canada at the Fantasia Film Festival in Montreal. It screened at the Los Angeles Film Festival in the same year.—Emil Marmol

Bibliography
Fukasaku, Kenta, dir. *X-Cross*. X-Cross Film Partners, 2007. Film.

· Y ·

YAKUSHO, KŌJI (1956–)

Kōji Yakusho is one of the most active actors in Japanese cinema and television. He was born in Isahaya, Nagasaki Prefecture as Kōji Hashimoto into a large family as the youngest of five brothers. After graduating from Nagasaki Prefectural High School of Technology in 1974, he moved to Tokyo to commence his career as a civil servant in a municipal ward office called in Japanese *yakusho*, from which he took his acting name. Due to his growing interest in drama, in 1978 he enrolled at the prestigious and exclusive Mumeijuku Acting Studio created and managed by the great actor Nakadai Tatsuya. After three years of an intense training program he made his professional debut as an actor in a TV drama from NHK Television called *Nacchan no Shashinkan* about the Second World War. Soon after this Yakusho became an acclaimed actor while playing the historic role of Oda Nobunaga in 1983 NHK's drama *Tokugawa Ieyasu* and Miyamoto Musashi in 1984 NHK's drama *Miyamoto Musashi*.

The notoriety gained in TV dramas helped him to make his first film debut in Itami Juzo's film *Tampopo* (1986) in the nameless role of Man in White Suit, a character who defies social conventions regarding food, sex, and violence. In 1988, Yakusho began his international career, playing his first main character in *Another Way* directed by Kōsaku Yamashita. By 1996, when he played the leading role in the Japanese hit *Shall We Dance*, Yakusho was a well-known actor, thanks to the numerous televised dramas and movies and theatrical films he made in the late 1980s and early 1990s. Yakusho's natural, but passionate, acting style earned him many awards and professional recognition, and in 1998 he received a special governmental award for his contribution to Japanese cinema and his support for expanding Japanese culture abroad.

After starring in films such as Imamura Shohei's *The Eel* (1997), a film that won the Palm d'Or at the Cannes Film Festival, he began a collaboration with famous cult horror-film director Kurosawa Kiyoshi. The pair's collaboration resulted in several supernatural, detective thriller and drama films for cinema and television. *Cure* (1997), one of the most celebrated works made by Yakusho in association with Kurosawa, is a detective horror story about a serial killer who seems to use hypnosis to force people to commit murders. Detective "Kenichi Takabe," played by Yakusho, investigates these bizarre and apparently disconnected murders with the help of a psychologist named Sakuma (Tsuyoshi Ujiki). Kurosawa earned a great deal of international attention for his horror and thriller films, most of which starred Yakusho. After *Cure*, Yakusho played in seven other Kurosawa films, which made him an internationally recognized actor in the new wave of Japanese horror in the 1990s.

Yakusho won the Best Actor Award at the Chicago International Film Festival for his leading role in the second-last film directed by Shōhei Imamura, *Warm Water under the Red Bridge* (2001). This allowed Yakusho to participate in several additional international productions, such as *Memoirs of a Geisha* directed by Rob Marshall in 2001, and *Babel*, directed by Alejandro González Iñárritu in 2006. In 2009, Yakusho made his debut behind the camera directing and starring in the film *Gama no abura* (*Toad's Oil*). In addition, he began a new collaboration with one of the most famous contemporary directors in Japan and abroad, Takashi Miike. Yakusho participated in two samurai films directed by Miike, *Yūsannin no Shikaku* (*13 Assassins*, 2010) and *Ichimei* (*Hara-Kiri: Death of a Samurai*, 2011). Both of them were box office hits.

In 2012 Yakusho received the Imperial Purple Ribbon medal for his outstanding achievement in the artistic field. Since his first television drama, Yakusho has acted in more than eighty-five films, television movies, and television dramas.—Nieves Moreno Redondo and Fernando Ortiz-Moya

YUMEJI (1991)
DIRECTOR: Seijin Suzuki
SCREENPLAY: Yōzō Tanaka
SPECS: 128 minutes; color

Yumeji (1991), made a decade after *Zigeunerweisen* (*Tsigoeneruwaizen*, 1980) and *Kagerō-za* (*Heat Haze Theatre*, 1981), is the concluding work in Seijin Suzuki's (b. 1923) Roman Taisho trilogy. All three films freely mix reality with fantasy. They are slow-paced, esoteric ghost stories set in the exuberant and intense Taisho era (1912–1926), the transforming period in which the West's raucous Jazz Age was introduced into a rapidly modernizing Japan. The dreamlike *Yumeji* is capricious and eerie, as absurdist as it is surreal, and as unconstrained in crossing social and stylistic boundaries as was the real-life painter and poet Yumeji Takahisa (1884–1934), its protagonist. Yumeji, a self-trained artist, is particularly known for his *bijinga* (pictures of beautiful women), willowy beauties in natural poses with slightly melancholic expressions. They were popular with the general public, but not the cultural elite. Little is known about Yumeji's early artist life, so Suzuki felt he could depict his subject as freely as he wished, and created a portrait of a whimsical painter madly engaging with his subjects.

The first few minutes of *Yumeji* are completely undisciplined. Yumeji, played by Kenji Sawada (b. 1948; he is most famous as "Julie," the lead singer for the rock band the Tigers) wears a kimono patterned with loud swirls. He attempts to escape from a crowd of people in formal Western-style clothing, who are bouncing colorful beach balls in the air. Meanwhile, a kimono-clad woman whose face is hidden from him floats suspended midair. Unable to reach the balls, and thus fit in, Yumeji mimes the throng's actions. He shoots a man in his hand, then wakes up and falls back in his chair just before the man can return his fire. That absurdity continues as Oyo, a model, accompanies him to the train station so that he can travel to Kanazawa and elope with his fiancée. As he taps the station's wooden pillars while waiting, sketches of attractive and sometimes naked women appear. Oyo then raps on his trunk, and more images jump out. Yumeji tells Oyo that Hikono, his fiancée, is ill, so he will meet her in Kanazawa. They then return to his dwelling to indulge in *l'amour fou*. When Yumeji eventually finds Hikono, acted by *Bee Bop High School* star

Masumi Miyazaki (b. 1968), she assures him that she will join up with him in Kanazawa shortly.

In Kanazawa Yumeji meets Tomoyo Wakiya, recently widowed after Onimatsu (Matsu the Devil) discovered her husband bedding his wife. She searches the lake every day for her husband's unrecovered body. Yumeji, constantly seeking a model of ideal beauty, becomes intrigued with the compliant Tomoyo. The action heats up when Oyo arrives with a message that Hikono's arrival has been delayed, as she has vomited blood. Oyo then leads him to a raucous party where he meets and initially bonds with the recently deceased Sekichi Wakiya, who is wearing a blonde wig. Soon afterward Onshu Inamura, Yumeji's acquaintance and rival artist, portrayed by Kabuki legend Tomisaburo Bando (b. 1950), joins them. After Wakiya returns home and introduces his friends to his wife, he jealously realizes his wife's infidelity. From here the situation becomes more bizarre. Yumeji's fiancée Hikono finally arrives in Kanazawa but is too ill to meet him, so she must stay at Wakiya's villa. A vindictive Wakiya throws a mad homecoming party while plotting to kill Yumeji after getting him to paint his wife's portrait. Meanwhile Onimatsu attempts to bludgeon Wakiya with his scythe once again. Yumeji, who attempts to experience and paint everything, must now struggle to stay alive. As he becomes haunted by both the natural and the supernatural, he has to deal with multiple aspects of himself. In the end the young romantic receives too severe a dose of reality's hardships for his nature, but he nonetheless pushes forward with his painting.

Suzuki is less interested in narrative than he is in Yumeji's character and his own stylistic experiments. His Yumeji always strives to locate alluring women, and desires to make love to them in order to understand their nature and thus paint them better. Apart from his relationship with his fiancée, who appears only infrequently, his affairs are transient. Wakiya adroitly analyzes Yumeji's character in relation to his wife when he says, "She married me, but she was a doll without a soul. You took her soul, put it in a closet, and forgot it." Yumeji initially rejects Oyo's request to become his model, telling her that since she had posed for her boyfriend for four years, he couldn't remodel her so easily. Then he reconsiders.

Yumeji views women interchangeably, but may not realize that he does. He speaks with the slightly older madam managing the Kanazawa ryokan about the pleasures of atmosphere and his enjoyment of rain. The artist then creates a special mood by telling her he feels as if he had been with her before at a place like her inn. Enticed, she adds that it doesn't need to be Kanazawa, any place will do. Hoping he is attempting to seduce her, she is deflated when he adds that the woman doesn't need to be her. Yumeji is a romantic who paints a bevy of woman, but never fully considers their inner qualities.

Suzuki styles *Yumeji* both gently and vulgarly. Like Yumeji, Suzuki uses a pallet of colors for his images. Red garners special attention as it is the color of blood and lips. For Tomoyo it recalls her husband's lambasted body, which she initially believes lies unrecovered in the lake. Soft pastels also adorn many of Yumeji's works. Suzuki's film progresses slowly, his scenes cheerful at times, funereal during others. He establishes Tomoyo's double nature using just a few shots, as she changes from a demure widow refusing to pose for his vulgar works to someone suggestively posing, draped only by her long dark hair. Suzuki's rhythms are slow and arty, whether he is depicting quiet scenes in natural settings or hedonistic reveries with psychedelic images.

Suzuki's Taisho era is an illusory period, and the three films in his trilogy are filled with contradictions and nihilism. Suzuki takes an anti-intellectual approach when discussing his works, contending they have no deeper meaning beyond what is shown on the screen. Yet there is consistency in his unencumbered liberal and romantic approaches to the era through his surrealistic re-creations. His Taisho may be as much about the 1980s, when he filmed the trilogy, as they are about the earlier age. Oyo, for example, modeled for her artist boyfriend for four years. She justifies breaking up with him by arguing that even models have human rights, a more contemporary concern.

The Japan National Railroad may have indirectly contributed to the popularity of Suzuki's trilogy. During the 1970s and 1980s it promoted tourism in Japan through nostalgic re-creations of Japan's earlier roots. This helped to generate a new wave of interest in the stories of Hyakken and Kyoka, the two authors whose stories were adapted for *Zigeunerweisen* and *Kagerō-za*. Their work had fallen out of vogue by then, as was the case with Yumeji's artwork. Suzuki's films, however, cannot be seen as pieces of nostalgia as they depict chaos and decadence. Nonetheless, they strongly evoke the atmosphere of the bygone era.

Yumeji won Best Supporting Actress and Best Art Direction awards at the 1992 Yokohama Film Festival. Produced by Genjiro Arato (b. 1946) and his Cinema Placet company, which had produced the two earlier Taisho trilogy films, it also played at the 1991 Cannes International Film Festival's Un Certain Regard section and several other festivals. Its score is equally famous as "Yumeji's Theme," providing original music for a key sequence in Wong Kar Wai's (b. 1956) *In the Mood for Love* (*Fa Yeung Nin Wa*, 2000).—Bill Thompson

See also: *Kagerō-za*; *Zigeunerweisen*

Bibliography

Suzuki, Seijun. *Yumeji*. Kino on Video/KimStim, 1991. DVD.

· Z ·

ZIGEUNERWEISEN (1980)
DIRECTOR: Seijun Suzuki
SCREENPLAY: Yōzō Tanaka
SPECS: 144 minutes; color

A director whose stylistic experiments with time and space in action-film contract assignments caused him to be fired for making "incomprehensible" works, Seijun Suzuki (b. 1923) was blacklisted from Japan's commercial film studios during the late 1960s and 1970s. *Zigeunerweisen* (*Tsigoineruwaizen*, 1980), *Kagerō-za* (*Heat Haze Theatre*, 1981), and *Yumeji* (1991), ferociously demiurgic works commonly called his Taisho trilogy, allowed him to reinvent himself more than a decade later. All are set in Japan's Taisho era (1912–1926). This was a period of intensity intertwined with a rising assimilation of many aspects of Western civilization, expanding liberalism, and chic materialism. Three imaginative artistic innovators from that time, the writers Hyakken Uchida and Izumi Kyoka, and the artist Takehisa Yumeji, figure prominently in these works. Suzuki's trilogy, made and distributed independently, carefully recaptures the settings and fashion of the period. Whereas his earlier action efforts typically ran around ninety minutes, these films are leisurely paced and last more than two hours. Stylistic innovations predominate, and all three contain elements of surrealism, focusing not upon political events but atmosphere, hedonism, and decadence. Nonlinear and transcending genres, they incorporate dreams or dream-like structures and ghosts, defying easy interpretation. While they are difficult to fathom, collectively they illuminate Taisho's pervasiveness. Although complete understanding may not be possible, a viewer must instead draw from their pieces, attempt to decipher some of their parts, and allow them to flow.

Zigeunerweisen, also called *Gypsy Airs*, is a virtuoso gypsy violin piece composed by Pablo de Sarasate in 1904 that was popular during the Taisho era. The film begins with a 78-rpm record spinning on an old gramophone, its static-filled music hovering over the film credits. As the director credit for Suzuki appears, the player's arm is raised, but the music continues to flow. The recording's conceit is that it contains a voice, said to be Sarasate providing indistinguishable instructions to his orchestra.

A scruffy-looking Tadashi Nakasano, played by Yoshio Harada (1940–2011), is on the run from the locals for having enticed and then betrayed a woman in a coastal resort town. He determinedly munches on a roasted ear of corn, surrounded by an angry crowd with movements stylized into a frenzied dance. The fisherman's wife, from whose vagina six huge red crabs strangely appear, either committed suicide or had been murdered by Nakasano. The bearded bohemian is rescued when Toyojiro Aochi, a senior professor of German at the military academy, played by director Toshiya Fujita (1932–1997), arrives and vouches for his friend and former colleague. Aochi is spiffily attired in a Western suit and sports a trimmed mustache, while Nakasano wears a tattered kimono. They reminisce that night and hire Oine, played by Naoko Otami (b. 1950), a "geisha in mourning" over the death of her brother. Both men are infatuated with her, Nakasano particularly so after Oine describes how her brother's suicide led to his bones becoming tinged with pink. Three blind and itinerant musicians are also introduced in this scene, which ends the next morning with Nakasano following the musicians to travel around Japan while Aochi remains.

The narrative extends over several years. Nakasano marries Sono (also played by Otami), a woman from a wealthy family whose appearance is identical to that of Oine. Meanwhile Nakasano continues his wanderings. Sono dies a year after giving birth to a daughter Toyoko, having caught the Spanish fever that Nakasano had contracted on his journeys. Aochi is shocked when he discovers Oine then serving as Nakasano's wet nurse and apparent second wife. Nakasano dies from a drug overdose sometime afterward while traveling in a mountainous region, yet several years later Oine believes that he is talking to Toyoko nightly.

Several threads introduced in the opening scenes are expanded upon throughout the film, but not fully clarified. Aochi serves as the film's narrator, but at times he cannot differentiate between dreams and reality. His wife, Shuko, may be having an affair with Nakasano. Her sister Taeko is hospitalized. When Shuko's allergies derail her, Aochi visits Taeko on Shuko's behalf. Taeko describes an earlier visitation to him in which Nakasano arrived with Shuko. When Nakasano had something caught in his eye, Shuko very sensuously licked it. Aochi attempts to follow up this story during a second visit, but Taeko is too feverish to even remember Nakasano. Shortly before Taeko's death, she tells Aochi that this incident had occurred in a dream that she and Aochi shared together, totally befuddling Aochi. *Zigeunerweisen* inexplicably cuts to Nakasano stopping by Aochi's house immediately after Aochi's first conversation with Taeko, a scene whose objectivity and point of view are unclear. With Aochi gone, Nakasano attempts to seduce Shuko. As she flees, he appears to be omnipresent, so she finally acquiesces. Shuko explains her illness to Nakasano, who responds that slightly rotted fruits taste the best. Sometime later, when her husband inquires her about her allergies, she sumptuously sucks a peach skin and tells him that they have receded, that her body must have matured.

There are implications that Aochi and Sono also have an affair. Sono is initially introduced confidently preparing a *konnyaku* dinner for Aochi and Nakasano in the Nakasano home. Its warm aroma permeates the scene, and Aochi suggestively enjoys the feast. While Nakasano is away, Aochi again visits Sono, who nervously prepares this tantalizing dinner hot pot again. She becomes quite upset as Aochi prepares to leave, expressing her loneliness, and eerily draws Aochi into a darkened room containing a mirror and other surrealistic images. Toyoko, the daughter, is named after Aochi, whose first name is Toyojiro and who may actually be her biological father.

Toyoko is also associated with the supernatural. While alive, Nakasano had become obsessed with bones and colors of red due to Oine's description of her brother's suicide and tinted bones. Nakasano forces a reluctant Aochi to agree that when the first of the two dies, the other should take possession of the bones, and we later see Aochi awkwardly attempt to open Nakasano's urn to examine them. When Shuko first learns of his death, she and Aochi are imaginatively portrayed through pinkish cherry blossoms.

Oine, believing that Nakasano died in order to join his wife, Sono, desires to possess all of his earthly properties. She visits Aochi's home late at night several times, always asking Aochi to return an obscure book or object Nakasano had lent him much earlier. She finally acknowledges that Toyoko converses with her late father, even though the little girl was too young to have any memory of him when he died. Oine had overheard Toyoko repeat the loaned items during those talks. The film ends with Aochi returning the *Zigeunerweisen* recording, which Shuko had hidden in the back of a picture frame (apparent proof of an affair with Nakasano). Aochi later encounters Toyoko waiting for him near a pedestrian bridge. Speaking as a surrogate for Nakasano, Toyoko demands his bones. She insists that her father is still alive, but that Aochi merely thinks that he himself is alive, but is dead.

Suzuki loads his film with notions of doppelgängers (doubles) and pairings. Sono and Oine's identical appearances confuse even Aochi. Director Suzuki often repeats images and dialogues, playfully providing slight variations. When Aochi brings the recording back to Oine, she repeats actions from an earlier scene in which Aochi had visited Sono. At one point she leaves the room, then rapidly reemerges in Sono's clothing. She exits again, immediately reappearing in her old clothes. When she plays the recording that Aochi is returning, she becomes anxious about Toyoko. The voice, previously muffled, now clearly states, "She will not return."

The stylish Shuka, a Japanese *moga*, or "modern girl," contrasts strongly with the more traditional Sono/Oine. While Aochi and Nakasano appear to be quite different in appearance and disposition, Aochi admires Nakasano's freedom, and his desire to emulate his friend's double life may be stronger than is initially apparent. Although Aochi dresses in Western clothing while Nakasano's wardrobe is traditional, both have taught at the conservative Japanese military academy and frequently shift between the contemporary and the traditional.

Zigeunerweisen cuts between reality and dreams, sometimes indistinguishably. Doppelgängers, ghostly presences, unidentified voices, and bones all play into the concept of *ero guro nansensu* (erotic grotesque nonsense) in vogue in the 1920s and 1930s. *Zigeunerweisen* combines several stories by Hyakken Uchida (1889–1971), whose modernistic works innovatively explore mysterious realms of the living and the dead. Uncredited in the film, these stories originally were not linked and were even more enigmatic than Suzuki's work. Hyakken is best known in the West as the free-spirited German professor honored by his affectionate students in Akira Kurosawa's 1993 *Madadayo*.

Zigeunerweisen's distribution is likewise fascinating. Film companies own Japanese theater chains. Because Suzuki was blacklisted, they all refused to book his cryptic independent production. As a result, producer Genjiro Arato set up a giant inflatable tent near the Tokyo Dome, successfully screening it for twenty-two weeks. He then used the tent to distribute it throughout Japan. It received nine Japanese Academy Award nominations, and beat out Kurosawa's *Kagemusha* as Best Film, Best Director, Best Art Direction, and Best Supporting Actress (Michiyo Okusu [b. 1946] as Shuko). It also garnered these four awards plus one for Best Actress from *Kinema Junpo*, Japan's leading film magazine. Following a sneak preview at the Japan Society in New York, the film was presented at the Thirty-First Berlin International Film Festival in 1981, where it received an Honorable Mention, and the Chicago International Film Festival. Suzuki attended the Berlin Film Festival, and was willing to discuss technical details but refused to assist confused critics in unraveling its enigmatic plot.—Bill Thompson

See also ero guru nansensu genre; Kagerō-sa; Yumeji

Bibliography

DiNitto, Rachel. "Translating Prewar Culture into Film: The Double Vision of Suzuki Seijun's *Zigeunerweisen*." *Journal of Japanese Studies* 30, no. 1 (2004): 35–63.
Suzuki, Seijun. *Zigeunerweisen*. Kino Video/KimStim. DVD.
Uchida, Hyakken. *Realm of the Dead*, translated by Rachel DiNitto. Chicago: Dalkey Archive Press, 2006.

ZOMBIE SELF-DEFENSE FORCE (2006)

DIRECTOR: Naoyuki Tomomatsu
SCREENPLAY: Naoyuki Tomomatsu
SPECS: 75 minutes; color

Zombie Self-Defense Force, known as *Zonbi jieitai* in Japanese, is a 2006 zombie comedy. It references a Romero-esque sardonicism while incorporating a more modern level of high-intensity gore. The film is directed by Pink Grand Prix award winner, Naoyuki Tomomatsu (b. 1967). The film revolves around the convergence of separate groups of survivors of a zombie outbreak caused by the release of radiation from a crashed UFO.

The film begins with the voice-over of a heavy-handed diatribe decrying America's need for violence and the scores of Japanese civilians slaughtered during World War II. The voice-over urges Japan to stop kowtowing to America and form its own superior military. The narrator does state, however, that there are some aspects of American culture that deserve praise—most notably, acclaimed zombie-film director George A. Romero.

The first visual scene is of a comically poor-quality flying saucer precariously waffling through the clouds; it is engulfed in fire and billowing smoke. The story then diverges into the separate narratives of different groups witnessing the descent of the UFO from what appears to be a somewhat remote region in the woods. All watch in awe as the ship crashes and emits a green haze that engulfs everyone.

One of the groups is comprised of Kenzaki, a member of the yakuza, and his brother Hiroshi who have brought an unwitting victim to the woods to be assassinated. After the kill, Kenzaki injects himself with a celebratory drug while Hiroshi digs the grave. While Kenzaki is enjoying his high, the person he has recently murdered reanimates and attacks him. Thinking it is a drug-induced hallucination Kenzaki merely laughs. Hiroshi, though, panics and screeches that this is no hallucination. As Kenzaki struggles with this corpse, a group of zombies descend upon them. Hiroshi runs off as Kenzaki is devoured by this rabid pack of the undead.

Another group is comprised of Hitomi, played by Mihiro Taniguchi (b. 1982), a petulant pop star in the middle of a photo shoot, and her film crew. She is implacable and monstrous to the members of the film crew. Their shoot is interrupted by a horde of zombies that quickly devour everyone except Hitomi, who launches the last remaining crew member into the horde to facilitate her escape.

In another region of the woods, the Kibara Unit of soldiers is on a training exercise and encounters a woman who has inexplicably hanged herself. The captain, played by Kenji Arai (b. 1978), commands his radio specialist, Miyato, to contact HQ, but communications are down. Hayakawa, played by Jun Yamasaki (b. 1973), suggests visiting the crash site immediately. As they bag the hanging victim, Hayakawa ribs fellow soldier Takamitsu about the legend of a World War II serviceman, named Officer Kidota, who committed hara-kiri nearby and who still haunts those very same woods. While he is speaking, an image is shown of the decrepit but well-enough-preserved serviceman sitting meditatively in a cave. Shortly after this discussion, the corpse of the dead woman reanimates and rips through Miyato's neck. Before the zombie can do any further damage, Yuri, played by Miyu Watase (b. 1979), incapacitates the monster. The group leaves the scene with Hayakawa further discussing the fabled serviceman and how his corpse has managed to remain fresh throughout the decades; he opines that his hatred for America is what has kept his corpse intact. Yuri pauses during this conversation and holds her head in pain while she has a fuzzy memory of doctors seemingly experimenting on her.

The last group is that of a couple in a remote hotel near the woods. The hotel owner is having an extramarital tryst, but his lover, Akemi, is acting malignantly. Akemi expresses her discontent over the affair, while he ministers to her whining and waspish behavior. To his dismay, she reveals that she is four months pregnant. When he does not respond delightedly to the news, she snaps and threatens to sue him unless he gets a divorce. She expresses disquieting pleasure as she outlines how she can methodically ruin his life. While on this tirade, she slips, slams her head on the coffee table, and dies. As the owner attempts to dispose of the body, Akemi reanimates and attacks him. He barely survives the struggle, which ends with a shotgun blast to Akemi's head.

Both fleeing, Hiroshi and Hitomi encounter each other in the woods. She makes many sexual insinuations about what she will do to be kept safe. This pleases Hiroshi and they form a quick alliance. They quickly converge with the Kibara unit. Hayakawa immediately recognizes Hitomi and is star-struck, which pleases her greatly. Hitomi switches her affections to Hayakawa, which does not sit well with Hiroshi. The group decides to regroup at a hotel that the captain has located on his map. They start traveling toward the location with Hitomi riding piggyback on Hayakawa. As they walk to the hotel, Yuri is troubled again by a vision of doctors hovering over her. As the military unit is approaching the hotel, the owner is once again trying to dispose of his dead lover's body. He conceals the body quickly and greets the strangers. The captain asks to use the phone, and Hitomi runs off to the bathroom to clean off. When confronted about the blood on his face, the hotel owner says that it was from slaughtering a sow, a pregnant one at that.

Akemi's loudly twitching body alerts the group that there is someone else in the hotel. They walk in on her body shaking from a swollen stomach, which explodes, and a projectile flies out. The hotel owner comes into the room, upset that they are wandering about, and his zombie fetus attacks him. This zombie fetus starts by choking him with its umbilical cord and then proceeds to bite him to death.

The soldiers attempt to kill the swift moving zombie fetus. Yuri deftly catches it by its umbilical cord saving Takamitsu from certain death. The fetus runs off toward Hitomi in the bathroom. Meanwhile, the hotel owner reanimates and attacks Takamitsu.

The group splits in two. Hiroshi and Hayakawa go to save Hitomi while the captain and Yuri assist Takamitsu. The zombie fetus quickly bites Hiroshi but Hayakawa manages to shoot the monster fetus in the head. In the other room, Yuri manages to put down the hotel owner, saving Takamitsu. As they are doing this, though, the corpse of Miyato and the still-active corpse of the hanging victim appear outside of the home opposite a glass door. Kezaki and the film crew arrive shortly thereafter.

It becomes clear that these zombies cannot be killed. Yuri commands the survivors to seal up the hotel, which is being surrounded by the undead. In the process of locking up, Yuri is attacked by the once again reanimated Akemi. Yuri empties her sidearm into Akemi but is knocked out by the strain and falls back into another flashback of being experimented on.

She awakens to find Takamitsu tending to a very sick Hiroshi. The bodies of Akemi and the hotel owner have been tied up and still are very much a potential threat. It is now night and the hotel is completely surrounded by the undead. While the captain, Yuri, and Takamitsu stare into the crowd of zombies, Hiroshi rises from the couch to check on Hitomi and Hayakawa who are flirting in the kitchen. In a fit of rage, Hiroshi raises his gun on Hayakawa. Hearing the argument in the kitchen, the others storm in and disarm Hiroshi. Hiroshi is returned to the couch, but his symptoms worsen significantly. It takes the strength of Yuri and Takamitsu and an injection of sedatives to subdue him.

A remark made by Takamitsu brings Yuri to the bleak realization that she has no memories prior to this day. She confides in Takamitsu that she is having troubling memories that she does not understand. They return to the group, who have decided to try to lure the zombies to one side of the house and escape in the hotel owner's vehicle. Hayakawa distracts the zombies while Yuri, the captain, and Takamitsu run through the back door to find the vehicle.

After distracting the zombies, Hayakawa goes back to Hitomi to evacuate her and Hiroshi. Rather than moving, she tries to seduce Hayakawa and asks him to entertain her with a story. He starts telling the story of Officer Kidota. While he is recounting the tale, Hiroshi becomes a zombie and attacks Hayakawa.

Meanwhile, zombies besiege the troops en route to their vehicle. Yuri runs out of bullets and pulls out her samurai sword. She finds that she is preternaturally adept with the blade. Takamitsu reaches the vehicle but is attacked by Miyomi; in his struggle he accidentally shoots the captain in the head. Yuri saves the bitten Takamitsu and they escape with the vehicle.

Back at the hotel, Hayakawa is still engaged in a life and death struggle with Hiroshi. Despite being a zombie, Hiroshi still has the capacity to use a gun and the two engage in a gunfight. During the fight, Hitomi escapes to a bedroom only to be bitten by the reanimated corpse of the crew member she sacrificed to escape. Hitomi fights off the zombie and sprints back just in time to see Hiroshi killing Hayakawa. Hitomi attempts to escape but is attacked by Hiroshi and a reanimated Hayakawa.

At the car, Takamitsu knows he is doomed. He confides in Yuri that he was part of the science division that created Yuri, the first living cyborg. She ignores him as she drives back to the hotel. They reach the hotel and she gets out of the car and sprints inside. Takamitsu also gets out but only long enough to holler to Yuri the truth while making no effort to save himself. Takamitsu informs her that she is a reanimated corpse that was turned into a cyborg and that today was her first field exercise. As zombies bring him down, he yells that she has the power to be a patriotic super soldier, which she can engage by pressing down on one of her molars. His final words are that if she is successful that they will mass-produce soldiers like her to invade America as retribution for World War II.

Meanwhile, Yuri is back at the hotel watching Hitomi struggle for her life with Hayakawa and Hiroshi. Yuri decapitates Hitomi putting her out of her misery. She pauses in thought long enough for all of the zombies to reach her when she presses the special molar with her tongue. The molar engages cyborg vision and abilities. She unleashes all of her abilities and destroys the horde.

At this point, the much-talked-about serviceman appears in Yuri's new cyborg mind. The serviceman is now a zombie and is on a collision course with her. Yuri and the zombie serviceman meet in a field and engage in an elaborately choreographed fight sequence. Their skills and technique appear equal. Yuri has one of her arms ripped off during the fight, and she retreats deeper into the woods and stumbles upon the crashed spaceship. There, a friendly and cartoonish mushroom-shaped alien appears stating that he comes in peace. Yuri summarily cuts him in half without a second thought. After killing the alien, she reengages the serviceman and tears him asunder. Inexplicably, splitting him in two causes him to explode.

The voice-over returns with a mixed message about Yuri being Japan's last hope of patriotism, as well as an inhuman force that represents the evils of war. Yuri struggles through the forest to a road leading into a nearby town. She is met by the corpse of Hitomi carrying her own head and a group of schoolgirls. Before she can engage them, though, another alien ship arrives and crashes into Mount Fuji causing a volcanic eruption killing everyone in the vicinity.

This film received mixed to negative reviews. It premiered at the Dead by Dawn Film Festival in Edinburgh with what some critics dubbed a lukewarm response. The film was released directly to DVD and later distributed to the United States.—Evan Marmol

Bibliography
Tomomatsu, Naoyuki, dir. *Zombie Self-Defense Force*. GP Museum Soft, 2006. Film.

Index

About the Editor and Contributors

Salvador Murguia is associate professor of sociology at Akita International University and Paul Orfalea Center Fellow in Global Studies at the University of California, Santa Barbara. His research interests include popular culture, deviant behavior, and food and foodways among prison populations. Professor Murguia is currently working on four books including *Diets of the Disrepute: Control and Resistance within Prison Dining.*

★ ★ ★

Kimiko Akita is an associate professor at Aichi Prefectural University in Aichi, Japan. From 2005 to 2014, she was an associate professor in the School of Communication at the University of Central Florida. Her research interests are in gender, intercultural communication, and anime.

Rea Amit is assistant professor of modern languages, Japanese, at Illinois College. He holds a BA degree in philosophy and comparative literature from Tel Aviv University, and an MA degree in aesthetics from Tokyo University of the Arts. His research interests include comparative Asian cinemas (with special interest in India), non-Western philosophical aesthetics, and theories of popular culture.

Joel Neville Anderson is a filmmaker and scholar with research interests in personal documentary, experimental film/video, Japanese cinema/visual culture, and film programming. He is pursuing a PhD in the University of Rochester's graduate program in Visual and Cultural Studies where he received the Celeste Hueghes Bishop Award for Distinction in Graduate Studies, expecting to complete his dissertation in 2018. Joel curates JAPAN CUTS: Festival of New Japanese Film at Japan Society in New York, and his article "Cinema in Reconstruction: Japan's Post-3.11 Documentary" is available in *Film on the Faultline* (2015).

Rebecca Bacheller is the collections assistant at the Intrepid Sea, Air & Space Museum. She is a graduate of George Washington University's Museum Studies Program and has worked at the Costume Institute at the Metropolitan Museum of Art, the Smithsonian National Air and Space Museum, New York Historical Society, and Harper's Ferry National Historical Park. She resides in New York and is an avid fan of Asian extreme cinema.

William Bamberger has published book, film, and art reviews, as well as essays and translations in a number of magazines and research volumes and on websites. His primary interests include science fiction, late twentieth-century art, German Expressionist fiction, comics as literature, and contemporary poets. His

Riding Some Kind of Unusual Skull Sleigh (1999) was the first book-length study of Don Van Vliet ("Captain Beefheart").

Peter Bernard is a fourth-year PhD candidate in the Department of East Asian Languages and Civilizations at Harvard University. He specializes in modern Japanese literature. He is interested in the history of *kaiki gensō bungaku* ("weird and fantastic literature") in modern Japan, and in the formation of an aesthetic of rural horror through the intersection of *kaiki* and *chihō* ("regional") literatures spanning from the late 1880s to the present. He is also interested in the relationship between literature and *minzokugaku*, or "studies of the folk," and in locating *kaiki gensō bungaku* within a transnational Gothic mode.

Joanne Bernardi is associate professor of Japanese and Film and Media Studies at the University of Rochester. She has published on Japanese cinema, literature, and culture; silent cinema, moving image, and media history and historiography; film preservation; Godzilla and nuclear culture in Japan and the United States; visual and material culture; and digital humanities. She is author and editor of *Re-Envisioning Japan: Japan in 20th Century Visual and Material Culture*, a critical online archive of travel and educational ephemera that provides a lens to investigate changing representations of Japan and its place in the world in the early to mid-twentieth century.

Nicholas Bestor is a graduate student at the University of Texas at Austin, where he is pursuing a PhD in Media Studies. Nicholas graduated from Middlebury College in 2009 with a BA in Japanese Studies and received his MA in Film and Media Studies from Emory University in 2012. His research interests include contemporary American television, animation, and table-top gaming.

William Blick is a librarian and assistant professor at Queensborough Community College in Bayside, New York. He has published work on film, music, literature, and popular culture. He has presented papers at the University of Gdansk, Poland, and the University of Leeds, England. He is also a prolific writer of genre and literary fiction that has been featured in several journals and anthologies. As artist and critic, Bill has also tried to combine his librarian skills and his love of the arts into a synergistic blend of creativity and information dissemination.

Jeffrey Bullins is an assistant professor of communications at the State University of New York, Plattsburgh. His research interests include sound design for film and television as well as genre studies, particularly horror. His essay, "Hearing the Game," examining sound in the *Saw* film franchise, is featured as a chapter in *To See the Saw Films* (2014). Jeffrey is also a freelance sound designer and has worked on various horror features and shorts.

Jennifer Coates is an assistant professor at the Hakubi Center for Advanced Research at Kyoto University. She completed a PhD in Japanese Cinema at the School of Oriental and African Studies, University of London, in 2014. Her research interests include Japanese cinema, audience studies, conflict studies, gender, affect, and Japanese philosophy. She is currently preparing a manuscript on repetitive tropes in postwar Japanese film titled *Making Icons: Female Representation in Japanese Cinema 1945–1964.*

Michael Crandol is a visiting assistant professor of Japanese studies at the College of William and Mary. He recently completed his doctoral dissertation on the history of horror cinema in Japan during the prewar and early postwar eras. His publications include an article on the films of Nakagawa Nobuo and a chapter on the history of Japanese horror film in the British Film Institute's forthcoming *Japanese Cinema Book.*

Josh Dawson is currently a PhD student in the Comparative Literature department at SUNY Buffalo (2015–2019), having completed previous graduate degrees in philosophy and studies in comparative literature and the arts at Brock University in St. Catharines, Ontario. Dawson's primary research interests are film aesthetics and trauma, and his dissertation will refine this focus into a study of national narration and trauma through a comparative analysis of ancient Hebrew texts and contemporary Israeli films.

Mike Dillon received his PhD in critical studies from the USC School of Cinematic Arts and is an instructor at California State University at Fullerton. His research interests include transnational cinema and genre studies (especially horror, science fiction, and yakuza films), focusing particularly on cinema's engagements with human mobility and violence in the global era. His current projects include a chapter in the forthcoming anthology *Transnational Horror and the Global Grotesque.*

Amitabh Vikram Dwivedi is assistant professor of linguistics at Shri Mata Vaishno Devi University, India, and author of three books—two on lesser-known Indian languages: *A Grammar of Hadoti* (2012) and *A Grammar of Bhadarwahi* (2013); and one poetry collection in Hindi titled *Chinar ka Sukha Patta* (Dried leaves of Chinar) (2015). As a poet, he has published more than one hundred poems in different anthologies, journals, and magazines worldwide. His poem "Mother" has been included as a prologue to *Motherhood and War: International Perspectives* (2014).

Erica Joan Dymond is a professor at Marywood University. Her research interests include horror film, independent film, art film, anime, manga, Japanese culture, and Gothic literature. Dr. Dymond's many publications include "From the Present to the Past: An Exploration of Family Dynamics in Stephen King's *Pet Sematary*" in *Journal of Popular Culture* 46, no. 4 (2013).

Leena Eerolainen is a PhD candidate at the University of Helsinki. Eerolainen is currently working on a thesis titled "Metamorphosis and Personification of the Monstrous" and anticipates completing this doctorate in 2018. In addition to research in metamorphosis and transformation, Japanese horror and *kaiki* stories, and magical realism and the fantastic in Japanese film, Eerolainen is completing a manuscript titled *100 Years of Japanese Cinema* (in Finnish).

Joseph P. Elacqua is presently an adjunct professor at Mohawk Valley Community College in Utica, NY, where he teaches courses on Japanese language and ancient world history. Trained in the various religious traditions of East Asia, his research focuses on two main areas: Esoteric Buddhism and Onmyōdō, a Japanese tradition based on Chinese concepts of yin-yang and the five phases. He is currently working on an extensive examination of the god Taizan Fukun—a key deity within both Japanese Esoteric Buddhism and Onmyōdō—which he first encountered in the 2001 film *Onmyōji*.

Daniel Fandino is a graduate of the University of Central Florida. His academic interests include history, anime, American and Japanese pop culture, the virtual worlds of massively multiplayer online games, and the relationship between technology and nationalism.

Sabrina Vaquerizo González holds a BA in translation and interpreting from Autonomous University of Barcelona. Additionally, she holds an MA in editing at Open University of Catalonia and an MA in Japanese economics and politics at the same university. González is currently pursuing a third MA in contemporary China and Japan at the Open University of Catalonia—anticipating completion in 2017. She will then go on to pursue a doctorate through research on Japanese cinema, culture, its literature, and its philosophy.

Jeff Hammond is a PhD candidate at the Courtauld Institute of Art, University of London, researching modern art in Taisho-era Japan (1912–1926). He received his BA in visual and performed art from the University of Kent and his MA in film studies from the University of Exeter. Hammond's research interests are identity, modernism, and contemporary twentieth-century Japanese (and Asian) art and cinema.

Jim Harper is a writer and film critic specializing in cult cinema from around the globe. He is the author of *Legacy of Blood: A Comprehensive Guide to Slasher Movies* (2004) and *Flowers from Hell: The Modern Japanese Horror Film* (2008). His work has appeared in many publications and websites, including *Midnight Eye*, *MYM*, *Electric Sheep*, *Necronomicon*, *V-Cinema*, *Deranged*, *Alternative*, and *Scream*, and he has contributed to the *Directory of World Cinema* series. Currently Harper is preparing the first English-language book about the German Edgar Wallace films of the 1960s.

Alejandra Armendáriz Hernández is a PhD student at University Rey Juan Carlos in Madrid. Her research interests include the study of women filmmakers and theories and representations of gender in Japanese cinema and visual culture.

Seán Hudson is a PhD candidate currently studying Japanese visual media and popular culture at Kyushu University. For his master's thesis, he examined the aesthetics of Kurosawa Kiyoshi's horror films through the lens of queer theory, in line with his interest in horror as a culturally permitted, anti-ontological force in societies.

Gavin F. Hurley is assistant professor of English at Lasell College in Newton, Massachusetts, where he teaches composition, English, and interdisciplinary humanities courses. In 2014, he received his PhD in English from the University of Rhode Island. Dr. Hurley has published essays in *The Cinema of Rob Zombie: The Social and Political Philosophy of Horror* (2015) and *The Generic Turn: The Contemporary Novel and the Poetics of Genre* (2015). His research interests include spiritual/religious rhetoric, composition pedagogy, and postmodern stylistics of horror cinema.

Yoko Inagi is an assistant professor and librarian at the City College, City University of New York. She earned her MA in library and information studies at the University at Buffalo in 2008 and an MA in literature at the City College of New York in 2014. Her research interests lie in comparative studies of Eastern and Western utopian and dystopian literature, as well as cultural and historical studies of citation practices, academic integrity, library classification systems, and subject headings used in academic institutions overseas.

Zachary Thomas Ingle is a PhD candidate in film and media studies at the University of Kansas. His research interests include African American cinema, horror, religion in film, and the work of Robert Rodriguez. He recently defended his dissertation on Rodriguez and graduated in 2015.

Frank Jacob is assistant professor in the History Department of the City University of New York's Queensborough Community College. His major fields of research are Japanese history, German history, and global history. He is the editor of the open access journal *Entertainment—Journal of Media and Movie Studies*.

Jason Christopher Jones is a lecturer in Japanese studies at Monash University. His research centers on visual representations of contemporary Japanese popular culture, international adaptations thereof, and the "Japanization" of Western cultural elements. He examines cultural adaptation as represented in Japanese film, television, animation, manga, and other texts. He is also an active translator, interpreter, and subtitler.

Daniel F. Joseph is a student of medieval Japanese literature, focusing on the short narrative prose forms *otogi-zōshi* and *setsuwa*, in particular tales of monks, warriors, and monsters. He has also recently begun working with *emaki* illustrated scrolls. His primary interest is in translation, and he is currently preparing manuscripts of a number of his translated tales for future publication. Joseph will receive his MA from Harvard University in 2016.

Rick Kenney is chair and professor in the Department of Communications at Georgia Regents University–Augusta. His research specialties are in media ethics and Japan studies. Dr. Kenney coauthored "A 'Vexing Implication': Siamese Cats and Orientalist Mischief-Making," in *Diversity in Disney Films: Critical Essays on Race, Ethnicity, Gender, Sexuality, Disability*.

Boleyn Key is a PhD student in history at Georgia State University. Research interests include the cultural and intellectual history of Depression-era United States and Brazil, modernism, aesthetic theory, and, on occasion, horror films. He holds a BA from the University of Southern Mississippi and an MA from the University of Alabama. He lives in Atlanta, Georgia.

Kyu Hyun Kim is associate professor of Japanese and Korean history at the University of California, Davis. He is the author of *The Age of Visions and Arguments: Parliamentarianism and the National Public Sphere in Early Meiji Japan* (2008) and has contributed many articles on Japanese and Korean history, cinema, and popular culture to *The New Korean Cinema* (2005), *The Korean Popular Culture Reader* (2014), and *East Asian Film Noir* (2015), among other publications. He also serves as an academic adviser and contributing editor to Koreanfilm.org.

Paula S. Kiser works as the Instruction and Electronic Resources Librarian at Mary Baldwin College. She holds a master's in history from James Madison University and a master's in information science from the University of Tennessee at Knoxville. Her interests include connecting people to research related to science fiction, fantasy, romance, and horror genre fiction as well as library history and digital humanities.

Edwin Lohmeyer is a PhD student in the Communication, Rhetoric, and Digital Media program at North Carolina State University. He is currently exploring new ways in which a body interacts with and generates new sensory and perceptual experiences through digital video and sound from a Deleuzian perspective. To this end, his interests also comprise the study of affect experienced by a spectator when engaging with forms of digital cinema, gaming, remix culture, and new media art.

Emil Marmol is a PhD student at the University of Toronto/OISE. He expects to complete his degree in 2017. His research focuses on the use of noncommercial news media to foster critical thinking and engaged citizenship among secondary and postsecondary students. Emil has professional film and radio production experience and has published several papers on the effects that neoliberalism has had on students, faculty, and labor unions within the higher education sector. For more on his work in critical media literacy, please see www.comparenews.org.

Evan Marmol is a graduate student in the Master of Social Work program at California State University, Sacramento. He is a member of the 2018 cohort. Marmol's research interests include the concurrence of the sexualization of deities with the rise of patriarchy and the impact of law enforcement argot in reference to the disadvantaged and its capacity to further dehumanize the marginalized.

Carolyn Mauricette has loved the morbid and fantastic from a young age. With a healthy diet of the Brothers Grimm, Saturday-morning sci-fi, classic horror, and ghost stories from the Caribbean, she has explored many a métier in her life. Starting with dance, going on to a BA in English from the University of Toronto, and ending up in a fifteen-year career as a makeup artist, she finally refocused on her first love—writing—and, inspired by her favorite film, *Rosemary's Baby*, founded her blog, *rosemary's pixie* (www.rosemaryspixie.com), highlighting independent and Canadian horror, women in horror, and the representation of people of color within the genre.

Mark N. Mays, JD is a freelance media critic specializing in visual media, music, and Japanese pop culture. He has written on the Japanese horror boom of the late 1990s and the films of Akira Kurosawa and Kiyoshi Kurosawa and has published interviews with Japanese filmmakers including Mamoru Oshii. His writing is featured in the booklet included in the special edition DVD of *Jin-Roh: The Wolf Brigade* and various periodicals.

Jay McRoy is professor of English and Cinema Studies at the University of Wisconsin, Parkside. He is the editor of *Japanese Horror Cinema* and the author of *Nightmare Japan*.

Jared Miracle is a lecturer in the College of Foreign Languages at Ocean University of China. His professional interests include East Asia, folklore, martial arts, popular culture, foodways, and space studies. He is the author of *Now with Kung Fu Grip! How Bodybuilders, Soldiers, and a Hairdresser Invented Martial Arts in America*.

Monir Hossain Moni is a permanent research professor and director of the Program on Global Japan Studies at the Asia Pacific Institute for Global Studies (APIGS) based in Dhaka, Bangladesh. He is currently a visiting research scholar at the International Research Center for Japanese Studies (*Nichibunken*) in Kyoto. His field of scholarly expertise is Asia Pacific international interdisciplinary studies, with Japan as a single-country concentration. He has authored many globally useful journal articles, encyclopedia entries, and books.

Lindsay Nelson holds a PhD in comparative literature from the University of Southern California. She is currently a project lecturer in the Department of Global Communication Strategies at the University of Tokyo. Her research interests include Japanese horror films, contemporary Japanese literature, Japanese pop culture, and the depiction of monsters, cyborgs, and the virtual in Japanese cinema. Her work has appeared in the *Electronic Journal of Contemporary Japanese Studies*, *Cinemascope Independent Film Journal*, *Midnight Eye*, and the *East Asian Journal of Popular Culture* (forthcoming in 2016).

Senjo Nakai is a lecturer of communication studies at Chulalongkorn University in Thailand. Before joining Chulalongkorn, he taught Japanese studies and communication studies in both Thailand and Japan. His areas of expertise include Thai and Japanese media industries, grapevine communication, and popular culture. His recent articles include "Breaking the Silence of the Atomic Bomb Survivors in the Japanese Graphic Novel *Town of Evening Calm, Country of Cherry Blossoms* and the Film Adaptation" (2015); "Thai Civil Society" (2014); and "The Contested

Meanings of the Postwar Show in Cinematic Reflections of Tokyo Tower," *Chulalongkorn University's Journal of Communication Arts* (2012).

Yuki Nakayama is a PhD candidate at the University of Michigan, Screen Arts and Cultures department scheduled to graduate in May 2018. She is currently working on a dissertation project about 1980s and 1990s Japanese variety programs and their relationship to the educational function of television. Her research interests are postwar media culture and industry, education and entertainment media, race and gender representation, issues of audiovisual translations, and moving image preservation and archiving.

Megan Negrych obtained her BA in Japanese language in 2012, with a minor in history, and her MA in history in 2014 from the University of Regina. Her thesis, "In the Shadow of Anxiety: The Detective Fiction of Akimitsu Takagi and Seichō Matsumoto and the Japanese Post-War Experience," focuses on the ability of Japanese detective fiction to serve as a secondary historical account. Her academic research interests include colonialism and change in twentieth-century Japan; memory, trauma, and the legacy of WWII in Japan; folklore and horror; and the social and cultural history of horror in Japanese pop culture.

Fernando Ortiz-Moya is assistant professor of architecture and built environment at the University of Nottingham in Ningbo, China. His research interests lie in the area of urban studies, ranging from theory to planning practices. More recently, together with his colleague Nieves Moreno, he has approached the study of cities from a cinematic perspective, analyzing how social and cultural aspects of the urban realm are represented in cinema.

Alex Pinar is assistant professor of intercultural communication and Spanish at Akita International University, Japan. He holds a PhD in applied linguistics and an MA in research in language and literature from the University of Barcelona. He has taught at different universities in several countries and is author of textbooks of Spanish as a foreign language. His research interests are second language acquisition in the study-abroad context, intercultural communication, cultural studies, and world literature.

Laura Montero Plata holds a PhD in history of cinema from the Autonomous University of Madrid, and is a member of the editorial staff of the film review magazine *A Cuarta Parede*. She is programmer and co-organizer for Contemporary Japanese Film Week at Madrid's Official Language School. Her main research interests lie in the field of East Asian cinemas, anime, and contemporary Japanese cinema. She has published in a large variety of books and journals about Japanese animation. In addition, she wrote the book *El mundo invisible de Hayao Miyazaki* [The invisible world of Hayao Miyazaki] (2012); it is currently undergoing its fifth reprint.

Nieves Moreno Redondo is an advanced PhD candidate in film history and research fellow (PIF) in the Faculty of Letters at the Autonoma University of Madrid. Her research interest lies in the area of film studies and Japanese studies, particularly Japanese cinema and Japanese silent films. She is also researching, together with her colleague architect Fernando Ortiz-Moya, about the cinematic perspective of cities in Japan and the relation of national identity and urban landscapes in contemporary Japanese cinema.

Aimee Richmond recently obtained her PhD from the University of Sheffield, for which she examined how contemporary Japanese horror film functions transnationally, particularly in terms of how UK audiences understand and create meanings from the films, and the formation of a UK-constructed "Japanese horror film" genre. Her research primarily focuses on transnational and cross-cultural elements, and her research interests include Japanese popular culture, audience research, genre formations, cultural geography, and fan studies.

Elisabeth Scherer is a lecturer and research associate at the Department of Modern Japanese Studies at the Heinrich-Heine University in Düsseldorf. Scherer studied Japanese studies and rhetoric at the University of Tübingen and Dōshisha University (Kyoto). She obtained her PhD in Japanese studies from Tübingen University with a dissertation on female ghosts in Japanese cinema and their origins in Japanese arts and folk beliefs. Scherer's areas of research include Japanese popular culture (especially film and TV series), rituals and religion in contemporary Japan, gender studies, and the reception of Japanese art and popular culture in the West.

Sara L. Sumpter is a PhD candidate at the University of Pittsburgh. Sara's research interests include Heian- and Kamakura-period hand scrolls, the impact of sociopolitical strife on visual and material culture, supernatural creatures in Japanese literature, the development of Japanese horror iconography, theories of the grotesque, narrative and sequential art, and comic books.

Bill Thompson is a New York–based freelance writer and former film programmer. During the 1980s, he created "Spectrum of Japanese Cinema" featuring weekly double features of Japanese films presented at the Bleecker Street Cinema, which he programmed for five years. He also edited the *1000 Eyes Magazine/Focus*. After receiving an MA degree from the University of Michigan, he studied film at New York University and East Asian culture at Columbia University. He has written about Japanese cinema and culture for several books and a variety of publications for nearly forty years.

Till Weingärtner received his PhD in Japanese studies from Freie Universität Berlin in 2012. During his PhD research, he was active as a professional comedian in Japan for eighteen months. He was teaching at Freie Universität Berlin and the University of Manchester before commencing his current position as lecturer in East Asian Studies at University College Cork, Ireland. His research focuses on Japanese comedy, performance, media, and film.

James A. Wren holds a PhD in comparative literature from the University of Washington, a DPhil in modern Japanese literature and cultural studies from

Niigata University (Japan), and a DSc in immunogenetics and Silk Road Studies from the Chinese University of Mining and Technology (PRC). He pursued a career in medicine in Japan before moving into literature at Rhodes College and the University of Hawai'i and has widely published on modern Japanese and Indonesian literature, medical history, and narrative theory. He retired as professor of modern Japanese and comparative literature and languages at San José State University.

Marc Yamada is an assistant professor in the department of Comparative Arts and Letters at Brigham Young University. He received a PhD in Japanese literature and culture from UC Berkeley in 2007 and has published several articles on modern Japanese literature, film, and manga and is currently working on an article on Japanese filmmaker Kore-eda Hirokazu as well as a book on the cultural reactions to Japan's "lost decades" of the 1990s and 2000s.